Professional Data Warehousing with SQL Server 7.0 and OLAP Services

Sakhr Youness

Wrox Press Ltd. ®

Professional Data Warehousing with SQL Server 7.0 and OLAP Services

wrox

Published by Wrox Press Ltd, Arden House, 1102 Warwick Road, Acocks Green,
Birmingham, B27 6BH, UK
Printed in the United States
ISBN 1-861002-8-15

Trademark Acknowledgements

Wrox has endeavored to provide trademark information about all the companies and products mentioned in this book by the appropriate use of capitals. However, Wrox cannot guarantee the accuracy of this information.

Credits

Author
Sakhr Youness

Technical Reviewers
Steve Danielson
Robin Dewson
John Granade
Tony Greening
Hope Hatfield
Michiel Leji
Paul Morris
Sumit Pal
Gary Vartamoff
Helmut Watson

Development Editor
Dominic Lowe

Technical Editors
Chris Goode
Robert FE Shaw

Managing Editors
Joanna Mason
Dominic Lowe

Project Manager
Tony Berry

Design/Layout
Mark Burdett
Jonathan Jones
John McNulty

Figures
William Fallon
Jonathan Jones

Index
Michael Brinkman
Andrew Criddle

Cover
Chris Morris

About the Author

Sakhr Youness, PE, MCSD is a senior software architect at AppNet, Incorporated in Southeast Michigan. Sakhr has been a professional engineer since 1996 and a Microsoft Certified Solution Developer since 1997. He has extensive experience using Microsoft and Oracle tools to develop client/server and n-tier applications. As part of his work at AppNet, Sakhr provides consultation to and develops solutions for AppNet's clients to help them develop Web-based multi-user applications based on Microsoft DNA architecture.

Sakhr has written and contributed to many books including Professional SQL Server 7.0 Programming by Wrox Press, as well as helping with many technical reviews on topics ranging from Oracle 8 and SQL Server 7 to Visual Basic 6 and Visual Studio 98. He is also the main author of the SQL Unleashed book, and a contributor to SQL Server 7.0 Programming Unleashed, published by Sams Publishing.

Sakhr enjoys spending time with his wife, Nada, and 2-year old daughter, Maya. His hobbies include swimming, playing basketball, reading, and watching sporting events. He can be reached by email at: syouness@home.com

Dedication

To my wife, Nada, my daughter, Maya, and my parents.

Author Acknowledgments

This is the first time I've written a whole book from start to finish. It has been such an incredible experience. An experience with its ups and downs, and without the support of the closest people to me, it would never have succeeded. I would like to thank my wife, Nada, and my daughter, Maya, for their support and putting up with the long nights and ruined weekends as I worked on the book. I would also like to thank my parents who helped make me what I am.

Writing this book has been a great experience for me. What made it really great was working with a team of highly professional and dedicated people at Wrox Press who work hard, and value the hard work of an author. I would like to thank Chris Goode, Robert Shaw, Tony Berry, Dominic Lowe, and all the Wrox team members who worked extra hard to make this book a success. It has been a real pleasure to work with these people.

Table of Contents

Introduction

Computer applications and systems are the most prominent aspect of the last quarter of the 20th century. No matter where you go or what you do, chances are that you will interact with them either directly or indirectly. Sometime after (it could be immediately after) you pay for clothes you buy at the mall, the department store's inventory database gets updated, and its accounting system updates the account balances for you and the store. When you make a phone call, be it from your home phone or a cell phone, the phone company's computer system updates your account data with the number you called, time of the day, and the duration of the call (among other things) so that the bill you receive will accurately reflect your phone call.

Companies have become aware of the importance of using the latest technical advances in computer technology and embarked on developing computer-based systems that help them get a competitive edge in today's highly competitive market. One way to do this is to use existing data collected from their everyday transactions and analyze it to help them make the right strategic decisions for their organizations.

Decision Support Systems (DSS) grew from the need to analyse and make sense of the data accumulated by companies through their computer-based applications. Companies realize that such systems give them a competitive edge allowing them to respond to market trends and customer needs, cut costs, and increase their profits.

Decision Support Systems consolidate the existing data, summarize it, scrub it, and group it. The resulting consistent and "clean" data is then used to produce meaningful reports that give insights into what factors affect the company's performance and what could make it more profitable. Special software tools can be used to produce these reports and to extract information that immediately obvious to the decision makers, through a process known as **Data Mining**. These reports can eventually help decision makers come-up with the best decisions possible.

Microsoft realized the importance of building decision support tools, and embarked on doing so since the mid 1990's. Microsoft used its superiority in graphical user interface design to produce tools that are easy to learn and use. Some of the tools that have been used for a few years for decision support include Microsoft Excel's pivot table and Microsoft Access' cross-tab queries. Many of these tools will work with any backend database.

The previous versions of SQL Server were thought of as inadequate in supporting large data warehousing needs. This was based on the fact that the previous versions lacked the ability to support large data stores, and the database engine, at the time, did not effectively support analytical processing of large data sets. However, with the release of SQL Server 7.0 these conceptions started to change. SQL Server 7.0 proved to be impressive in handling the large amounts of data accumulated by companies over the years. Many new improvements and tools were added to the new release that really made the difference. These tools include:

- New architecture that allows for vast storage support (terrabytes of data)
- Improved database engine that supports querying large data sets.
- New Data Transformation Services (DTS)
- New On-Line Analytical Processing (OLAP) services.
- Microsoft Repository.
- Support for OLE DB and the introduction of OLE DB for OLAP and ActiveX Data Objects (ADO).
- Desktop decision support tools, such as OLAP Manager, English Query, and the new multidimensional expressions language (MDX) aimed at manipulating multidimensional databases.

Who is this book for?

If you are a database administrator or developer who is anxious to learn about the new OLAP and data warehousing support in SQL Server 7.0, then this book is for you. It doesn't really matter if you have previous experience with SQL Server or not. This book is not about teaching you how to use SQL Server. Many books are available on the market that would be more appropriate for this purpose. This book specifically handles OLAP and data warehousing support in SQL Server 7.0, giving you all you need to know to learn these concepts and become able to use SQL Server to build such solutions.

If you have experience in data warehousing and OLAP using non-Microsoft tools, but would like to learn about the added support for these kinds of applications in SQL Server 7.0, then this book is also for you.

If you are an IS Professional who does not have experience in data warehousing and OLAP services, then this book will help you understand these concepts. It will also provide you with the knowledge of one of the easiest tools to accomplish these tasks nowadays so that you can instantly start working in the field.

If you are a client-server application developer or designer who worked on developing many on-line transaction processing (OLTP) systems, then this book will show you the differences between such systems and OLAP systems. It will also teach you how to leverage your skills in developing highly normalized databases for your OLTP systems to develop dimensional databases used as back-ends for OLAP systems.

What Does the Book Cover?

This book covers a wide array of topics, starting with an introduction to the world of data modelling with emphasis on dimensional data analysis. The book also covers in detail the different aspects of the Microsoft OLAP Services: OLAP database storage (MOLAP, ROLAP, HOLAP), OLAP cubes, and how they are built, cube dimensions, measures, etc.

The new Multidimensional Expressions (MDX) language that was introduced with the first release of Microsoft OLAP is discussed in Chapters 8 and 9 with a long appendix listing all the built-in functions and statements. Many examples are included to enrich the book and make the content easier to read.

Chapter 7 discusses in detail Microsoft Data Transformation Services (DTS) and how it can be used in the Microsoft data warehousing scheme. Client tools are also discussed; in particular, the PivotTable service and its integration with Microsoft OLAP and other Microsoft tools, such as MS Excel.

Other topics covered in the book include an introduction to data marts and data mining and how these concepts fit with the overall Microsoft data warehousing strategy. Security, optimization and administration issues are covered in the last three chapters of the book. I hope that in reading this book you will get a very good handle on the Microsoft data warehousing framework and strategy, and be able to apply most of what is in it to your specific projects.

What Do You Need to Use to Use This Book?

All you need to use this book is to have basic understanding of data management. Some background in data warehousing would be helpful.

As for software requirementst, you need to have the following:

- Access to the latest SQL Server release and have Microsoft OLAP Services installed.
- Windows NT 4.0 or 2000 (Windows 9x will work, but only in a very limited capacity without support for OLAP Services)

Most of all, you need to have the desire to learn this technology that is new to the Microsoft world.

Conventions

To help you get the most from the text and keep track of what's happening, we've used a number of conventions throughout the book.

For instance:

> **These boxes hold important, not-to-be forgotten information which is directly relevant to the surrounding text.**

While the background style is used for asides to the current discussion.

As for styles in the text:

- When we introduce them, we **highlight** important words.
- We show keyboard strokes like this: *Ctrl-A*.
- We show filenames and code within the text like so: `OLAP_Example`
- URLs and text on user interfaces is shown as: Menu.

We present sample code in two different ways:

```
In our code examples, the code foreground style shows new, important,
    pertinent code
```

```
while code background shows code that's less important in the present
    context, or has been seen before.
```

Tell Us What You Think

We've worked hard to make this book as useful to you as possible, so we'd like to know what you think. We're always keen to know what it is you want and need to know.

We appreciate feedback on our efforts and take both criticism and praise on board in our future editorial efforts. If you've anything to say, let us know on:

feedback@wrox.com

Or via the feedback links on:

http://www.wrox.com

1

Overview of OLAP and Data Warehousing in SQL Server

If you are new to data warehousing and on-line analytical processing, you must be asking yourself the inevitable question, Just what are OLAP and Data Warehousing, and why the big fuss about them? This chapter introduces you to the OLAP and data warehousing concepts in general and to the Microsoft contribution to this field in particular.

If you are a seasoned data warehouse professional, you may want to skip the introductory information in this chapter and move to Appendix B, which discusses the installation process of the Microsoft OLAP services, or to Chapter 2, which discusses the Microsoft OLAP architecture. However, if you are new to the data-warehousing world, or would like to read a refresher about it, then this is the chapter for you.

This chapter contains an overview of:

- What is On-Line Analytical Processing (OLAP), what are its benefits, and who will benefit from it most?
- What is data warehousing, and how does it differ from OLAP and operational databases?
- Microsoft SQL Server 7.0 new OLAP and data warehousing capabilities.
- The architecture of the Microsoft OLAP service including the data collection, transformation, analysis and presentation tools.

What is OLAP?

Let's answer the first question that probably comes to mind about OLAP – what is OLAP, and what are its benefits?

Why use Data Warehouses?

Relational databases have gained great popularity since the mid 1980's. Many corporations adopted these databases for their mission-critical data needs. Many database vendors supported relational databases and produced state-of-the-art products that would make using such databases easy, efficient, and practical.

As a result, many corporations migrated their data to relational databases, which were mainly used in areas where transactions are needed, such as operation and control activities. An example would be a bank using a relational database to control the daily operations of customers transferring, withdrawing, or depositing funds in their accounts. The unique properties of relational databases, with referential integrity, good fault recovery, support for a large number of small transactions, etc. contributed to their widespread use.

The concept of data warehouses began to rise as organizations found it necessary to use the data they were collecting through their operational systems for future planning and decision-making. Assuming they use the operational systems, they had to build queries that summarized the data and fed management reports. Such queries, however, would be extremely slow because they usually summarize large amounts of data, sharing the database engine with every day operations, which in turn adversely affected the performance of operational systems. The solution was, therefore, to separate the data used for reporting and decision making from the operational systems. Hence, data warehouses were designed and built to house this kind of data so that it can be used later in the strategic planning of the enterprise.

Relational database vendors marketed their databases as tools for building data warehouses. Therefore, you see companies like Oracle, Sybase, Informix, and IBM among the leading companies in offering data warehouse capabilities in their databases. Data accumulated in a data warehouse is used to produce informational reports that answer questions like "Who?" and "What?" about the original data. For instance, in the bank example above, a data warehouse can be used to answer a question like "Which branch yielded the maximum profits for the third quarter of this fiscal year?" Or it could be used to answer a question like "What was the net profit for the third quarter of this fiscal year per region?"

OLAP and Data Warehouses

While data warehouses are usually based on relational technology, OLAP uses a multidimensional view of aggregate data to provide quick access to important information for further analysis. OLAP enables analysts, managers, and executives to gain insight into data through fast, consistent, interactive access to a wide variety of possible views of information. OLAP transforms raw data to useful information so that it reflects the real factors affecting or enhancing the line of business of the enterprise.

The basic advantage of OLAP systems is that they can be used to study different scenarios by asking the question "What if?". If we take the bank example, a sample question would be, "What if the bank charges an extra $1.00 for every automatic teller machine (ATM) transaction done by a user who is not a current bank customer? How would that affect the bank revenue?". This unique feature makes OLAP a great decision making tool that could help determine the best courses of action for the company's business. OLAP and data warehouses complement each other. The data warehouse stores and manages the data, while OLAP converts the stored data into useful information. OLAP techniques may range from simple navigation and browsing of the data (often referred to as slicing and dicing), to more serious analyses, such as time-series and complex modeling.

The timeline of business data in a data warehouse/OLAP system is presented in the figure below. The figure shows that raw data is collected, stored and managed into a data warehouse, and OLAP converts the data to information. Advanced OLAP analyses and other tools, such as data mining (explained in detail in Chapter 11), can further convert the information into powerful knowledge.

The timeline of corporate data in decision support systems

Dr. Codd, the inventor of relational databases and one of the most prominent database researchers, first coined the term OLAP in a white paper entitled "Providing OLAP to User Analysis: An IT Mandate" which he published in 1993. The white paper defined 12 rules for OLAP applications. Nigel Pendse and Richard Creeth of the OLAP Report (http://www.olapreport.com/DatabaseExplosion.htm) simplified the definition of OLAP applications as applications that should deliver **fast analysis of shared multidimensional information** (**FASMI**). This statement means:

- Fast: The user of these applications is an interactive user who expects the delivery of the information they require at a fairly constant rate. Most queries should be delivered to the user in five seconds or less.
- Analysis: OLAP applications should performs basic numerical and statistical analysis of the data. These calculations could be pre-defined by the application developer, or defined by the user as ad hoc queries.
- Shared: The data delivered by OLAP applications should be shared across a large user population. This stresses the need for implementation of the security requirements necessary for keeping the data confidential and safe.
- Multidimensional: OLAP applications are based on multidimensional databases, which is an essential characteristic of OLAP.
- Information: OLAP applications should be able to access all the data and information necessary and relevant for the application. The data may be located in different sources and be large in volume.

What are the Benefits of OLAP?

ComputerWorld magazine reported in February 1998, that Office Depot, one of the largest office equipment suppliers in the US, significantly improved its sales due to the improved on-line analytical processing (OLAP) tools it used in its different stores. This result came at a time when the financial markets expected Office Depot's sales to drop after the failure of the merger with Staples, a competitor to Office Depot, due to the loss of many people whose job was to conduct such analyses. ComputerWorld reported that the improved OLAP tools used by Office Depot helped increase sales a respectable 4% for the second half of 1997. For example, Office Depot found that it was carrying too much fringe stock in the wrong stores. Therefore, the retail stores narrowed their assortment of PCs from 22 to 12 products. That helped the company eliminate unnecessary inventory and avoid costly markdowns on equipment that was only gathering dust.

It seems that the 80/20 rule applies to many aspects in life. One of these aspects has to do with retailers. Retailers usually make most of their sales and profits (around 80%) from the sales of around 20% of the goods they stock. Goods that fall into the 80% with least sale and profit potential are usually referred to as fringe stock.

The Office Depot example is a strong indication of the benefits that can be gained by using OLAP tools. OLAP tools can improve the productivity of the whole organization by focusing on what is essential for its growth, and by transferring the responsibility of the analysis to the operational parts of the organization. In the Office Depot example, by moving the analyses to the store level, the company empowered the store managers to make decisions that made each of these stores profitable. The inherent flexibility of OLAP systems allowed the individual stores to become self-sufficient. Store managers no longer rely on the corporate information systems department (IS) to model their business for them.

Developers also benefit from using the right OLAP software. Although it is possible to build an OLAP system using software designed for transaction processing or data collection, it is certainly not a very efficient use of developer time. By using software specifically designed for OLAP, developers can deliver applications to business users faster, providing better service that in turn allows the developers to build more applications.

Another advantage of using OLAP systems is that if such systems are separate from the On-Line Transaction Processing (OLTP) systems that feed the data warehouse, OLTP systems performance will improve due to the reduced network traffic and elimination of long queries to the OLTP database.

In a nutshell, OLAP enables the organization as a whole to respond more quickly to market demands. This is possible because it provides the ability to model real business problems, make better decisions for the conduct of the organization, and use people resources more efficiently. Market responsiveness, in turn, often yields improved revenue and profitability.

Who will benefit from OLAP?

OLAP tools and applications can be used by a variety of organizational divisions; sales, marketing, finance, and manufacturing, to name but a few.

The finance and accounting department in an organization can use OLAP tools for budgeting applications, financial performance analyses and financial modelling. With such analyses, the finance department can determine the next year's budget to accurately reflect the expenses of the organization and avoid budget deficits. The department can also use its analyses to reveal weak points in the business that should be eliminated, and points of strength that should be given more focus.

The sales department, on the other hand, can use OLAP tools to build sales analysis and forecasting applications. These applications help the sales department to realize the best sales techniques and the products that will sell better than others.

The marketing department may use OLAP tools for market research analysis, sales forecasting, promotions analysis, customer analysis, and market/customer segmentation. These applications will reveal the best markets and the markets that don't yield good returns. They will also help decide where a given product can be marketed versus another product. For instance, it is wise to market products used by a certain segment of society in areas where people belonging to this segment are located.

Typical manufacturing OLAP applications include production planning and defect analysis. These applications will help determine the effectiveness of quality assurance and quality control (QA/QC), as well as determining the best way to build a certain product, and the source for its raw materials. Information delivered by an OLAP system in this case may lead to the discovery of problem areas for a company, that are hidden behind numbers that may be misleadingly indicating good performance.

For all the types of OLAP users above, OLAP will deliver the information they need to make effective decisions about their organization's line of business and future directions. The information delivered by the OLAP tools is delivered quickly, and just in time when needed. This rapid delivery of information is the key to successful OLAP applications. Time is the critical piece to really making effective decisions.

The information delivered by OLAP applications usually reflects complex relationships and is often calculated on the fly. Analyzing and modeling complex relationships is practical only if response times are consistently short. In addition, because the nature of data relationships may not be known in advance, the data model must be flexible, so that it can be changed according to new findings. A truly flexible data model ensures that OLAP systems can respond to changing business requirements as needed for effective decision-making.

What are the Features of OLAP?

As we saw in the previous section, OLAP applications are found in a wide variety of functional areas of an organization. However, no matter what functions are served by an OLAP application, it must always have the following elements:

- Multidimensional views of data (data cubes).
- Calculation-intensive capabilities.
- Time intelligence.

Multidimensional Views

Business models are multidimensional in nature. Take the Office Depot example: several dimensions can be identified for the business of that company; time, location, product, people, etc. For example, sales can differ in time from quarter to quarter, or from year to year. The time dimension, therefore, has several levels within it. The location, or geography dimension, can also have multiple levels such as city, state, country, etc. The product dimension is no different from the previous two dimensions. It can have several levels, such as categories (computers, printers, etc.), and more refined levels (printer cartridge, printer paper, etc.).

This aspect of OLAP applications provides the foundation to slice and dice the data, as well as providing flexible access to information buried in the database. Using OLAP applications, managers should be able to analyse data across any dimension, at any level of aggregation, with equal functionality and ease. OLAP software should support these views of data in a natural and responsive fashion, insulating users of the information from complex query syntax. After all, managers should not have to write structured query language (SQL) code, understand complex table layouts, elaborate table joins, and summary tables.

The multidimensional data views are usually referred to as **data cubes**. Since cubes have three dimensions in Newtonian physics, this maybe a misnomer. In reality data cubes can have as many dimensions as the business model allows. Data cubes, as they pertain to Microsoft SQL Server 7.0 OLAP services, will be discussed in detail in Chapter 2.

Calculation-intensive

While most OLAP applications do simple data aggregation along a hierarchy, some of them may conduct more complex calculations, such as percentages of totals, and allocations that use the hierarchies from the top down. It is important that an OLAP application is designed in a way that allows for such complex calculations. It is these calculations that add great benefits to the ultimate solution.

Trend analysis is another example of complex calculations that can be carried out with OLAP applications. Such analyses involve algebraic equations and complex algorithms, such as moving averages and percent growth.

OLTP (On-Line Transaction Processing) systems are used to collect and manage data, while OLAP systems are used to create information from the collected data that may lead to new knowledge. It is the ability to conduct complex calculations by the OLAP applications that allows for successful transfer of the raw data to information, and later to knowledge.

Time Intelligence

Time is a universal dimension for almost all OLAP applications. It is very difficult to find a business model where time is not considered an integral part. Time is used to compare and judge performance of a business process. As an example, performance of the eastern region this month may be compared to its performance of last month. Or, the profits of a company in the last quarter may be judged against its profits the same quarter of the last year.

The time dimension is not always used similar to other dimensions. For example, a manager may ask about the sales totals for the first two months of the year, but is not likely to ask about the sales of the first two computers in the product line. An OLAP system should be built to easily allow for concepts like "year to date" and "period over period comparisons" to be defined.

Another interesting concept that should be considered in OLAP applications when time is considered is the concept of balance. A balance of the computers built in a quarter will be the sum of the computers built in the individual months of the quarter. So, if the company built 20 computers in January, 10 in February, and 25 in March, the balance of computers built for the first quarter will be 55 computers. On the other hand, the balance of cash flow for a quarter will usually be the ending balance at the end of the quarter regardless of cash flow balance of the individual months in the quarter. So, if the balance at the end of January is $20,000, at the end of February is $15,000, and at the end of March is $25,000, the balance for the end of the quarter will be $25,000. Lastly, the balance of employees in a quarter will usually be the *average* balance of the number of employees in the company in the individual months. So, if the number of employees in January is 10, in February 8, and in March 15, the balance of employees for the first quarter will be (10 + 8 + 15)/3 or 11:

Month/Quarter Balance	Number of Employees	Number of Computers Built	Cash Flow at the End of the Month
January, 1999	10	20	$20,000
February, 1999	8	10	$15,000
March, 1999	15	25	$25,000
First Quarter, 1999	11 (Average)	55 (Summation)	$25,000 (End value)

The variation of the concept of balance with time

What is a Data Warehouse?

As you have already seen in the previous sections about OLAP, a data warehouse is a central repository that stores the data collected in the enterprise's business operations. Originally, a data warehouse was located on a mainframe server, although nowadays, increasingly you will find data warehouses built on PC-based servers. Data from various OLTP applications and other sources is selectively extracted and organized into the data warehouse. The data is used by OLAP systems and user queries to aid in decision-making.

A data warehouse integrates data from several diverse, heterogeneous sources. It consolidates this data and stores it in a step-by-step fashion. The data warehouse organizes and stores the data needed for informative analytical processing over a long historical time perspective. The data is thus stored as snapshots of the corporate business in time, and once stored, it does not change.

Not only does the data warehouse store the data collected and "scrubbed" (data scrubbing is explained later in the chapter in the Data Transformation section) from the corporate OLTP applications, but also may store the data generated by the OLAP reports. This data is canned as snapshots at a certain point in time and stored in the data warehouse to facilitate quick retrieval when needed.

How Does a Data Warehouse Differ from Traditional Operational Data Stores

The data warehouse differs from operational database systems in many ways. One of the main differences between these two types of systems is the data collected in each of them. In operational systems (OLTP systems), the data is called "operational data", and in the data warehouse, the data is usually referred to as decision-support data. The table below summarizes the main differences between operational data found in OLTP systems and decision support data found in a data warehouse.

Operational Data	**Decision Support Data**
Application-oriented: data serves a particular business process or functionality.	Subject-oriented: data serves a certain subject of the business, such as customer account, customer information, etc.
Detailed data.	Summarized or refined data.
Structure is usually static.	Structure is dynamic where new data cubes can be created as needed. Existing cubes can also be modified by adding new dimensions, or dimension levels.
Targets data-entry people.	Targets managers and decision makers.
Volatile (can be changed).	Non-volatile (is not changed after it is inserted).
Requirements are usually known before the design of the system.	Requirements are not totally understood prior to the design of the system.
Follows the classical development life cycle.	Completely different life cycle.

Table Continued on Following Page

Operational Data	Decision Support Data
Performance is important because of the large number of concurrent users that may access the data.	Performance issues are more relaxed, since a far smaller number of people are expected to access the data simultaneously, thus there are no serious concurrency issues to worry about.
Transaction-driven.	Analysis-driven.
Must be highly available for the end-users (back-up and recovery plans are very well planned).	Does not have the same degree of high availability requirement, and plans for back-up and recovery are more relaxed.
Usually retrieved in units or records at any given time. This leads to processing only a small amount of data in any given process (transaction).	Usually retrieved in sets of records. This leads to processing large amounts of data in one single process (such as finding out a particular trend based on data collected over several years).
Reflects current situation.	Reflects values over time (historical).
When managed (administered), it is usually managed as a whole.	Usually managed in pieces, or smaller sets.

The major differences between data warehouse data and operational OLTP data are summarized and presented in the following sections below.

Purpose and Nature

The data warehouse is subject-oriented, that is it's designed around the major subjects of the enterprise business. Traditional operational databases, on the other hand, are usually process-oriented based on the functionality provided by the applications accessing them. For example, an operational system may be designed around processes like bank savings, loans, and other transactions, while a data warehouse may be organized around subjects like customer data, vendor data, activity data, etc.

The subject-orientation of the data warehouse makes its design different from the design of an operational database. As a result, the data warehouse design involves data modeling and database design. The business processes, which are the heart of the operational database design, do not affect the design process of the data warehouse.

The data warehouse may exclude data that is not directly relevant to the decision support process. This data may be essential for the daily activities taking place in operational databases and are therefore included in them. For example, a banking OLTP database may include a lookup table about available statuses of a customer account. This table may be linked to other tables lending them its primary key as a foreign key, which makes maintaining status information easy by maintaining only the lookup table. The next figure shows a sample of the data that may be contained in the status lookup table. The figure shows different fields that are important for the OLTP system, such as the description of the status and the last two fields that keep track of who last updated the table, and when. In the data warehouse, data is not expected to change, and the different fields in the status table may not be needed. Instead, the `StatusName` field may be stored in the fact table

The fact table is the table that holds the facts of the business that need to be analysed, such as sales, profits, amount of storage at hand. etc. For more details on fact tables, please refer to Chapters 2 and 3.

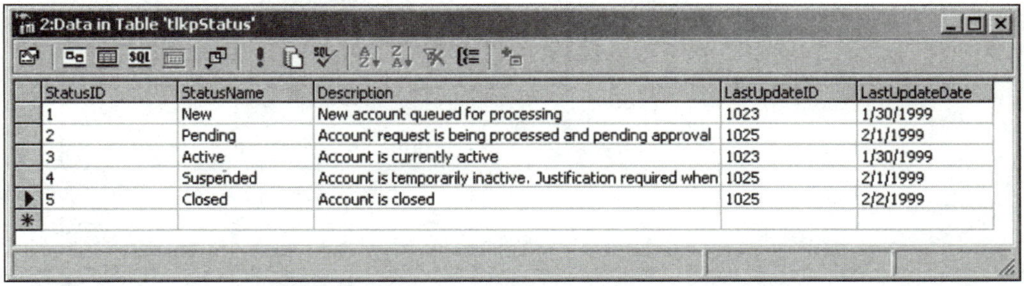

StatusID	StatusName	Description	LastUpdateID	LastUpdateDate
1	New	New account queued for processing	1023	1/30/1999
2	Pending	Account request is being processed and pending approval	1025	2/1/1999
3	Active	Account is currently active	1023	1/30/1999
4	Suspended	Account is temporarily inactive. Justification required when	1025	2/1/1999
5	Closed	Account is closed	1025	2/2/1999

The lookup table tlkpStatus in an OLTP system

Data Structure and Content

Operational databases also differ from the data warehouse in their structure. Operational systems are usually designed to allow a large number of small transactions (OLTP systems). This requirement makes it necessary to optimise the database for data inserts, updates and deletions. The most efficient way to do so is by normalizing the database tables to at least the third normal form (3NF) according to Dr. Codd's rules.

Dr. Edgar F. Codd is considered to be the father of relational databases. His paper 'A Relational Model of Data for Large Shared Data Banks' was a seminal paper, in a continuing and carefully developed series of papers by him since 1970. This paper is considered the trigger that brought relational database management systems into existence. Dr. Codd provided the momentum for widespread research into numerous related areas, including database languages, query subsystems, database semantics, locking and recovery, and inferential subsystems.

A table is said to be in third normal form (3NF) if all the following conditions below are met:

- It's in first normal form (1NF), which means that it does not have any repeating groups, and each field is an atomic (scalar) value.
- It's in second normal form (2NF), which means that it has a key that determines all non-key attributes in the table.
- In addition to being in 1NF and 2NF, all non-key attributes are mutually independent, and fully dependent on the primary key.

To understand the normal forms, consider this example: in the old days, a company kept a master file that included data collected for employees. The file included fields like `emp_number`, `first_name`, `last_name`, `dept_number`, `dept_name`, `dept_description`, etc. as shown in the table below:

emp_ number	first_ name	last_ name	dept_ number	dept_ name	dept_description
00001	John	Doe	100	Finance	Control financial activities
00002	Mary	James	110	Marketing	Marketing Department

To put this file in 1NF form, you need to eliminate repeating groups. Notice that the repeating group in this example is the department information. To eliminate the repetition, you need to create a new `Department` table that holds the department information fields and holds an ID field that is kept in the original file to link the two tables. The two tables will then look like:

Employee table:

emp_Number	first_name	last_name	dept_id
00001	John	Doe	1
00002	Mary	James	2

Department Table:

Dept_ID	dept_number	dept_name	dept_description ...
1	100	Finance	Financial Department
2	110	Marketing	Marketing Department

If we consider the employee number to be the primary key of the employee table, then we notice that the two tables are normalized to the 3NF form. The employee table has each record identified by the primary key, `emp_number`. The identification makes each record unique in itself. The third condition for 3NF listed above is also true for this example. For instance none of the non-key fields, like the `first_name` and `last_name` (Having Doe in the `last_name` field does not really depend on having a John in the `first_name` field), in the employee table are dependent on each other. Also, all non-key fields depend on the key column, employee number.

The data warehouse, on the other hand is not expected to be subject to updates and deletions, however inserts may happen periodically when data is exported to it. Therefore, there is no need to keep the tables normalized to 3NF. Improving the query performance against the data warehouse may require that its tables be de-normalized leading to acceptable redundancies.

Another aspect of the data structure in a data warehouse stems from the very nature of OLAP systems. Specifically, OLAP's multidimensional database that stores data represented by multidimensional views (see OLAP Characteristics earlier in the chapter), and the complex calculations that take place in such systems.

Most OLAP applications are intended for interactive use, and users of these applications expect to get a fast response to queries (ideally, not more than a few seconds). This is simple to achieve if queries only have to retrieve information from a database, reformat it and present it to a user, but gets slower and more complicated if a significant amount of calculation work has to be done to service the query. This might include hierarchical consolidation, calculations of variances, analyzing trends, deriving computed measures, and so on. As the amount of calculations performed on the data increases, so does the time it takes to get the query results. This becomes more apparent as calculations involve a larger number of items retrieved from the database.

Thus, in order to get a fast response, all large multidimensional applications need to pre-calculate at least some of the information that will be needed for analysis. This might, for example, include high-level consolidations needed for reports or ad hoc analyses, and which involve too much data to be calculated on the fly. In multidimensional databases, the storage of pre-calculated data is usually automatic and transparent. Some OLAP systems that store the data in the same OLTP system, usually referred to as relational OLAP (ROLAP) systems, use summary tables. The summary tables store similar pre-calculated and pre-aggregated information to that stored by a multidimensional database. Again, although the details of the implementation differ, there is no difference in principle between multidimensional databases and ROLAP products in this regard.

The diagram opposite shows samples of customer transaction data as it makes its way from an OLTP system to a data warehouse, and finally to an OLAP system where a report may be generated.

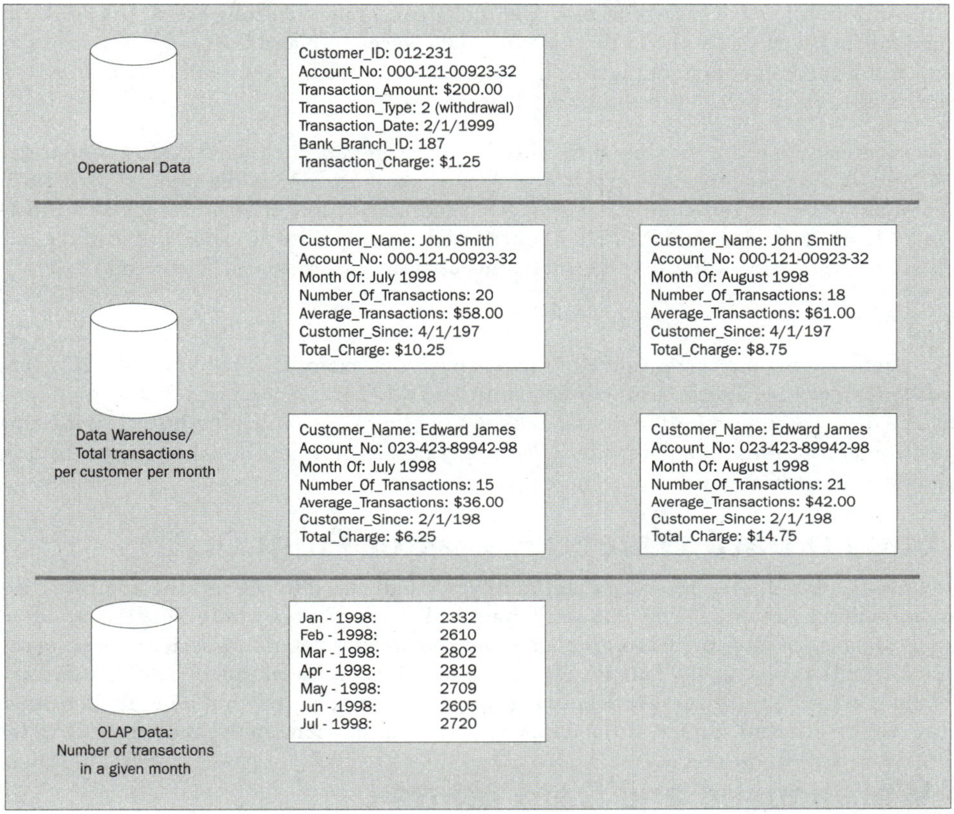

Data migration from operational systems to analytical systems

This diagram shows that the OLTP system holds detailed information about the transaction. What we are not able to see is that the transaction table is linked to many other tables according to certain relationships. The data warehouse stores the collective transactions over time after selecting the important pieces of data to store, and performing some transformation on it. In the figure, we see that the data warehouse stores each customer with the date since she/he opened an account, the total amount of transactions, and the total bank charges as a result of these transactions. The data in the data warehouse is used to generate the OLAP data, which shows the number of transactions for the bank customers for each month. The information the bank managers draw from this analysis is whether their bank is serving more transactions or not over time.

Data Volume

OLTP systems are designed to be small in size to allow for efficient updates, inserts and deletions. Once some data is recognized to become static and not likely to change, the data is archived from such systems into the data warehouses. The archived data can then be deleted from the OLTP system leaving room for new data to be collected.

The data warehouse is designed to hold large amounts of data. While an OLTP system can rarely exceed the 100 GB limit, a data warehouse is likely to be measured in the TB ranges. The data stored in the data warehouse is organized in a way that optimizes query performance.

This rule is not always the case. You may find that a corporation is using their OLTP system as the backend for their analysis tools. In this case, the data warehouse and the OLTP have the same size. This practice is not recommended, because optimising the database for transaction processing will degrade its performance in analytical processing, and vice versa.

Data storage volume is not the only difference between operational OLTP systems and data warehouses. The volume of data processed when retrieval occurs is also extremely different. With OLTP systems, a small amount of data is retrieved for every performed transaction. In data warehouses and OLAP systems, a large set of data may have to be processed when queries are issued against the data store. The data is retrieved in sets, rather than in small units as is the case with OLTP systems.

Timeline

OLTP systems depict the current state of the business. For example, a banking OLTP system will hold records that show the current customer accounts, and the daily transactions that take place around them. The data warehouse for the same bank, on the other hand, will store historical information about bank customers, accounts, and activities over a long period of time. Data is retrieved from the data warehouse as snapshots in time.

How Does a Data Warehouse Differ From OLAP

As we have discussed, OLAP services and tools are usually used to convert the enterprise raw data into information and knowledge. The data warehouse is the storage area where OLAP may tap into to do its analyses. Data is fed into the data warehouse over time from operational systems using many techniques. In the process, the data is said to be scrubbed and transformed. This transformation and scrubbing is done because the raw data in the operational system may not be in the format and shape that can lead to efficient storage in the data warehouse, or efficient analyses by the OLAP tools.

Data Warehouses and Data Marts

Today's corporations strive to conduct their business on a national and global basis. We see companies that originated in the US expanding their business across the oceans to Europe, Asia, and Africa. Business expansion created the need to access the corporate data from different geographical locations in a timely manner. For example, a salesperson who is working in Texas for a company based in California may need instant access to the enterprise database to identify names of potential customers in Texas, or to retrieve certain information that would help in selling the product to an old Texas customer when meeting with them.

The solution to this problem was to create smaller versions of the data warehouse based on certain criteria, called **data marts**. The data marts in this salesperson's case could hold corporate data for customers in Texas. Being of a manageable size, the data mart can fit on a mobile PC, such as a laptop that the salesperson may carry with them. Data marts created a new way of thinking when designing corporate data repositories:

- Some corporations completely replaced the concept of having a data warehouse with that of having smaller data marts that can be fed with the data they need from the operational systems.
- Other companies decided to use data marts to complement their data warehouses by moving data into them from the data warehouse allowing for more efficient analysis based on criteria like department, geographical area, time period, etc.
- Finally, some corporations decided to use their data marts as the first stage into which operational data is stored. The data is then replicated from all of the corporate data marts into a central data warehouse.

The diagram below shows a typical data warehouse/OLAP system architecture. The next three figures show how this architecture changes to accommodate the introduction of data marts according to the strategies discussed above.

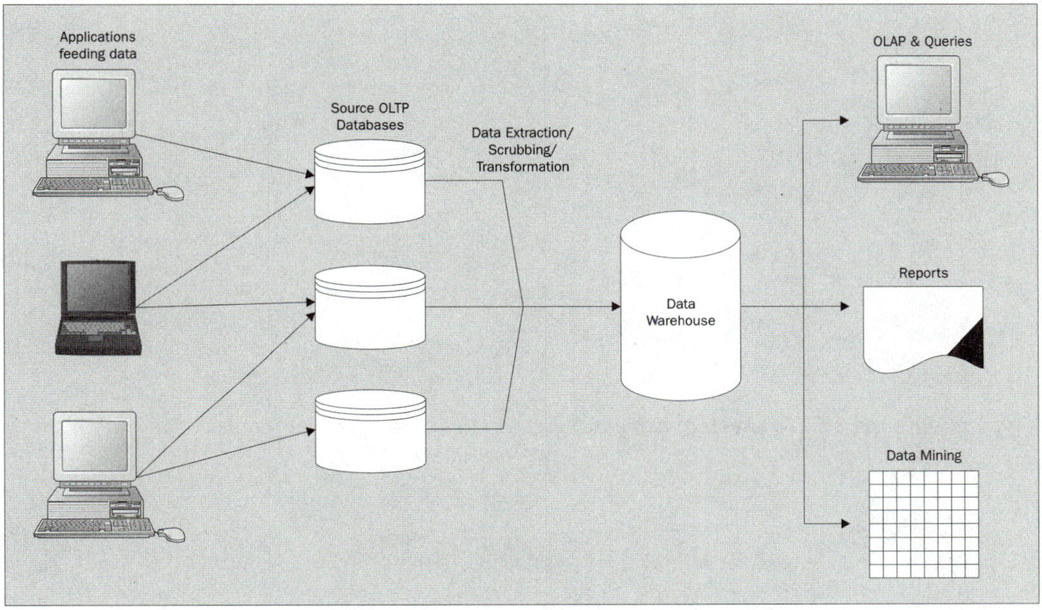

A typical data warehouse/OLAP system architecture with no data marts

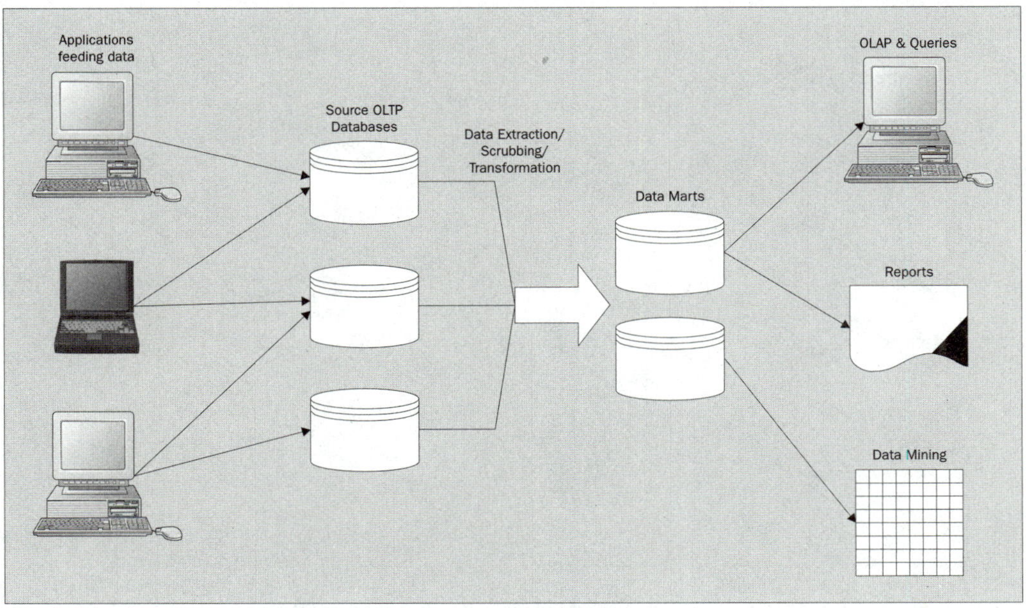

A typical data mart/OLAP system architecture with the data marts replacing the data warehouse

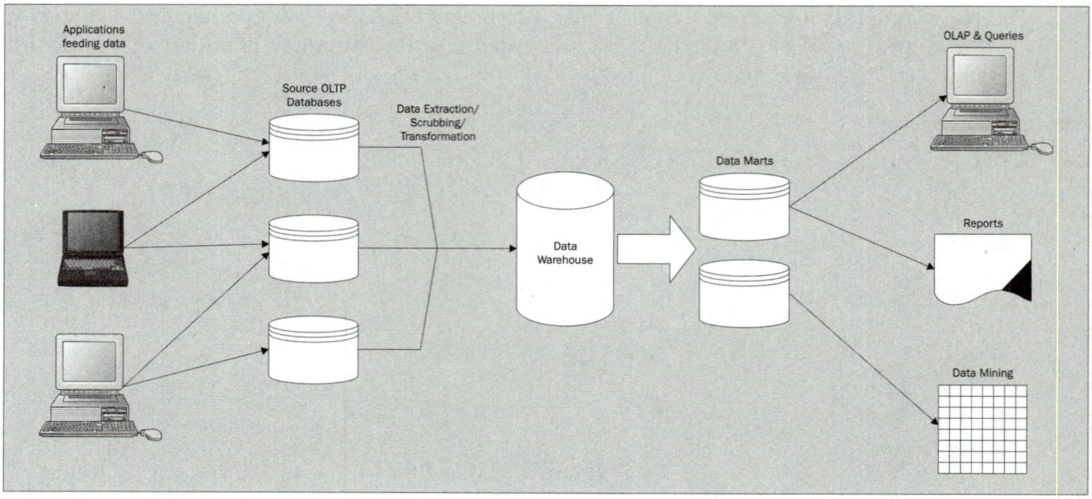

A typical data mart/OLAP system architecture with the data marts populated with data from the data warehouse

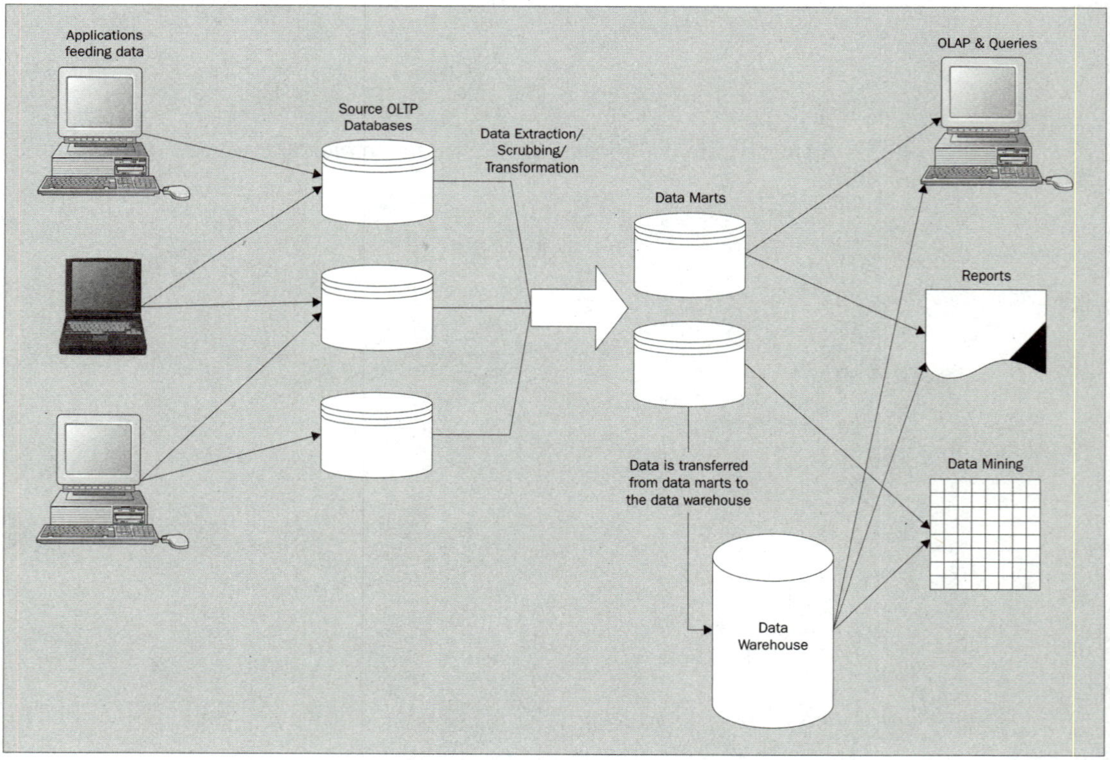

A typical data mart/OLAP system architecture with the data mart data used to populate the data warehouse

Each one of these solutions has its relevant advantages and disadvantages to the companies that adopted them. No matter what the solution is, data marts usually have similar characteristics to those of the data warehouse, except for the data volume. Actually, due to the smaller data volume, queries are usually faster to run in data marts as opposed to the data warehouse.

Data Mining

Many corporations accumulate the data they collect in the process of their daily operations in a data warehouse and data marts for analysis reasons. The analyses they conduct on the stored data helps the managers in the decision making process. One relatively new, but powerful, concept that has started to gain popularity in the business world is data mining. With data mining, managers find out aspects and facts about their business that may not be evident otherwise. Data mining establishes relationships between business elements that may seem completely unrelated.

As an example, managers of a grocery store decided to distribute free coupon cards. When a customer pays for groceries, the cashier scans their card to see if any coupons apply to the customer's groceries. This actually makes the customer happy since they don't have to manually search for the coupons, clip them and argue with the cashier about their validity. On the other hand, as the cashier scans the customer's card, the database is updated with whatever has been bought from the store. The data collected for all the customers can then help the managers decide which products are selling the most, or which ones that are located near the cashiers really get the most attention among "compulsive" buyers. This is possible because managers have access to a wide range of data about the customers and their purchases. They also know which products are located near the cashier from their serial number. Linking these pieces of information will help them design their product displays at the checkout stations better.

In general data mining leads to the following results:

- Discovering unknown associations. Such associations can be found when one event can be correlated to another event that **seems** completely unrelated (for example, beer buyers are likely to purchase peanuts)
- Sequences, where one event leads to another later event (for example, customers who purchase curtains are likely to come back to purchase rugs from the same store)
- Recognizing patterns which lead to classification, or new organization of data (for example, certain profiles are established for customers based on what they purchase)
- Finding groups of facts not previously known. This process is known as event clustering.
- Forecasting, or simply discovering patterns in the data that can lead to predictions about the future.

Overview of Microsoft OLAP and Data Warehousing

One of the biggest problems for OLAP tools in the early 1990s was that these tools were not too easy or intuitive for the end-user to use. The end-user is usually the person who will make the decisions based on analyzing the historical data collected in the data warehouse. Previously, developers had to build costly applications around these tools to make them easier to use and to cut down on the learning curve for the end-users.

Microsoft recognized the importance of providing a better database system that can be used for data warehousing. Microsoft also recognized the importance of providing tools that would make the data analysis an easy and enjoyable process. With the release of Microsoft SQL Server 7 and the tools that accompanied it, Microsoft was able to deliver a viable solution to the problem. This section briefly introduces these tools and their effectiveness. A detailed description of each of these tools, and their use is presented in the balance of this book.

The diagram below shows a schematic of the architecture of the Microsoft SQL Server data warehousing and OLAP services. In the figure, several tools are shown, and each tool has a unique function. The tools can be divided into several major parts: data source, data transformation and export, data storage, data analysis, and data presentation. The remainder of this chapter will present an overview of the different parts shown in this schematic.

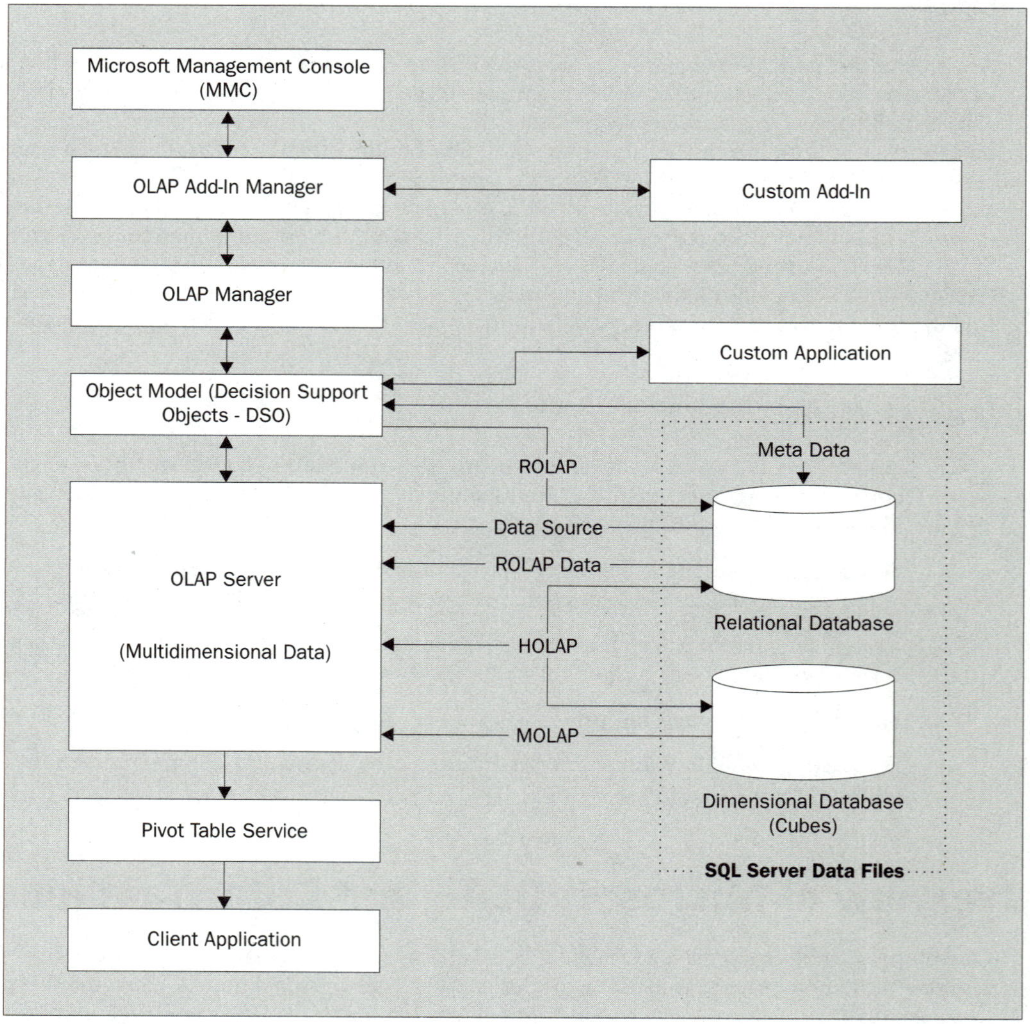

Schematic of Microsoft OLAP and Data Warehousing Architecture

Features of Microsoft OLAP Services

Microsoft OLAP Services came with some good features that address the complexity of the OLTP systems. These features are:

- **Ease of use**. The Microsoft OLAP Services are easy to use. Many wizards, editors, and help materials are available to help the user in every step of the way. The OLAP Manager user interface is a great tool that will give you access to metadata views and cube data, amongst other things. The OLAP Manager also provides you with wizards to create and edit cubes, dimensions, and levels. Other wizards include a usage analysis wizard and usage-based optimisation wizard.
- If you are not an advocate of using wizards, like me, then you will find several editors that allow you to perform the tasks that the wizards are capable of doing, and more.
- **Flexibility**. Several storage modes are available through the Microsoft OLAP Server. These include storing cube data into multidimensional cube files (MOLAP), relational databases (ROLAP), or a hybrid of the two (HOLAP). Cubes can also be partitioned, with each partition stored in different storage mode. Cube partitioning and storage modes will be covered in more detail in Chapter 2.
- **Scalability**. Microsoft OLAP services support both the Intel-based servers and existing DEC Alpha servers (future DEC Alpha servers will not support Windows NT/2000) The OLAP client can run on Windows 9x, Windows NT, and Windows 2000. The OLAP services have been also designed to address a variety of data warehousing scenarios, such as customized aggregation options, usage-based optimization, data compression, and distributed calculations. All these features make the Microsoft OLAP services highly scalable.
- **Integration,** OLAP services are integrated with the Microsoft Management Console (MMC), SQL Server and Windows NT. This integration allows for shared security, powerful usage of OLE DB data sources as a result of having an OLE DB provider for OLAP services, and client and server side cache.
- **Widely supported APIs and functions**. The OLAP Server and Microsoft PivotTable service support OLE DB, ADO, user-defined function, and decision support objects (DSO).

These are only a few of the features that make Microsoft OLAP Services a powerful contender in the data-warehousing world. If you would like to learn more about the features of MS OLAP services, refer to the product documentation.

The Foundation: Microsoft SQL Server 7.0

SQL Server 7.0 is the foundation of Microsoft data warehousing and OLAP. SQL Server is a relational database management system (RDBMS) and one of the best database systems for the Windows NT platform. SQL Server scales from the Windows 9x platforms to the Windows NT and Windows 2000 data server platforms. It can be used on Intel-based machines as well as Alpha-based workstations running Windows NT as their operating system.

As the foundation of the Microsoft OLAP and data warehousing, Microsoft SQL Server provides many advantages to decision makers, including:

- Low price and high performance that lead to a great reduction in the total cost of ownership.
- SQL Server is compatible with many other software components and tools used in the deployment of data warehouses.
- SQL Server is integrated with the Internet. Web sites can be easily built based on SQL Server data using the Internet Wizard.
- A wide variety of technologies can be used to easily connect to SQL Server, which makes data access for analysis an easy task.
- SQL Server Enterprise Manager makes system administration easy, even for non-database administrators.
- SQL Server is designed to provide optimal performance on the Windows NT and Windows 2000 platforms, which gives it a great advantage over other RDBMS running on the same platforms.
- Data replication is built-into the SQL Server engine, which cuts down on the cost of using third-party tools, or additional tools to conduct the replication.
- SQL server data can be easily exported to other desktop office applications such as Microsoft Word, Microsoft Excel, Microsoft PowerPoint, and e-mail.
- Scalability is another important feature of SQL Server 7.0. SQL Server 7.0 scales up from the Windows 9x platforms to the Windows 2000 Advanced Server, providing high portability and availability to a wide customer base.

Data Transformation Services (DTS):

SQL Server relational databases serve as the main data source for the OLAP and data warehousing services. Naturally, the data source could be any other database, such as Oracle, or even the mainframe. However, in this book, we will be assuming that the whole data warehousing architecture is based on Microsoft technologies.

Microsoft introduced data transformation services (DTS) into SQL Server 7.0 to facilitate the collection and transfer of data from their OLTP sources to the OLAP system. DTS provides a means to moving the data from the source to the destination data warehouse. In the process, DTS performs data validation, cleanup, consolidation, and transformation the data when needed.

DTS is installed automatically with the SQL Server 7.0 Standard and Enterprise installations, but not with the Desktop installation, which means they are not installed on the Windows 9x platform.

Data Validation

Data validation is an essential task that has to be conducted during or after extracting the data from the source OLTP databases and transferring it to the destination data warehouse. If the data is not valid, the integrity of the business analyses conducted based on it will be in question. For example, in the case of a currency field where the OLAP system may exist in different countries, one has to make sure that the data in this currency field is always converted appropriately according to the currency of the destination data warehouse.

Other things you need to pay close attention to when validating the data is information related to geographical regions. You need to make sure that the referenced cities are in the right countries as the country field states. Yet another example refers to validating data; you need to make sure that products are represented in a consistent manner in all data sources.

Data Scrubbing

Data reconciliation has to take place between multiple sources feeding the same data warehouse. The reconciliation process is referred to as data scrubbing. For example, if a product is classified as beverage in one OLTP system, and soft drink in another system, the two different classifications must be reconciled during the data transformation process before the data related to them can be aggregated and stored in the data warehouse. Failing to do so will yield inaccurate results in the final reports that are generated based on the data warehouse.

Data scrubbing can be achieved in different ways. These ways are described in more detail in later chapters, but are summarized here.

- Using DTS import and export wizards to modify data as it is copied from the source to the destination data store.
- By writing a Microsoft ActiveX script or program. This kind of script or program may use the DTS API to connect to the data source and scrub the data. This method is not the easiest method to perform data scrubbing, but it provides a great deal of flexibility, because it uses the power of the scripting or programming language to access the data, which often can provide a tremendous amount of control and manipulation across heterogeneous data sources.
- DTS Lookup provides the ability to perform queries using one or more named, parameterized query strings. This allows for building custom transformation schemes to retrieve data from locations other than the immediate source or destination row being transformed.

Data Migration

Ideally, when migrating data from OLTP data sources to a data warehouse, data is copied to an intermediate database before it is finally copied to the data warehouse. This intermediate process is necessary to allow for data scrubbing and validation to occur.

Special care should be taken when performing the data migration. The migration process should be performed during periods of low activities at the operational OLTP systems to minimize the impact on the performance of these systems. If the data migration is done from multiple data sources that are replicas or share in replication processes, the migration must happen when all these sources are synchronized to make sure consistent data is copied from these sources.

A commonly deployed strategy is to execute data migration procedures after the nightly database backups occur. This ensures that if a migration procedure crashes the system, there are backups available.

Data Transformation

When you move the data from the source OLTP databases to the destination data warehouse, you may find yourself performing many transformations of existing data to make it more operational and practical when used in the destination store. Below are examples of data transformations you may want to consider when moving data from the OLTP databases to the data warehouse:

- You may break a column into multiple columns, such as dividing a date or timestamp field into its date components, day, month, quarter, and year.
- You may also find yourself having to calculate new fields based on the values in source fields, such as creating a total price field in the destination database, which is a result of multiplying the unit price by the quantity sold fields in the source database.

- You may need to merge separate fields into one field, such as merging the first name and last name fields in the source database in one name column in the destination data warehouse.
- You may also want to map data from one representation to another, such as translation of code to literal values and converting values from decimal numerical values (1, 2, 3, etc.) to Roman numerals (I, II, III, etc.).

DTS Components

Data transformation services (DTS) is comprised of the import wizard, the export wizard, and COM programming interfaces that allow for the creation of custom import/export and transformation applications. A detailed discussion of these topics is presented in Chapters 6 and 7 of this book.

Metadata and the Repository

Metadata is, by definition, data about data. In other words, the information about the way storage is structured in the data warehouse, OLAP and DTS services is all kept as metadata, which is stored in the Microsoft Repository. The repository is built to maintain such technical information about the data sources involved with the services mentioned above.

SQL Server stores repository information in its msdb database, which is a relational database. As you will see in Chapter 6, Microsoft Data Transformation Services, three storage types are available for DTS packages: Repository, SQL Server, and external files. Repository is the preferred means of storing DTS packages in a data-warehousing scenario because it is the only method of providing data lineage for packages. DTS packages are discussed in more detail in Chapter 6.

Access to the repository is possible through the interfaces exposed by the OLAP manager's graphical user interface (GUI). The OLAP manager is discussed in detail in Chapter 5. Metadata can also be accessed through the decision support objects (DSO), and through programs that use interfaces to the repository. Microsoft recommends only using DSO or OLAP manager's GUI to access the metadata because the repository is subject to change in future releases of SQL Server

Decision Support Services (DSS)

Microsoft decision support services (DSS) consist of the DSS analysis server, also referred to as the OLAP server, and the pivot table service. Below is an overview of these components. Detailed discussion of them is provided in later chapters.

DSS Analysis Server

Often referred to as the OLAP server, the DSS analysis server is the heart of Microsoft OLAP. The DSS server extracts data from heterogeneous sources across the organization for analysis and querying. The DSS server stores aggregated and processed data in the multidimensional database for quick access when needed. It can also utilize data stored in summary tables in the OLTP database as well. Decision support objects (DSO) can be used to access the DSS server and create custom applications that provide custom reports to the end-user.

The Pivot Table Service

The pivot table service was added to SQL Server 7.0 after being tested for quite a long time in Microsoft Excel and Access. This service allows the user to create cross-tab tables on the fly by specifying the columns and rows on which aggregations should be made.

DSS Server can work with several tools on the OLAP client side, such as English Query, Microsoft Office (especially, MS Excel and MS Access) allowing these tools to access its cube data through the pivot table service. This gives the user a great advantage, because she/he is most likely familiar with these tools, and can use them efficiently for the data analysis.

The OLAP Manager

The OLAP Manager is a graphical user interface (GUI) that allows the user to build an OLAP solution based on existing data sources. This section will is not meant to teach all about the OLAP manager, since this is covered comprehensively in Chapter 5. The screenshot below shows the OLAP Manager main screen when you first open it.

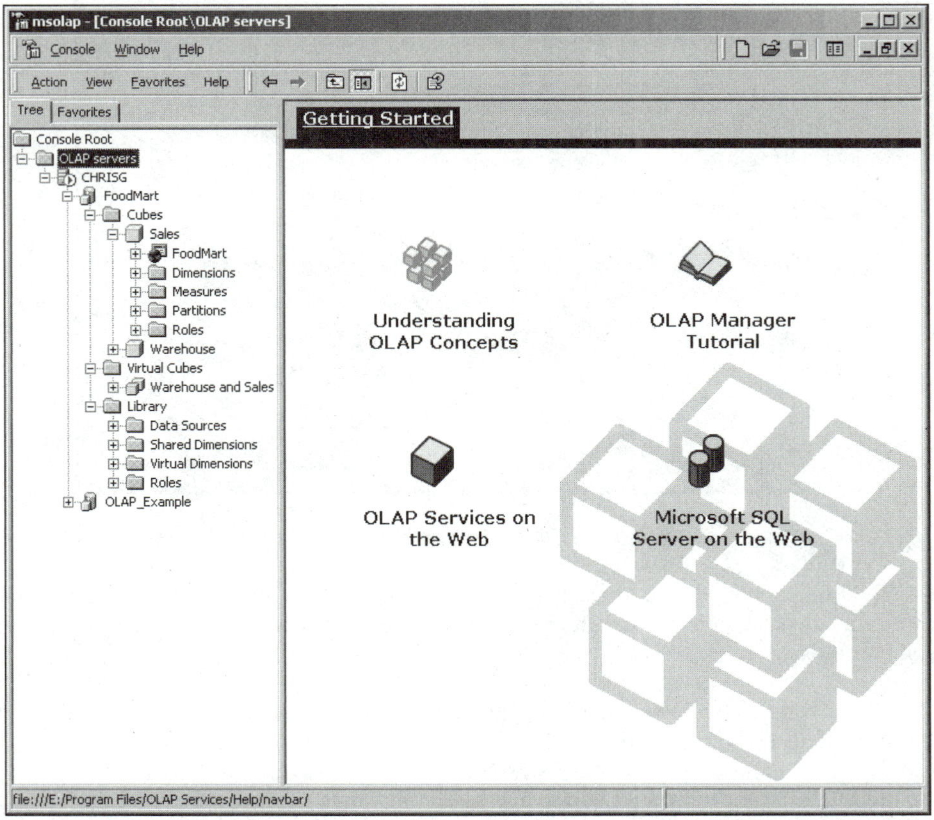

The OLAP Manager

OLAP Manager is opened as a snap-in into the Microsoft Management Console (MMC). MMC is a graphical tool that allows you to access several Microsoft (and recently non-Microsoft) services in the Windows NT environment. These services are added as snap-ins using the add-in manager. This actually allows you to open the Microsoft OLAP Manager if you are working with other tools that are opened as MMC snap-ins as well. For example, if you are working with Microsoft Transaction Server (MTS), you can select the Add/Remove Snap-in command of the Console drop-down menu of MMC, then select the Add button on the resulting dialog. The screen you see would look like the screenshot below. You can highlight Microsoft SQL Server OLAP Services in the Dialog list box, and click the Add button to open the OLAP Manager.

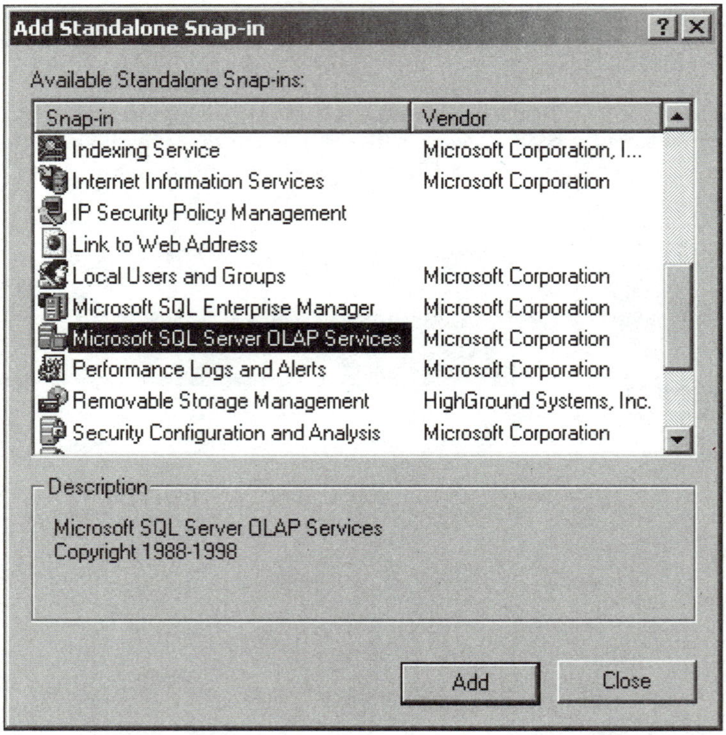

Adding the OLAP Manager MMC Snap-in Dialog

The OLAP Manager allows you to easily manage your OLAP databases. It provides you with wizards to add new data cubes, change the structure of existing cubes by adding or changing dimensions and their levels of complexity.

The OLAP Manager also allows you to manage the security of your cubes so that you can guarantee only authorized access to their data.

Finally, the OLAP Manager allows you to access the metadata of your cubes and their components. As you select an element that has representation in the metadata from the left-hand pane of the OLAP Manager Screen (for example, a cube), you be able to click the Metadata menu on the top of the right-hand pane to access the metadata for the selected cube:

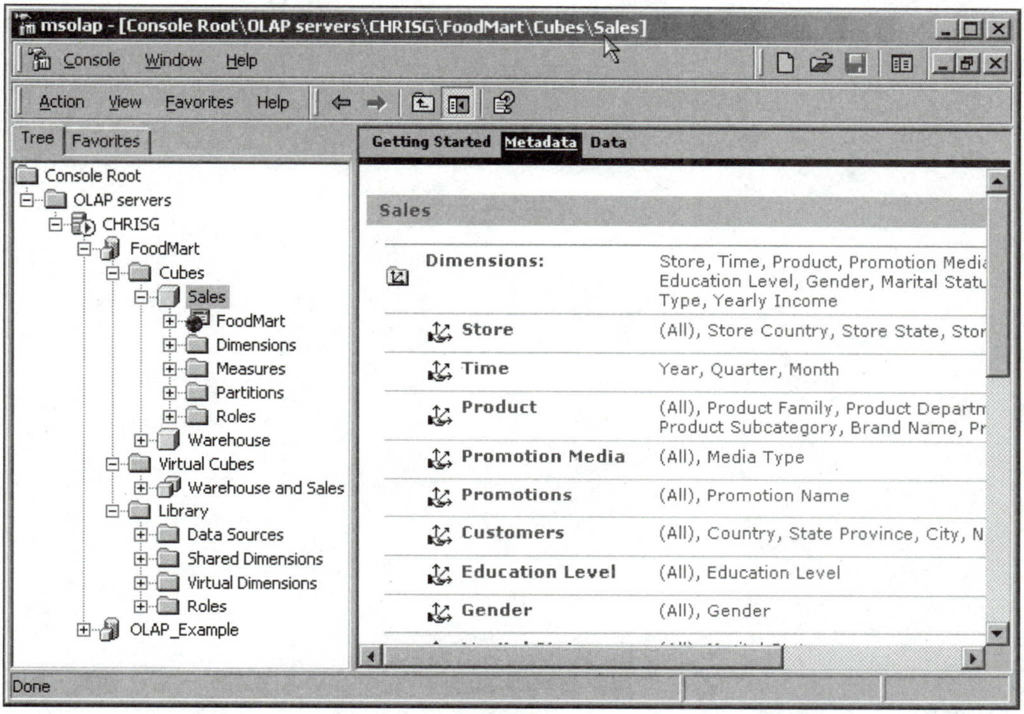

Accessing the OLAP cube metadata from the OLAP Manager

Client Architecture

The diagram below shows a schematic of the client architecture of the Microsoft OLAP Services. The Client architecture is based on the Pivot Table service, which was incorporated into SQL Server 7 after years of testing and enhancement with Microsoft Excel and Access. Data access abstraction technologies, such as OLE DB and ActiveX Data Objects (ADO) may be used in combination with the Pivot Table service to build custom client applications. These applications are responsible for presenting the information extracted from the data warehouse to the end-user. Standard tools can also be used instead of custom applications. These tools include the powerful Microsoft Excel spreadsheet program and Microsoft Access.

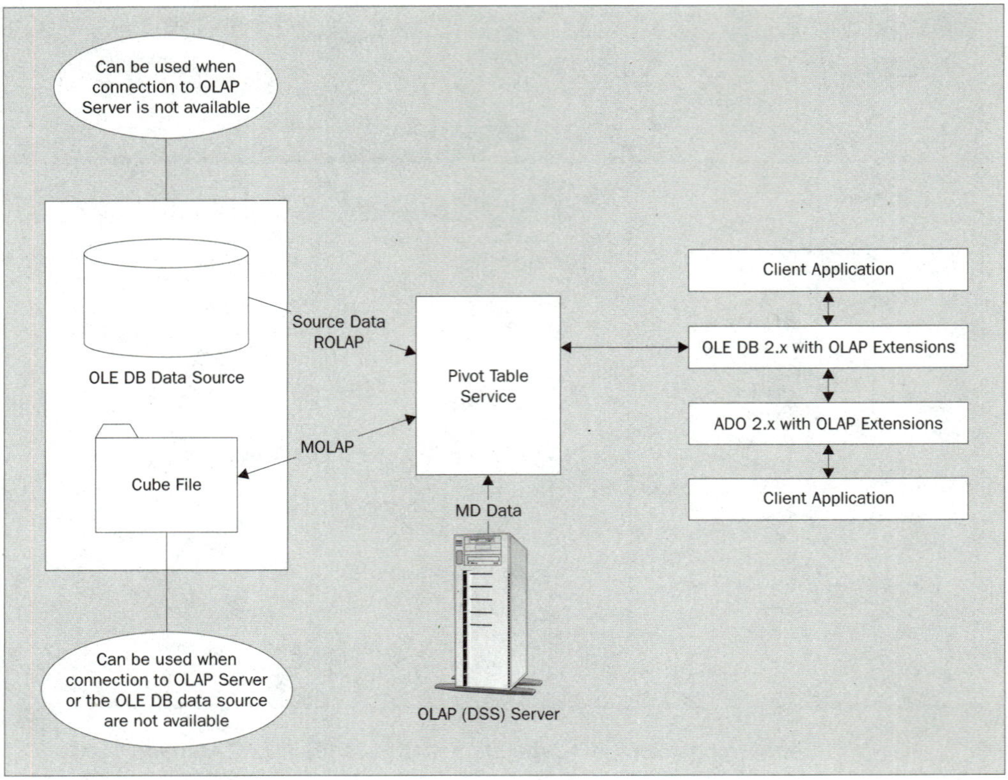

One unique feature of the Microsoft OLAP client architecture is that the user can work with the information off-line. If a connection is not available to the OLAP server, the user can access the operational database, which includes summary tables that mimic the OLAP database. These summary tables can then be used by the client applications to generate the needed reports. If a connection to the OLE DB source is not available, the user can still use stored cube files to do their analyses. These cube files can be saved locally when the cubes are created and viewed in the OLAP Manager screen against the OLAP database.

Summary

Data warehousing and OLAP is gaining great attention among information technology professionals, companies and clients. It is a natural step in the evolution of data management, where large amounts of data are being collected by the organization everyday. The data can yield tremendous benefits when analysed. Microsoft recognized this trend, and as a result embarked on enhancing its enterprise database management system, SQL Server, to handle data warehousing needs. It augmented the database management system with its OLAP services, which make data warehousing easier and more cost-effective.

Appendix B will show you how to install Microsoft OLAP services and start using them for your data warehousing needs. The next chapters will go into more detail about the architecture of these services and exactly how they can be utilized to build optimal data warehousing solutions.

2

Microsoft OLAP Services Architecture

In the previous chapter we looked at a quick overview of the Microsoft Data Warehousing and OLAP services. In this chapter, we will take an in-depth look into the architecture of Microsoft OLAP, looking mainly at the server and client architecture.

The topics covered in this chapter include:

- OLAP cube architecture including cube dimensions and dimension levels.
- The metadata that stores information about the cubes and their components.
- Relational OLAP (ROLAP), versus, Multi-dimensional OLAP (MOLAP), and Hybrid OLAP (HOLAP)
- Star and snowflake schema used in the multi-dimensional database
- Decision Support Objects
- The Pivot Table service

Overview

In Chapter 1 we looked at a brief overview of the Microsoft data warehousing and OLAP services' architecture. Let's do a quick recap of some of the general concepts before diving into the details of the architecture.

The diagram below summarizes the different parts of the Microsoft OLAP services' architecture. In this figure, different levels can be identified in Microsoft OLAP, the data source, the data storage and the OLAP server, and the client part. The next figure, "*an overall schematic of the Microsoft OLAP Services architecture*", zooms in into the architecture and shows how the components of each of these levels interact with each other.

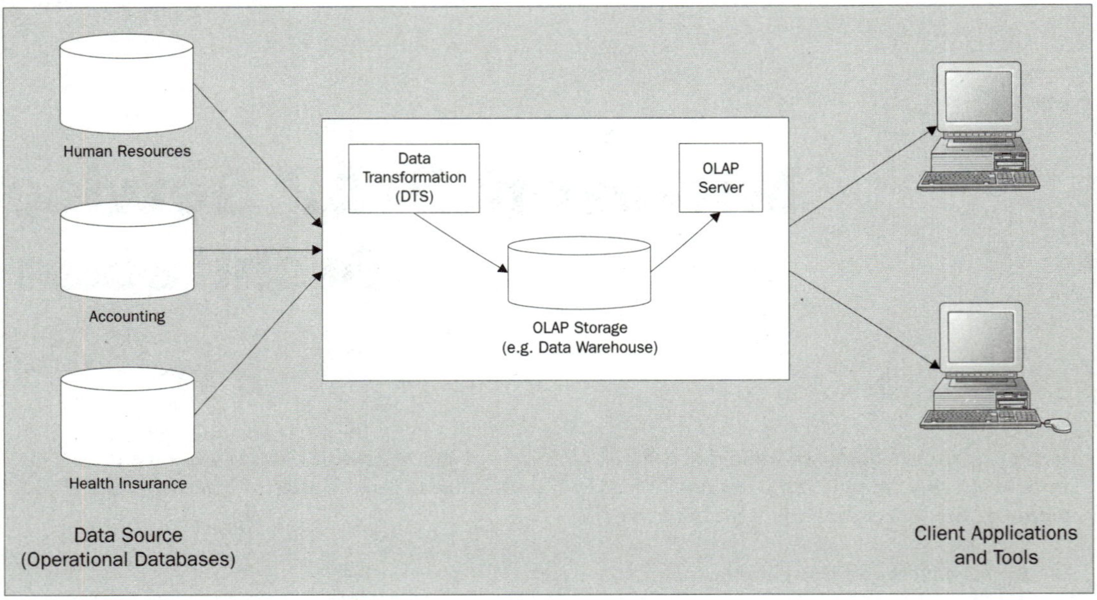

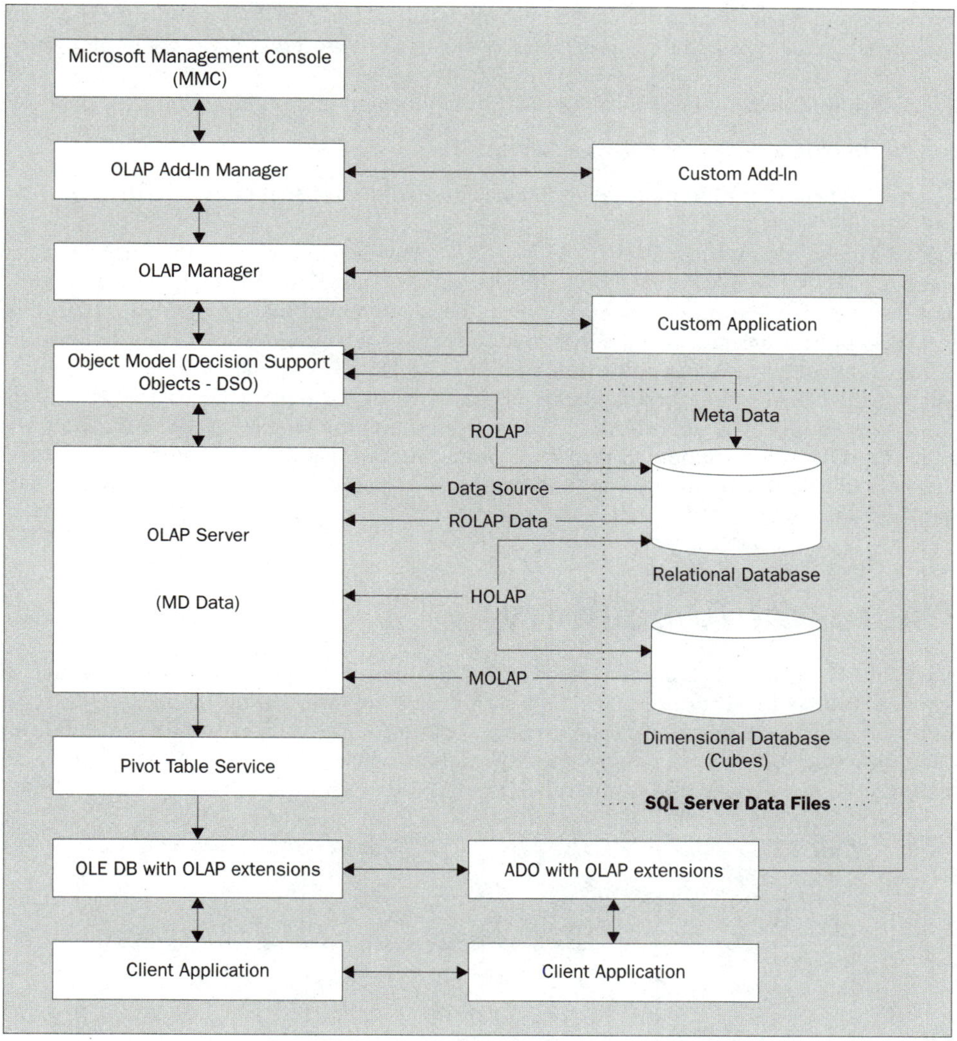

This diagram shows the OLAP server, which creates and manages multidimensional data cubes. (Multidimensional data cubes will be explained in more detail later in the chapter.) The OLAP server provides OLAP data to the PivotTable service, which in turn provides this data to client applications. The PivotTable service uses multidimensional Microsoft ActiveX Data Objects (ADO MD) and the OLE DB provider for Microsoft OLAP services.

The source data for the OLAP system, specifically for the multidimensional cubes, is usually relational databases. The structure of the data in these databases is usually transformed into a star or snowflake schema typically used in OLAP data warehouse systems (star and snowflake schemas are explained later in the chapter in the Dimensional Databases section). Data can be fed into the data warehouse database from multiple sources, such as legacy databases, OLTP systems, etc. These data sources need to support connection via ODBC or OLE DB. The Data Transformation Services (DTS) of SQL Server version 7.0 provide a means to manage the data warehouse, importing data into it from these heterogeneous sources. The OLAP server uses the data in the data warehouse to create the data cubes.

Cube definition and specification is called cube metadata. The OLAP server stores cube metadata in a repository. As we mentioned in Chapter 1, data cubes can be stored in a variety of modes:

- As multidimensional database files (MOLAP) located in a multidimensional database
- As tables in a relational database (ROLAP)
- As a hybrid of multidimensional database files and relational tables (HOLAP)

The OLAP Manager Graphical User Interface (GUI) provides control over the OLAP manager. Custom applications can also be developed, using the Decision Support Objects (DSO) object model, to control the OLAP server. DSO applications may control the creation and management of data cubes by the server. DSO applications also may be designed to manage the cube metadata in the repository. The OLAP Manager program is an application based on the DSO object model to provide the needed control over the OLAP server and the cube metadata. The OLAP manager is used as snap-in to Microsoft Management Console (MMC). Popular programming languages, like Microsoft Visual Basic, can utilize the DSO object model to provide custom programmatic control of the OLAP server. DSO can also help developers build custom applications that interact with the OLAP Manager user interface. You can find an overview of DSO in Appendix A.

The Microsoft Repository

The Microsoft Repository is a place to store and share objects between software tools, such as development tool add-ins, services, system descriptions (tool information models, or TIMs), instances of system objects, and custom reusable components. It is used in SQL Server 7.0 to store information about the different objects presented by the SQL Server services and tools. As an example, the figure below shows the metadata stored in the repository for a data cube.

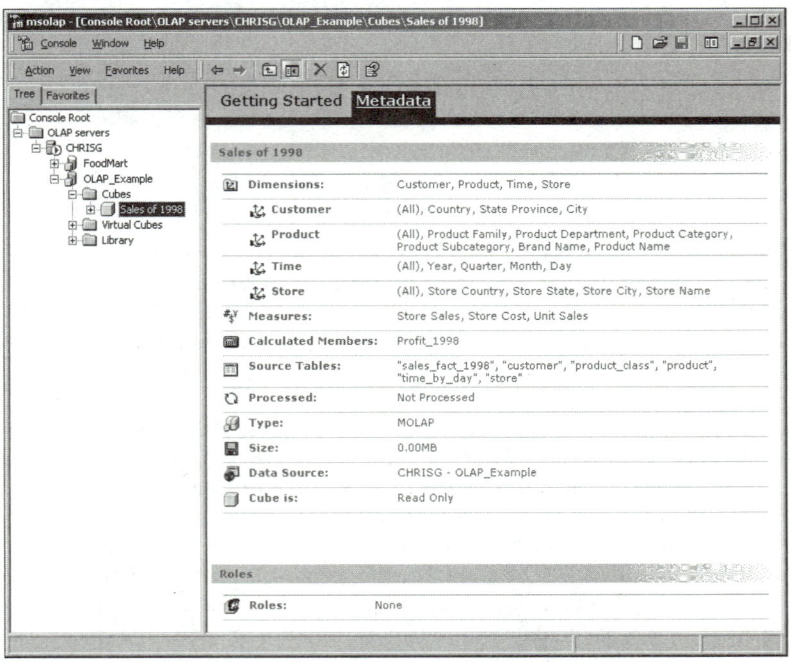

Almost all of the new releases of Microsoft development and data management tools support and allow access to the repository. Some of the benefits achieved by using a central location to store information about the different objects and tools are:

- Reusability: With the storage of such information in the repository, the information can be organized in a way that allows for its reuse, if needed.
- Dependency tracking: The repository not only stores information about the different objects used by the software tools, but also facilitates establishing and querying relationships between stored objects.
- Tool interoperability: this facilitates the use of these tools in different systems.
- Data resource management: The repository stores global metadata for an enterprise data warehouse, and a resource library of available services and components, which makes managing such data easier and more efficient.
- Team development: the repository can store metadata about a development project's source control, which facilitates the management of concurrent activities on different versions and configurations of project design and development.

The heart of the repository is an engine, which is a set of component object model (COM) and OLE Automation interfaces. These interfaces provide access to the repository allowing browsing its data and writing data to it. The repository data is stored in a relational database, in the SQL Server case it is msdb. With other development tools, this database can be a SQL Server database, or a Microsoft Access database.

Architecture of the Microsoft Repository

The following figure shows the different parts that constitute the Microsoft Repository:

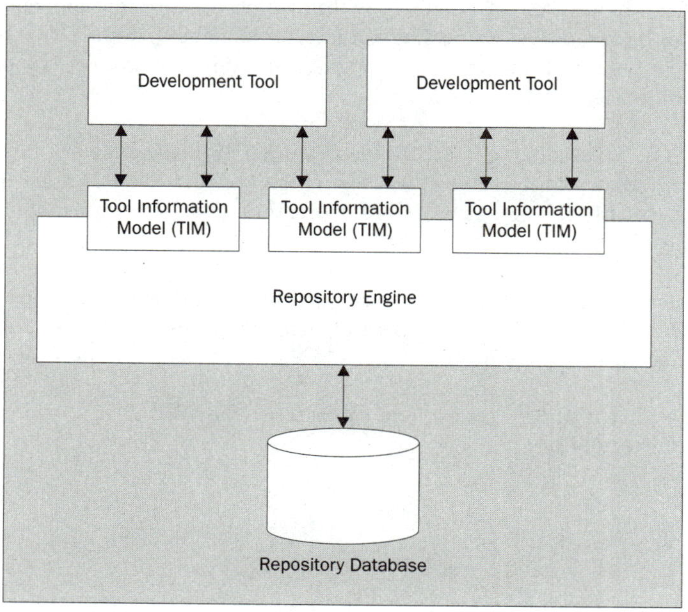

The figure shows four tiers in the repository architecture. These tiers are:

- **The Repository database**: a relational database, usually a SQL Server or Microsoft Access database. Queries can be issued directly against this database (though writing directly to the database isn't recommended). Several tools can be used to do this and can interact with the repository engine, which makes the necessary updates.
- **The Repository engine**: a COM-based tool that manages data in the repository. The engine provides basic functions to store and retrieve repository objects and the relationships among them. An elaborate object model is provided for the repository engine. This object model allows developers to create their own applications that provide custom access to the repository.
- **Tool Information Model**: This model is a combination of an object model that specifies the types of information of interest to one or more tools, and a Type Information Model. For example, Data Transformation Services Information Model (DTS IM) specifies the types of data of interest to data transformation services users, such as package structure and objects. This information model allows database administrators and developers to create custom repository-aware tools to analyze the structure of the DTS packages. DTS architecture is discussed later in this chapter. The type information model specifies the types of information of interest to information model creators.
- **Application Development tools**: Software application development tools are software tools for managing the process of developing, deploying, and maintaining software applications. Other tools include the services and tools used by SQL Server developers and administrators to build custom solutions to specific issues. As an example, DTS is used by these people to perform data transformation and conversions.

Microsoft Repository in Data Warehousing

The Microsoft repository can be used as a framework within which the different tools used to design and build a data warehouse can be assembled into a single data warehousing system. These tools can be created by different vendors, which allows software designers and developers to create data warehousing solutions combining the strengths of these various tools.

The tools introduced by SQL Server that are readily incorporated in this framework include the operational database system, data extraction and transformation services (DTS), OLAP services which allow for dimensional analyses of the aggregate of the historical data, and end-user tools, such as English Query and the Pivot Table.

The repository provides a shared facility that can be accessed by all of those who are developing any of the parts of the data warehousing application. This facility also expresses the inter-relationships among the various parts of the data warehousing application.

For examples on using the Microsoft Repository, you can refer to the Web site: http://msdn.microsoft.com/repository.

The OLAP Data Source

The data sources in the Microsoft OLAP and data warehousing architecture are comprised of the heterogeneous operational sources that provide the data to the data warehouse, and the services that transform data from these sources to a form that can be stored in a data warehouse, data mart, or a multidimensional cube.

This section discusses these elements in some detail starting with the operational data sources ending with the data warehouse and data cubes.

Operational Data Sources

With the Microsoft OLAP services, an operational data source is usually a relational database. However, any data source that can provide connection to its data through open database connectivity (ODBC), or through OLE DB, can be used as a source for the Microsoft OLAP system. Microsoft Data Transformation Services (DTS) can be used to transfer the data from these sources to the OLAP system.

A department store may have many stores in different cities around the country. These stores may use relational databases for their everyday activities. These databases will hold information about the customer, especially if the customer has a credit card that they obtained through the department store. The database will also store inventory information as well as information about the employees, or financial information. When a customer purchases an item from a store, the inventory table, the transactions table and the customer table will be updated.

Business rules may be put in place to trigger some actions or prevent other actions. For instance, when a new transaction is processed, the inventory table will be updated by subtracting the number of purchased items from the available inventory. The inventory of the purchased items will then be evaluated against the order threshold limits to decide whether new items should be ordered to replenish the stock.

Operational systems are designed to handle the daily operations of the on-line transaction processing system. They inherently have business rules and conducted a large number of small transactions. The following diagram shows a typical database schema.

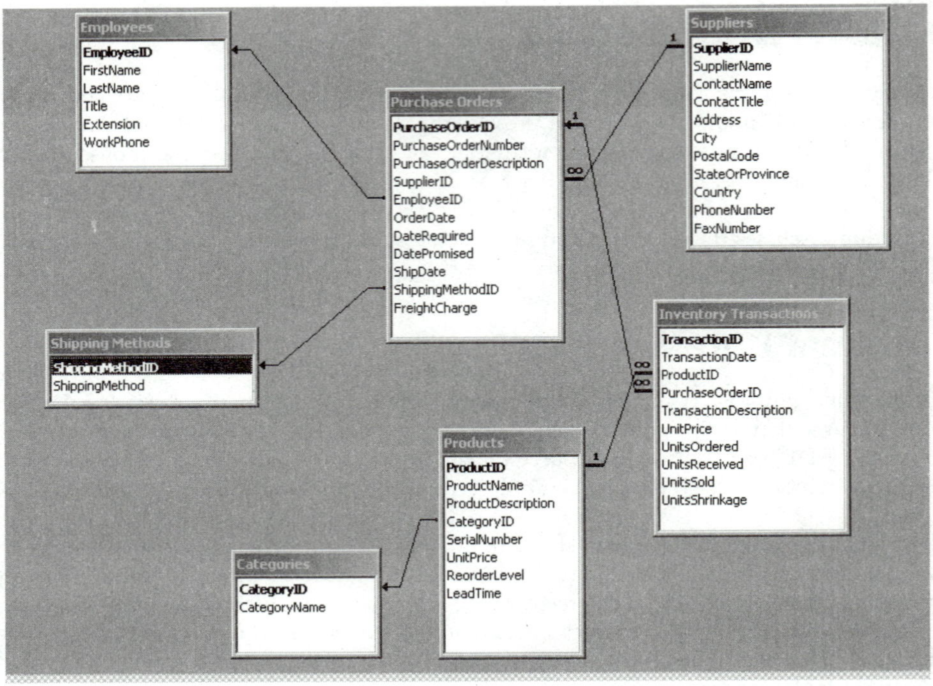

You notice in this system that the tables are highly normalized and related to one another. This leads to fragmentation of the data. A purchase order, for example, is stored over four different tables.

As the number of small transactions increases, the data volume increases to a level that could affect query performance in these systems. Therefore, the data volume should be periodically reduced to maintain the desired system performance. The data reduction is usually done through backing up and then deleting the old data, or by exporting historical data to the data warehouse and then deleting it from the local database. Data export to the data warehouse is not simply moving the old records as is to their new home, but consolidating, scrubbing and transforming the data in the process. This can all be done with the Microsoft Data Transformation Services. The reason for this transformation is that the data structure in the data warehouse is different from that in the operational system. The data warehouse data structure is optimized for query performance, rather than for transaction processing, as is the case in the operational systems. As an example of transforming data from the operational system to the data warehouse, think of timestamp fields in the operational systems, stored in a time format. It is better to transform these fields into regular datetime data types because we may never need the fine resolution of the time values when we build reports based on the data warehouse data. The smallest level we would be likely to need to go to is the day level. Also, if you are extracting data from more than one source, you may find one source saving the data for the same field that needs to be consolidated among the sources as a short date, while another source saving it as a long date. By transforming the data, all these differences will be levelled and the data will be stored in the data warehouse in a consistent manner.

Data Transformation Services

SQL Server 7's data transformation services are designed to allow for import, export, and transformation of data. A basic object, called a package, stores information on these processes and when they need to be launched. A package includes one or more tasks that are executed as steps defining a workflow process. This section outlines the architecture of the DTS package and shows the types of objects, tasks and steps that can be included in it. It also outlines the informational model of DTS and how it interacts with the metadata.

DTS Package Tasks

The following illustrates the tasks that could be found in a DTS package. These tasks include:

- Copying data from one source to another,
- Transform data using Microsoft ActiveX scripting technologies,
- Execute SQL statements at the database server,
- Run an external program that performs certain data manipulation and transformation, and
- Transfer database objects from one machine to another, given that the machines are running SQL Server 7.0.

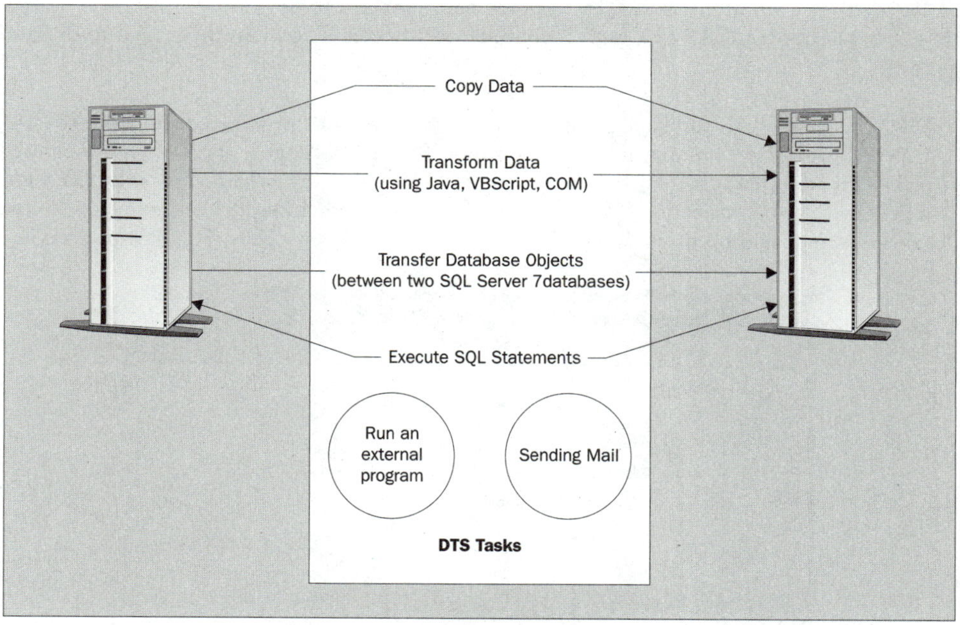

Three kinds of objects can be found in a DTS package (see following figure), a connection object, a task object, and a step object. The connection object defines an OLE DB data source that connects to a source or a destination data store. The task object includes the details of the tasks that constitute the workflow process, such as copying data, running certain SQL statements, or running certain programs, etc. Step objects define the sequence for executing the task objects. Constraints are associated with these objects that allow enforcing precedence rules on task executions. For example, an on-success constraint for task 1 will prevent task 2 from execution unless task 1 has been finished successfully.

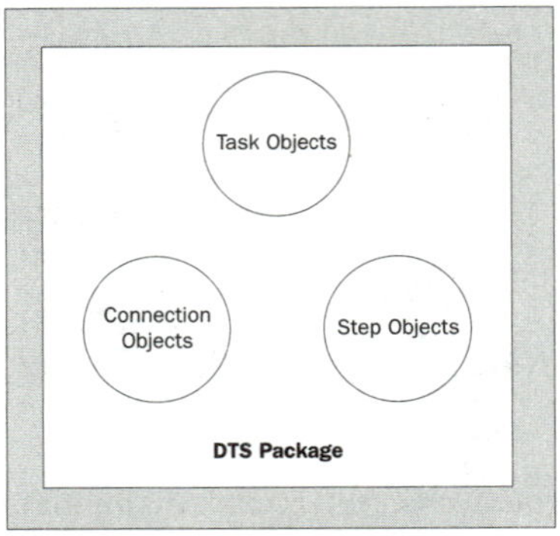

Defining DTS Package Components

You can define the components in a DTS package using several tools. These tools are installed with SQL Server, but support OLAP and building a data warehouse. The main tools used to define DTS packages are:

- DTS Designer: This tool is a graphical user interface that can be accessed from the SQL Server Enterprise Manager to create and modify DTS packages, and define the connection, tasks and steps associted with these packages. The following screen shows the DTS Designer screen with two connections, two tasks and an arrow indicating the sequence of the two steps. DTS designer will be discussed in detail in Chapter 6, Using Data Transformation Services.

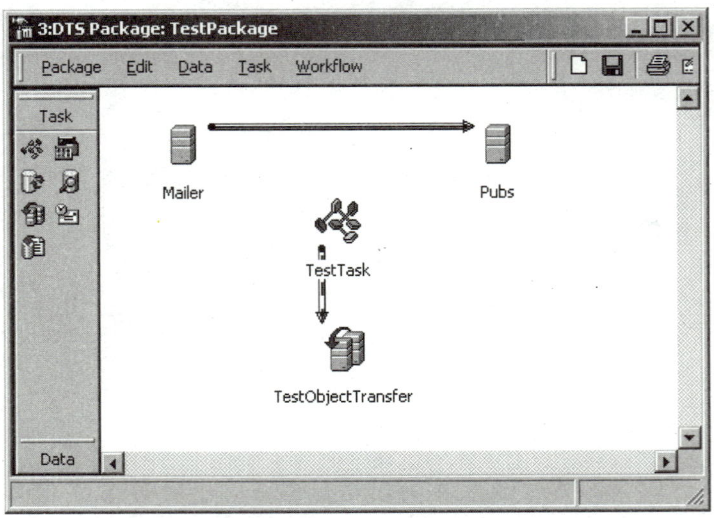

- DTS Import/Export wizard: These are sequences of screens that lead the user into creating and running DTS packages to export and import data between two OLE DB compliant data sources. The wizards allow for performing data transformation during the import/export process. These wizards can be accessed through the SQL Server Enterprise Manager, or can be run from the command line using the `dtswiz` utility. The DTS export/import wizards are discussed in more detail in Chapter 6. The figure below shows how these wizards can be accessed from the Enterprise Manager's Wizards dialog box.

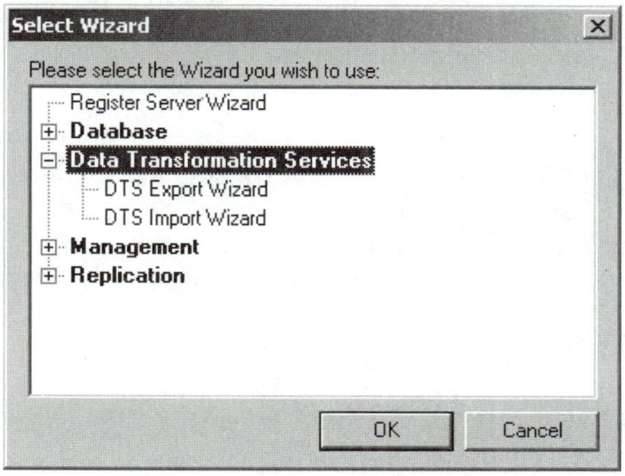

- DTS programming interface: DTS services expose a set of COM (component object model) interfaces, and provide a set of OLE automation-compliant interfaces that allow developers to create custom export/import and data transformation programs. The DTS object model includes objects, properties, methods, and collections used to write programs that copy or transform data from an OLE DB source to an OLE DB destination. DTS programs using these interfaces can range from simple Microsoft Visual Basic or Microsoft JScript scripts to complex C++ applications.

  This feature is especially important in data warehouse projects. In these projects, data transformation can become rather complex because the data has to be transformed to fit a different schema from the original operational database schema. Also, data imported into the data warehouse has to undergo aggregation and validation. With the flexibility provided by the COM interfaces, all of these requirements can be achieved.

OLE Automation and the Component Object Model (COM) are technologies that allow developers to write encapsulated re-usable code according to the object-oriented programming principles. With these technologies, developers don't have to deal with the internal complexities and data of such objects; instead, they only deal with the interfaces they exhibit. These interfaces are a set of properties, methods, and sometimes events exposed to the outside world to allow interaction and use of the objects. Numerous books, available from Wrox Press deal with these subjects covering the theories behind and practical application of these technologies.

Executing the DTS Package

After a package is defined, the information related to its definition and objects is stored in the repository as part of the DTS metadata. The package will not perform what it was intended to do until it is executed. Several tools can be used for this purpose. These tools include:

- DTS Designer GUI: you can execute the package from the DTS Designer user interface by selecting the Execute command in the Package pull-down menu.
- SQL Server Agent: you can create a scheduled job with the SQL Server Agent that executes the package when it runs.

The SQL Server Agent is a service that comes with SQL Server to allow for the scheduling of periodic activities on Microsoft SQL Server or the notification to system administrators of problems that have occurred with the server. For example, you can use this service to schedule nightly backups of the server, or execution of a DTS package that transfers data from several sources to the data warehouse or data mart. A detailed explanation on how this service can be used with DTS packages is presented in Chapter 6.

- The DTS Export and Import Wizard will also give you the choice to execute a DTS package.
- You can use the DTS Package object's `Execute` method in a custom application that uses the DTS object model.
- You can use the `dtsrun` command prompt utility.

These methods and tools are discussed in detail in Chapter 6, Microsoft Data Transformation Services.

One advantage of DTS architecture is that it implements a pass-through architecture. This will ensure that all the functionality of source and destination OLE DB data sources is available to the developer. DTS transmits all SQL statements specified in DTS tasks without changing them to the source or destination OLE DB data sources. Statements or stored procedures tested against an OLE DB provider work the same way in a package as they do from an OLE DB-based application or utility.

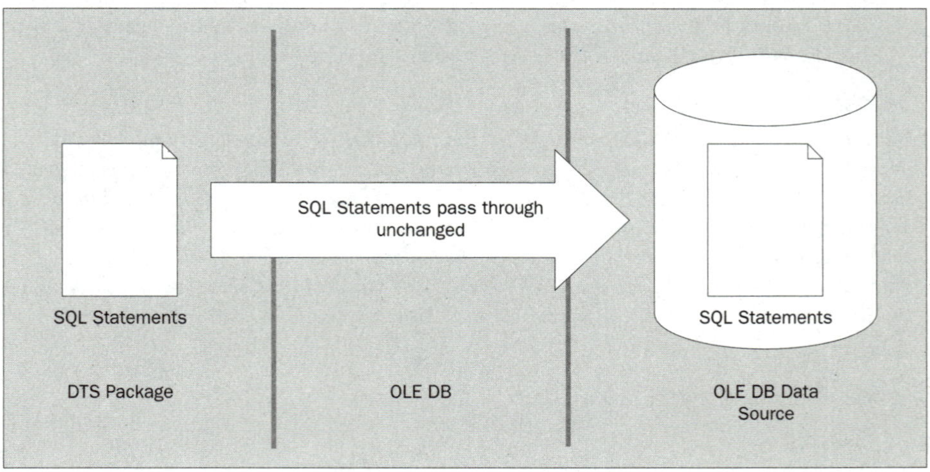

DTS Information Model

The DTS information model (DTS IM) defines what data transformations are needed, and defines their groupings into larger execution units if needed. For example, DTS IM may define that customer data has to be summarized based on certain criteria before transformation to the data warehouse can take place. DTS IM also defines the types of data accessed, the source of that data, and the mechanism by which it will be accessed and transferred.

DTS metadata may include data about the databases referenced in a DTS package, such as primary and foreign keys, column type, size, precision, scale, nullability information, and table indexes.

Because DTS IM allows for the storage of data transformation metadata in a central, well-defined location, the repository, and because many data transformations are generic, this storage allows for reusing existing transformations if the data warehouse or data marts are to be rebuilt.

DTS IM is built to be flexible allowing the sharing of data transformation information across multiple tools. This allows the use of tools from different vendors during the building and maintenance of data warehouses. The advantage of this is that if a company is using specific tools to access certain data sources, the company can still use these tools.

The OLAP Server

The OLAP manager is the engine that drives the data analysis and management in the OLAP database. As we saw in Chapter 1, in general, operational databases may not be feasibly used to generate reports based on historical data. This led to the new concepts of "flattening" the operational databases, eliminating some of the relationships among its tables, and creating databases with dimensional schemas.

This section discusses the structure of dimensional databases and the structure of the Microsoft OLAP server, including the data cubes, which are generated, based on the analysis needs.

Dimensional Databases

Although the relational database schema model allows for great flexibility in defining ways to look at and process the data in the database, in a business situation we often find that the way data is processed is different, especially by decision makers. Decision makers are not interested in the details of every single transaction recorded in the database – instead they are interested in looking at the "big" picture. For instance, instead of looking at individual customer records in the operational database, which may include data about the customer's phone, address, etc; they are interested in knowing the number of customers per quarter or at the end of each month. As an example, let's take a look at the transaction table in an operational banking database.

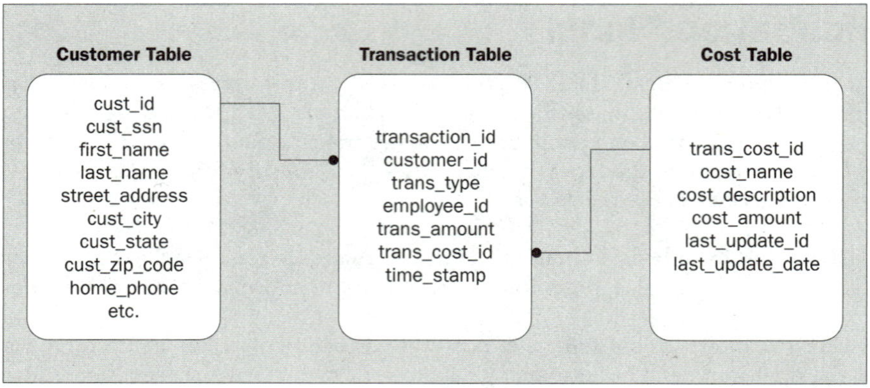

Notice how the transaction table is linked to many other tables through relationships. In the figure, only the links to the customer and cost tables are shown, however all but two fields in the transaction table are foreign keys that link to other tables. The two non-foreign key fields are `trans_amount` and `trans_type`.

As the OLTP system is used over time, the table grows in size and becomes full of transaction data, sometimes for the same customers, conducting similar transactions with different amounts and at different costs. Because of the large amount of data it holds and the versatility of the types of activities stored, the table becomes a good candidate for business analysis.

The business analyst may be interested in finding out the effect the transaction cost of ATM withdrawals had on the revenue. In this case, they would be looking for the results in a table or even graph format similar to the chart below:

Cost	Num of Trans	Revenue
$1.50	7,000	$10,500
$1.00	3,500	$3,500
$2.00	2,500	$5,000
$2.50	2,000	$5,000

To get these results, the business analyst may ask a SQL developer to write a complex query for them that could extract the data from the OLTP system and put it in the format they want. This query may look like the code presented below.

```
SELECT   cost_amount as Cost,
         Sum(transaction_id) as [Num of Trans],
         cost_amount * sum(transaction_id) as revenue
FROM     transaction, cost
WHERE    cost.trans_cost_id = transaction.trans_cost_id
AND      transaction.trans_type = 'ATM'
GROUP BY cost_amount
```

It is needless to say how time and resource-consuming it is to follow this path whenever the business analyst wants to get some summaries and aggregations of data. This is a simplified version of what could happen in the real world. In production OLTP systems, a query like this may be much larger, involving many table joins that would affect the speed at which the results get returned and affect the performance of computers used by people accessing the operational database for everyday important business transactions.

To solve this problem, a separate database would be built to represent the business facts more accurately. This database will be fed from the operational database, but after the data has been transformed to fit the new structure. This is because the schema of this database will not be relational; instead, it will be dimensional. This database can have what is called a **star** or a **snowflake schema**, or combination of both. In these schemas, a fact table is usually joined to a number of "dimension" tables. For our example, we may build a transaction table to record daily transactions of products offered by a given store. This table is referred to as the **fact table**. The transaction table includes the facts of the business activities identified by dimensions. The facts are measures of activities. In our example, transaction amount is the only measure of facts in the transaction table, just as it usually is in a typical relational database. Dimensions help put the facts in context and represent such things as time, service, customer, and location. In our example, these dimensions include time, branch, customer, and service. The following figure shows a representation of the star database schema. More details about dimensional analysis, including star and snowflake schemas, are included in Chapter 3, Dimensional Analysis and OLAP Cubes.

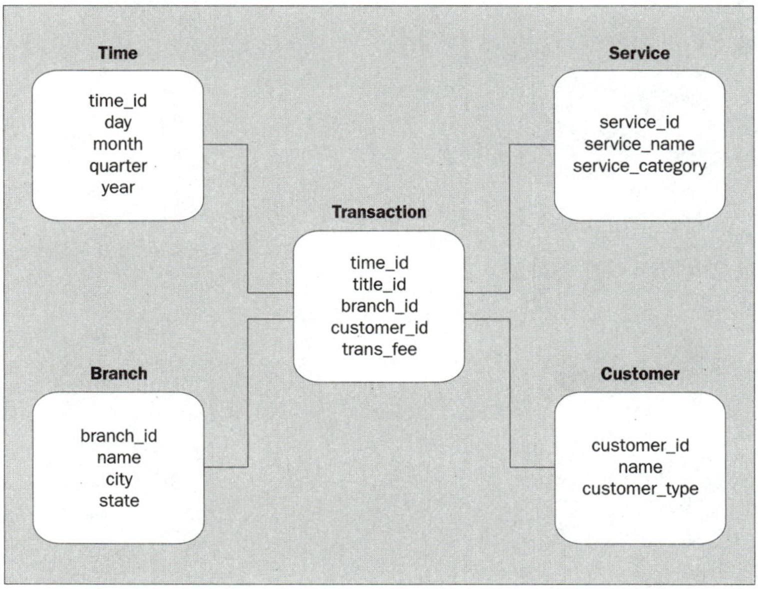

In the above diagram we notice that the fact table, sales, captures transactions on a daily level for each branch, for all customers, and for all services. This table, therefore, will grow to be very large. To improve the efficiency at which data is retrieved from the database, aggregates are pre-computed at different levels and stored in the database or in an optimized format, as we will see in later chapters.

The tables linked to the fact table are called dimensions. They are used to generate the aggregations from the fact table. For instance, you can find the total monthly transaction fees of all services to all customers by all branches when you query the transaction table grouping by month of the year. Or you can find the total transaction fees by state at all times, for all customers, and for all services when you query the sales table grouping on state. You can have aggregations on a combination of the dimensions in the sales fact table. For example, you can find the total fees for a particular service by state on a monthly bases for a certain type of customers by grouping on state and month and adding the appropriate criteria in the `WHERE` clause for the customer and book category.

Data Cubes

The previous section introduced us to the concept of dimensional databases and dimensional analysis. Let's get back to the OLAP Server architecture now. The most important part of the OLAP server architecture is the OLAP data cubes. These cubes usually represent the data in the example we saw in the previous section. The dimensions of the cube represent the dimensions of the fact table. Each cell in the cube represents a fact corresponding to a level of detail for the different dimensions of the cube. Although the graphical representation of the cube can only show three dimensions, a data cube can have up to 64 dimensions when using SQL Server's OLAP services. The following figure shows a representation of a data cube for the transaction table with the branch, service, and time dimensions shown.

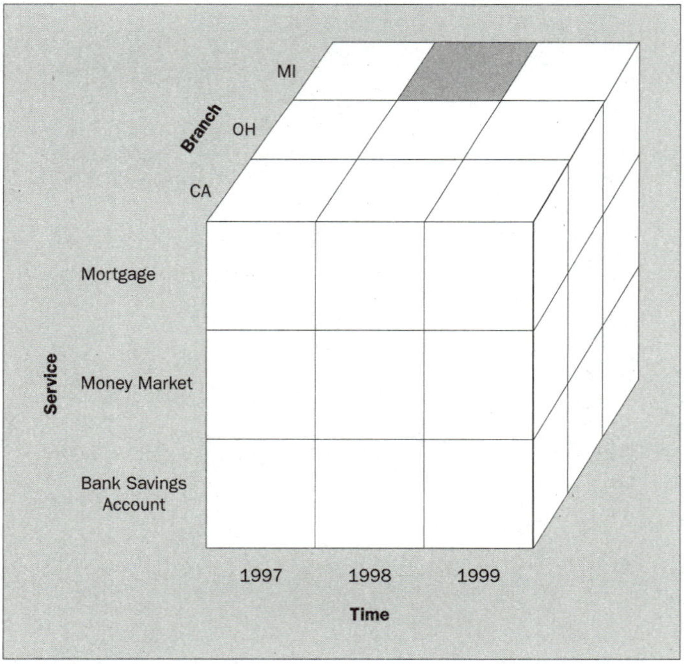

If you want to use this cube to find out the total mortgage transaction fees collected for branches in Michigan during 1998 for the mortgage service category, you need to look at the shaded cell in the figure, which is the resulting cell from the intersection of the three mentioned dimensions. That cell should contain the total fees for mortgages collected in 1998 in the state of Michigan. In other words, this value is the sum of the mortgage fee fact along these dimensions in the fact table.

The OLAP server works with the Microsoft decision support services (DSS) to allow you to build your cube from any source of data that has an OLE DB provider. This source can be a relational database in any database management system that has an ODBC driver, such as Oracle or Sybase SQL Server, or has a native OLE DB provider, such as SQL Server, or MS Access. The data source for the cube can also be a dimensional database, text files, LDAP data source, etc.

Cube Partitions

Partitions represent logical divisions of cube data broken down by the values of a particular dimension or the data source. For example, you can have a partition on the transaction cube based on the state values creating partitions for regions like Midwest, Northeast, etc. Alternatively, you may want to create a partition that stores transaction data based on a three-year basis.

A partition can be saved separately on a different disk drive from the original cube. This allows you to place data that is not used or queried frequently on slower storage media. A detailed description of partitions is presented in Chapter 3.

Virtual Cubes

As I mentioned in the previous section, OLAP data cubes are comprised of dimensions and measures. One feature of the OLAP server is that it allows linking two or more OLAP cubes that share common dimensions. This process creates the virtual cubes. An example of shared dimension is time. The time dimension can be used, like we saw in the previous example, for the transaction cube, or it can also be used for an employee cube, and so on.

Virtual cubes take advantage of the shared dimensions to create links among data sets that seem unrelated. Virtual cubes require no additional storage needs, and can link cubes based on different storage types. For instance, you can create a virtual cube that links the employee and transaction cubes, even if the employee cube is stored in the relational database and the transaction cube in the multi-dimensional database.

With the virtual cube proposed above, bank managers and decision makers can establish the relationship between the average number of bank teller, or mortgage officers in a branch and the total revenue of the branch related to their services. This information will give these managers insight into this complex relationship and help them decide the optimal average number of employees for a particular service per branch. It is worth warning that going over board with these relationships may be counterproductive. Many of the relationships established may make no sense and have no value. e.g. the number of ATM transactions and the number of cheque books ordered. The validity of these relationships is closely associated with the quality of the raw data that supports them.

OLAP Storage Types

Three options of storage are supported by the OLAP server and the decision support services that ship with SQL Server 7.0 based on the data cube storage method. These options are, multi-dimensional OLAP (MOLAP), relational OLAP (ROLAP), and a hybrid of the previous two options (HOLAP). Each of these options provides certain benefits, depending on the size of your database and how the data will be used. These options are discussed in the following sections:

MOLAP

MOLAP is a high performance, multidimensional data storage format.The data supporting the cubes is stored with this option on the OLAP server as a multi-dimensional database. MOLAP gives the best query performance, because it is specifically optimized for multidimensional data queries. Performance gains stem from the fact that the fact tables are compressed with this option and bitmap indexing is used for them.

Since MOLAP requires copying all the data converting its format appropriately to fit the multi-dimensional data store, MOLAP is appropriate for small to medium-sized data sets. Copying all of the data for such data sets would not require significant loading time or utilize large amounts of disk space.

ROLAP

Relational OLAP storage keeps the data that feeds the cubes in the original relational tables. A separate set of relational tables is used to store and reference aggregation data in this OLTP system. These tables are not downloaded to the DSS server. The tables that hold the aggregations of the data are called materialized views. These tables store data aggregations as defined by the dimensions when the cube is created.

With this option, aggregation tables have fields for each dimension and measure. Each dimension column is indexed. A composite index is also created for all of the dimension fields. Due to its nature, ROLAP is ideal for large databases or legacy data that is infrequently queried. The only drawback to these systems is that generating reports from them or processing the cube data may affect users of the operational database reducing performance of their transaction processing.

HOLAP

A combination of MOLAP and ROLAP is also supported by the DSS server. This combination is referred to as HOLAP. With HOLAP, the original data is kept in its relational database tables similar to ROLAP. Aggregations of the data are performed and stored in a multidimensional format. An advantage of this system is that HOLAP provides connectivity to large data sets in relational tables, while taking advantage of the faster performance of the multidimensional aggregation storage. A disadvantage of this option is that the amount of processing between the ROLAP and MOLAP systems may affect its efficiency.

OLAP Client Architecture

The following figure shows a schematic of the client architecture of the Microsoft OLAP Services. The heart of the client architecture is the Pivot Table service. Pivot Table service interacts with the OLAP server and provides COM-based interfaces for use by client applications accessing OLAP data on the server. Depending on the language the client applications are written in, these applications connect to Pivot Table Service using OLE DB 2.0 with the optional OLAP support extensions, or Microsoft ActiveX Data Objects (ADO 2.x) with the OLAP extensions too.

The Pivot Table service is an in-process desktop version on the OLAP server. This service is designed to provide online and offline data analysis and online access to OLAP data. The Pivot Table Service functions as a client of OLAP Services. In other words, this allows the Pivot Table service to access OLAP data on-line, perform analyses on the data, including building data cubes, perform some cache management for off-line analyses, and conduct off-line analyses of cached data on the client. In addition to this functionality, the Pivot Table service provides COM interfaces to other client applications to access the OLAP server, the OLAP data, and the client cache.

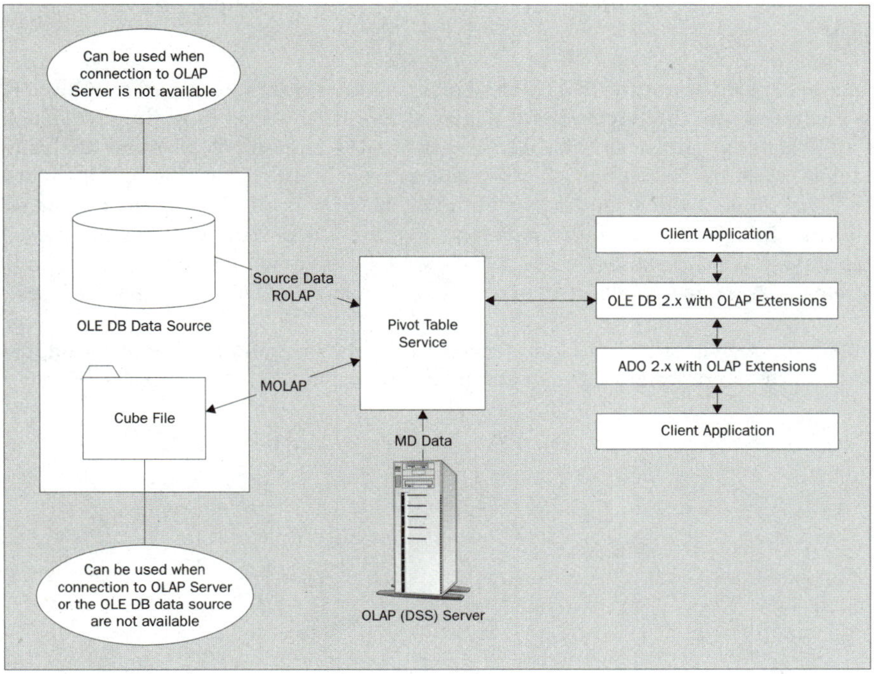

In a nutshell, the PivotTable Service serves the following functions:

- Serves as a shared connection point to the OLAP server for all of the client applications, for both on-line and off-line analyses.
- Allows for building data cubes using relational data by functioning as a service provider to implement multidimensional functionality and expose the OLE DB interfaces with OLAP extensions.
- Serves as a tabular data provider by supporting a subset of SQL. This allows the presentation of the data returned from the SQL statement as a pivot table.
- Supports multidimensional expressions (MDX), which makes it a multi-dimensional data provider. MDX is the structured query language used for Microsoft OLAP data. It allows access to data cubes, their dimensions, etc. from SQL statements.
- Enables client applications to create a local cube directly from a relational data source.
- Allows users to download data from data sources and store the data in a multidimensional structure on a local computer for offline analysis.

As you will see in Chapter 9, the Pivot Table service can work only with one cube. Performance of this service is directly related to the amount of data it manages because it does not implement an internal aggregation management system for defining or storing data aggregations.

You can build your own applications that use the Pivot Service to access OLAP data, or you can use Microsoft or third party applications that already support this service for access to multi-dimensional OLAP data. Microsoft Excel and Microsoft Access (Office 2000) support the Pivot Table service and can use it to connect to an OLAP server to retrieve and analyze data, and to create and use local cube files.

Summary

In this chapter, we talked about the Microsoft OLAP and data warehousing architecture. This architecture is divided into three main parts, source data, OLAP server, and the Pivot Table service used with OLAP client applications. The OLAP server is the main mechanism for analyzing multi-dimensional data, creating data cubes, building data aggregations, connecting to the client and data sources. The Pivot Table is the essential part of the client architecture having the unique and important feature of allowing both on-line and off-line analyses of the OLAP data. Off-line analyses are possible thanks to this service's cache management that allows users to download data from the multi-dimensional data sources and use it off-line to build a data cube or conduct other analyses.

In the next chapter, we will talk about the lifecycle of the data warehousing application, from the requirement gathering and design to the deployment phases.

3

Dimensional Modeling – OLAP Cubes

The previous chapter outlined the Microsoft OLAP and Data Warehousing architecture. The main component of the Microsoft OLAP architecture is the OLAP server. The OLAP server's main architectural element is the OLAP cube. These cubes are built as a result of dimensional analysis and modeling of the data available through business activities over a long period of time. OLAP applications are designed around building these cubes and analyzing their data. Therefore, it is important to understand these structures before you can proceed to the next topics.

The topics covered in this chapter include:

- Representing hierarchies in the Microsoft OLAP services
- Cube Dimensions
- Dimension members and their properties
- Calculated members
- Cube measures
- Virtual cubes
- Representing cube elements in the OLAP database schema

Hierarchical Structures

When dealing with data, many relationships can be established between different data elements. One type of relationship is very common in business applications. This type is hierarchical structures. The following figure shows how an employee in an organization XYZ belongs to a hierarchy that starts with the employee level at the bottom, and ends up with the company level at the top. In this hierarchy, employees belong to departments. A number of departments, such as Human Resource, Sales and Engineering, belong to a regional office. Many regional offices belong to a division, such as Europe versus North America divisions. These divisions collectively form the company. Understanding these hierarchies is essential when designing a data warehousing solution. These hierarchies describe relationships among business entities, which are essential in defining the cube dimension levels, as you will see later in the chapter.

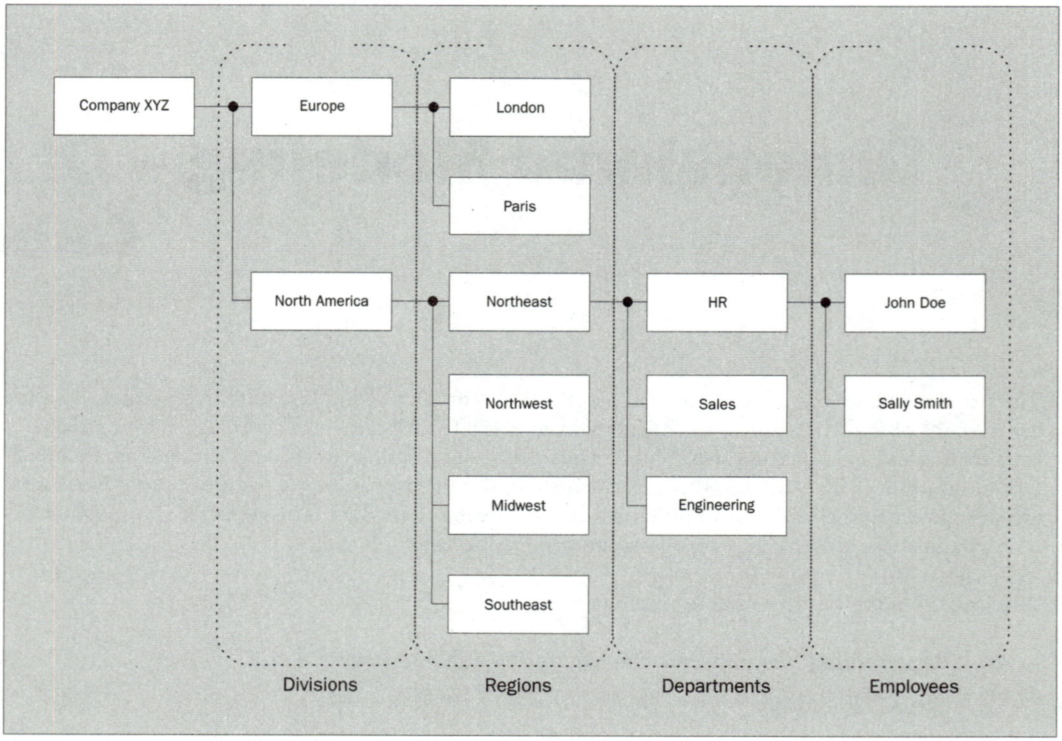

A representation of a simple hierarchy

Several forms of hierarchies can be identified. Some are regular and some irregular. The following figure illustrates some of these forms. In diagrams (a) and (b) on the next page, the hierarchies are regular. Notice that every parent has the same number of children on the same level. Also notice that even though the top levels in (b) have no parent entities, they are still treated as siblings. Diagram (c) shows an example of an irregular hierarchy.

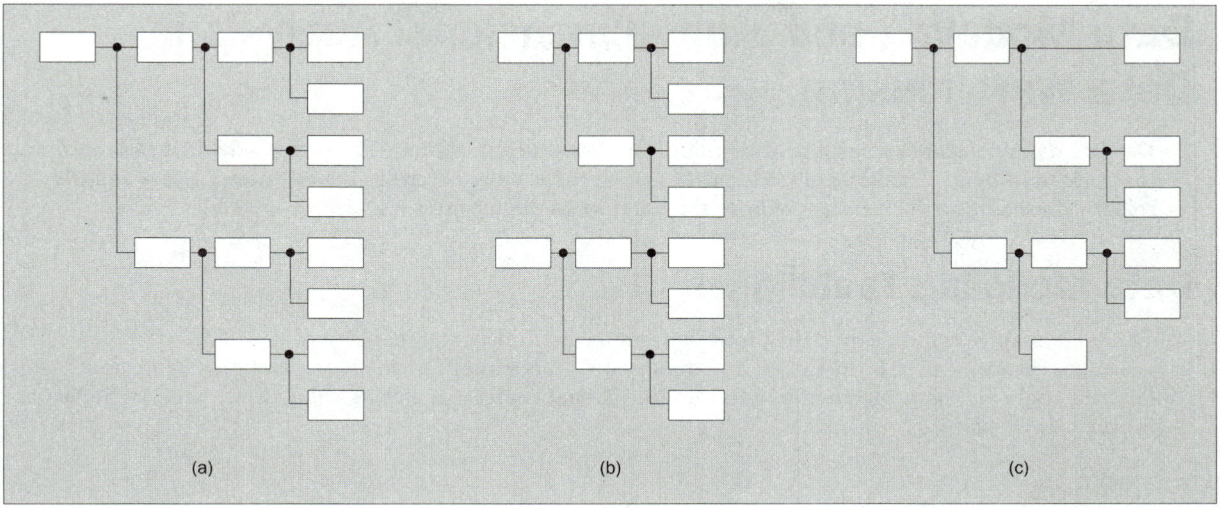

Some hierarchies are regular, and some are not.

The degree of irregularity of a hierarchy is an indication of the level of its complexity. The more complex hierarchies are, the more irregular they will be. No matter how irregular a hierarchy is, there are always three levels that define it. These levels are the root, the middle, and the leaf levels. Let's take as an example the simple hierarchy shown in the first figure shown; the root level is the company XYZ level. All other levels start with this parent entity. The leaf level of the hierarchy is the farthest level from the root. In our example, it represents the individual employees of the company. All the levels between the root and the leaf levels are called the middle levels of the hierarchy. The following figure shows a generic representation of the structure of the levels of a hierarchy.

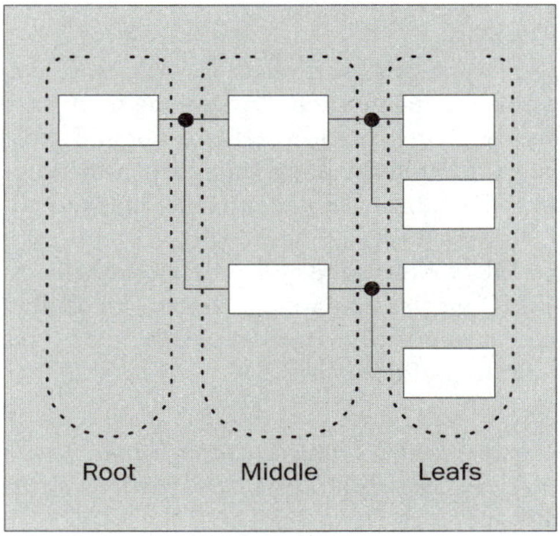

The structure of the hierarchy

Now that you have a basic understanding of hierarchies, you will be able to see how they are utilized in the Microsoft OLAP architecture.

Data Modeling and Multi-dimensional Analysis in Data Warehousing

Data modeling is an essential step in building any database application. The data model is the blueprint that is used to build and create the database. The model usually describes the business process and the relationships among the different entities that interact in the business world.

Data Modeling Techniques

There are mainly two data modeling techniques relevant to data warehousing design. These techniques are entity relationship (ER) modeling and dimensional modeling. The following sections define and describe these techniques with emphasis on dimensional analysis, which as you will see later, is the basis for the OLAP cubes.

ER Models

The ER model is an abstraction tool because it can be used to understand and simplify the ambiguous data relationships in the business world and complex systems environments. ER modeling is based on two basic concepts: **entities**, and the **relationships** between those entities. ER models are used to produce a data model for the specific area of interest. The next figure shows a representation of a typical ER diagram.

An entity represents real world objects that can be observed and classified by their properties and characteristics. An entity has its own business definition and a clear boundary definition that is required to describe what is included and what is not. In the detailed ER model, it is critical to find out the unique identifier of an entity. These unique identifiers are called **candidate keys**. Candidate keys are used to select the key that is most commonly used to identify the entity. This key is usually referred to as the primary key.

Attributes are defined as part of the entities and relations. Attributes describe the characteristics of properties of the entities. An attribute name should be unique in an entity and should be self-explanatory. For example, simply saying field1 or field2 is not allowed, we must clearly define each attribute with a descriptive name. Simply speaking, an entity in the logical model maps to a database table in the physical model of the database, and an attribute maps to a table column.

Another important concept in ER models is the concept of a domain. A domain consists of all the possible acceptable values and categories that are allowed for an attribute. Simply, a domain is just the whole set of the real possible occurrences. As an example, the data type, such as integer, date, and character, provides a clear definition of domain.

An attribute is said to be a primary key if it uniquely identifies the record in the table and cannot be null. A primary key can be composed of one attribute, or multiple attributes. In the latter case, it is called a composite primary key.

A foreign key in a table identifies the relationship between the entity represented by the table and the entity that has the same attribute as its primary key. Foreign keys allow the storage of information in related tables eliminating the need of repeating groups of columns in the main table.

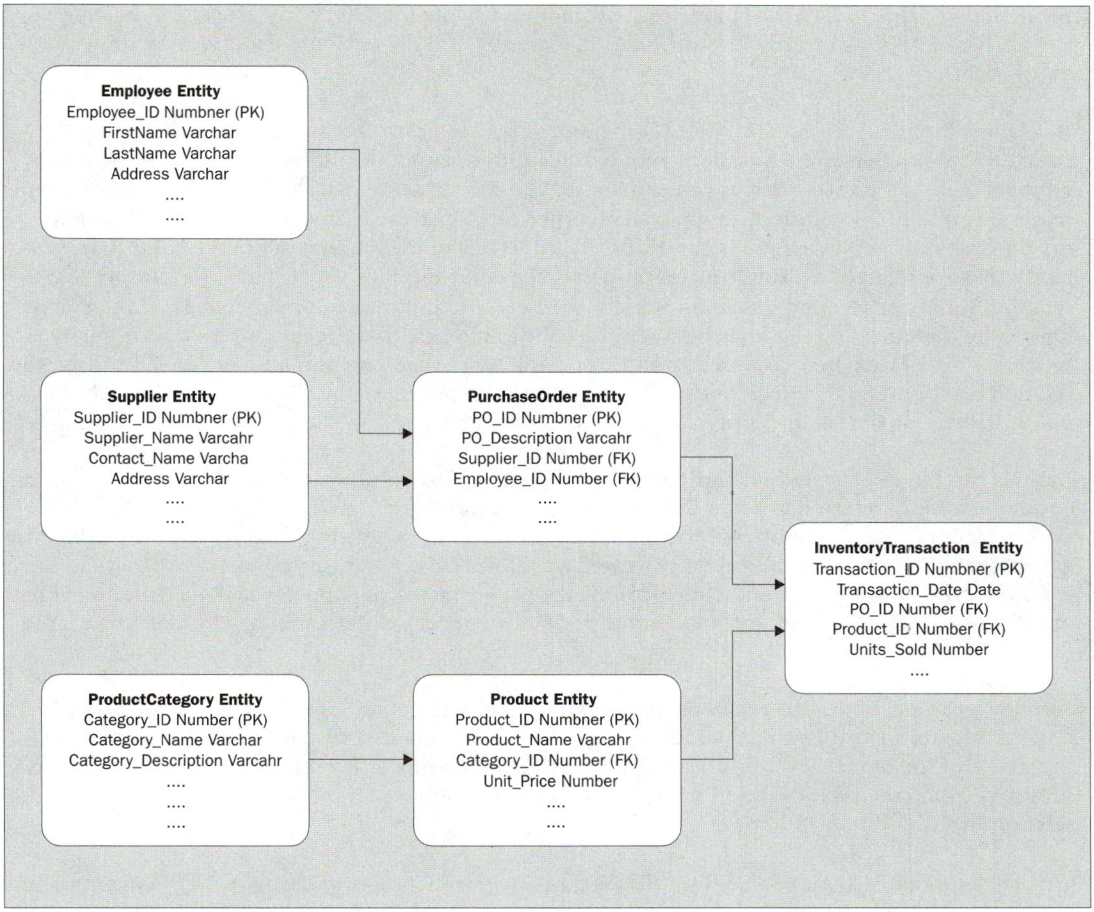

An example of an Entity Relationship (ER) Model

The above diagram depicts a typical inventory control system. It shows several entities and the relationships between these entities. For example it, is obvious from the diagram, that the inventory transaction entity is directly related to the purchase order and the product entities. The relationship is expressed in terms of the shared attributes between the two entities that participate in the relationship. For example, the relationship between inventory transaction and products is expressed in terms of the attribute `product_id`, which serves as a primary key in the product entity and a foreign key in the inventory transaction entity.

ER modeling is a vast subject and we do not intend to cover it in too much detail in this book. Many relational database design and data modeling books discuss this topic in great detail. I found the following two books to be excellent in handling database models in general, including ER Models: "The Data Modeling Handbook: A Best Practice Approach to Building Quality Data Models" by Gregory W. William, and published by John Wiley & Sons, Inc.; and "Database Modeling & Design" by Toby Teory, published by Morgan Kaufmann.

As an added value to database modeling, ER-models usually identify many aspects of the database design. These aspects include key attributes in an entity and the attribute data types as shown in the above figure.

A relationship is represented in the ER diagram with lines drawn between entities. It depicts the structural interaction and association among the entities in a model. A relationship is designated grammatically by a verb, such as owns, belongs, and has. In our example, we can say that an employee wrote several purchase orders, or a purchase order can cause many inventory transactions. The relationship between two entities can be defined in terms of the maximum number of instances of one entity that are related to a single instance in another table and vice versa. Thus, we can say that a relationship is one-to-one (1:1), one-to-many (1:M or 1:∞), and many-to-many (M:M). In the above figure, the directions on the lines between the entities indicate the direction of the one-to-many relationships. For example, an employee can handle more than one purchase order. Therefore, the relationship between the employee entity and the purchase order entity is one-to-many with the arrow pointing towards the "many" side, the purchase orders entity.

Entities can have subtypes and supertypes. The relationships between a supertype entity and its subtype entities is usually referred to as an ISA relationship. An ISA relationship defines one entity as a generalization of several more specialized ones. For instance, a beverage category for a product can be a generalization for a soft drink category as well as coffee and tea category; thus we say that the beverage is a supertype of soft drinks and coffee/tea drinks. Supertypes and subtypes make a data model more expressive of the real world and enable the model to support the database development in a more flexible manner.

Another example of an ISA relationship is students entity (category) on one hand and graduate, undergraduate, special learning students categories on the other hand. The student category is a supertype of the other three. It is also said that if a subtype (lower level category or entity) has only one supertype, then the relationship is a hierarchy. If a subtype has more than one supertypes, then the relationship is said to be a lattice.

One concept that is avoided in ER models for on-line transaction processing (OLTP) systems is the concept of **derived attributes**. This concept is widely utilized when building ER models for a data warehouse. Data warehouse models tend to include more derived attributes explicitly in the model. As a matter of fact, all summarized attributes in the data warehouse are derived, because the data warehouse collects and consolidates data from source databases. As a consequence, the metadata should contain all of these derivation policies explicitly and users should have access to it. As an example of a derived attribute, total sales may be derived from units sold and unit cost attributes. This derived attribute will be derived at a certain frequency if it were to be aggregated or summarized. For instance, weekly sales should be aggregated on a weekly basis, and so on.

Dimensional Modeling

Dimensional modeling is a technique for conceptualizing and visualizing data models as a set of measures that are described by common aspects of the business. It is especially useful for summarizing and rearranging the data and presenting views of the data to support data analysis. Dimensional modeling focuses on numeric data, such as values, counts, weights, balances, and occurrences. In data warehousing, dimensional modeling is simpler, more expressive, and easier to understand than ER modeling. ER modeling, however, has been around much longer and is more established. More research is still needed in the area of dimensional modeling, which has only been around for a decade or so.

Dimensional modeling uses three basic concepts: **measures**, **facts**, and **dimensions**. These concepts serve in the Microsoft OLAP services as the basic components of the cube structures. Data cubes and dimensional modeling are powerful in representing the requirements of the business user in the context of database tables.

The following are definitions of the main concepts in dimensional data modeling.

Fact

A fact is a collection of related data items, consisting of measures and context data. Each fact typically represents a business item, a business transaction, or an event that can be used in analyzing the business or business processes. When you want to view the sales of the company by store by quarter, you usually look at the total revenue and net profits. These are the facts you are interested in. In the Microsoft OLAP services, facts are implemented in the core tables of the OLAP database in which all of the numeric data is stored. These tables are referred to as the fact tables, and are usually derived from the raw data in the operational database systems.

Dimension

A dimension is a collection of properties along which we conduct our analysis of the facts. Dimensions allow us to view the fact in different contexts. For instance, the total sales can be viewed in terms of store, city, or region. These three levels are members of the geographical dimension of the sales process. In a dimensional model, every data point in the fact table is associated with one and only one member from each of the multiple dimensions. This becomes clear if you look at the following figure, where the cell that has a measure value of 400 corresponds to a unique set of dimensions: Q3 (3rd quarter), Pita Bread, and Detroit. Many analytical processes are used to quantify the impact of dimensions on the facts. To clarify the relationship between the facts and the dimensions, think of a record in the fact table. The record has many links to the dimension tables. These links identify the record as unique. Keep this in mind and don't worry if you cannot visualize it yet. This will all make sense as you read on about the OLAP cubes later in the chapter.

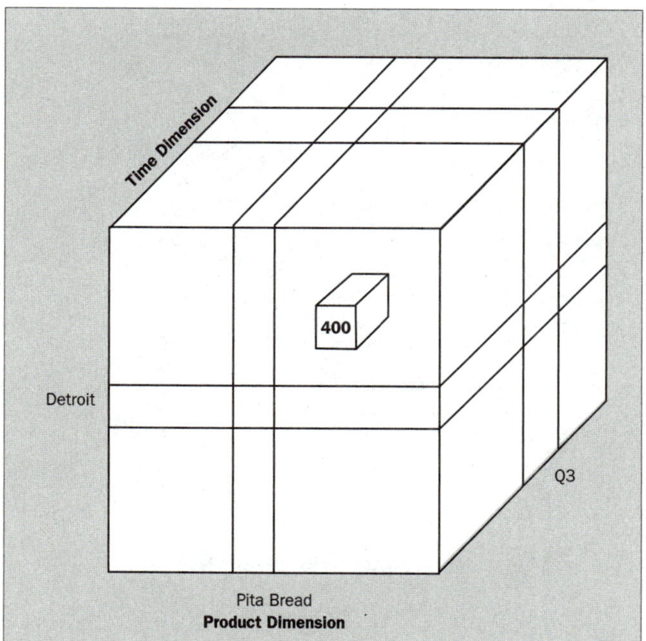

Common dimensions used in sales-related data warehouses include:

- Time
- Geography
- Customer
- Salesperson
- Scenarios such as actual, budgeted, or estimated numbers

Dimension Members: Take the time dimension as an example. The dimension consists of several levels, such as day, week, month, quarter, and year. Each one of these levels consists of members. For example, the members of the day level would be Monday, Tuesday, etc., or Day1, Day2, ... Day7. As for the month dimension, the members would be January, February, etc. or Month1, Month2, ... Month12. Therefore, you may assume that a dimension contains many dimension members organized in levels inside the dimension. When you combine these concepts with the fact table records, you find that the dimension member determines the position in the dimension with which a certain record in the fact table is associated.

Dimension Hierarchies: We can arrange the members of a dimension into one or more hierarchies. Each hierarchy can also have multiple hierarchy levels. A member of a dimension may be located on more than one hierarchy structure. An example to consider is the time dimension hierarchy as shown in the following figure. Two hierarchies are defined in the figure for the time dimension because the week member does not follow the first hierarchy. If data is to be aggregated on a weekly basis, the second hierarchy has to be used. This is because a week can span two months. Thus, the time dimension is a good example of multiple hierarchies of a dimension.

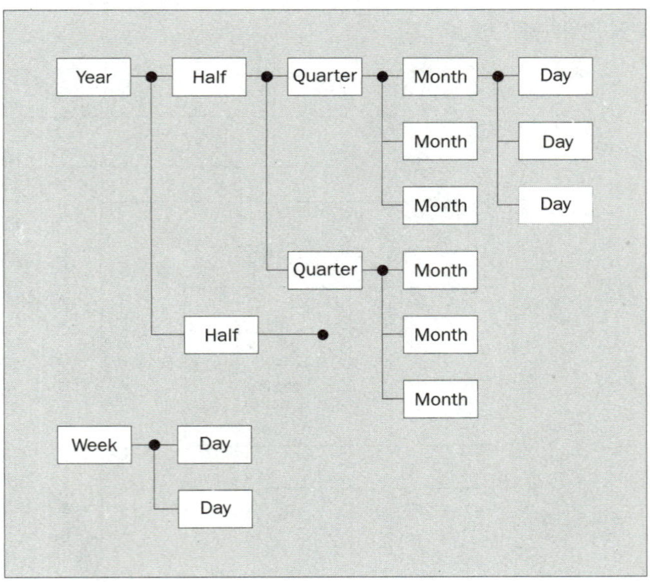

Time dimension hierarchies

Measure: A measure is a numeric attribute of a fact, representing the performance or behavior of the business relative to the dimensions. The actual numbers are called as variables. For example, measures are the sales in money, the sales volume, the quantity supplied, the supply cost, the transaction amount, and so forth. A measure is determined by combinations of the members of the dimensions it is associated with and is located in the fact table of the OLAP database.

Importance of Data Modeling

Data modeling is an important step in the building of a data warehouse because modeling gives us the ability to visualize systems before they are built. After all, a model is an abstraction and reflection of the real world. The goal is to make this reflection as close to the real-life situation and relationships between the different business elements that it describes. This will make the data model more useful, and the database that is built based on the model will be more stable and efficient.

The data model plays the role of a guideline, or plan, to implement the data warehouse. Traditionally, ER modeling has primarily focused on eliminating data redundancy and keeping consistency among the different data sources and applications. Consolidating the data models of each business area before the real implementation can help assure that the result will be an effective data warehouse and can help reduce the cost of implementation.

Data Cubes

One effective way to visualize the data model and the dimensional hierarchies and facts is to build a cube. The dimensions of the cube will be the dimensions of the fact table. We can represent a three-dimensional model using a cube. Usually a dimensional model consists of more than three dimensions, and is referred to as a hypercube. However, a hypercube is difficult to visualize, so a cube is the more commonly used term. In the following figure, the measurement is the volume of sales in hundreds of units for a chain of auto dealerships. This measurement is determined by the combination of three dimensions: geography, product, and time. The geography dimension and product dimension have their own two levels of hierarchy. For example, the geography dimension has the region level and state, while the product has the levels of make and model.

The time dimension shows the time levels down to the quarter level. Assuming that the data presented is for 1999, the cube will help us read that this chain of dealership sold 1700 Taurus vehicles in Wisconsin in the first quarter, and 1800 Mercury Sable vehicles in New Jersey for the same quarter. In other words, the cube is a great tool to visualize the data summaries and aggregations in a most useful way.

If you are thinking to yourself that this is not an ideal way to represent data to end-users, don't worry. The cube representation in the following figure is only meant for visualization purposes. It is the simplest form possible, with only three dimensions. If we had more than three dimensions, we probably would have trouble trying to represent the cube in that figure. Actually, cube data is represented in tabular forms with multiple column and row headings that correspond to the cube dimensions as you will see later.

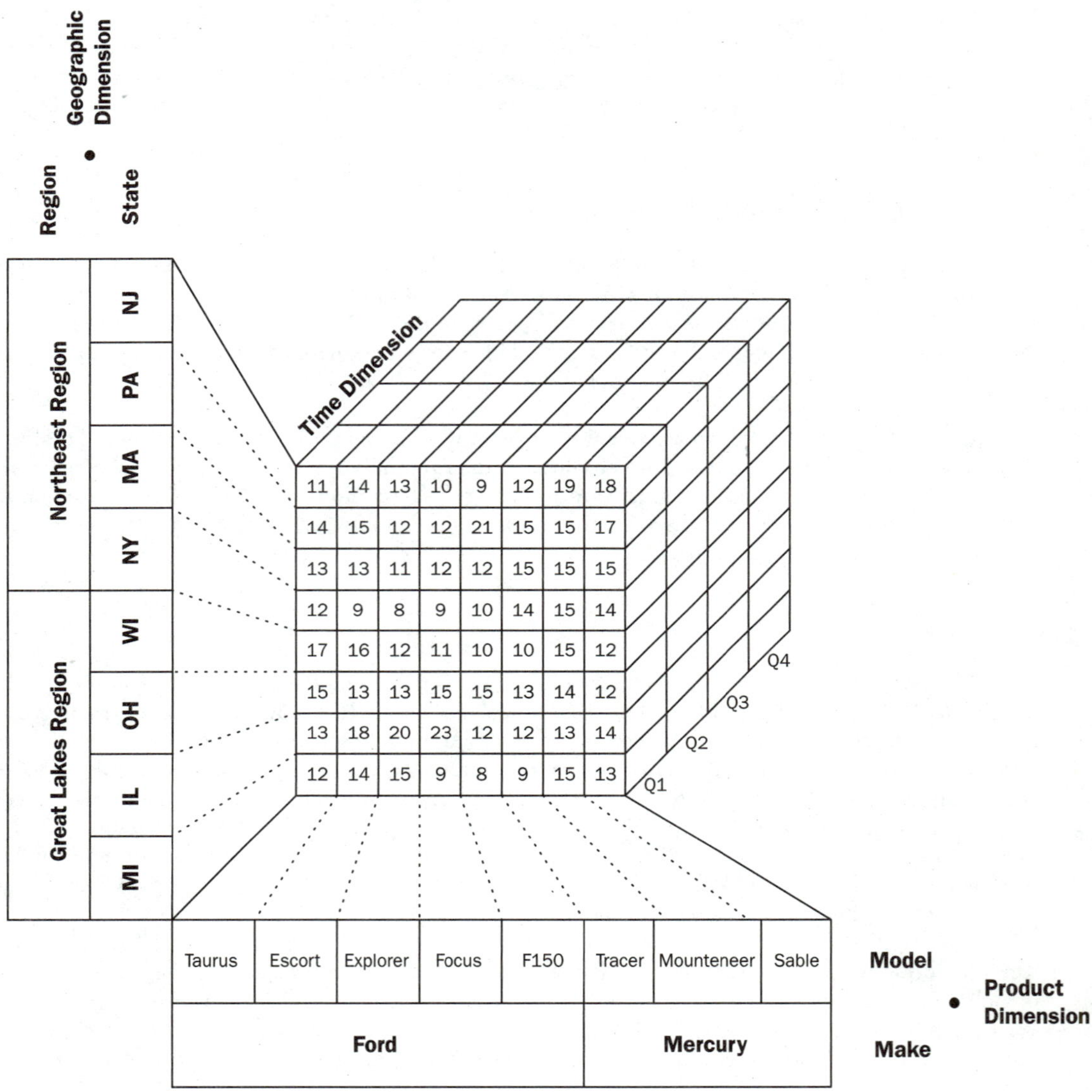

The data cube, a representation of the dimensional model

OLAP Operations

Data modelers use dimensional modeling to primarily support on-line analytical processing (OLAP) and decision-making. Data analysis in OLAP services involves four main operations: drill-down, roll-up, slicing, and dicing. These operations are decided based on the granularity of the data at hand and the dimensions used in the analysis. Granularity determines drill-down and roll-up operations. Dimension browsing determines slice and dice operations.

Data granularity actually depends on which level you are at in a dimension. For instance, if you are looking at sales facts for the months of 1998, your facts are more granular than if you were looking at them for the quarters of 1998. In other words, you will be looking at more data points (granules) when you look at a lower level than when you look at a higher one.

Drill-Down and Roll-Up

Drill-down and roll up are the operations for moving the view down and up along the dimensional hierarchy levels. Drilling down leads to higher levels of detail, while roll-up leads to the opposite. These two operations are analogous to zooming in and out of the data view along the dimension hierarchies. These hierarchies determine the navigation path. The following table explains the meaning of these two operations:

	Quarter	**Ford**	**Mercury**
ABC - Autos	Q1 - 1998	120	89
	Q2 - 1998	123	91
	Q3 - 1998	101	75
	Q4 - 1998	99	73
Roll Up ↑ Drill-Down ↓			
	Month	**Ford**	**Mercury**
ABC - Autos	Oct- 1998	40	31
	Nov - 1998	35	29
	Dec - 1998	24	13

Illustration of Drill-down and Rollup operations.

The measurement in this case is the number of cars sold at a dealership. It was noticed that the number of sales in the fourth quarter had declined at the particular dealership. Drilling down into the data for the fourth quarter along the time dimension reveals that the sales for December, in particular, were pushing the downward trend, and that this was perfectly natural due to the extended holidays during that month which affects the overall results for the fourth quarter.

Slicing and Dicing

These two types of OLAP operations are used to focus the view of the data along some dimension. With slicing, the cube is cut-off along one dimension to focus on a specific perspective. With dicing, the slice is rotated to take place along a different dimension. As an example, the table below shows the same auto dealership chain sales cube.

1998 Sales		Ford		Mercury	
	Quarter	Escort	Taurus	Tracer	Sable
Midwest	Detroit	21	39	13	33
	Cleveland	19	40	9	35
Northeast	Philadelphia	8	26	3	19
	New Jersey	9	19	5	12

1998 Sales		1998 Ford and Mercury			
	Quarter	Q1	Q2	Q3	Q4
Midwest	Detroit	119	134	128	110
	Cleveland	104	124	120	101
Northeast	Philadelphia	99	110	109	89
	New Jersey	65	79	78	69

1998 Sales		1998 Ford Only			
	Quarter	Q1	Q2	Q3	Q4
Midwest	Detroit	73	80	73	70
	Cleveland	65	79	79	59
Northeast	Philadelphia	33	59	49	38
	New Jersey	36	45	49	38

Example of slicing and dicing the data cube

In the above tables, the data for our dealership chain is presented along three dimensions, geographic location, time, and product (automobile). The first view shows a slice of the data cube focusing on auto sales for specific Ford and Mercury models in four major cities in the Midwest and Northeast regions for the 1998 fiscal year. Dicing means rotating the view along a different dimension. This is shown in the next pane of data. Time now becomes the main dimension along which data is summarized and presented. Finally, the third pane shows a good example on slicing the data cube where the view in the middle pane is sliced across the auto make to focus only on sales of the Ford division.

The four OLAP operations described above are extremely important in dimensional analysis of data warehouses. However, in order to be able to conduct such operations, a special kind of database schema has to be used. This schema is often referred to as the **Star** schema. The following section will introduce you to this concept and to some extensions that were added to it later, namely, the **Snowflake** and the **Constellation** models.

OLAP Database Schema

Two main schemas are used with OLAP databases, star and snowflake schemas. A third model, the constellation model is also used but it is actually only a multiple star schemas. This section will discuss in detail the theoretical background of these two types of schemas and explain when and where each can be used.

Star Schema

Looking at the model we have discussed so far in this chapter, the dealership chain model, we see that we mainly have three dimensions of the data in the model. These dimensions are geographic location, time, and automobile. The fact table, which includes the measures, such as sales, inventory, number of customers, etc. also includes foreign keys that point to the dimensions in the dimension table. The collection of the fact table and the dimensions linked to it are usually referred to as the star schema.

The classic star schema is characterized by the following:

- A single fact table containing a compound primary key, with one segment for each dimension, and additional columns of additive, numeric facts.
- A single dimension table for each dimension with a generated key, and a level indicator that describes the attribute level of each record. For example, if the dimension is VEHICLE, records in the dimension table might refer to MAKE (Ford, Mercury), MODEL (Taurus, Crown Victoria), MODEL YEAR (1999, 2000), etc. We might assign a level number to these (such as 1=make, 2=model, 3=model_year) and put that value in the "level" column.
- The single fact table will contain detail (or "atomic") data, such as sales dollars, for a given dealership, for a given model, in a given time period.
- The fact table may also contain partially consolidated data, such as sales dollars for a region, for a given make/model for a given time period.

> **You need to be extra careful when building aggregations for your fact table. For example, in the auto dealership OLAP system, if data is consolidated only to the model level, a query for Vehicle Make information will bring back no records and, hence, report no sales activity. In other words, in general, aggregations that are not pre-calculated will not be returned when you query for them. For this reason, simple star schemas MUST contain either ALL of the combinations of aggregated data or at least views of every combination. Of course, Microsoft OLAP Services compensates for aggregations that are not pre-calculated by calculating them at runtime, which affects performance compared to having them pre-calculated.**

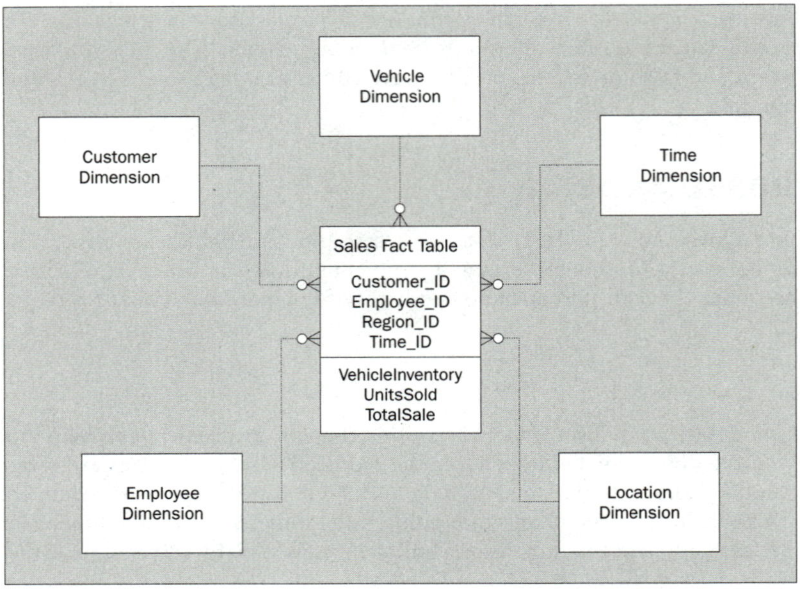

The simple Star Schema

In the star schema, the level indicator is needed in the dimension table whenever aggregates are stored with detailed facts. For example, the SQL statement below will retrieve the sales amount for Ford Taurus cars in the Midwest dealerships sold during the third quarter of 1998. Dropping the level indicator in the query will cause it to retrieve all Ford sales for the Midwest for that period of time.

```
SELECT  s.Region_ID,
        s.Vehicle_ID,
        s.Time_ID
FROM    Sales_Fact_Table s
WHERE   s.Vehicle_ID IN(SELECT v.Vehicle_ID
                     FROM Vehicle_Dimension v
                     WHERE Model="Taurus" AND Level = 2)
AND      s.Time_ID IN(SELECT t.Time_ID
                     FROM Time_Dimension t
                     WHERE DATEPART('Y', t.Date) = '1998'
                         AND DATEPART('Q', t.Date) = '3')
```

Therefore, the level indicator is an important concept in the star schema.

Constellation Schema

A new type of schema, the constellation schema, was introduced to avoid errors caused by neglecting the level indicator. The following figure shows an illustration of a constellation model. In this model, facts have been aggregated for the region and state levels in two additional fact tables. These fact tables still link to the other dimensions, but to save on complexity, these links are not shown in this diagram.

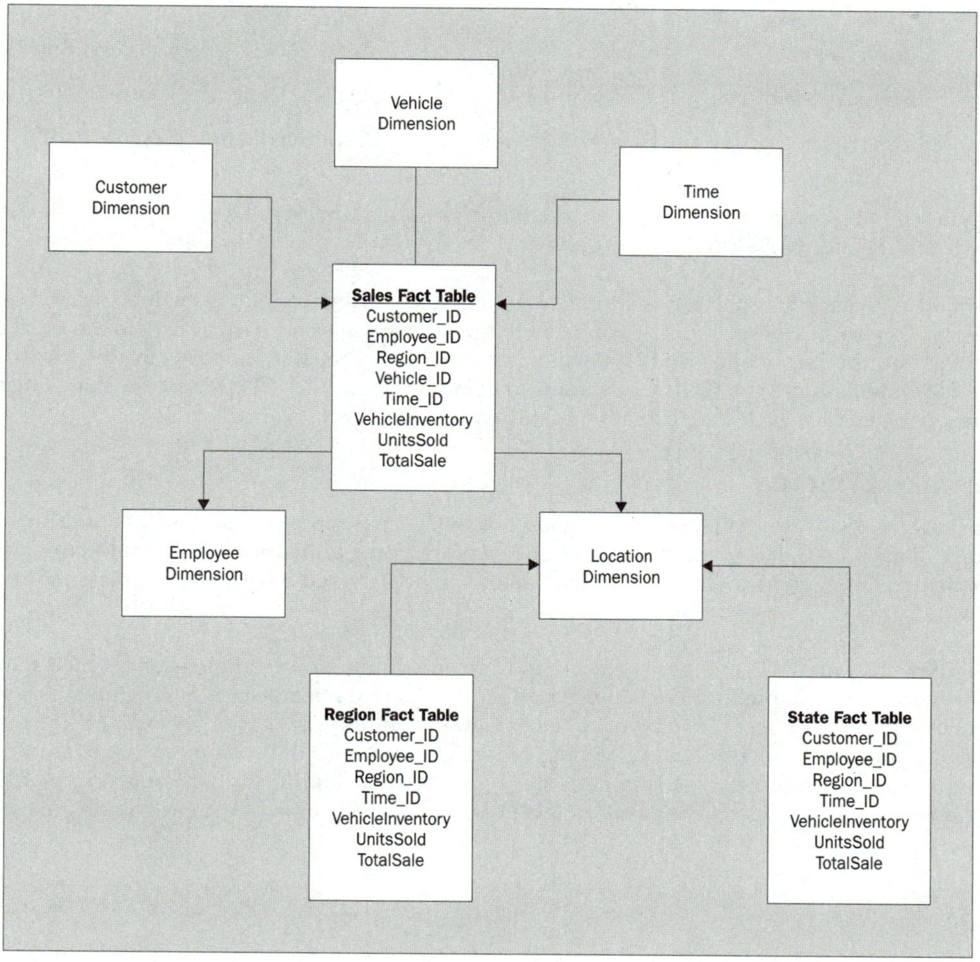

The Constellation Model

Based on this diagram, if you need to find data summaries for a state or a region, you need to only select from the corresponding fact table. This will allow you to avoid using the level indicator for that dimension.

Constellation models are not the best answer to dimensional modeling needs because they quickly become complex, especially if you involve more than one dimension. The number of fact tables will grow to match the number of possible combinations of the desired dimensions and their levels. For instance, if you want to build a constellation model based on vehicle and dealership location, you will need fact tables corresponding to the following combinations:

Ford/Region	Ford/State	Ford/City	Mercury/Region	
Mercury/state	Mercury/City	Taurus/Region	Taurus/State	
Taurus/City	Explorer/Region	Explorer/State	Explorer/City	...etc.

As you see, this becomes very unpractical and may be a nightmare to keep track of all the fact tables needed as a result of the combinations above.

Another drawback for constellation models is that multiple SQL statements will be needed to answer the same question. For example, if you need to find out the sales for Taurus cars in the third quarter of 1998 in both Michigan and Ohio, you will need to write two separate queries, one for Michigan, and one for Ohio, and use the UNION operator to combine the results. The reason for that is that the fact data aggregated for each state is in a separate fact table.

Snowflake Schema

The star schema is the simplest representation of the business entities and their relationships in the dimensional model. However, sometimes one or more of the dimension tables could grow in size to become a very big table, which prompted database modelers and developers to create the snowflake schema.

The snowflake model is the result of decomposing one or more of the dimensions, which sometimes have hierarchies themselves. We can define the many-to-one relationships among members within a dimension table as a separate dimension table with a hierarchy. Let's take for example the automobile dealership sample we have been discussing so far. The customer dimension may be composed of two sub-dimensions, customer type, and customer region. Other sub-dimensions could also be included in the analysis, such as customer education level and customer income (see Figure on next page)

The decomposition of the customer dimension makes the model look a bit like a snowflake, hence came the name for this kind of data model.

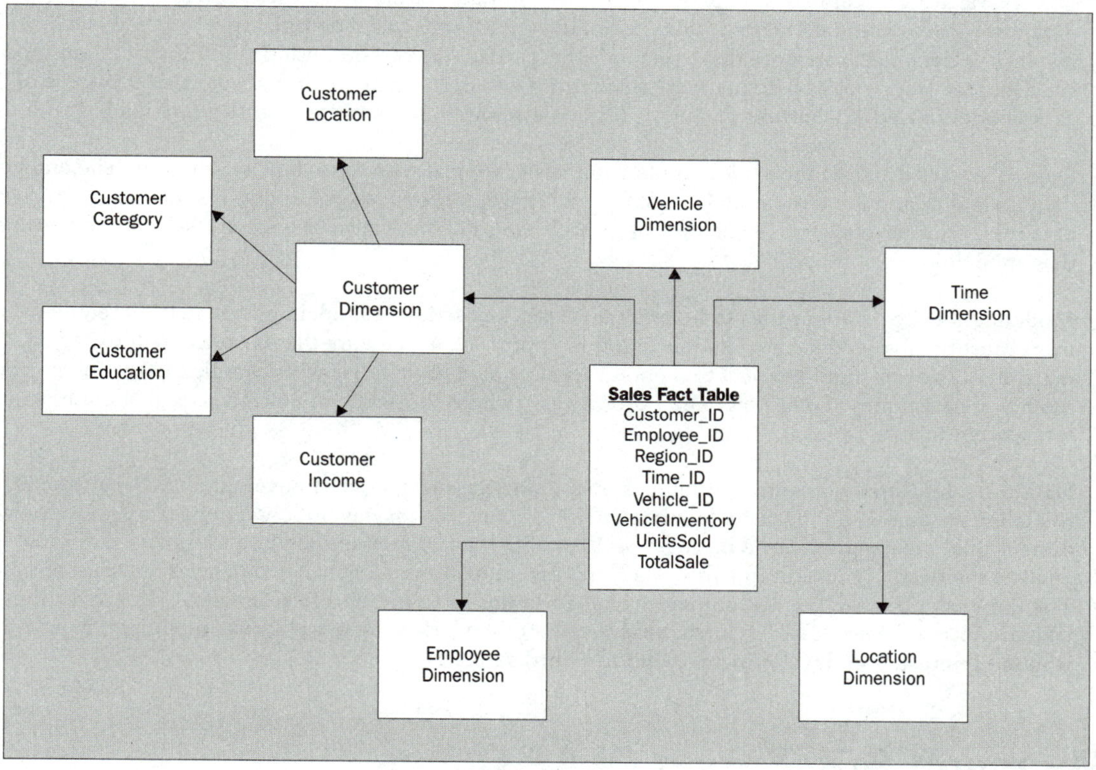

The Snowflake schema

The advantage of the snowflake schema generally is that it saves disk space by eliminating redundant text records in the dimension table. However, the amount of saved space is usually very small compared to the size of the fact table, and many developers and data modelers don't consider this to be a great advantage.

The snowflake schema adds a little more complexity to the dimensional model, which causes many users to prefer to use the simplistic star schema instead.

Data Consolidation

End users care about performance. To them, a fast response to their queries is highly appreciated, and the slow response can be very frustrating. To satisfy this need, database designers usually consolidate the data by pre-aggregating and pre-summarizing it and storing the consolidated data in the database as separate fact tables. This works great as long as the data modeler is aware of how the users will query the data and what response time they expect. Based on this awareness, the data modeler can design the dimensions in a way that makes their drilling-down, rolling-up, slicing and dicing as effective as possible.

Data Modeling for Data Marts

Data marts are very similar in structure and nature to data warehouses. The essential difference between data warehouses and data marts is that data marts are more focused on one aspect of the business. For instance, a data mart can store departmental data, or data for certain periods of time or certain products, etc. Chapter 10 discusses data marts in much more detail, and Chapter 1 presented an overview of data mart models based on their interaction with the data warehouse and the way they are loaded with data.

Data marts are usually much less complex and easier to deal with than data warehouses. The amount of data is smaller and the data model is smaller with fewer tables to worry about in some cases. However, data marts still have to be designed properly with their database structure established after extensive data modeling.

Modeling for the data mart has to be more end-user focused than modeling for a data warehouse. End users must be involved in the data mart modeling process, as they are the ones who will use the data mart. Because you should expect that end users are not at all familiar with complex data models, the modeling techniques and the modeling process as a whole should be organized such that complexity is transparent to end users.

Data mart developers recommend dimensional modeling for data mart development. Dimensional modeling, as a powerful data modeling technique, is suitable for developing data marts that support dimensional data analysis for a business problem. Such analysis could include using an OLAP tool to analyze the data, organize it in cubes, slice and dice it to come up with the data aggregations necessary. The dimensional modeling techniques presented in this chapter, therefore, are also suitable for those who are primarily interested in a narrower scope of the work of data warehouse modeling, that is, those who are interested in developing data models for data marts.

Microsoft SQL Server OLAP Cubes

After the lengthy background about dimensional analysis and OLAP cubes, lets take a look at how Microsoft OLAP Server deals with the issues discussed so far in this chapter. Specifically, let's look at how OLAP cubes are built and used in the Microsoft OLAP services.

Cube Creation

Cubes are data structures that store subsets of the data warehouse data for quick uniform response to user queries. Cubes usually store aggregations and summaries of the data in the data warehouse or even the OLTP database. Cubes return the values of attributes that affect the decision making process in the organization, such as sales amount, inventory, etc. These attributes are called measures. Measures are usually defined in the fact table of the OLAP database. The values of these measures are usually summarized or aggregated along other attributes called dimensions.

In Microsoft OLAP, cube creation is usually conducted in three steps: cube definition, specifying summarization strategy by designing aggregations, and loading the cube by processing it. These three steps are briefly discussed below.

Cube Definition

Defining a cube is done through dimensional data modeling of the warehouse data. To define a cube, you need to do the following:

- Create a data model based on multi-dimensional modeling of the warehouse data.
- Include one or more fact tables and many dimension tables in the data model you create.
- Once you have your data model, you need to select a fact table and define some measures in it.
- Select your dimensions, which are usually one or more columns from the dimension tables. Dimensions provide the categorical descriptions by which the measures are separated for analysis by cube users. For example, a vehicle fact table for an auto dealership may include fields like `vehicle_price`, `vehicle_dealer_invoice`, `inventory_of_vehicles`, etc.
- Dimensions would include attributes describing vehicle make or model, dealership location, time, customer, salesperson, etc.

Defining Aggregations

Dimensions usually contain hierarchies of levels that specify the categorical breakdown of the data. For example, vehicle location may include levels like, country, state, city, etc. Dimension levels allow users to ask questions at different levels beginning with high-level, more general questions, and then drilling down to more detailed aspects of the hierarchy. For example, a user may ask about the sales of Ford cars in the Midwest region, then drill down to find out sales by model and year, such as 2000 Taurus's in each state and city of the Midwest region. This will tell the analyst which models are selling well and which are not, pulling the overall sales down. It is these hierarchies in the dimension levels that determine the way aggregates are constructed. In the Microsoft OLAP a cube can have up to 64 dimensions, including the Measures (which count as one dimension, making the actual maximum number of dimensions in a cube 63).

Loading (Processing) the Cube

After designing the cube and determining its measures, dimensions, and dimension levels, you need to process it , which results in creating and loading the data aggregates according to the specified dimensions and measures. Loading the cube actually stores the calculated aggregations across its measures and levels in its storage schema. The different options available for cube storage are discussed later in the chapter.

> **OLAP Services requires that you process the cube, which will result in creating the aggregations from the fact table and dimensions specified in the cube. After the aggregations are created, they are loaded into their storage area according to the storage methodology used. Chapter 5 covers in detail the way this is conducted.**

Microsoft SQL Server OLAP Services includes a user-friendly, graphical tool, called the OLAP Manager that makes defining cubes, their aggregations, and loading them easy. This tool includes a cube wizard providing an easy way to design cubes, and a cube editor that offers additional flexibility for creating and modifying cube structures. These tools are described in detail in Chapter 5, The OLAP Manager.

Cube Measures

Cube measures include the data elements that the end user is interested in. Data aggregation is conducted based on these measures across the different dimensions of the cube. Based on the OLAP system's goal, these measures may include things like sales, unit cost, total cost, number of units, etc.

Measures are stored in the fact table, and since in Microsoft OLAP a cube can have only one fact table, all these measures for the cube have to be stored in the same table. A measure can be one field or a combination of several fields, such as net profit, which is an expression of the sales and cost fields.

Fact tables include additive and non-additive fields. Additive fields are fields you can perform arithmetic operations upon, such as adding them. An example would be `inventory_units`, or `unit_sales`. Non-additive fields do not allow such operations, and hence are not suitable as cube measure. An example would be `vehicle_id`, or `transaction_id`. However, non-additive fields can be parts of a calculated member (explained later in this chapter), which allows them to be part of the cube measure indirectly. As an example, in a banking data warehouse application, you may be interested in finding out the number of particular transactions in the bank. In this case, you may use the non-additive field, `transaction_id` with an aggregation function, such as COUNT to build a calculated member that can be used as a cube measure.

Cube Dimensions

Cube measures are analyzed based on several factors or categories, called dimensions. For example, if a cube's measure is cars sold, and its dimensions are time, dealer location, and vehicle type, users of the cube can find out which vehicles sold in terms of the categories identified by the measures, dealer location, time, and vehicle type.

A dimension can be used in an individual cube, called a private dimension, or multiple cubes, called a shared dimension. As you will see in Chapter 5, private dimensions are located in the dimensions folder under the cube for which they were created. Shared dimensions, on the other hand, are located in the shared dimensions folder in the library folder for a database in the OLAP Manager view. Shared dimensions also appear in the dimensions folders under the cubes that include them.

Microsoft OLAP allows you to use shared dimensions within any cube in the database avoiding the time-consuming alternative of creating duplicate private dimensions within each of the cubes that need to use them.

One great benefit of using shared dimensions is enabling the standardization of business metrics among cubes. For example, using the same standardized shared dimensions for time and geographical location ensure that data analyzed from different cubes is summarized and organized in a similar fashion.

Defining Cube Dimensions

Cube dimensions are stored in the dimension tables of the cube schema. Therefore, before you can define these dimensions, you need to create this schema using whatever data modeling technique you like. Once you create the cube schema, you can define a dimension by selecting one or more related fields in a dimension table. When selecting multiple fields, you have to make sure that the fields are related and form a hierarchy. This hierarchy defines the dimension levels from the general to the more specific level. Take the time dimension, for instance, you can define this dimension based on the hierarchy: decade, year, quarter, month, and day.

The selected columns in the dimension table correspond to different levels of the dimension. Since a dimension level forms a single hierarchy, these levels allow for moving up and down the hierarchy and finding the cube measures at these different levels. This is what is referred to as drill-down and roll-up operations, with drill-down providing more specific and detailed information about the measure and roll-up providing more generalized summary information.

The records in the dimension table define the level members. For example, the quarter level typically has four members in a year. However, if the dimension table includes several years, 1997, 1998, and 1999 for example, then the number of measures will be 4 x number of year members (3 in our case, which yields 12 member quarters).

In Microsoft OLAP services, the hierarchies represented by the cube dimensions should be regular and uniform. In these hierarchies, each parent has one or more children, and each child has only one parent node. A leaf is the last node in the hierarchy and has ancestors that trace back up the hierarchy to the top level, which is usually referred to as the ALL level.

There are several ways to graphically represent the hierarchies of the cube dimensions. The method I find more useful is the pyramid or triangle representation. According to this representation, the top of the pyramid will represent the highest level in the hierarchy, and as you go down the pyramid, you will encounter the lower levels. The nice thing about this representation is that as you go down the pyramid, the number of members of the hierarchy levels, which is represented by the area of the pyramid between each level and the level above it, grows and becomes larger. Take the following figure, for example; you see that the members of the levels in the time hierarchy increases as you drill down the hierarchy. Assuming that the year is the top level, a year has one member; a quarter level will have 4 members, and a month level will have 12 members.

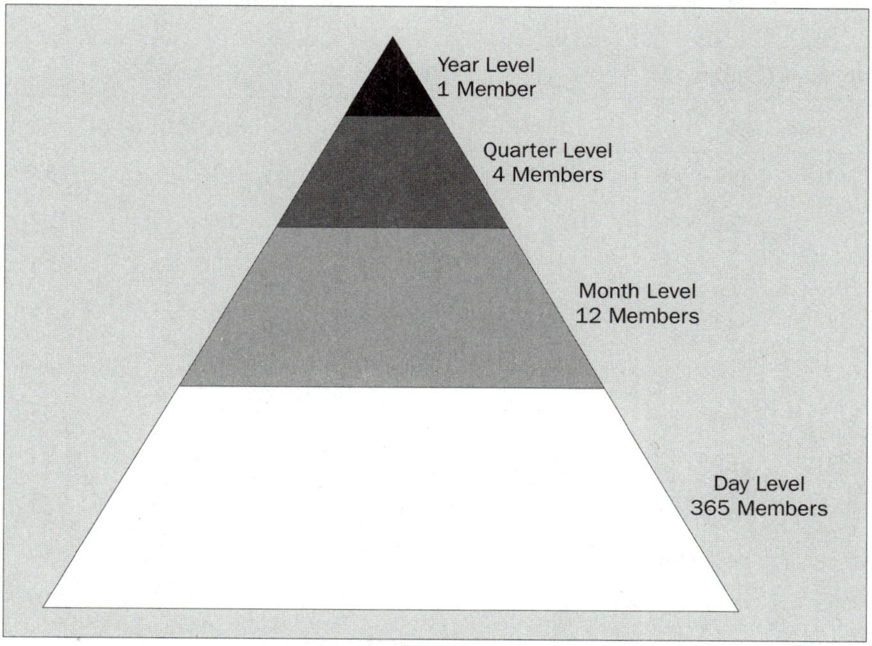

Graphical representation of dimensions, levels, and members

In tabular representations of cube data, members provide the column headings, row headings, and subheadings by which measures are separated and displayed to cube users. The following table shows that the members of the location dimension are shown as the headings and sub-headings of the rows of the tabular representation. The figure also shows that the members of the vehicle type dimension are the headings and sub-headings of the columns of the table. All level members of the dimensions are shown in bold in the following table, whereas the measure values are shown as the cells of the table, and are in regular text format.

1998 Sales		**Ford**		**Mercury**	
		Escort	**Taurus**	**Tracer**	**Sable**
Midwest	**Detroit**	21	39	13	33
	Cleveland	19	40	9	35
Northeast	**Philadelphia**	8	26	3	19
	New Jersey	9	19	5	12

Tabular representation of the cube dimension members

Multiple hierarchies are supported by Microsoft OLAP services. Multiple hierarchies provide similar but alternate views of the cube data. For instance, the following table shows the total sales in millions of dollars per region over the calendar months of 1998 and 1999. A similar view shown in the next table represents the total sales in millions of dollars per region for the fiscal months of 1998 and 1999. You can see that the two views look similar, yet represent different data sets.

Total Auto Sales (Millions $)			**Ford**		**Mercury**	
			Midwest	**Northeast**	**Southwest**	**Southeast**
1998	**Q1**	**Jan**	21	39	13	33
		Feb	18	16	15	27
		Mar	25	43	20	39
	Q2	**April**	24	42	16	37
		May	23	38	16	36
		June	19	40	9	35
	Q3	**July**	22	39	15	33
		August	18	17	16	27
		September	26	45	20	40
	Q4	**October**	24	43	18	39
		November	24	39	18	36
		December	20	40	11	37

Total Auto Sales (Millions $)			Ford		Mercury	
			Midwest	**Northeast**	**Southwest**	**Southeast**
1999	**Q1**	**Jan**	23	41	16	35
		Feb	20	17	17	27
		Mar	26	45	22	40
	Q2	**April**	25	45	20	40
		May	25	41	18	38
		June	22	40	11	37
	Q3	**July**	24	42	17	36
		August	21	19	18	28
		September	27	45	22	41
	Q4	**October**	26	46	21	40
		November	26	43	18	40
		December	9	19	5	12

Total auto sales for dealership chain per region for the calendar months

Total Auto Sales (Millions $)			Ford		Mercury	
			Midwest	**Northeast**	**Southwest**	**Southeast**
1998	**Q1**	**Oct, 1997**	18	19	11	25
(Fiscal)		**Nov, 1997**	21	19	13	27
		Dec, 1997	19	17	11	25
	Q2	**Jan, 1998**	21	39	13	33
		Feb, 1998	18	16	15	27
		Mar, 1998	25	43	20	39

Total Auto Sales (Millions $)			Ford		Mercury	
			Midwest	Northeast	Southwest	Southeast
	Q3	Apr, 1998	24	42	16	37
		May, 1998	23	38	16	36
		Jun, 1998	19	40	9	35
	Q4	Jul, 1998	21	41	14	35
		Aug, 1998	19	17	15	29
		Sep, 1998	26	43	21	40
1999	Q1	Oct, 1998	25	42	16	37
(Fiscal)		Nov, 1998	25	40	16	36
		Dec, 1998	20	40	11	36
	Q2	Jan, 1999	21	41	14	37
		Feb, 1999	21	17	17	31
		Mar, 1999	26	44	22	41
	Q3	Apr, 1999	26	42	17	37
		May, 1999	27	41	16	37
		Jun, 1999	20	42	11	38
	Q4	Jul, 1999	21	41	15	39
		Aug, 1999	21	19	19	32
		Sep, 1999	28	46	22	41

Total sales for the dealership chain in millions of dollars for fiscal months of 1998 and 1999.

In Microsoft OLAP, each multiple-hierarchy dimension is defined as two or more dimensions. These dimensions have names that share the same prefix followed by a period but have different suffixes. For example, dimensions with names of `Time.Calendar` and `Time.Fiscal`. The suffix should not equal any current or future level name or member name in the dimension because queries using the dimension may be ambiguous. For instance, you may not say: `Time.Quarters` and `Time.Year`, etc.

The OLAP Manager, as you will see in Chapter 5, includes a dimension wizard, which enables you to create dimensions quickly and easily. This wizard can be used from within the cube creation wizard to create private dimensions, or can be used separately to create a shared dimension. One thing worth noting is that the wizard makes defining the time dimensions especially easy. This dimension is based on the `datetime` data field in the data warehouse. Standard time hierarchies are available, and the levels associated with a selected hierarchy are automatically extracted from the `datetime` field.

Processing Dimensions

After defining a dimension, it needs to be processed before it becomes available for use. Processing means saving its structure and loading it with the appropriate data. Microsoft OLAP allow for two kinds of processing for the dimension, complete rebuild, and incremental processing.

With the total rebuild option, the dimension is re-created according to the new definition, and loaded with data. This option is usually performed when a structural change takes place, such as adding a level, eliminating a level, or moving some members from one level to another. In other words, this option is required for processing the dimension in the case of a structural change, or a change in the relationships between members of the dimension hierarchy.

Incremental processing is warranted only when new members are added to the dimension. For example, if a new city is added to the location dimension under the same city level, or a new state is added, and so forth. This type of processing is not possible when a member of the dimension moves from one level to another, or is dropped all together.

With the complete rebuild processing, cubes using the dimension become unavailable for use until they are re-processed. However, in the case of incremental processing, the cubes referencing the dimension remain available for use where users can issue queries against them.

Please note that if a shared dimension is defined and saved without processing it, the dimension will be processed automatically once any cube referencing it is processed.

Dimensions can be processed in the OLAP Manager by right-clicking on the dimension name in the tree pane, and selecting "Process". This will be explained in more detail in Chapter 5.

Member Properties

Member properties provide users with additional information about level members. A member property is an attribute associated with a member of a dimension level. For example, each member of the Day level of the time dimension has an associated Boolean member property called "holiday". If the day is a holiday then the value for this property is True, otherwise it is False.

A member property is stored in a column in the same table as the dimension level containing the members. So, for example, Holiday is stored in the same table as the Day level.

OLAP Storage

Fact tables are usually large tables. Aggregations and summary operations conducted on these tables require enormous amounts of resources, such as RAM and CPU power. Given the bandwidth available in today's networks, and the power of database servers, OLAP vendors, including Microsoft, prefer to have all the aggregations and operations on the data conducted in the backend, utilizing the processing power of the database server, and the database engine which is optimized for such operations.

Storage Models

Multidimensional databases usually take data from other sources, such as legacy systems, relational databases or desktop tools, such as spreadsheets. Sometimes the data is input directly from end-users, perhaps via a spreadsheet interface. In a ROLAP, the data is still physically stored in an RDBMS, usually in some form of star or snowflake schema, whereas in an MDB (multidimensional database), the data is physically stored in a different file structure, optimized for multidimensional processing. There are also hybrid OLAP products, which allow both direct access to relational data for multidimensional processing, as well as having their own optimized multidimensional disk storage. Regardless of the storage method used for multidimensional data, it is very rare indeed for the multidimensional processing to be based directly on data in operational systems, so almost all OLAP applications work on extracted copies of data that came from other systems. The extracted copies are always held in a form that is to a greater or lesser extent optimized for multidimensional processing

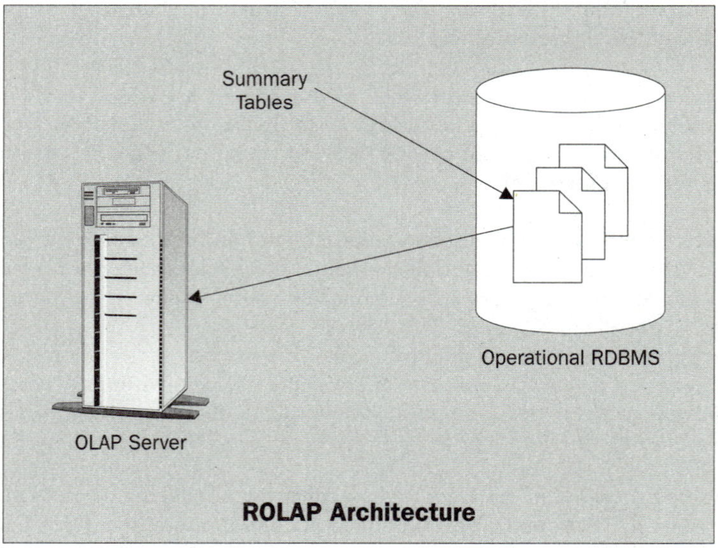

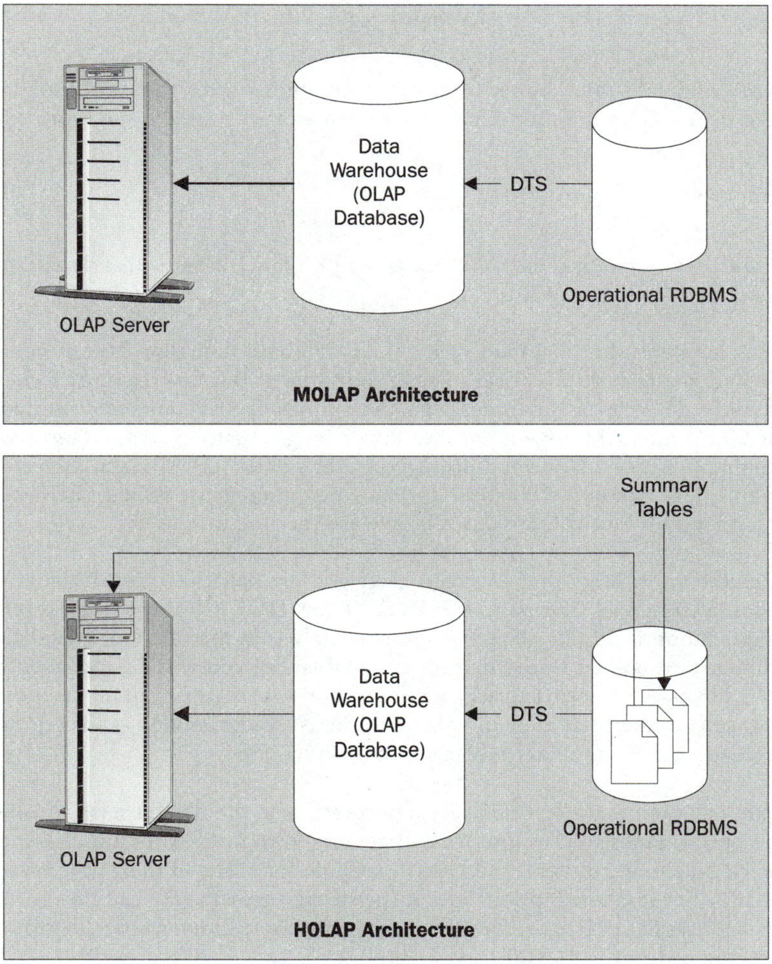

Storage models in Microsoft OLAP services

The figures above shows the differences in the three storage models. They show that in the ROLAP case, multi-dimensional data is aggregated and stored in the relational database. As for MOLAP, the summary data and aggregations are stored in the same multi-dimensional database. Finally, HOLAP systems, data in the relational database can be accessed while some data is aggregated into the multi-dimensional database.

The Potential of Database Explosion

When data is extracted from production systems to be stored in the OLAP system, the data is likely to take much less space in its new multi-dimensional home. Actually, it is estimated that the same amount of data stored in an OLAP system takes one-third to half the storage it took in the relational database. These are many reasons for this, including:

- The keys, indexes and dimensional structures are either not required at all or take far less space.
- The sparsity of data is often better suppressed. In other words, data is consolidated and not distributed over a large number of tables, or even a many pages in the same table in some instances.
- The data may even be compressed.

Given the points above, you might then say, what is the problem? What is this database explosion you are talking about in the title of this section?

Well, consider what happens after you load your OLAP database. Usually, these systems are designed for interactive use and fast response for user queries. But, how is this fast response to be achieved if the queries usually issued against these databases involve complex aggregations and summarization, which require enormous CPU and RAM power, and can take a long time to execute? The answer to this question is conducting pre-calculations and pre-aggregations of the OLAP data, then storing these pre-calculated and aggregated data in the database so that when queries are issued, the results will be readily available, and the queries will look as if they were running on-the-fly.

If the MOLAP architecture is used, the new aggregates and pre-calculated results will be stored in the same database automatically and transparent. If ROLAP (or, HOLAP) is used, the results of this pre-calculation and aggregation is usually stored in summary tables in the relational database. Usually, each combination of dimensions will be stored in a separate table. So, you will have a table that includes data for first quarter of 1998 sales of Ford Taurus cars in the Midwest region, and another one for storing the first quarter sales results of the same type of vehicle in the Northeast region, and so forth. This might end up with a large number of summary tables, as you can imagine.

One might think that storage space for the aggregation results in the database is a small price to pay for excellent run-time performance of user queries and generated reports. After all, disk space is cheap these days, and most machines, servers, and clients, are idle for much of their time, particularly overnight. The answer to these assumptions is that the storage growth rate can be enormous and lead to counter-productive consequences. Based on the number of sparse dimensions, the growth factor for the database can be on the order of 10's, 100's, even 1000's.

To understand this principle, we need to visualize how sparsity affects the volume of the database. The following figure shows a representation of the detailed data and the aggregations of such data along the different combinations of dimensions. The dark shaded cells along the detail section show the first and second level aggregations along combinations of the two dimension levels. The dotted cells show aggregations of the previous aggregations. The solid black cell shows a third level aggregation of the detail combinations. The two dimensions represented in the figure are vehicle type and geographic location. The location shows a hierarchy that goes across division (North America, Europe), and region (Midwest, Northeast, Southwest, Southeast, Canada in North America, and England, France, Germany, Spain, and Italy in the European division). If we were to show the state or city level, the detail section would grow even more.

By sparsity, I mean that some combinations are not valid, even if represented in the detail section and aggregated later in the aggregated data section. For instance, some models, such as Mercury Mountaineer, may not be available in a region like, Spain. Or, maybe a whole car division, like Mercury, may not be available in a region like Italy. This leaves many cells in the detail section with NULL values and creates the sparsity I have been talking about.

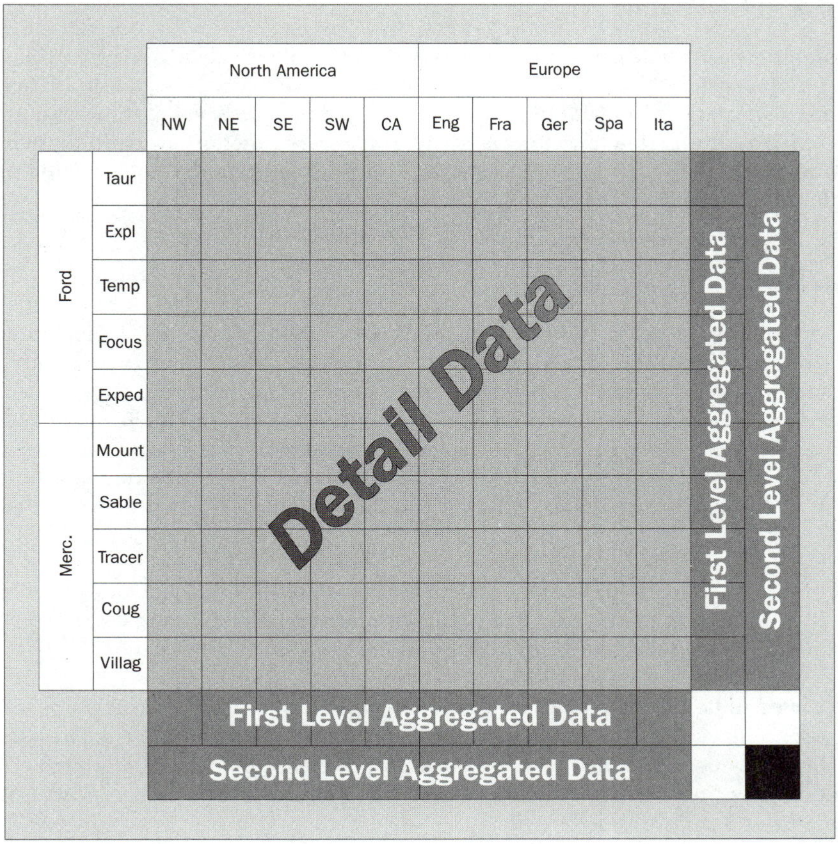

An Illustration of the effect of two dimensions with only two levels each on the volume of detailed and aggregated data

The number of cells in the aggregated area grows rapidly with more dimensions added in the picture. This growth becomes worrisome with five or more dimensions, especially if you take into account that the likelihood of consolidated cells to be populated is much greater then that of detail cells. Therefore, the growth of the database storage can grow in a tremendous fashion.

So, how can we avoid getting into this situation? How can we maintain acceptable query and reporting performance without leading to this database explosion? Here are two answers:

1. Microsoft OLAP does not pre-calculate all possible combinations of dimension levels. Instead, it only pre-calculates the aggregations of the first level, which is usually the one that takes longest to create.

2. Reduce sparsity of the data objects by implementing a good design. As a rule of thumb, try to minimize the number of dimensions in a cube, and create multiple cubes, instead.

Calculated Members

Calculated members are members in dimensions with their values calculated at run-time. The calculated members definition is stored but its data is calculated when the query is issued. In Microsoft OLAP, calculated members allow for the addition of members to dimensions without increasing their storage requirement. Microsoft OLAP allows for the use of 100 library functions to build these members, and also allows you to add your own functions as well. You will see examples of calculated members, how they are built and used in later chapters of this book.

Virtual Cubes

Just like views in relational databases combine other views and tables in new logical units, virtual cubes combine two or more cubes into one logical cube. Virtual cubes don't hold any measure data within themselves; rather, queries against them retrieve data stored in the underlying regular cubes. Actually, virtual cubes only store their own definition and require no physical storage for the data they represent. A virtual cube can also be based on only one regular cube to expose a subset of its measures and dimensions. For instance, you can build a virtual cube based on a sale cube that has dimensions like product, location, time, store, customer, etc. The virtual cube may only expose the product and location dimensions.

One benefit of virtual cubes is similar to a benefit that is offered when using views in relational databases, which is limiting the measures and dimensions of regular cubes that can be seen by the users. This is considered a great security feature that promotes using such virtual cubes.

Virtual cubes need to be processed before they can be used. Processing a virtual cube establishes the links to its underlying cubes, dimensions, and measures. Processing a virtual cube also triggers the processing of underlying cubes that have not been processed yet. Therefore, although establishing the internal links of the virtual cube is a fast process, it may still take a long time to process it if any of the base cubes have not been processed before.

Member Properties

Dimension members have attributes that describe them and provide detailed information about them. These attributes are called member properties. The information provided by such attributes is usually less important than the levels themselves, and the properties do not qualify as separate levels. In addition to providing information about a member, member properties can be used in queries and thus provide end users with more options when analyzing cube data. Member properties are also the basis of virtual dimensions, which are discussed in the next section of this chapter.

To create a member property, you need to add a column in the same dimension table that holds the dimension member of interest. Then, you need to associate the value of this column with the level that contains the members. For example, each member of the `Month` level has an associated boolean member property called `Review Month`. This property records whether the given month is a review month or not. The value of the boolean is 1 (TRUE) for months that are review months, and 0 (FALSE) for days that are not. The `Review Month` property is stored in the same level as `Month` in the same `Time` dimension table.

To understand why member properties do not qualify as separate levels, think about the `Review Month` member property. Before this property was introduced, the `Time` dimension had a natural hierarchy of `Year/Quarter/Month/Day`. However, review months needed to be pointed out, because some queries may need to retrieve them. If review months were added as a level in the time dimension, the natural hierarchy of this dimension will be disrupted. Think of users having to drill through the hierarchy to the `Day` level – these users would have to go through `Month` and `Review Month` before they get to the `Day` level, which is unrealistic and inaccurate to say the least.

Viewing member properties is usually done in the OLAP Manager by right-clicking a level member.

Virtual Dimensions

Sometimes you may need to do some analysis based on a member property of a dimension level, rather than on the dimension level. For instance, in an employee dimension, you may want to analyze the data in terms of the employee salary, which is a property of the staff level of the employee table. In this case, you may create a virtual dimension based on the salary field in the employee dimension and use this new virtual dimension in any cube that can utilize it. Just like regular dimensions, virtual dimensions can be used in virtual cubes.

Before you may add a virtual dimension to a cube, you need to make sure that the dimension that supplies its member properties is also included in the cube. Virtual dimensions do not increase the storage requirements of the cube because the physical data is still stored in the cube that includes the member level that supplies its member properties.

Write-enabled Cubes

One nice feature about Microsoft OLAP services is that it allows you to create write-enabled cubes. These cubes give you the chance to study different scenarios while doing your analysis by changing some values in the cubes. The new values are stored separate from the cube data, but are incorporated with the query results. These changes are usually referred to as write-backs.

One condition for making changes to cube values is that changes can only be made to cells at the lowest level, that is, cells that do not contain aggregated information, or cells which are at the leaf level. For example, you may change the sale value of sale transaction, but not the total sales for a week, month, etc. When queries are performed, the individual changes are applied to the summary information in the upper levels of the dimension hierarchies so that the user can see the effect of the changes on these aggregations.

When a user makes changes to a value in a cell, the difference between the new and old values is stored in the write-back table. For instance, if a cell is changed from 10 to 12, the value 2 is stored in the write-back table along with the change time, end-user information, and a pointer to the cell in the cube. An audit trail is usually recorded in the write-back table, and the original value in the cube is preserved.

Chapter 5 will show how you can create write-enabled cubes along with the security requirements for such changes.

Partitions

Client applications and queries may see the cube data as one integral entity. However, the fact is that cube fact data is stored separately from cube aggregations and those are stored separately from cube dimension data. The cube's fact and aggregation data are usually stored in separate partitions that follow the OLAP storage modes discussed earlier: multi-dimensional (MOLAP), relational (ROLAP), and a hybrid of the previous two modes (HOLAP).

Partitions provide great flexibility and power in managing OLAP cubes, especially large cubes. For example, a large cube containing auto sales information can contain partitions that include sales data from previous years, and partitions for each quarter of the current year. Having these quarterly partitions allows for dumping new data only in a small portion of the cube that corresponds to the most recent quarterly partition, leaving the other quarterly partitions completely static. This results in easier maintenance of the cube and its aggregations. When the year ends, the four partitions for the ending year can be merged together in one partition for the year. Also, partitions can have several storage modes, source data locations, and aggregation designs, providing great flexibility in designing your cube storage strategy to fit your needs.

In Microsoft OLAP, a cube has at least one partition. A partition is a separate region of physical storage of part of the cube's data. Cubes may have multiple partitions to optimize physical access to the data. Although cube partitions are not visible to the client queries, database administrators (DBA) can use them to manage storage of data within the cubes. As an example of cube partitions, a sales cube may be partitioned to store a year's worth of sales fact and aggregation data. The partitions can be designed so that they store the data for each quarter of the year, and at the end of the year the quarter partitions can be merged to form a big partition for the whole year.

It is very important to pay special attention the way partitions are defined and created. Duplicate fact data in more than one partition may lead to incorrect results when summarizing and aggregating the data.

Aggregation design of a partition stores the definition of the aggregations in the cube. Aggregation designs can be shared between cube partitions, and may be copied from one cube partition to another. This allows for smooth merging of the cubes when needed, because one condition for such merging to happen is that the merging partitions have the same data storage mode and aggregation design.

Although a partition can be based only on a single fact table, the same fact table can be used as the basis for the design of multiple partitions.

Note that, in the first release of SQL Server 7.0 OLAP Services, you need to run the Enterprise Edition before you are able to define multiple partitions for a cube. Installing the Enterprise Edition of SQL Server 7.0 requires running the Enterprise Edition of Windows NT 4.0 with service pack 4 or higher, or Windows 2000 Advanced or Data Server.

Defining, or creating a partition, is done in one of three ways:

- Specifying a data slice
- Using a different fact table for the partition

- Filtering data in a fact table which is used by multiple partitions

You have to be aware that no matter what method you use to create your partitions, it is your responsibility to ensure that no duplicate detail fact data exists in the different partitions.

Specifying a Data Slice

Creating a data slice is done using the OLAP Manager's partition wizard. The wizard attempts to create a filter on the data in the fact table to include only the data you need to include in the partition. If you specify your own filters, these filters that you create will join the filter created by the partition wizard in one big filter. Creating your own filter will always be a safe way to ensure that you include only the data you need to include in the partition. In some cases, when the data source includes only the data that will be stored in the partition, there may be no need for such a filter.

The following figure illustrates how a slice can be taken out of the cube data for sales in New York State for the whole year and for all products. You just need to make sure when you take this slice and use it as a basis for a partition, that New York data don't show up in other partitions of the cube. The safest way to do so is by applying filters on the remaining partitions to exclude New York data.

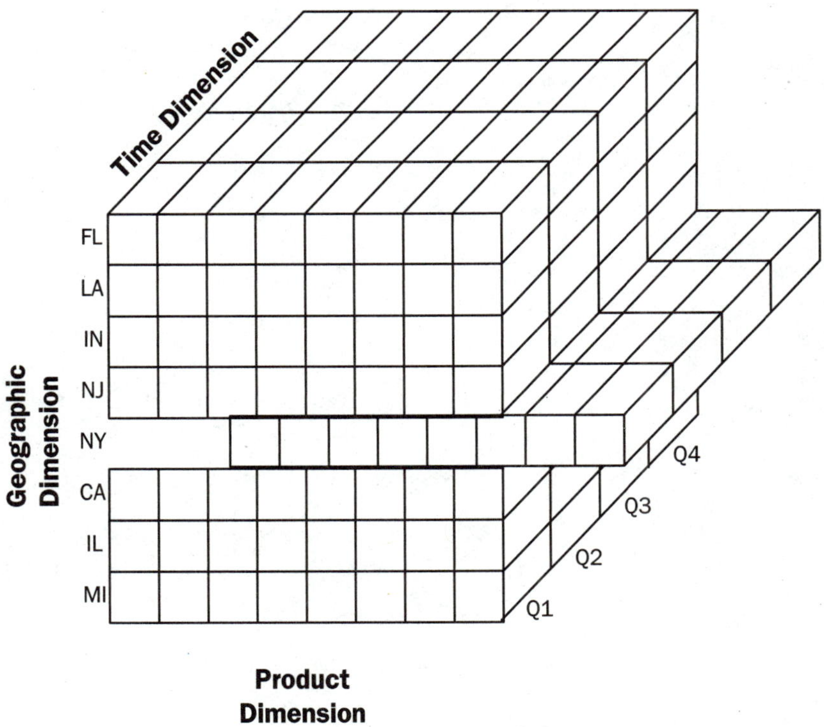

Taking out a slice of the cube representing the sales data in New York state for all products and quarters in the fact table.

Using a Different Fact Table

You may create your partition be basing it on a different fact table. The fact tables in the cube should have the same structure but include different fact data. For example, one fact table may include this year's data, and another fact table may include last year's data, and so on. This method is a good way to ensure integrity of the data in the partitions by eliminating duplication of fact data among them.

The following figure illustrates how two fact tables, one for 1998 fact data and one for 1999 fact data can be used as basis for two different partitions of the same cube. Note that the two partitions share the same dimension tables, except for the time dimension. The 1998 partition uses a time dimension table that has only one member at the year level, that is 1998. Similarly, the 1999 partition has a time dimension table that has one member only at the year level, that is 1999.

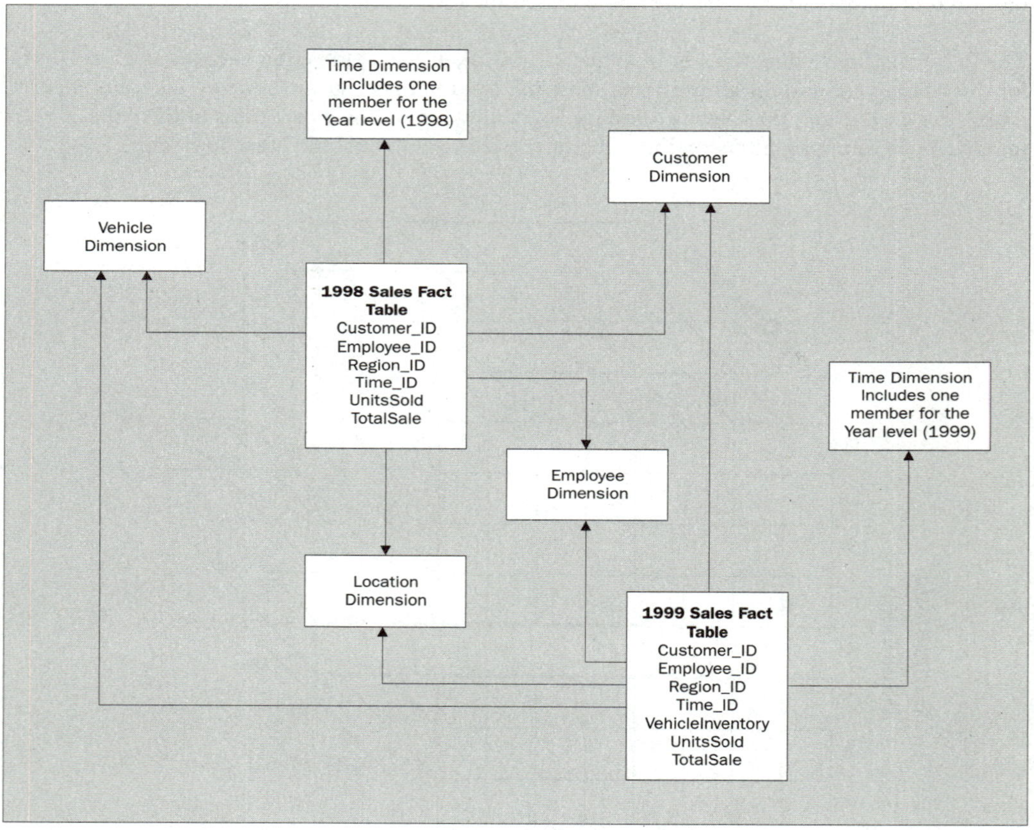

Using different fact tables for the different dimensions in cube

Filtering the Data in the Fact Table

The last method for creating a partition is by filtering the fact data in the fact table. With this, the same fact table can be used for all partitions in the cube, if desired. You need to make sure of two things to ensure integrity of your partition data:

- Design your filters in a way that eliminates duplicate fact data among cubes.
- Design your filters so that the collection of all partition data returns the whole fact data set for the cube.

To learn more about filters and how you can apply them when creating the partitions, refer to Chapters 7 and 8 about the Multi Expression language (MDX), the language Microsoft introduced with OLAP services to access and manipulate cube data.

Merging Partitions

As we discussed previously, merging partitions is a powerful tool introduced by Microsoft OLAP services. The merging however, has to be conducted carefully in order to ensure accuracy of processed data and integrity of aggregated results.

Merged partitions have to fulfill the following two conditions before they can be merged:

- Their storage mode is the same (MOLAP/ROLAP/HOLAP).
- They have the same aggregation design.

If you are merging partitions based on slices of the cube data, you need to pay special attention to use the right filters before processing the resulting partition. If you don't do so, you will run the risk of having duplicate data. For example, if an inventory cube has three partitions of types of vehicles, Cadillac, Chevrolet, and Pontiac. Let's assume that the data pertaining to each vehicle type is stored in a separate partition, partition 1, partition 2 and partition 3 respectively. Let's say you merged partition 2 and 3. The new partition will hold the correct data until you process it. Once you process the partition, data for all three vehicle types will be stored in the merged partition causing the Cadillac data to be duplicated in the cube, once by Partition 1 and once by the merged partition. The reason this duplication takes place is that Microsoft OLAP Services will specify the contents of the merged partition by the parent of the three partitions, which could be the manufacturer (General Motors in this case) causing the data related to the three Makes, Cadillac, Chevrolet, and Pontiac to be pulled into the merged partition instead of pulling just the data for Chevrolet and Pontiac makes. This will happen unless you have a filter specified to exclude the Cadillac data when the cube is processed. Thus, the final cube will eventually have two partitions, the Cadillac partition and the merged partition with the Cadillac data redundant in both partitions.

To avoid this situation, you need to explicitly apply a filter that excludes the Cadillac data from the merged partition before you process it (Vehicle="Chevrolet" OR Vehicle="Pontiac") or (Vehicle <> "Cadillac" if the parent level includes only GM and the vehicle type level only includes these three members).

Another thing to watch for when you merge partitions using different fact tables, is that fact tables are not merged automatically; you have to manually do so. When you merge partitions using the same fact table, a filter is created to store the data for both partitions available in the fact table into the merged partition.

When you merge partitions based on the MOLAP storage mode, their facts data is also merged. This results in an internally complete and consistent partition. However, the facts stored in MOLAP partitions are copies of facts in the fact table. When the partition is subsequently processed, the facts in the multidimensional structure are deleted and data is copied from the fact table as specified by the partition's filter. If the source partition uses a different fact table from the target partition, there is a chance you will get an incomplete data set in the MOLAP structure. To avoid this situation, you need to manually merge the fact table with the target partition's fact table.

There is no limitation on which should be merged first – fact tables, or partitions. However, the aggregations will not accurately represent the underlying facts until both operations have been completed. When merging HOLAP or ROLAP partitions that access different fact tables, try to perform the merge when users are not connected to the cube containing these partitions in order not to affect the performance and accuracy of the queries they are running against the fact table.

Summary

In this chapter, we discussed dimensional analysis and OLAP database design principles. These principles include OLAP cubes, and their components. We also introduced OLAP operations, such as slicing and dicing, drilling down and rolling up data. These concepts are crucial for the design of any decision support system (DSS). After the background of OLAP and dimensional analysis, we talked about the Microsoft OLAP cubes and their components in some detail. This should give you a good background to prepare you for when we delve into the design of the data warehouse system in the next chapter, which includes designing the decision support system as well.

4

Designing the Data Warehouse and OLAP Solution

The previous chapters discussed the background to the Microsoft Data Warehousing and OLAP tools and strategy. This background is essential if you are a newcomer to the world of data warehousing, since you need to understand these concepts before you can proceed with the next steps of building the data warehouse. The background is also useful if you are a seasoned data warehousing professional, but have not yet gained experience using Microsoft Enterprise Data Management tools and technologies.

This chapter deals with the design of the Data warehouse and OLAP solution. It discusses the pre-requisites for a successful design and the tools needed, ending up with the detailed design ready for implementation. In the process of presenting these issues, we look at how to build a data warehouse and OLAP application for a typical sale and inventory system. This example is similar in many areas to the Food Mart sample that is installed with the Microsoft OLAP Services.

Several issues will be covered throughout the chapter, including:

- Pre-requisites for a successful design: data, people, and tools
- Understanding the business model and its importance in the design process
- Using Rapid Application Development (RAD) for prototyping
- The importance of metadata
- Star schema design and its variants
- Specifying the need and strategies for data extraction and migration
- Production and delivery issues

Pre-requisites for a Successful Design

As an engineer, I have always believed that the design phase of any project is the most important phase. This is true in any project and applies to any discipline. When you design a software project, it is essential to start it in the right way, even if it means spending more time and resources than you would think are necessary. The better your design, the better your product will be. Because a good design minimizes the number of iterations that a project will go through during its life cycle, you will end up saving time and precious resources.

A data warehousing project has its own life cycle. The first step in this cycle, which is illustrated in the diagram below, is defining and gathering requirements. Once the requirements for the project at hand have been defined, prototypes can be developed to select the best design, then the data analysis and design stages can begin, along with the development, testing, and documentation. After these steps, the application is tested by the client (which also forms part of the construction phase). Once testing is complete, and bugs ironed out, the project is ready for rollout and to be used by the client. At this stage, the project isn't yet completely finished. Once the project has been released, issues will be raised either through maintenance, or through the needs of the clients, that may require modifying the project. This may lead to additional analysis and development of the new desired functionality, or fixing issues raised during the first few days of real-time operation.

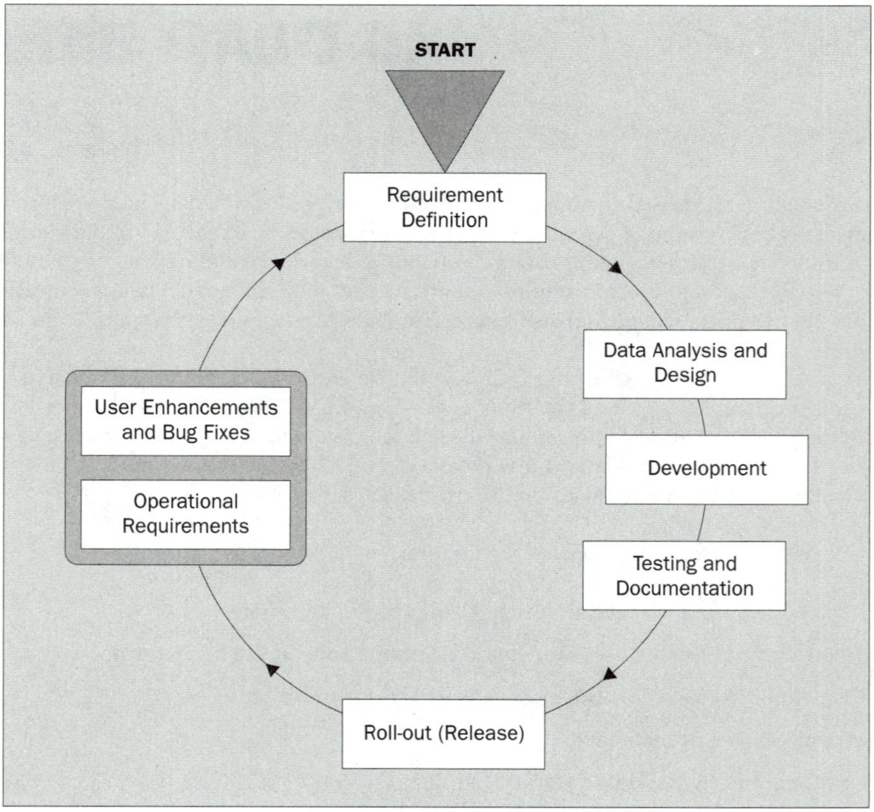

An illustration of the life cycle of a data warehouse project

A good data warehouse design will cut down on the number of iterations the project may be subjected to in its life cycle. It will anticipate the added requirements as much as possible and be flexible enough to accommodate them beforehand, or at least make adding them later inexpensive. As users start using the data warehouse, they might come up with what are called "operational requirements" which were not thought of during the requirement gathering stage. It is therefore important to gather details about all possible operational requirements and arrangements, such as user interface changes that might affect the data structure, who will be using the data warehouse, and where it is to be deployed, etc. in the design stage.

So, if the design phase of the data warehousing project is so important, how do we make sure the design is really good? The answer to this question lies in the following sections.

Customer Management

Customer management (end user and client) simply means collecting the data you need from the customer in an adequate manner. When you gather the data required for your design, you need to make sure you talk to the right people. Knowing the audience who will use your application and talking to them directly will help you obtain accurate information about what functionality is really needed.

Your first step is to talk to the executives, and convey to them of the importance of a data warehousing project. Then speak to these executives about how they use the system. You will probably find that these executives know the system best via the reports that they receive that help with every-day decision making and planning.

The next logical step is to talk to the people who produce these reports. These users are not necessarily members of the IT department, or computer wizards. They could be (in addition to the business analysts) secretaries that prepare current reports from compiling data given to them by analysts in a spreadsheet format, or clerks who feed data to the analysts. These users are the ones who usually give you the best information about the business, and what data is being collected. These people are the future intelligent users of the data warehouse and the OLAP solution

You also need to communicate with the information technology (IT) people in the client's organization. This will allow you to gather information about the client's systems, their infrastructure, tools, etc. This knowledge is essential in the selection of the technologies to be used for the data warehouse project.

Other people you need to interact with on the client side are people using the current production systems. These systems will feed the data warehouse, and it is essential to know their data structure, size, and even samples of the data stored in them. This is important for the successful design of your data transformation system that will scrub, transform, and transfer data from their data stores to the data warehouse.

In your investigation of current production systems, you need to investigate all possible sources that may feed the data warehouse in the future and plan to include them in the design. Frequently, the customer will come back to you with a fifth request after you fulfill the four they asked for during the requirement gathering. Knowing all possible sources of data that might feed the data warehouse may make meeting these additional requirements easier and less costly in the future.

The Project Team

Building a successful data-warehousing project requires the right people who are dedicated and enjoy doing what they do. You need to have experts on your team, even if they are outside consultants, including "domain experts" who have worked on projects handling similar situations before. The expertise these people will bring may make a big difference in the design specifications and throughout the different stages of the project. Because of their experience, they know what should be included and what to avoid. This would probably become apparent at the later stage of the projects, but then it may be too late to take care of. Also, their experience would help in project scoping, phasing and execution.

> ***Project scoping* – setting the functionalities that need to be covered or handled by the project, and also setting the functions that will not be handled to avoid raising undue expectations.**
>
> ***Phasing the project* – dividing the tasks into groups that will be carried out in phases.**
>
> ***Execution of the project* – designing and building the data warehouse based on the scope, and phases of the project.**

However, in building your project team, you should try not to rely solely on outside consultants. If you do, you may quickly find that supporting the project after its release will be a big problem, since these people may not be available quickly enough to help with the support. Ideally you need to have a balanced team of in-house professionals and outside experts who will work together and share their knowledge and experiences to ensure adequate support of the application at all times.

Once the team is assembled, try to make sure it stays intact for the duration of the project. You don't want to use the revolving door policy with people joining the team late and others leaving it for other projects at will. Doing so is a recipe for failure because each phase of the project requires special expertise in different areas. Losing someone who has already acquired the knowledge and has been working on the project for some time is a big loss to the project. Replacements for such people will need to be trained and brought up to speed before they can contribute to the project, which may adversely affect the timetable of the deliverables during the different phases of the project.

The skills required by different team members needed during the life-cycle of the data warehousing project include:

- **Project Management**: a team member who will be responsible for managing the project and communicating with the client regarding progress and day-to-day issues.
- **Technical Leadership**: this is someone who knows the technical aspects of the project and has leadership skills that allows them to lead other team members to do their work the best way possible.
- **Senior Analysis Skills**: this is someone who will communicate with the customer, gather information about their business, their systems, and learn about all potential sources of data that may end up in the data warehouse. This team member's role is crucial in the design phase, and in phases where changes to the project scope are considered.
- **Database Design**: a team member who will be responsible for the data modeling and database design for the data warehouse. This person should have experience in data warehouse database design, due to the unique nature of these databases as you have already seen in the previous chapters.

- **Data Transformation**: This person will be responsible for the transfer and transformation of the data from its sources to the destination warehouse, and possibly to the query processing system, which contains the tables of pre-calculated and pre-aggregated data.
- **Database Administration**: a team member who can perform database administration duties for the development databases. This person will be helpful in identifying operational needs for the data warehouse database that can be planned for in the design phase.
- **Development**: these are team members who will develop the different parts of the data warehousing solution. They are the ones who will design the cubes and build them. They are the ones who will also design the strategies and tools for data transformation and loading into the warehouse.
- **Quality Assurance/Testing**: this person is responsible for testing the project to insure that it meets the specific quality requirements of the business every step of the way.
- **Technical Writing**: this team member will work closely with other team members to document the data warehouse solution throughout its stages.
- **Other**: these include system administrators, secretaries, intern personnel who help with testing, and data population of the development environment. The role of these people is essential for the success of the testing and debugging processes.

Although all the skills and positions mentioned above are important, they don't mean that you have to have separate people with each one fulfilling only one need; rather, you can have one person that covers more than one needed skill, just like you may need several people performing the same task which requires more than one person to fulfill.

The Tools

The last element for a successful data warehouse solution is the tools used to build and operate the data warehouse. The tools include everything you use in terms of hardware and software to build your warehouse. The hardware should be adequate to store immense amounts of data collected and transferred to the data warehouse, and the software should be adequate for running the data warehouse in the most efficient and fault-free fashion possible.

Hardware

Hardware spans a long list of elements used in the building and operation of the data warehouse system. First, the computers that house the data warehouse should have great processing power and vast disk storage. Fault-tolerance should be planned for by having redundancy and backup servers, and backing up the data in the warehouse to other media that can be kept and protected off-site, for use when database recovery is needed.

The OLAP server should also be powerful with a great amount of RAM and CPU power to allow for fast processing of the queries issued against the data warehouse data, and rapid generation of the desired reports.

The network elements, routers, cables, switches, hubs, etc. should allow for broad bandwidth to facilitate fast transfer of the data from its origins to its destinations. The network is one of the most important pieces that can ensure successful delivery of the solution to the end user. With robust networks, data will be transferred quickly from operational databases and other sources to the data warehouse, and data will also be transferred quickly after its processing at the OLAP server.

When you set the hardware budget for your project, you need to look at real life situations where Microsoft OLAP Services and SQL Server 7.0 were used to build a data warehousing solution, then compare these situations with the one you are dealing with. You also need to do some prototyping that will allow you to scale up what you really need in production environments. The basic requirements as stated by Microsoft should only be seen as guidelines.

The following are two examples of actual hardware used in case studies presented on the Microsoft web site. You can find these case studies and others at the Microsoft web site: *http://www.microsoft.com/sql/bizsol/datawarehousing.htm.*

A case study with Shoney's Inc.

Micro Computer Solutions conducted a study to build a business intelligence system for Shoney Company, a leading family dining restaurant chain in the USA, early last year. The study was conducted to help marketing, sales, and inventory managers to analyze point-of-sale data to help them respond quickly and accurately to market opportunities. Some of the specs in this case study included:

- Database size: 50-gigabyte database,
- Server: Compaq ProLiant server
- Operating System: Windows NT Server
- Number of Processors: 4 PentiumPro 200 MHz with 512 KB cache CPUs
- RAM: 1.8 GB RAM,
- RAID controllers: 2 Compaq Smart-2DH RAID Controllers
- Storage systems: 2 Compaq ProLiant U2 Storage Systems
- Backup Drive: 1 Compaq DLT 35/70 GB Tape Drive.
- Storage configuration: A total of 220 GB disk storage configured as 2 RAID5 arrays each with seven 7 18.2 GB 10K RPM WideUltra SCSI-3 disk drives, and 1 RAID1 array with 2 4.3 GB WideUltra SCSI-3 disk drives.

The system was designed to support the following:

- Initial load in the fact table of more than 120 million rows of data, which corresponds to two to three years of historical data
- More than 120,000 rows of nightly incremental updates
- Integrate with client/server and Web-based Cognos business intelligence tools for end-user access
- Integrate with Microsoft Exchange Server to keep the system administrator informed of performance issues

For more information on this case study, visit the Microsoft web site at: *http://www.microsoft.com/sql/bizsol/Shoney.htm.*

A case study with HarperCollins:

HarperCollins, one of the oldest English language publishers in the World, wanted to build a system that allows it to use its myriad of data to accurately forecast demand, keep returns to a minimum, and effectively manage the supply chain. The system allows for immediate access to point of sale information: units shipped, dollar cost to retailers, cost to produce, and how many units actually sell to customers. This access is a requirement that was cumbersome and costly to meet within HarperCollins' complex, legacy systems environment. Some of the specs in this case study included:

- Databases supported: a 92-gigabyte trade sales database; a 35-gigabyte database for HarperCollins' religious book publishing division, Zondervan; a 20-gigabyte database with pooled cost information for both divisions; a 50-gigabyte data warehouse; a 10-gigabyte Publishing Information Exchange database; and the company's General Ledger system
- Number of servers: 2 Windows NT–based servers
- Processors: 4 processors per server
- RAM: 1 GB of RAM per server
- The system used Silvon DataTracker, which is an application foundation that supports the development and deployment of powerful supply-chain applications

For more details on this case study, you can visit the web site: *http://www.microsoft.com/sql/bizsol/Harper.htm.*

Software

Software also spans a wide range of components starting with the operational database systems, to the data warehouse database management system (DBMS), to the OLAP services used and the data transformation tools and finally reporting tools used at the client machines.

The operational database should allow for fast access and querying of its data when feeding the data warehouse. The data warehouse DBMS should be optimized for data retrieval, and should be powerful and capable of handling potentially huge amounts of data. The data transformation tools should be efficient to allow for smooth transformation of the data from the sources to the destination data warehouse. The OLAP service should be powerful and capable of performing aggregations and summary tables quickly. Finally, the presentation tools should be user-friendly and allows powerful tables and graphs of the data to be built in response to the user's ad-hoc queries. This is important to accurately reflect the nature and findings of the data summaries in a robust fashion.

Given that you have the right hardware in place, Microsoft software and tools present a perfectly integrated set of software tools for building a successful data warehouse. The Windows NT/2000 Server operating system serves as the networking software and the software on which the databases will be based. SQL Server is a proven relational database that can be used efficiently for operational systems, and with the release of version 7.0, SQL Server became a good candidate for very large databases (VLDB), which are usually needed for data warehousing solutions. SQL Server 7.0 also includes an integrated set of tools for data transformation between the origins and the destination data warehouse. These tools utilize other Microsoft technologies that are designed specifically for the Windows environment, such as ActiveX technologies.

Microsoft OLAP server serves as a good solution for conducting OLAP operations, because it is tightly integrated with other Microsoft tools and with SQL Server. OLAP client tools, such as the pivot table service, are also a great choice for data presentation because they are also integrated with other popular tools, such as Microsoft Office, and can utilize the ActiveX technologies.

In short, the Microsoft solution for data warehousing not only includes the OLAP service, but also the operating system, the database management system, the networking system, the presentation tools, and the technologies that bind these components, such as ActiveX and component object model (COM).

Designing the Data Warehouse

After meeting the pre-requisites for the data warehousing project, and as a first step in the design of the data warehousing and OLAP solution, a strategy has to be laid out for the data warehouse project design and construction. The core components of this strategy include:

- **Policy**: rules that will determine how the data warehouse will be managed and used after its construction. These policies include the goal and scope of the data warehouse, rules that govern operational issues like loading and maintenance frequency, and organizational issues, such as security determination.
- **Transformation**: The data stored in the data warehouse is not likely to be the same raw data generated by OLTP systems. Instead the data has to be scrubbed, cleansed, transformed, and migrated, then the data may need to be summarized, filtered, refined, etc. Chapters 6 and 7 discuss in more detail how these operations can be conducted.
- **Metadata**: this is a repository of information about the data structures, applications, objects, and business rules in the data warehouse. This data is constructed once and centrally located for potential reuse in the future.
- **Storage**: After transformation the raw data is moved to its final destination – the data warehouse database. Data storage in the warehouse has to be optimized for easy accessibility, manageability, and flexibility.

The strategy mentioned above should be the guidance throughout the different phases of the project. We will now move on to discuss the different steps involved in the design process of our data warehousing solution for a typical sale and inventory system.

In the following sections, we will discuss the design steps for the data warehousing application in general without using the Microsoft OLAP Manager. We will see how the latter can be used in the different stages of design process in the next chapter, The OLAP Manager. The steps in the following sections of this chapter include:

- Analyzing the business, user, and technical requirements
- Designing the data warehouse database
- Designing the metadata
- Designing the data transformation strategy
- Designing the data warehouse policy and long-term maintenance and operation
- Designing the user interface tools

Analyzing The Requirements

Let's assume that a client representative contacted your company to perform an analysis and feasibility study for building a sale and inventory data warehouse solution, that would allow them to generate reports to assist them in the decision making and planning for future products, marketing, and sales strategies.

As a result, you establish a plan for gathering the requirements from the client. The plan includes interviewing the top managers at the client company, to find out about their specific vision and expectations from the data warehouse. The plan also includes identifying and meeting with all people who can provide valuable input to the design process.

It is important to ask the right questions when gathering the requirements; questions that increase your knowledge of the data and enhance your familiarity with the business issues and rules involved. Knowing the data will allow you to find the measures you need to represent in your OLAP solution. It will also allow you to identify the dimensions that you need to use to assess these measures. Finding the right measures and dimensions and identifying their relationships from the start will save you a great deal of time and effort later on after you have built your solution. Let's say that, after building your warehouse and OLAP application, you found out that a measure relates to some dimensions in a different way from the way represented in the design. This will mean modifying your design, and probably modifying your data transformation schemes, and re-importing the data into the data warehouse. Identifying the right relationships at design time will spare you from doing all of that.

We looked at the schema of the OLAP database in Chapter 3. We are using the term OLAP database here as a reference to the repository of the OLAP cube data. This schema includes a fact table with multiple dimension tables linked to it. The fact table has the measures that represent the issues of interest that you want to identify. Designing the OLAP solution starts by identifying these measures, and the dimensions related to them.

To identify the measures used in your OLAP solution, you need to ask the business analysts the kind of questions that would lead you to the purpose they want to use the data for. For instance, the client management and/or business analysts will tell you that they are interested in knowing about total sales by region, data, salesman, customer, etc. They may also tell you that they are interested in knowing their inventory and its relationship to the number of orders at any given time.

Gathering requirements for your data warehouse design involves identifying several types of requirements. These types include:

- Business requirements: owner requirements
- Architect requirements
- Developer requirements
- End user requirements

Business Requirements

Identifying the business requirements can be a complex and tricky task. This task includes identifying the objectives of the data warehouse or the data mart, determining the scope of the solution and any special requirements by the customer among other things. Therefore, when you set out gathering business requirements, you need to look into the following areas:

Business objectives

In our example, these objectives may include broad objectives like organizing the corporate data that is collected through the production OLTP systems in a way that may produce meaningful information that can be used for the decision-making and planning for the company's future. The objectives also include more specific needs like knowing the sales by region, time, and customer. Examples of broad objectives would be something like improving vendor assortments, or improving customer service, etc. A more specific goal would be the average weekly rate of sales for each family of products per region over last quarter.

Solution scope and objectives, customers, and stakeholders

In our example the scope will include the sales and inventory areas of the company business. Other areas, such as accounting, human resources, etc. will not be handled by this solution at this time. The door will, however, be open for expanding the solution to cover the other areas in the future, if needed. The customer of this solution will be the company's decision makers and business analysts. This includes the management, some of the IT department personnel, and the owners of the company. The owners and shareholders, if the company is traded publicly, will be stakeholders as well because they will benefit from the solution in learning about the performance of the company and the status of its business.

Sources of data

One of the important business and customer requirements is identifying the data sources that can contribute to the data warehouse and establish the optimal plans for collecting the data and sorting out what is beneficial and should be stored in the data warehouse and moving it into the data warehouse database.

For instance, a company may be migrating from legacy systems to the more modern PC-based systems. In the process, the company wants to salvage the data it collected over the years with the old system, and probably will continue to collect through the same system in place for some time in the transitional phase of the migration process. A basic requirement is to transform and transfer the data to the new system with a high degree of accuracy and efficiency.

Another concern customers have is when their data is hosted by different sources. Customers want their data to be well consolidated and transferred to the data warehouse. For instance, a company may have the payroll system based on a Unix-based Oracle database, the production and inventory data in a DB2 database on the mainframe, and the sales data in a SQL Server database, or possibly one branch only uses spreadsheets to keep track of timesheet information. The processes used to transfer the data and transform it should be well defined and polished. In cases like these, you need to identify all possible sources that can contribute to the data warehouse, study the data structure of these sources, and decide on what to keep and what to ignore. All this can be done by asking the customer and their agents the right questions.

Planning, budgeting, scheduling, and allocating resources

Another concern the customers will have has to do with the plan and implementation of the data warehouse, the budget they need to allocate for it, and the schedule and resources necessary for building it. All these are requirements that have to be identified early in the planning process. Failing to assess these elements with some degree of accuracy will eventually lead to difficulties that would probably fail the whole project.

As a result of identifying good business requirements, specifications for the data warehouse can be defined in terms of the following:

- Subject Areas: topics of interest to various business functions. As an example, the marketing department may have interest in one or more of the following topics: market research, competitive analysis, buyer behavior, market segmentation, product (market matching), pricing and budgeting decisions, product decisions, promotion decisions, channel decisions, and forecasting trends.
- Prototyping: this is an important step that will yield specific subject areas for the marketing department, such as orders, promotions, markets, sales, and time cycle.
- Granularity: the higher the granularity, so the amount of detail increases. This is defined by increasing the number of levels in the dimensions.
- Dimensions: Based on the analysis of the requirements, the following dimensions could be recognized:
  - Time with a calendar hierarchy (day, week, month, quarter, year)
  - Customer groups (customer, market segment, market, industry)
  - Product families (product, product family, product line)
  - Geography and location (sales rep, territory, district, country region, country, international region, corporate)
  - Organization structure (department, business unit, division, strategic business unit, subsidiary, corporation)

Architect's Requirements

Besides business and customer requirements, you need to identify architect requirements. In many cases, corporations use specific tools offered by certain vendors. The architect should be aware of the options that can be explored and the tools available. Also, the architect should be able to look at previous project catalogs, which would provide a great deal of information of how things were done. The architect, however, may still find that they need to use some tools that have not been used in previous projects, or that are not offered by the company's vendors. In this case the architect has to build a good case to present to the management for approval to obtain the required tools when they are not provided by the conventional vendors.

Developer's Requirements

Developer requirements should also be taken into consideration when gathering the requirements for the data warehousing solution. These requirements include specific applications, interfaces, computers, databases, communications, and user-interface screens. They also include technology requirements, deployment requirements, data warehouse production readiness requirements, and other requirements for development and deployment such as personnel, their skills, and availability.

End-user Requirement

It is extremely important to collect the requirements of the end-users because they are the ones who will be working with the system on a daily basis. These users will be mostly concerned with workflow. In other words, how does the functionality offered by the data warehouse fit into the end user's daily workflow? Other end-user requirements include query and reporting requirements, data analysis requirements, and types of activities including slicing and dicing separate data items in various ways, drilling down progressively exposing more details about the data, data mining to look for hidden patterns, and data surfing to browse the data warehouse data in an undirected manner. End users also want to be able to download and make local modifications, build business models, for example, using spreadsheets, data viewing in the form of two-dimensional views like spreadsheets, relational and relational tables, multi-dimensional views, reports and charts, and sample databases. Finally, it is very important to build a user-friendly GUI that the user approves of, and finds easy to use.

Design the Database

Microsoft OLAP services require an OLE DB data source. The data source contains one or more fact tables from which cubes can be built. The database also requires defining numeric measures based on certain fields in the fact table (such as unit price). Dimension tables should also exist to be used for analysis of the fact table measure data. These dimensions include things like, customer, time, product, store, etc. Dimension tables contain a minimum of two columns, one of which should be a key column. Other columns describe and define individual attributes of the dimension, such as product brand category and sub-category. Dimension tables could also include keys to other dimension tables, for instance the product dimension may include the product category key, which is the key of the product category dimension table. The relationships between the fact table and dimension tables, specified by the joins of these tables, follow the star or snowflake schema.

In this section, we will look more closely at the design of a sales and inventory database as the basis for our data warehouse. The schema of this database is presented in the following diagram. Looking at the schema, we notice that there are two facts to analyze: sales and inventory. Each one of these facts has a fact table of its own. The fact tables are joined by dimension tables forming a star schema in each case.

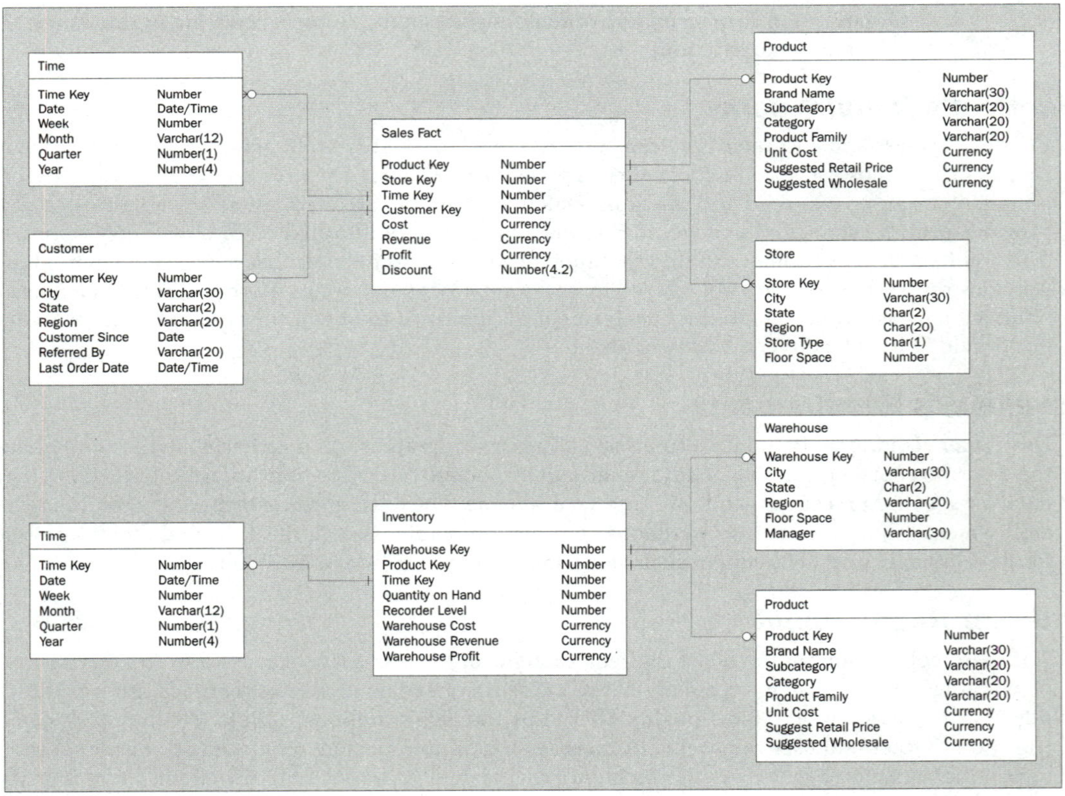

Schema of the Sales and Inventory database

When designing an OLAP solution with the Microsoft OLAP services, you need to make sure that the logical and physical design of the database meet the following conditions:

OLAP Services Uses Only Certain Aggregation Functions

What you should do is calculate the measure by getting the total profits and dividing that by the total sales at the aggregation level (year for instance).

Be Aware of Pre-Calculations

Another thing you need to be aware of is that sometimes you need to do some calculations before you do the aggregation. For example, if you have in your fact table the cost, unit price and sale amount, you can calculate the profit by subtracting the cost from the product of the unit price and sales amount. This new value has to be calculated before you do any aggregation on it, in order for the aggregation to be accurate. The new value can be saved as a calculated measure, or in some cases a calculated member.

Dimension Data Must Appropriately Exist in Dimension Tables

Dimension tables in Microsoft OLAP services should have columns representing level members as member key, name, and properties. With this, each level in the hierarchy is represented in its own table. This is not the only way hierarchical data is represented in relational databases. Sometimes you may find hierarchies represented in one table with self-joins of a key field to a parent key field. These tables provide great benefits in that they allow for unbalanced hierarchies to be represented where the leaf levels can be located at different distances from the root. Another benefit these tables provide is that they allow you to move subtrees easily in the hierarchy by changing the parent key for the root of these subtrees. However, these tables will not work with Microsoft OLAP services and have to be converted to a series of snowflaked tables that represent a balanced hierarchy before using them. The following diagram shows the difference of the two representations.

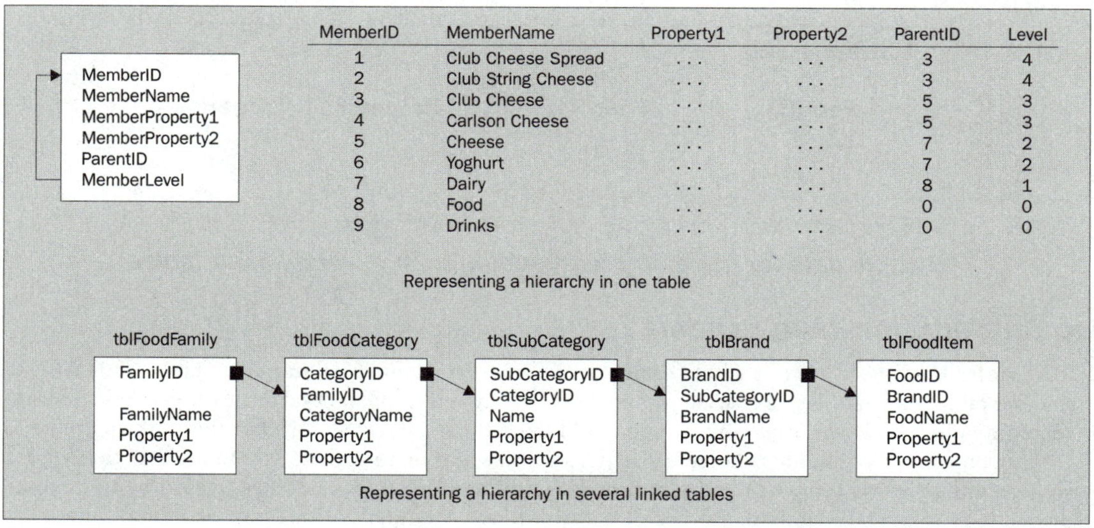

MemberID	MemberName	Property1	Property2	ParentID	Level
1	Club Cheese Spread	...	...	3	4
2	Club String Cheese	...	...	3	4
3	Club Cheese	...	...	5	3
4	Carlson Cheese	...	...	5	3
5	Cheese	...	...	7	2
6	Yoghurt	...	...	7	2
7	Dairy	...	...	8	1
8	Food	...	...	0	0
9	Drinks	...	...	0	0

Two different ways to represent hierarchies in relational databases

tblFoodFamily			
FamilyID	**FamilyName**	**Property1**	**Property2**
1	Food	...	...
2	Drinks	...	...

tblFoodCategory			
CategoryID	**CategoryName**	**Property1**	**Property2**
1	Dairy	...	...
2	Meet	...	...

tblSubCategory			
SubCategoryID	**Name**	**Property1**	**Property2**
1	Cheese	...	...
2	Milk	...	...

tblBrand			
BrandID	**BrandName**	**Property1**	**Property2**
1	Food	...	...
2	Drinks	...	...

tblFoodItem			
FoodID	**FoodName**	**Property1**	**Property2**
1	Food	...	...
2	Drinks	...	...

Sample data for hierarchy representation in several linked tables

Use Star or Snowflake Schema ...

Microsoft OLAP Services can create dimensions from one or more columns in a table. This table can be the fact table, or could be a separate dimension table linked to the fact table through a key column. It is recommended, however, that you use separate linked dimension tables, rather than the fact table to create your dimensions. This choice usually results in a star or snowflake schema. Using this kind of schema enhances visibility of the dimension data, while optimizing its storage according to the basic principle of relational database models. It is easier to see the relationships between the different dimensions and the fact table with this representation. Storage need is optimized due to the possibility of using smaller key columns in the fact table that join to the dimension table, which includes the descriptive name column of the dimension and its levels. This is because name columns are usually of the character data type, which requires more storage than the numeric data type of the key columns. Indexes related to the dimension member keys in the fact table will also be smaller in this case, which not only improves the storage situation, but also improves the speed at which data is retrieved from the table in queries.

To get a better grasp on this concept, assume that the fact table includes 3 million records. Assuming that the table has three dimensions, let's see the difference in storage needed for each case: either including the dimensions in the fact table, or separating them out in their own tables. In the first case, let's assume that the dimension name field is a character field of length 30 characters. That means the storage needed for the three dimension columns in the fact table, not considering the indexes related to them is calculated according to the following formula:

Needed Storage = `3,000,000 x 3 x 30/(1,024 x 1,024) = 257.5MB`

> **The formula above simply multiplies the number of columns in the fact table corresponding to the dimensions by the size of the columns, and the result is multiplied by the number of rows in the table. The division by (1024 x 1024) converts the result from Bytes to MB.**

In the second case, the storage needed for the same dimensions if they are separated out in their own tables and joining them to the fact table through a 4-byte numeric key column is calculated according to the formula:

Needed Storage = `3,000,000 x 3 x 4/(1,024 x 1,024) = 34.3MB`

The benefit becomes even more obvious when you add the storage needed for the indexes on the fact table in both cases. The added storage needed to accommodate the separate dimension tables is usually minimal and negligible compared to the space savings in the fact table. This is because these dimension tables are usually small in size and include only a few records to several hundred records in extreme situations.

Another benefit of using the star or snowflake schema is that maintaining the dimensions becomes much easier. Dimensions are processed by OLAP services by performing `SELECT DISTINCT` on the dimension column in the fact table. If this column is a long character field, it will take much longer to process this query than if it is a numeric value. This leads to even better performance.

Finally, by separating dimension tables out from the fact table, you ensure that all members at the different levels of the dimension exist even if they are not represented in the fact table. For example, if the fact table for December 1998 sales does not include brand XYZ of food, this brand will still exist as a member of the brand level of the product dimension table.

How About Dimension Members?

When it comes to dimension members, several rules have to be fulfilled in your design for the Microsoft OLAP Services database. These rules are described below.

Member Names

Member names need not be unique within a level. However, within the hierarchy the member names should be unique. In other words, you may have the member name Jackson for a city in the state of Mississippi and for a city in Michigan at the same time. The member name here is not unique to the overall city level. However, for the hierarchy it is unique because there is only one Jackson in Mississippi and only one Jackson in Michigan.

One thing you may want to consider in the design stages of your dimension members is converting numbers to textual types filling in the left places with zeros, because if you do not do this, OLAP Services will. This is because OLAP Services can only sort text values. For instance, if you perform the transformation, 1 becomes "01" and 2 becomes "02". If OLAP services does the conversion on its own, you will have difficulties sorting the numbers correctly. When OLAP Services converts the numbers to text types the 1 becomes "1" and the 2 becomes "2". Sorting the numbers from 1 to 20 will then yield something like: 1, 10, 11, 12, 13, 14, 15, 16, 17, 18, 19, 2, 20, 3, 4, 5, 6, 7, 8, 9, which probably isn't the way you want the sort to happen.

Members and Aggregate Levels

Microsoft OLAP Services requires that hierarchies be fully connected. In other words, any member at a non-leaf level should have at least one child member in the next lower level. If this next level is a leaf level, then the child will be at that leaf level and this child will not have any more children. What this means is that dimension members should exist at all aggregate levels, and you cannot have a level that is void of members. If a hierarchy is irregular and not fully connected, members have to be filled in at the leaf and other missing levels. These members could be empty, as long as the hierarchy is transformed into a fully connected hierarchy. One way to accomplish this practically is to use outer joins to create views on the snowflake tables defining the dimension to return all members of the dimension. The dimension would then be based on the view, rather than the original snowflake tables.

Let's present an example to make this clearer. Look at the following figure. It represents a simple irregular hierarchy representing different monthly expenses: insurance, payroll, and utility bills. The insurance shows payments for life, health, and auto insurance. The leaf level is supposed to be the types of insurance. However, this level is missing for the payroll and utilities categories. In order to make this hierarchy work in Microsoft OLAP Services, we need to construct a view based on the tables of the hierarchy using outer joins. Assuming we have an Expense Category table and an Expense table with the structures shown in the following figure, we can write the SQL (as shown after the diagram) to create the view.

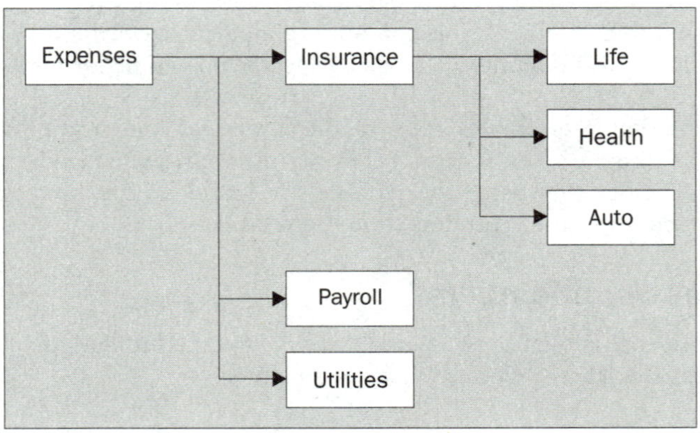

A simple irregular hierarchy

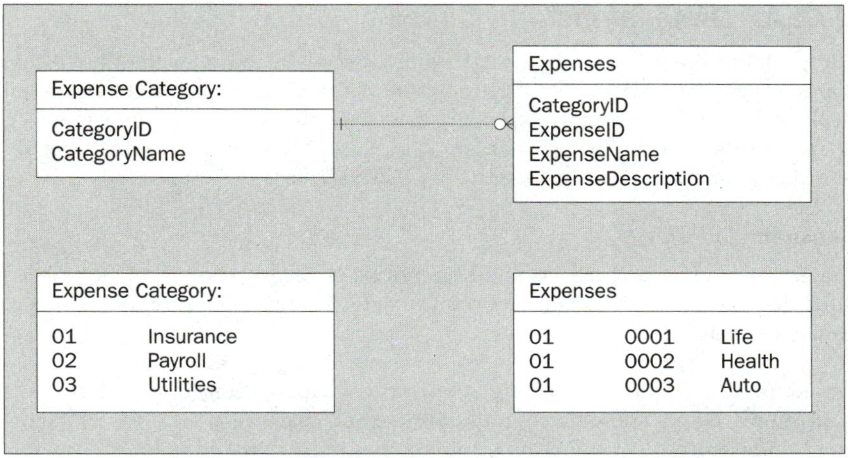

Tables of the hierarchy shown in the previous figure

```
CREATE VIEW vwExpenses AS
SELECT  [Expense Category].CategoryID,
        [Expense Category].CategoryName,
         Expenses.ExpenseID, Expenses.ExpenseDescription
FROM    [Expense Category] LEFT JOIN Expenses ON
        [Expense Category].CategoryID = Expenses.CategoryID;
```

As a result the view will have the values in the table below:

CategoryID	CategoryName	ExpenseID	ExpenseDescription
01	Insurance	0001	Life
01	Insurance	0002	Health
01	Insurance	0003	Auto
02	payroll	Null	Null
03	Utilities	Null	Null

You notice that the view will have empty cells for the missing leaf levels for the payroll and utilities categories.

One more thing to consider when designing dimensions and hierarchies in Microsoft OLAP Services is that each fact should relate to a single member in the lowest level used by each dimension in the cube. For instance, in our sales and inventory example, the `sales` fact should relate to the lowest member in the dimensions involved: `time`, `product`, `store`, and `customer`. In other words, the facts should be at the levels: `day`, `product name`, `store`, and `customer name` of these dimensions respectively. You cannot have a fact at the `day`, `product name`, `state`, and `customer name` levels of these dimensions because the `state` level of the `store` dimension is not the lowest level in that dimension.

Designing OLAP Dimensions and Cubes

The most important step in designing the multidimensional database for the OLAP solution is designing the cubes and dimensions. Microsoft OLAP solutions provides a wide variety of options when it comes to these designs. You can build shared, private, or virtual dimensions, or you can also choose to make your cube either a stored cube or a virtual one. So let's look at how we design cubes and dimensions in a way that utilizes the many powerful aspects of OLAP services.

Naming Dimensions and Cubes

Once a dimension or cube is saved, its name cannot be changed. Therefore, pay special attention when naming these objects, especially when you want to define multiple hierarchies, which can only be done through dimension names.

Naming a cube or dimension follows the general naming conventions in OLAP services. That is, the name can have only letters and digits in addition to some characters, such as, "@" and "#", in addition to spaces and underscores. Cube and dimension names must start with a letter. Any leading or trailing spaces to the name are truncated by OLAP services. Dimension names allow a maximum of one period, which is used to represent multiple hierarchies in the dimension.

Choosing Between Shared and Private Dimensions

Private dimensions are used exclusively by the cube they are created in. Shared dimensions, on the other hand, can be used by multiple cubes in the database. Private dimensions require that the cube be processed if they or their data ever change. With this, private dimensions do not allow for incremental processing. Also, virtual dimensions cannot be formed from member properties of private dimensions. However, private dimensions can participate in multiple hierarchies with other private or shared dimensions in the cube, as long as the names of these dimensions are unique.

Unless it is absolutely necessary to use a dimension exclusively with a cube, it is recommended that you build your dimensions to be shared. Private dimensions don't really offer any benefits over shared dimensions.

Multiple Hierarchies

Microsoft OLAP Services define multiple hierarchies in terms of the name of the dimension that they are part of, by introducing a period in the name that separates the name of the dimension from that of the hierarchy. For example, to create two hierarchies for the `Time` dimension, `fiscal` and `calendar`, you can create two dimensions and give them the names: `Time.Fiscal` and `Time.Calendar` respectively. Therefore, as you see, multiple hierarchies are treated as separate dimensions in OLAP services. One undesirable side effect of this is that OLAP services will create aggregates between the two dimensions representing the hierarchies. These aggregates are usually meaningless and only consume disk space and processing time for the cube.

If you want to design multiple hierarchies in your OLAP solution, make sure the naming of the dimensions participating in the hierarchy is correctly established and make sure you set the properties of the dimensions and their members appropriately, because these properties don't have to be the same between the two dimensions forming the multiple hierarchy.

Member Properties

As we discussed in the previous chapter, Microsoft OLAP services allow you to create member properties for members of a certain level of a dimension. These member properties are defined by any field in any of the tables that make up the dimension. This feature provides you with the flexibility and ability to build virtual dimensions and filter MDX query results (see Chapters 7 and 8).

Member properties are not automatically aggregated in the same way measures are. OLAP services do not group query results based on member property values. Such grouping has to be done in a view. Member property values are treated as text values by OLAP services regardless of the type behind these values. Therefore numbers, string values, and dates are all considered text values. If you use member properties in SQL queries and you want to express them in the resultset in terms of their true type, you need to use SQL conversion functions, such as `CAST` and `CONVERT` to explicitly convert them to the type they are supposed to have. This conversion allows the client that is issuing the query to format the values in the proper way. For instance, dates can be formatted to show day/month/year instead of month/day/year, and currency values can be formatted to show a currency sign, separating comas, and decimals.

In your design, you need to highlight all these points so that when the development of the client queries and reports takes place, these issues can be accounted for.

Virtual Dimensions and Virtual Cubes

As we discussed in the previous chapter, member properties can be used to create virtual dimensions. The next chapter will illustrate how this can be done with the OLAP Manager. Virtual dimensions act like views. They add valuable analysis capabilities, as well as security among other benefits, but they increase query processing time compared to regular dimensions. Virtual dimensions have only two levels, the ALL level and a base level, and can be used to break a dimension on multiple display axes. For example, for the `Time` dimension, if you create a virtual dimension that includes only the month level together with the ALL level, you can use the *virtual* `Time` dimension with the *regular* `Time` dimension to display a matrix in which the column headings are years and the row headings are months as shown in the table below.

Sales in $1,000	**1997**	**1998**	**1999**
Jan	20	19	23
Feb	18	17.6	22.2
Mar	19.5	22	17
Apr	21	22.1	20.5
...	...	...	...

When you design virtual dimensions, you need to weigh the benefits of saving storage space against the disadvantage of increased query processing time. If the benefits outweigh the losses, then virtual dimensions become a good option to include in the design of your data warehouse.

Virtual cubes are another feature offered by OLAP services, to allow for better dimensional analysis and reporting. They allow you to view data from multiple cubes across any dimensions, shared or private that are part of these cubes, and they may contain calculated members and other definitions. Virtual cubes can also offer a viable solution for analysis of a situation that is much more difficult to analyze with a single regular cube.

Designing Partitions

In the previous chapter we discovered that multiple partitions are allowed on a single cube in the Enterprise edition of Microsoft OLAP. Partitions are considered a great feature because they physically implement logical segments of data, and therefore can be used for optimization and maintenance purposes of the system. Designing partitions has to be done with extensive care to avoid duplicating data or eliminating data in some cases.

The previous chapter presented many guidelines for creating these partitions and working with them. The next chapter shows you how to use partitions in the OLAP Manager, the GUI tool provided with Microsoft OLAP services to design, manage, and maintain the system. However, things to be careful about when dealing with partitions include overlapping partitions and incomplete partitions. These concepts are discussed in some detail below.

OLAP services do not track overlapping partitions, which may lead to duplicating data in the partitions resulting in incorrect aggregations. To illustrate how this can take place, let's consider the sales and inventory database example we have been using so far. If we design our partitions so that each will include data for one quarter of the year and still have a partition for the whole year, then if the year partition uses the same fact tables as the quarter partitions, your values will be counted twice. The solution to this problem is merging the quarter partitions to form a year partition instead.

Incomplete coverage of the cube with the partitions will yield empty cells. Therefore, when you suspect that empty cells are encountered where they shouldn't be, examine your partitions to see if they are incomplete and don't cover the whole cube. Just like overlapping partitions, incomplete partitions lead to erroneous aggregation results.

Metadata and the Microsoft Repository

In the first two chapters, we met the Microsoft repository, and discovered how it is used to store the metadata describing the different aspects of the data warehouse and OLAP services. In this section, we will re-iterate the ideas discussed previously, and add more explanation to them in light of the new information introduced in this chapter.

When you create any objects in OLAP services, data about the object is called metadata and is stored in the Microsoft repository. Metadata describes the object, its properties and all aspects related to it. You can view some of the metadata in the OLAP Manager by selecting the metadata tab (where available) in the detail pane. The screenshot on the following page shows an example of the metadata display in the OLAP Manager. The following is a metadata summary for different components and objects of the OLAP services.

Data Source

The data source used for the OLAP database and for the individual cube has its own metadata that describes it. As you will see in Chapter 5, The OLAP Manager, as we define a data source for a cube, when you prepare your design for the OLAP database, you need to specify the name of the data source, the source data store (a SQL Server database for example), the location of the data store (server name), and OLE DB Provider name that facilitates the connection to the data source. When you create the data source, you will see these items listed as part of the metadata for it in addition to the status which indicates whether the connection to the source is established or not.

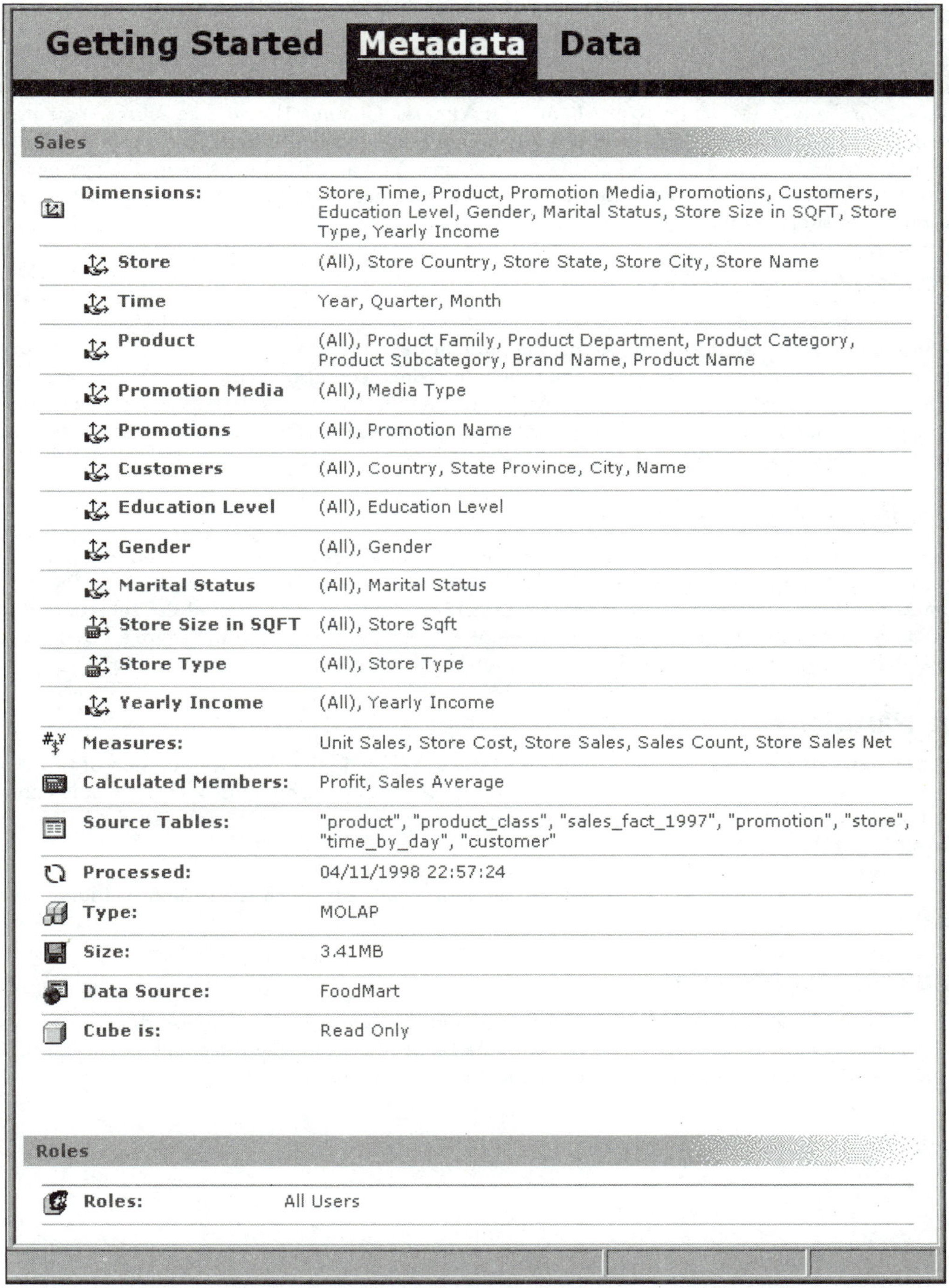

Cube metadata as it shows in the OLAP Manager

OLAP Cubes

In the process of designing your data warehouse and OLAP solution, you need to define the metadata for OLAP cubes. This includes specification of the dimensions, measures, calculated members, source tables, storage type (MOLAP, ROLAP, or HOLAP – see Chapter 1), and data source. You also need to identify the security of this cube and possibly create separate roles to limit access to it. Each of these items has to be identified in detail and with great care. You also need to estimate the aggregation sizes and storage need for the cube so that the customer takes necessary measures to have the needed resources to support them.

Dimensions

When it comes to dimensions, you need to specify the number of dimensions you will be using in your solution, the names of these dimensions, the number of levels in each one, and the type of each dimension – whether it is a standard or a time dimension. You also need to specify for each dimension whether it is a private dimension or a shared one. Finally, you need to specify when you need to have each of the dimensions processed, whether before the cube processing (for shared dimensions) or during the cube processing.

Individual Dimensions

Metadata for individual dimensions includes information about the levels included in the dimension, the source table for the dimension, the source columns for the levels of the dimension, and the member count. You may find it difficult to predict the member count for each level of the cube dimension, but a rough estimate will help determine the degree of aggregation and size of the aggregates that you can get away with. Also defined as part of the dimension metadata are the cubes it is used in.

Cube Partitions

As you have already seen, cube partitions are only available in the enterprise edition of OLAP Services. The Standard edition allows for only one partition for the cube, which includes the whole cube. Metadata for the partition defines its name, data source, storage type (MOLAP/ROLAP/HOLAP), and the slices for the partitions.

SQL Server stores repository information in its `msdb` database, which is a system relational database that ships with SQL Server.

Sample Model Metadata

The following is an example of a specification of metadata for a data warehouse design for a typical sales and inventory data warehouse system we had looked at earlier in the chapter. The specification shows the kind of information you need to ideally keep track of in the metadata.

Defining the model goals (inventory and sales)

Inventory	
Name:	Inventory
Definition:	This model contains inventory data for each product model in each warehouse, on a daily basis.
Purpose:	The purpose of this model is to facilitate the analysis of inventory levels and warehouse profits.
Contact Person:	Warehouse Manager.
Dimensions:	Warehouse, Product, and Time.
Facts:	Inventory
Measures:	Quantity on hand, reorder level, cost, revenue, profit.
Calculated Members	Floor space in sqft

Sales	
Name:	Sales
Definition:	This model contains sales data for each product model, on each order, on a daily basis.
Purpose:	The purpose of this model is to facilitate the analysis of product sales.
Contact Person:	Regional Sales Manager
Dimensions:	Customer, Product, Store, and Time
Facts:	Sales
Measures:	Cost, revenue, profit, amount sold, and discount amount
Calculated Members	Floor space in sqft, and store type

Fact Metadata

Inventory	
Name:	Inventory
Definition:	This fact contains inventory data for each product model in each warehouse, on a daily basis as well as cost and profit data for the warehouse.
Load Frequency:	Daily
Load Statistics:	Last load date: N/A
	Number of rows loaded: N/A

Inventory	
Usage Statistics:	Average number of queries/day: N/A
	Average rows returned/query: N/A
	Average query runtime: N/A
	Maximum number of queries/day: N/A
	Maximum rows returned/query: N/A
	Maximum query runtime: N/A
Archive Rules:	Data will be archived after 24 months, on a monthly basis.
Archive Statistics:	Last archive date: N/A
	Date archived to: N/A
Purge Rules:	Data will be purged after 48 months, on a monthly basis.
Purge Statistics:	Last purge date: N/A
	Date purged to: N/A
Data Quality:	Inventory levels may fluctuate throughout the day as more stock is received into inventory from production and stock is shipped out to retail stores and customers. The measures for this fact are collected once per day and thus reflect the state of inventory at that point in time, which is the end of the working day for a plant.
Data Accuracy:	The measures of this fact are "some value%" (preferably as close to 100% as possible) accurate at the point in time they represent. This is based on the results of physical inventories matched to recorded inventory levels. No inference can be made from these measures as to values at points in time not recorded.
Time Granularity:	The measures of this fact represent inventory levels on a daily basis.
Key:	The key to an inventory fact is the combination of the keys of its dimensions: `Warehouse`, `Product`, and `Time`.

Sales:	
Name:	Sale
Definition:	This fact contains sale data for each transaction that has been recorded in the sales systems at each retail store.
Load Frequency:	Daily
Load Statistics:	Last load date: N/A
	Number of rows loaded: N/A

Sales:	
Usage Statistics:	Average number of queries/day: N/A Average rows returned/query: N/A Average query runtime: N/A Maximum number of queries/day: N/A Maximum rows returned/query: N/A Maximum query runtime: N/A
Archive Rules:	Data will be archived after 24 months, on a monthly basis.
Archive Statistics:	Last archive date: N/A Date archived to: N/A
Purge Rules:	Data will be purged after 48 months, on a monthly basis.
Purge Statistics:	Last purge date: N/A Date purged to: N/A
Data Quality:	It is possible for errors to be made by staff completing a transaction. However, the numbers recorded represent what is actually contracted with the customer and must be honored.
Data Accuracy:	The measures of this fact should be 100% accurate in that they represent what was actually sold.
Time Granularity:	The measures of this fact represent sales of a given product on a given transaction.
Key:	The key to a sale fact is the combination of the keys of its dimensions: `Customer`, `Stores`, `Product`, and `Time`.
Key Generation Method:	The time portion of the key is simply the date the sale takes place. The `product` key is retrieved from the product tables in the operational system. The `store` key is retrieved from the store tables in the operational systems using the `region ID` and `store ID`. The seller key is retrieved from the seller translation table using the `region ID`, `outlet ID`, and `salesperson ID`. The `customer` key is retrieved from the customer translation table using the `customer ID` and `customer location ID`. The `order ID` from the original order is used as the `order` key for the sale fact.
Source:	`Order` Table in operational system database Conversion Rules: Rows in each order table are copied into the sale fact on a daily basis. You may add some scrubbing and cleansing, conversion rules for the copy process.
Selection Logic:	Only rows for the current transaction date are selected.

Dimension Metadata

Customer	
Definition:	A customer is any person or organization who purchases goods from the client company or any of its subsidiaries. A customer may be associated with many business locations (hence the geography aspect or hierarchy of the dimension).
Hierarchy:	Data can be summarized at three levels for a customer. The lowest level of summarization is the customer city appearing in the ship-to address. Data from each location (ship-to address) can be further rolled up to be summarized by state, then by region.
Change Rules:	New customer locations are inserted as new rows into the dimension. Changes to existing locations are updated in place.
Load Frequency:	Daily
Load Statistics:	Last load date: N/A
	Number of rows loaded: N/A
Usage Statistics:	Average number of queries/day: N/A
	Average rows returned/query: N/A
	Average query runtime: N/A
	Maximum number of queries/day: N/A
	Maximum rows returned/query: N/A
	Maximum query runtime: N/A
Archive Rules:	Customer data is not archived.
Archive Statistics:	Last archive date: N/A
	Date archived to: N/A
Purge Rules:	Customers who have not purchased any goods from the client or any of its subsidiaries in the past 48 months will be purged on a monthly basis.
Purge Statistics:	Last purge date: N/A
	Date purged to: N/A
Data Quality:	When a new customer is added, a search is done to determine if we already do business with another location. In rare cases separate branches of a customer are recorded as separate customers because this check fails. Until such time as the customer notices separate locations dealing with us, these occurrences remain as originally recorded. The region attribute was not originally in the operational system. It is added based on a matrix that shows the regions based on zip codes in the ship-to-address attribute.
Data Accuracy:	Incorrect association of locations of a common customer occurs in less than "x%" of our customer data. The value of "x" will be based on some research of the operational data.

Customer	
Key:	The key to the customer dimension consists of a system-generated number.
Key Generation Method:	When a customer is copied from the operational system, the translation table is checked to determine if the customer already exists in the warehouse. If not, a new key is generated and the key along with the `customer ID` and `location ID` are added to the translation table. If the customer and location already exist, the key from the translation table is used to determine which customer in the warehouse to update.
Source:	
Name:	`Customer` table
Conversion Rules:	Rows in each `customer` table are copied on a daily basis. For existing customers, the name is updated. For new customers, once a location is determined, the key is generated and a row inserted. Before the update/insert takes place a check is performed for a duplicate customer name. If a duplicate is detected, a sequence number is appended to the name. This check is repeated until the name and sequence number combination are determined to be unique. Once uniqueness has been confirmed, the update/insert takes place.
Selection Logic:	Only new or changed rows are selected.
Name:	`Customer Location` Table
Conversion Rules:	Rows in each customer location table are copied on a daily basis. For existing customer locations, the ship-to address is updated. For new customer locations, the key is generated and a row inserted.
Selection Logic:	Only new or changed rows are selected.

Customer Attributes:	
Attribute 1:	Customer key
Definition:	This is an arbitrary value assigned to guarantee uniqueness for each customer and location.
Change Rules:	Once assigned, the values of this attribute never change.
Data Type:	Numeric
Domain:	1 - 999,999,999
Derivation Rules:	A system-generated key of the highest used customer key +1 is assigned when creating a new customer and location entry.
Source:	System generated

Table Continued on Following Page

Customer Attributes:	
Attribute 2:	Name
Definition:	This is the name by which a customer is known to the client.
Change Rules:	When a customer name changes it is updated in place in this dimension.
Data Type:	Char(30)
Domain:	Derivation rules: To ensure the separation of data for customers who have the same name but are not part of the same organization, a number will be appended to names where duplicates exist.
Source:	Name in Customer Table
Derivation Rules	Name is derived by concatenating first name, middle initial, and last name of the retail customer, or by copying the company name for business customers.
Attribute 3:	City
Definition:	This is the city part of an address where the client ships goods to a corporate customer. It is possible for a corporate customer to have multiple ship-to locations, hence multiple `City` member values. For retail customers no `City` is kept because no ship-to-address is kept in the source table. Therefore, there can only be one entry in the customer dimension for a retail customer.
Change Rules:	When a `City` changes it is updated in place in this dimension.
Data Type:	Char(60)
Domain:	All valid cities within the client's service area.
Derivation Rules:	The ship-to (City) is derived from the ship-to-address in the operational table.
Source:	Ship-to address in the `Customer Location` Table
Facts:	Sale
Measures:	Cost, revenue, quantity sold, and discount amount
Attribute 4:	State
Definition:	This is the state part of an address where the client ships goods to a corporate customer. It is possible for a corporate customer to have multiple ship-to locations, hence multiple `State` member values. For retail customers no `State` is kept because no ship-to-address is kept in the source table. Therefore, there can only be one entry in the customer dimension for a retail customer.
Change Rules:	When a `State` changes it is updated in place in this dimension.

Customer Attributes:	
Data Type:	Char(60)
Domain:	All valid states within the client's service area.
Derivation Rules:	The ship-to (State) is derived from the ship-to-address in the operational table.
Source:	Ship-to address in `Customer Location` Table
Facts:	Sale
Measures:	Cost, revenue, quantity sold, and discount amount
Attribute 5:	Region
Definition:	This is the region in which an address where the client ships goods to a corporate customer. It is possible for a corporate customer to have multiple ship-to locations, hence multiple `Region` member values. For retail customers no `Region` is kept because no ship-to-address is kept in the source table. Therefore, there can only be one entry in the customer dimension for a retail customer.
Change Rules:	When a `Region` changes it is updated in place in this dimension.
Data Type:	Char(60)
Domain:	All valid regions within the client's service area.
Derivation Rules:	The ship-to (Region) is derived from the ship-to-address' zip code based on a matrix the client establishes to define regions.
Source:	Ship-to address' zip code and client's region/zip code matrix
Facts:	Sale
Measures:	Cost, revenue, quantity sold, and discount amount

You can actually continue with this specification adding to it the remaining dimensions, measures, member properties, virtual dimensions, etc. This specification will eventually serve as the blueprint for the design and policy of your OLAP solution.

Data Loading and Transformation Strategy

Part of the design of the data warehouse is the design of the data loading and transportation strategy. SQL Server 7 includes Data Transformation Services (DTS), which make this task much easier than it would have been.

Loading the data into the data warehouse goes through several stages. These stages are: data capture, data transformation, and data application. The designer has to focus on all three stages determining the techniques to use for each one and the physical storage for the data during each stage.

Capturing the Data

The data warehouse receives data captured from the operational systems and other external sources. Capturing the data means collecting it from these capture sources, which include various file formats and both relational and non-relational database management systems. The data can be captured from many types of files, including extract files or tables, image copies, changed data files or tables, DBMS logs or journals, message files, and event logs. The technique used for capturing the data varies with the type of the data being captured, as you will see below. Data capturing techniques include source data extraction, DBMS log capture, triggered capture, application-assisted capture, timestamp-based capture, and file comparison capture. Let's discuss the application and use of each of these techniques.

Source Data Extraction

Source data extraction provides a static snapshot of source data at a specific point in time. This technique is suitable for a static temporal data model that doesn't require a continuous history. Source data extraction works best when files, tables, or image copies are sought from the capture process. This technique may be best used when a whole block of data is to be loaded into the data warehouse, maybe replacing some data in the warehouse that is related to the same source, but at a different snapshot in time. As an example of using this method, a school that usually updates its data warehouse with the year data at the end of the year, while archiving the data of the last year.

DBMS Log Capture

Log capture enables the data to be captured from the DBMS logging system. It has minimal impact on the database or the operational systems that are accessing the database. This technique requires that DBMS logging is supported and turned on, as well as a clear understanding of the format of the log records and fairly sophisticated programming to extract only the data of interest based on what is logged in the log files. This method is not directly possible with SQL Server since the format of the log files generated by the SQL Profiler is internal to SQL Server, and cannot be easily read outside the SQL Profiler. A work around this is to have the SQL Profiler log the traces to a table in the database, and then you can use Triggered Capture (see below) to extract data from it.

Triggered Capture

Many database management systems, such as SQL Server and other SQL92 compliant systems, support triggers and stored procedures. Triggers are procedures that provide for the execution of SQL or complex applications when specific events in the database take place, such as inserting new records, updating or deleting existing ones. These triggers can enable any type of capture. The trigger itself simply recognizes the event and invokes the procedure. It is up to the user to actually develop, test, and maintain the procedure. This technique must be used with care because it is controlled more by the people writing the procedures rather than by the database management system. Therefore, it is open to easy access and changes as well as interference by other triggering mechanisms.

Application-assisted capture

Application-assisted capture involves writing programs that include the logic to capture the data from almost any operational source. This implies total control by the application programmer along with all the responsibilities for testing and maintenance. Microsoft data abstraction technologies, such as OLE DB and ADO, allow for writing such applications to access a wide variety of data sources using the programming language of your choice. Although a valid technique, it is considered better to have application-assisted capture performed by products developed specifically for this purpose, rather than to develop your own customized application unless you sufficiently test and verify that your application will do what it is intended to do without unwanted side effects.

One benefit of DBMS log capture, triggered capture, and application-assisted capture is that each of these techniques can produce an incremental record of source changes, to enable use of a continuous history model. Each of these techniques typically requires some other facility for the initial load of data.

Timestamp-based capture

Timestamp-based capture is a simple technique that involves checking a timestamp value to determine whether the record has changed since the last capture. If a record has changed, or a new record has been added, it is captured to a file or table for subsequent processing. This technique may require structural changes to existing operational systems to ensure that timestamp fields exist in each table participating in the capture process of such systems.

File Comparison

A technique that has been used for many years is file comparison. Although it may not be as efficient, it is an easy technique to understand and implement. This technique involves saving a file that includes a snapshot of the data source at a specific point in time of data capture. Then, at a later point in time, the current file is compared with the previous snapshot file. Any changes and additions that are detected are captured to a separate file for subsequent processing and adding to the data warehouse databases. As an example, an auto manufacturer wanted to create a Web-based application that allows potential customers to search all dealer inventories and factory inventories on the Web to find the car they like, and possibly buy it on-line. The database supporting the search engine is a SQL Server 7.0 data warehouse. Data is extracted from thousands of individual dealer's databases and consolidated in an ASCII format file. The data is compared to factory data, with new built cars that are not in dealer inventory being added as well. The resulting file is then uploaded into the database every week. However, every night, the file is compared to the previous nights upload to check for differences. These differences are then loaded appropriately when found.

It seems at first that timestamp-based capture and file comparison capture, with their comparison technique, produce a record of the incremental changes that enables support of a continuous history model. However, this may or may not be accurate. Care must be exercised because more than one change of a record may occur between capture points resulting in not recording all changes to the operational system, which may lead to losing some of these changes that took place between capture points. Therefore, the history captured would be more accurately described as a history based on points in time, rather than a record of the continuous change history.

As a data warehouse designer, you need to take all these techniques into consideration when planning your data capture based on the sources you are capturing data from, the kind of data you need to capture from these sources, and the nature of capture history, continuous versus based on point in time. It is possible, for instance, to use a mixture of these extraction techniques e.g. you may use 'Application Assisted Capture' to produce records in an intermediate database which is then 'Source Data Extracted'. This can be especially useful for remote data sources or where the security and integrity of the raw data is an issue. The table below will help you to quickly find the proper techniques you want to consider for a specific situation.

	Best Use Scenario		
Data Capture Technique	Initial Load	Incremental Load with Continuous Change History	Incremental Load with Periodic Change History
Source data extraction	X		
DBMS Log Capture		X	
Triggered Capture		X	
Application-based Capture		X	
Timestamp-based Capture			X
File Comparison Capture			X

Comparison of data capture techniques

Transforming the Data

Transforming the data to the data warehouse involves several processes. These processes should be designed to ensure validity and integrity, adequacy and usefulness, and in some cases aggregation and calculation of new values based on data source values. These functions are usually classified as data validation, data scrubbing, and data transformation. The following paragraphs briefly describe these functions. A detailed discussion of these issues is available in Chapter 6, Microsoft Data Transformation Services.

Data validation involves ensuring data integrity and validity. For example, it ensures that the cities mentioned are in the right states, or countries. It also ensures that when working with currency fields, the data is transformed to the right currency for the country in which the data mart or data warehouse will be used. Validation also ensures referential integrity in terms of primary and foreign keys in the database.

Data scrubbing reconciles data coming from different sources to feed the same destination table in the target data warehouse database. For example, if an product is classified as beverage in one source and spirit in another, one of these two classifications will be accepted and the other dropped to ensure that the product will always fall under the same classification in the data warehouse. Microsoft SQL Server allows you to use several techniques to perform data scrubbing. These techniques include: the data transformation services import/export wizard, writing custom ActiveX-based script or programs to do the scrubbing, or using DTS lookup. These techniques are discussed in greater detail in Chapter 6.

Data transformation process converts the captured source data into a format and structure suitable for loading into the data warehouse. Metadata is usually used to store the mapping characteristics used to transform the source data in the Microsoft repository. Metadata defines any changes that are required prior to loading the data into the data warehouse. The data transformation process will help to resolve the anomalies in the source data and produce a high quality data source for the target data warehouse. Transformation of data can occur at the record level or at the attribute level. Three basic techniques are used for the transformation in general and include structural transformation, content transformation, and functional transformation.

Structural transformation changes the structure of the source records to be similar to that of the target database. This technique transforms data at the record level. Which means that the whole record is transformed to match the structure of the record in the target database.

Content transformation changes data values in the records. This technique transforms data at the attribute level. Content transformation converts values by use of algorithms or by use of data transformation tables.

Functional transformation creates new data values in the target records based on data in the source records. This technique transforms data at the attribute level. These transformations occur either through data aggregation or enrichment. Aggregation is the calculation of derived values such as totals and averages based on multiple attributes in different records. Enrichment combines two or more data values and creates one or more new attributes from a single source record or multiple source records that can be from the same or different sources.

The transformation process may require processing through the captured data several times because the data may be used to populate various records during the apply process. Data values may be used in a fact table as a measure, and they may also be used to calculate aggregations. This may require going through the source records more than once. The first pass would be to create records for the fact table and the second to create records for the aggregations. Finally, the update interval is closely related to the time it takes to perform data transformations. Some transformations involve complex processes and huge amounts of data, not to mention having to go through the data more than once. Therefore, processing these transformations can take long hours, which will affect the frequency of their occurrence.

Applying the Data

When the data warehouse model is being created, consideration must be given to the plan for populating the data warehouse. Limitations in the operational system data and processes can affect the data availability and quality. In addition, the populating process requires that the data model be examined because it is the blueprint for the data warehouse. The modeling process and the populating process affect each other.

The data warehouse model determines what source data will be needed, the format of the data, and the time interval of data capture activity. If the data required is not available in the operational system, it will have to be created. For example, sources of existing data may have to be calculated to create a required new data element. In the case study, the `Sale` fact may require `Total Cost` and `Total Revenue`. However, these values do not reside in the source data model, therefore they must be calculated. In this case, `Total Cost` is calculated by adding the cost of each component, and `Total Revenue` is calculated by adding all of the Order Line' s `Negotiated Unit Selling Price` times `Quantity Ordered`. The model may also affect the transform process. For example, the data may need to be processed more than once to create all the necessary records for the data warehouse.

The populating process may also influence the data warehouse model. When data is not available or is costly to retrieve, it may have to be removed from the model. Or, the timeliness of the data may have to change because of physical constraints of the operational system, which will affect the time dimension in the model.

OLAP Policy and Long-Term Maintenance and Security Strategy

OK, now you have completed the database design for the data warehouse, you even designed the data loading strategy for it. Now you have to take care of important issues that will have a great impact on the success of the data warehouse. Some of these issues, such as security and maintenance, are discussed in this section. Other issues, such as, user interface design and choosing reporting tools are discussed in the following section.

What is the OLAP Policy?

Designing the data warehouse does not stop at designing the database, data loading strategies, and metadata for the OLAP solution. It is important that the design take into account on-going maintenance and security issues while the data warehouse is in use. Establishing what I call the "OLAP Policy" is actually meant to help make this task as easy and smooth as possible. The OLAP Policy means creating rules and policies regarding the use of the data warehouse, maintaining it, and establishing the security strategy.

When you wrote the requirements and specifications documents for your data warehouse, you probably included sections about how the data warehouse will be used, how the use will be monitored and what kind of statistics will be generated to help refine it in the future. Hopefully you also remembered to document the frequency at which the data is loaded into the data warehouse, and the frequency and rules of archiving data out of the data warehouse. You probably also added rules for backing up the data warehouse's database, and rules for handling customer requests, in case the customer still wanted to add feedback after they started using the thing, and maybe rules for what actions to take in cases of emergency, that is when the data warehouse is down or suffered major disaster and recovery efforts need to be underway to recover the data up to the latest backup. If you have done all these tasks, then you have already written your OLAP policy rules.

What Rules Does the OLAP Policy Contain?

The OLAP policy includes rules that should be incorporated in the OLAP and data warehouse metadata. These rules are designed to handle situations detailed below:

Security Plan

A very important component of the policy is the security plan for the data warehouse. Security in SQL Server data warehousing spans over several levels, the OLAP cubes, the SQL Server data warehouse database, and the operating system level. OLAP Services provides security through roles that can be defined at the cube level. These roles are tightly integrated with Windows NT users and groups. The purpose of a security plan is to identify which users can see what data and perform what activities in the database. To develop your security plan, you need to list all the items and activities in the database that must be controlled through security, identify the individuals and groups in the company, and cross-reference the two lists to identify which users can see what data and perform what activities in the database.

SQL Server provides a sophisticated security model that, if used well, prevents unwanted access to the data and the database objects. Although sophisticated, the security model in SQL Server is easy to understand and manage. SQL Server Enterprise manager provides the tools to establish and manage security. You can also perform the same tasks, and more by using security-related system and extended stored procedures, or SQL Server's distributed management objects (SQL DMO). The security model allows for two modes of authentication, NT authentication only, and mixed (SQL Server and NT) authentication. After the user is authenticated, the security mechanism is the same for both modes.

The security model allows for implementation of security at the Windows NT domain level, Windows NT computer level for the computer hosting the SQL Server, the SQL Server level through login accounts, and database and application level through the use of roles and permissions and assigning them to the database object level. A detailed description of the SQL Server security model and how it can be integrated with OLAP Services security is described in Chapter 12, Data Warehouse Security.

Database Backup and Recovery

As you probably know, a common practice in the database administration world is backing up the databases. Backups allow for recovery of the data in disaster cases. Backup and recovery plans should be an important part of the OLAP Policy and the OLAP and data warehouse solution metadata. SQL Server provides tools for to perform backups, which, in turn, provides a safeguard for protecting critical data stored in the data warehouse databases. Backing up and restoring a database allows for the complete restoration of data over a wide range of potential system problems. These problems include:

- Media failure: If one or more of the disk drives holding a database fail, you are faced with a complete loss of data unless you can restore an earlier copy of the data.
- User errors: If a user or application, unintentionally or, maliciously, causes invalid modifications to a large number of records of data, maybe deleting many records or changing the value of a table field with an erroneous UPDATE SQL statement to one value for all records. In these cases, the best way to deal with the problem may be to restore the data to a point in time before the modifications were made.
- Permanent loss of a server: If a server is disabled permanently, or a computer is lost to a fire or flooding, you may need to activate a warm standby server or restore a copy of a database to another server.

Additionally, backing up and restoring databases is useful for other problems, such as moving or copying a database from one server to another. Backing up a database from one computer, and restoring the database to another can make a copy of a database quickly and easily on the target computer.

Backing up a database makes a copy of a database, which can be used to restore the database if it is lost. Backing up a database copies everything in the database, including any needed portions of the transaction log. The transaction log is used during recovery operations to commit completed transactions, and roll back uncompleted transactions. Backing up a transaction log backs up only the changes that have occurred in the transaction log since the transaction log was last backed up.

Restoring a database backup returns the database to the same state it was in when the backup was created. Any incomplete transactions in the database backup, (transactions that were not complete when the backup operation completed originally), are rolled back to ensure the database remains consistent.

Backup, recovery, and replication (when needed) are some of the administrative tasks that will be discussed in Chapter 13.

Auditing

Auditing allows you to recognize all activities that happened in the database and who did these actions. This is an important requirement, since if, for any reason, unwanted events happen, auditing can tell you when the event took place, and can probably tell you who conducted the activity. Auditing is implemented in SQL Server as part of security and is described in more detail in Chapter 12.

Statistics Gathering

It is important to monitor how the users are using the data warehouse and OLAP tools. Knowing the number of queries and type of these queries issued against a particular fact cube, for example, will allow you to make modifications accordingly to either make such queries more efficient, or maybe change them to be more attractive if they are hardly ever used. Therefore, your initial design should plan to add monitoring of such statistics to the metadata of the project. Some examples of these statistics may include:

- Average and maximum number of queries against a certain fact.
- Average and maximum rows returned per query.
- Average and maximum query run time.
- Last archive data
- Last backup date
- Last load data
- Number of rows loaded in number of rows returned.
- Last archive data
- Date archived to
- And other stats as needed.

Archiving and Data Distribution Plans

As the data warehouse receives more and more data from operational sources, its size grows and queries against it become slower. To maintain high query performance, you will need to separate the data in the fact tables according to the data field (dimension) to multiple fact tables (for example sales fact table for 1999 and sales fact table for 1998, etc.). Hence the cut-off point at which you start separating the data has to be estimated as part of your design. Also, at some point, when you notice that some of the fact tables that relate to a few years in the past are sparsely used, you may want to consider archiving them out of the database into a different location to preserve the space they occupy for newly added data. The design should estimate the point at which the data is archived, with plans to retrieve it quickly when needed.

Data distribution is encountered when the operational data goes directly into small data marts. Data mart data is then replicated into the data warehouse. This is another issue that has to be taken into account in the design stages of the data warehousing solution. If the data marts are fed from the data warehouse, then you need to determine the frequency at which you load data into the data marts from the data warehouse.

User Interface and Querying Tools

Data presentation and query tools are some of the most important parts of the data warehousing solution, mainly because they are accessed directly by the end users and are designed to meet their display requirements. Microsoft SQL Server OLAP Services is integrated with the Pivot Table service, which acts as the engine that transfers the data requested by the queries from the cubes and aggregate tables to the user interface elements. These elements could be custom made using any programming language, or a well-established reporting or spreadsheet application, like Microsoft Excel.

Pivot Table and user interface tools are discussed in great detail in Chapter 9, Data Analysis and Presentation.

Summary

This chapter dealt with the design of the data warehouse and OLAP solution. We discussed the pre-requisites for a successful design, the tools needed, ending up with the detailed design plan ready for implementation. In the process of presenting these issues, we discussed the issues involved with the design of a data warehousing solutions, beginning with the pre-requisites for a successful design, to analyzing the requirements, and ending with establishing a policy for long term maintenance.

The next chapter describes the OLAP Manager I have been talking about repeatedly, and shows you how it can be used to do a variety of tasks in a user-friendly and easy way.

5

The OLAP Manager

Microsoft OLAP Services includes a graphical, user-friendly tool to manage the OLAP server, called the OLAP Manager. The OLAP solution developer can use the OLAP Manager to build the data cubes and their components. They can also use it to view the metadata for the cubes and their component objects. The OLAP Manager may help the developer analyze the data in the cubes in different views.

This chapter will describe the OLAP Manager in detail and illustrate how it can be used to accomplish these goals.

Topics covered in this chapter include:

- Describing the OLAP Manager screens
- Building an OLAP Database with the OLAP Manager, Including:
  - Creating and editing shared dimensions
  - Creating a cube
  - Using the Cube Editor
- Creating new taskpad views in the OLAP Manager

Overview

Microsoft introduced the Microsoft Management Console (MMC) a couple of years ago to serve as a hosting application for a variety of tools and administrative applications for Back Office products. MMC allows such tools and applications to be added as "snap-ins" to the MMC window as we will see later. The OLAP Manager is a snap-in in the Microsoft Management Console that includes two main panes, the tree pane, and the detail pane. The detail pane is based on hypertext markup language (HTML). The following figure shows the two panes when you first start the application.

Microsoft Management Console (MMC) is a common console framework for server and network management applications known as snap-ins (such as the OLAP Manager). These snap-ins allow developers and administrators to more effectively manage the resources represented by these snap-in applications.

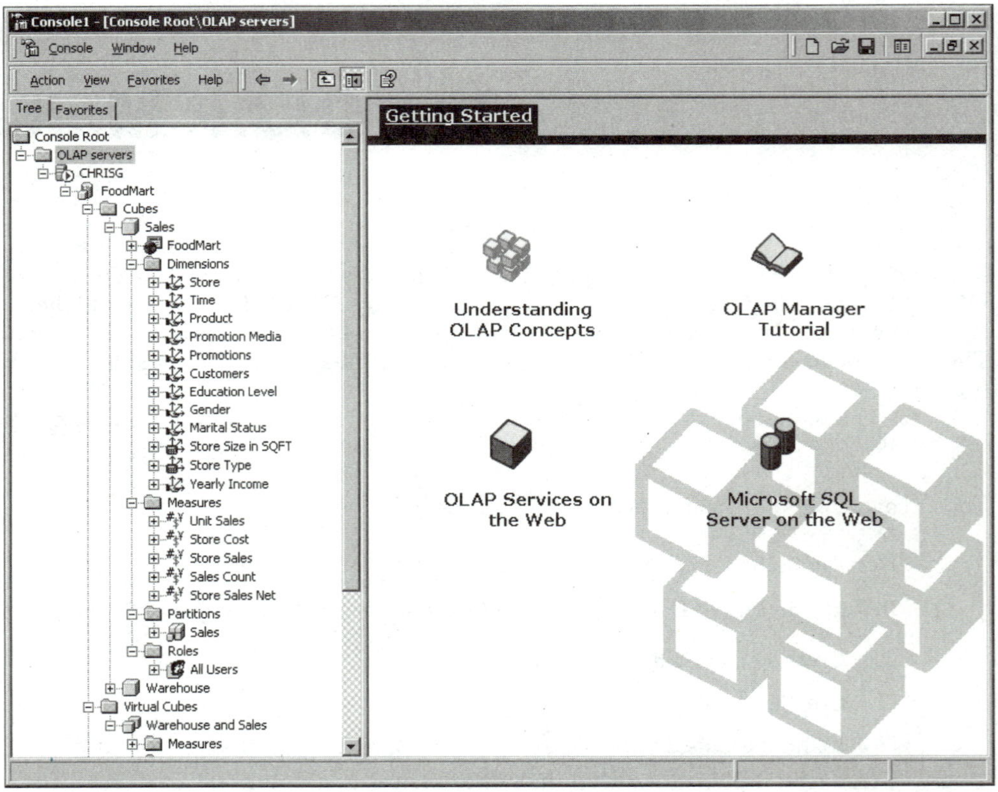

The OLAP Manager's tree and HTML-based detail panes

Starting the OLAP Manager

To start the OLAP Manager, from your desktop, you can select Start|Program Files|Microsoft SQL Server 7|OLAP Services|OLAP Manager.

However, if you are already working with another MMC application, such as Microsoft Transaction Server (MTS), or Internet Information Server (IIS), or even the SQL Server Enterprise Manager, you can add the OLAP Manager snap-in, which will open it for you so that you can easily switch back and forth between the snap-ins. For example, if you are using IIS, you can use the Console menu to select the Add/Remove Snap-in menu command to add other MMC snap-in applications, such as the OLAP Server.

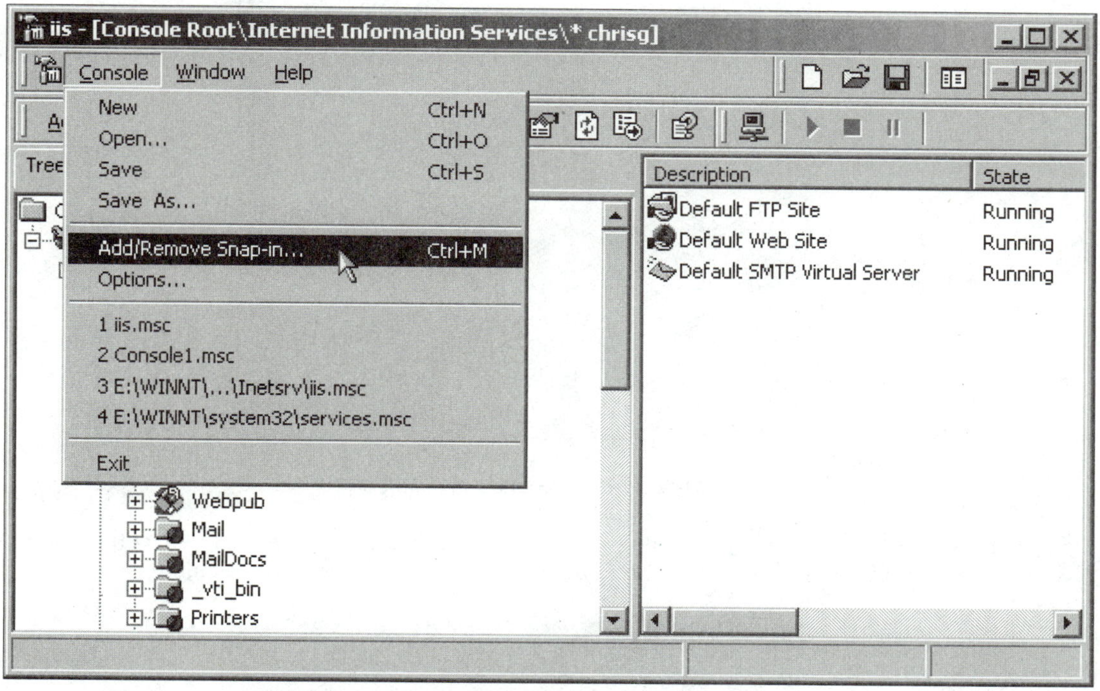

Using the Console Menu in MMC to add new snap-in applications

Selecting the command shown in the above figure will open the Add/Remove Snap-in dialog box shown in the following screenshot. The box shows a list of already available snap-ins in the MMC screen. You may select one of them and remove it from the list, or click the Add button to open a new dialog, which will allow you to choose from a list of snap-in applications installed on your machine that you could add to the MMC.

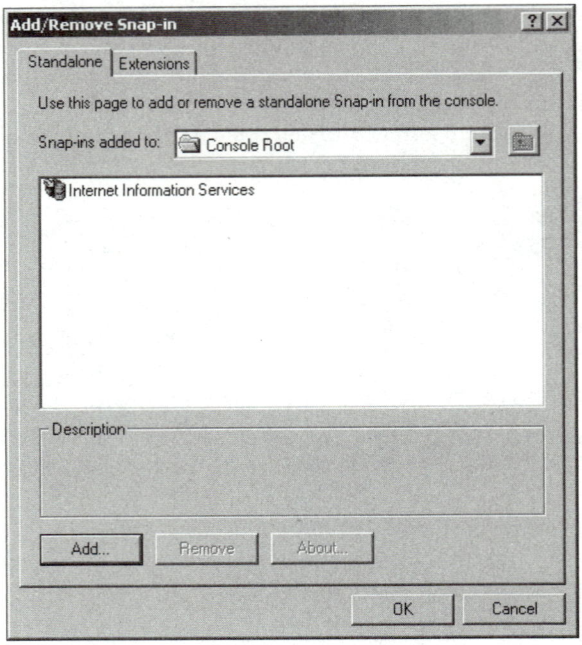

The Add/Remove Snap-in dialog box

From the Add Standalone Snap-in dialog shown in the following figure, you can select the Microsoft SQL Server OLAP Services and click the Add button to open it in the MMC window.

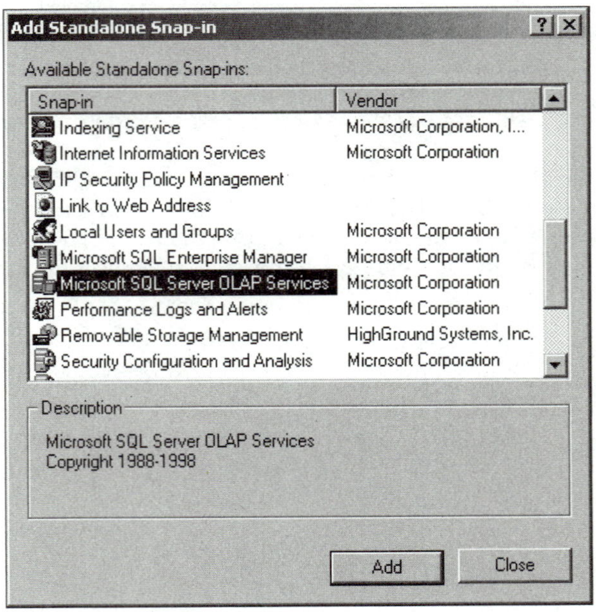

Adding the Microsoft OLAP Manager snap-in to the MMC window

When you close the dialog boxes, you will see that the MMC window includes both IIS and the OLAP Manager snap-in applications.

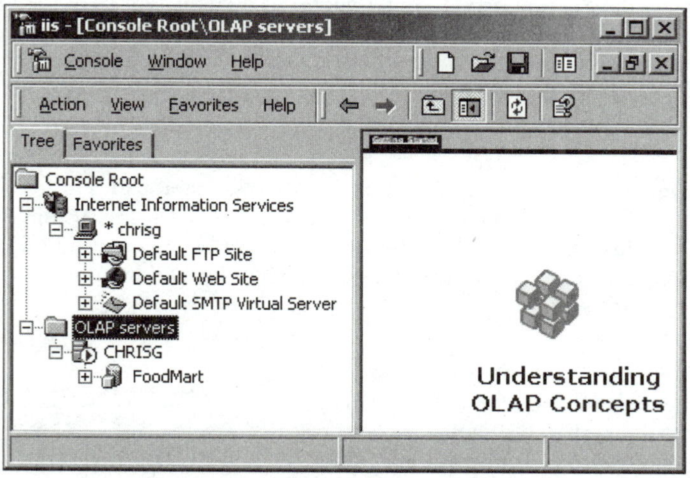

The MMC Screen after adding the OLAP Manager snap-in

The OLAP Manager Panes

The OLAP Manager has two panes, the tree pane and the HTML-based detail pane. Just like other MMC snap-in applications, the tree view allows you to navigate through the different objects and functions available through the resource represented by the snap-in. In the OLAP Manager case, it allows you to view the cubes and their elements. The detail pane shows details of the element selected in the tree pane in an HTML format that allows you to navigate even further from one topic to another.

The Tree Pane

The tree pane presents a hierarchical view of many of the objects and functions available through the OLAP Services. The following are the different nodes and their representation in the tree view:

Registered OLAP Servers

The first node in the tree represents registered OLAP server folders. The OLAP server name is the name of the machine on which the OLAP Services are installed. Two OLAP Servers are shown in the tree view in the following figure, C491805-A and C491805-C.

Databases

Each OLAP server can have multiple databases, in the following figure, the FoodMart and the Pubs databases are examples of such entities. A database can have many OLAP cubes, virtual cubes, or library items. A folder represents each one of these components on the tree. Opening the folder will show its components.

Cubes

The cubes are represented as the next level below the databases level. Examples of these cubes in the following figure include the Sales and Warehouse cubes. The cubes represent the OLAP cubes created during the dimensional analysis of the data. Expanding any of the cubes (by clicking the + sign next to it) will show its elements: data source, dimensions and measures. Two more items can also be shown under the OLAP cubes, partitions, and roles.

Virtual Cubes

Each database contains a Virtual Cubes folder that represents virtual cubes in the database. A virtual cube is a combination of two or more cubes in the database that allow for custom viewing of the data by mixing it from several cubes. Underneath each virtual cube node you can find folders that contain information defining the virtual cube. These folders include information about the virtual cube's measures, dimensions, and roles.

Library

The library folder includes information about the data sources, virtual dimensions, shared dimensions, and roles in a database. Each database has its own library folder.

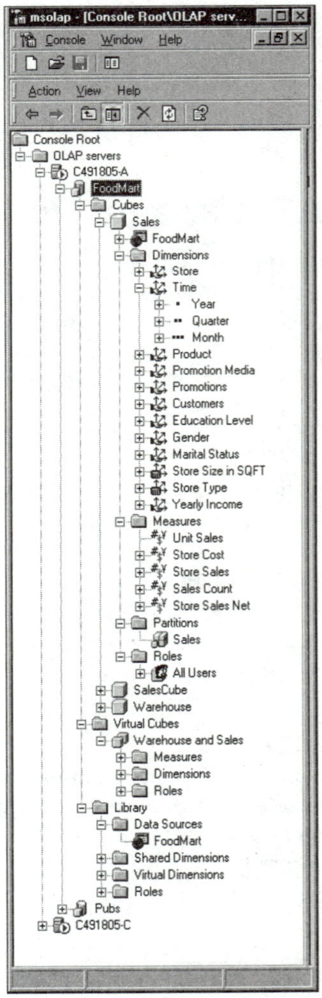

The tree pane of the OLAP Manager

Data Source

Each cube has a folder underneath it in the tree hierarchy that includes information about the OLE DB provider, such as connection information, network settings, connection time-out, and access permissions. This folder is called the data source.

Dimensions

The cube's Dimensions folder contains a node for each dimension in the cube. Several types of dimensions are available, cube-specific (private), shared, or virtual. Private dimensions are available only to the cube they fall under. Shared dimensions are available for all cubes in the database, and they are also located in the library's shared dimensions folder. Virtual dimensions, which are defined in Chapter 3, are also available to all cubes in the databases and are also found in the virtual dimensions folder in database's library folder. As examples of dimensions available in the above figure, the store and time dimensions can be seen underneath the sales cube.

Each dimension has nodes underneath it representing the levels of the dimension. A number of dots representing the level appear to the left of the level name in the tree view. For example, the quarter level in the time dimension of the sales cube is the second level in that dimension. Therefore, two dots appear to the left of the name of the level name.

Measures

A measures folder exists underneath each cube in the tree view. This folder includes data about the cube's measure. The measure represents the data we are seeking from the dimensional analysis summarized along the cube's dimensions. Unit sales and store cost are two examples of measures of the sales cube in the previous figure.

Roles

A node in the roles folder represents each group of users that have access privileges to the cube. This folder appears underneath all types of cubes including the virtual cube. The roles folder also appears in the library folder of the database, and includes all the groups that have access to any of the database's cubes.

The HTML Pane

The HTML pane includes an HTML-based representation that changes dynamically to reflect the selection made in the tree view pane. Since the information presented in the HTML pane is highly variable, it is not feasible to describe all possible views of it here. However, the figure below shows a metadata view of the store dimension of the sales cube in the FoodMart database.

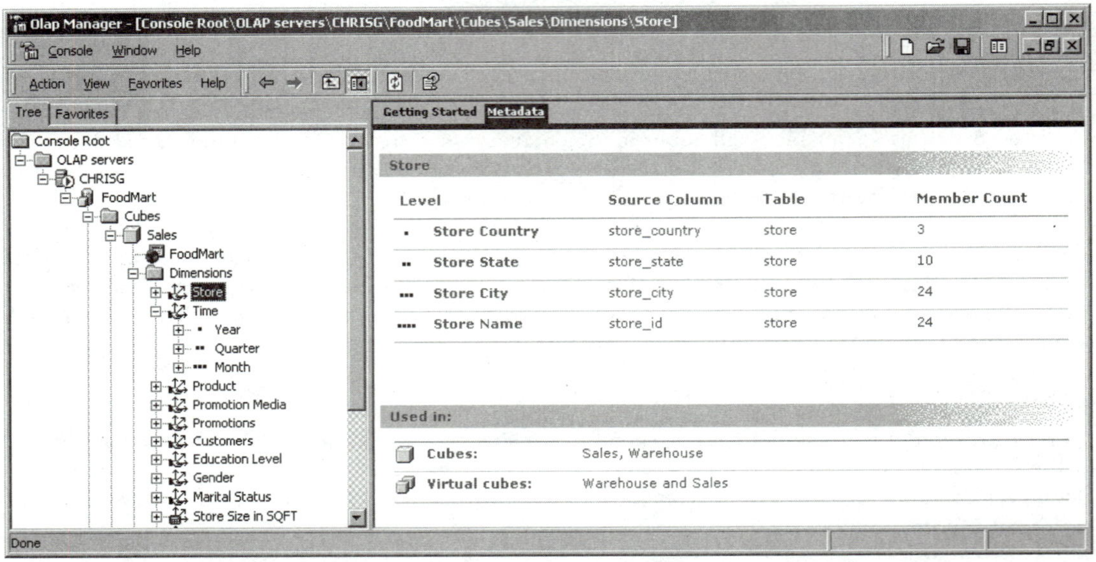

Metadata view of the store dimension in the HTML-styled detail pane

Registering and Unregistering OLAP Servers

The OLAP Manager allows you to register remote OLAP servers and administer such server from your own machine giving you access to their cubes and cube metadata. This feature is similar to the feature of registering remote SQL Servers in the SQL Server Enterprise Manager. This functionality is highly convenient for remote problem solving, analysis and administration of OLAP servers.

To register a new OLAP server in your MMC window, right click on the OLAP Servers folder, and select the Register Server command from the context-sensitive menu. This will open the Register OLAP Server dialog box. Type the name of the remote OLAP server and click OK:

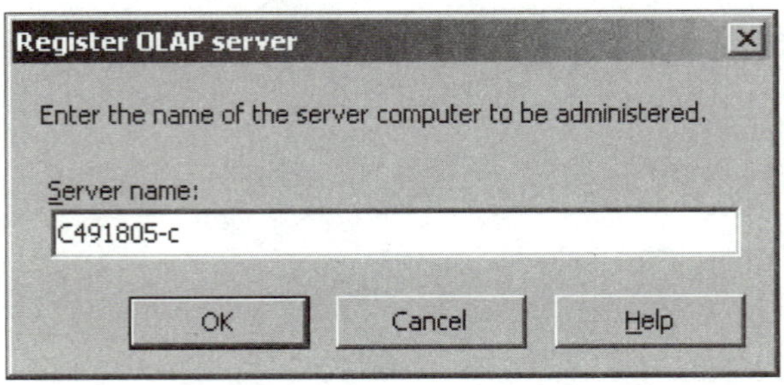

The Register OLAP Server dialog box

You must be able to authenticate to the remote server before you can access the OLAP server installed on it. Once registered, a new folder in the tree view will represent the remote server.

You may unregister an OLAP server by right-clicking on its name in the MMC window and selecting the Unregister Server command from the context-sensitive menu.

Building The Database

Now you are familiar with the Microsoft OLAP Manager screens, let's build the OLAP database for the sales and inventory solution discussed in the previous chapters. As a pre-requisite for this work, you need to have a star/snowflake schema representing the data warehouse tables available.

To create a new database, you need to select the OLAP server on which the database will reside from the tree pane. Then, you can select the menu option "Action|New Database" in the Microsoft OLAP Manager's screen. You can also right-click the server name and select "New Database" from the context-sensitive menu. The New Database dialog appears prompting you for a name for the database you are creating. Type the name in the Database Name field, and a brief description in the description field:

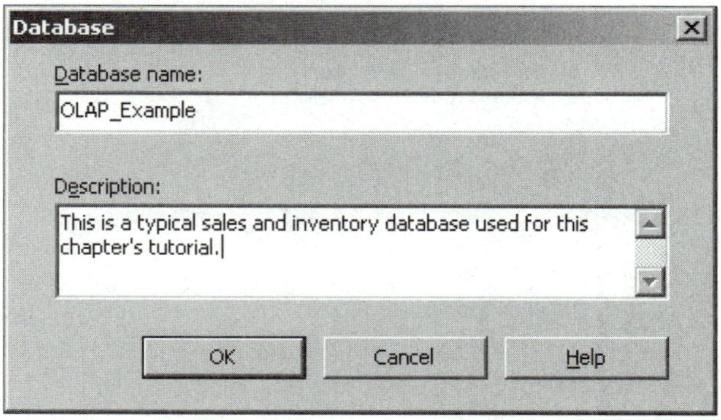

The dialog that allows you to create a new OLAP database

Pressing the OK button will create a new OLAP database for you on the specified server.

Identifying the next steps, such as, data source measures, dimensions, etc. can all be illustrated by building a cube. However, in the next sections, you will read about building most of these pieces separately from the cube first, then putting them all together to build the cube. We start by setting up a data source which points to the location of the schema, which will be used as the basis for the cubes in the OLAP database. The schema we will use is the same schema used in the previous chapters and is based on the sample database that ships with SQL Server OLAP Manager, the Food Mart database. The only difference is that we scaled-up the Food Mart database, which is a Microsoft Access database, to be a SQL Server 7 database. The next section will show you how this is done using the SQL Server Enterprise Manager.

Scaling Up the FoodMart Database

The FoodMart database is an Access database that exists in the `[DriveLetter:]\OLAP Services\Samples` folder. In this section, we will upscale it to a SQL Server database 7.0 database before we use it throughout the book.

Creating the New SQL Server Database

1. In the SQL Server Enterprise Manager, create a new database by right-clicking the Databases tree item in the tree view and selecting New Database:

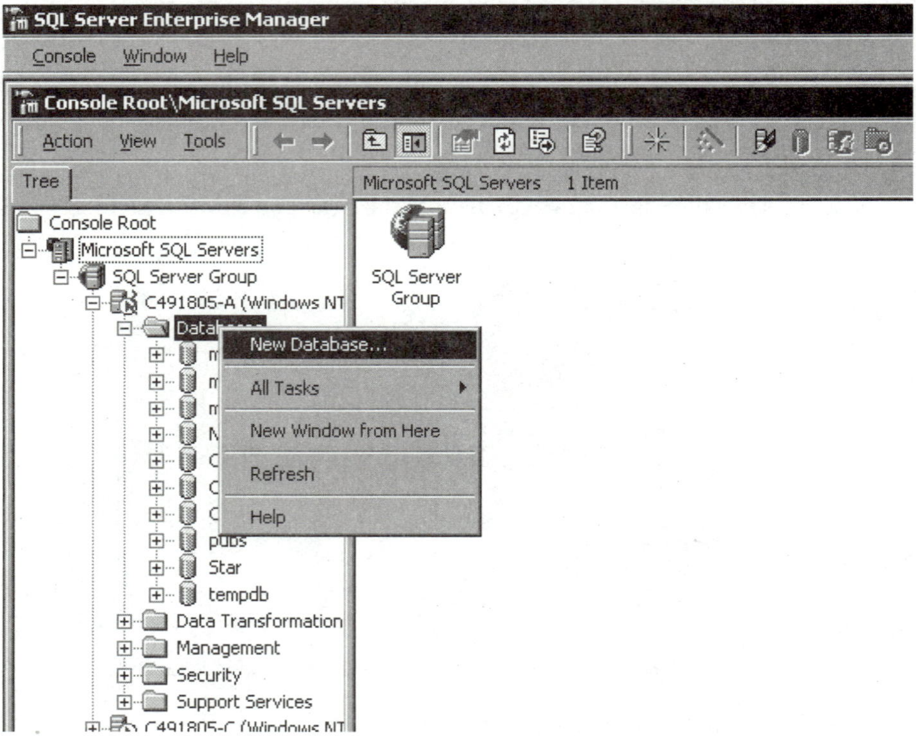

Creating a new database in the Enterprise Manager

2. In the **Database Properties** dialog box, type the name of the database as OLAP_Example and click the OK button.

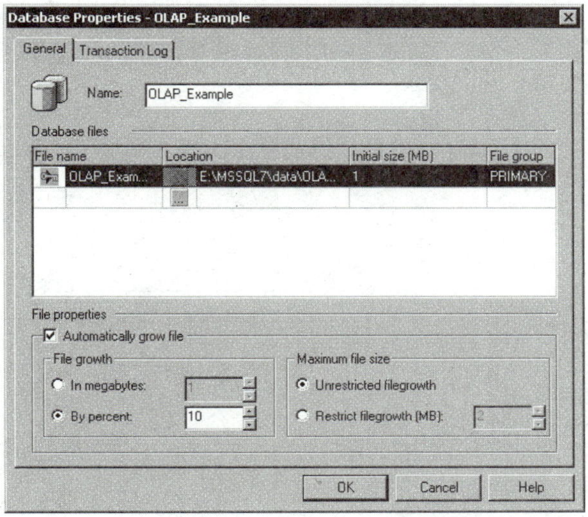

The Database Properties dialog box

Importing the FoodMart Database

The next step is to use the data transformation services in the SQL Serve OLAP Manager to import the FoodMart database.

3. In the Enterprise Manager, right-click the **Data Transformation Services** tree item in the tree view, and select the **Import Data** command. This will launch the Data Transformation Import Wizard as shown in the figure below.

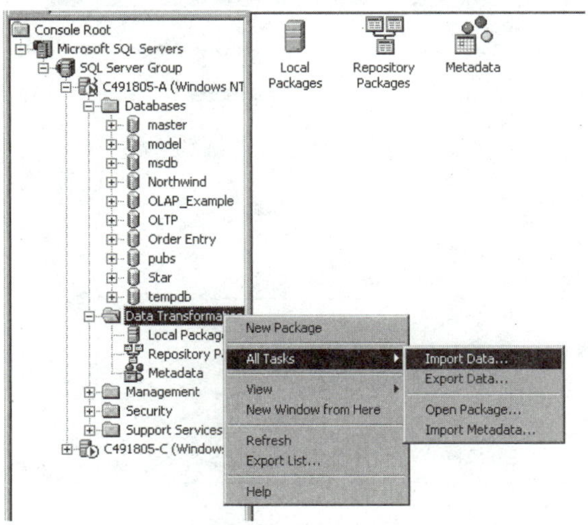

Staring the database import process

4. Skip to the next screen "Choose a Data Source" of the Import wizard. In this screen, shown below, select "Microsoft Access" in the Source drop-down list, and the FoodMart.mdb file in the File Name text box. Click the **Next** button.

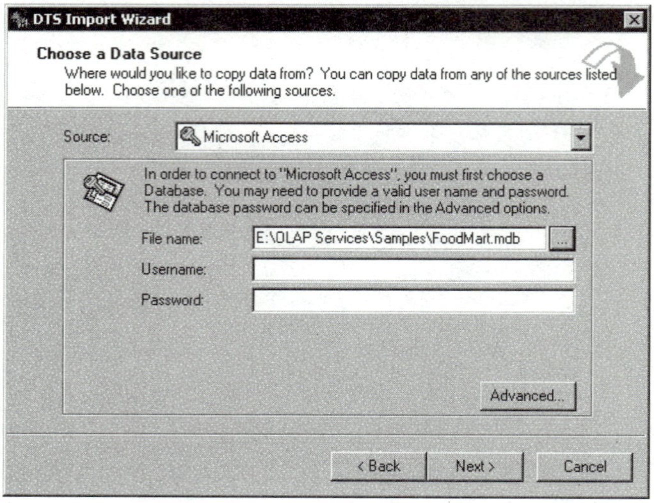

Selecting the Import Source

5. In the next screen "Choose a Destination", select the Microsoft OLE DB Provider for SQL Server in the Destination drop-down list, select the `OLAP_Example` database in the Database drop-down list, make sure the server drop-down points to the right SQL Server, and fill in the server authentication information as shown in the figure below. If the `OLAP_Example` database does not show in the list of available databases, click the `Refresh` button to refresh the list. Once done, click the **Next** button.

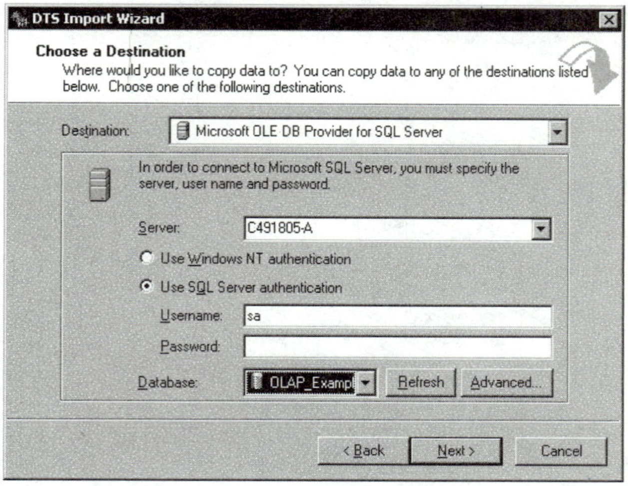

Selecting the DTS Import Destination

6. In the next screen, "Specify Table Copy or Query", select the `Table Copy` option, and click the **Next** button.

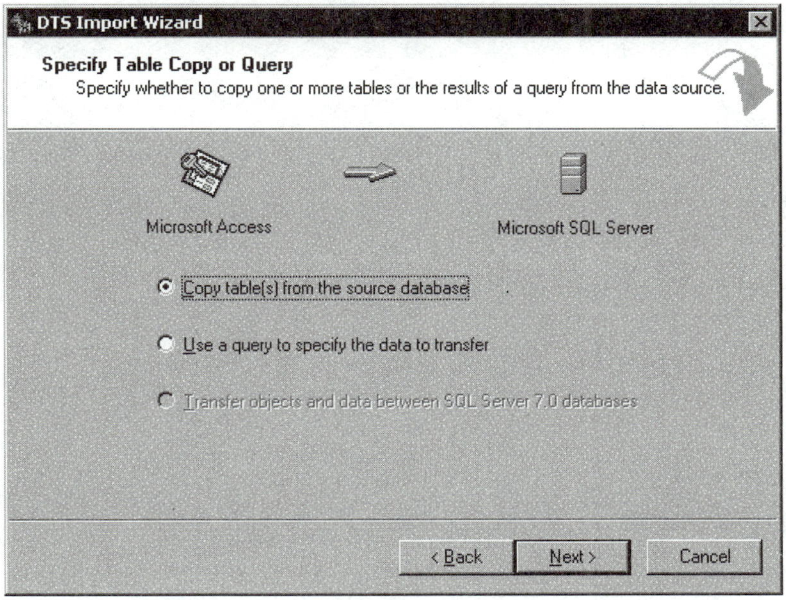

Selecting the DTS Import Option

7. In the next screen, select all tables from the FoodMart database, and click the **Next** button.

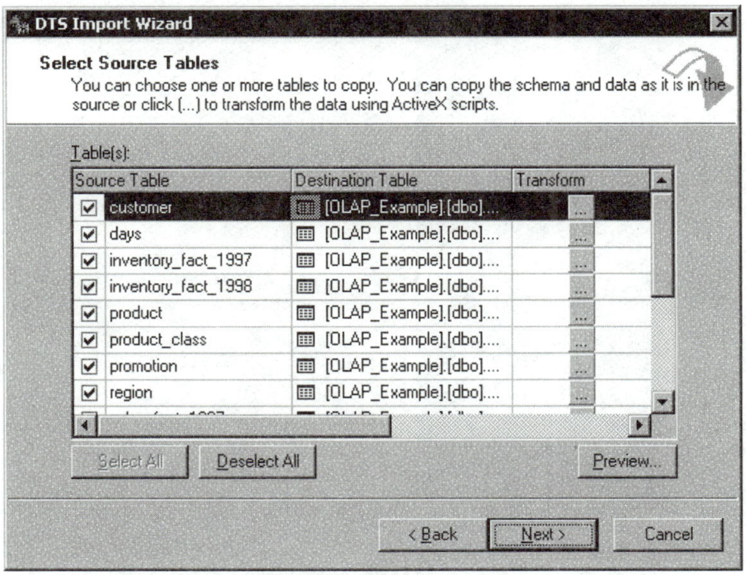

Selecting the tables to import

8. Next, you can choose to run the import process immediately, create a DTS packge, or schedule a DTS package to run later. DTS Packages will be explained in detail in the next chapter. Make sure the Run Immediately option in selected and click the Next button.

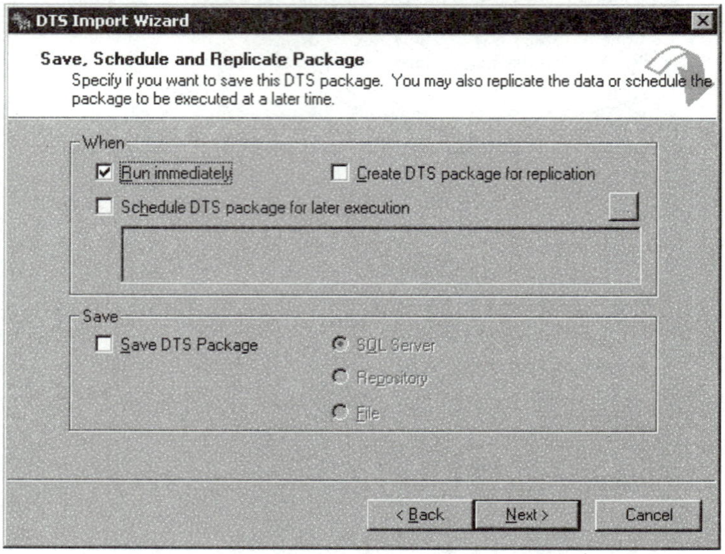

Choosing the Run Immediately option

9. The next screen of the wizard shows you a summary of the options that you have chosen so far. You can go through these options to make sure your selections were correct. If everything looks fine, click the Finish button to start the Import process.

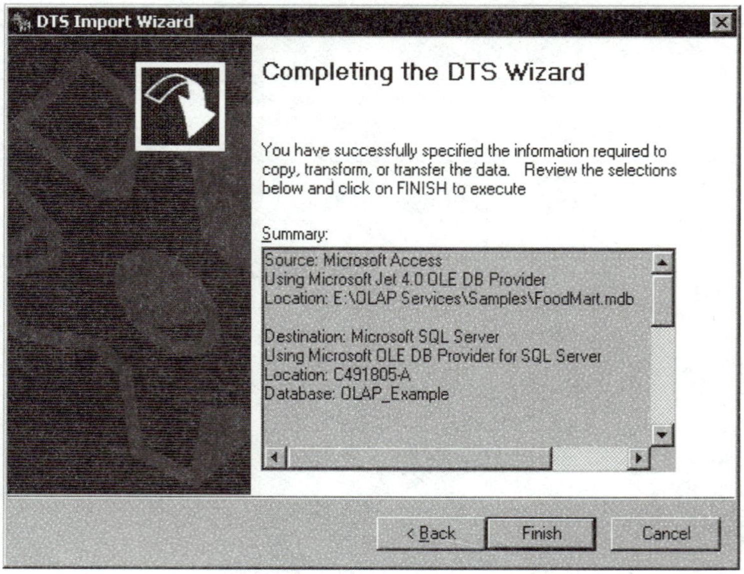

Summary of the DTS Import options

10. When you click the Finish button, the wizard start the import process while showing you the progress in the import process in the screen below.

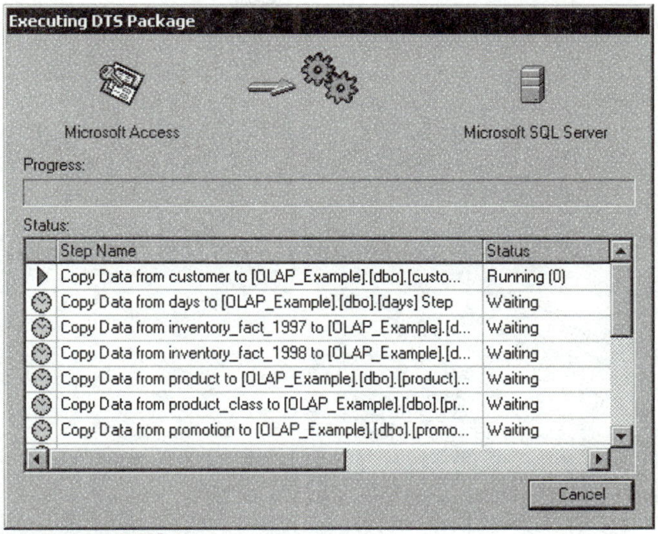

Executing the DTS Import

Defining the Data Source

To define a data source, you need to expand the tree structure of the database and select the "library" node. "Data Sources" is a branch that can be seen once you have expanded the "library" node as you can see in the following figure. To create a new data source, you can right-click "Data Sources" and select "New Data Source", or select the menu option: "Action|New Data Source". Once you have done so, the Data Link Properties dialog is displayed. This wizard dialog guides you through selecting an existing data source, or creating a new one.

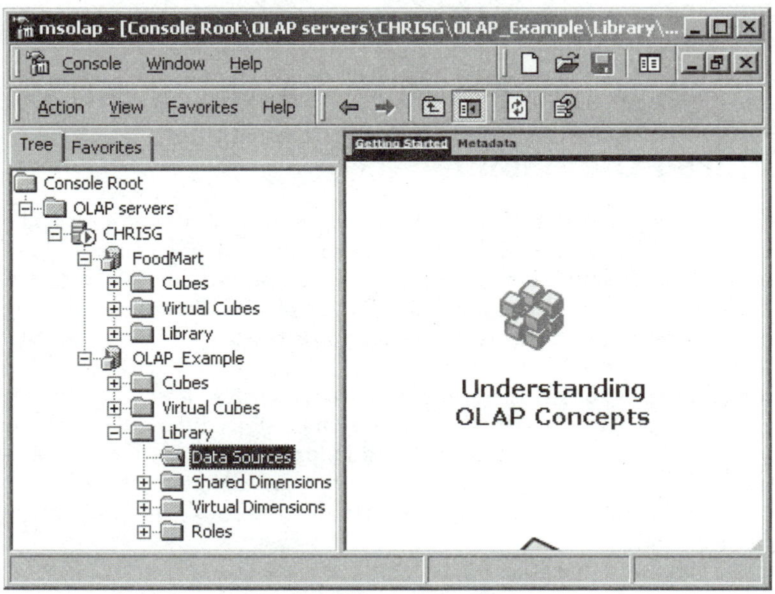

Setting up a new data source

Start by selecting the OLE DB provider for Microsoft SQL Server as shown in the following figure, then click the "Next>>" button. This will lead you to the connection tab of the dialog, also shown in the following figure, allowing you to specify the Microsoft SQL server name that hosts the database of interest. In this dialog, you can also specify the authentication mode to the SQL Server and the name of the database you want to connect to. Once you have entered all the necessary information in the dialog box, press the "Test Connection" button to make sure you can safely connect to the database with the settings you selected.

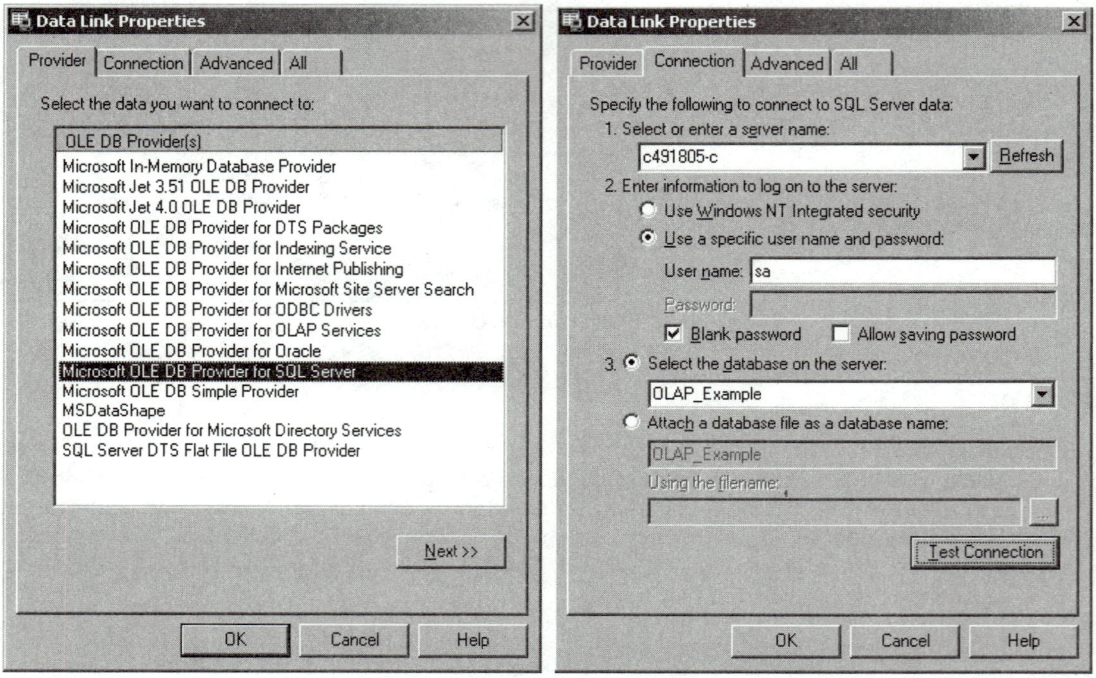

Data source wizard dialog

Creating Shared Dimensions

OLAP services allow you to create two types of dimensions, private dimensions and shared dimensions as we have seen in Chapter 3. Private dimensions are specific to a given cube and can only be used by it. Shared dimensions, on the other hand, are stored in the library folder of the tree structure and can be used by more than one cube. In this section, we will build shared dimensions, leaving private dimensions to the section in which we create the cube structure.

The classification of a dimension as a private or a share dimension determines the scope in which the dimension can be used. OLAP Services also classifies dimensions differently based on the information they hold. According to this classification, a dimension (private or shared) can be a standard dimension, or a time dimension. The reason for this distinction is the unique nature of the time dimension. The time dimension has predefined multi-hierarchies (calendar and fiscal), and building aggregations for this dimension requires special handling.

In the next sections, we will first start building two standard dimensions then build a time dimension. In any case, creating these dimensions involves selecting one or more dimension tables in the data source, identifying the type of the dimension, defining the dimension levels by selecting the appropriate columns from the tables, and providing a name for the dimension.

Creating a dimension can be done with the OLAP Manager's Dimension wizard or with the OLAP Manager's Dimension Editor. We will build the first dimension using the wizards, while we build the second one with the dimension editor.

Creating a Standard Dimension with the Dimension Wizard

In this section, we will learn how to use the Dimension wizard to create the `Customer` shared dimension. To start the wizard, select the Shared Dimensions folder from the tree pane of the OLAP Manager screen and right-click. This will present you with a context sensitive menu, select New Dimension|Wizard from this menu.

The first screen of the wizard, shown below, gives you the option to select one table to base your dimension on, or multiple tables. The selection you make depends on whether you use the star or snowflake schema for your OLAP database respectively. For the `Customer` dimension, we will use a single table and click the Next button.

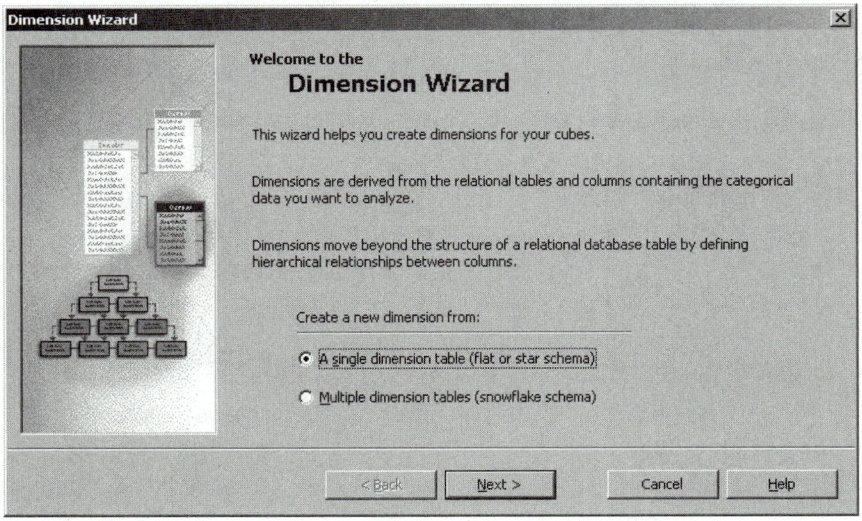

First screen of the Dimension wizard

The next screen you are presented with is shown in the figure below. This screen lists available data sources. Clicking the "+" sign next to the data source name will expand the data source to show all the tables underneath it. Selecting a table will display details of its fields in the Details list box. For our purposes, let's select the Customer table.

In the figure below, you notice the field "Name". I added this field to make it easy to refer to a customer directly by name, rather than to concatenate the fname and lname fields every time we refer to them. The way this field is added and populated is with the following T-SQL statements. These statements can be run in the SQL Server Query Analyzer.

```
USE OLAP_Example
ALTER TABLE Customer
    ADD Name Varchar(150)
GO
UPDATE Customer
    SET [Name] = fname + ' ' + lname
Go
```

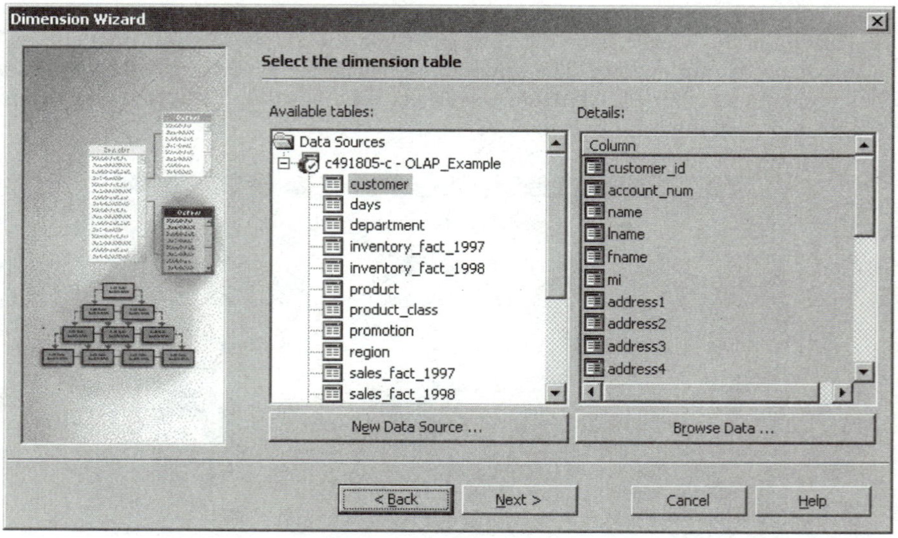

Selecting the Customer table for the Customer dimension

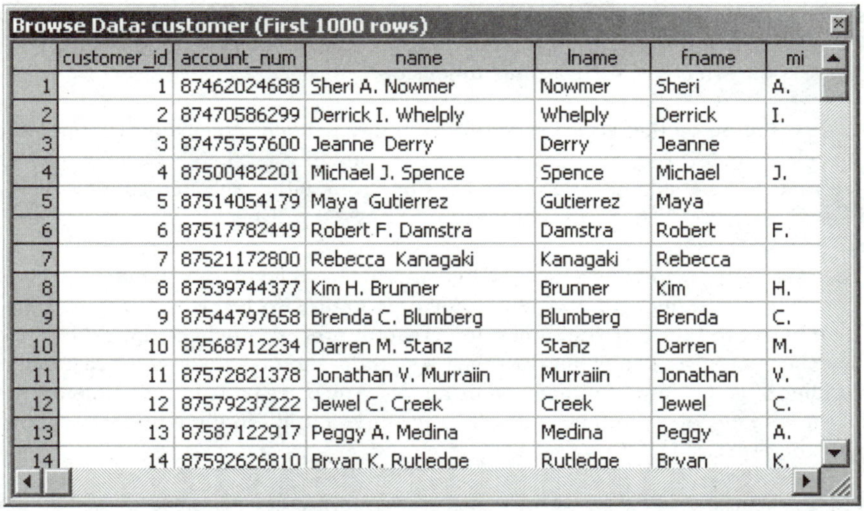
Browse Data: customer (First 1000 rows)

	customer_id	account_num	name	lname	fname	mi
1	1	87462024688	Sheri A. Nowmer	Nowmer	Sheri	A.
2	2	87470586299	Derrick I. Whelply	Whelply	Derrick	I.
3	3	87475757600	Jeanne Derry	Derry	Jeanne	
4	4	87500482201	Michael J. Spence	Spence	Michael	J.
5	5	87514054179	Maya Gutierrez	Gutierrez	Maya	
6	6	87517782449	Robert F. Damstra	Damstra	Robert	F.
7	7	87521172800	Rebecca Kanagaki	Kanagaki	Rebecca	
8	8	87539744377	Kim H. Brunner	Brunner	Kim	H.
9	9	87544797658	Brenda C. Blumberg	Blumberg	Brenda	C.
10	10	87568712234	Darren M. Stanz	Stanz	Darren	M.
11	11	87572821378	Jonathan V. Murraiin	Murraiin	Jonathan	V.
12	12	87579237222	Jewel C. Creek	Creek	Jewel	C.
13	13	87587122917	Peggy A. Medina	Medina	Peggy	A.
14	14	87592626810	Bryan K. Rutledge	Rutledge	Bryan	K.

Browsing the dimension table data

It is worth mentioning that on the second screen of the Dimension wizard, you can select a different data source from the one you are using by default. You can also click the Browse Data button to see a live view of the data in the selected table, as shown in the above figure.

The next screen of the wizard will allow you to specify whether the dimension you are building is a standard dimension or a time dimension. In our case, the `Customer` dimension is a standard dimension as shown in the figure below.

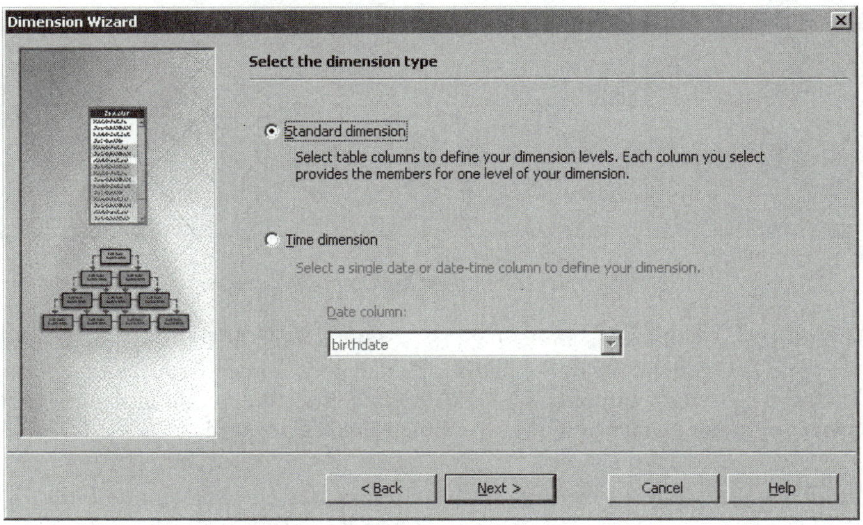

Selecting the dimension type from the Dimension wizard

If we had selected a time dimension, the Data Column drop-down list would have been activated and, we would have been able to select the data field to use in the dimension. You will see how this is done in a following section when we create a time dimension.

Clicking the Next button on the wizard screen shown in the above screenshot will open the screen that allows you to select the levels of the dimension you are building. In this screen, you can select from the list on the left that shows available columns in the dimension table. Selected columns will move to the Dimension Level list box.

The default setting in this step allows for members of a selected level to be counted. Counting members is required for cube processing and may take some time to process levels with a large number of members. If you want to speed up the dimension creation process, uncheck the Count Level Members Automatically check box (see following figure). If you choose to do so, you must manually enter an estimated number of levels for the dimension using the Properties pane in the Dimension editor later on. If, again, you prefer not to do this, you will be prompted to fill in the numbers of the individual levels during cube processing.

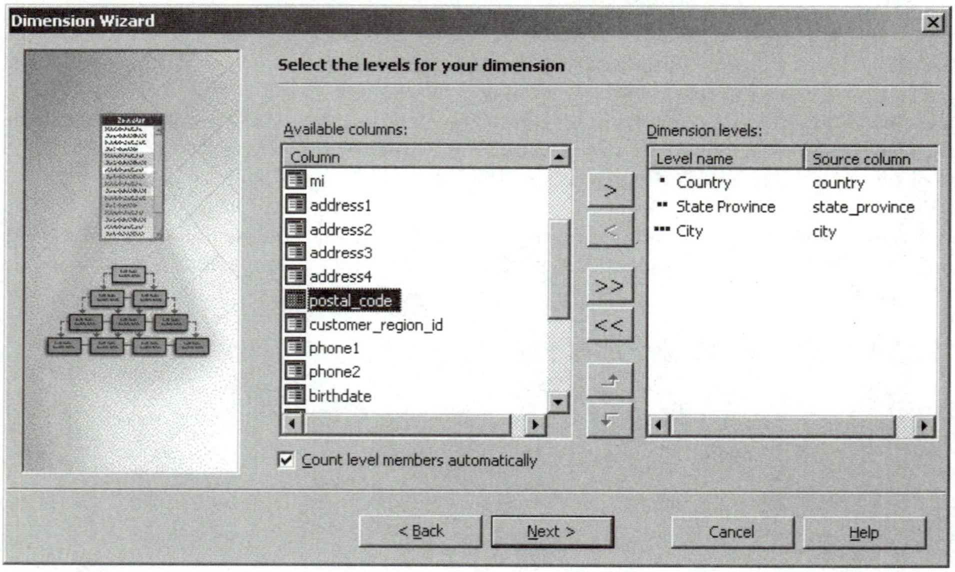

Selecting levels for the Customer dimension

Clicking the Next button will lead us to the final step of the wizard. In this step, you can name the dimension and preview its data (see figure below). The name you choose for the dimension must not exceed 24 characters in length and must start with a letter. Also, keep in mind that the name you choose for your dimension cannot be changed once the dimension is processed.

Please note that the Dimension wizard can be started from within the Cube wizard (discussed later). If you choose to launch the Dimension wizard from the Cube wizard, you will be able to specify whether you want to share the dimension or not in this last step.

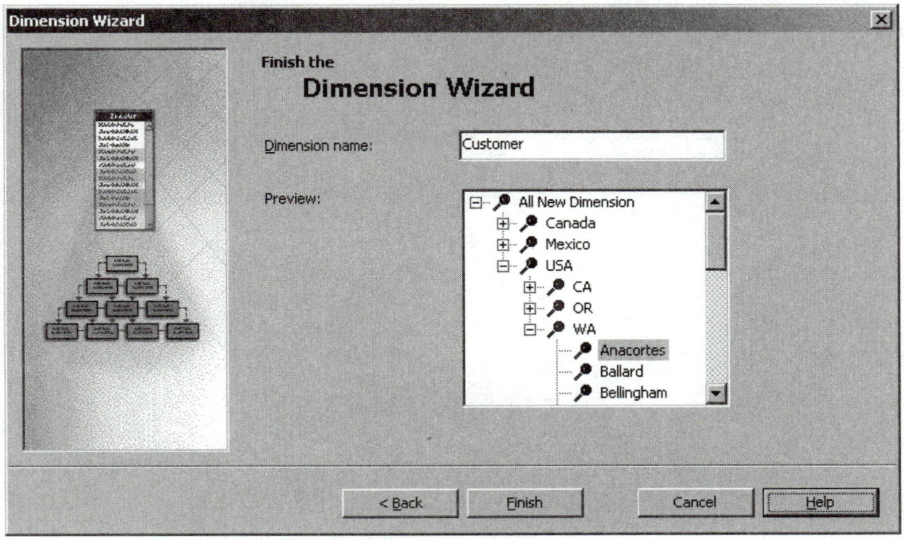

Naming the dimension and previewing its data.

As you notice in the Preview section of the figure, the members of the top level are displayed first. Expanding one of these members will reveal the members of the next level underneath it, and so on.

Once you have finished creating the dimension with the dimension wizard, the dimension editor is opened to allow you to edit it and add any final touches that the wizard did not give the chance to do. We will discuss the dimension editor and its use in the following sections.

Creating a Standard Dimension with the Dimension Editor

Now that you have seen how to create a dimension using the OLAP Manager's dimension wizard, let's create the product dimension with the dimension editor. The Dimension Editor gives many advantages over the wizard. Some of these advantages are:

- More flexibility in designing your dimension. You don't have to design the dimension according to the steps assigned to you by the wizard.
- You can assign properties values of the dimensions that you could not have done in the wizard.
- Allows you to control the joins between the dimension tables (if the dimension references more than one table)

The Dimension Editor is launched by right-clicking on the Shared Dimensions folder in the Library folder and selecting New Dimension|Editor, as shown in the figure below. You can also use the console's menu bar, specifically, the Action menu when the Shared Dimensions folder is selected to issue the same command.

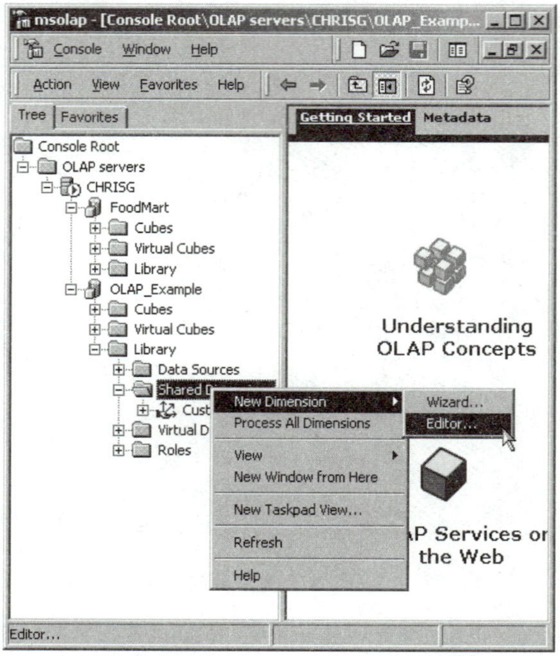

Launching the Dimension Editor

When you launch the Dimension Editor to create a new dimension, a starting dialog appears asking you to select a table that will be used as a basis for your dimension (see below). This dialog shows a list of available data sources. Expanding a data source by clicking the "+" sign next to it will show the tables belonging to the data source. Selecting a table from the list will show the details of its fields in the Detail list. For our purposes, let's select the `Product` table from the list and click OK.

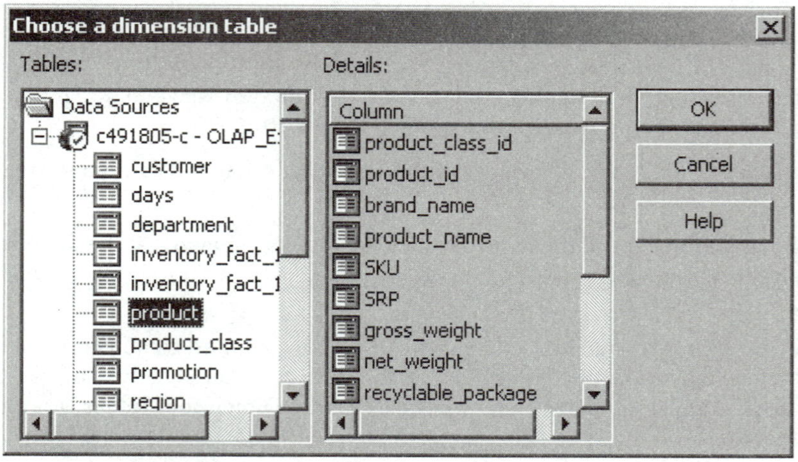

Selecting a base table for the New Dimension

After selecting the Product table in the opening dialog, the Dimension Editor opens showing an ER-type representation of the table in the right pane of the screen (see below). The product dimension will have levels corresponding to the levels of the product dimension. These levels include product_name and brand_name. However, we are also interested in having other product-related attributes, such as subcategory, category, department, and product family, as part of the dimension levels. These attributes are located in the product_class table, therefore adding them requires adding this table to our dimension base tables.

Adding the product_class table can be done by right clicking in the detail pane of the Dimension Editor and selecting Insert Tables. The same command can be achieved by using the Insert menu of the Dimension Editor. Once added, the product_class table can be seen in the detail pane of the Dimension Editor screen joined to the product table through the product_class_id field (see following figure).

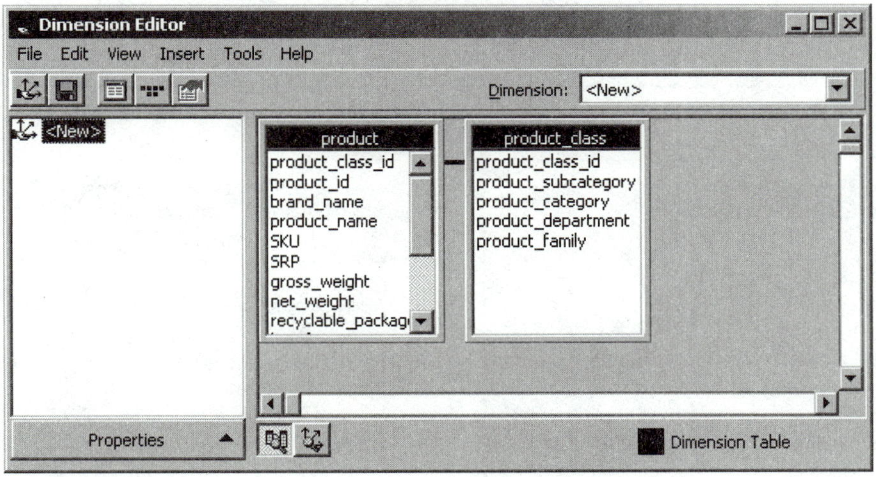

Dimension editor screen with the product and product_class tables added

Please note that you can add the join between the product and product_class tables manually by dragging and dropping the joined fields from one table to the other. An alternative would be to right-click the field you want to join from one of the two tables, and selecting Insert Join from the context-sensitive menu. From the Select Column dialog, you can select a column to join to.

Removing a join can be done by right-clicking the join line in the schema pane and selecting the Remove command. This can also be accomplished by right clicking the field name participating in the join and selecting Remove Join from the pop-up menu.

Adding the levels of interest is accomplished by using the Insert|Level menu command, or by right clicking the <New> item in the left pane and selecting New Level, as shown in the figure below. Doing so will open the Select Column dialog shown in the second figure below. The dialog shows the two tables on which the dimension is to be based with all of their fields. Selecting the appropriate check boxes to the right of the field list will limit the fields presented to the types checked. For instance, if we only check "text" and uncheck the remaining fields, we get a partial list of the fields in the two tables including the ones shown in the third figure below.

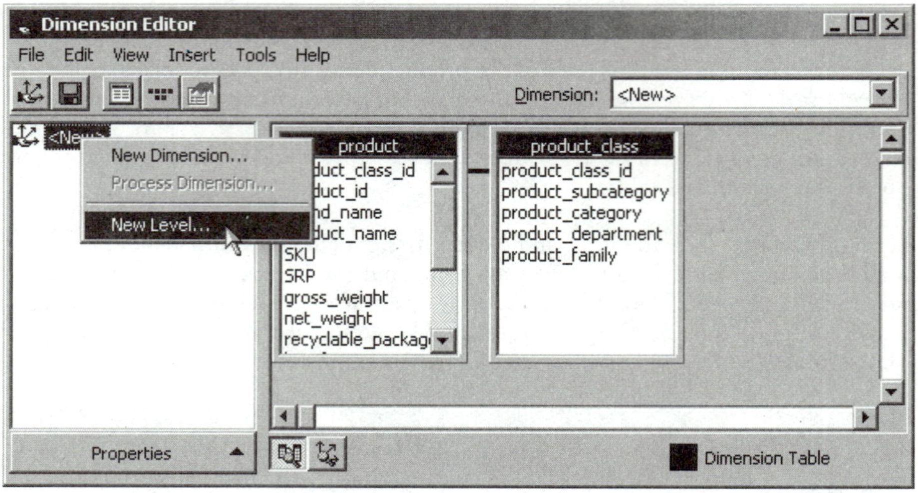

Creating a new level

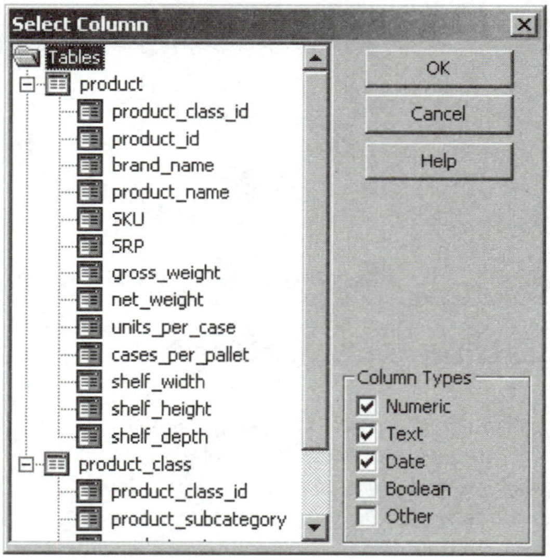

The Select Column dialog

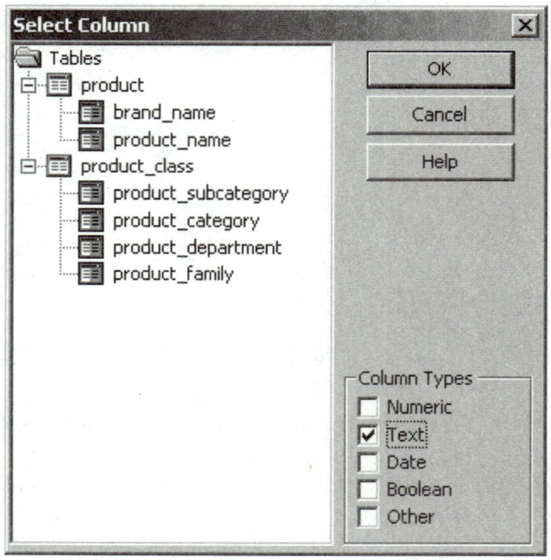

The Select Column dialog showing only text fields

Let's start with the highest level of the `Product` dimension hierarchy, the product_family. To add the corresponding level, select it and click OK. Repeat the same process for the remaining levels in the descending order of the hierarchy (`Product_Department`, `Product_Category`, `Product_subcategory`, and `Product_Class_id`) until you have added all the needed levels to the `Product` dimension. Newly created levels are shown in the Dimension Editor's left pane.

We can now add member properties to the levels in the dimension. Let's add the SKU, gross_weight and net_weight fields as member properties of the product_name level. To do this, select the product_name level and choose the Insert|Member Property from the menu bar. Once you have done this, the Select Column dialog opens, and you can now select the fields corresponding to the required member properties one at a time. When you have finished, your Dimension Editor screen should look like the following figure.

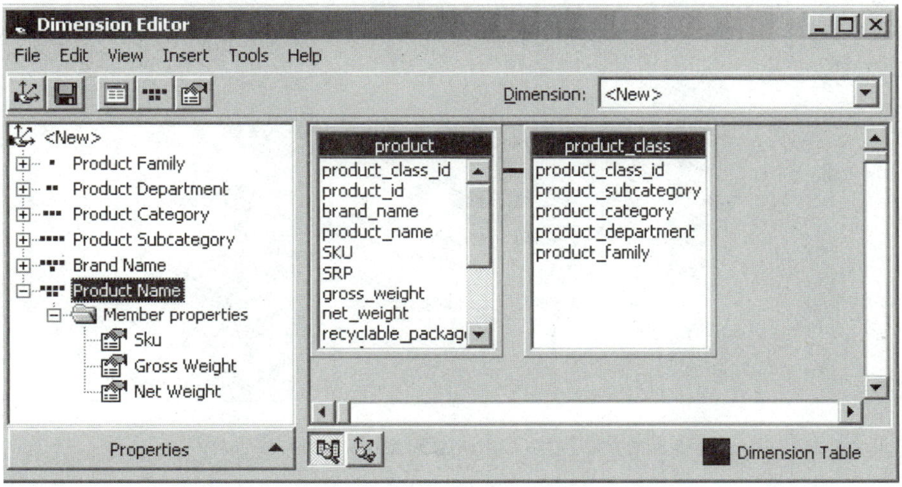

The Product dimension levels and member properties

The last step in creating the dimension is saving it. To do this, you need to select the File|Save menu item, which will pop-up the New Dimension Name dialog (see following figure), if this dimension is a new dimension.

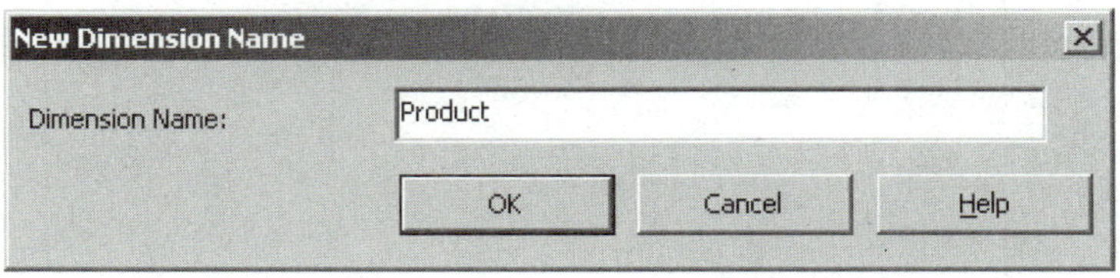

Naming the new dimension

Notice that all the levels selected for the product dimension are text fields. In general, it is more efficient to use the field with the smallest data type. For instance, for the `product_name` level, using the `product_id` field for express this level will be more optimal for the dimension storage.

Creating a Time Dimension

OLAP Manager makes creating a time dimension an extremely easy task by using the dimension wizard. As you have already seen, the dimension wizard can be used to create a standard dimension as well as a time dimension. The time dimension can be based on a number of time-defined fields in the time dimension table, or on one field. The wizard will take care of the complex formulas used to create the time hierarchies.

Run the wizard like you saw in the "Creating a Standard Dimension with the Dimension Wizard" section until you get to the step where you select the dimension table. Select the `time_by_day` table as shown in the figure below.

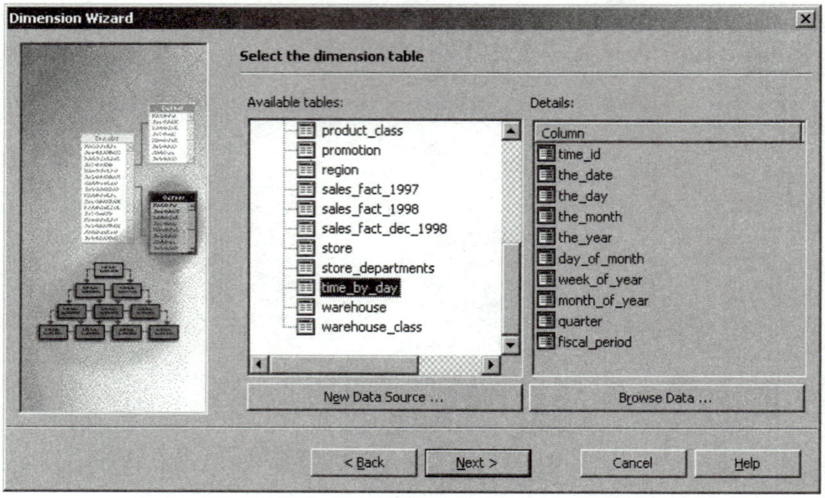

Selecting the Time Dimension table "time_by_day"

In the next step, the wizard prompts you to select the type of the dimension. Select the `Time` dimension and select the column of the table that includes time values (`the_date`) as shown in the figure below. The values of this column will be used to extract the level values of the time dimension. For example, a date, such as February 24, 2000, would yield the following values for the time levels when the dimension is processed.

Level	Value
Day	55
Week	8
Month	2
Quarter	1
Year	2000

OLAP Services obtains these values by implementing the `DatePart()` and `Format()` function in the SQL Statements it uses to extract the level values. An example of this would be:

```
SELECT DISTINCT
    DatePart('yyyy',time_by_day.the_date),
    "time_by_day"."quarter",
    DatePart('m',time_by_day.the_date),
    Format(time_by_day.the_date,'mmmm'),
    Format(time_by_day.the_date, 'yyyy-mm-dd'),
    Format(time_by_day.the_date, 'd')
FROM time_by_day
```

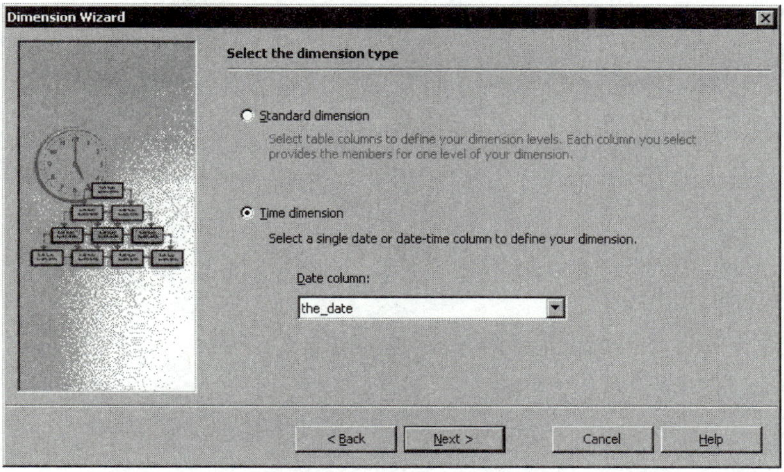

Selecting the Dimension type (time vs. standard)

The next step prompts you to select what time hierarchy you want to use. The available hierarchies are:

- Year, quarter, month, day
- Year, quarter, month, day, hour, minute
- Year, quarter, month
- Year, month, day
- Year, month, day, hour, minute
- Year, month
- Year, week, day
- Year, week, day, hour, minute
- Year, week

Even though the wizard provides you with the large selection of hierarchies listed above, you can still create your custom hierarchy by selecting one of the available ones that is closest to what you want, and adding other levels to it using the dimension editor or some decision support objects (DSO) program.

Decision Support Objects (DSO) is a COM-based application programming interface with an object model representing the Microsoft OLAP Services. DSO enables you to create applications that enhance, augment, and automate OLAP services. These applications would be used, as an example, to control the OLAP server, create and maintain OLAP objects, and establish data source connections.

During this step of the wizard, you also need to select the starting data of the year by providing a month and day. This is a powerful feature that saves you a great deal of thinking and work by accurately implementing fiscal years. The wizard will automatically calculate the correct labels for all the level members based on your selection.

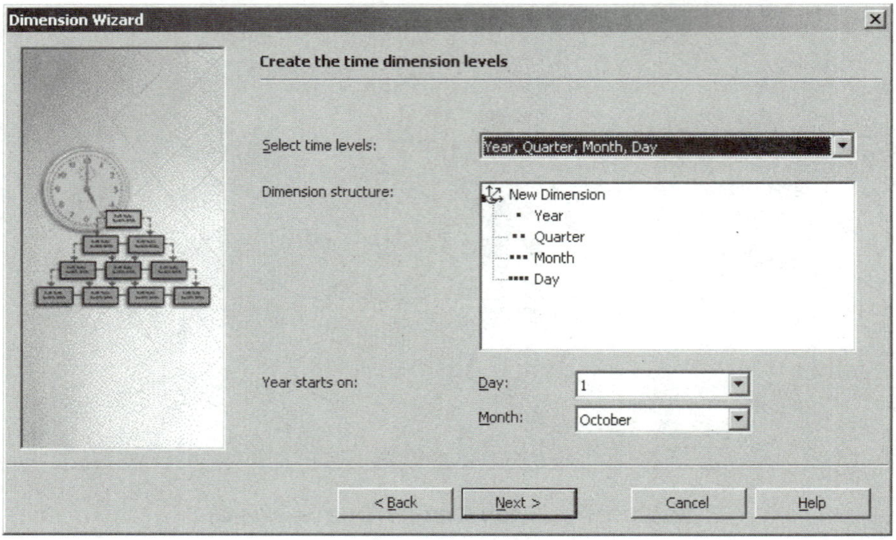

Selecting the time hierarchy and start date of the year level

The next step is similar to the standard dimension step in which you provide a name for the dimension and you can view the hierarchy you selected. The figure below shows how the wizard calculates the correct labels for the time levels (quarter, month, etc.) based on the start date of the fiscal year. In this example, the start date is October 1, and the wizard clearly shows that the first quarter includes the months, October, November, and December.

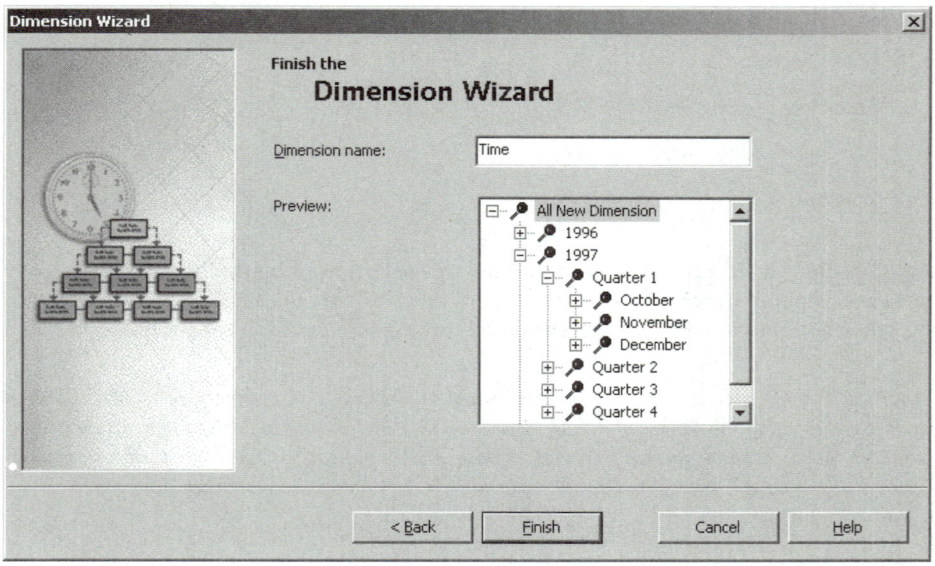

Naming the dimension and viewing its hierarchy

Editing the Dimensions

You might think that once a dimension is created it cannot be edited or changed. However, this isn't the case since OLAP Manager allows you to use the dimension editor to edit the dimension properties. Actually, you should learn how to use the editor because it provides you with added flexibility by creating the dimension quickly with the wizard, then using the editor to add the flavors and functionalities that were not possible to add with the dimension wizard alone.

You can view the properties of the dimension in the dimension editor by selecting the View|Properties from the menu bar, or by clicking the "Properties" button on bottom of the editor's window. This selection will make the properties window visible as shown in the figure below. Hiding this window is done by doing the same action that made it visible, that is selecting the View|Properties command from the menu bar, or again clicking the "Properties" button, which is located on top of the properties window when it is visible.

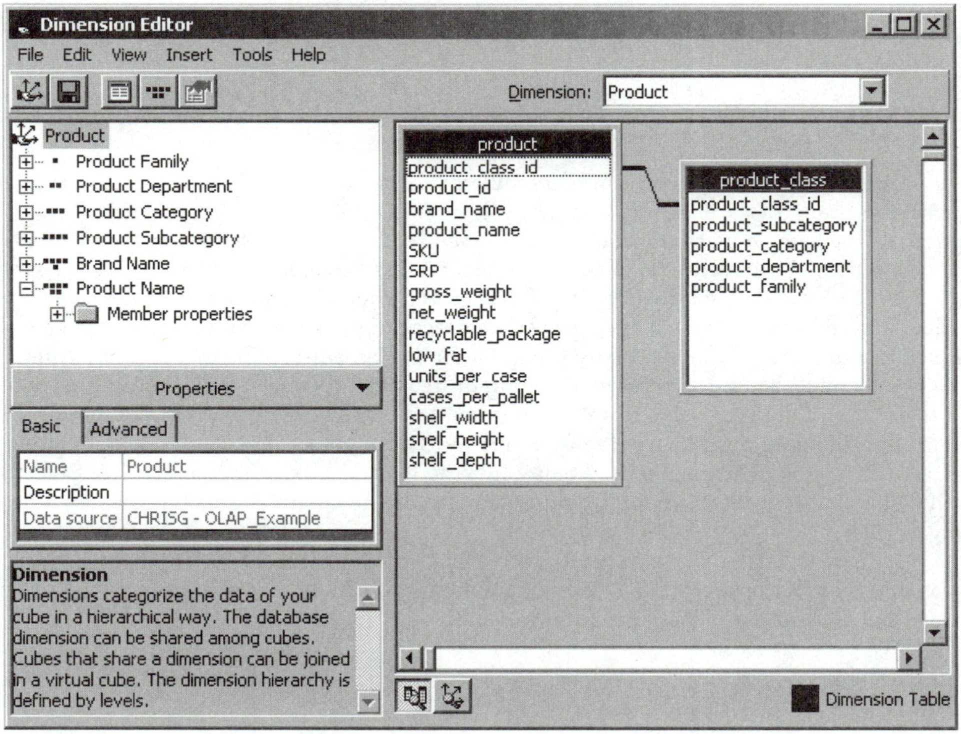

The dimension editor with the properties window displayed

The properties window can be used to edit any properties of the dimension or its elements (levels, members, member properties). However, you cannot change the dimension name or data source. The properties window provides two tabs, basic and advanced. In the following sections, we will look at the most important properties of the dimension, levels, and members.

Basic Properties

The basic properties for a dimension, as the previous figure shows, are:

- name
- description
- data source

The name and data source cannot be changed after the dimension is created. The description, however, is editable and should be provided to reflect the purpose of the dimension and a brief description of its elements.

The basic properties of a dimension level are:

- name
- description
- member key column

All these properties are editable and can be modified after the dimension is created. Although the name and description properties are self-explanatory, it is useful to provide meaningful names and descriptions of the level you are working with. Frequently, the wizard provides you with a name that corresponds to the field name in the database (`cust_id`, for example). You may need to change that to a more meaningful name. Also, the description serves as a good reminder in the future to what the level means. The wizard does not allow you to provide a description, nor does it provide one. Therefore, it is a good idea to add a description manually using the dimension editor. The member key column property, on the other hand, can refer to a column or to a value derived from a column, such as a formula that extracts the year value from a date-formatted column. However, the column or the value derived from the column must be a string or a number. Editing this value can be done by typing in the text box next to it, or by clicking the "..." button next to the text box, which opens the "Select Column" dialog allowing you to select a column from the dimension table that will serve as the key for the member.

When you add member properties to a level of a dimension, you notice three basic properties in the properties pane (or window). These properties are:

- name,
- description, and
- source column

The source column property points to the table column of the dimension table that represents the value of the member property. Editing this value can be done by typing in the text box next to it, or by clicking the "..." button next to the text box, which opens the "Select Column" dialog allowing you to select a column from the dimension table that will serve as the source for the member property.

Advanced Properties

Advanced properties of the dimension can be found on the Advanced tab of the Properties window when the dimension is selected, and include:

- All level,
- All caption, and
- Type

The `All level` property is used to decide whether you want to specify an "All" level (a level which includes everything) in the dimension hierarchy. The value of this property is either "`Yes`" or "`No`". The `All` caption includes a description or name of the `All` level. You can enter any valid name for this caption that follows the naming conventions for dimensions and cubes. By default, a dimension has an `All` level with the caption of "`All`" and the dimension name. For example, if the dimension is the Product dimension, the default caption for the `All` level would be "All products". Hierarchical dimensions usually need an `All` level to aggregate the data over the members of each level. If you don't include the `All` level for a hierarchical dimension, the aggregations will stop at each member of the top level. On the other hand, for non-hierarchical dimensions, you need to set this property to `No`, because leaving the default value of `Yes` will result in an aggregation that does not have any significant meaning and will only waste storage and processing time.

The `Type` property specifies the type of the dimension and can be either "`regular`" or "`time`". When using the wizard, this value is set to "`time`" when you create a time dimension and to "`regular`" when creating non-time dimensions. This property can be accessed by MDX time functions to identify the dimension as a time dimension.

Advanced properties of a dimension level can be found on the Advanced tab of the properties window when a level is selected, and include:

Member Name Column

The Member Name Column property indicates the name of the column that includes member names. Microsoft OLAP Services stores dimension information and cube aggregations internally based on the key column (explained in the basic properties section). However, externally, OLAP Services allow for the use of a different column that includes a valid name or SQL function for display purposes. This makes it easy to understand the results of the aggregations when generating reports based on the OLAP data. By default, when you create a level, the member name property is the same as that of the member key property. However, by all means, change the member name property to something more descriptive. For example, in a product dimension, the product level may have a key based on the product SKU or `product_id` field. Displaying the aggregation results based on the product name, such as Idaho Potatoes is much more understandable than using the `product_id` of 001231. After all, the purpose of the OLAP processing is to simplify the data and present it in an understandable fashion.

One advantage of differentiating the two column rather than using the descriptive column for both the key and name properties is that the key column has to be indexed to optimize query performance. Indexing a numeric or "ID" column is much easier and more efficient than a longer text field. So, while the OLAP server uses the indexed key column to do the querying and bring back the results, the descriptive column will be used for display purposes.

Editing the Member Name Column property is allowed. However, you need to pay close attention to the syntax. Use the same syntax as the one you see created by default, that is, use the dimension table name followed by a dot and the column name surrounding the names by quotation marks, such as: `["table name"."column name"]`. An example of using a valid SQL function for this property would be using the customer full name based on the first, middle, and last name fields in the customer dimension table: `"Customer"."cust_fname" + ' ' + "Customer"."cust_minitial" + ' ' + "Customer"."cust_lname"`.

One advantage of the Member Name Column property is that you can use it to create multiple levels based on the same column using the dimension editor. The key here is that you have to use the dimension editor to create these dimensions, rather than using the wizard. A good example would be the date dimension. For this case, you can use the date field in combination with some date functions to create the different levels you need. As an example, to create a `Year` level, you can create a new level based on the `Date_id` field of the time dimension table, `tblDays`, and name `"Year"`, then change the `Member` key and `Name` column properties according to the functions below:

```
Member Key Column: DatePart('yyyy', "tblDays"."Date_id")
Member Name Column: Format("tblDays"."Date_id", 'yyyy')
```

Repeating the process above for the month, day, and other levels, you can create the whole hierarchy based on one field, `data_id`.

Member Count

As the name implies, this property indicates the number of members available in the selected level. For example, if the dimension is geographic location, the state level may have 50 members representing the 50 states. The number of members is updated by OLAP services when a level is added.

Unique Members

This property indicates whether the member key column values for the dimension level are unique. Based on the determination of uniqueness, this property can be set to `Yes` or `No`. If you create your dimension with the dimension wizard, the value is set automatically. However, the set value is not always accurate, and you need to verify it and change it if needed in the dimension editor.

Level Type

As the type property that applies to the dimension, the level type property applies to the dimension levels. The property specifies the type of the dimension level as standard if the dimension is not a time dimension, and as either one of the values below, if the dimension is a time dimension:

- Years
- Half years
- Quarters
- Months
- Weeks
- Days
- Hours
- Minutes
- Seconds

Key Data Size

This property indicates the size of the key column in bytes.

Key Data Type

This property indicates the type of the key column.

Order By Key

The default of this property allows you to order dimension level by the member key column. Setting this property to false, orders the members according to the member name column. This is very useful when you want to order the results in terms of the names, rather than the keys. For example, it makes more sense to order by city name, rather than city key. Using the name will make it easy to locate members you are looking for.

Processing the Dimensions

After you design your dimensions, you need to process them to populate their tables with the appropriate data. For example, as we saw in the earlier time dimension example, the dimension levels are not calculated and populated from the date field until you process the dimension.

To process a dimension in the OLAP Manager, right click the shared dimension in the OLAP Manager's tree view and click the Process command. This action will bring up the Process a Dimension dialog box, shown in the figure below. We have used the `Product` dimension in our example.

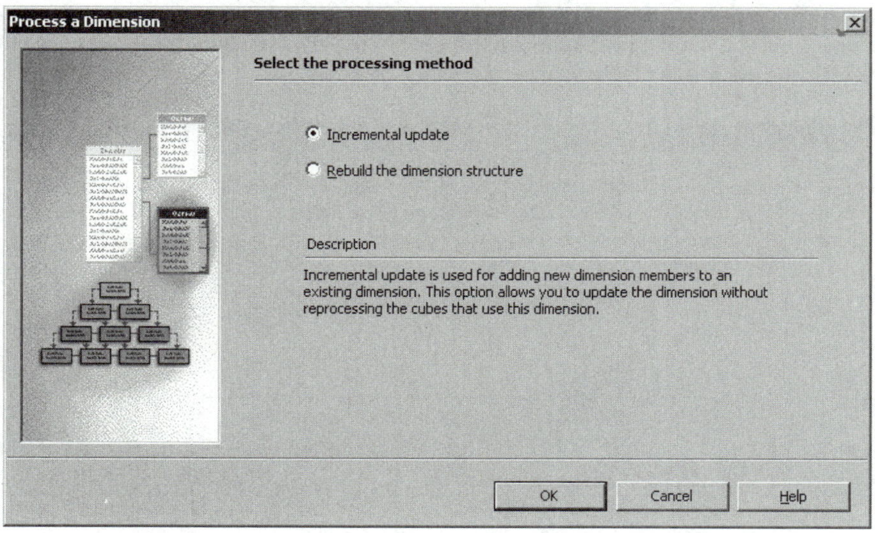

Process a Dimension dialog box

As the dialog box shows, two types of dimension processing are available: rebuilding the dimension, and incrementally updating it as acceptable changes are made. The first type of processing is required when the structure of the dimension is changed, such as removing a level in the dimension hierarchy or adding a new one. Rebuilding the dimension is also required when the relationship between members in the dimension hierarchy changes.

Be careful when you process a dimension with the rebuild option. This option makes all cubes that incorporate the shared dimension unavailable to users. These cubes will only become available when processed again. Also, if you change the structure of a dimension, or make a change that warrants processing it with the rebuild option, and you don't process it, the dimension will be processed automatically when any cube incorporating it is processed.

You might ask the question, if my dimensions will be built anyway when the cube using them is processed, then why bother processing the dimensions individually? The reason you need to process the dimensions individually when you can is to speed up the cube processing. If the dimensions in the cube are not processed before the cube is processed, the cube will take considerably longer time to process.

The second type of dimension processing is by incrementally updating it. This option is warranted when you add new members to the dimension without causing any structural changes to it. As an example, when you add a new product category to the category level of the product dimension, you will not be changing the structure of the dimension, and only an incremental update is needed to process the dimension.

With the incremental update option, cubes incorporating the dimension remain available after the change to the dimension has been made. However, the change will not become available until the dimension has been processed. Also, processing a cube incorporating the dimension that changed will also automatically process it.

Once you select the type of processing you intend to do for your dimension, and click the OK button in the Process a Dimension dialog box, a Process screen appears showing you the progress of the dimension processing as shown in the following figure. This screen also allows you to view details of steps you select by clicking the Detail button.

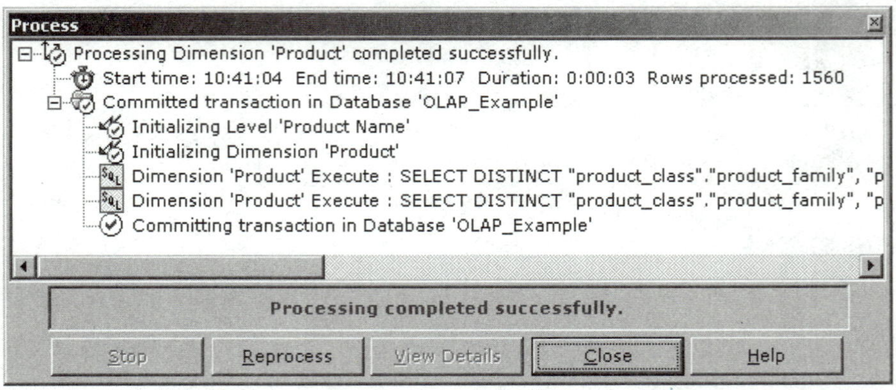

The Process dialog box showing the steps conducted by the OLAP server to process the dimension

Creating Member Properties

We discussed in Chapter 3 that member properties are attributes associated with the members of a dimension level. For instance, the customer level of the customer dimension has members, for example, XYZ. A member property would be something like a field identifying the customer type to be a company or an individual, etc. In Chapter 2 we talked about the importance of member properties in building virtual dimensions. Now you will see how you can create member properties using the OLAP Manager. To create a member property for a dimension level member:

1. Right-click on the shared dimension from the library folder in the tree view of the OLAP Manager and select the Edit command from the context-sensitive menu. (We have used the `Product` dimension in this example.) This action will launch the dimension editor.

2. In the dimension editor, select the level that includes the members you want to add the property to and click on the Insert Member Property toolbar button (you can just right-click the level and select New Member Property). We have used the `Product Name` level. This action will open the Select Column dialog box, which we saw earlier in the chapter.

3. Select the "`Low Fat`" field and click OK.

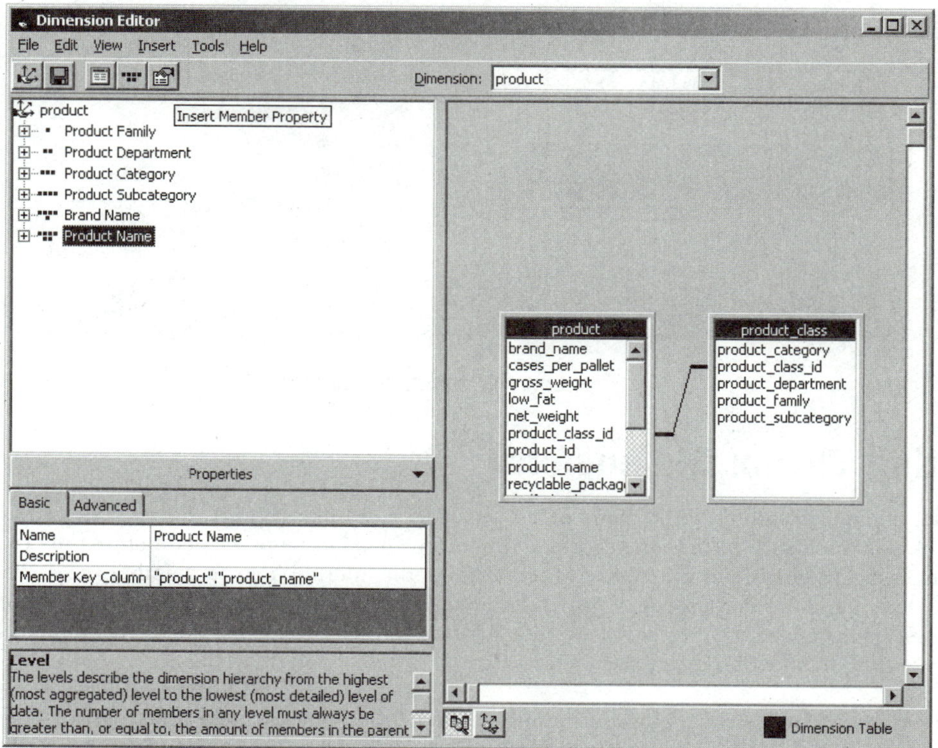

The Insert Member Property button on the dimension editor's toolbar.

4. This will add the `Low Fat` field as a member property of the `Product Name` level in the `Product` dimension (see following figure). After adding the member property, you have to process the dimension (or cube) with the incremental updates option. The member properties are not accessible from the OLAP Manager, you have to use the dimension editor to access them.

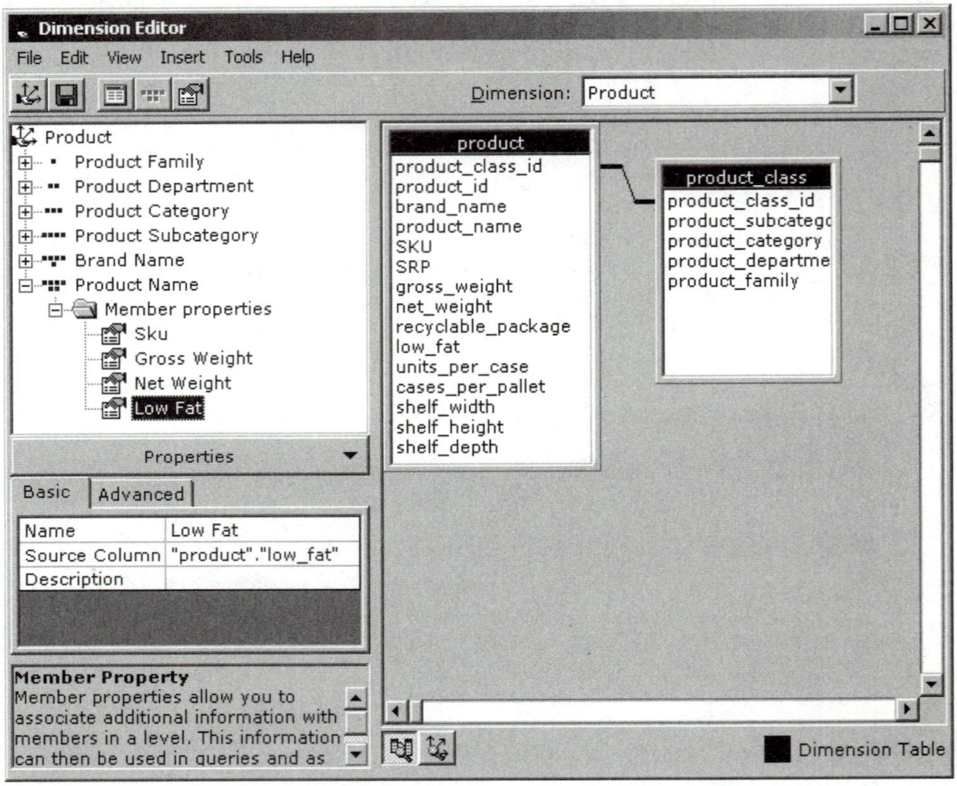

The "Low Fat" member property

Creating Virtual Dimensions

Virtual dimensions are useful in many cases for security, storage savings and reduced cube processing time. As we discussed in Chapter 4, virtual dimensions need to be processed before they can be used. However, processing them is a matter of establishing the internal links to member properties it is composed of and is a fast process if the underlying dimensions and cubes have already been processed. If these dimensions and cubes have not been processed, then processing the virtual dimension incorporating them will trigger their processing too.

Virtual dimensions are not required for building data cubes, but are often used to display relations that are not clearly visible or to conduct some trend analysis based on some dimension members and a member property. For example, you can create a member property that describes whether a product is recyclable and build a virtual dimension based on it. Once the virtual dimension is incorporated in the cube, you can cross-reference it with the members of other dimensions establishing relationships between recyclable products and sales, for example.

Virtual dimensions are created from member properties. You can add a virtual dimension to a cube only if the dimension that supplies the member property is also included in the cube and all virtual dimensions are shared, not private. You can use the virtual dimension wizard to create a virtual dimension. The wizard allows you to select the member property that defines the virtual dimension.

1. Start the wizard in the OLAP Manager tree view by right clicking the virtual dimension folder in the tree view of the OLAP Manager and selecting New Virtual Dimension from the context-sensitive menu.

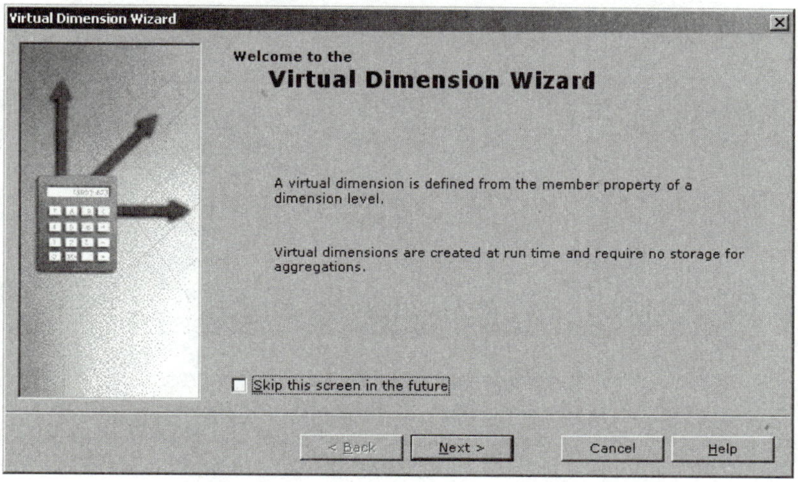

The opening screen of the virtual dimension wizard

2. The next screen of the wizard allows you to select the member property to base the virtual dimension. Select "Product Name.Recyclable Package" and move to the next screen (see figure below).

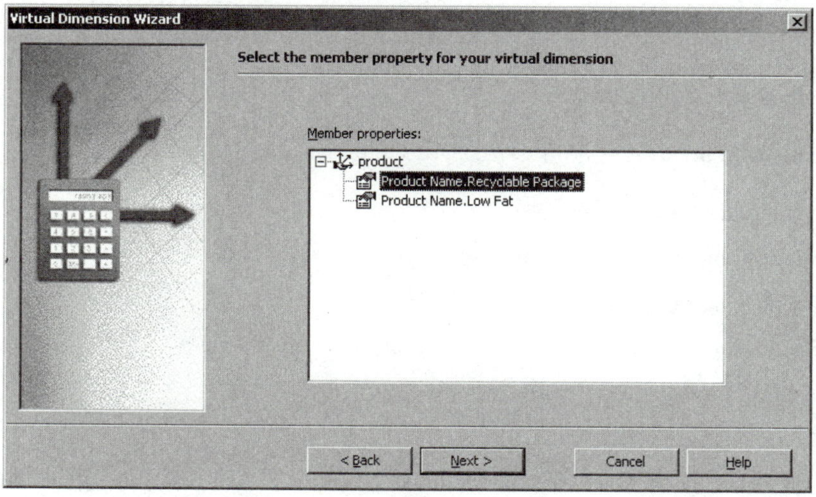

Selecting the member property for the virtual dimension

3. In the next screen assign a name to the virtual dimension. Name this new virtual dimension `vd_Recyclable` and click the Finish button:

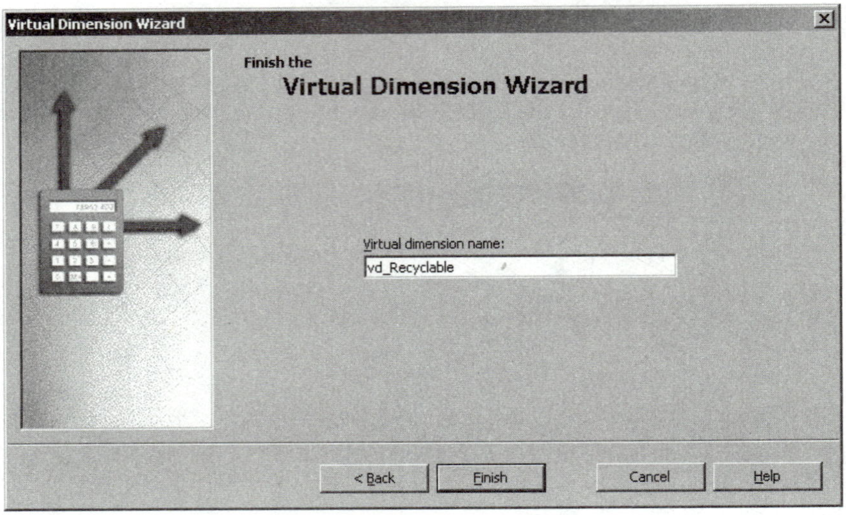

Selecting a name for the virtual dimension

That's it, you've just created a virtual dimension. Later in the chapter we will add this dimension to one of the cubes we build, and use it to view the data according to the relationship between the member property and other dimensions in the cube.

Creating a Cube: Putting It All Together

Building the cubes is the most important step in the building of your OLAP solution. People who want to use your solution end up using these cubes analyzing their data to get to what they want. In the previous sections, you saw how some components of the cube could be built. These components included shared dimensions, virtual dimensions, and member properties. In this section, you will see how these components fit with the scheme of building the cube and how you can build other components that complete the picture.

Building the cube involves several steps. These steps are outlined below:

- Specifying the data source
- Identifying the cube fact table
- Identifying the cube measures
- Identifying the cube dimensions, both private and shared
- Adding partitions if needed
- Processing the cube

Some of these steps, such as defining the data source, have already been discussed earlier in the chapter. Some have been partially discussed, such as shared dimensions. Let's discuss the remaining steps in some detail showing how the OLAP Manager can be used to accomplish them.

Identifying the Fact Table

The cube we are building in this chapter is based on the `OLAP_Example` database, which is based on the `FoodMart` sample OLAP database that ships with the Microsoft OLAP Services. Before you can build the cube, you need to build the dimensions that will comprise it. These dimensions include: `Customer`, `Product`, `Time`, and `Store`. You have already seen different ways to create the first three of these dimensions; you can either use the dimension wizard, or the dimension editor to create the last dimension, the `Store` dimension. Remember that this dimension has the following levels:

- Store Country
- Store State/province
- Store City, and
- Store name

Just like the dimension, the cube can be created with the wizard or with the cube editor. To start the cube wizard, select the Cubes folder in the tree view of the OLAP Manager, then select the menu command: Action|New Cube|Wizard as shown in the following figure. You can also right-click the Cubes folder and select the pop-up menu command: New Cube|Wizard.

The following steps will lead you into building the cube:

1. Just like any Microsoft wizard, a welcoming screen appears describing the wizard.
2. The next screen, shown in the following figure, presents you with the data sources that you can pick from. It also gives you the option of creating a new data source by clicking the New Data Source button below the Data Sources and Tables list box. Clicking this button will lead you to the Data Link Properties screen, which we saw earlier.
3. Select the OLAP_Example data source and expand it by clicking the "+" sign next to it. This will show you the list of available tables in this data source. Select the `sales_fact_1998` table to use as our fact table for this cube. As soon as you select the table, the Detail list box gets populated with the field names of the selected table. If you want to view the data in the table, you can click on the Browse Data button located below the Detail list box.

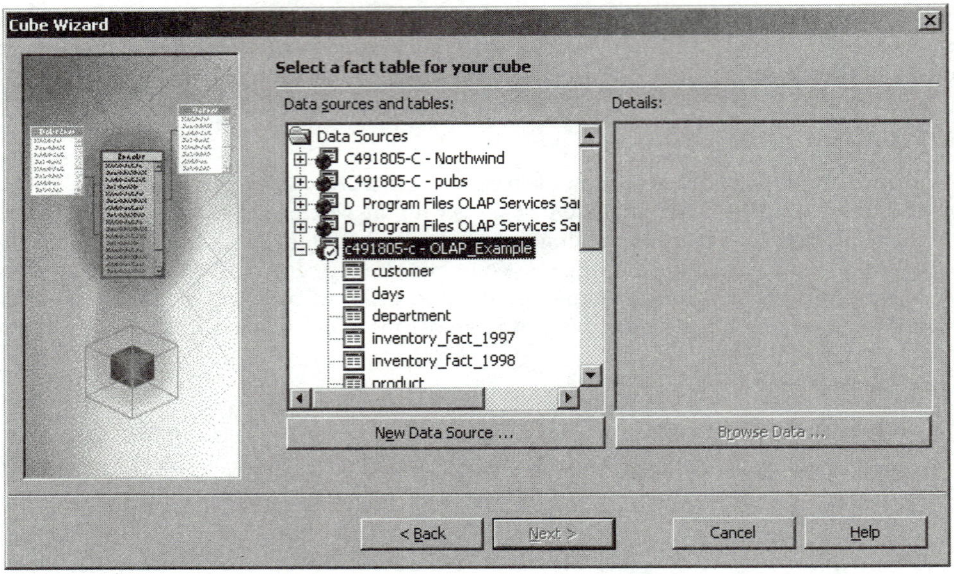

Selecting the data source for the cube from the existing data sources

Once a cube definition is saved in OLAP services, the name and data source cannot be changed.

Selecting the Measures and Dimensions

4. Clicking the Next button leads to the cube wizard step that allows you to select the columns from the fact table that will serve as the cube measures as shown in the figure below.

5. Individually select `store_sales`, `store_cost`, and `unit_sales` fields from the fact table, and for each field, click the ">" button to move it from the Fact Table Numeric Columns list box to the Cube Measures list box. You can also move these fields by individually double clicking them. You may notice that the field labels in the cube measure list box change and don't keep the same names as the table columns. The names given to the measures by OLAP servies are: Store Sales, Store Cost, and Unit Sales respectively. This is OLAP Services way of giving default descriptive names of these measures.

   Although the cube wizard allows you to select multiple columns in the fact table numeric columns list, you can move only one column at a time, or all at once to the cube measures list in this version of OLAP services.

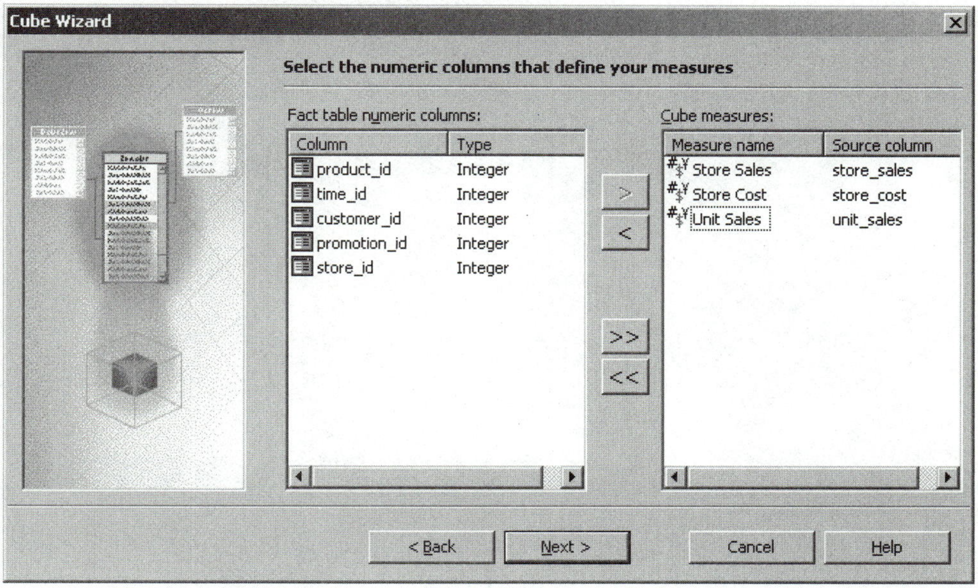

Selecting the Cube Measures in the Cube Wizard

6. The next step of the wizard shows you available shared dimensions to pick from. The figure below shows the four dimensions, `Customer`, `Store`, `Product`, and `Time`. Select the first four dimensions and click the ">" button to include them in the cube. Notice that in this step, you can launch the dimension wizard that you saw earlier in the chapter by clicking the New Dimension button. This will allow you to create a dimension that is private and not shared by other cubes.

7. In the next step you will be able to name the cube with any valid name ("Sales of 1998" in our example), and even view the structure of the cube in the Cube Structure pane. You can also view a sample of the cube data by clicking the Browse Sample Data button. This will only show you a sample, not the real cube data. To see the cube data, you have to process it first.

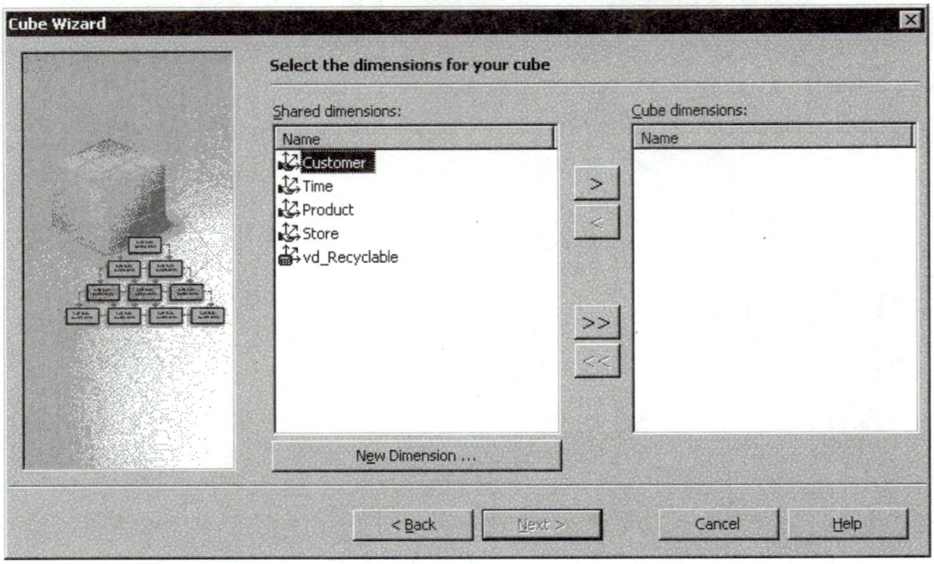

Selecting the cube dimensions

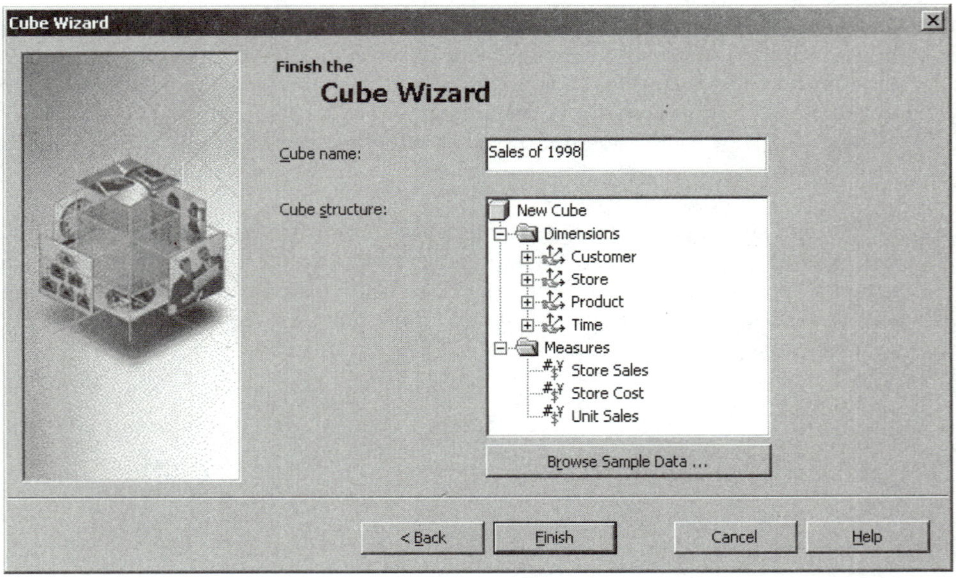

Naming the cube and viewing its structure

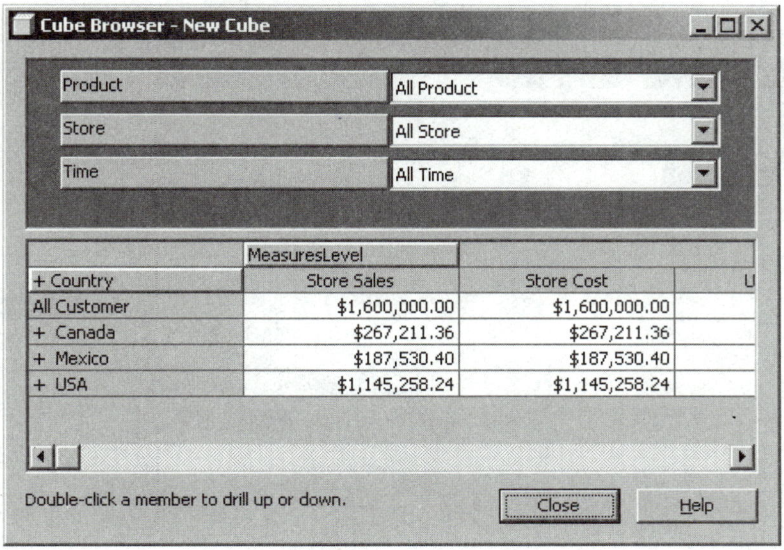

Browsing sample cube data

Clicking the Finish button ends the wizard and opens the cube editor. Just like the dimension editor, the cube editor allows you to refine the cube definition. The following section describes the cube editor and the main functions it provides.

Cube Editor

The cube editor (shown in the figure below) is a graphical tool that accompanies the OLAP Manager and can be launched at will with the Action|Edit menu command when you have a cube selected, or with the Edit command on the pop-up menu that shows when you right-click the cube name in the tree view.

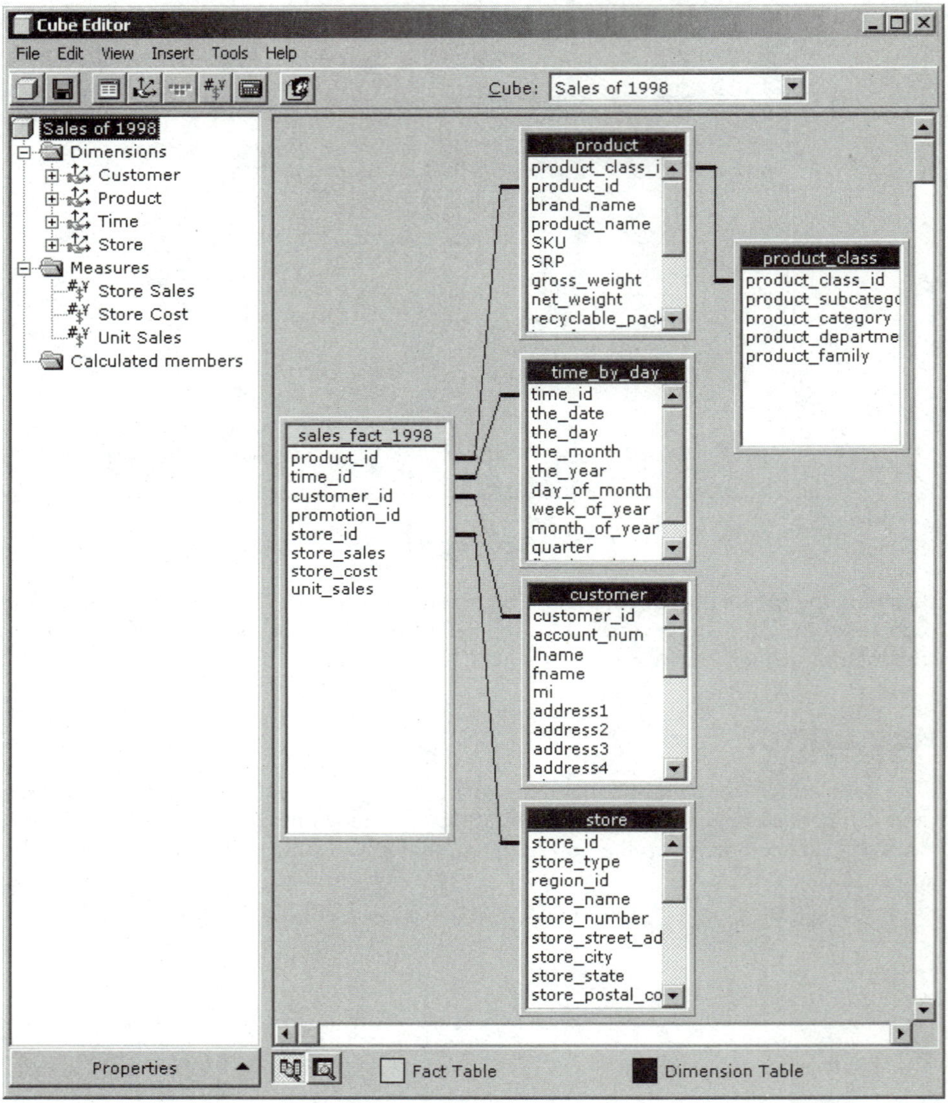

The cube editor screen

Using the cube editor, you can specify any table joins that the wizard did not specify, or wrongly-specified in some cases when you created your cube. An example of this is the wizard selecting one of two available join options for some tables that you don't want selected. You can also use the cube editor for a variety of tasks, such as:

- Adding calculated members
- Inserting new measures
- Inserting new dimensions
- Inserting new tables (this is if you are building the cube from scratch because OLAP services allows only one fact table per cube in the current version)
- Specifying table joins in the cube schema
- Design cube storage
- Process the cube
- Validate cube structure
- Optimize cube schema
- Manage roles and their access privileges to the cube data and elements
- Browse cube data
- Set cube properties

The cube editor is composed of several panes:

- A tree pane showing the structure of the cube with its dimensions, measures, and calculated members
- A properties pane that shows the properties of a selected item in the tree view, and
- A main pane that shows the cube schema by default. This pane can also show the cube data if you select the View|Data menu command.

Adding Calculated Members

OLAP services allow you to create new measures based on simple or complex calculations, which gives you a great flexibility to manipulate the data and get meaningful insights from it. In order to make good use of this feature, you need to have a basic knowledge of the new multi-dimensional extensions language, MDX. MDX is introduced in Chapter 7 and discussed in more detail in Chapter 8

Calculated members are not stored in the OLAP database. Instead, they are calculated at runtime and held in memory each time you request them. Therefore, it is recommended that you keep the calculations simple and short to avoid performance degradation as a result of conducting these calculations.

You can use the Insert Calculated Members toolbar button, or you can right-click the Calculated Members item in the tree pane and select New Calculated Member from the pop-up menu to add a new member. Once you do so, the Calculated Member Builder dialog box appears as shown in the following figure. In this dialog, you can select the measure or dimension, and even the dimension member that will be used as a basis for the calculated member. The Value Expression box is where you enter the calculation in MDX format. If you, like me, frequently make mistakes while typing, you can use the expression-building tools below the value expression box to build your expression. These tools allow you to drag and drop data members and functions to the value expression box, and then use the calculator-type buttons to build your expression. I am not going to go into the detail of using this tool because it is meant to be intuitive and easy to understand. You can refer to the product documentation or help screens for detailed description on how to use this tool.

For our purposes, let's now create a new member based on the measures of the `"Sales of 1998"` cube. The calculated member will give us the profits by subtracting the costs from the sales values: `[Measures].[Store Sales] - [Measures].[Store Cost]`. To save the new member, click OK.

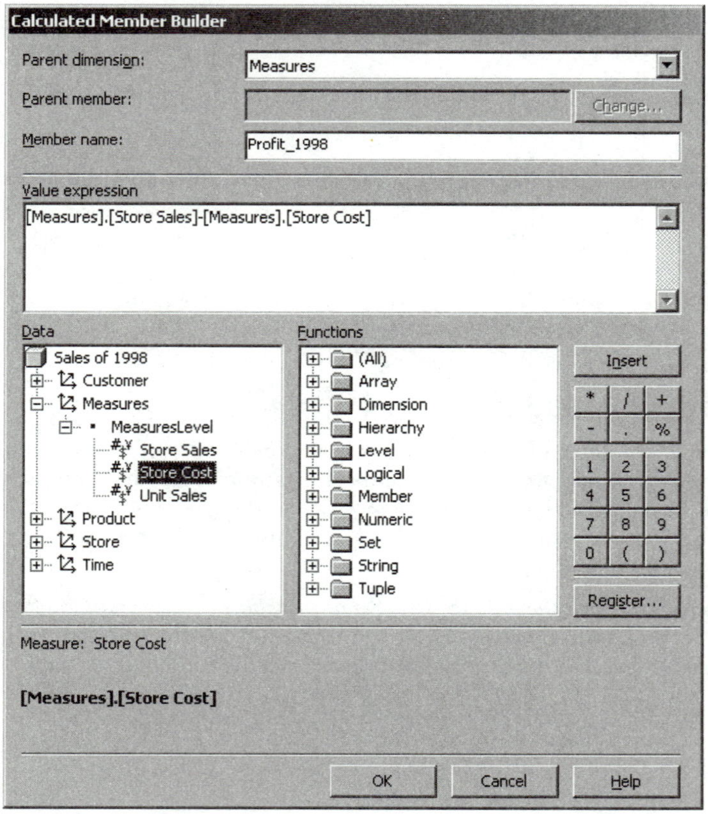

Calculated Member Builder screen

It is worth mentioning that the calculated member builder screen allows you to add your own functions that you can write in the language of your choice to the list of functions that can be used to create the calculated member. The Register button on this screen opens up a Register Function Libraries dialog (see figure below) allowing you to navigate to the location on your computer or network nodes that includes the functions or libraries you want to add.

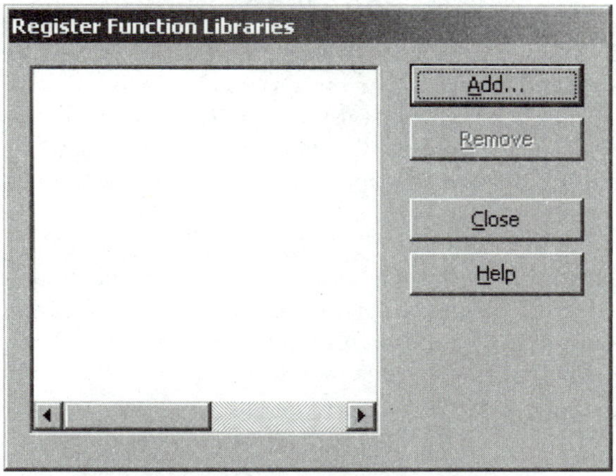

Registering a new function library

Adding your own user-defined functions enables client applications to extend the OLAP Services internal function library. If an OLAP function conflicts with a user-defined function, the OLAP Services internal function always takes precedence over the registered function. A user-defined function can be developed on any tool capable of generating Microsoft ActiveX libraries, such as Visual C++, Visual Basic, or Visual J++. The types accepted as registered libraries include:

- Type libraries (`*.olb, *.tlb, *.dll`)
- Executable files (`*.exe, *.dll`)
- ActiveX controls (`*.ocx`)

The order of the libraries in the list defines the precedence of function name resolution in cases of conflicts. For instance, if two libraries contain the same function name, the first library takes precedence. Two libraries are already registered by default: the Visual Basic for Applications Expression Services function library (VBA332.dll), and the library that supports the Microsoft Excel worksheet functions. The Excel libraries have to be installed prior to the OLAP Services installation.

Supported functions should include arguments of string or numeric data types only. If the arguments are arrays or variants, then these should be arrays or variants that include only string or numeric types. The return values of the supported functions should follow the same rule, that is, they should be string or numeric, or an array or variant of strings and numeric values.

After registering a library or function, it is treated like any other function in OLAP services. Calling it would be the same way you call any other function. For example, let's say that we added a library that includes a function that calculates number of salespeople needed and is defined as:

```
Public Function NumberOfSalespeopleNeeded() As Integer
```

This function can then be used in defining a new calculated member that returns the number of sales reps needed for a region.

Inserting New Tables, Measures, and Dimensions

The OLAP Manager's cube editor can be used to insert new tables, measures and private or shared dimensions. The Insert menu and some toolbar buttons can be used to insert new tables, measures, or dimensions. You can also right-click the Measures item in the tree view and select New Measure to add a new measure. This will open the Select Column dialog that we saw earlier in the chapter, allowing you to select a column for your new measure. Keep in mind that Microsoft OLAP Manager allows only one fact table for each cube.

Right-clicking the Dimensions item in the tree view gives you the choice to add a private dimension, or open the dimension manager. The dimension manager allows you to manage existing dimensions, or add new ones. The dimension manager is shown in the figure below. Clicking the New Dimension button on the dimension manager screen will launch the dimension wizard that will lead you into adding the new dimension.

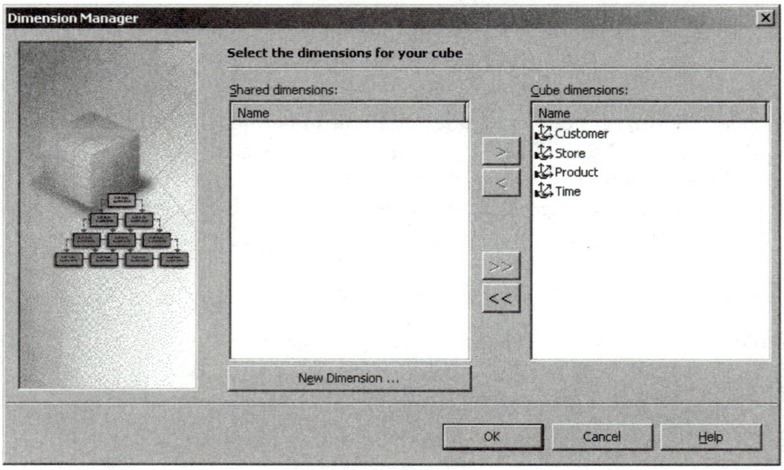

The dimension manager screen allows you to remove or add dimensions to your solution

Designing Cube Storage

Aggregations are pre-calculated summaries of the data that provide a mechanism for rapid query response. Cube data and aggregation can be stored in a variety of ways. In Chapter 3 we looked at the storage problem and its relation to sparsity. OLAP Services addresses these issues by implementing the following:

- No storage is allocated for empty cells
- Data compression is applied to stored aggragations
- OLAP services provides a complex algorithm for optimizing storage and performance needs

- Several storage modes are available providing you with flexibility of where to keep the data and how to manage it
- You can create the storage strategy that fits your needs.

Cube data can grow in size in an out-of-control fashion unless well designed. Sparsity is defined by the amount of empty cells in a cube. For example, if one dimension contains products and another dimension contains store regions, cells at the intersection of the Midwest stores and product family XYZ could probably be empty. In other words, Product XYZ is not being sold in the Midwest region.

The OLAP Manager's cube editor allows you to specify the storage options for your cube data and aggregations. Storage options are covered in detail in Chapters 3 and 4. I will only show how you can use the cube editor to specify these options.

Selecting the menu command Tools|Design Storage will launch the storage design wizard. After the customary the Welcome screen, you will be able to select the type of data storage: MOLAP, ROLAP, or HOLAP (see following figure). The MOLAP option stores the cube data and aggregates in multidimensional structures. The ROLAP option will leave your cube data in its relational structure and store the aggregates in summary tables in the same relational database. The HOLAP option is a hybrid of the previous two options allowing you to store the cube data in the relational structure and the aggregates in multi-dimensional structures. For the purposes of this example, select the MOLAP option.

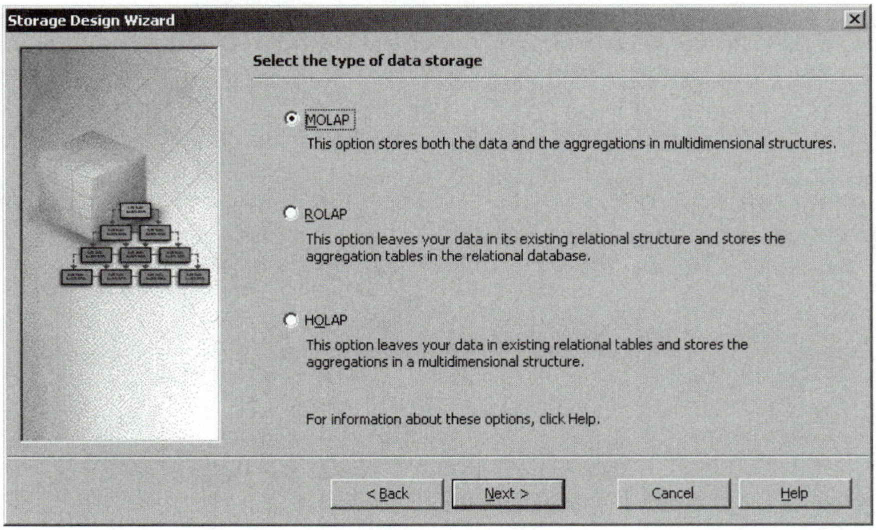

Selecting the storage type for the cube

The next step will allow you to set aggregation options. These options are based on the relationship between the size of such aggregates and the performance of the OLAP system. As the size of the aggregates increases, performance increases because you will be storing the answers to most queries. However, at a certain range, performance gains with the added aggregation start to diminish reaching the point of diminishing returns. At that range, increasing the size of aggregates by 50% may only yield a few percentage points of gain in performance.

The figure below shows the step that allows you to specify the aggregation option. These options include:

- Estimated storage reaches x amount of MB
- Performance gains reach x%
- Until I click stop

The first option adds aggregates until a certain point where the storage amount reaches a preset amount in MB. The second option ends the aggregates at the point where a preset target of performance gains is reached. The last option leaves it to you to decide when to stop the process.

To start creating the aggregates, click the Start button after making your aggregation option choice. This will cause the button caption to change to Stop (as shown in the figure below). The storage design wizard will start crunching and processing for a few minutes until it reaches the target set by the option, or you click the Stop button if you selected the third option. If you wish to redo the aggregations using a different option, you need to reset them with the Reset button. Resetting the aggregates will remove them from storage. The graph on this wizard screen helps visualize the gains you achieve, as more aggregates are stored. Click the Next button to move onto the next stage.

The next step of the storage wizard asks you whether you want to process the cube or just save the aggregates and process the cube later. Processing the cube involves processing any unprocessed or changed dimension incorporated in the cube. Processing the cube also fills it with data from the fact table by executing SQL queries. The processing of the cube takes some time to finish, possibly a few minutes after which the cube is populated, and the aggregations specified in the aggregates option step are created. (You can also process the cube directly from the cube editor by selecting Tools|Process.)

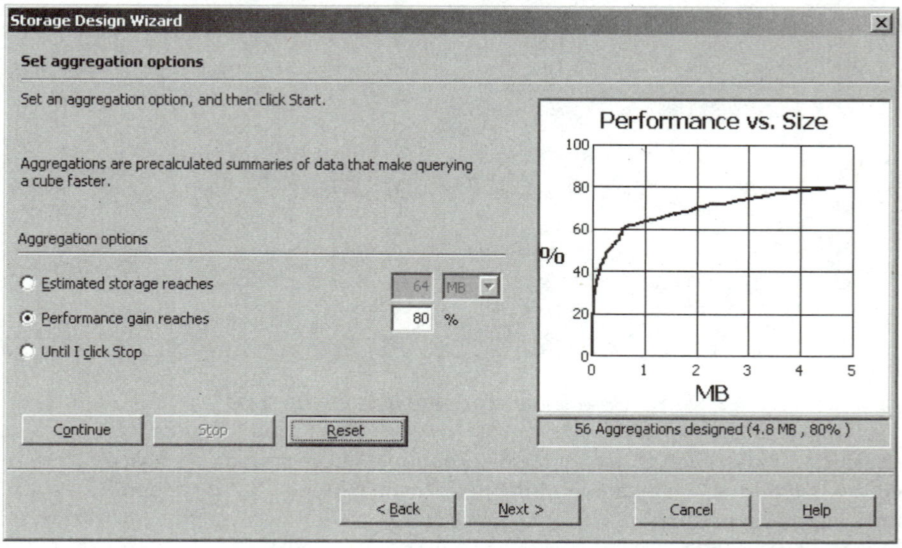

Selecting aggregation options in the storage wizard

When you process the cube, the Process screen will appear showing you what steps OLAP services is executing. Once it is done, you can double click the lines with the SQL statements used to create the dimensions (if not processed), or the partitions. Doing so will pop-up the View Trace Line screen, which shows you the SQL statement used by OLAP services to perform the indicated step. The following figure shows this screen with the SQL statement used to create the primary partition of the cube.

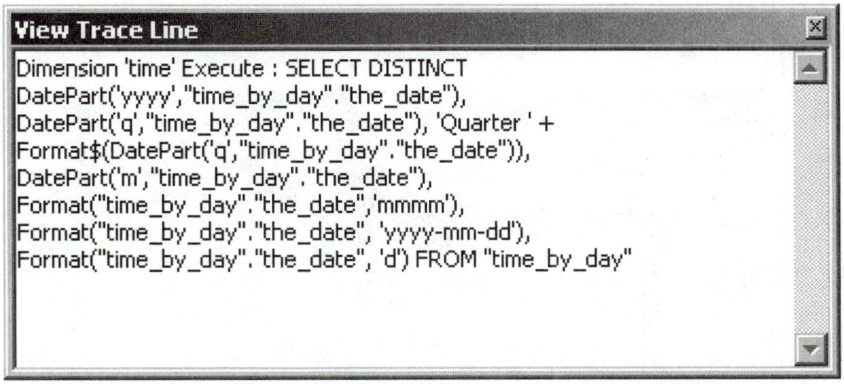

Viewing the SQL statements used in processing the cube

Setting Cube Properties

The cube editor also allows you to set cube properties in the Properties pane. If it is not visible, this pane can be made visible by selecting the menu command: View|Properties with a cube selected in the tree view. You can also click the Properties button to toggle between showing and hiding the properties pane. The properties pane has two tabs showing basic and advanced properties. The following are the properties you expect to see for a cube in this window.

Name and Data Source

These two basic properties are read-only. Once the cube has been created, you cannot change its name or data source. The name has to be a unique name for the cube in the OLAP database. The data source, as we saw earlier, point to the database where the cube schema (fact table and dimension tables) exists.

Description

Description is a useful basic property that allows you to enter descriptive text for the cube. This text helps remind you of things in the future after not working with the cube for some time.

Fact Table

This is another basic property of the cube that allows you to set the fact table for the cube. If the cube has more than one partition, the fact table assigned by this property is the one used for the primary partition. In the enterprise version of OLAP services, you can create additional partitions that can have different fact tables. Changing the fact table for the primary partition is allowed, but the new table has to be picked from the same schema.

When I changed the fact table for the Sales of 1998 cube to a different fact table in the schema, the customer and product dimensions were deleted. Also, the joins between the new fact table and the dimension tables: product and time, where lost. Of course, I used the dimension manager to add the missing dimensions again, and the schema pane to fix the table joins.

Please note that if the new fact table does not include some of the measures in the previous table, these measures will be dropped.

To change the fact table, you can type the name of the new fact table in the text box corresponding to this property, or you can click the "..." button that appears when you select the property to bring up a Choose a Fact Table dialog (see below). In this dialog, you can select the new fact table that will replace the existing one and click OK.

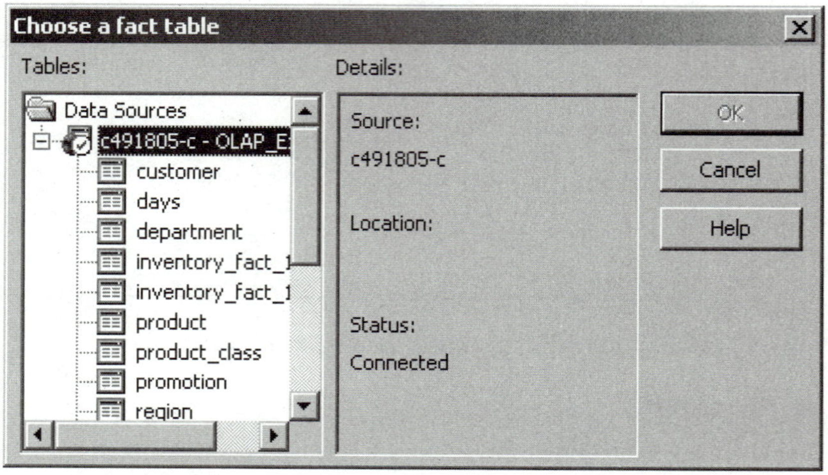

Choose a Fact Table dialog box

Fact Table Size

This is an advanced property that appears on the Advanced tab of the cube property pane. Fact table size indicates the number of rows in the fact table. OLAP services use this property to calculate aggregations when processing the cubes. You can use this property when you optimize the performance of your OLAP solution. By changing it you can influence how aggregates are calculated. Detailed discussion of performance optimization is presented in Chapter 13, Administration and Optimization of the Data Warehouse and OLAP.

Aggregate Prefix

This is also an advanced property that indicates the prefix to be used for aggregate tables in the ROLAP storage solution. The general syntax for these table names is: `prefix_cubename_aggregationID`.

Cube Dimension and Dimension Level Properties

The properties seen in the dimension editor for dimensions and dimension levels appear in the cube editor's properties pane when selecting a dimension. These properties, however, are read-only and cannot be edited from here. There are a number of properties that do not show up in the dimension editor, but some of them can be set in the Cube Editor. These properties are important when you optimize the OLAP solution and include:

Aggregation Usage:

This property is located on the advanced tab of the properties pane and allows you to limit building aggregations in a certain way. The aggregation usages allowed include: Standard (all levels), which is the default value, top-level only, bottom-level only, and custom (see figure below). When you select the custom option for this property, you will be able to generate aggregations for a particular level by setting the `Enable Aggregation` property for that level to `Yes`. The latter property does not become active unless you select the custom option for the dimension's `Aggregation Usage` property.

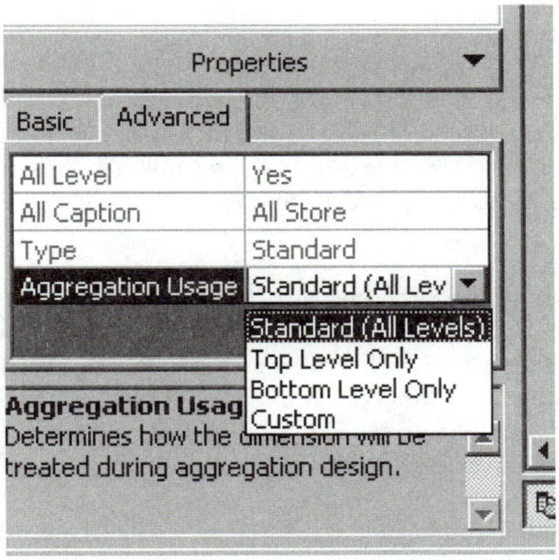

Setting the Aggregation Usage property

Disabled Level Property:

This property indicates whether the indicated level is disabled. Disabled levels are not visible to users in the OLAP manager screen. It has to be set in code using decision support objects (DSO). The default for this property is `No`. Setting this property to `Yes` allows you to enter data for the cube at the level above the disabled level. This is how you can enter cube data above the leaf (bottom level) level. Disabling a level prevents it and the levels below it from being used by MDX (see Chapter 7, Introduction to MDX), and from appearing in dimension metadata in clients through OLE DB for OLAP.

Enable Aggregation

This is another advanced dimension level property. As you saw in the Aggregation Usage property, this property does not become active until you select the Custom option for the Aggregation Usage property. If the property is set to `Yes`, aggregations for the corresponding level will be calculated.

Member Key Column

This is another advanced property for the dimension level. The property indicates the field of the table that will serve as the member key for the dimension levels. This property can be used for optimization purposes.

Measure Properties

Measures also have their own specific properties that show up in the cube editor when selecting a measure. Just like the cube, dimensions and levels, measure properties are classified as basic and advanced, and include:

Name

Name, is a basic property of the cube measure. The fact that you can set this property allows you to give the measures more descriptive names for the end users instead of the default names OLAP services chooses based on the table columns.

Description

This basic property is very useful in conveying information to the user that was not possible with the wizard. You can also specify attributes relating to the measure that do not have properties that define them, such as unit. For example, if a dimension indicates quantity of items sold, you may say in the description that the measure indicates quantity sold, etc.

Source Column

This is another basic property of the cube measure. It identifies the column in the fact table that serves as the source for the measure. The source column property is editable, which allows you to change the value or even enter an expression for it. This becomes very handy when creating calculated measures, which is different from calculated members. For example, you can create a new measure for total sale price based on quantity sold and unit price. The total sale price measure's source column would look like: `"sales of 1998"."quantity" * "sales of 1998"."unit price"`.

The benefit of using this calculated measure versus using a calculated member is that with the measure, the values will be calculated before the aggregations, which allows us to aggregate the results at any level, not just the leaf level. With calculated members, aggregates are conducted first, which give us accurate aggregations only at the leaf level.

Aggregate Function

This is another basic property that defaults to the `SUM` function, meaning that all measures are additive. You can, however, change this property to any of the values: `MAX`, `MIN`, or `COUNT`. An example on using these functions is an OLAP solution that deals with rainfall distribution by location and time. You may want to create a measure that shows the maximum rainfall amounts by location using the `MAX` function, the minimum rainfall amounts using the `MIN` function, the total rainfall amounts using the `SUM` function, and another dimension using the `COUNT` function. Finally, you can create a calculated dimension to return the average rainfall amount by location by dividing the `SUM` measure by the `COUNT` measure.

Data Type

The default data type is based on the data types of the columns referenced by the measure. As you know, data types have different storage requirements. A long data type, for instance takes 4 bytes of storage capacity, while an integer takes only 2 bytes. Therefore, if you want to optimize storage, you can play with this property as long as the data is adequately represented in the fact table. You have to be specifically careful when dealing with calculated members. These members may be based on columns of multiple data types. OLAP services may pick the wrong type for the result and convert the aggregations to that type, and sometimes you may receive an error as a result of the cube processing. For instance, if the calculated member is the result of multiplying the number of overtime hours worked (which is an unsigned integer) by a fixed percentage (which is a decimal) and by the hourly rate (which is a decimal), OLAP Services will pick the type of the result to be both unsigned integer or decimal. Therefore, you need to watch the resulting calculated member, and make sure it has the data type you want.

Data types accepted by OLAP services include:

- Big Integer
- Binary
- Boolean
- String (Unicode)
- Char
- Currency
- Date
- Date
- Time
- Date & Time
- Decimal
- Double
- Integer
- Numeric
- Single
- Small Integer
- Tiny Integer
- Unsigned Big Integer
- Unsigned Integer
- Unsigned Small Integer
- Unsigned Tiny Integer
- Char (Unicode)
- Text

Display Format

This advanced property contains a string that defines the format of measure values when displayed by front-end applications, such as Microsoft Office products. For example, if the measure is a date, you can set this property to any acceptable formatting string by the client application. In the case of MS Office VBA, something like `format ("facttable"."measure", "mm/dd/yyyy")` would be acceptable. If this property is not set, it defaults to "standard".

Is Internal

This is an advanced property of cube measures and, if set to `Yes (Default is No)`, indicates that the measure is used internally by the cube and is not visible to the end users. This is, however, different from when you set a level's disabled property to `Yes`. The difference is that the measure will still be available for MDX calculations and cube aggregations. Also, when this property is set to `Yes`, the cube measure will not show up as part of the OLE DB for OLAP metadata. Accessing it requires using decision support objects (DSO), or something similar. For more information on DSO, please see Appendix A.

Managing Roles

Managing roles can also conducted in the cube editor as well as the general OLAP Manager screen. To manage roles for a cube, you can select the Tools|Manage Roles menu command, or click the Manage Roles toolbar button. As the name implies, this functionality allows you manage existing roles and create new ones assigning them permissions to access the cube data. The Manage Roles dialog appears when you click the Manage Roles toolbar button or select the corresponding menu command. This dialog is shown in the figure below. I am not going to discuss in detail how to manage roles here. I just want to mention that cube roles are integrated with Windows NT security. The roles can be made parts of system user groups. A detailed description of cube security and roles is available in Chapter 13, Data Warehouse Security.

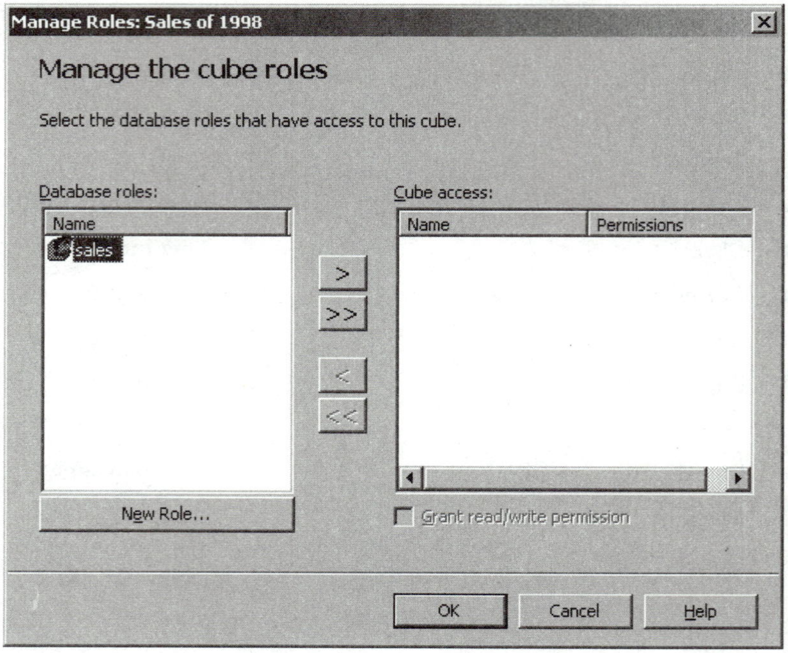

The Manage Roles dialog box

Validating Cube Structure and Optimizing Its Schema

Other tasks you can accomplish with the cube editor include validating cube structure and optimizing its schema. These commands can be run from the Tools menu of the cube editor. Validating cube structure verifies that the cube structure doesn't contain invalid components that would prevent processing of the cube. Invalid components include invalid joins between the fact table and the dimension tables, or an invalid member of a dimension. The optimizing cube schema command simplifies a cube's schema for maximum performance by removing unnecessary joins and other inefficient processes.

Viewing Cube Data

The last task we will discuss of the cube editor is viewing cube data. With the cube successfully processed, you can select the menu command View|Data to display the data of the cube in a nice way that allows you to expand and contract the view according to the cube dimension levels. The figure below shows an example of the data in the Sales of 1998 cube for the time and product dimensions. You can select the time dimension level you want to view the data for from the drop-down list at the top of the HTML pane, and then expand the product levels as you wish to view the measure data in the data grid. This view along with other front-end tools will be discussed in more detail in Chapter 10, Data Analysis and Presentation.

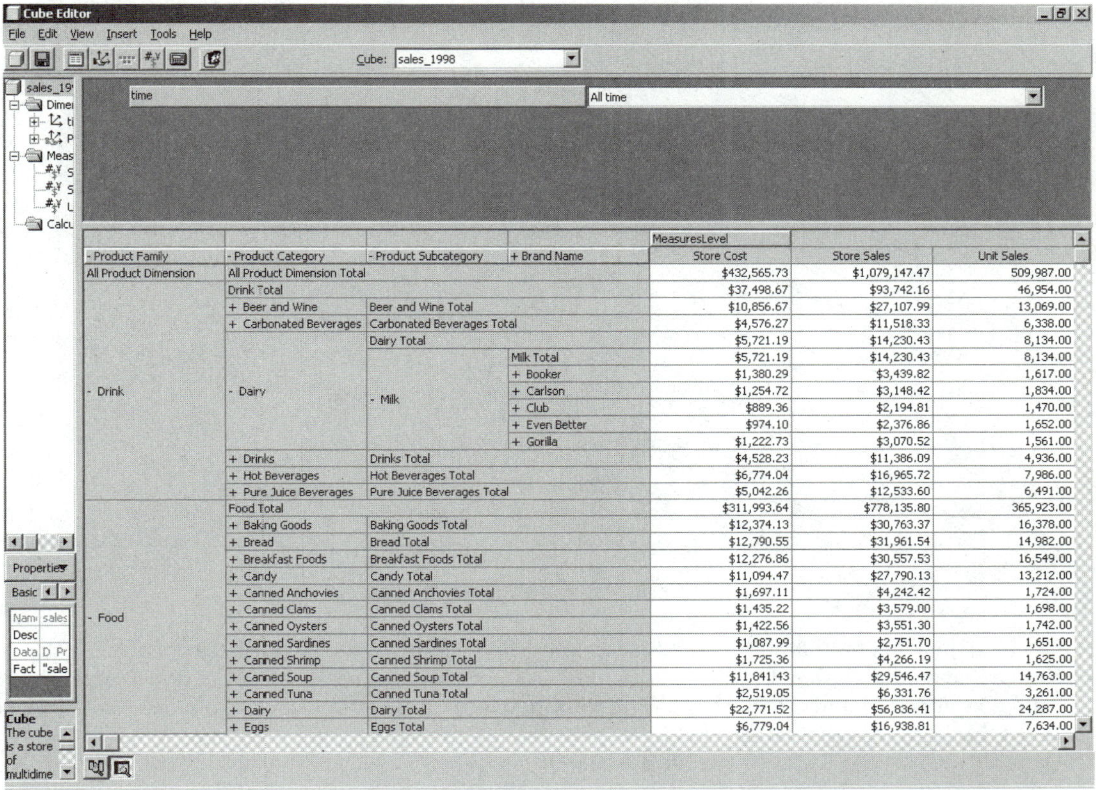

Viewing cube data with the cube editor

Creating Partitions

The Enterprise edition of SQL Server OLAP services allows for the creation of multiple partitions for the same cube. The standard edition only allows for one partition, the primary partition, to be created for the cube. Actually, the partition wizard is also absent from the standard edition. In this section, you will see how you can create several partitions for the same cube that can be used to logically divide the data.

In our example, if we want our cube to show the data in the fact tables for sales of 1998 and 1997, we need to create another partition for the 1997 data. We could have put the data for both years in the same fact table and thus in the same partition. However, since most queries are likely to be against the recent year rather than the year before it, it makes sense to use a separate partition for the 1997 data. Also, for performance purposes, when we create partitions separating the data by year, the OLAP will ignore the large data for the years not included in the query, which will enhance the query performance.

If you expand the partitions folder under the cube in the tree view, you will notice that the primary partition already exists for the cube. To create a new partition, right click the partitions folder and select New Partition from the context-sensitive menu, or select the OLAP Manager's menu item Action|New Partition. This will launch the partition wizard:

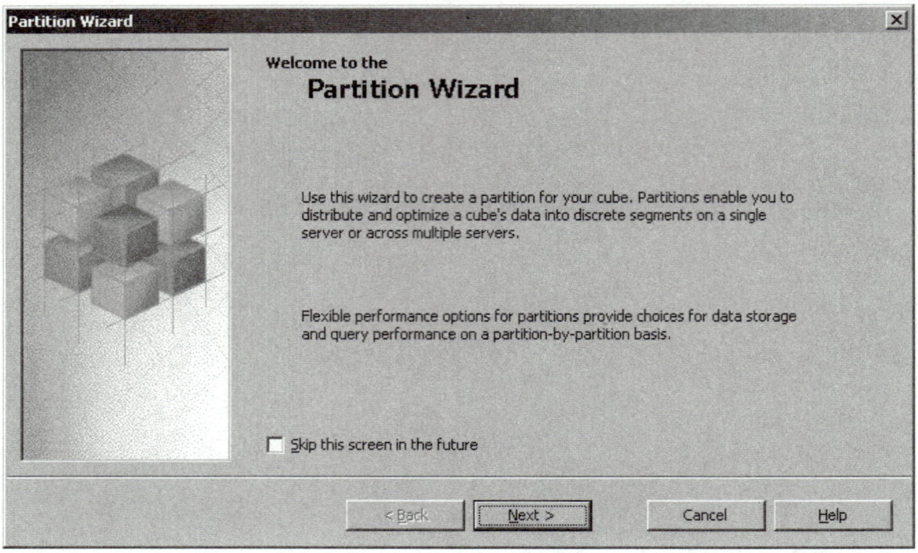

The partition wizard welcome screen

Clicking the Next button on the welcome screen will lead you to the page where you specify the data source and fact table. The Change button on this screen allows you to select the data source (the same source in our case) and the fact table from the Choose a Fact Table dialog. From this dialog, we can select the 1997 sales fact table. The dimensions required for this partition are shown below.

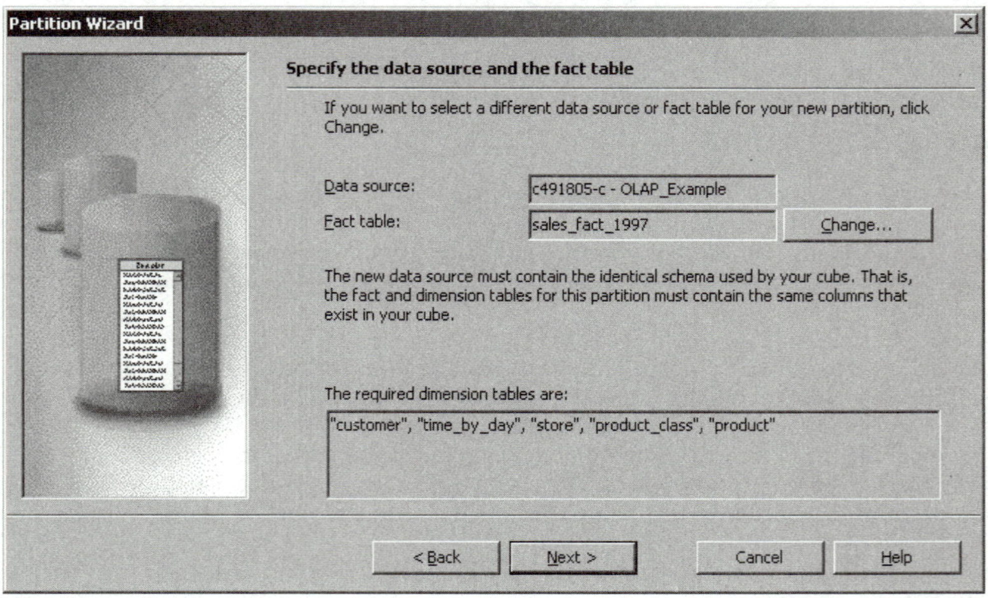

Specifying the data source and fact table for the new partition

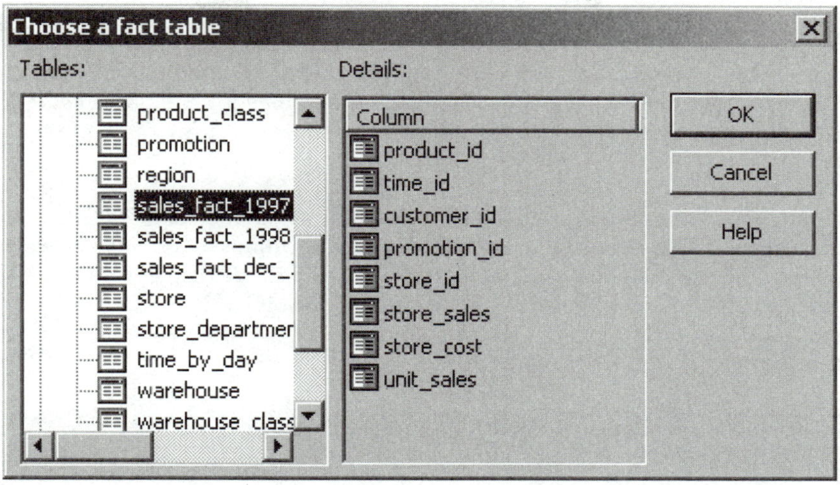

Selecting a fact table for the new partition

After specifying the data source and fact table, the next screen allows you to optionally select the data slice. A slice defines a subset of the cube's data and is determined by the intersection of a maximum of one member from each dimension. For instance, had we chosen to use the same fact table for both partitions, we would have created a slice that includes only the 1997 member of the year level of the time dimension, with all other dimensions completely included. But, since we chose to have two separate fact tables for the primary and the new cube we are creating, there is no need to define a data slice.

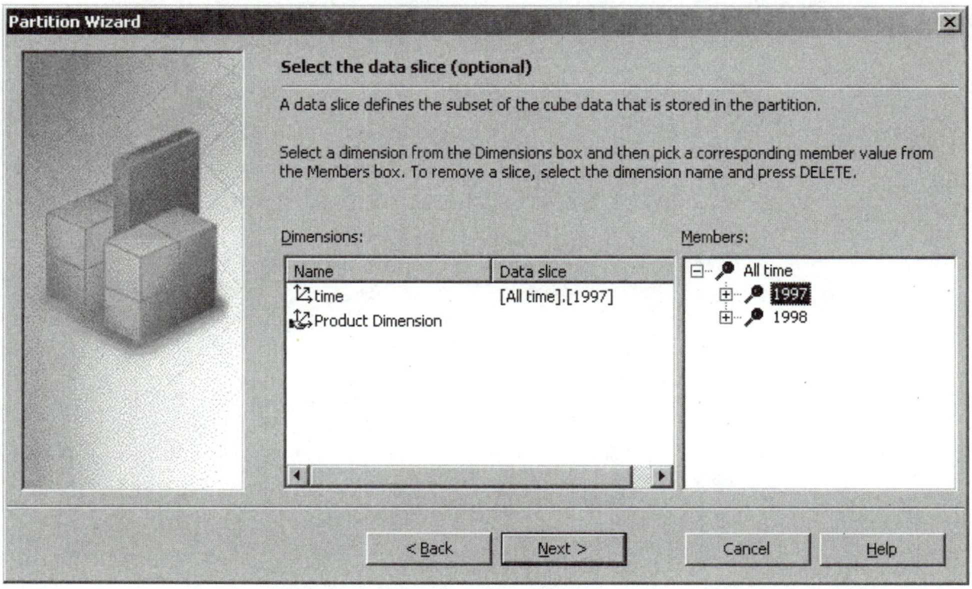

Selecting a data slice in the partition wizard

The next step in the wizard allows you to name the partition and design its storage. If you select the radio button box corresponding to "design aggregations for your cube now", the design storage wizard, which we saw earlier in the chapter, will start when you click the finish button. You can choose to design the aggregations later, or even copy aggregations designed for another cube. If you know the data will not be queried as much, it makes sense to design fewer aggregations that the primary cube to save storage.

Clicking the Advanced button will open a dialog that allows you to enter a WHERE clause to filter the fact table even further. This limits the data populating the partitions to a smaller set saving even more storage. You can also use this screen to enter a prefix to use with the names of the aggregations. This, however, applies to ROLAP storage and is not warranted for MOLAP and HOLAP storage. In ROLAP storage, it is a good idea to separate the tables holding the aggregations for a partition by prefixing their names with such prefix.

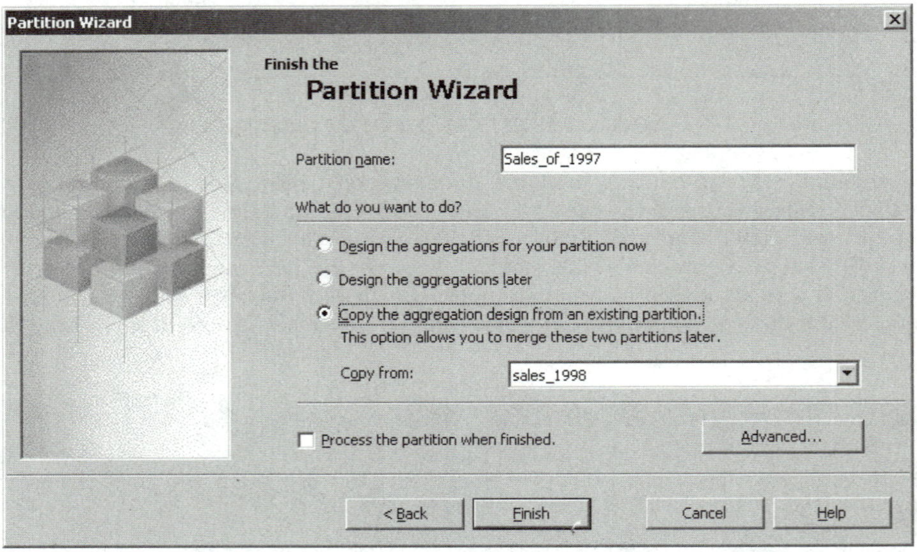

Naming the partition and designing its storage

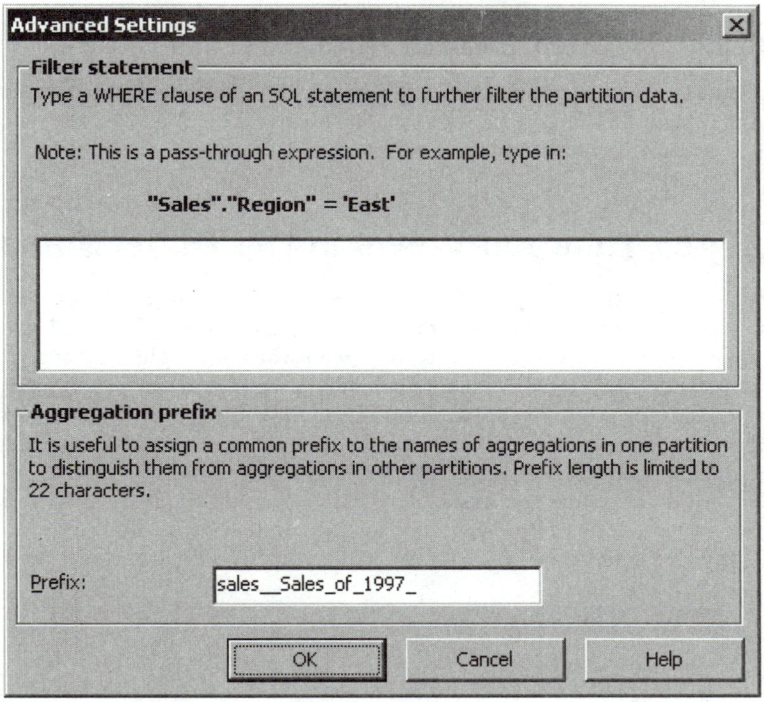

Advanced partition settings

Creating a Cube Without the Wizard

Could you have created the cubes we saw from scratch without any help from the cube wizard? The answer to this question is yes, if you know how to use the cube editor. Using the cube editor will give more flexibility in your cube design and control over which steps to do first. To create a cube from scratch using the cube editor:

- Right click on the Cubes item in the tree pane and select New Cube and Editor from the pop-up menu.
- Select a data source and fact table for the cube from the list of data sources and fact tables in the Select a Fact Table dialog box.
- Enter a name for the cube in the Name property located on the basic tab of the properties pane. Notice that the Name property is editable at this stage. It will become read-only when you save your cube. You may also want to enter a meaningful description at this point as well.
- Add shared dimensions by opening the dimension manager. The latter can be opened by right-clicking the Dimensions folder in the tree view of the OLAP Manager and selecting "Dimension Manager". You can also use the Insert|Dimension|Manager menu command. Once open, you can select the shared dimensions available in the dimension manager to add to your cube.

- Adding tables is also easy and can be done by selecting Insert|Table then dragging and dropping the table and establishing their joins as we have already seen earlier in the chapter.
- To insert measures, you can select the menu command Insert|Measure, or drag and drop a column from the schema tables to the measures folder. You can also select a column, right click, and select Insert As Measure command.

Creating New Taskpad Views in the OLAP Manager

One feature of the OLAP Manager is that it allows you to customize the detail window for certain tree view items, or groups of items. The way this is accomplished is by selecting New Task Pad View from the Action menu, or from the context-sensitive menu when you right-click some of the tree view items. The New Taskpad View Wizard is then launched and walks you through creating the new custom view for the selected item or group of similar items. The following figure shows the second screen of this wizard, where you can specify the style of the details pane and a style for task descriptions. The default style for the details pane is a horizontal list. You can change this style to either vertical list or no list. The style for task descriptions defaults to "Info Tip" where descriptions are displayed in large medium, or small icons. An alternate option is to choose a text style for such descriptions. The wizard shows you an example of how the items will look as you make your selections on the screen.

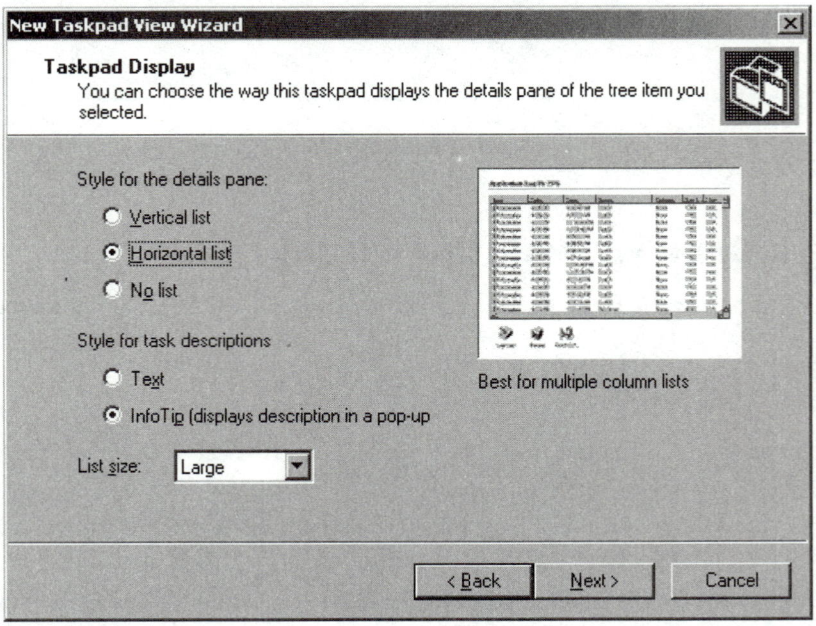

Selecting styles for the details and task description sections in the taskpad wizard

The next screen in the wizard allows you to specify whether you want to apply this screen view to only the selected item in the tree view, or to all similar items. You can also set this view to be the default for these items.

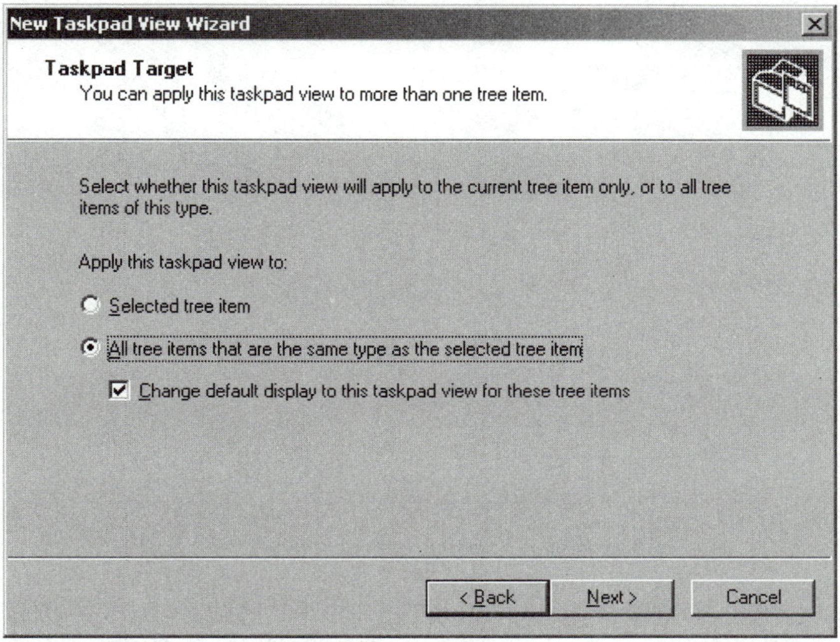

Selecting the items to apply the view to

The next screen will allow you to name the view and add a description. Following this screen, the last screen asks you whether you want to add any tasks to the view. If you choose to add new tasks, the New Task Wizard will help you through the process.

The New Task Wizard

This wizard allows you to create a task for the taskpad. The screen following the welcome screen is shown in the following figure. This screen allows you to identify the type of command you want to run. You can select any of the following types of commands:

- Menu command: allows you to add a menu item to the task view.
- Shell command: allows you to add a command that is executed from the Shell, or you may open a web page by providing a URL.
- Navigation command: allows you to add a command that navigates to a view selected from the favorite tab.

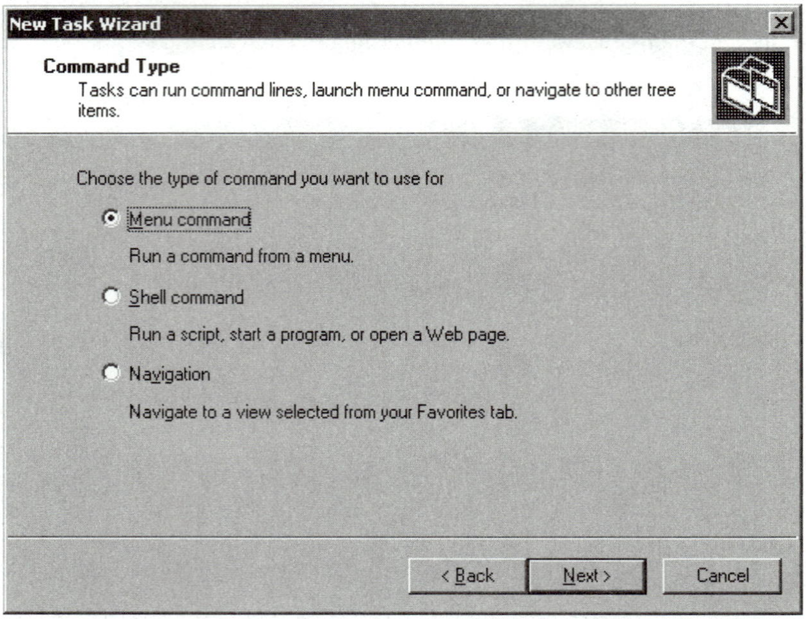

Choosing the command type in the new task wizard

Selecting the menu command and clicking the Next button leads to the screen shown in the following figure. In this screen, you can select the source of the command to be an OLAP manager tree item, or an item from the Details pane. Selecting the tree option from the Command Source drop-down list, the Console Tree and Available Commands lists get populated. You can then select an item from the tree and a corresponding command. For example, let's select the Edit Cube command. The next screen allows you to name the command and add a description to it. Based on the style you selected for the description, the description will either show up in the view as text or as tooltip text. The next screen allows you to select an icon for the command from a list of provided icons. At the end of the wizard, your command is added to the Detail pane. Clicking the icon will open the cube editor, and bringing the mouse close to it will show the description you entered in the wizard as a tool tip.

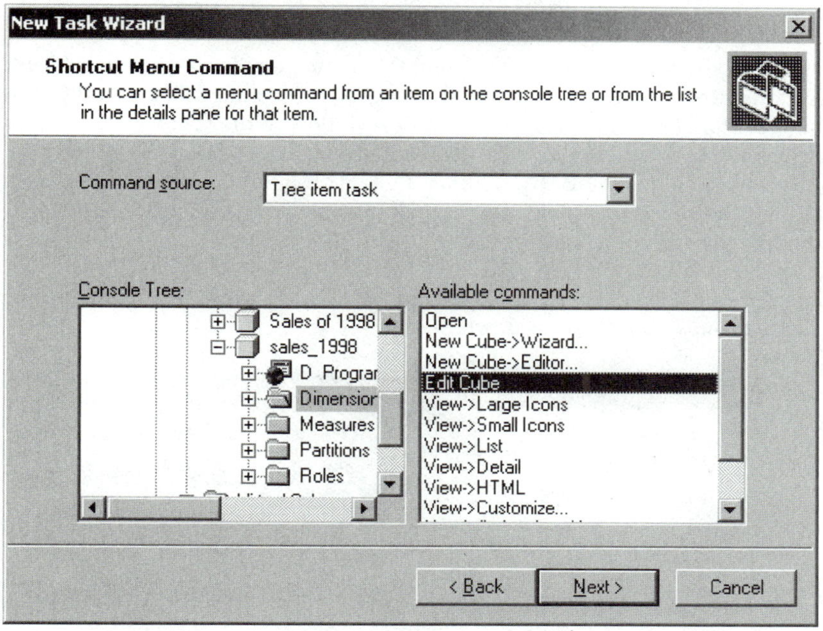

Selecting a tree view command to add to the task view

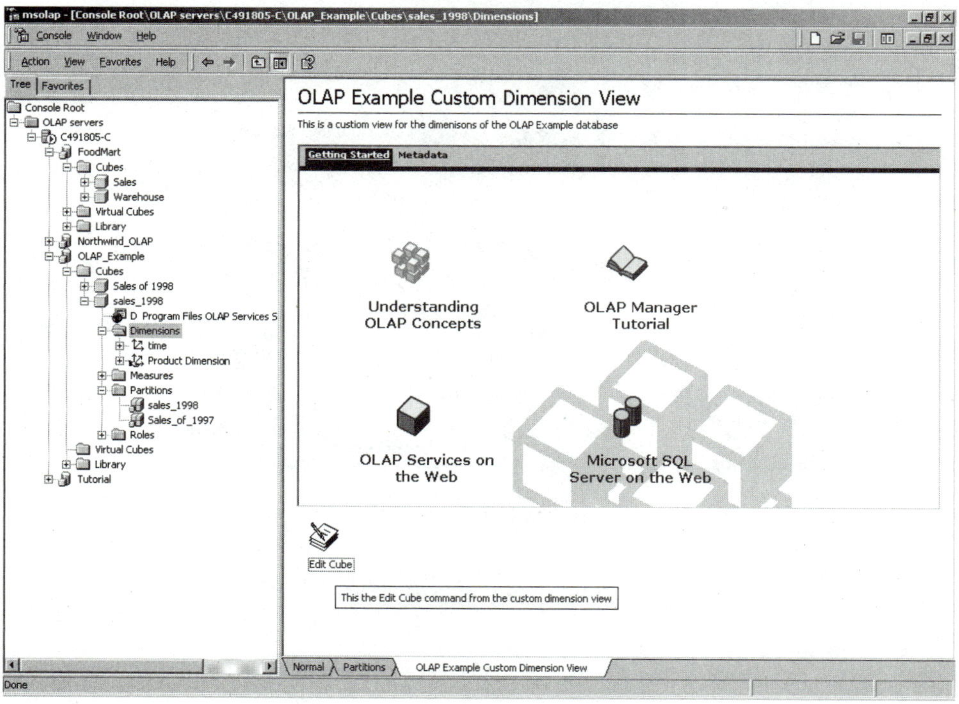

The OLAP Example database custom dimension view and the Edit Cube command

Editing A Task View

You can edit an existing task view by selecting the menu command Action|Edit Taskpad View or by right clicking the tree item represented by the view and selecting Edit Taskpad View from the context-sensitive menu. Doing so will open the properties window of the task view as seen in the figure below. The properties window has two tabs, General and Task. The general tab allows you to change the styles of the pane and task descriptions. By clicking the Option button, a dialog opens up to allow you to reset the items to which this view applies. You can set the view to the selected item alone, or to all similar items in the tree view of the OLAP Manager.

The Task tab presents you with a list of existing tasks for the view. You can select a task and modify it, add new tasks, or move a task up or down the list.

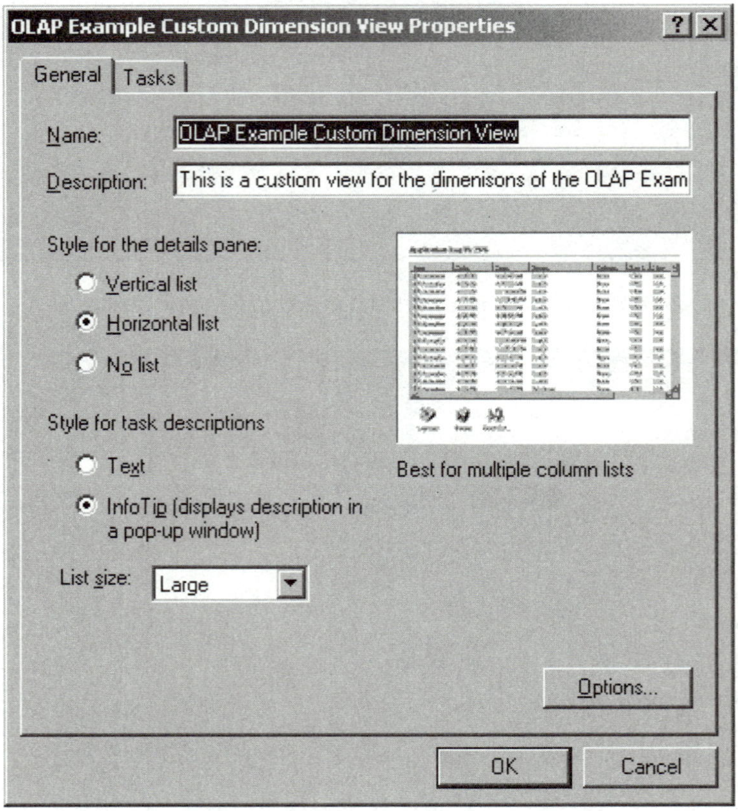

The Properties Window of the task view

Summary

The OLAP Manager is a great graphical easy-to-use tool that allows you to perform most of the tasks you need to perform with Microsoft OLAP services. In this chapter we discussed the main features and functions that can be accomplished by using the manager. We started with a description of the OLAP Manager's environment and the Microsoft Management Console (MMC), which the OLAP Manager runs in its environment. We then learnt how the tool could be used to create the OLAP database, the OLAP cube, dimensions, measures, etc. The next chapter will discuss another useful tool that accompanies SQL Server 7 and that is essential to the success of the data warehouse design and implementation, that is Data Transformation Services (DTS).

6

Microsoft Data Transformation Services (DTS)

One of the most challenging issues with building a data warehouse is populating it with data after its construction. The warehouse is usually expected to accommodate data from multiple heterogeneous sources. The data has to go through several stages of extraction, validation, scrubbing, cleansing, transformation, and transfer. Microsoft SQL Server 7.0 offers a technology that can help throughout these stages. This technology is called Data Transformation Services (DTS). DTS can handle all of these stages because it is integrated with the Microsoft Universal Data Access technologies and the Microsoft ActiveX technologies. As you will see in this chapter, DTS packages can be used to extract data from OLE DB and ODBC compliant data sources. They can also be used to run scripts and programs written in other languages to perform the needed tasks of data handling before storage into the warehouse.

We discussed Microsoft DTS to some extent in the earlier chapters of this book, and by now you probably have an idea of what it is and what it is used for. In this chapter, we take a closer and more detailed look at these services and how they can be utilized in the overall Microsoft OLAP and data warehousing strategy.

The issues you will read about in this chapter include:

- Overview of DTS: this is an overall look at the DTS technology and the basic functionalities that it can be used for, and how these apply to data warehousing.
- DTS architecture: including the components and objects from which DTS is composed and how they interact with each other and other ActiveX components to perform the required tasks.
- Using the DTS Wizards: It is these wizards that facilitate many of the simple and straightforward functions, such as importing and exporting data, etc.
- Using the DTS Package Designer to create packages and tasks that would allow for more advanced manipulation of the data before transferring it to the destination database.

Overview

In the process of creating your OLAP and data warehouse solution, you will design the data warehouse, even build it and create the database and the tables that will host the data to be kept in the warehouse. You may then ask yourself a question: "Did my design take into account the population plan of the data warehouse?" You may be in a situation whereby you need to get data from at least seven different incompatible sources. For example, imagine a scenario where some of the data is in an accounting system, which resides in an old proprietary system developed by IBM for the mainframe computer twenty years ago. Other information is available in an Oracle database that holds the information about all of the products produced by the company, and keeps track of a transaction and sales record. Other sources include daily dumps from remote servers to an FTP directory that can be accessed, etc.

The next question you will probably ask is: "What technology can I use to perform all these daunting data transfer tasks, and can this technology perform some transformations to the data before populating the data warehouse? Does SQL Server offer this service?" The answer to these questions is yes; you can use SQL Server 7.0's data transformation services (DTS) to do the job. DTS is a technology that was introduced in SQL Server 7.0 to consolidate many tools that already existed in previous versions and add new tools that perform new functionalities that were not available before. DTS will answer your questions allowing you to do the transfers and transformations necessary for a successful population of the data warehouse.

What Exactly Can DTS Do For Me?

DTS is the best technology you can use to populate the data warehouse and data marts with the data coming from multiple heterogeneous sources interactively or automatically on a regularly scheduled basis (see figure below). DTS can schedule these jobs for you because it is integrated with SQL Server 7.0, which allows it to use the SQL Agent service to do the scheduling. DTS can be used to perform data validation before populating the data warehouse. It can also be used to create custom transformation objects that can be integrated into third-party products. Finally, DTS can be used to access applications using third-party OLE DB providers. This allows applications, for which an OLE DB provider exists, to be used as sources and destinations of data.

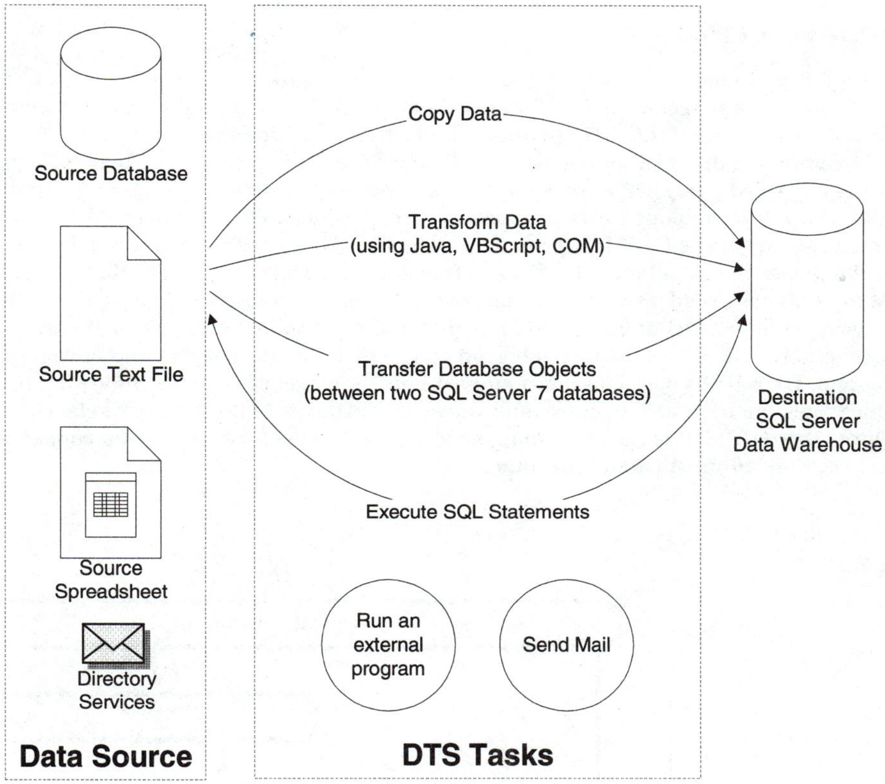

An illustration of DTS roles and functions

DTS facilitates access to native OLE DB providers such as SQL Server, Microsoft Excel, Microsoft Access, Oracle, and more recently IBM's DB2. DTS also facilitates access to ODBC data sources for which no native OLE DB providers are available yet. This is done using the Microsoft OLE DB Provider for ODBC. This provider still uses an ODBC driver to access the ODBC data source.

OLE DB is the Universal Data Access (UDA) technology adopted by Microsoft. It is the data abstraction technology of choice for Microsoft. OLE DB allows access to virtually any data source (relational databases, text files, directory services, mail data stores, etc.), and Microsoft is putting a great deal of support behind it. It is also useful to note that using native OLE DB providers will provide you with faster access to data sources than using ODBC.

DTS also allows you to access ASCII fixed-field length text files and ASCII delimited text files using the built-in DTS Data Pump flat file OLE DB provider (`Dtsffile.dll`). This provider makes it easier to access ASCII files and retrieve information from them by assuming that the data follows a certain pattern (fixed length fields, or delimited fields).

What is an OLE DB provider, by the way?

OLE DB providers are pieces of data abstraction software that give you access to a variety of data sources, such as databases, email and LDAP directories, file system objects, etc. Hence, OLE DB providers can be used to define the source and destination for the DTS job. Some OLE DB providers are created by Microsoft, and others by third party software companies or even rival database vendors who want to use OLE DB technology to allow access to their products. OLE DB providers are an essential part of the OLE DB technology, which is the core of the universal data access technologies (UDA) adopted by Microsoft as the data access method of the future. Many database vendors and third party companies began to create native OLE DB drivers, similar to what happened to ODBC in the not so far past. This will only strengthen OLE DB as the technology of choice to define the sources and destinations of data. OLE DB is based on the component object model (COM). the following figure illustrates the UDA architecture, and where OLE DB fits in it. The figure clearly shows that OLE DB is the core component of this architecture facilitating connection between the application and the data sources.

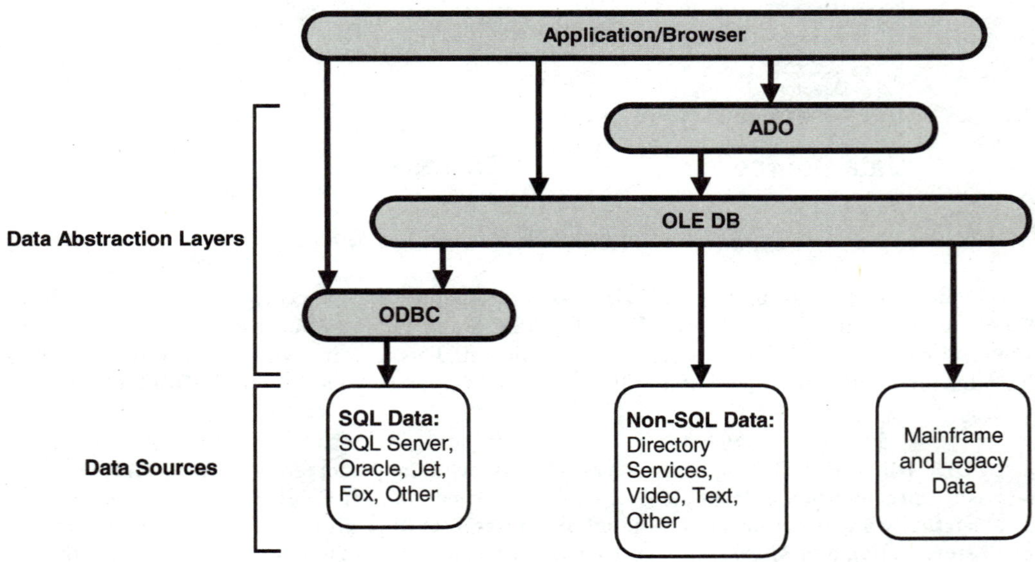

An illustration of the Microsoft Universal Data Access Architecture

The following points highlight the importance of DTS as the data transfer and transformation technology for use with Microsoft Datawarehousing:

- DTS supports the high-speed non-logged bulk copy program (BCP) inserts into the SQL Server database. This is so far the fastest method to move large amounts of data into the SQL Server tables. BCP is explained in more detail later in the chapter.
- DTS supports the creation of customized transformations with script, such as VBScript, Windows Scripting Host (WSH), or JavaScript. It also allows the creation of such customized components with full programming languages, such as Visual Basic, Visual C++, and Visual J++, by accessing and running programs written in these languages.
- DTS also supports the transferring of complete database objects between source and destination data sources, as long as these sources are on SQL Server 7.0. A DTS task, **Transfer SQL Server Objects**, can be used to transfer all of the metadata and data for some or all of the objects in one SQL Server 7.0 database to another SQL Server 7.0 database. For example, the Transfer SQL Server Objects task can be used to move a table with all of its associated index, constraint, rule, default, and trigger definitions and the existing rows in the table. The Transfer SQL Server Objects task can also be used to transfer the definitions of objects such as views and stored procedures between the SQL Server data sources. This feature makes it easy to transfer a database in the development environment to a developer's laptop so that they can continue to work against a real database when they are disconnected from the team development environment.

In other words, the main tasks that are performed by DTS can be classified in one or more of these categories:

- Importing and exporting data
- Transforming data (including validation, scrubbing, and cleansing)
- Transferring database objects

The following sections discuss these categories in more detail explaining what is involved in each of them.

Data Import and Export

Importing and exporting data is the process of exchanging data between applications by reading and writing data in a common format. For example, DTS can import data from an ASCII text file or Access database into SQL Server. Alternatively, data can be exported from SQL Server to an OLE DB data destination, such as an Excel spreadsheet. In other words, data import and export involves a source and destination and the data in between. DTS provides easy-to-use wizards that guide you through the process of importing and exporting data, as you will see later in the chapter.

The following DTS features make DTS a great tool to perform imports and exports through a DTS package:

- **Ability to use OLE DB provider's advanced properties:** this is especially true when using native OLE DB providers. These providers will allow you to use features and functions specific to the data source you are trying to access, which add a great deal of flexibility and power when extracting the data for import from the source, or preparing it for export to the destination. For instance, using the OLE DB provider for Oracle will allow you to use some of the Oracle features that the OLE DB provider for ODBC, or simply ODBC, cannot provide.
- **Column mappings:** DTS import/export wizards allow you to map database table field names to the names of the fields in the destination database. You no longer have to live with naming conventions that don't conform to your standard naming conventions. For instance, if you were importing data from a legacy system on the mainframe, you would have to use the column names defined on the mainframe for the fields in your destination database if you were conducting this transfer in prior versions to SQL Server 7.0.
- **Data transformation scripts:** As part of the import/export package, you can define scripts to perform data transformations.
- **Advanced transformation properties**: that allow for complex data scrubbing and cleansing before dumping it into the destination database.
- **Transferring data and database objects**: between computers running Microsoft SQL Server 7.0: These objects include tables, fields, constraints, referential integrity and relationships, indexes, stored procedures, views, etc.
- **Saving the DTS package:** The DTS package can be prepared and saved as part of the database, allowing it to be re-used as a template in the future.
- **DTS package scheduling:** With this feature, you don't always have to perform the DTS import or export tasks right after you create the DTS package. The package can be prepared and executed repeatedly later interactively or on a scheduled basis

Data Transformation

A data transformation is the set of operations applied to source data before it is stored in the destination database. Examples of data transformation are:

- DTS allows the calculation of new values from one or more source columns, such as calculating the profit based on the sales and cost fields.
- DTS allows for breaking a single column into multiple values to be stored in separate destination columns, such as breaking the `CustomerName` field into a `FirstName`, `MiddleInitial`, and `LastName` fields.
- DTS may also be used to combine several fields into one value and to store the result of the combination in a separate field in the database, such as combining the area code and phone number fields to produce a long phone number.
- DTS also allows for data validation, such as making sure the city of London belongs to the right country, England, or that Mr. Jones, the human resources manager, belongs to the human resources department.

This transformation feature makes DTS a perfect fit for Microsoft OLAP Services and data warehousing. Transformations make it easy to implement simple and complex data validation, scrubbing, and enhancement during import and export. Because of the importance of this particular process in building a successful data warehouse, we will discuss different aspects of it in more detail later in the chapter.

Database Objects Transfer

DTS can transfer database objects between heterogeneous data sources, such as transferring objects between an Oracle database and a SQL Server database. Obviously, DTS can also transfer database objects between SQL Server databases. When using heterogeneous data sources, the built-in facilities of DTS only move table definitions and data. To transfer other objects such as indexes, constraints, and views you must use methods such as specifying tasks that execute the SQL statements needed to create these objects on the destination data source. As an example, if you want to transfer the UNIQUE constraint on the `CustomerName` and `CustomerPhoneNumber` fields from an Oracle database to a SQL Server database table, you need to write a statement similar to the one below after transferring the table.

```
ALTER TABLE customer
CONSTRAINT u_customer_unique  NONCLUSTERED (CustomerName, CustomerPhoneNumber)
```

The code above ensures that the combination of customer name and address is unique in the customer table. The NONCLUSTERED keyword is not absolutely necessary since this is the default value that SQL Server uses. However, because the source is an Oracle database, where the concept of clustered indexes has a completely different meaning than in SQL Server, I wanted to ensure that the created index as a result of the constraint is nonclustered.

Tasks and steps are explained in detail later in the chapter. However, if both the source and destination are SQL Server 7.0 data sources, you can define a Transfer SQL Server Objects task to transfer indexes, views, logins, stored procedures, triggers, rules, defaults, constraints, and user-defined data types in addition to transferring the data.

Support for Multiple Data Sources

DTS supports multiple data sources as its source and destination. You don't always have to use DTS to import data to a SQL Server database, nor do you always have to use it to export data from such a database. DTS source and destination can be any valid OLE DB or ODBC compliant data source, including Relational Database Management Systems (RDBMS), text files, spreadsheets, directory services such as LDAP, etc.

Sources and destinations are defined in the DTS package or wizards by specifying a connection. In the case of a SQL Server connection, the following figure shows the information needed to establish such connection. You need to specify the OLE DB provider, which in this case is the OLE DB provider for SQL Server. You also need to specify the server on which the database you need to link to is located, in addition to the security authentication mode to use. You can specify using NT authentication, or SQL Server authentication using a login name and password. Of course, don't forget to specify the database you want to link to as well.

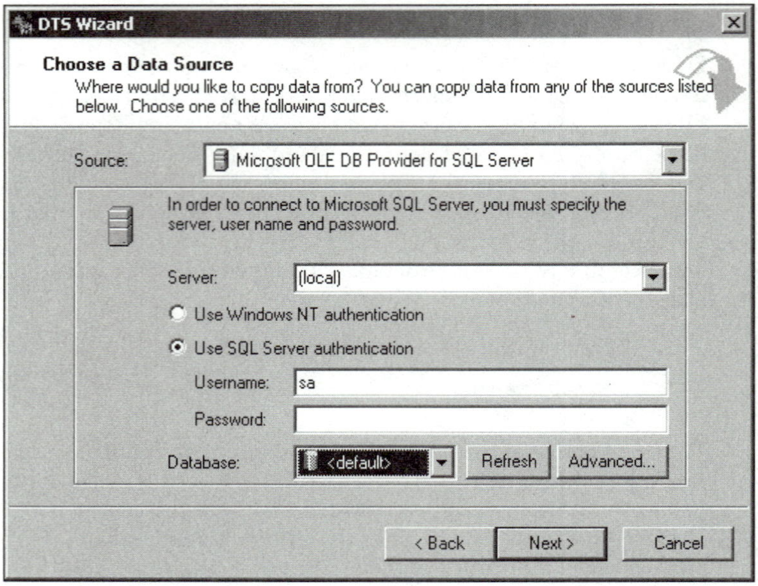

Connection information to SQL Server using the native OLE DB Provider for SQL Server

The information required to connect to a different data source can very different, depending on the connection mechanism. For instance, connecting to the same SQL Server database using the OLE DB Provider for ODBC with the Microsoft ODBC driver for SQL Server may require providing an ODBC data source name (DSN), which is not required when using the native OLE DB provider for SQL Server. Also, connecting to a file data source, such as an Excel spreadsheet will also require different information from that provided for the connection to a SQL Server, as shown in the screenshot below.

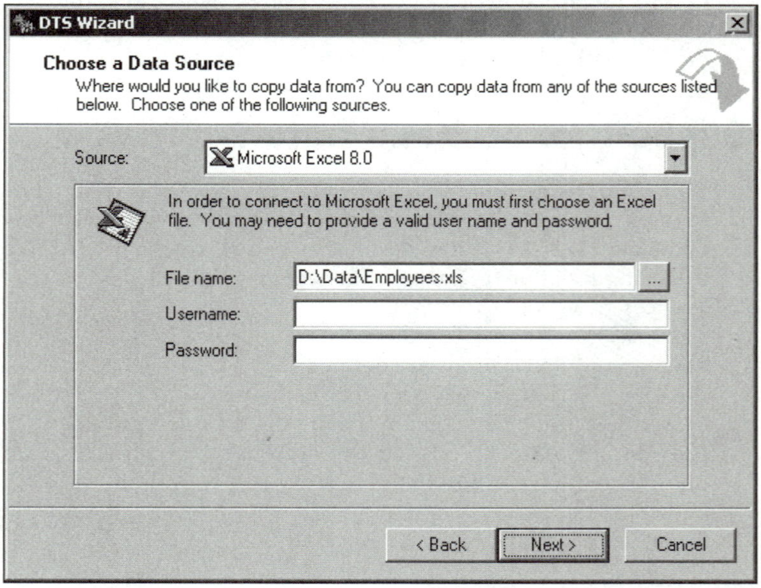

Specifying information needed to connect to an Excel spreadsheet

In the above example, you notice that you can specify the source to be the appropriate version of Microsoft Excel, and the file path and name. If you have security set up for the file, you also need to provide the username and password.

The following is a list of the different data sources that can be connected to through native OLE DB providers provided by Microsoft:

OLE DB Provider for Microsoft SQL Server

OLE DB Provider for Oracle

OLE DB Provider for OLAP Services

OLE DB Provider for Internet Publishing

OLE DB Provider for IBM's DB2

OLE DB Provider for Text Files

OLE DB Provider for ODBC data sources

The last provider (OLE DB Provider for ODBC) leaves the door wide open for a variety of data sources to connect to as long as these data sources are ODBC compliant and have ODBC drivers.

Data Transformations

Although mentioned in the overview section above, I think data transformation is a big reason why DTS is an important (even integral) part of the Microsoft data warehousing strategy. Therefore, I would like to expand on the discussion of data transformation in this section with detailed definitions and some examples on data validation, scrubbing, transformation, and migration.

Data Validation

Before data is entered into the data warehouse, it has to be validated. Data validation ensures the quality of the information in the data warehouse. After all, your data warehouse is only as good as the data stored in it. Validating the data also increases the integrity of the data warehouse and the confidence in the information extracted out of it later. The validation process can be time consuming and difficult, but still necessary. Microsoft SQL Server 7.0 helps you automate some of the validation tasks by implementing constraints in the data definition language (DDL). DDL is the part of the SQL language used to create database objects, such as tables, views, etc. SQL Server also allows you to implement your own complex validation algorithms in the form of scripts, stored procedures, or extended stored procedures. The following sections explain how simple and complex validation can be achieved using SQL Server's features.

Simple Validation

As I mentioned in the previous section, SQL Server provides several features that allow for simple validation of the data. Such validation includes integrity insurance through constraints on database object creation and data insertion. Simple validation is usually done through data definition, which includes table, column and constraint definitions. Triggers can sometimes be used for simple validation. Examples of simple validation include:

Constraints ...

```
ALTER TABLE customer ADD CONSTRAINT
u_customer_unique  NONCLUSTERED (CustomerName, CustomerPhoneNumber)
```

The uniqueness constraint on the customer table presented in the code sample above ensures that each record in the table is unique. No two records in the table will have the same values of customer name and phone number. When a user tries to insert a record that violates the constraint, an error is generated and the record will not be inserted.

```
ALTER TABLE customer
customer_name VARCHAR(30) NOT NULL
ALTER TABLE customer
ADD CONSTRAINT state_check
CHECK (state IN ('MI', 'OH', 'IL', 'IN', 'MN', 'WI'))
```

The check constraint above ensures the state field can only have states in the Midwest. This check constraint can be sued when a table is partitioned based on the state field. The resulting partitions can be used in separate data marts.

"NULL" and "NOT NULL" ...

The NOT NULL condition ensures that the customer name field cannot be left blank, and will always have a value. The DEFAULT keyword can also be used to ensure having a default non-NULL value for a column. If a user tries to insert a NULL value in a field that does not accept NULLs, an error will be generated and the record will not be inserted.

Data Types ...

Data types also dictate the kinds of data accepted for the fields in the database. Hence, you cannot store simple numbers or string values in a date/time field.

Complex Validation

DTS allows you to take validation beyond the simple validations mentioned in the previous section. DTS allows you to reference database scripts, stored procedures, or even external programs in the DTS package that perform complex validation and return the results that will determine whether to accept or reject the data.

In case you are not familiar with them, stored procedures are procedures created using Transact SQL (T-SQL), compiled and saved in the database. These procedures add a great value in that they use the power of the database engine, and they are pre-compiled, therefore they run fast. Triggers are a special case of stored procedures. Triggers run automatically when events take place at the database tables level. For instance, when a delete happens to a record, a trigger may run to perform certain tasks, such as maintaining integrity by making sure no orphan records of the deleted record are left.

As an example of a trigger used in data validation, the following trigger ensures that the inserted record in the sales fact table of a sales and inventory data warehouse solution has a product associated with it in the product dimension table. If no product is found, the record is written to a log file with an error message. A different stored procedure is called to perform the error logging to centralize this process, which could be accessed by more than one trigger in the database.

```
USE OLAP_EXMAPLE
IF EXISTS (SELECT name FROM sysobjects
         WHERE name = 'verifyProductCost' AND type = 'TR')
         DROP TRIGGER verifyProductCost
GO
CREATE TRIGGER verifyProductCost
ON sales_fact_1998
FOR INSERT, UPDATE
AS
DECLARE  @product_id int,
         @sales_id int
SELECT   @product_id = product_id,
         @sales_id =sales_id
FROM     sales_fact_1998 s
         INNER JOIN inserted i
         ON s.sales_id = i.sales_id
         JOIN products p
         ON p.product_id = i.product_id
IF (@product_id IS NULL)
BEGIN
logError('product does not exist in the product table for transaction: ' +
@sales_id)
         ROLLBACK TRANSACTION
END
```

Of course, stored procedures give you a great flexibility, through raising exceptions, in what to do when your validation fails. For instance, you can raise an exception that causes another step in the package to log the failure in a log file or the Windows NT event log. ActiveX scripting can also be used to perform complex validations. This is discussed in more detail later in the chapter.

Data Scrubbing

Data coming from different sources may not be consistent even if it pointed to the same entity. For example, a national grocery store chain company is building a data warehouse. Data about inventory of the individual stores around the country is gathered and consolidated before it is transferred to the data warehouse to allow for searching on a national level. However, the stores don't all use the same system to keep track of their inventories, especially since the company acquires new stores almost every month. These new stores take some time before they can really start using the tools and applications provided by the corporate offices. As a result, the same data could be represented differently in the different databases of the individual stores. You may see some refer to the item "Italian salad dressing" as "Italian Dressing", or just "Italian" knowing that the category they belong to is salad dressing. Some stores may refer to reduced fat milk as:

Milk (reduced fat)

Reduced fat milk

Redc'd fat milk

2% fat milk

98% fat-free milk

All of these representations point to the same item and have to be consistently represented in the data warehouse, and this is where data scrubbing comes into play. When the data is received from various sources, it is examined for such inconsistencies in representing the same thing. The examination can be by building queries that separates these items in separate resultsets, then examining these result sets to collect all the different forms of something. If the values were not made consistent, any queries using the data would probably evaluate the values as different products. If the detail data in the data warehouse is to produce consistent information, the product name must be made consistent for all values.

Data scrubbing can be achieved in several ways:

- Using the DTS Import and DTS Export wizards to modify data as it is copied from the source to the destination. These wizards are discussed later in the chapter.
- Writing a Microsoft ActiveX script, executed by a program that uses the DTS API, to connect to the data source and scrub the data.
- Using a DTS Lookup.

As an example on using DTS Lookup, the data in the system should be scrubbed, such as the values for the State field should always be a two-character value, such as "MI" instead of "Michigan", "Mich", or even "mi". DTS lookup allows for searching for the right values based on a named parameterized query that you provide. The query can retrieve data from sources that are not immediately involved in the transformation process. DTS Lookup is explained in more detail later in the chapter.

Data Transformation

Let's say we made our data look consistent. Are we ready yet to move it into the data warehouse? Not yet. You may still find some columns needing some change or transformation, examples:

- Calculating new values based on existing data, including data aggregation and summarization.
- Changing all alphabetic characters to uppercase or vice versa.
- Breaking up a single value into multiple values, such as a product code in nnnn-description format into separate code and description values, or a date value in MMDDYY format into separate month, day, and year values.
- Merging separate data values into a single value, such as concatenating a first name value with a last name value.
- Mapping data from one representation to another, such as converting data values (1, 2, 3, 4) to (A, B, C, D).
- Data transformation also involves formatting and modifying extracted data from operational systems into merged or derived values that are more useful in the data warehouse.
- Another example is converting numeric representations for decimals from European to US or vice versa (123.45 in US is written as 123,45 in Europe).

The transformation process usually takes place during the migration process: when data is copied either directly from the operational sources or from an intermediate database, because the data has been scrubbed.

In addition to performing insert-based transformations of data, DTS provides data-driven-queries, in which data is read from the source and transformed, and a parameterized query is executed at the destination, using the transformed values in the destination row. Data-driven queries are explained with examples later in the chapter.

Note: When using DTS to create fact tables for use with Microsoft SQL Server OLAP Services, you don't really need to create any aggregations while migrating the data. OLAP Services is specifically designed to create the optimal aggregations after the data warehouse has been populated with DTS. Also, you don't really need to segment a date into individual time levels, such as week, month, quarter, or year columns in the `Time` *dimension table. The OLAP Services Dimension Wizard provides an automated facility for this type of time transformation (see Chapter 5, The OLAP Manager).*

Data Migration

Like the name suggests, this process copies large amounts of scrubbed, transformed, and cleaned data from the source to the destination data warehouse. This is the last step of the data transformation and takes place after the cleansing and scrubbing has been done. Data migration can either be conducted through the Import/Export wizards, or through the Bulk Copy Program (BCP). In either case, since the data processed is usually large, you can choose to do full or incremental updates. These updates must be conducted when there is little activity on the SQL server to minimize the impact on the users.

As a rule of thumb, use BCP when you don't have validations and transformations taking place during the migration process. BCP will give you the fastest migration you can possibly want. This is because BCP is just a data dump utility that is optimized for dumping data with little if any logical processing. If you are conducting some logic or processing during this last migration process, don't use BCP; instead, use the import and export wizards, or ActiveX scripting.

Using the DTS Package

The most prominent feature that DTS offers to interact with is the DTS Package. Interaction with DTS packages can be accomplished through the Microsoft SQL Server Enterprise Manager, or through applications using the DTS API. The DTS package is an entity that includes all the information needed to connect to the data store, both the source and destination, and perform the necessary transformations. The DTS package, not only houses this information, but also controls how and when the connections, validations, and transformations are conducted. As part of the definition of the DTS package, you can choose to do one or more of the following:

- Define connections to the data sources representing the source and destination for your transformation.
- Define task objects that define certain actions within the package.
- Define step objects to define the sequence of execution of the task objects.

Once the DTS package has been defined, you can:

- Run the package immediately.
- Create a DTS package for replication.
- Schedule the package to be executed at specific times.
- Schedule certain tasks of the package to be executed at different times.

A DTS package can be stored in one of the following forms:

- DTS COM-structures storage files.
- In the msdb database of Microsoft SQL Server.
- In the Microsoft repository (see Chapters 1 and 2 for explanations of the Microsoft Repository).

Anatomy of the DTS Package

The DTS package is primarily composed of three types of objects (see figure below), the connection object, the task object, and the step object. While the connection object defines the connection properties and conditions to the source and destination data source, the DTS task object defines a particular course of action to be taken as part of the transformation. The DTS step determines the order of execution of the DTS tasks.

The following figure shows clearly that the relationship between the components of the DTS package is functional and not hierarchical. There are three tasks represented in the diagram which use either one or both of the two connections. Task 1 uses connections 1 and 2, task 2 uses only connection 1, while task 3 uses only connection 2. The tasks represent a situation similar to executing an ActiveX component, dumping data into the database, or sending email. The connections may be to two SQL Server databases. Task 1 has only one step, step 1, while task 2 has both steps 1 and 2, and task 3 has step 2 only. The task objects use the connection objects to establish connection to the data sources. The steps objects determine what order the task objects will be executed, and what order actions within the task should be carried out.

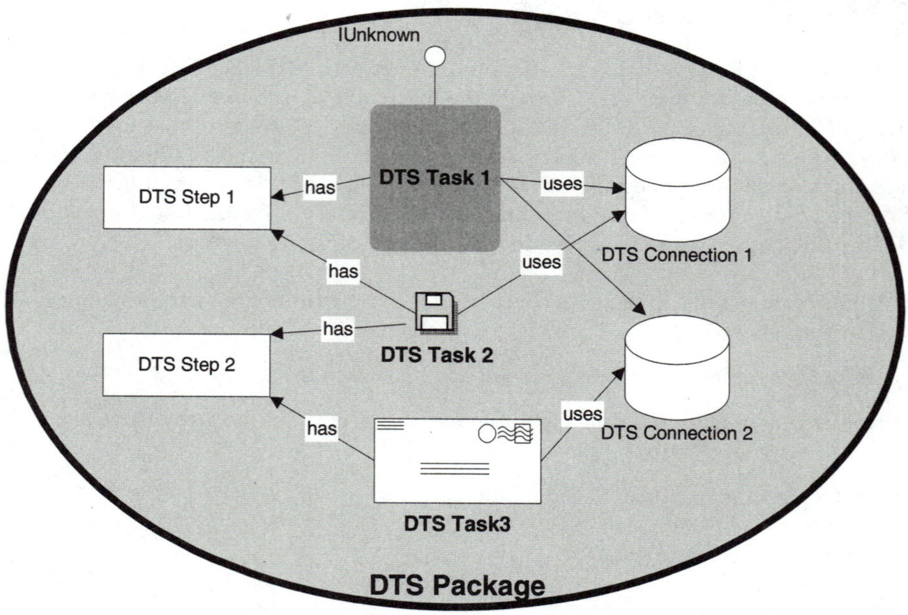

Illustration of the DTS package component objects

DTS Connection

Each DTS task may have zero or more connection objects. These connection objects store the information needed to connect to the respective data source when the package is executed. There are three types of connection objects available: data source connections, file connections, and Microsoft data link connections.

Data source connections specify information about the source and destination OLE DB or ODBC data sources as we have already seen earlier in the chapter. The way the information is requested in the DTS wizards and screens varies based on the data source. However, the connection object stores the following information for most data sources:

- Server name.
- Data format and location, including database name (catalog) and table name if applicable.
- User name and password.
- ODBC data source (DSN) if the OLE DB provider for ODBC is used.

File connections specify information about source and destination files, data format, file names and locations. Microsoft file connection settings are stored in the data link file (extension .udl). This occurs when you set up the connection through OLE DB. Once saved in the data link file, the connection can be established by loading this file.

DTS Task

The most prominent object within the DTS package is the task, which defines a work item to be performed as part of the transformation process. SQL Server version 7.0 includes several built-in tasks. Each performs a different type of work item. SQL Server also provides the DTS object model with which you can create custom tasks. Creating custom tasks is beyond the scope of this book. For more information about this topic, see "DTS Programming" in SQL Server 7.0 Books Online.

You can create packages in the DTS Designer, which is a part of SQL Server Enterprise Manager, as described later in the chapter. Tasks must be installed and registered on the machine on which you want to use it. The built-in tasks included with SQL Server 7.0 are registered automatically during installation. Custom and other tasks are installed and registered separately. All created and registered tasks are available for addition to the DTS package in the DTS Designer.

The seven original built-in tasks that come with SQL Server 7.0 DTS services are listed below:

- ActiveX Script: this task executes scripts written in scripting languages, such as VBScript, Perl Script, or JScript, allowing you to use the full capabilities of the scripting language. ActiveX scripts can access data using ActiveX Data Objects (ADO) or invoke any object that supports OLE Automation.
- Execute Process: Enables you to launch a separate batch file or executable program.
- Execute SQL: Allows you to write one or more SQL statements to be executed. The SQL task is associated with a `Connection` object. The SQL statement(s) must use valid syntax for the OLE DB provider of the `Connection` object it's associated with.
- Data-Driven Query: Implements advanced data transformation functionality. It's often used as a tool to update information in a data warehouse by scanning rows in the source data and by executing a query based on the value of the rows.

- Transfer SQL Server Objects: Moves SQL Server objects between the specified data source and destination. Both the source and destination must be running SQL Server 7.0.
- Send Mail: Allows you to send e-mail including email attachments in the form of attached data files. You can also execute the tasks of sending mail using the generic Execute Process task.
- Bulk Insert: Provides a way to transfer large amounts of data into the data warehouse. Its flexibility is limited, but this task is the best choice when you need to load data into the warehouse very fast.

Microsoft recently released a new built-in task for DTS – the OLAP Services Processing task. Since this new task is relevant to the discussion in this chapter, I will discuss it in some detail later in the chapter.

DTS Data Pump

The DTS data pump is the engine behind DTS functionality. It is an OLE DB service provider that allows for moving data at a high speed between heterogeneous data sources and the destination data source. A task is actually an instance of this in-process COM-based server. At least two connections are needed for the data pump to do its work. More than two connections are needed if more than one data source are involved as being the source for the task at hand.

Being an OLE DB provider, the data pump is extensible and allows for performing complex transformations and validations of the data as it transfers it. The data pump instance or DTS task requires the following three elements to be defined:

- Source rowset, which is usually a table or the result of a SELECT query returning records from one or more tables in the source databases.
- Destination, which is usually a table in the destination data warehouse.
- Transformation mappings, which are usually mappings of columns from the source rowset to the destination table. The mapping can be one to one, one to many, many to one, or many to many. In other words, You can have three columns in your source rowset that represent a customer name, with each one of them coming from a different connection. The three customer name fields in the source are mapped to one such field in the destination table.

With the data pump, you can simply copy the data as it is from the source rowset to its destination, implement ActiveX scripting driven transformations, or even implement highly complex custom transformations using advanced programming languages, such as C++.

The different types of tasks can be created with the data pump. Hence, whether you create and execute a SQL task, or a data-driven query task, you will be using the data pump behind the scenes, because all of these tasks are basically instances of the data pump.

DTS Object Transfer

This component uses the SQL Distributed Management Objects (SQL-DMO) interfaces to move database objects between one SQL Server database and another. Almost all objects you can think of can be transferred with this task:

- tables
- views
- stored procedures
- defaults
- rules
- user-defined data types
- logins
- users
- roles
- indexes
- constraints

When transferring tables, you can choose to transfer only the definition of the tables, the data only, or both the definition and data.

DTS Step

The last component of the DTS package we will discuss is the DTS step. Steps establish a workflow scheme that control the processing of the tasks in the DTS package. Every task must be associated with at least one step. If no such association exists, the task will never be executed. Since steps define the sequence of execution of the tasks in the DTS package, these sequences are usually logical. For example, you have to perform the task of creating a connection to the data source (step 1) before you can query the data source for a source rowset (step 2).

Steps are not explicitly defined in the DTS package designer. Instead, they are implicitly created to do certain tasks when you create workflows between different tasks in the DTS package designer. You can however create step objects using the DTS API from your application.

Steps contain constraints that help determine precedence. What this means is that you can use a constraint that prevents a step from starting until another step has already completed. It is those constraints that control the flow of execution of the package tasks in the end. There are three types of precedence constraints that can be defined on a step:

Completion:	This means the step will execute as soon as the prior step is complete regardless of its success or failure.
Success:	This constraint will allow the step to execute only if the prior step has completed execution successfully.
Failure:	This constraint will allow the step to execute only if the prior step has failed. If the prior step completes execution successfully, the step will not be executed.

As an example of precedence constraints, let's assume that you are loading data from a text file into a table. The first step is creating the table in the destination database. The second step is loading the data into the table. The second step will not execute until the table has been created successfully. Therefore, a success constraint is placed on the second step. Assuming that the table is created and the data is loading, if a failure happens, you want to cancel the loading deleting the rows that have already been loaded and sending an email message to the database administrator informing them of the problem. This third step will not execute unless the table loading (step 2) fails.

Later in the chapter, you will see examples on building a DTS package and tasks within the package. You will then see how these constraints are applied.

Storing the DTS Package

The DTS package can be stored in one of three forms, the repository, the database, or in external COM-structure files. It is worth noting that database storage of the DTS package puts it in the msdb database. This database is also used for storing the metadata. However, packages stored in the database and those stored in the repository are placed in separate sets of system files.

> **When SQL Server is installed, several system databases get installed, including: master, msdb, model, and tempdb. All of these databases, except for tempdb, need to exist when the server is restarted. The msdb database stores metadata information and information about DTS packages. For more information about msdb and the other system databases, see the Warehouse Backup and Recovery section in Chapter 13.**

How are DTS Packages Stored in SQL Server?

Packages stored in SQL Server are stored in the msdb database as binary large objects (BLOB). These packages are stored in the `sysdtspackages` table, and are displayed in the SQL Server Enterprise Manager's DTS subtree. The following figure shows two local DTS packages in the Detail pane with the Local Packages folder selected in the tree pane of the SQL Server Enterprise Manager. The packages are viewed by those who have sufficient security privileges to view them. These packages, however, must have unique names. If your server is set with in-sensitive sort order, the case of the name is stored, and a package names as `mypackage` is the same as `MYPackage`.

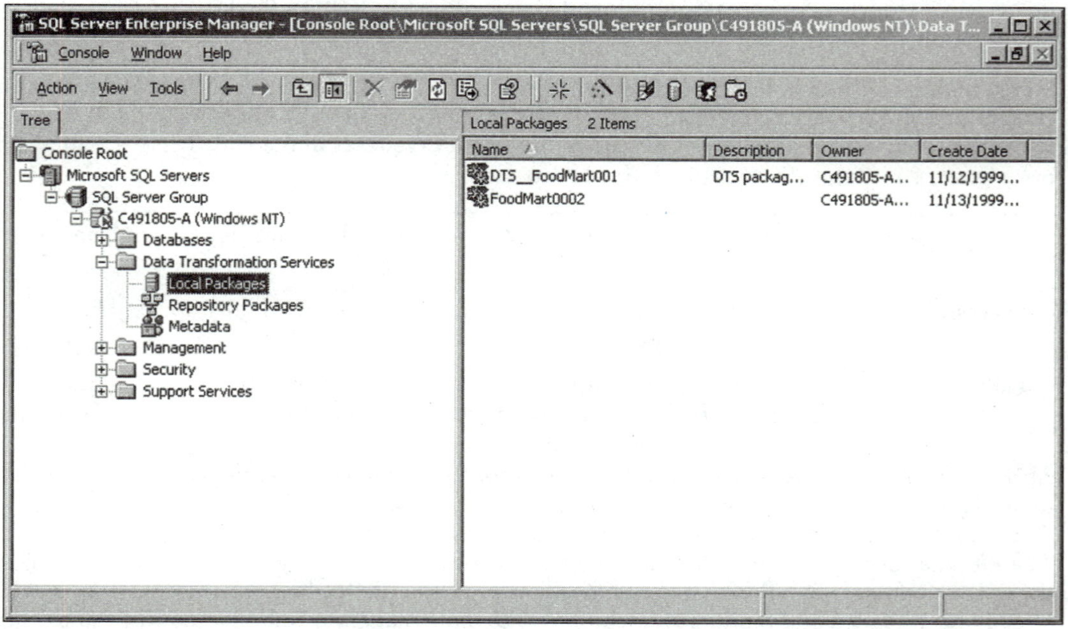

The Local Packages viewed in the Enterprise Manager's window

DTS Package Storage in the Repository

DTS packages can be stored in the repository, which is stored in the msdb database. This is the preferred way to stored DTS packages in data warehousing because it is the only storage method that provides data lineage for the packages. Data lineage allows you to record where the data came from, how it was calculated, and when it was stored among other things. This falls in line with the Microsoft data warehousing strategy of providing meaningful way to integrate multiple products through shared metadata.

Given that multiple repositories can exist on a SQL Server, DTS only supports one repository, the one stored in msdb. Packages stored in the repository can be viewed by those who have sufficient server privileges to view the repository. Just like packages stored in the SQL Server msdb, repository DTS packages must have unique names.

DTS Package Storage in COM-Structured Files

If you want to save your packages outside the database and make them mobile so that you can install them on other servers anytime you want, you can use this type of storage. DTS packages can be saved in COM-structured files. Each one of these files can contain one or more packages. It can even hold different versions of the same package. The files can be located on the SQL Server box, on the client, or simply on a file server. These files cannot be viewed automatically in the SQL Server Enterprise Manager. To view them and their packages, you need to open the file using the menu commands shown in Figure 7.7. This is done by right-clicking the Data Transformation Services folder in the SQL Server Enterprise Manager, selecting All Tasks, then Open Package. This will open a dialog box that allows you to browse the directory and network to find the DTS package file.

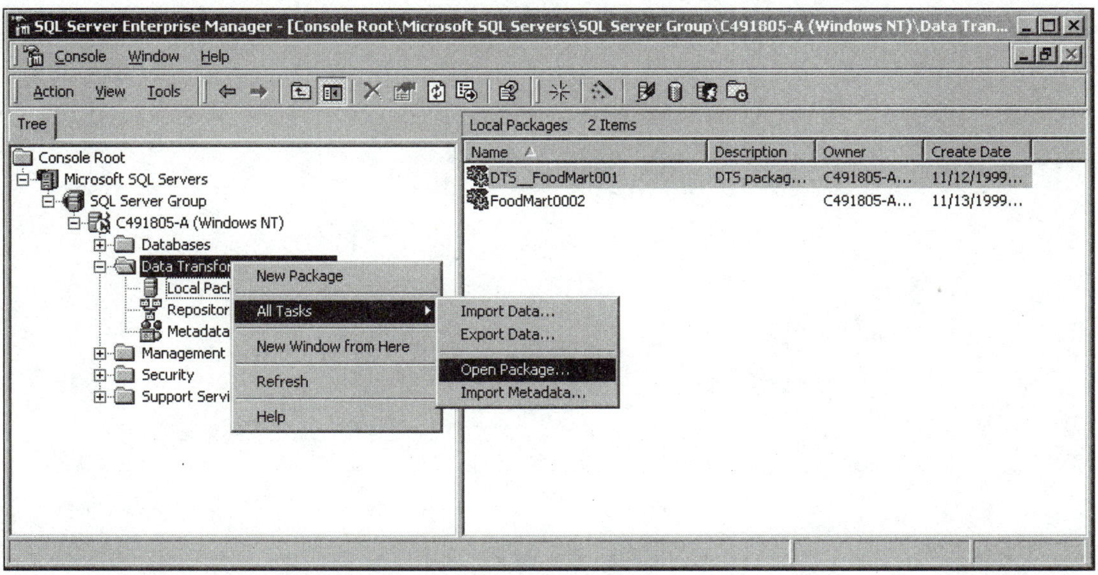

Opening a DTS package file

Packages stored in COM-structured files do not have to have unique names. You can use the same name for more than one DTS package.

DTS package are uniquely identified by the combination of package IDs assigned when the package is first created, and version IDs re-assigned every time the package is saved or executed. Both the package ID and version ID's are Globally Unique Identifiers (GUID). When a package is saved to a COM-structured storage file, each package version is saved in a separate storage area as substorage under the package ID. Each package version contains substorage for the package components: tasks, steps, connections, and global variable collections (collection of variables available to all tasks within the package). The COM interface `IStorage` is used to accomplish this. The following figure illustrates how packages and their components are stored in COM-structured files.

The Component Object Model's (COM) `IStorage` interface supports the creation and management of structured storage objects, allowing hierarchical storage of information within a file. `IStorage` interface is often referred to as "a file system within a file."

Elements of object following a structured storage scheme are divided into storages and streams. Storages are analogous to directories, and streams are analogous to files in a file system. Within a structured storage there will be a primary storage object that may contain substorages (which may be nested), and streams. Storages provide the structure of the object, and streams contain the data, which is manipulated through another COM interface called the IStream interface.

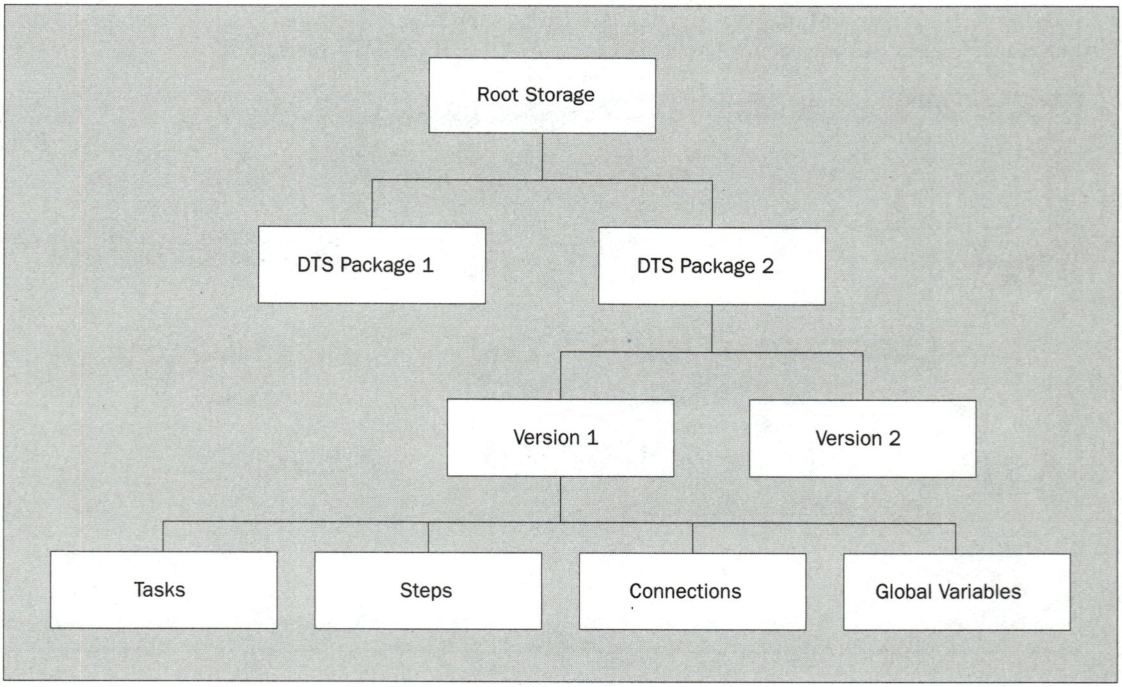

Illustration of COM-structured storage of DTS Files.

The DTS Designer

Microsoft introduced the DTS Designer as a graphical tool that is easy to learn and use to make it easy to perform the DTS tasks. The DTS Designer provides:

- The ability to perform a chain of actions as part of a DTS package in a transactional manner. These actions allow for easy import/export and transformation of the data as it is moved from heterogeneous sources to the destination data warehouse, or a destination database.
- Integration of OLE DB as the data movement mechanism, allowing access to many types of data stores and sources. These sources range from text files, Excel and other Microsoft office documents, MS Access databases, to Oracle, SQL Server, and DB2 databases.
- Access to the Microsoft repository allowing for the sharing of metadata and data lineage information.
- The ability to create, save, and manage DTS packages.

Although other tools exist to work with DTS, such as the Import and Export wizards, the `dtsrun` and `dtswiz` command utilities, and the Microsoft SQL Server Enterprise Manager, the DTS Designer still stands as the most important of these tools when handling DTS packages. This importance comes from the fact that it has been designed to make the handling of such packages as easy as possible. Therefore, you can obviously see that the DTS Designer is used to do the following tasks:

- Establish one or more OLE DB connections to the data sources and a connection to the destination source. A list of available OLE DB providers can be accessed through the designer screens.
- Perform data transformation between the data sources allowing for the transfer of the data from the source data source to the destination data source while performing built-in, or custom tasks that validate the data, scrub it, and transform it.
- The designer allows for the creation of the DTS packages which package the tasks needed for the transformation in one entity that can be saved, reused, and managed with ease.
- DTS Designer also allows forthe use of precedence constraints on the steps that control the flow of execution of the DTS tasks as you have already seen earlier in the chapter.

Many of these points have already been discussed earlier in the chapter, but not within the context of the DTS Designer. In this section, I will show you how these concepts fit with this designer.

DTS Designer Window

The DTS Designer window, shown in the following figure, provides many tools that can be used for the design and management of the DTS package. The Designer screen is integrated into the Microsoft Management Console (MMC) window. The designer still has its own menu bar consisting of five menus: Package, Edit, Data, Task, and Workflow.

- The Package menu allows for saving the package, executing it, controlling the layout of the designer screen, and viewing and setting package properties.
- The Edit menu includes regular Windows editing commands, such as Copy, Cut, Paste, etc.
- The Data menu lists available OLE DB providers to choose from when creating new connections to data sources. This list usually includes: OLE DB Provider for SQL Server, Microsoft Access, Excel, desktop databases, such as dBase 5 and Paradox, text files for both the source and destination, Microsoft ODBC driver for Oracle, Microsoft Data Link, and other connections that you might be able to specify based on what drivers and providers you have installed on your SQL Server box.
- The Task menu lists the seven built-in tasks (explained earlier in the chapter) that can be accomplished with DTS in addition to two menu items to register and unregister new custom tasks. If you register new custom tasks, they will be added to this menu as well.
- The Workflow menu allows you to add a transform between connection objects. It also allows you to set precedence constraints on the steps used to execute the DTS tasks.

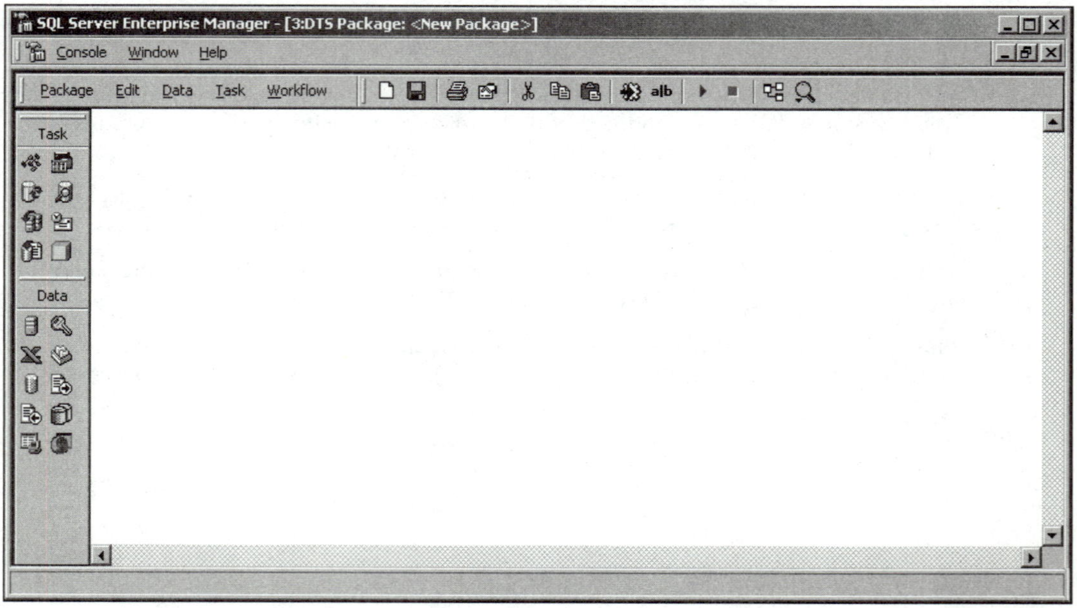

The DTS Designer window with a new blank DTS package

Three toolbars are also available from the designer providing shortcuts to the menu commands. These toolbars are the main toolbar which allows for quick access to the functions of the Package, Edit, and Workflow menus; the Task toolbar and the Data toolbar allow quick access to the commands found in the Task and Data menus respectively.

DTS Package Management

The most important functionality performed by the DTS Designer is allowing for DTS package management. This management starts from the early stages of planning the package and deciding on the tasks that should be included in it, creating it, saving it, editing and possibly deleting it, and executing it. Securing the package and setting its properties is also an essential part of package management.

Creating and Saving the DTS Package

Package creation can only be done through the SQL Server Enterprise Manager's DTS tree element. To create a new DTS package right-click the "Data Transformation Services" on the tree view in the Enterprise Manager (see Figure below).

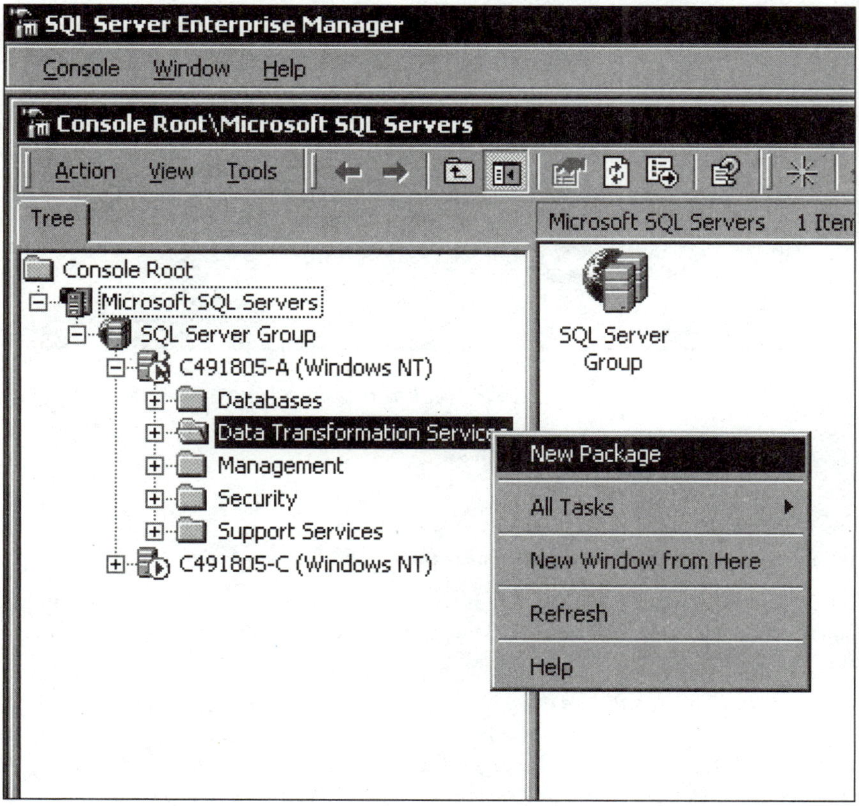

Creating a New Package

In the figure above, select the New Package menu item from the context-sensitive menu. This will open the DTS Designer window as shown in the above figure.

To save a DTS package, select the Save or Save As menu item from the Package menu. This will open the Save DTS Package dialog box, shown in the following figure:

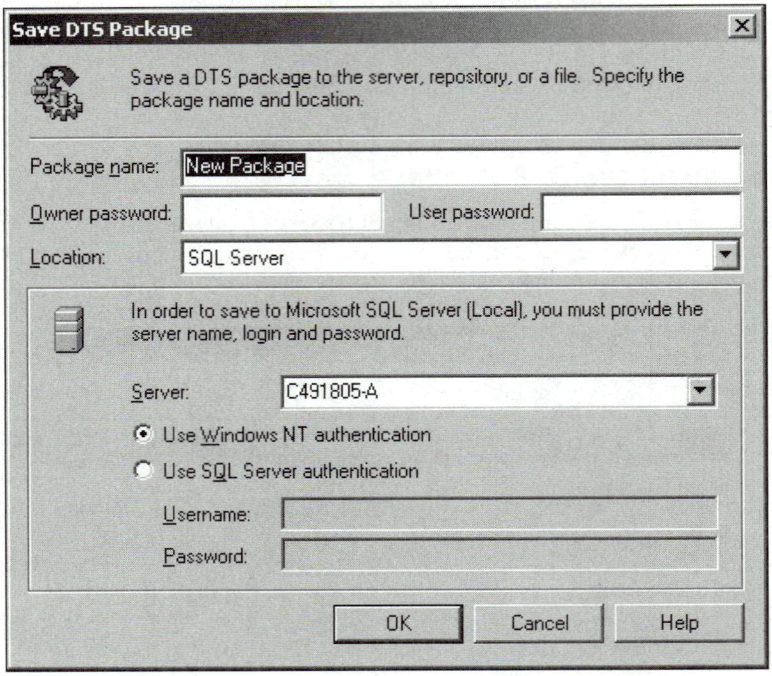

Save DTS Package dialog box

With this dialog, you can do the following:

- Provide a name for the package.
- Set the owner's password, and the user password if necessary.
- Set the location where the package is to be saved. The three options available from the Location drop-down list are SQL Server, which is the default; SQL Server Repository, and File.
- If you choose to save the package in msdb (SQL Server package storage or SQL Server repository storage options), you will need to provide the server name, and authentication information. If you save the package to a file, you need to specify an existing DTS package file or a new one and the location where the file is to be saved. The DTS file extension is ".dts".
- Once a DTS package is created, you can start designing it by adding OLE DB connections to the source and destination data stores, tasks and defining workflow transformations and precedence constraints. Conducting these functions from the DTS Designer window is described in the next section.

Saving the DTS package to the Microsoft SQL Server Repository allows you to provide lineage information, which is information on where the data came from, and can be on a row-by-row basis, if needed.

Designing the DTS Package with the DTS Designer

In this section, I will generically present how to use the DTS designer to design a DTS package. A detailed example on using DTS to perform a data transformation from an online transaction processing (OLTP) system to an online analytical processing (OLAP) system, including designing a DTS package, is presented in a latter section of this chapter.

The following figure shows a designed DTS package consisting of a connection object that points to a Microsoft Access order entry database, a connection to a SQL Server database containing the sales and inventory data for an OLAP solution, data transformation task, and precedence constraints.

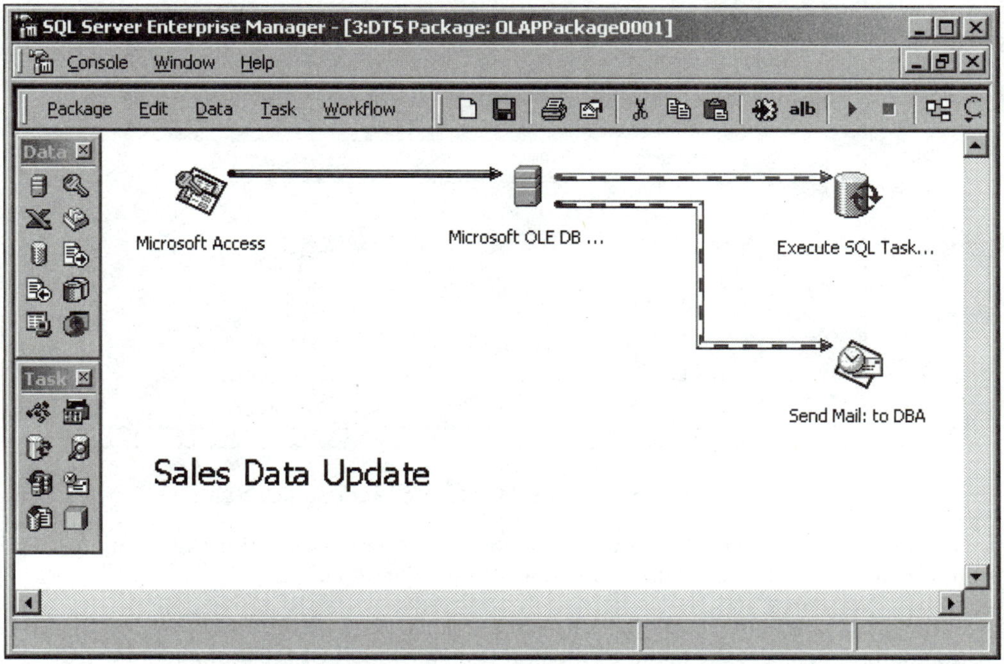

The Design of a sample DTS package

Adding the Connection Objects

Two connection objects have to be added to the designer, a connection to a Microsoft Access database used as the online transaction database (OLTP) for order entry to the system, and the SQL Server database serving as the database for the sales and inventory data warehouse.

To add the connection to the MS Access database drag the MS Access icon from the Data toolbar to the designer main area and drop it (you can just click the MS Access icon in the Data toolbar, or select the Microsoft Access item from the Data menu). This will open the Connection Properties dialog shown in the following figure.

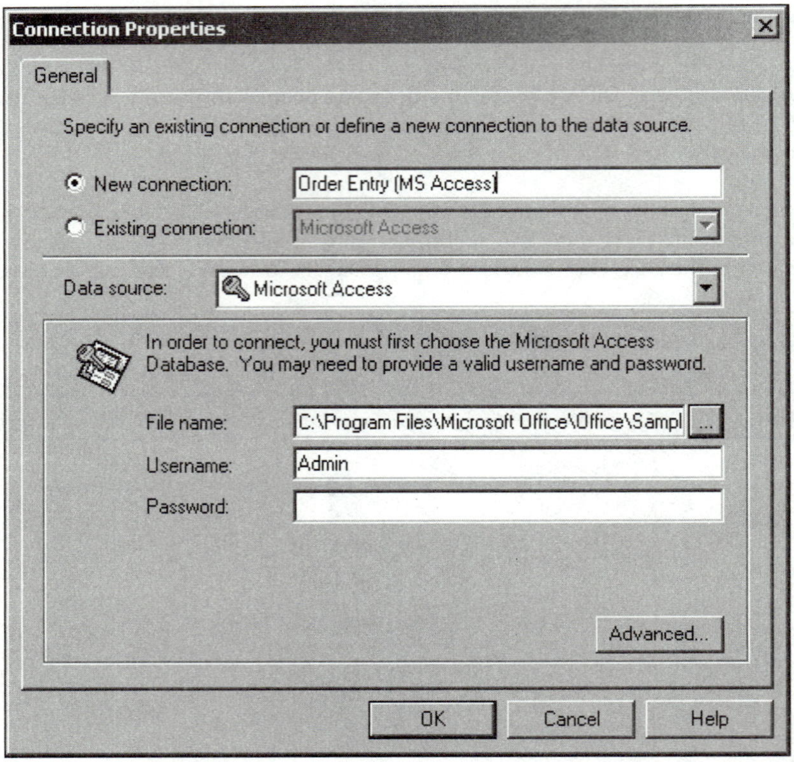

Connection Properties for the MS Access database

In this dialog you can specify the name of the connection, the path and file name of the database you want to use, and the credentials used to connect to the database.

To add the connection to the SQL Server database, click the OLE DB Provider for SQL Server icon in the Data toolbar, or select the menu command, Data|Microsoft OLE DB provider for SQL Server. This will open the Connection Properties dialog shown in the following figure. In this dialog, you can specify the name of the connection, the SQL Server that hosts the database, the database name, and the credentials used to authenticate to the SQL Server.

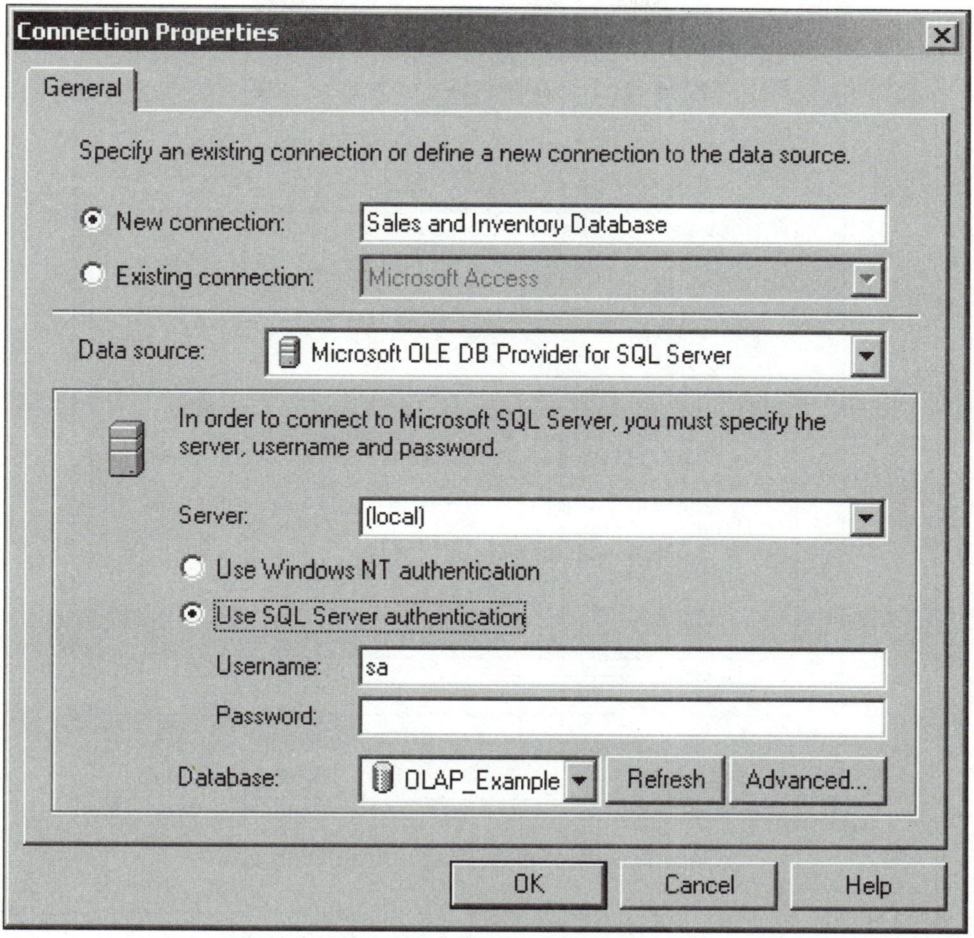

Connection properties for the SQL Server connection

Next, you need to add the transformation between the two connections. To do so, select the MS Access connection, hold down the *Ctrl* key and select the SQL Server connection, then select the Add Transform command from the Workflow menu. This will open the Data Transformation Properties dialog box shown in the following figure.

The Data Transformation Properties dialog box is rich with functionality that allows you to define the source, destination, and the transformation type, among other things. So, let's take a closer look at this dialog.

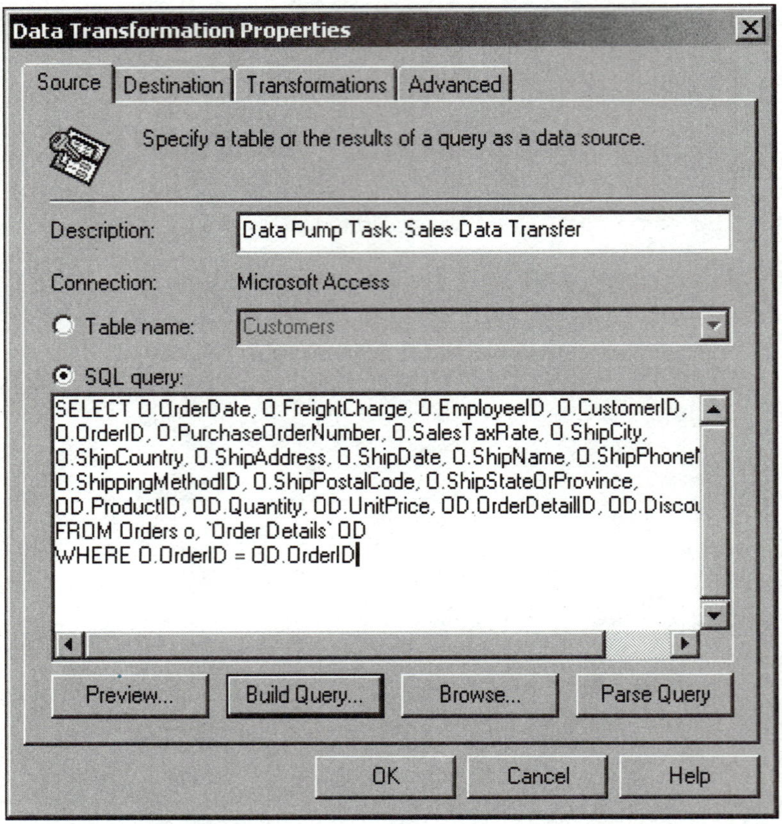

Data Transformation Properties dialog box

The dialog is composed of four tabbed pages; Source, Destination, Transformations, and Advanced. In the Source page, you can specify the source of the data from the Access database we are using. The source can simply be a table, or it can be a query. You can type the query in the SQL query area, or you can have the dialog help you build it by pressing the Build Query button. This button launches a utility that helps you graphically build the query. If you are ever familiar with using the Query By Example (QBE) tools in Microsoft Access, you will find this utility very similar. The following figure shows the utility as it is used to build the source query for our example transformation. This utility is referred to as the DTS query designer.

The Browse button on the dialog in the figure above allows you to open a text file that holds the SQL code for your query to execute. The Parse button checks the syntax and validity of the query and reports any errors. The Preview button allows you to view the data resulting from running the query.

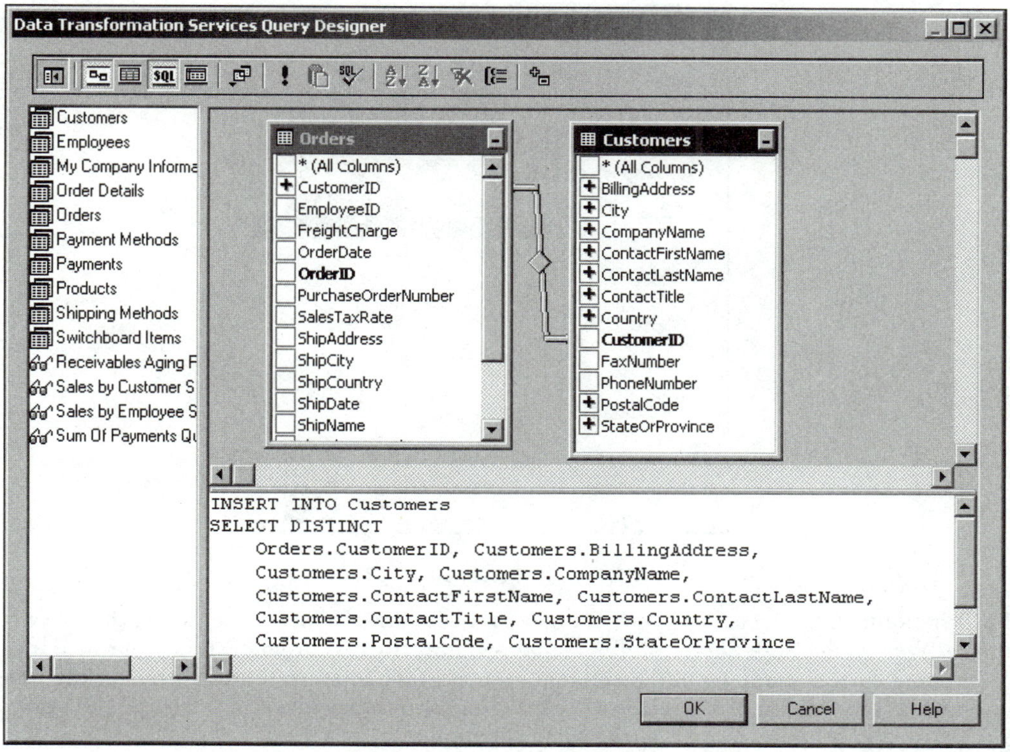

Building the source query with the DTS query designer

The Destination page on the Data Transformation Properties dialog is shown in the following figure. This page allows you to specify the destination table that will store the data. This table may be an existing table in the database, or a new table you create by pressing the Create New button. The destination table does not have to have the same structure as the source table. Pressing this button opens a dialog with a template for a SQL statement for creating a table. By modifying the statement, you can create a new table and define the fields and their data types. Selecting an existing table from the Table Name drop-down list, will show the details of its attributes in the grid below the drop-down list.

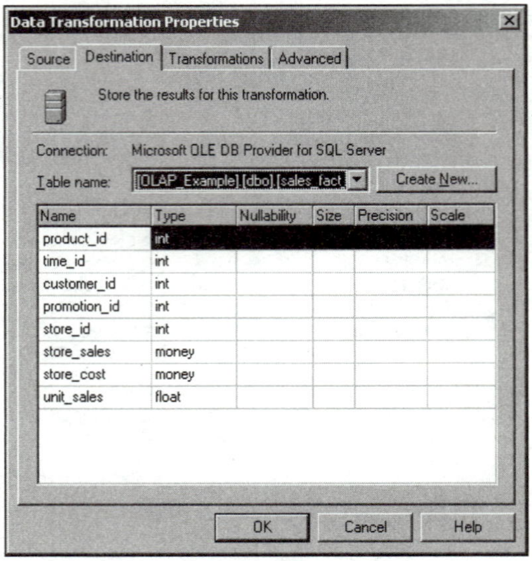

Setting the destination table.

The **Transformations** tab is the tab where database columns are mapped between the two data sources. You can let SQL Server do the mapping automatically, or you can do your own mapping. When doing custom mapping of the columns, you can add columns to the list by clicking the **New** button when the column of interest is selected. You can remove a column pair from the mapping list by selecting the column pair and clicking the **Delete** button.

Two types of transformations are supported through this page, column copy, and ActiveX scripting. The column copy does exactly what the name implies, that is copying column values from the source to the destination. The ActiveX option gives you more flexibility performing some validations and transformations before moving the column values.

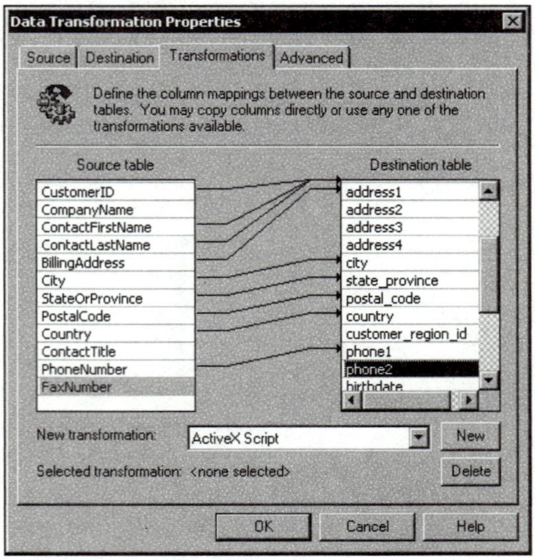

The Transformation tab of the Data Transformation Properties dialog

For example, to create a Copy Column transformation, select the source and destination columns, make sure the New Transformation drop-down list shows the Copy Column option, and click the New button.

As an example of creating an ActiveX Script transformation, select the source and destination columns: Fax and Phone2 respectively, select the ActiveX Script option from the New transformation drop-down menu, and click the New button. This should bring up the window shown below:

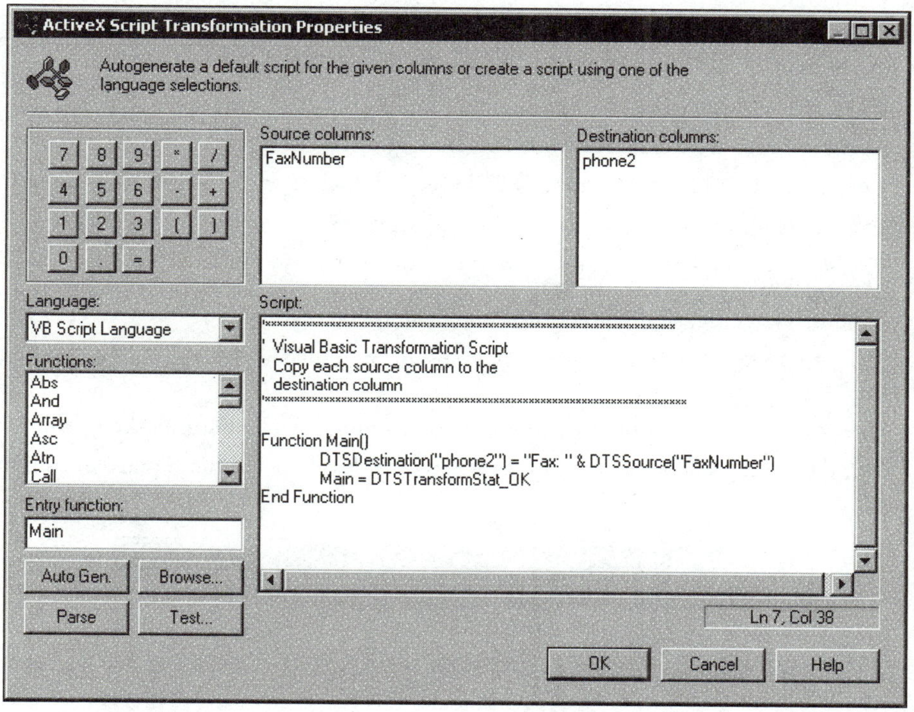

Creating an ActiveX Script transformation

In the script area, modify the script so that the word "Fax: " appears before the fax number in the field to indicate that you are mapping the fax number from the source to the Phone2 field in the destination table.

```
Function Main()
  DTSDestination("phone2") = "Fax: " & DTSSource("FaxNumber")
  Main = DTSTransformStat_OK
End Function
```

The Advanced tab in the dialog, shown below, allows you to specify advanced options for the transformation, including:

- **Max error count:** indicates the maximum number of errors at which the task execution stops. The Use Fast Load option, if selected, will cause the transformation to fail at the first error, even if Max error count is set to a value not equal to 0 or 1 as long as Insert commit size option in the dialog is set to 0. Therefore, if you want to log more errors to the exception file, either clear Use fast load or set Insert commit size to another value, such as 1.

- **Exception file name:** indicates the name of an exception log file.
- **Row delimiter:** indicates the delimiter used to separate rows of data for the exception file. The default is a carriage return/line feed delimiter {CR}{LF}.
- **Column delimiter:** indicates the delimiter used to separate columns of data for the exception file. The default is a vertical bar delimiter.
- **Insert commit size:** indicates the size of the data to commit to the destination during data movement.
- **Fetch buffer size:** indicates the number of rows of data being fetched at the source during data movement.
- **First row:** indicates the first row of data moved.
- **Last row:** indicates the last row of data moved.
- **Lookups:** Allows for performing DTS Lookup, which is explained later in the chapter.
- **Use fast load:** this option supports bulk-copy processing.
- **Enable identity:** if selected, this option allows you to insert explicit values in the identity column. Identity columns in SQL Server are counter that are incremented by the server by default. They are usually used for ID fields in tables.
- **Keep NULLs:** this option specifies that empty columns will retain a null value during the fast load operation.
- **Check constraints:** causes the table constraints to be checked during the loading operation.
- **Table lock:** if selected, this option causes a table-level lock to be in place during the fast copy operation.

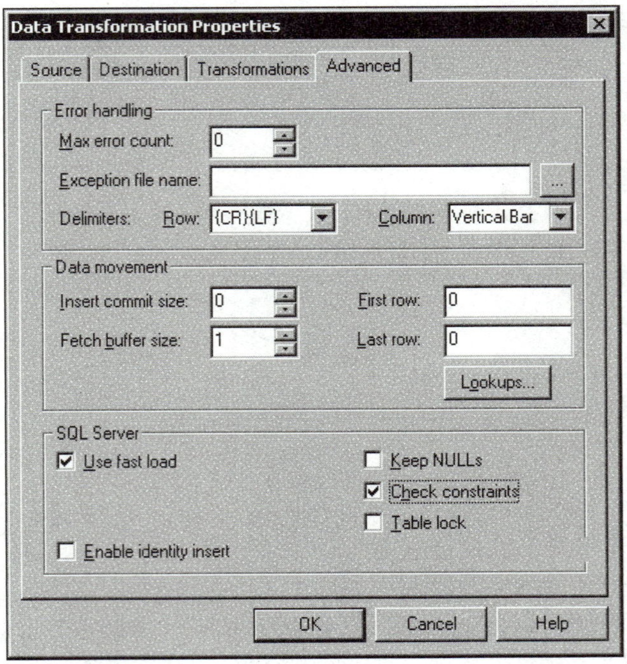

Specifying advanced transformation options

The next step in designing a DTS package is adding tasks and precedence constraints. In this example, two tasks are added, a SQL query task that is executed on success of the transformation, and an email task that is executed when the transformation fails. This task sends email to the database administrator informing them of the problem and asking them for their intervention to help straighten out the situation.

To add the email task click the Send Mail button on the Task toolbar. Set the properties appropriately in the Send Mail Properties dialog box as shown in the following figure.

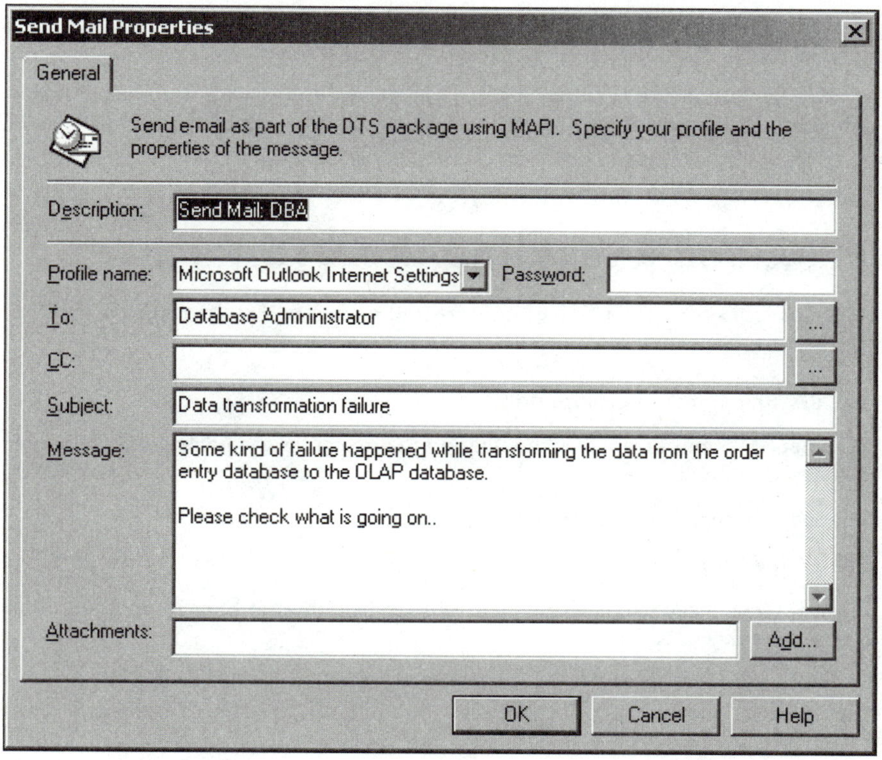

Send Mail task properties

In the figure above, you can set a description of the SendMail task, for instance "send mail to the DBA", you can choose an email profile on the SQL Server machine and enter the password for the profile. You can also specify the recipients and add the message subject and text. The ellipsis (...) buttons to the right of the To and CC text boxes will open your address book allowing you to select the recipients of the message directly from it. Finally, the Add button allows you to browse your file system for files you need to attach to the message.

In summary, the DTS Designer allows you to add as many connection objects as possible. It also allows you to add tasks and precedence constraints that determine the order by which the tasks will be executed. For an example on doing a DTS package design, see the "Data Transformation Example" section later in the chapter.

Editing and Deleting the DTS Package

To edit an existing DTS package that is saved in SQL Server or the repository, double click it in the SQL Server Enterprise Manager Detail pane, or right click on its name and select the Design Package menu item from the context sensitive menu. This will open the DTS package in the DTS Designer allowing you to conduct design changes and other management tasks.

To delete a DTS Package, right-click its name in the SQL Server Enterprise Manager, and select the Delete menu item from the context-sensitive menu.

Executing the DTS Package

Executing and scheduling the DTS package can be considered part of the package management process. The next section presents in detailed description the different methods to execute the package.

Scheduling and Executing the DTS Package

A DTS packages that is created and built, or created correctly, can be run in several different ways, including:

- The **dtsrun** command prompt utility.
- SQL Server Agent to run a scheduled job that executes the package. SQL Server Agent is explained in detail in Chapter 13.
- The DTS Designer user interface.
- The DTS Export and Import Wizard user interfaces.
- If the DTS package is created in a custom application, the Execute method of the package can be used for this purpose.

In all of the methods above, the DTS package is loaded into the client application process and executed from that process.

Using the dtsrun Utility

Packages run using this command prompt utility will run in the context of the command prompt window. The syntax for this command is:

```
dtsrun [{/? | {/[~]S server_name {/[~]U user_name [/[~]P password] | /E}| {/[~]F
filename/[~]R repository_database_name} }{/[~]N package_name [/[~]M
package_password] |[/[~]G package_guid_string] | [/[~]V
package_version_guid_string]}[/!X] [/!D] [/!Y] [/!C]}]
```

Arguments available to this command are listed below:

Argument	Description
/?	Similar to help utility for this command. When issued, it displays the command prompt options listed in this table.
~	Specifies that the parameter to follow is encrypted and its value is represented in a hexadecimal text format. Can be used with the /S, /U, /P, /F, /R, /N, /M, /G, and /V options. Using encrypted values increases the security of the command used to execute the DTS package because the server name, password, and so on, are not visible.
/S server_name	Network name of the computer hosting the SQL Server that you are connecting to.
/U user_name	Login ID used to connect to the NT machine hosting the SQL Server that you are connecting to.
/P password	Password for the `user_name` login account.
/E	Specifies that a trusted connection is used where no password is required.
/N package_name	Is the name of a DTS package to execute.
/M package_password	Is an optional password assigned to the DTS package when it was created (see Package security later in the chapter).
/G package_guid_string	The GUID representing the package ID.
/V package_version_guid_string	The GUID representing the version ID assigned to the DTS package when it was first saved or executed. A new version ID is assigned to the DTS package each time it is modified or executed.
/F filename	Used in the case of executing COM-file DTS packages. It represents the name of a structured storage file containing DTS packages. Interestingly enough, if the `server_name` argument is also specified, then the contents of filename are overwritten with the DTS package retrieved from SQL Server.
/R repository_database_name	Is the name of the repository database containing DTS packages. If no name is specified, the default database name is used.
/!X	Retrieves the DTS package from SQL Server, and overwrites the contents of the DTS file specified by the filename argument, without executing the package. If this option is not specified, then the DTS package is executed immediately.

Table Continued on Following Page

Argument	Description
/!D	Deletes the DTS package from SQL Server and the package is not executed in this case. It is not possible to delete a specific DTS package from a structured storage file. If you want to delete a DTS package from such file, the entire file needs to be overwritten using the combination of the /F and /S options.
/!Y	This argument is used when the ~ argument is used. It displays the encrypted command to be used to execute the DTS package without executing it.

As an example, if you want to execute a package called DTSPackage0001, which is stored in the SQL Server's msdb database, you can issue the command:

```
dtsrun /myServerName /U sa /P saPWD /N DTSPackage0001 /M packagePWD
```

Scheduling the DTS Package for Execution

A DTS package can be scheduled in one of two ways to be executed at a particular point in time. The two ways include, using the DTS Designer, which is explained in detail in the next section, or using the SQL Agent. A DTS package can be scheduled for execution once, or at recurring intervals.

Using the SQL Agent to Schedule DTS Packages

To schedule execution of a DTS package through the SQL Server Agent, you need to create a new job after making sure that the SQL Server Agent service is running. To create a job using the SQL Server Enterprise Manager, expand the Management folder in the tree pane, expand the SQL Server Agent item. Then right click the Jobs item and select New Job from the context-sensitive menu as shown in the following screenshot:

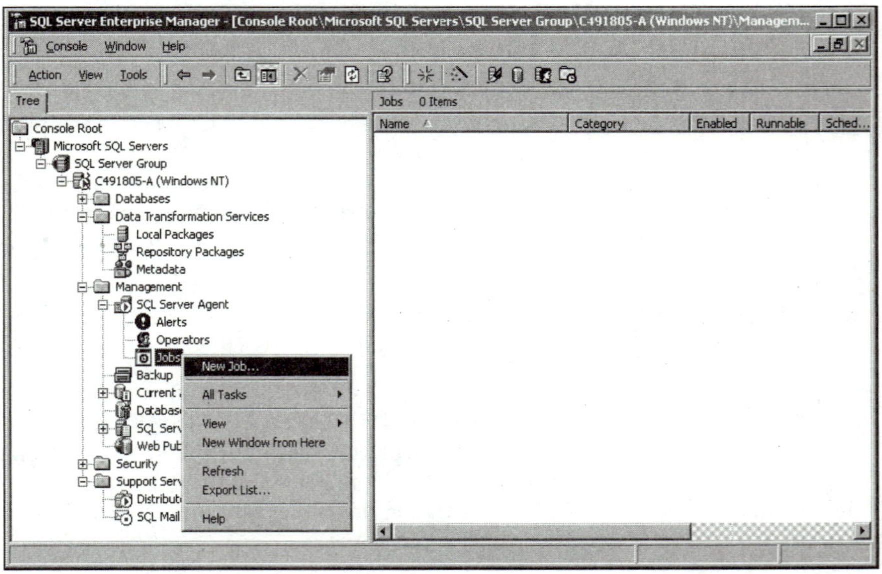

Creating a new job in SQL Server Agent to schedule a DTS package execution

Selecting the New Job menu command will open the New Job Properties dialog box, shown in the figure below. The dialog box shows 4 different tabs, the general tab, the steps tab, the schedules tab, and the notifications tab. In the general tab, you can specify a name for the job, select from a list of categories to categorize the job, set the owner of the job, provide a description for it, and set the target server on which the job will be executed.

The Step tab allows you to create one or more steps to be executed with the job. Clicking the New button in that page will open the New Job Step dialog. In this dialog, shown in the figure below, you can specify the step name, step type, the database used for the step and add the commands you want to be carried out. The step type to be used when executing a DTS package from the SQL Server Agent is Operating System Command (`CmdExec`). The command you enter is a `dtsrun` command, which is explained earlier in the previous section.

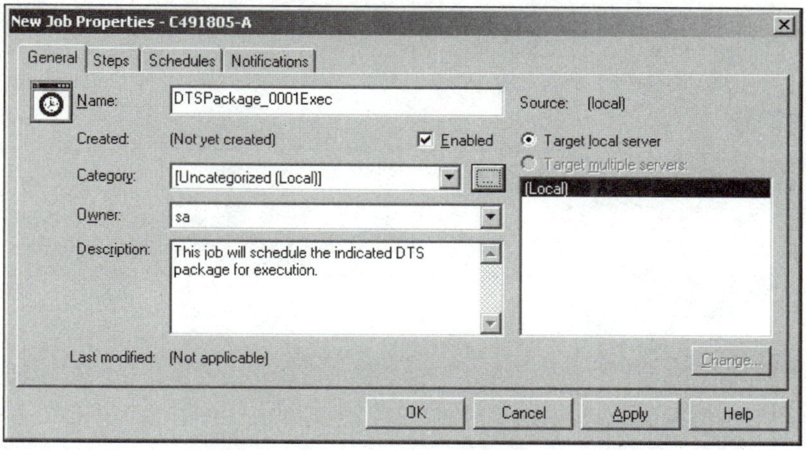

The SQL Server Agent New Job Properties dialog box

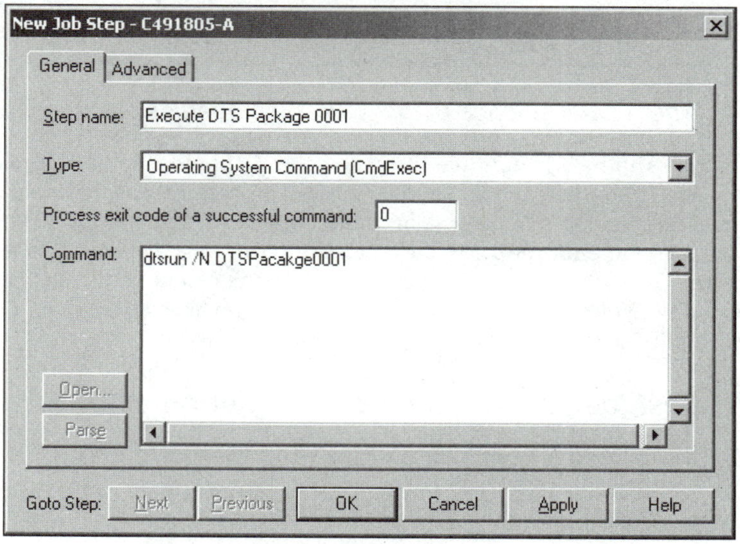

The New Job Step dialog of the SQL Server Agent

The New Job Step dialog provides some powerful options on the Advanced tab that allow you to decide what to do in case of success or failure. It also allows you to set the number of attempts for running the step. You can also output the results to a file you specify in this screen. As an example, you can specify that you want the SQL Server Agent to proceed to the next step in case of success of the step execution after a maximum of 10 trials. If the step fails, you can specify that you need to quit the job and report the failure and the error messages. The following figure shows the Advanced page of the New Job Step dialog box.

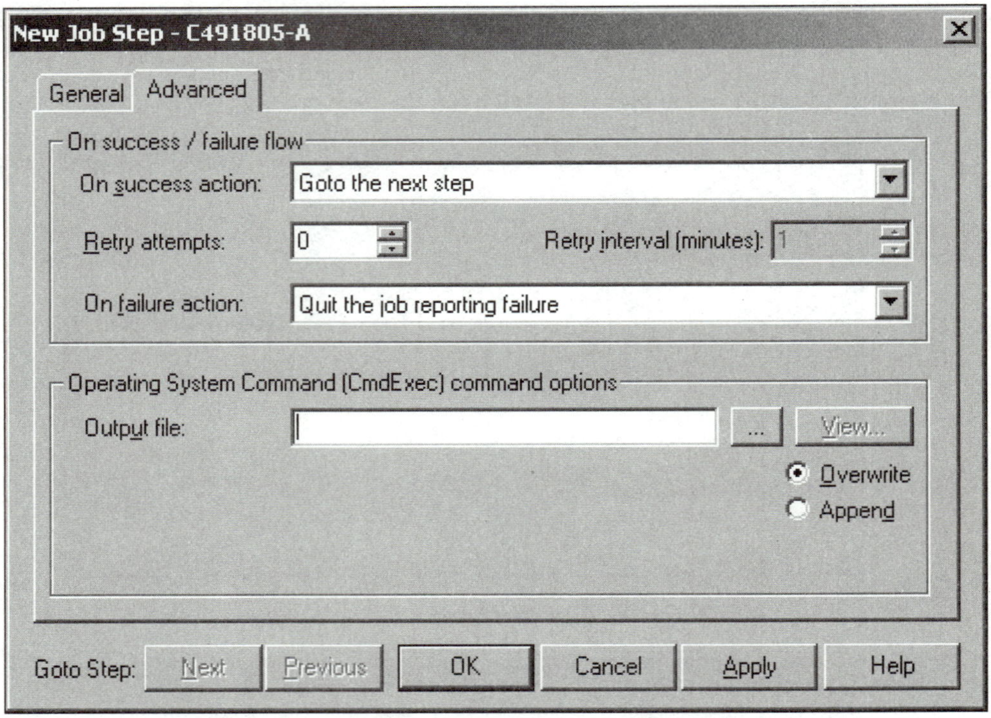

The Advanced page of the New Job properties dialog box.

Once saved, the step will be added to the list of steps available for the SQL Agent job in the Step page of the New Job Properties dialog. In that dialog, you can still specify the schedule to be followed for executing the DTS Package. The Schedules tab of the New Job Properties dialog box is used to add a new schedule for the DTS package. The series of screens used to specify this schedule are straightforward. You can also specify alerts based on the results of the execution of the DTS package. For example, you can have the system administrator paged in case of failure so that they can perform some remedial actions.

Using the DTS Designer to Schedule the Execution of DTS Packages

Unless you are already familiar with the DTS designer, I recommend that you read the next section, which will familiarize you with it before you proceed.

To schedule a DTS package to be executed using the DTS designer, right click the name of the package you want to schedule in either the Local Packages or Repository Packages folders, and select the Schedule Package command as shown in the following figure.

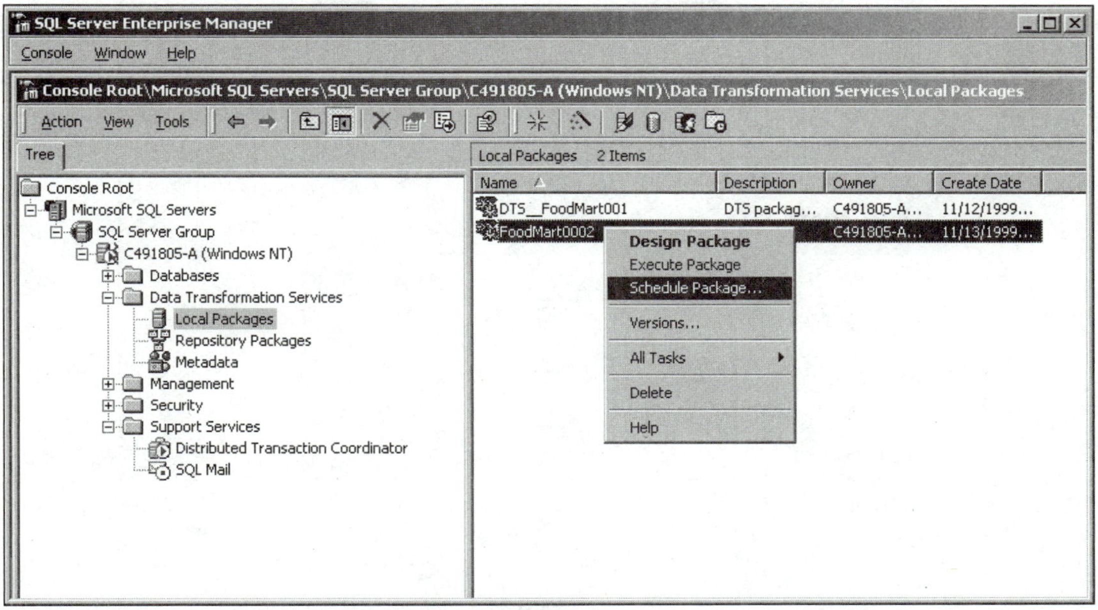

Scheduling a Package to be run with the DTS Designer

The action described in the above figure will open the Edit Recurring Job Schedule dialog box, shown in the following figure. The options provided in this dialog are clear and allow for establishing a flexible schedule for the execution of the DTS package. For instance, you can set your package schedule to execute:

- Daily: With this option, you can specify which days to skip, if you want to do so.
- Weekly: With this option, you can specify which day of the week you want to have the DTS package executed. For example, you can set it to be executed every Sunday at midnight.
- Monthly: With this option, you can specify which day of the month and the frequency in months to execute the package. You can also specify something like, execute the package on the last Sunday of the month every two months.

You can also specify the daily, weekly, or monthly frequency, and the start and end dates of the schedule.

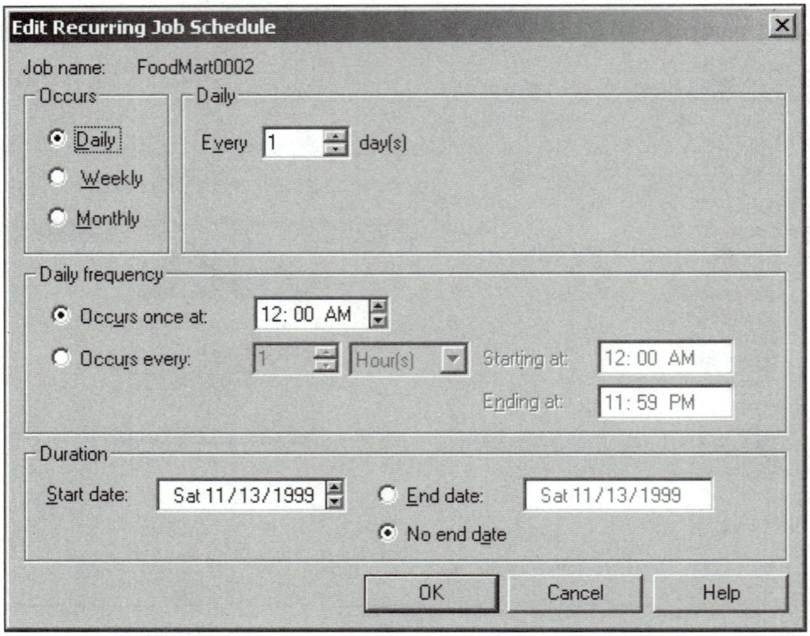

The Edit Recurring Job Schedule dialog box

DTS Import and Export Wizards

The Data Transformation Services (DTS) import and export wizards allow you to interactively create DTS packages that can be used to import, export, validate, and transform heterogeneous data using OLE DB and ODBC. DTS can also copy schema and data between relational databases. Using the DTS object transfer capability, you can also copy indexes, stored procedures, referential integrity constraints, and other database objects between computers running Microsoft SQL Server version 7.0. Such object transfer is not possible between older versions of SQL Server and the current version 7.0. To perform such transformations between the prior versions and the new one, you need to generate the SQL code from the source database, edit it as appropriate, and run it at the destination database.

The DTS Import and DTS Export wizards allow the user to:

- Establish connection to the source and destination databases by setting the properties of these OLE DB and ODBC connections.
- Copy an entire table, or the results of an SQL query, such as queries involving joins of multiple tables, or even distributed queries.
- DTS Import/Export wizard comes with a Query Builder tool that allows you to build queries interactively if you are not quite proficient at building such queries.
- Alter several properties of the table fields, such as name, data type, size, precision, scale, and nullability, when copying the source to the destination.
- Specify transformation rules that govern how data is copied between columns of different data type, size, precision, scale, and nullability.

- You can also execute a Microsoft ActiveX script that can modify (transform) the data when copied from the source to the destination, or perform any operation supported by the Microsoft JScript or Microsoft Visual Basic Scripting Edition languages.
- Transfer database objects such as users, roles, views, and stored procedures between computers running SQL Server 7.0
- Save the DTS package to the SQL Server msdb database, Microsoft Repository, or a COM-structured storage file.
- Specify whether destination tables are to be used for replication.
- Schedule the DTS package for later execution.

In this section, I will briefly present the DTS Import and Export wizards, and how these wizards can be used in data warehousing transformations.

The Import Wizard

Let's transfer the tables and data in the Order Entry MS Access database to an Order Entry database in SQL Server 7.0. To do this, you must create the destination database in SQL Server. Since this book does not cover creating a database in SQL Server, I recommend referring to the SQL Server Books On Line if you need help with this step.

You can launch the Import/Export wizards in many different ways. For now, let's right click on the Data Transformation Services item in the tree view of the Microsoft Enterprise Manager, and select All Tasks|Import Data. This will launch the first window in the wizard. Followed by the Choose a Data Source page, as shown below.

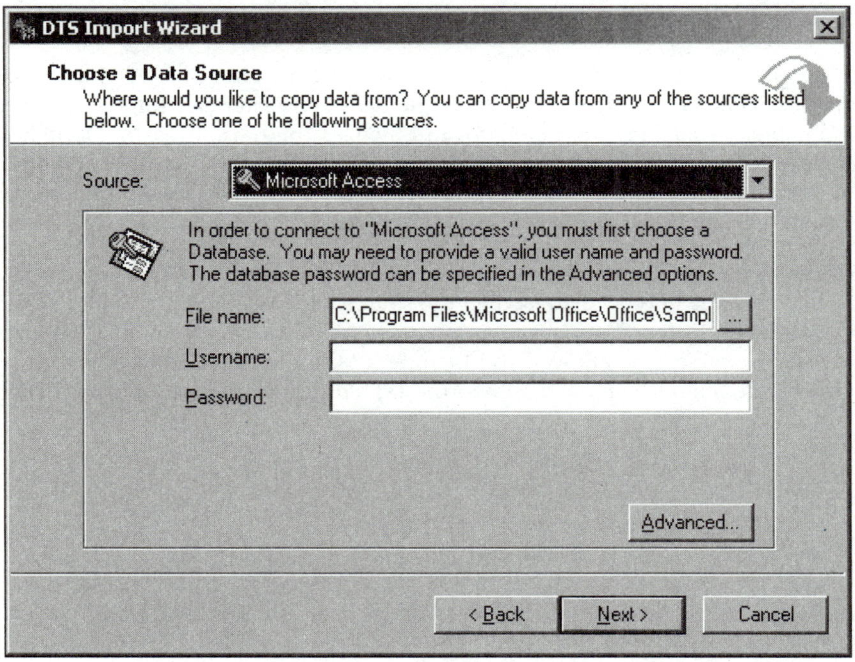

The data source page in the DTS Import wizard.

In the data source page, select the Order Entry MS Access database used as a source for this import. The next page is similar to this page, except it allows you to specify the destination of the import, which is the still blank Order Entry database in SQL Server 7.0 as shown in the figure below:

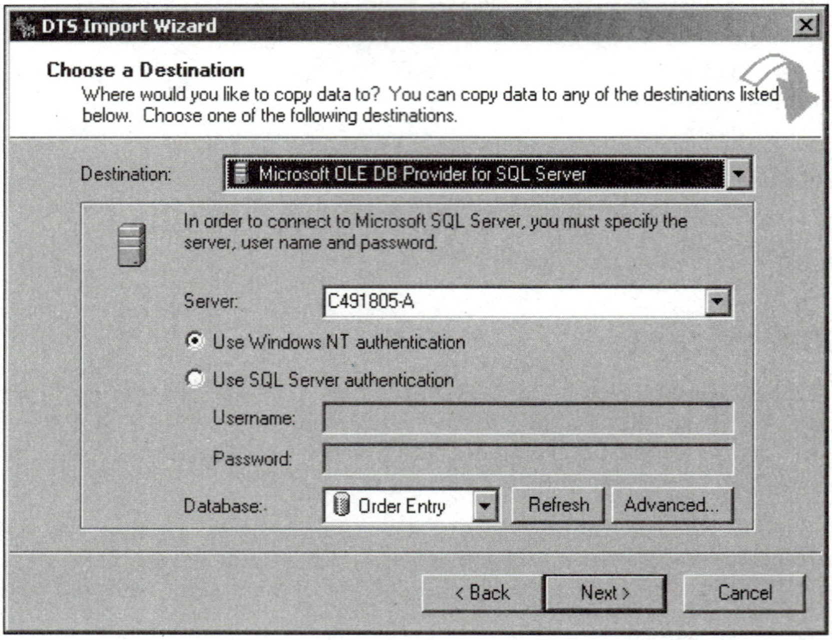

Specifying a destination in the DTS Import wizard.

The next step allows you to specify whether you want to copy tables between the source and destination, or execute a SQL query to specify the data to transfer (see following figure). For our case, let's copy all tables by clicking the Select All and the Next buttons. The Transform button shown on this screen of the wizard allows you to perform column mapping and transformation through the dialog that combines the Transformation and Advanced tabs of the Transformation Properties dialog which we saw earlier in the chapter.

Notice that the Transfer Objects option is not available because the source is not a SQL Server 7.0 database. This option is only available when the source and destination are both SQL Server 7.0 databases. Had you selected the query option, you would have been presented with a screen shown in the third figure following, that allowed you to enter a SQL query, or build one using a query builder similar to the query builder you have seen in the DTS transformation properties dialog earlier in the chapter.

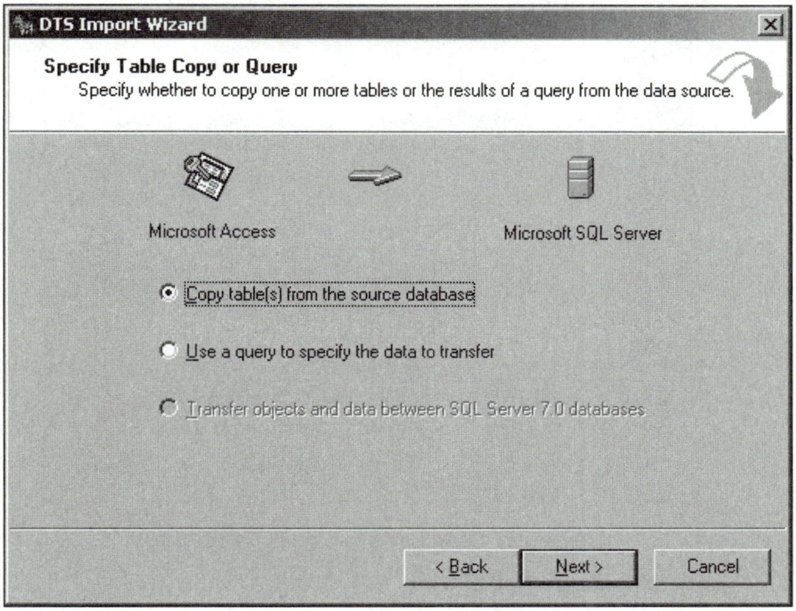

Selecting what to import in the DTS Import Wizard

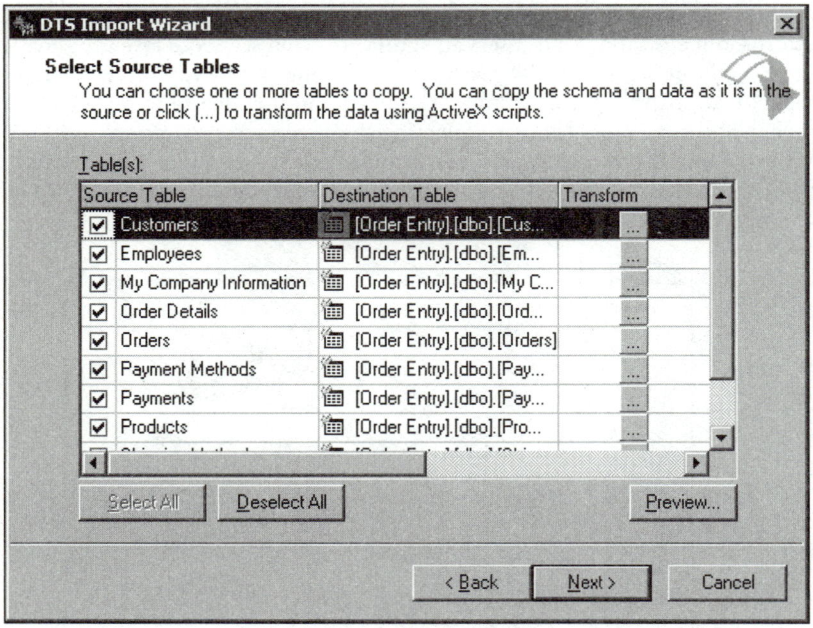

Selecting the tables to import

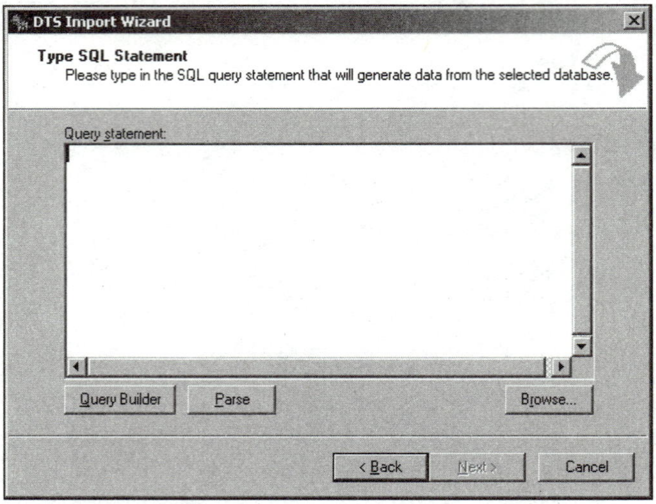

Selecting data to import using a query

The next screen in the wizard is shown in the following figure, and allows you to schedule the package for execution, save, and replicate its data. If you choose to run immediately, the import process will start immediately when you press the **Next** button. If you choose to schedule the execution of the import package at a later time, perhaps to avoid affecting other user's performance on the server,you can press the ellipsis (...) button to bring up a scheduling screen. This allows you to schedule it to run once or at a fixed interval, similar to what we have already seen with scheduling DTS package execution using the DTS Designer. Selecting the **Save DTS Package** option will save the import specifications in the wizard in a DTS option in the location you select, the SQL Server, the SQL Server repository, or in a DTS file. Selecting the save package option also makes the next screen prompt you for a name for the package, description, and password for the package owner. Authentication credentials to the SQL Server where the package will be saved are also requested on this screen.

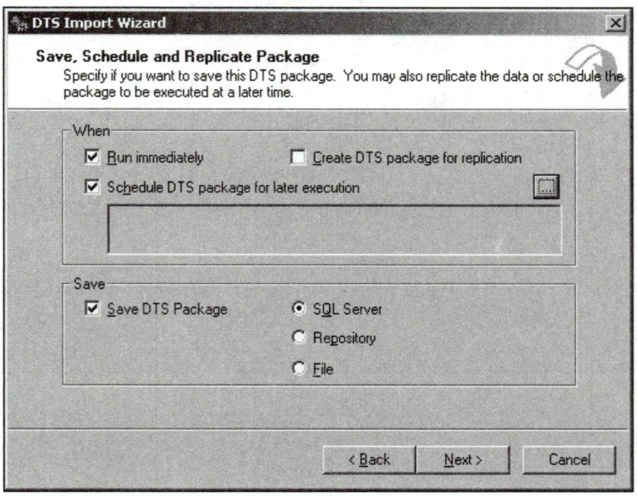

Scheduling, saving, and replicating the DTS package

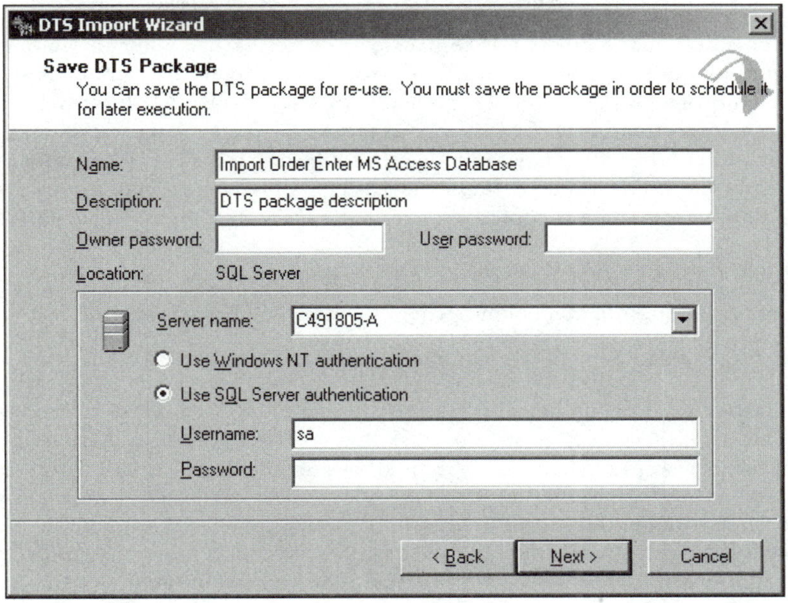

Specifying a name and other properties for the package for saving it.

The next step will execute the package and show you the progress of these executions as shown below. Please note that the execution of the import package requires that the SQL Agent service be running.

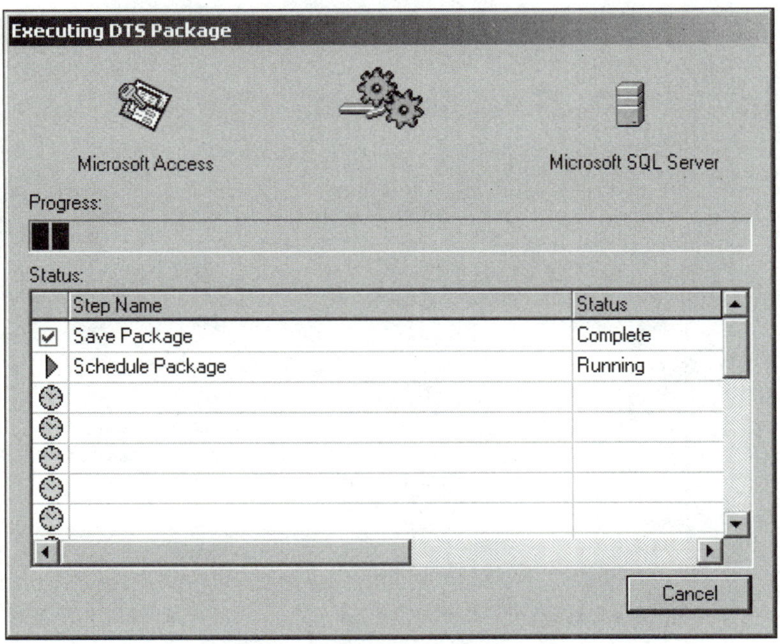

DTS Import Package execution progress

As a closing note, the DTS Import and DTS Export wizards act in a similar way to the DTS Designer in that both tools design and create a DTS package. To verify this, you can see the design of the package created by the DTS Import wizard in the following figure by right clicking its name in the SQL Server Enterprise Manger screen and selecting Design DTS Package from the context-sensitive menu. The DTS Import and DTS Export wizard are not just a trucking operation that hauls data from one data source to another, they have intelligence built in that makes them similar to the DTS designer in many ways. For instance, these wizards can allow you to map a source column to a destination column as the data is copied similar to the DTS Designer. This is done by:

- Specifying which source columns to copy.
- Specifying the destination column where the data will be copied.
- Changing the data type of the data if needed and if a valid data conversion is applicable.

Notice that, in the figure, a number of tasks equal to the number of tables transferred exist in the DTS package. Each one of these tasks has a SQL task that creates a transferred table in the destination database. An on-success precedence constraint allows for the transformation between the Access table and the corresponding SQL Server table to take place. Each of these transformations defines a source table and fields, destination table and fields, and a mapping between the source and destination. The beauty of this is that you can schedule the package for execution later, and in the mean time, you can modify its design in a way that makes your import process more customized and flexible.

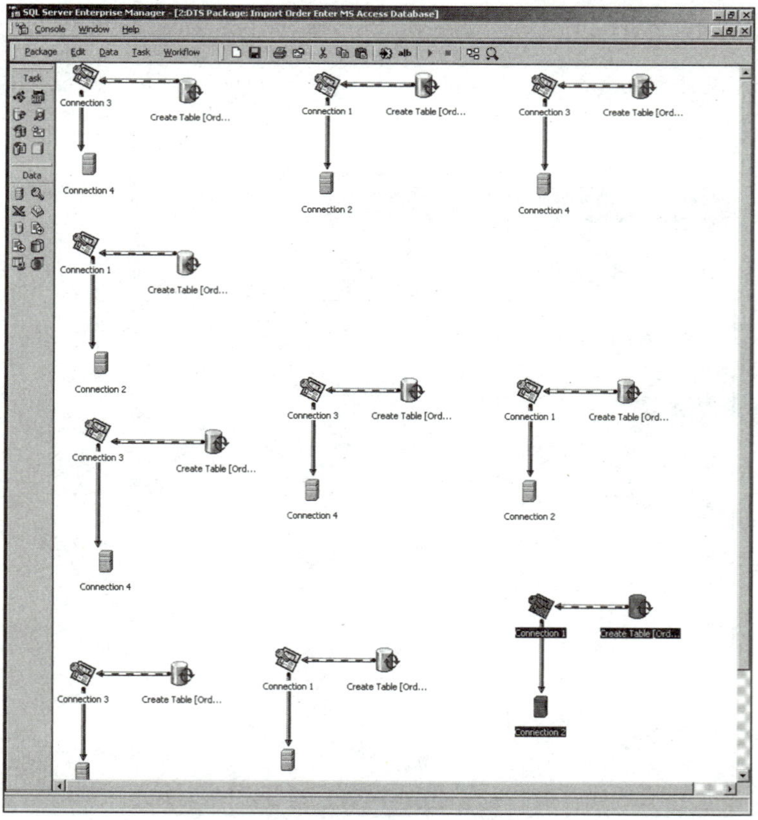

The design of the DTS Import package

Advanced DTS Topics

DTS is an extremely powerful tool that you can use to satisfy your data transformation needs in a very flexible way. Some of the aspects that make DTS such a powerful tool include data driven queries, DTS lookup, and viewing package metadata among other things. In this section, I will briefly discuss these issues and also touch on performance issues with DTS.

Data-Driven Queries (DDQ)

Ideally, you would like to be able to select data from a source, transform it, and dump it in a destination table. However, real life situations require more flexibility in the way you design and run your queries. Data-driven queries (DDQ) are one of the tasks that you can select in the DTS Designer that provide you with much higher flexibility than regular SQL queries used in SQL tasks.

The data-driven query is row-based. It loops through the resultset of a query and takes action as determined by conditions defined in an ActiveX script. This makes these queries perform their inserts row by row as opposed to the bulk inserts of regular queries. The ActiveX script determines which one of up to four different types of queries is to be executed on the row. These four types include an insert, update, delete, and a user-defined query

DDQ is used when extensive business logic is implemented while transforming the data. It can be implemented in populating data marts on an incremental basis, for instance. DDQ allows you to log errors based on the processed rows to a file you specify, and even skip certain rows from the insert process, or quit the whole process if a certain error took place.

As a quick example of using the DDQ in a data warehouse situation, let's say that a task of updating the `Customer` dimension is required to run every night. The complexity of this task comes from the fact that in the operational OLTP system feeding the data warehouse, the region field is not available or is not populated. Also, when updating the `Customer` dimension table, you need to loop through the rows and find out if the row already exists. If it does, you need to skip it – if it does not, you need to insert the new row. However, before you insert the new row, you need to lookup the value for the region of the customer based on the state and city values. This can be done by using DTS Lookup, which is explained in the next section.

So, to implement this example select the task Data Driven Query from the task menu in the DTS designer of your DTS package, and select the query shown in the figure below as the source for the transformation.

The DDQ Task screen looks similar to the SQL Query task dialog in that it has a source, destination, and transformations tabs. These tabs function in a similar fashion to the ones in the SQL Query task, which you saw before.

The Options tab can be used to create the two lookups needed for our DDQ example. The second figure shows the two lookups, and the third and fourth figures show the details of their SQL queries.

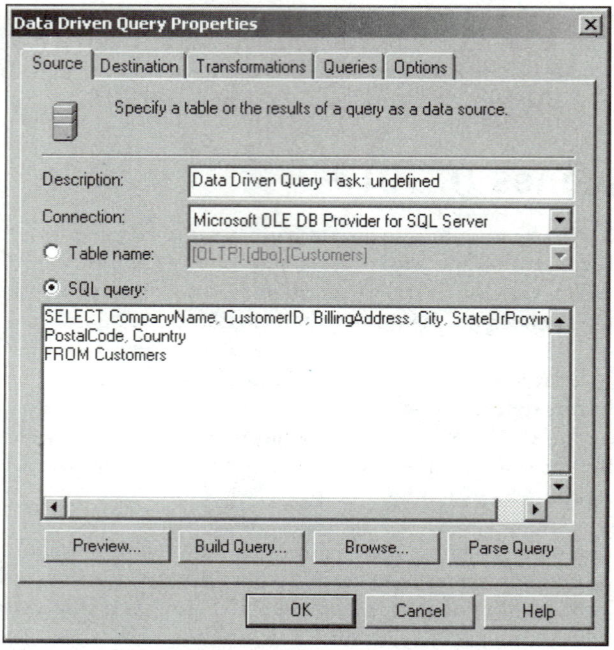

The DDQ task screen

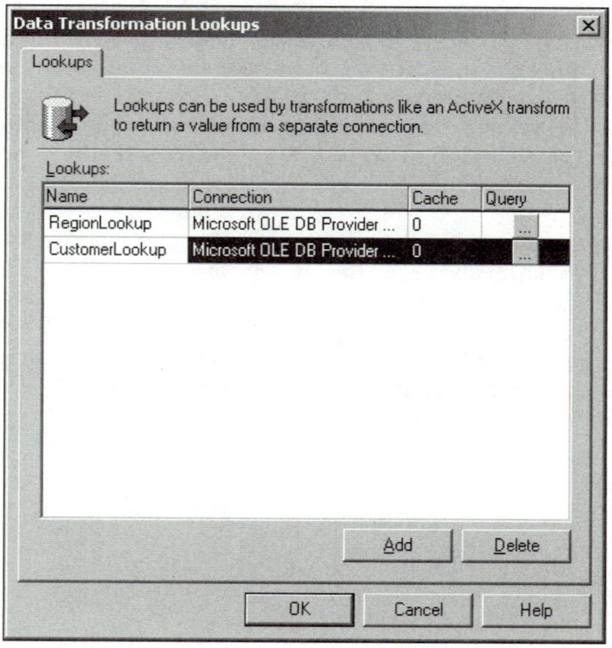

Lookups used for the DDQ example

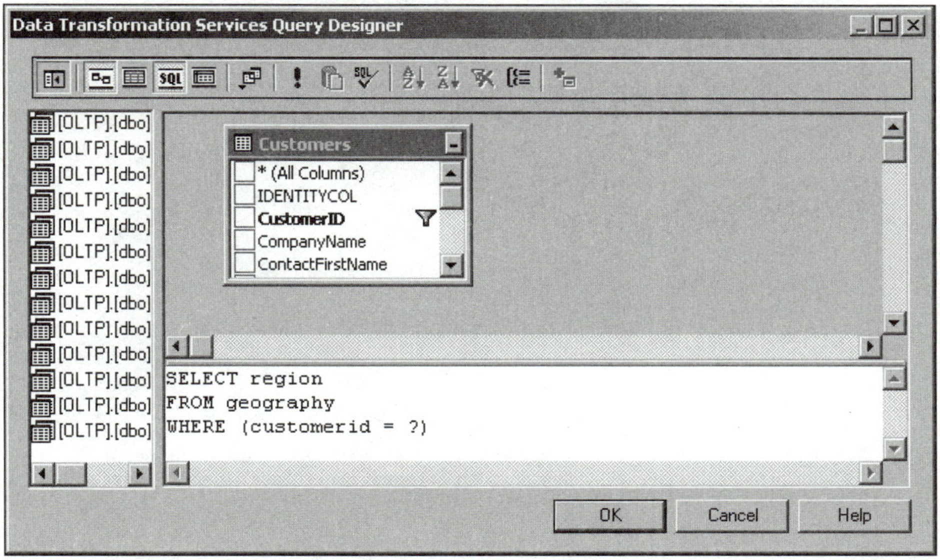

The region lookup query

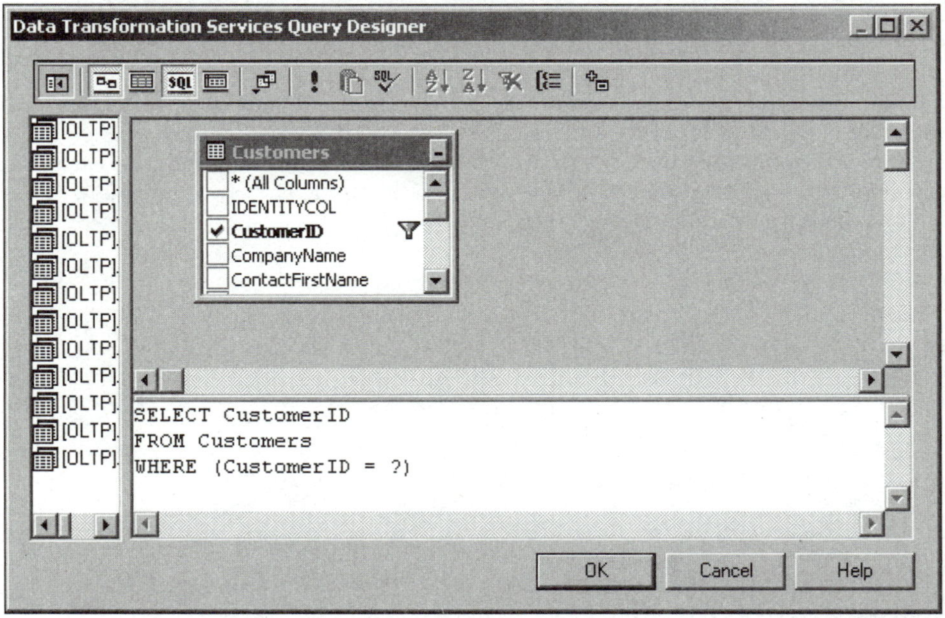

The customer lookup query

The queries tab is where you can specify the queries to use as the basis for your data-driven query task. Let's for example specify an insert query with several parameters corresponding to the fields in the destination table. The following figure shows this query.

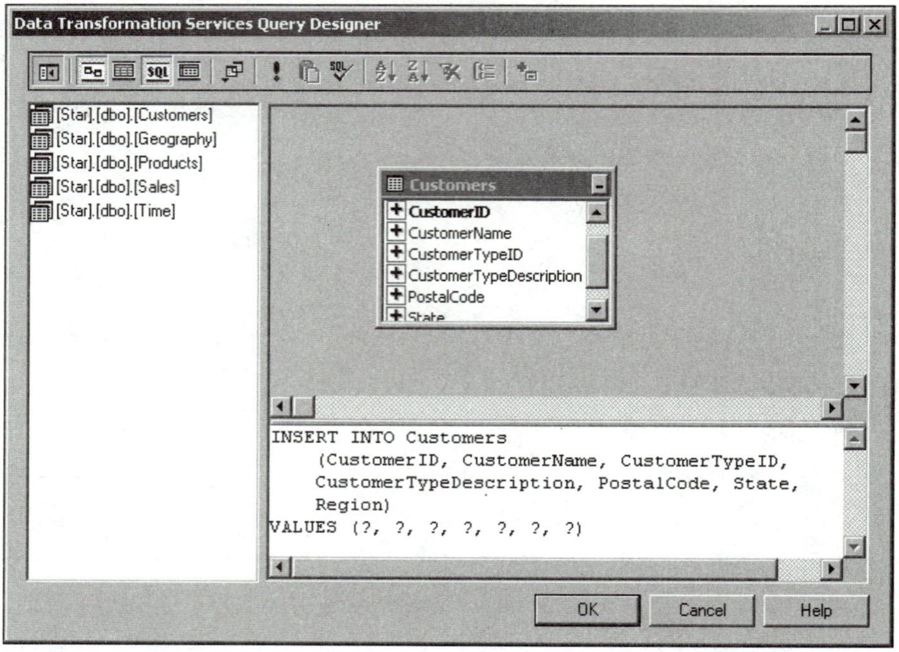

The parameterized insert query to be used in the DDQ task.

You can add other queries, such as a delete query and an update query. Then in the transformations tab (of the Date Driven Query Properties dialog we saw earlier), you need to change one of the mappings to a script passing back the desired value of `DTSTransform_Stat` for each condition. The Script will decide, based on some business logic, whether to delete a row, update it, or insert it using any of the queries you defined in the Queries tab.

A sample script looks like:

```
Function Main()
  If DTSLookups("CustomerLookup") . _
    DTSExecute(DTSSource("CustomerID")) <> "" then
    Main = DTSTransformStat_DeleteQuery
  Else
    DTSDestination("CustomerID") = DTSSource("CustomerID")
    DTSDestination("CustomerName") = DTSSource("CustomerName")
    SDestination("CustomerTypeID")= _
        Source("CustomerTypeID")
    DTSDestination("CustomerTypeDescription") = DTSSource _
        ("CustomerTypeDescription")
    DTSDestination("PostalCode") = DTSSource("PostalCode")
    DTSDestination("Region")DTSLookups _
        ("RegionLookup).Execute(DTSSource("CustomerID"))
  End if
End Function
```

In the script above, notice how the value of the DTS Lookup is retrieved with the `Execute` method of the appropriate DTSLookup object. The method has the syntax:

```
DTSLookups("LookupName").Execute(Parameter).
```

Where `Parameter` is the parameterized source field in the DTS Lookup query.

DTS Lookup

We have already seen how DTS Lookups can be used in combination with DDQ, hence, DTS lookups allow a custom transformation to retrieve data from locations other than the immediate source or destination row being transformed. DTS Lookups are objects grouped in one collection, `DTSLookups` collection, which is available in `DataPumpTask` and `DataDrivenQueryTask` objects in the DTS Designer. The main advantage of using DTS Lookups as opposed to COM objects or other programs is that DTS Lookups use a connection that is already open in the DTS Designer. Whereas COM objects and other programs need to open a connection to the data source before they can perform the work, which adds a performance hit when such connection is created. Therefore, using DTS Lookups will give you an edge in performance.

> *The `DataPumpTask` and `DataDrivenQueryTask` are two objects that represent the data pump and data-driven queries respectively. These objects allow for programmatic control of the data pump and the DDQ.*

A DTS Lookup is defined by several attributes:

- Name: which should be unique per collection. For instance a DTS Lookup object can have the same name in each of the `DTSLookups` collections associated with the `DataPump` task and the DDQ task.
- Parameterized query: as you saw in the previous section.
- Connection ID: related to the source or destination.
- Maximum number of rows to be cached: Such caching is designed to improve performance of the lookup actions.

DTS Package Metadata (Viewing the Repository)

The DTS designer allows you to browse the metadata of the DTS package and see its data, structure, and lineage. The DTS Designer's information model is used as a template for storing metadata information related to DTS packages. To browse the metadata information and lineage data generated by the DTS Designer you can:

- Use the DTS Repository Browser and SQL Server Enterprise Manager's metadata viewing tools. These will allow you to see the schema of the database and properties of its objects. You can also view metadata and version history of the DTS Packages using these tools.
- Write your own custom repository viewing tool after getting familiar with the repository and the API's used to access it.

When you save your package to the SQL Server repository, you store information about the database in the package's metadata. This information includes primary and foreign keys, indexes, column data type, size, scale, nullability, etc.

We will not go into more detail about the DTS Package metadata, because it is beyond the scope of this book. If you need to know more about it, you can consult the SQL Server Books On-Line.

Improving DTS Performance

DTS transformation performance can be improved by using several techniques. These techniques are outlined below. A detailed discussion of these techniques is presented in Chapter 14 – Performance Optimization of the Data Warehouse.

Using ActiveX Scripts

Using scripting languages may slow down data transformations and data pump operations by up to four times. The choice of the language to use for scripting is also important. VB Script is found to be faster than JScript, and JScript was found to be faster than Perl Script.

Using ordinal values when referencing columns is faster than using their names. Hence, it is faster to use DTSSource(1) than DTSSource("CustomerID") because this will save the database engine the step of transforming the names into ordinal values.

Using Data Pump and Data Transformations

Although the Data Pump task is designed for speed and can compete with command prompt BCP (Bulk Copy Program) when copying data, this task can be slowed considerably with custom transformations. To minimize this effect, it is recommended that you avoid mapping a separate transformation function for each column involved in a data pump operation. Also, consider mapping as many like transformations into a single script and function as possible, rather than allowing each column to have its own transformation invocation method.

Using Data-Driven Queries versus Transformations

If no transformations are used and only direct one-to-one mapping of columns is done with the data pump task, this task is much faster than DDQ. However, if transformations are involved, DDQ proves to be faster due to the COM interface it is using behind the scenes to transform the data, which is faster than that used for data pump transformations.

Using Bulk Inserts and BCP

The T-SQL BULK Insert command is supported by OLE DB provider for SQL Server and is faster when used with import files than BCP. Therefore, if no transformations are involved, consider using this command.

Using DTS Lookups

As you saw earlier, DTS Lookups can be invoked from within the data transformation allowing for use of the same connections to the source and/or destination. This gives DTS Lookups an edge over global variables and COM objects. However, if the transformation can use a direct SQL statement as opposed to DTS Lookup, performance will improve significantly.

Other SQL Server Techniques

When moving data between SQL Server sources without the need for complex transformations, the fastest way to do so is by SQL: statements. Also, try to use the SQL Server performance tuning and monitoring tools, such as SQL Server Profiler as much as possible when building your queries.

The New OLAP Services Processing Task

A new tool was released by Microsoft a few months after the release of SQL Server 7.0, and is called the OLAP Services Processing Task. This tools fits as a new built-in task in the DTS Designer Task menu. The tool is available for download from the Microsoft Web site at: http://www.microsoft.com/sql/productinfo/olap.htm. In this section, I will introduce this new task and show you how it can be used with OLAP Services.

How Can You Use It?

The main dialog for this task can be launched by selecting the OLAP Services Processing Task from the Task menu in the Designer. The task is used to process one or more objects in OLAP Services from within the DTS Designer. In this main dialog, you can specify a name for the task and provide a description for it.

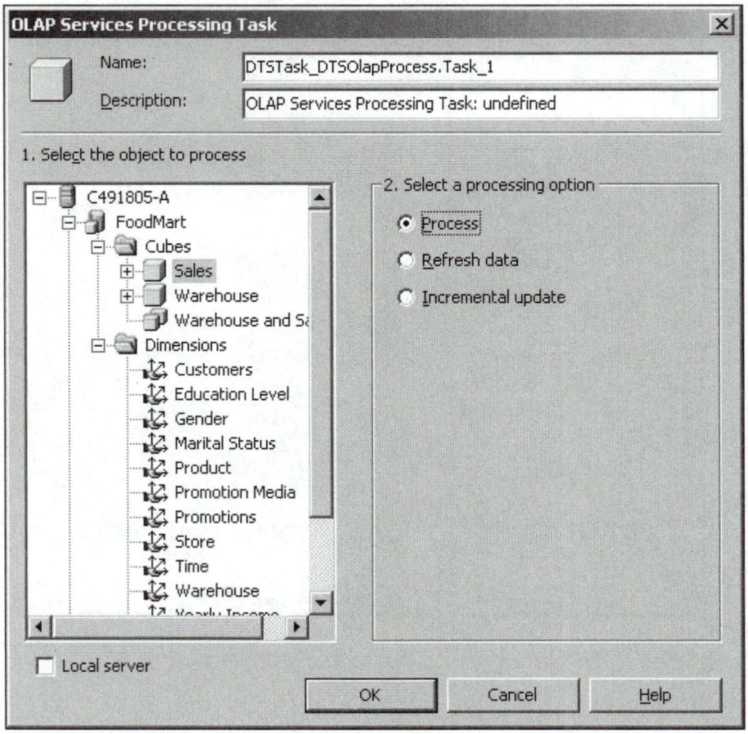

The OLAP Services Processing Task dialog box

You can then select an OLAP object from the tree view. The objects you can select include:

- Database: If selected, all cubes, partitions, virtual cubes, and dimensions in the database will be processed.
- Cubes folder: If selected, all cubes and virtual cubes in the folder will be processed.
- Cube: You can choose to process the cube, refresh its data, or conduct an incremental update.
- Partition: You can either process the partition, or conduct incremental updating of it.
- Virtual cube: Same processing as the cube.
- Dimensions folder: All dimensions in the folder will be processed.
- Processing includes all dimensions in the folder.
- Shared dimension: Dimension will be processed or incrementally updated.
- Virtual dimension: Same processing as the shared dimension.

When selecting the incremental update processing option for a cube, the dialog shows three additional fields (see following figure): Data Source, Fact Table, and Filter:

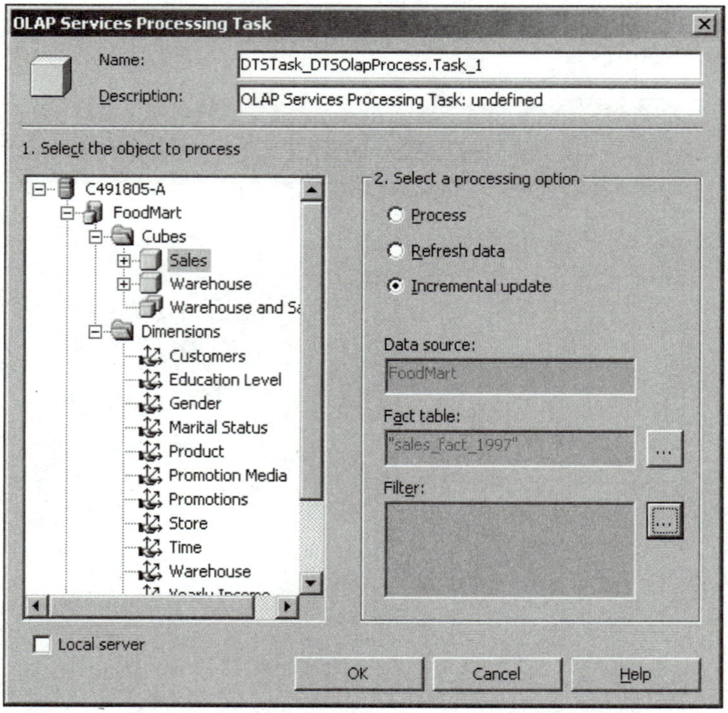

The dialog for the OLAP Services Processing Task with Incremental Update selected

- **Data source**: This text box displays the data source for an incremental update of a cube or partition. You can change the data source by clicking the ellipse (...) button next to the Fact table box which launches the Choose Fact Table dialog box.

- **Fact table**: This text box displays the fact table for an incremental update of a cube or partition. You can change the fact table by clicking the ellipse (...) button next to it as mentioned in the Data Source section above.
- **Filter**: This text box displays the filter for an incremental update of a cube or partition. A filter limits the fact table records used in the incremental update. You can add or change a filter by clicking the ellipse (...) button next to it, which launches the Filter Expression dialog box.

Benefits Of Using OLAP Services Processing Task

The benefit of using this tool is that it allows you to make the process of data transfer and processing the OLAP objects a seamless and integrated one. You can also benefit from DTS Designer's features when processing OLAP data by imposing some precedence constraints, such as preventing a dimension from processing until data transfer to its table is completed successfully.

Data Transformation Example

The following is a presentation of an example on how data transformations can be conducted using packages designed inside the DTS Designer. This example is available with SQL Server 7.0 in the directory where the developer tools are located. This folder is usually located at: [Drive Letter]:\MSSQL7\DevTools\Samples\DTS\dtsDemo.EXE. This is a self-extracting zip file that, when it is run, will expand several files. To install the sample, you need to run the file `OltpStar.bat` located in the Designer subfolder.

Database Schemas

This sample application shows how data can be transferred from an order entry online transaction processing system (OLTP) to a dimensional database for an online analytical processing (OLAP) system. Two SQL Server 7 databases are installed with the sample application, the OLTP database simply called (OLTP), and the OLAP database called (Star). The schemas for these two databases are presented in the following two figures respectively.

The OLTP database is fully normalized to optimize the order entry by multiple salespersons. This database consists of thirteen (13) tables the most important of which are the orders and order details tables. The remaining tables, basically link to these two tables to ensure the normalization we discussed earlier. The Star database, on the other hand, consists of five tables, one fact table called the Sales table and four dimension tables, called Customers, Product, Time, and Geography.

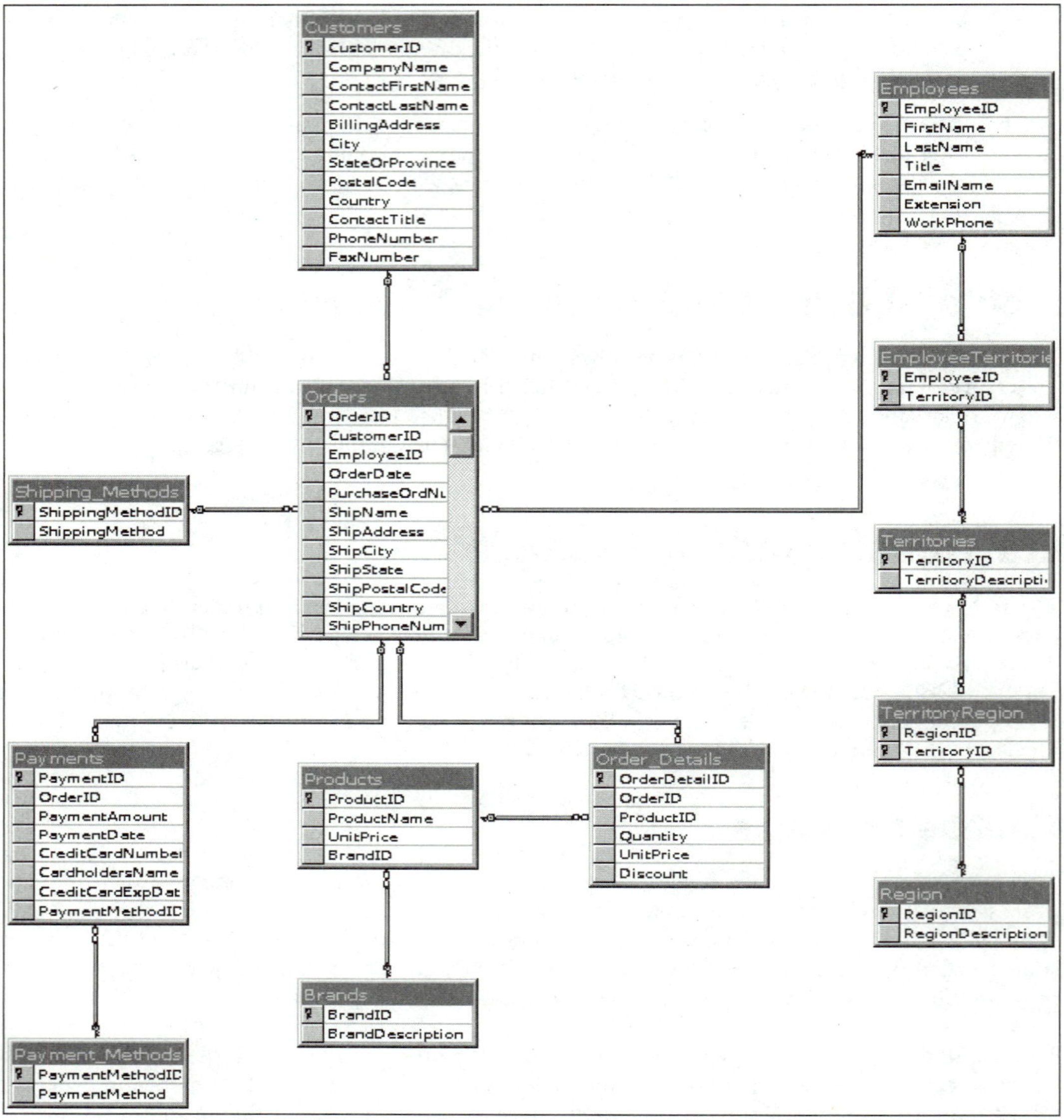

Schema of the order entry "OLTP" database

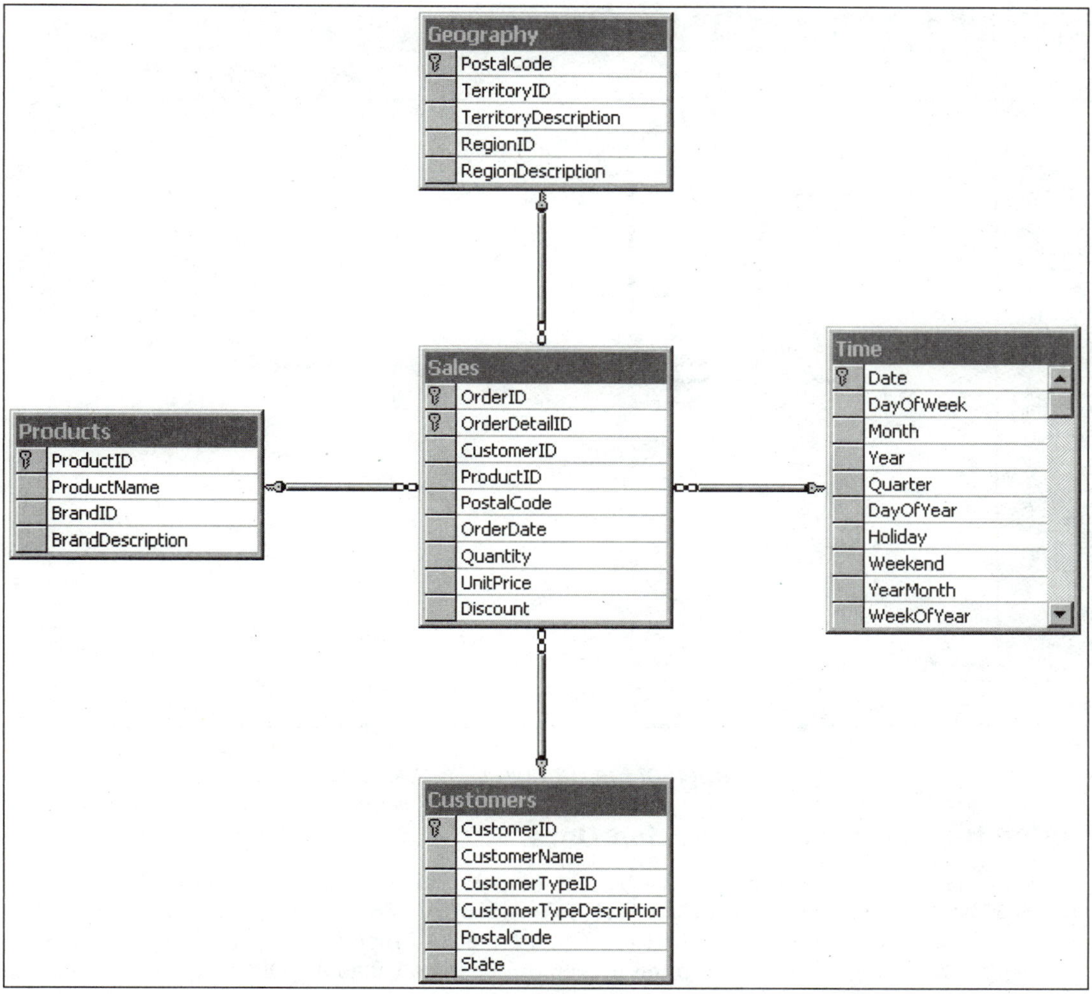

The star schema of the "Star" OLAP database

DTS Package Design

Next, we need to design a DTS package that can perform the transformation from the source OLTP database to the destination Star data mart. The following figure shows the design of the DTS package. The design includes five connections to the OLTP database (OLTP1 through OLTP5), and two connections to the Star database (Data Mart1 and Data Mart2).

In this design, you can see 5 transform data tasks and one on-success precedence constraint. You should start by laying out this design before setting the properties of the different items in it. Please note that the precedence constraint has to be added last. Adding it before adding the final transform data task between OLTP5 and Data Mart2 will generate an error and it will not work. A precedence constraint always connects between two tasks in the DTS Designer. The first four transformations are used to transform dimension data from the OLTP database to the Star database (Data Mart).

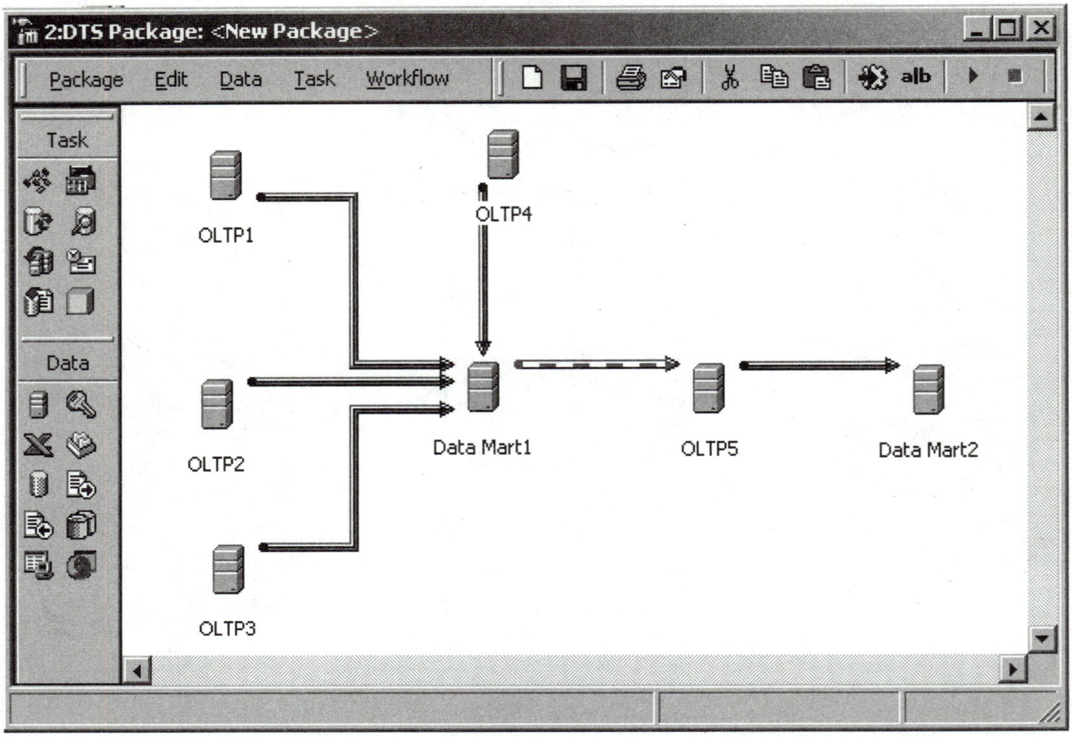

Design of the Sample DTS package

Loading the Customer Dimension Data

Let's now see how we can configure loading the customer dimension data from the OLTP system into the Star database. The Transform Data Task linking OLTP1 and Data Mart1 will be used for this purpose. Double click it to launch the Data Transformation Properties dialog box (see the next figure below). In the dialog, set the description text box to Loading Customer Dimension Data. Then, in the SQL box, type the following SQL code:

```
SELECT CustomerID = CustomerID, CustomerName=CompanyName,
    CustomerTypeID = (CustomerID % 4),
    CustomerTypeDescription = CASE (CustomerID % 4) WHEN 0
        THEN 'Excellent' WHEN 1 THEN 'Good' WHEN 2 then 'Average'
        WHEN 3 THEN 'Poor' ELSE 'Average' END,
    PostalCode=PostalCode, State=StateOrProvince
FROM Customers
```

The modulus operator divides two numbers and returns the remainder of the division. Thus, 10%6 = 4

In the Destination page of the Data Transformation dialog, select the Star database and the Customer table as the destination. Make sure the mappings of the columns from the source SQL statement to the destination Customer table are accurate and close the dialog.

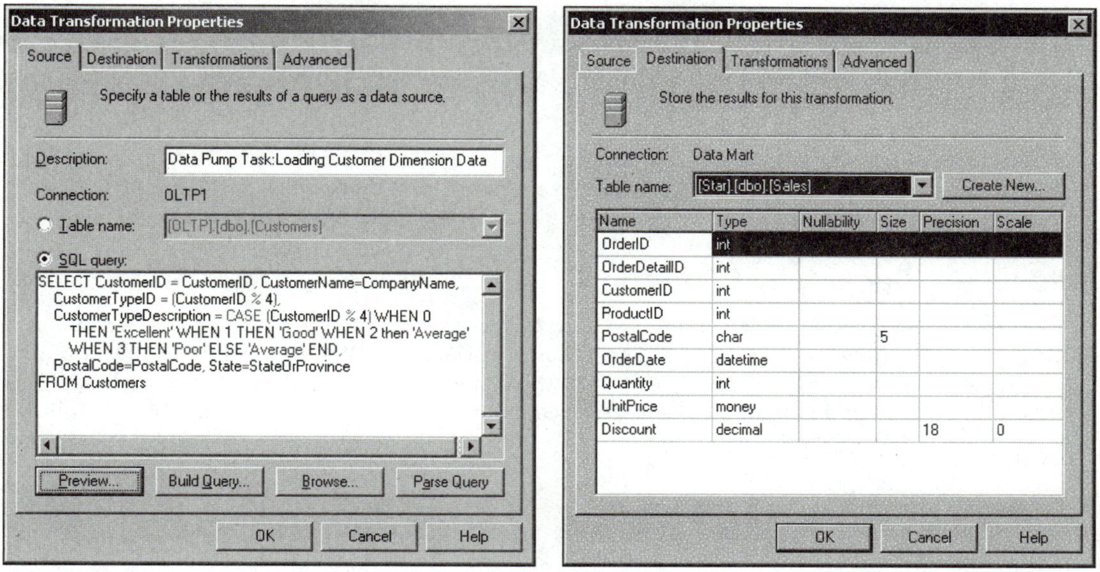

Configuring the Data Transformation task to load the customer dimension data

Building the Time Dimension

Building (or loading) the `Time` dimension in the data mart is similar to loading the `Customer` dimension, except for the source and destination. The Transform Data Task linking OLTP2 and Data Mart1 will be used for this purpose. In the source page of the Data Transformation Properties dialog, set the description to Loading Time Dimension Data, and in the SQL Query box, type the following SQL code:

```
--Use the DatePart function to separate out the different
--parts of the data field that you want to use in the dimension.

SELECT DISTINCT
    DATE=O.OrderDate,
    DayOfWeek=DATENAME(dw,O.OrderDate),
    Month = DatePart(mm,O.OrderDate),
    Year = DatePart(yy,O.OrderDate),
    Quarter =DatePart(qq,O.OrderDate),
    DayOfYear= DatePart(dy,O.OrderDate),
    Holiday='N',
    Weekend = CASE DATEPART(dw,O.OrderDate)

WHEN (1) THEN 'Y'
    WHEN (7) THEN 'Y' ELSE 'N'
        END,
        YearMonth = DATENAME(month, O.OrderDate) +
              '_' + DATENAME(year,O.OrderDate),
        WEEKOFYEAR=DATEPART(wk,O.OrderDate)
    FROM Orders O
```

Notice in the code above, the use of date functions to create the values needed for the additional fields in the `Time` table in the Star database that do not originally exist in the `Orders` table in the OLTP database. For example, to get a quarter field value, the function: `DatePart(qq,o.OrderDate)` was used.

In the Destination page of the indicated dialog, set the destination table to be the `Time` table of the `Star` database. Verify the column mappings in the Transformations page of the dialog box, and verify the query syntax and validity by pressing the Parse Query button in the Source page.

Building the Geography Dimension

Building the `Geography` dimension in the data mart is similar to loading the `Customer` dimension, except for the source and destination. The Transform Data Task linking OLTP3 and Data Mart1 will be used for this purpose. In the source page of the Data Transformation Properties dialog, set the description to Loading Geography Dimension Data, and in the SQL Query box, type the following SQL code:

```
SELECT PostalCode = T.TerritoryID, TerritoryID= T.TerritoryID,
    TerritoryDescription = T.TerritoryDescription, RegionID = R.RegionID,
    RegionDescription = R.RegionDescription
FROM Territories T, Region R, TerritoryRegion TR
WHERE T.TerritoryID = TR.TerritoryID AND TR.RegionID = R.RegionID
```

In the Destination page of the indicated dialog, set the destination table to be the `Geography` table of the `Star` database. Verify the column mappings in the Transformations page of the dialog box, and verify the query syntax and validity by pressing the Parse Query button in the Source page.

Building the Product Dimension

Building the `Product` dimension in the data mart is similar to building the `Customer` dimension, except for the source and destination. The Transform Data Task linking OLTP4 and Data Mart1 will be used for this purpose. In the source page of the Data Transformation Properties dialog, set the description to Loading Product Dimension Data, and in the SQL Query box, type the following SQL code:

```
SELECT ProductID = P.ProductID, ProductName = P.ProductName,
    BrandID = B.BrandID, BrandDescription = B.BrandDescription
FROM Brands B, Products P
WHERE B.BrandID = P. BrandID
```

In the Destination page, select the `Products` table from the `Star` database as the destination table for this transform data task. In the Transformations page, click ActiveX Script, and then select all columns in the source and destination tables by holding the *Shift* key while you select them. Make sure ActiveX Script is selected in the New Transformation drop-down list. Then unmap and remap the columns using the Delete and New buttons respectively. The ActiveX Script Transformation Properties dialog appears. Set the language to VB Script and modify the script in the script area changing the case of `ProductName` and `BrandDescription` columns to uppercase using the UCASE() function. The ActiveX script should then look like:

```
Function Main()
DTSDestination("ProductID")=DTSSource("ProductID")
    DTSDestination("ProductName")=UCase(DTSSource("ProductName"))
    DTSDestination("BrandID")=DTSSource("BrandID")
    DTSDestination("BrandDescription")=
    UCase(DTSSource("BrandDescription"))
    DTSDestination("ProductID")=DTSSource("ProductID")
    Main = DTSTransformStat_OK
End Function
```

On the Transformations tab, notice the many-to-many relationship indicated by the mapping diagram (see following figure). Click OK to save the transformations and exit the transform data task.

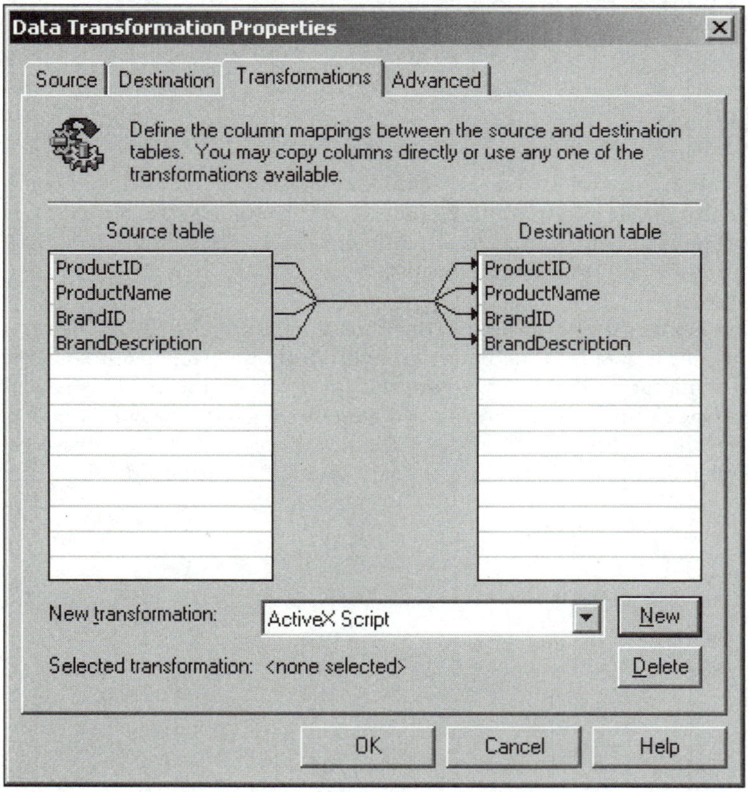

Many-to-many mapping of the product dimension columns

Building the Sales Fact Data

Building the sales fact data in the data mart is similar to building the `Customer` dimension, except for the source and destination. The Transform Data Task linking OLTP5 and Data Mart2 will be used for this purpose. In the source page of the Data Transformation Properties dialog, set the description to Loading Sales Fact Table Data, and in the SQL Query box, type the following SQL code:

```
SELECT OrderID = O.OrderID, OrderDetailID = D.OrderDetailID,
    CustomerID = C.CustomerID, ProductID = D.ProductID,
    PostalCode = C.PostalCode, OrderDate = O.OrderDate,
    Quantity = D.Quantity, UnitPrice = D.UnitPrice, Discount = D.Discount
FROM Orders O, Order_Details D, Customers C
WHERE O.OrderID = D.OrderID AND O.CustomerID = C.CustomerID
ORDER BY OrderID, D.OrderDetailID
```

In the Destination page of the indicated dialog, set the destination table to be the `Sales` table of the `Star` database. Verify the column mappings in the Transformations page of the dialog box, and verify the query syntax and validity by pressing the Parse Query button in the Source page.

With this, the package is designed and ready to run. To run the package, refer to the section earlier in the chapter on executing DTS packages.

Summary

Data Transformation Services is a great technology that makes transforming and loading data into data warehouses an easier and more flexible task. DTS is another feature of Microsoft SQL Server and a presentation of the integration of the different tools and technologies that come with it to work in tandem to produce the best possible results.

Now that we have talked about designing the data warehouse, the OLAP database and cubes, how to transfer and transform data into the data warehouse from heterogeneous sources, you still need to learn about presentation of the data warehouse data in a useful form. This is where Chapter 9 comes in handy. In the mean time, the following two chapters introduce you to a new programming language for the Microsoft OLAP Services, called Multidimensional Expressions (MDX). Learning about this language is a must if you want to learn and apply Microsoft OLAP Services in your projects.

7

Introduction to MDX

With the introduction of the OLE DB Provider for OLAP, which enables access to multidimensional and tabular data, came Multidimensional Expressions (MDX). MDX forms the querying language used by SQL Server OLAP services to manipulate multidimensional data. MDX is installed when you install Microsoft OLAP services and provides a powerful syntax and semantics for querying and manipulating data stored in server-based and local OLAP cubes.

OLAP functions provide the ability to query cube data, define calculated members, and build local cubes. These functions allows for interaction with the PivotTable service and other OLE DB providers to query the cube data and return meaningful resultsets. MDX also allows you to develop your own functions that you can register and operate on multidimensional data accepting arguments and returning values in MDX syntax.

This chapter introduces you to the syntax and semantics of this language and to the powerful features it provides. The areas that we will cover in this chapter include:

- Using SQL when handling dimensional data
- MDX and Metadata
- MDX object model
- MDX construction
- Calculated members
- Named sets
- MDX query syntax

How Good is Good-Old-SQL?

This happens in the same way that the Structured Query Language (SQL) can be used to query data in relational databases, and perform several types of operations on the data in these databases, (OLE DB for OLAP extensions, specifically MDX, can be used to provide similar functionality on multidimensional data.) SQL queries, however, always return two-dimensional resultsets from the OLAP cubes. If you need to return multi-dimensional resultsets, you need to play a number of tricks using views and the like. Even then, the job is anything but easy. It involves several steps of building temporary tables and views before you can reach your destined solution. If you want to easily return multi-dimensional resultsets, you have to use MDX, because MDX does not return a spreadsheet-like resultset; instead, it returns a cube.

Please don't conclude from this that you cannot use regular SQL queries to query OLAP data. You can not only query data with regular SQL, but also execute some data definition language statements (DDL) to create dimension tables or fact tables used in building cubes. Actually, Microsoft added support for SQL in its data abstraction technologies (such as ActiveX Data Objects) to allow access to OLAP data through these technologies by passing regular SQL statement. One thing worth noting with this regard is the introduction of OLE DB provider for OLAP and ADO Multi-Dimensional or ADO MD. The OLE DB for OLAP reference, along with the product documentation discusses these issues in detail. Therefore, I am not going to cover them here, and if you want further information about them, you may refer to the references indicated above.

Could SQL Tricks Do the Job?

As we just discovered, you can use regular SQL queries against the multidimensional database that holds the cubes and their data to return resultsets for your reports. But, how useful are these resultsets, and, if they are not in an optimal form, how can you make them as useful as possible? To illustrate this concept, consider the following example on using regular SQL queries with OLAP cubes. In the example, a query is required to return the total store sales by state and by product category. The schema we are going against is shown in the following figure:

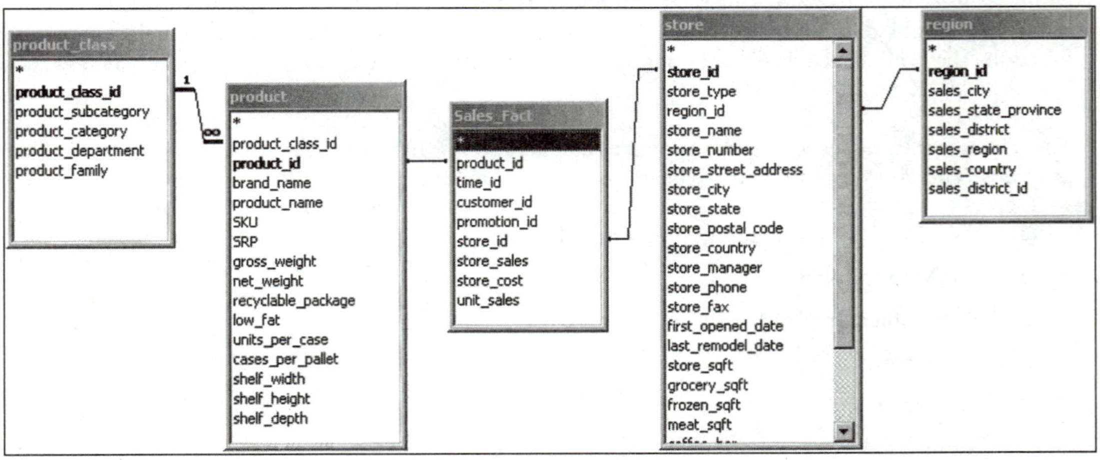

Schema used to retrieve sales by state and product category

The query would look like:

```
SELECT  Sum(sf.store_sales) AS Total_Sales,
   pc.product_category,
   r.sales_state_province
FROM  region r
   INNER JOIN (store s
   INNER JOIN (product_class  pc
   INNER JOIN (product p
   INNER JOIN sales_fact sf ON
      p.product_id = sf.product_id) ON
      pc.product_class_id = p.product_class_id) ON
      s.store_id = sf.store_id) ON
      r.region_id = s.region_id
GROUP BY  pc.product_category,
   r.sales_state_province;
```

The table below represents a partial resultset of this query:

Total_Sales	product_category	sales_state_province
$2,965.62	Baking Goods	BC
$4,400.84	Baking Goods	CA
$2,592.14	Baking Goods	DF
$1,319.59	Baking Goods	Guerrero
$99.87	Baking Goods	Jalisco
$3,624.91	Baking Goods	OR
$4,466.08	Baking Goods	Zacatecas
$2,478.10	Bathroom Products	BC
$3,761.57	Bathroom Products	CA
$2,408.50	Bathroom Products	DF
$1,297.05	Bathroom Products	Guerrero
$6,247.63	Bathroom Products	WA
$1,916.51	Bathroom Products	Yucatan
$3,591.43	Bathroom Products	Zacatecas
$2,575.52	Beer and Wine	BC
$4,016.16	Beer and Wine	CA
$2,245.23	Beer and Wine	DF
$1,415.64	Beer and Wine	Guerrero
$101.47	Beer and Wine	Jalisco
$2,036.28	Beer and Wine	Yucatan
$3,554.12	Beer and Wine	Zacatecas
$2,826.24	Bread	BC
$4,499.86	Bread	CA
$2,601.79	Bread	DF

In the example above, the data returned from the query is represented in tabular form. A more useful form that would be even more readable and multi-dimensional would look like the next table. To reach this representation using SQL, we need to play some tricks in addition to some limiting assumptions as shown below.

The tricks start with building a working storage table from which the desired multi-dimensional representation will be built.

```
CREATE TABLE Total_Sales
        (Sale_State_Province        Varchar(8000) NOT NULL,
         Baking_Goods               Money,
         Bathroom_Products          Money,
         Beer_Wine                  Money,
         Bread                      Money)
Go
```

Notice that this working table does not have a primary key, and the product columns are "nullable". Also notice that we have to know in advance the number of different products that we need to represent in the table. Adding a new product in the future will cause this solution to be re-designed.

Total_Sales	**product_category**			
sales_state_province	**Baking Goods**	**Bathroom Products**	**Beer and Wine**	**Bread**
BC	$2,965.62	$2,478.10	$2,575.52	$2,826.24
CA	$4,400.84	$3,761.57	$4,016.16	$4,499.86
DF	$2,592.14	$2,408.50	$2,245.23	$2,601.79
Guerrero	$1,319.59	$1,297.05	$1,415.64	$3,432.00
Jalisco	$99.87	$12,452.00	$101.47	$2,344.00
OR	$3,624.91	$14,234.60	$231.45	$3,452.00
WA	$2,245.60	$6,247.63	$643.22	$2,321.00
Yucatan	$3,556.87	$1,916.51	$2,036.28	$3,443.25
Zacatecas	$4,466.08	$3,591.43	$3,554.12	$2,312.12

Multi-dimensional representation of the SQL query results shown in the previous table

The next step is to fill the table we have just created with data relating to the different products using the following SQL statements.

```
INSERT INTO Total_Sales (Sale_State_Province, Baking_Goods)
    SELECT r.sales_state_province,
        Sum(sf.store_sales)
    FROM  region r
        INNER  JOIN (store s
        INNER  JOIN (product_class  pc
        INNER  JOIN (product p
```

```
          INNER  JOIN sales_fact_1997 sf ON
              p.product_id = sf.product_id) ON
              pc.product_class_id = p.product_class_id) ON
              s.store_id = sf.store_id) ON
             r.region_id = s.region_id
      WHERE pc.product_category = "Baking Goods"
      GROUP BY r.sales_state_province
GO

INSERT INTO Total_Sales (Sale_State_Province, Bathroom_Products)
      SELECT  r.sales_state_province,
          Sum(sf.store_sales)
      FROM    region r
          INNER  JOIN (store s
          INNER  JOIN (product_class  pc
          INNER  JOIN (product p
          INNER  JOIN sales_fact_1997 sf ON
          p.product_id = sf.product_id) ON
          pc.product_class_id = p.product_class_id) ON
          s.store_id = sf.store_id) ON
          r.region_id = s.region_id
      WHERE pc.product_category = "Bathroom Products"
      GROUP BY r.sales_state_province
GO

INSERT INTO Total_Sales (Sale_State_Province, Beer_Wine)
      SELECT r.sales_state_province,
          Sum(sf.store_sales)
      FROM    region r
          INNER  JOIN (store s
          INNER  JOIN (product_class  pc
          INNER  JOIN (product p
          INNER  JOIN sales_fact_1997 sf ON
              p.product_id = sf.product_id) ON
              pc.product_class_id = p.product_class_id) ON
              s.store_id = sf.store_id) ON
              r.region_id = s.region_id
      WHERE pc.product_category = "Beer and Wine"
      GROUP BY r.sales_state_province
GO

INSERT INTO Total_Sales (Sale_State_Province, Bread)
      SELECT r.sales_state_province,
      Sum(sf.store_sales)
      FROM    region r
           INNER  JOIN (store s
           INNER  JOIN (product_class  pc
           INNER  JOIN (product p
           INNER  JOIN sales_fact_1997 sf ON
               p.product_id = sf.product_id) ON
               pc.product_class_id = p.product_class_id) ON
               s.store_id = sf.store_id) ON
               r.region_id = s.region_id
      WHERE pc.product_category = "Bread"
      GROUP BY r.sales_state_province
GO
```

Of course, you might ask, what if one of the columns relating to the product categories includes null values? In this case, we need to change the way we are building the summary table by using a view that selects all states/provinces with the help of outer joins, and using this view to populate the left column of the working table. The next step would be to use the same view in our statements that populate the product category columns to ensure that values are inserted properly.

In summary, it can be increasingly difficult and tricky to accomplish a simple task like the goal we are trying to accomplish using only traditional SQL. Therefore, Microsoft introduced MDX as a powerful alternative that allows you to build views like the one discussed above with ease and allows you to manipulate multidimensional data stored in cubes in an easy fashion. In contrast to the previous SQL example, by the time you finish reading this chapter and the next chapter, you will see how the same problem can be solved with ease using MDX.

MDX Basics

As we saw in previous chapters, a sales and inventory solution can be represented in a multi-dimensional schema. The schema is composed of a set of cubes with each cube having measures and dimensions. You also saw that members of a dimension might be consolidated or aggregated along a hierarchy. Some dimensions, such as the time dimension, can have more than one hierarchy allowing members to roll up in multiple ways. Each hierarchy has levels, and each level is made up of a set of members. Understanding these hierarchies is essential to understanding MDX, because MDX is built to deal with these hierarchies. Where possible, in this chapter, I will introduce many examples, while explaining the different aspects of MDX.

Notes on the Syntax

Every programming language comes with unique syntax features that differentiate it from other languages. Historically, Microsoft tried as much as possible to unify the syntax of many of the languages used in its products. Hence, the VB/VBA/VB Script (VBS) family came about. VBA syntax used in MS Office applications is very similar to VB syntax. The syntax used in VBS is also very similar to VB. You can, sometimes, cut and paste code from one of these languages into a program written in another language. With MDX, however, the syntax is completely different from anything you have seen in other Microsoft products. This is mainly because of the nature of the language and what it represents, and also because it is still in its first release.

On MDX Functions

Functions and their operators are largely optional in MDX. You may choose to include the whole function call and its operators if you want, but this will create long code lines. Therefore, it is a good idea to leave out some of the unused operators when possible. The syntax of MDX functions is irregular. Two representations are used for functions, the standard VB-style format of calling a function as `Function(arguments)`, and the object-style representation in which the function is called as if it were a method of an object using the dot notation (`.Function()`). There are no standard rules for using these two representations, you just have to know which to use with which function. This is where code-generating tools become handy. The Visual Basic MDX sample application, covered in Chapter 8, which ships with OLAP services, is a good start.

An example on the first representation is the `Hierarchize(set)` function which returns the given set after putting the members of its dimensions into hierarchical order. An example on using object notation for MDX functions is the `member.Properties(property name)` function. This function returns the value of the given property, which is expressed or evaluated as a string, for each member of the dimension.

One final note on MDX functions is that the functions that don't take arguments don't take parentheses. This is similar to Visual Basic notation and unlike the syntax for Visual J++ or Visual C++ functions. For example, if a function does not have any arguments, it can be called as: `Call FunctionName` or `Call object.FunctionName`, and not as: `Call FunctionName()` or `Call object.FunctionName()`.

On Language Syntax

Let's take the simple query that retrieves the total sales for stores in the USA for the second and third quarter of 1998 (all products are included). Don't worry now about the syntax and knowing what everything in the query is. The remainder of the chapter covers all of these areas.

```
SELECT
    {[Measures].[StoreSales] } on columns,
    {[Time].[1998].[Q2], [Time].[1998].[Q3]} on rows
FROM SalesCube
WHERE ([Store].[States].[USA])
```

The different parts of this query are explained in the following diagram. Please note that the diagram corresponds only to this sample query. Other queries could very well have additional parts, or miss some of the parts shown in the diagram.

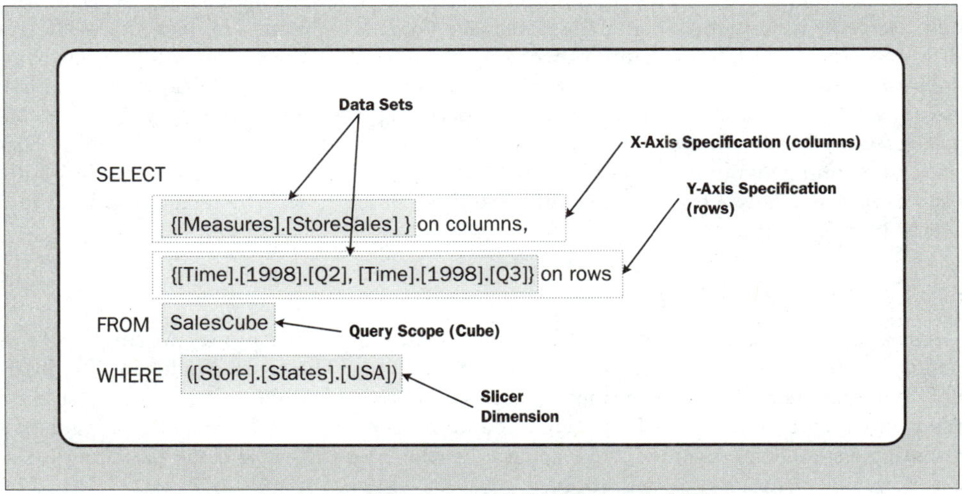

diagram showing the different parts of the first sample MDX query

The following may be concluded from the syntax of the query above:

- You notice that MDX uses curly brackets "{}" to represent a set of members of a dimension or group of dimensions. In the query above, the only dimension is the time dimension, besides the measure dimension, of course.
- You also may conclude that axes are defined in the query by mapping dimensions onto them. The first three axes of an MDX query are called rows, columns, and pages. If more than one dimension is mapped onto an axis, the axis will consist of tuples (elements) that include members of each of the mapped dimensions.

- The order of numbering of axes is columns, then rows, then pages. We will see what axes are, in more detail shortly.
- The FROM clause includes the name of the cube on which the query is based. Only one cube per query is supported in the current version of Microsoft OLAP Services.
- The WHERE clause includes slicer dimensions by specifying the one member included in these dimensions in the query. In our example, the slicer dimension is the geographic location dimension. The only member included on the State level is "USA".
- You, finally, notice some similarity between the general syntax of MDX queries and regular SQL queries. After all, the two kinds of queries use the clauses: SELECT...FROM...WHERE. However, as you learn more about MDX, you will also learn that it diverges significantly from regular SQL in many ways to allow it to support multi-dimensional data.

How About Some Definitions Before We Go Into The Details?

The following are definitions of terms used in this chapter. These terms identify the parts of an MDX statement and the returned cube among other things. These definitions identify what is referred to as the MDX object model. This model is very rich and is based on the OLAP services' dimension and cube. These definitions also are touched upon in several locations later in the chapter. A basic understanding of these concepts is very important. Therefore, unless you are already familiar with MDX grammar, you need to study these definitions before proceeding to the next sections. These definitions have to be considered in light of Chapters 3 and 4. In these chapters, the basics of multidimensional databases are discussed, which is what multidimensional expressions represent. The following diagram can be used to help understand these definitions. In this figure, part (a) represents a cube with three dimensions, product, time, and geography. A query against this cube yields a subset shown in part (b) of the figure. The subset includes only a few members of these three dimensions. The resulting cube is formed by the intersection of these dimensions.

Tuple

A tuple is a collection of members from different dimensions. For example, (Michigan, Q2) is a tuple formed by members of two dimensions: geography and time. The tuple (Michigan, Q2, food items) is formed by members of three dimensions: geography, time, and product. A tuple can have a single member, in which case it is called a degenerated tuple. For instance, Michigan is a degenerated tuple representing a state level member of the geography dimension. A tuple is the basic unit for forming an axis, as you will see in the next definition.

Axis

An axis is a collection of members from one or more dimensions organized as tuples. The axis is used to locate or filter specific values in a cube along the dimension members they represent. As an example, in a query returning sales by state and quarter for a product family, you may say a maximum of three axes can be used as a result of the query with each axis representing one of the three dimensions: geography, time and product. If some of these dimensions are nested, the number of axes can be reduced, for example, nesting the geography and product dimensions results in an axis with tuples, consisting of a member of each dimension projected on the axis. On the other hand, the time dimension, in this case, is projected on the other axis (y-axis). This axis holds tuples representing time values, like: first quarter of 1998, second quarter of 1998, etc.

OLAP Services supports a maximum number of dimensions in a cube of 63 in addition to one measure dimension. Therefore, the maximum number of axes possible in an MDX query is 64 axes, assuming no nesting of dimensions is taking place. However, in cellsets resulting from MDX queries, it is rare to have more than 4 axes at one time.

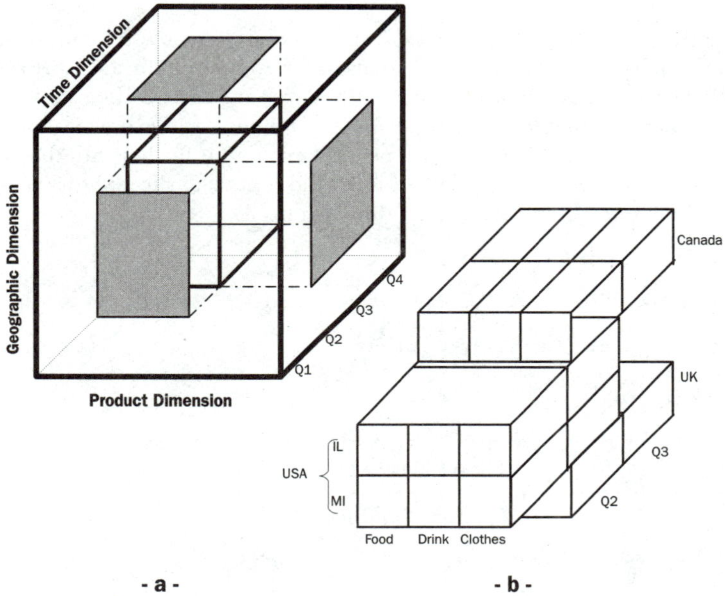

Understanding the basic definitions of MDX

Cellset

A cellset is the result of an MDX query on multidimensional data. It identifies a resulting cube that is a subset of the original cube. In the above figure, the smaller cube shown in part (b) is a cellset representing the results of the MDX query. A cellset consists of a collection of axes, usually no more than four axes and typically only two or three. The figure shows that the resulting cellset can have up to three axes corresponding to the three dimensions of the set.

Cell

A cell is an object positioned at the intersection of axis coordinates. Each cell has multiple pieces of information associated with it, including the data itself, a formatted string (the displayable form of cell data), and the cell ordinal value. (Each cell has a unique ordinal value in the cellset.) The ordinal value of the first cell in the cellset is zero, while the leftmost cell in the second row of a cellset, with eight columns would have an ordinal value of eight as shown in the following diagram.

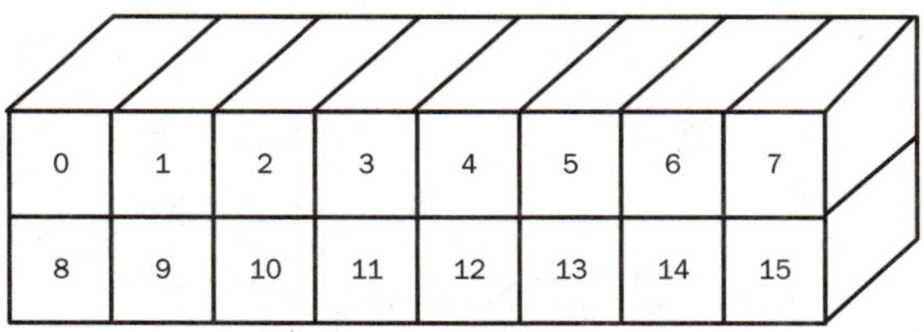

A cellset consisting of 16 cells

Slicer

Sometimes a dimension only contributes one measure to the MDX query. Such a dimension is referred to as a slicer dimension. This dimension appears in the WHERE clause of the MDX statement. In the figure shown previously (*Understanding the basic definitions of MDX*), the slicer dimension is the geography dimension where a slice containing US data only, is taken at the country level.

To make these concepts even clearer, let's look at the example below. The following table shows the results of an MDX query returning sales information for companies in the USA region over the quarters of 1998 and for several product families. This table represents the US slice shown in the figure shown previously (*Understanding the basic definitions of MDX*). Don't worry for now if you don't understand the query and its specific parts yet, since this will be explained a bit further into the chapter. Also, please note that the slicer in the query is represented in a bold font. The slicer shows that we only picked the USA country level member from the product dimension.

```
SELECT
    {[Product].[Product Family].Members} on columns,
    {[Time].[1998].[Quarters].Members} on rows,
    {[Measures].[Store Sales]} on pages
FROM SalesCube
WHERE ([Store].[All Stores].[USA])
```

	Total Sales in the USA		
	Product Families		
1998 Quarters	**Food**	**Drinks**	**Cloths**
Q1/1998	$12,525,452	$9,235,765	$11,455,874
Q2/1998	$14,142,343	$12,525,452	$12,525,452
Q3/1998	$15,123,042	$12,525,452	$12,525,452
Q4/1998	$11,002,002	$12,525,452	$12,525,452

In this example, the measure dimension is the total sales figure. There are three axes that represent the time, product, and sales measure dimensions. On the other hand, only one member, USA, represents the geography dimension. Therefore, the two dimensions, product and time are axis dimensions, while the geography dimension is a slicer dimension. An example of a cell is the cell resulting from the intersection of the x-axis (products) and the y-axis (time) for the members: Drinks, Q3/1998. The data value of this cell (shown in bold face) is $12,525,452. The ordinal value of this cell in the resulting cellset is 7. The ordinal value is calculated by considering the first cell in the first row as number 0, and adding one to this number as we move to the right and to the bottom of the cellset.

Let's Examine a Simple MDX Query ...

Just like the purpose of a regular SQL SELECT query is to specify a dataset (also referred to as resultset or recordset), the general MDX statement also specifies a dataset. However, in order for the MDX statement to do so, it must contain information about the following:

- **Scope (cube):** Each MDX query has a scope that is defined by one or more cubes. These cube(s) are a basic component of the MDX statement and determine what kind of data is the query expected to return. A query that includes the Sales cube for instance, is expected to return dataset about the sales facts such as profit, revenue, and cost, in terms of the sales cube dimensions (e.g. time, geography, customer, and product). Please note that the current release of MDX supports only one cube in the FROM clause. Future releases may support multiple cubes.
- **Axes:** The number of axes is another part of the MDX statement that has to be defined. Each axis defines one or more dimensions along which data is to be aggregated. For instance, an axis that includes the time and product dimensions will result in aggregations along these dimensions with each tuple including members of the two dimensions.
- **Dimensions:** Dimensions are projected on the axes with the possibility of nesting them, which makes such dimensions and the level of their nesting another essential part of the MDX statement.
- **Included members of projected dimensions:** The whole dimension isn't included all the time. Therefore, the included members of the dimension or included member tuples are another part of the statement, in addition to the sort order of such dimensions. As an example, the time dimension may have year members for 1997 and 1998. If we only include 1998, then 1998 represents an included member of the projected time dimension. 1997, on the other hand, represents an excluded member of the same dimension.
- **Non-projected dimensions:** Sometimes you need to filter members of projected dimensions based on non-projected dimensions. This also makes such members from a non-projected dimension part of the MDX statement. This will become more clear when you read about filtering members, wich is explained later in the chapter.

A basic form of the simple MDX query is:

```
SELECT <axis_specification> [, <axis_specification>...]
FROM <cube_specification>
WHERE <slicer_specification>
```

The following is a brief explanation of each part of this statement.

The axis specification includes the number of axes included in the statement and the members of each axis. This information is defined after the SELECT keyword in the MDX statement. Each one of the <axis_specification> parts specifies one axis. The number of the <axis_specification> clauses included in the MDX statement defines the number of axes.

To better understand the concept of the axis specification, consider expanding the example illustrated in the previous table, to include another dimension nested with the product dimension, that is the customer dimension. The expanded example is illustrated in the following table.

```
SELECT
    CROSSJOIN(
        {[Customers].[All Customers].[USA].[ABC Inc.],
            [All Customers].[Canada].[XYZ Ltd.]},
        {[Product].[Product Family].Members}) on columns,
    {[Time].[Year].[1998].Children} on rows,
    {[Measures].[Store Sales]} on pages
FROM
    SalesCube
WHERE
    ([Store].[All Stores].[USA])
```

In the query above, we are using several functions, such as: CrossJoin, Members, and Children. These functions are explained in detail in Chapter 8 and in Appendix A.

	Total Store Sales in the USA					
	ABC Inc.			**XYZ Ltd.**		
	Product Families			**Product Families**		
1998 Quarters	**Food**	**Drinks**	**Clothes**	**Food**	**Drinks**	**Clothes**
Q1/1998	$12,525,452	$12,525,452	$9,235,765	$4,655,874	$4,235,765	$5,455,874
Q2/1998	$14,142,343	$14,142,343	$12,525,452	$5,525,452	$5,525,452	$6,525,452
Q3/1998	$15,123,042	$15,123,042	$12,525,452	$5,525,452	$8,525,852	$7,525,452
Q4/1998	$11,002,002	$11,002,002	$12,525,452	$6,525,452	$7,553,452	$8,525,452

An expanded version of the example illustrated previously with the addition of the customer dimension

In this table, you can see that the horizontal axis (x-axis) includes two nested dimensions, customer and product families. The sales figures in the cells of the table show that the axis defines 6 tuples with each tuple having a member of each of these two dimensions. The tuples, therefore, look like this:

```
(ABC Inc, Food)
(ABC Inc, Drinks)
(ABC Inc, Clothes)
(XYZ Ltd, Foods)
(XYZ Ltd, Drinks)
(XYZ Ltd, Clothes)
```

Therefore, you may think of an axis as a set of tuples set in a linear form. If the axis has one dimension, each tuple will include a member of the dimension. If the axis has multiple dimensions, say n dimensions, then each tuple includes a member of each of the nested dimensions. To represent the tuples illustrated in this paragraph in the MDX statement, you need to use the unique names of the members included within these tuples. Thus, they become:

`([Company].[ABC Inc.], [Products].[Food]),`
`([Company].[XYZ Ltd.], [Products].[Food])`, and so on.

If the tuple is composed of members of more than one dimension, you should enclose the tuple in parentheses. However, if a tuple is composed of members of only one dimension, you don't need to use the parentheses.

Let's now look at the vertical axis (y-axis). There is only one dimension included in the y-axis, the time dimension at the quarter level. The tuples of this axis include the members of the dimension included in the table, that is:

```
Q1/1998
Q2/1998
Q3/1998
Q4/1998
```

Dimensions available in a cube are typically divided into two sets: axis dimensions, and slicer dimensions. Axis dimensions are dimensions for which data is retrieved for multiple members. With slicer dimensions, data is retrieved for only one member, and usually appears in the WHERE clause of the MDX query. The example illustrated in the table in the previous section explains this concept very well. Besides the measures, the geography dimension is the slicer dimension because only one member, USA, is included from it. As you can see, the components of the WHERE clause are surrounded by parentheses, even if only one element is defined in this clause.

The query discussed in this section is just the general form of a simple MDX query that is meant to familiarize you with the syntax of this language. MDX queries have many variations that add to their complexity. Some of these variations are discussed later in the chapter when more than one dimension and more than two axes are involved. Hence, before we discuss more complex forms of the MDX query, let's look at how metadata is represented in MDX. Knowing this will help us to gain a greater understanding of the syntax of the more complicated MDX queries discussed later in the chapter, and in the next chapter.

MDX Representation of Metadata

OLAP metadata includes information on OLAP cubes, measures, dimensions, levels, members, hierarchies, and member properties. All of these items are represented in some way or another in MDX queries. Therefore, it is important to study the relationship between OLAP metadata and MDX queries, because this study will help us learn about the representation of metadata.

Using Square Brackets

In MDX, you can refer to names of metadata items in one of two ways, delimited and non-delimited. The delimiting character is the square brackets "`[ ]`". As you probably know, naming dimensions, cubes, measures, and member properties follows some rules, such as starting with an alphabetic character. Naming dimension level members, however, does not follow any rules. If you choose not to delimit the names referring to metadata in your MDX queries, additional rules may have to be fulfilled, even for member names. One important rule, for instance, is that you cannot have spaces in the name.

If you use square brackets to delimit member and other metadata names, many of the rules are eased. Name-specific rules still apply for cubes, dimensions, measures, and member properties. If the name of the member includes a square bracket, the escape sequence "[[" or "]]" should be used. For example, if the member name is `Chocolate Milk with [Marshmallows]` then the representation of this member in MDX queries is: `[Chocolate Milk with [[Marshmallows]]]`. A member could also be empty which is represented simply as `[ ]`.

Using the Period in Metadata Representation

If an identifier has more than one name part, MDX uses periods to separate these parts. For example, to refer to the cheese level of the product dimension, you may write: `[Products].[Food].[Dairy].[Cheese]`, which identifies cheese as the food product family of the dairy category. The periods are placed between the brackets, not within. Hence, `[Products].[Food].[Dairy].[Cheese]` is not equal to `[Products].[Food].[Dairy.Cheese]`. The later represents a food product category named `Dairy.Cheese`. It does not represent the cheese subcategory of the dairy category of the food product family.

Establishing Unique Names

When referring to metadata names, it is very helpful to use unique names. For example, if you have a dimension called "`Time`", you can refer to it directly by its name if the name is unique. Otherwise, you will have to identify it by the cube name, then its name with a period in between, such as `[SalesCube].[Time]`. For an even better example, when you refer to a level of the time dimension, let's say the year level, specifically 1998, you need to write: `[Time].[Year].[1998]`. Generally speaking, the following rules can be used to establish unique names in MDX. These rules apply within the context of the cube. If you are building unique names outside the context of a certain cube, you need to prefix all these names defined below by the cube name in square brackets followed by a period.

Dimensions and Measures

Since dimension and measure names are unique within the same cube, you can uniquely identify a dimension or a measure, simply by using their name within the context of the cube. For example, the name `[Time]` or `[Store Sales]` uniquely identify the time dimension and the sales measure in the current cube.

Hierarchies

A hierarchy can be defined by prefixing its name, which is enclosed in square brackets, by the name of the dimension it belongs to (enclosed in brackets) and followed by a period. For example, to refer to the fiscal hierarchy in the time dimension, you may write: `[Time].[Fiscal]`. If only one hierarchy exists in a dimension, there is no need to represent its name. The name of the dimension will be the same as that of the hierarchy. For example, if there is no fiscal hierarchy in the time dimension, the implicit time hierarchy can be simply represented as `[Time]` instead of `[Time].[Time]`.

Levels

Continuing along the same path as the above two sections, the name of the level is identified by the name of the dimension in square brackets followed also by the name of the hierarchy in square brackets, then by the name of the level. Periods separate the names of the dimension, hierarchy, and level. For example, to identify the year level in the fiscal hierarchy, you can write: `[Time].[Fiscal].[Year]`, and to identify the State level of the geographic region dimension, you can write: `[Region].[State]` assuming that there is one implicit hierarchy in the geographic region dimension.

Members

Identifying member names is a little trickier than the previous names we have identified so far. The difference here is that you will have to literally go through the hierarchy adding the names of the members at all levels above the level of the member of interest. For example, to identify the first month of the third fiscal quarter of 1998, you may write: `[Time].[Fiscal].[All Time].[1998].[Quarter 3].[April]`, assuming that the fiscal year 1998 starts on the first day of October 1997. As another example, to identify the Detroit member of City level of the geographic dimension, you can write: `[Region].[All Regions].[USA].[Michigan].[Detroit]`.

Member Properties

To uniquely identify a member property, you need to add the name of the member property following the name of its level with a period between the two names. For example, the unique name for the customer contact's age, you write: `[Customer].[Contact].[age]`.

More On MDX Queries

As promised at the end of the simple MDX query section, we will now examine the construct of MDX queries in more detail. In this section, we will see how punctuation, operators, and functions are used in the MDX query, and then we will discuss the special keyword, `WITH`, which is used to define dimensional calculations in the query.

Constructing MDX Sets

MDX cellsets (or sets) are an important part of the MDX statement. They are often seen in the SELECT part where they reflect the cells of the cube that are to be returned from the query. Sets are usually surrounded by brace brackets "`{`" and "`}`". Like any programming language, MDX has a number of operators that it uses to identify these sets. You may, for instance use the comma and colon to separate members in cellsets. You may also use the period and the "`.Members`" operator to return the members in a dimension, level, or hierarchy. This section examines the basic operators, including the comma, colon, "`.members`", in addition to some of the basic function used in the MDX queries to identify data sets, such as `Crossjoin()`, `Order()`, and `Filter()`.

Separation of Set Elements (The Comma)

The comma (`,`) is one of the most widely used operators, which is present in almost every MDX query because it is an essential part of the set construction. The comma is the operator that separates the elements of such sets (tuples and subsets). For example, you can see how the comma is used to identify a set composed of the first three quarters of 1998.

```
{[Time].[Quarter1/1998], [Time].[Quarter2/1998], [Time].[Quarter3/1998]}
```

Another example is the set that holds three states, Michigan, Ohio, and Illinois, in addition to Canada along the `Store` dimension. In this example, the set is actually composed of two members at the country level, USA and Canada. The USA member is also composed of the three states mentioned above. The set, therefore, identifies members of two levels of the geographical dimension (Store).

```
{{[Store].[USA].[MI], [Store].[USA].[OH], [Store].[IL]}, [Store].[Canada]}
```

Identifying Ranges (Colon)

Sets may include ranges of members of a dimension, dimension level, or hierarchy. As we have seen before, OLAP services organize data in dimension data in different levels and according to certain hierarchies. The data may be ordered in a logical way to reflect a certain order of the members of the dimension level, or hierarchy. For example, in a time dimension, the members of the month level are usually ordered according to the months of the year beginning with January, and ending with December for a calendar hierarchy.

To express such ranges in MDX sets, you can use the colon operator ":". This is similar to how ranges of cells are defined in Microsoft Excel. Hence, to construct a set that includes all the quarters of 1998, you can write:

```
{[Time].[Calendar].[Quarter1] : [Time].[Calendar].[Quarter4]}
```

And to identify the months of fiscal 1998, assuming that the fiscal year starts on the first day of October, you can write:

```
{[Time].[Fiscal].[October 1997] : [Time].[Fiscal].[September 1998]}
```

Notice that the 1998 fiscal year actually starts with October 1997 in the example.

You need to be aware that OLAP Services handles ranges in one direction. That is a range given by: `{[Time].[Calendar].[July 1998] : [Time].[Calendar].[February 1998]}` will not return the expected range between February 1998 and July 1998. Instead, it will return the range starting with July 1998 and ending with the last member of the hierarchy at the year level.

Also note that we are including the hierarchy definition in constructing the set when the dimension has more than one hierarchy. This is because OLAP services will not find the dimension and will return an error if the hierarchies are not supplied in this case. If the dimension has one hierarchy that does not have a name, the name of the dimension will be enough to express the members of the set.

A range of one member will return a set with only that member. For instance, the set shown below includes only one member `[July 1998]`.

```
{[Time].[Calendar].[July 1998] : [Time].[Calendar].[July 1998]}
```

You can mix the comma and colon in constructing sets. For instance, if a cell is composed of the range July 1998 to October 1998 in addition to the month of February 1998, you can write the set as:

```
{[Time].[Calendar].[February 1998], [Time].[Calendar].[July 1998] :
[Time].[Calendar].[October 1998]}
```

Identifying the Set Members with the ".Members" Operator

We have so far seen how the comma and colon can be used to help construct a set. However, how can one refer to all members of a dimension, level, or hierarchy without including ranges and individual elements? This question arises when there are many members in a dimension level without a certain logical order. In a situation like this, it makes sense to refer to members of the dimension level altogether with one operator. The answer to this question is to use the "`.Members`" operator. This operator returns the members of the dimension, level, or hierarchy. For example, to return all the product categories in the category level of the product dimension, you can write:

```
{[Product].[Product Category].Members}
```

To build a query in which the members of the product categories level are laid across the columns of the resultset, you can write:

```
SELECT
    {[Product].[Product Category].Members}, …
FROM SalesCube
```

Again, you notice that if a dimension has more than one hierarchy, you need to append the hierarchy name to that of the dimension, otherwise, OLAP services will not be able to recognize the dimension. Of course, if there is only one hierarchy in the dimension, you have the choice of appending it to the name, or not. Finally, you need to keep in mind that when the ".Members" operator is used, it does not return calculated members of the dimension, level, or hierarchy. The solution to this is referring to these members by their names in the set, or using the MDX function AddCalculatedMembers(), which is explained later in the chapter.

CrossJoin()

In the examples we have seen so far, we only included one dimension in the cellset that the queries returned. However, chances are your cells will include members of more than one dimension. How would your MDX query look like to make this happen? The answer lies in the CrossJoin() function. The general syntax for this function is:

```
CrossJoin({Set1}, {Set2}) returns a set composed of all combinations of the
members of {Set1} and {Set2}
```

This function returns the cross product of the members of two different sets. Cross product means all possible combinations of these members. For example, to return the results shown in the table earlier, where both the customer and product families are laid across the x-axis, we can write:

```
SELECT
    CROSSJOIN(
        {[Customers].[All Customers].[USA].[ABC Inc.],
            [All Customers].[Canada].[XYZ Ltd.]},
        {[Product].[Product Family].Members}) on columns,
        {[Time].[Year].[1998].Children} on rows,
        {[Measures].[Store Sales]} on pages
FROM
    SalesCube
WHERE
    ([Store].[All Stores].[USA])
```

Just as a reminder, here are the results it produces:

	Total Store Sales in the USA					
	ABC Inc.			**XYZ Ltd.**		
	Product Families			**Product Families**		
1998 Quarters	**Food**	**Drinks**	**Clothes**	**Food**	**Drinks**	**Clothes**
Q1/1998	$12,525,452	$12,525,452	$9,235,765	$4,655,874	$4,235,765	$5,455,874
Q2/1998	$14,142,343	$14,142,343	$12,525,452	$5,525,452	$5,525,452	$6,525,452
Q3/1998	$15,123,042	$15,123,042	$12,525,452	$5,525,452	$8,525,852	$7,525,452
Q4/1998	$11,002,002	$11,002,002	$12,525,452	$6,525,452	$7,553,452	$8,525,452

The query construction above assumes that the product family level of the product dimension only includes the three members shown in the table: `Food`, `Drink`, and `Clothes`. However, if there are other members and we only wanted to show these three members, the query has to be changed as follows:

```
SELECT
    CrossJoin(
        { [Company].[ABC Inc], [Company].[XYZ Ltd] },
        { [Product].[Product Family].[Food],
          [Product].[Product Family].[Drink],
          [Product].[Product Family].[Clothes]}) on Columns,
    {[Time].[Calendar].[Year].[1998].Children} on rows
FROM SalesCube
Where ( [Store].[Country].[USA] )
```

This syntax goes in line with the discussion earlier regarding using the comma to express separate members of a dimension, level, or a hierarchy into a set.

It is worth noting here that it does not matter which order the sets are placed in the `CrossJoin` function. We could have, in the previous example, written the query in the following form without affecting the results:

```
SELECT
    CrossJoin(
        { [Products].[ Product Family].[Food],
          [Products].[ Product Family].[Drink],
          [Products].[ Product Family].[Clothes]},
        { [Company].[ABC Inc], [Company].[XYZ Ltd] } )
    on Columns,
    {[Time].[Calendar].[Year].[1998].[Quarters].Members} on rows
FROM SalesCube
Where ( [Store].[Country].[USA] )
```

The `CrossJoin()` function handles only two dimensions at a time. If you want to evaluate the cross product of more than two dimensions, you need to nest the call to this function. For example, if you want to nest the customer, product, and store dimensions and lay them all on the x-axis, you can use the `CrossJoin()` function like the example below:

```
CrossJoin(
  CrossJoin(
    { [Company].[ABC Inc], [Company].[XYZ Ltd] },
    { [Product].[ Product Family].Members }),
    { [Stores].[Countries].Members })
```

This would be the same as writing:

```
CrossJoin(
  { [Company].[ABC Inc], [Company].[XYZ Ltd] },
    CrossJoin(
      { [Product].[Product Family].Members },
      { [Stores].[Countries].Members }))
```

Another point to consider here is that the `CrossJoin()` function takes two sets as arguments. If one of the sets includes only one tuple, it would be a good practice to surround it by brace brackets to convert it to a set, even though not doing so will not produce any errors.

The "*" (asterisk) Operator

The asterisk operator "*" is an alternative to the `CrossJoin()` function. It also finds all possible combinations of the sets participating in the "`* product`". The general syntax for using this operator is illustrated in the example below, which is identical to the example in the `CrossJoin()` function section:

```
SELECT
    { [Products].[Product Family].[Food],
      [Products].[ Product Family].[Drink],
      [Products].[ Product Family].[Clothes]}
    *
    { [Company].[ABC Inc], [Company].[XYZ Ltd] }
    on Columns,
    {[Time].[Calendar].[Year].[1998].[Quarters].Members} on rows
FROM SalesCube
Where ( [Store].[Country].[USA] )
```

And in case there are more than two sets, this operator can still be used as illustrated in the example below:

```
    { [Company].[ABC Inc], [Company].[XYZ Ltd] } *
    { [Product].[Product Family].Members } *
    { [Stores].[Countries].Members }
```

Filter() Function

The `Filter()` function is also another function that helps define the set and its members. As the name implies, this function allows you to filter some values out of a set excluding them based on certain criteria. The function takes as parameters a set and a Boolean expression. The Boolean expression determines the values to include or exclude from the passed set.

```
Filter ({Set}, Boolean Expression) returns a {sub Set of the original set}
```

MDX allows several Boolean operators as part in the Boolean expression. These operators are listed in the table below.

Boolean Operator	Description
=	Equal
<	Less than
<=	Less than or equal
>	Greater than
>=	Greater than or equal
<>	Not equal
`IsEmpty(Expression)`	Checks to see if the "Expression", which is any valid MDX expression, returns an empty set
AND	Logical AND, the Boolean expression evaluates to True if both sides of the AND operator are True
OR	Logical OR, the Boolean expression evaluates to True if either side of the OR (or both) operator is True
NOT	Logical NOT: the Boolean expression evaluates to True if the expression to the right of the NOT operator evaluates to FALSE

Boolean operators used in MDX

As an example on using the `Filter()` function, let's return all the product families whose sales exceeded $8,000,000 in the USA in 1998.

```
Filter(
    { [Products].Members },
    ( [measures].[sales], [stores].[countries].[USA], [Time].[Year].[1998] ) >
8000000)
```

The results from a query containing the Filter function above would look similar to the results shown in the previous table, except that only sales values greater than $8,000,000 will show up:

	Total Store Sales in the USA				
	ABC Inc.			**XYZ Ltd.**	
1998 Quarters	**Product Families**			**Product Families**	
	Food	**Drinks**	**Clothes**	**Drinks**	**Clothes**
Q1/1998	$12,525,452	$12,525,452	$9,235,765		
Q2/1998	$14,142,343	$14,142,343	$12,525,452		
Q3/1998	$15,123,042	$15,123,042	$12,525,452	$8,525,852	
Q4/1998	$11,002,002	$11,002,002	$12,525,452		$8,525,452

You can actually move the countries and year specification to the set if you want, or just leave it as part of the Boolean expression. Also, this function, like most MDX functions, can be nested with another function, which provides a great flexibility in expressing and constructing the sets we want to construct. As an example on writing the same example above with the tuples defined in the set and nesting the `Filter()` and `CrossJoin()` functions:

```
Filter(
    CrossJoin(
        { [Products].Members },
        {[Stores].[Countries].[USA]}, [Time].[Year].[1998]),
    ( [measures].[sales] ) > 50000)
```

The Order() Function

Another function used in the construction of sets is the `Order()` function. This function helps to put the tuples in the set in a specific order. The function takes as arguments a set to order, a criterion for ordering, and an optional parameter that serves as a flag to whether the order will be ascending or descending. The syntax of this function is presented below:

```
Order ( {Set}, Criterion for Ordering, Flag (DESC, ASC, BASC, BDESC))
```

The function above returns a cellset ordered according to the criterion provided and based on the value of the optional flag, the set could be ordered in ascending or descending order. The ASC and DESC keep the ordering within the hierarchy, whereas the BASC and BDESC operators break the hierarchy boundaries and order the results as one unit. To understand the difference between ASC and BASC, the following example shows the results of the function when ordering the members of the following set:

```
Order(
    {[USA], [France], [California], [New York],
     [Italy], [Paris], [Los Angeles],
     [New York City], [Albany], [Rome], [Naples]},
    ([Time].[1997], [Store Sales]),
  DESC)
```

Set Member			Store Sales (x $1000)
Country	**State**	**City**	
USA			1200
	California		240
		Los Angeles	81
	New York		210
		New York City	121
		Albany	36
Italy			280
		Rome	110
		Naples	87
France			94
		Paris	88

As you can see from the table , using the DESC flag causes OLAP Services to sort the results in a hierarchy in terms of geographic location and sort the sales for each hierarchical category alone. The same function above would return the following results when using BDESC instead of DESC:

```
ORDER(
    {[USA], [France], [California], [New York],
        [Italy], [Paris], [Los Angeles],
        [New York City], [Albany], [Rome], [Naples]},
    ([Time].[1997], [Store Sales]),
    BDESC)
```

Set Member	Store Sales (x $1000)
USA	1200
Italy	280
California	240
New York	210
New York City	121
Rome	110
France	94
Paris	88
Naples	87
Los Angeles	81
Albany	36

Clearly, from the table above, the BDESC flag caused OLAP Services not to categorize the set and to treat it all as one unit when it sorted the results.

Again, this function can be nested with other functions to provide maximum flexibility in the resulting cellset. For example, let's write a query that does the same function as the last query, except that the returned cellset members correspond to store sales greater than $50,000. This condition is done using the `Filter` function:

```
ORDER(
FILTER(
    {[USA], [France], [California], [New York],
        [Italy], [Paris], [Los Angeles],
        [New York City], [Albany], [Rome], [Naples]},
        ( [Measures].[Store Sales] ) > 100000
        ),
    ([Time].[1997], [Store Sales]),
    DESC)
```

The results of the query above are shown in the table below. Compare these results to the results of the same query without the `Filter` function, which we saw earlier.

Set Member			Store Sales (x $1000)
Country	**State**	**City**	
USA			1200
	California		240
	New York		210
		New York City	121
Italy			280
		Rome	110

It is worth noting that the default sort order flag is ASC if no order flag is assigned.

Ordering sets in MDX is not a simple issue. We will revisit this topic in the next chapter when we discuss ordering sets. The complexity comes when you don't elect to break the orders of the hierarchies, which causes OLAP Services to sort the results within each hierarchy level as you have seen in the example above.

Dimensional Calculations in MDX

Multidimensional (MD) calculations in MDX carry a great deal of resemblance to two- and three-dimensional spreadsheet calculations. If you are familiar with such calculations in a spreadsheet program, like Microsoft Excel, you will find MDX calculations to be an easy topic. On the other hand, compared to SQL, MDX calculations are much easier to perform and understand. One aspect of MD calculations is that you can perform these calculations on ranges of cells, which spares you from repeating the calculations for each cell.

In SQL, if you were to perform any calculations, the calculations have to be embedded in the queries with the fields of the different tables that participate in the calculation explicitly or implicitly selected as well. As an example, to calculate the employment duration of all employees in a company, you may issue the query:

```
SELECT emp_name As EmployeeName,
               emp_start_date As StartDate,
               emp_end_date As EndDate,
               DateDiff(month, ISNULL(emp_end_date, GetDate())
                           , emp_start_date) As MonthsEmployed
FROM    EmployeeTable
```

You may notice in the query that we used three built-in SQL Server T-SQL functions, `DateDiff`, which takes the parameters, date part (month in our case), and the two dates we want to subtract one from the other; `IsNULL()`, which checks the value of the end data field, and replaces NULLs with the result of the third function we used, `GetDate()`, which retrieves the current system date. The calculation will be performed on each row of the resultset yielding the number of months of employment of the employees of the company. If you were to store this calculation in SQL, you may need to add a field to store its result. The added field value could then be calculated when a record is updated with a new end date value. This can be achieved in several different ways, such as an update trigger, or through the application that set the end date value. The other way to "pseudo" store the calculation in SQL is by creating a view based on the query presented above.

In MDX, calculations are placed in the axes of the query as new members of the dimensions, which fill in the cells with the calculation results. The keyword "`Member`" is used to indicate adding a new member to the dimension. The syntax generally looks like this:

```
Member: member_name AS calculation_formula
```

The `member_name` parameter in the general syntax formula above follows the same rules for defining unique members of a dimension. The dimension name (and possibly the hierarchy) along with the level name should be part of the name of the member. In MDX, calculated members are handled in one of two ways, they can be calculated privately to the query using the "`With`" operator, in which case, they are only available for the duration of the query run time; or they can be evaluated and made available for more than one query with the `Create Member` statement. These two methods will be explained later in the chapter.

Query-Defined Calculated Members (With Operator)

The `With` operator can be used in MDX queries to specify a calculated member. It can also be used to define named sets (discussed later in the chapter). The `With` operator comes before the SELECT clause of the MDX statement and defines a section in which the calculated member along with any named sets can be defined. The example below illustrates how this operator can be used to make accessing data and calculations so simple. In the example, we find out the duration of employment for the employees defined as a new member in the `With` section.

```
WITH
     MEMBER  [Measures].[Months Employed] AS
    '[measures].[EmpEndDate] - [measures].[EmpStartDate]'
SELECT
    { [Measures].[EmpStartDate],
      [Measures].[EmpEndDate],
      [Measures].[Months Employed] } on columns,
    { [Employee].[City].[Troy - Michigan].[EmpName] } on rows
FROM EmployeeCube
```

You notice that in this example, the member was added to the Measures dimension. Also, notice the syntax for the formula and how it is surrounded by single quotes. A sample of the results of the query is represented in the following table:

	Start Date	End Date	Months Employed
John Doe	1/1/1997	---	35.00
Janet Smith	7/15/1998	---	16.50
Mike Smith	1/1/1992	2/15/1998	73.50
Susan Davis	12/15/1988	1/15/1989	1.00
Yvonne Michaels	1/15/1990	---	118.50

A sample of the results of the MDX query calculating employment durations

The member added with this query to the measures dimension `(Months Employed)` is only available for the duration of this query and cannot be accessed or used by other queries.

Let's now go back to the sales and inventory samples. A query that retrieves the profits for the months of October and November of the 1998 calendar year for stores located in Troy, Michigan, along with the percent change in sales, cost, and profit between the two months may look like:

```
WITH
     MEMBER  [Measures].[Profit] AS
    '[measures].[Sales] - [measures].[Cost]'
     MEMBER  [Time].[October - November Change] AS
    '100 * ([TIME].[November-1998] - [Time].[October-1998])/[TIME].[November-
1998]'
SELECT
    { [Measures].[Sales],
      [Measures].[Cost],
      [Measures].[Profit] } on columns,
    { [Time].[Calendar].[October-1998],
      [Time].[Calendar].[November-1998],
      [Time].[October - November Change] } on rows
FROM EmployeeCube
WHERE ( [Stores].[City].[ Troy, Michigan ] )
```

The results of this query are presented in the following table:

	Sales	Cost	Profit
October, 1998	$120,000	$69,000	$51,000
November, 1998	$150,000	$71,000	$79,000
Percent Change	25%	3%	Is it 55% or 22% ?

Sales/Profit/Percent Change MDX query results

You notice from the previous example that we added two members in the WITH section, the profit member, and the October-November Change member. We projected the profit member on the x-axis making it a column; and the second member projected on the y-axis, making it a row in the table. You may be asking yourself "I wonder which calculation took place first, the profit or the change?" The reason this is a good question is the corner cell at the right and bottom of the table. This cell should represent the change in profit between the two months. The value of this cell is expected to be the same when calculated from the columns or from the rows. Surprisingly enough, these two values are not the same (55%) and (22%). So, which calculation takes precedence?

MDX solves this problem with what is called the `Member Solve Order` property, which is specified when the member is created. The member with the higher number is calculated based on the results of the calculation of the members with the lower number. This number can only be zero or higher. The number actually specifies precedence of calculation among the calculated members, and it is up to us to decide that precedence in the query. However, if no value is specified for this property, the value defaults to zero.

In our example, we need to find the change in profit between October 1998 and November 1998 rather than the difference of the sales and cost change. Therefore, we give a higher value to the October-November Change member than the `Profit` member to have the profits calculated first. With this the query becomes:

```
WITH
   MEMBER  [Measures].[Profit] AS
  '[measures].[Sales] - [measures].[Cost]',
   SOLVE_ORDER = 1
   MEMBER  [Time].[October - November Change] AS
  '100 * ([TIME].[November-1998] - [Time].[October-1998])/[TIME].[November-1998]',
     SOLVE_ORDER = 2
SELECT
  { [Measures].[Sales],
    [Measures].[Cost],
    [Measures].[Profit] } on columns,
  { [Time].[Calendar].[October-1998],
    [Time].[Calendar].[November-1998],
    [Time].[October - November Change] } on rows
FROM EmployeeCube
WHERE ( [Stores].[City].[ Troy, Michigan ] )
```

The results of this query are presented in the following table:

	Sales	Cost	Profit
October, 1998	$120,000	$69,000	$51,000
November, 1998	$150,000	$71,000	$79,000
Percent Change	25%	3%	55%

Sales/Profit/Percent Change MDX query results after assigning solve order values

It is worth noting the following things about the syntax of the WITH block when more than one member are specified.

- Members are not separated by any punctuation (comma, colon, semi colon, etc.). The keyword, MEMBER is the separator in this case.
- The SOLVE_ORDER property is separated from the definition of the member by a comma.
- The formula used to evaluate the calculated member is quoted in single quotes.
- SOLVE_ORDER values can be either zero or positive integers with a default of zero.

Non Query-Defined Calculated Members (CREATE MEMBER)

So far, you have seen how you can define a calculated member in an MDX query. Such members will be visible only to the query they are created in. MDX allows for defining calculated members on the server and client levels. Server-level calculated members are visible to all clients that can access the cube on which the member is defined. The tool that allows this to happen is the CREATE MEMEBR function. This function has to be used with the cube name and dimension name. The CREATE MEMBER command is not part of the query in which the member is used. Instead, it is a separate statement, which is executed separately from the SELECT query. The statement follows the same syntax as the definition of the calculated member in the WITH clause. The only difference is the addition of the cube and dimension names. The following statement created the two calculated members used in the last two examples above.

```
     CREATE MEMBER  [Sales Cube].[Measures].[Profit] AS
    '[Measures].[Sales] - [measures].[Cost]',
     SOLVE_ORDER = 5
     CREATE MEMBER  [Sales Cube].[Time].[October - November Change] AS
    '100 * ([TIME].[November-1998] - [Time].[October-1998])/[TIME].[November-
1998]',
     SOLVE_ORDER = 10
```

Using the CREATE MEMBER command adds the calculated member to the metadata allowing for the possibility to manipulate it via OLE DB for OLAP or Decision Support Object (DSO). Calculated members can also be defined using the OLAP Manager. These members are also visible to all clients that have access to the cube on the server.

Named Sets

One powerful feature of MDX is allowing for the definition of named sets. These are regular sets you defined using the rules and techniques we went through so far, to which names can be assigned. This has great benefits, such as holding certain values in sets of their own, giving the sets descriptive names that make it easy to refer to these items. Also, named sets make programming and writing SELECT statements easier, since you can only use the name of the set rather than the whole definition.

Just like calculated members, named sets are defined in the WITH block. The syntax for defining them is similar to that of calculated members, except that you use the SET keyword instead of MEMBER, and there is no need to specify the name of a cube or dimension. As an example on named sets, the following two queries produce identical results. The second one used a named set of "My Products".

```
SELECT
     { [Product].[Bread], [Product].[Cookies], [Product].[Cake] } on columns,
     { [Measures].Members } on rows
FROM InventoryCube

WITH
    SET  [My Products] AS
        '{ [Product].[Bread], [Product].[Cookies], [Product].[Cake] }'

SELECT
    { [My Products] } on columns,
    { { [Measures].Members } on rows
FROM InventoryCube
```

Like calculated members, named sets are also sensitive to the scope in which they are defined. Named sets defined in the WITH block of the SELECT query are local to the query and end with the execution of the query. However, you can use the command CREATE SET to create sets on the server or client. Sets created on the server will be available to clients accessing and querying the cube on which the sets were defined. Sets created by a client will only be available to the client and will go out of scope as soon as the client connection to the server is terminated or they are dropped.

An example of creating the same set in the example above with the CREATE SET command is shown below:

```
CREATE SET  [InventoryCube].[My Products] AS
        '{ [Product].[Bread], [Product].[Cookies], [Product].[Cake] }'
```

You notice here that the cube on which the set is defined has to be part of the name of the set. The dimension, however, does not have to be part of the set's name.

Unlike calculated members, named sets don't show up in the cube's metadata, and OLE DB cannot be used to manipulate them (at least for this release of OLAP Services). You can still, however, manipulate them programmatically using Decision Support Objects (DSO).

Named sets are evaluated the first time they are encountered and saved for subsequent use thereafter, until they go out of scope. This results in significant improvement in query processing, which is yet another benefit of named sets.

Axis Numbering and Ordering

One major part of the MDX SELECT statement is the axis definition. Axes are numbered from 0 to 64. If you choose 0 axes in the statement, then chances are you have a slicer dimension in the WHERE clause. If you don't, the global aggregate for the cube will be returned as a result, because you query will look like:

```
SELECT
FROM [SalesCube]
```

You have to be extremely careful when using numbered axes in your queries. The axes should be laid in the query according to their order and you cannot skip numbers. For instance, a statement like:

```
SELECT
    ... ON Axis(0),
    ... ON Axis(1),
    ... ON Pages,
    ... ON Chapters
```

is fine because it maintains the order of the axes. It is worth mentioning here that the first five axes are given the names: columns, rows, pages, chapters, and sections to look like a printed report. Continuing our example, the following two statements will generate errors because the first one does not maintain the order of the axes, and the second one skips axis numbers.

```
SELECT
    … ON Axis(1),
    … ON Pages,
    … ON columns

SELECT
    … ON Axis(0),
    … ON Pages,
    … ON Chapters
```

The first example has the axes in the order: 1, 2, 0 for rows, pages, and columns respectively; whereas the second example has the order of the axes as: 0,2,3 for columns, pages, and chapters axes respectively, skipping the rows axis (axis(1)).

In summary, if you are defining *n* axes in your query, you must number these axes from 0 to *n* -1 in an ascending order.

Selecting Member Properties

MDX queries allow you to select member properties defined on individual dimension levels or on the dimensions themselves. The properties are included on the statement axes. The keyword DIMENSION PROPERTIES is used to specify that member properties are to be retrieved. For example, the following code retrieves the birth date and gender member properties of the employees from the employee cube.

```
SELECT
     { [Employee].[Michigan].[Troy].Members },
       DIMENSION PROPERTIES
       [Employee].[BirthDate],
       [Employee].[Gender] on columns,
     { [Product].[Product Family].Members } on rows,
     { [Measure].[Store Sales]} on pages
FROM SalesCube
WHERE ( [Measures].[Sales], [Time].[July, 1998] )
```

The results of the query above would look like this:

	Employee Sales in Troy, Michigan				
	Birth Date	**Gender**	**Food**	**Drinks**	**Clothes**
John Doe	1/23/1959	M	$13,400	$15,005	$18,019
Janet Smith	11/5/1968	F	$10,300	$11,204	$13,112

The example above will retrieve the employees with their birth dates and gender and their sales in July, 1998 in Troy, Michigan.

Summary

This chapter introduced you to MDX. It is clear to see that MDX is a powerful language that allows you to query OLAP cubes in an efficient and powerful manner. Like SQL, MDX can be used in combination with other programming languages, which adds to its power and benefits. The next chapter discusses the more advanced features and issues with MDX in more detail, and presents the sample VB application that ships with OLAP Services, and allows for easy writing of MDX queries.

8

Advanced MDX Topics

In the previous chapter we talked through the basics of MDX. It is essential that these basics are understood so that you can use MDX confidently within your Microsoft OLAP projects. You will find that this chapter will be expanding on the topics we met in the last chapter, and adding new elements to the discussion that describe common use scenarios, special cases, and alternative actions. There will also be a host of new topics that we will meet specifically for advanced use of MDX

Topics covered in this chapter include:

- The Format String
- Empty Sets
- MDS Expressions: Set Value Expressions and Conditional Expressions
- An MDX Sample Application

The last thing we tackled in Chapter 7 was retrieving member properties. In this chapter, we will start with a more detailed presentation of the MDX statement, defining data and context for the different parts of the statement

Advanced MDX Statement Topics

Retrieving Cell Properties

Microsoft OLE DB Provider for OLAP supports several advanced properties for cells in OLAP cubes. Besides the value property, a cell can have properties that help customize its formatting and coloring. The table below lists cell properties supported by Microsoft OLE DB provider for OLAP, given that OLE DB providers may add their own properties that fit their systems.

Property Name	Mandatory/ Optional	Data Type	Description
value	Mandatory	DBTYPE_VARIANT	Actual value of cell.
formatted_value	Mandatory	DBTYPE_WSTR	Character string representing how the value is to be formatted.
cell_ordinal	Mandatory	DBTYPE_UI4	Ordinal number of the cell in the dataset.
format_string	Optional	DBTYPE_WSTR	The format string used to create formatted_value (see next section).
fore_color	Optional	DBTYPE_UI4	Forecolor of the cell for displaying the value.
back_color	Optional	DBTYPE_UI4	Backcolor used for displaying the value.
font_name	Optional	DBTYPE_WSTR	Font used to display the value.
font_color	Optional	DBTYPE_UI2	Font size to be used with the value.
font_flags	Optional	DBTYPE_ I4	Font flags that decide whether the value will be bold, underlined, struck out, or italic.

A list of Microsoft OLAP cell properties

The data types used in the table above are the types used by OLE DB specification. To understand these types better, let's map the ones used in the table above to the equivalent types in ADO, as shown in the following table:

OLE DB Type	ADO Type	Description
DBTYP_VARIANT	AdVariant	Indicates an automation variant.
DBTYPE_WSTR	AdWChar	Indicates a NULL-terminated Unicode character string.
DBTYPE_UI4	AdUnsignedInt	Indicates an unsigned integer (4 bytes).
DBTYPE_UI2	adUnsignedSmallInt	Indicates an unsigned small integer (2 bytes).
DBTYPE_I2	AdSmallInt	Indicates a 2-byte signed integer.

Explaining some OLE DB data types

As you might expect, a provider must support the mandatory cell properties listed in the first table – optional properties do not have to be supported. However, the provider may also add their own specific cell properties. Your application can be written to query what properties a provider supports by returning a `PROPERTIES` rowset, with the data type column restricted to `MDPROP_CELL`. Your application may also limit the properties returned by using the `CELL PROPERTIES` keyword in the `WHERE` clause of the query. As an example, the following query returns a dataset in which each cell has the properties: `VALUE`, `FORMATTED_VALUE`, `FORE_COLOR`, and `BACK_COLOR`.

```
SELECT NON EMPTY Products DIMENSION PROPERTIES Products.ID, Products.Name
   ON ROWS,
CROSSJOIN (Years, (Sales, ActualSales)) ON COLUMNS
FROM SalesCube
WHERE ([March-1998], SalesPerson.[All], Store.USA)
CELL PROPERTIES VALUE, FORMATTED_VALUE, FORE_COLOR, BACK_COLOR
```

Each provider has a default set of properties that includes the mandatory ones. For example, the default Microsoft OLAP cell properties would be: `VALUE`, `FORMATTED_VALUE`, and `CELL_ORDINAL`. If a provider has other mandatory cell properties, these properties will be part of the default set. Optional properties, on the other hand, are not returned unless the `CELL PROPERTIES` keyword is used to specify what properties to include in the `WHERE` clause. The latter case can include any properties, and may also exclude the mandatory ones. If the mandatory properties are not specified in the `CELL PROPERTIES` specification, they are not returned.

The Format String

As you have already seen in the table of OLAP cell properties, the format string is used to generate the `FORMATTED_VALUE` cell property. The format string varies based on the data type of the cell value. The following is a description of this string for three data type categories, character, numeric, and data/time data types.

Format String in Character Values

The format string can have one or two sections separated by a semi colon `";"`. If the string has one section, the string format applies to all strings in the cell value property. If the string is specified with two sections, then the first section applies to non-NULL, non-zero length string values, and the second section applies to NULL and zero-length string values. The format string may include the characters listed in the following table:

Character	Description
@	A character placeholder that either displays the character or a space character. If the string has a character corresponding to the position of the @ character, the character is displayed. Otherwise, a space is added. For example, when expressing the word "book" using the format string "@@@@@", we get " book" with a space at the beginning.
&	A character placeholder that displays either the character or nothing. If the string has a character corresponding to the position of the & character, the character is displayed. Otherwise, nothing is displayed. For example, when expressing the word "book" using the format string "@@&&&", we get "book" with **no** space at the end.
<	Displays all characters in lower case format. For example, when expressing the word "BoOk" using the format string ">", we get "book".
>	Displays all characters in upper case format. For example, when expressing the word "BoOk" using the format string ">", we get "BOOK".
!	Forces filling placeholder left-to-right instead of the default, right-to-left filling. For example, if "!" is used with the first example in the table: "!@@@@@" then the result would not be " book", instead, it would be "book ". And the additional space is to the right of the word.

Format string special characters for character type values

Format string in Numeric Values

The format string may include between one and four sections separated by semi colons. Depending on the number of sections, the format string will be interpreted differently according to the following table:

Number of Sections in the format string	Interpretation
One	The format expression applies to all values.
Two	The first section applies to positive values and zeros, the second to negative values.
Three	The first section applies to positive values, the second to negative values, and the third to zeros.
Four	The first section applies to positive values, the second to negative values, the third to zeros, and the fourth to null values.

For example, the format string "%##.#0;;\Z\E\R\O" has three sections, the first section applies to positive values, the second section is left blank, therefore, negative values will also use the first section for their display. And, the third section will display the word "ZERO" when a "0" is encountered. The following table specifies the characters that can appear in the format string for numeric values.

Character	Description
none	The numeric value has no formatting.
0	This character is a digit placeholder. If a numeric expression has a digit at the location corresponding to this character, the digit is displayed. Otherwise, a zero is displayed. If the number of zeros specified exceeds the length of the expression to the left or right of the decimal point, leading and trailing zeros are added. For example: using a format string of "0.0000" will express 7.345 as 7.3450, and using the format string "#.#00#" will express the same number as 7.345.
#	Similar to the 0 character, except that it either displays the digit or nothing (no zeros are displayed).
.	Decimal placeholder, and based on local settings of your system, it could be a comma ",". This character determines the number of digits to the right and left of the decimal point. If an expression evaluates to less than 1, and the # character is used for a placeholder, no digits will be displayed to the left of the decimal point. To display a leading zero, you need to use the "0" placeholder.
%	Percentage placeholder. The expression is multiplied by 100 and the % character is displayed. For example, using the format string "%###.####" to express the number 0.3453 will yield %34.53.
,	Thousand separator. Other characters may be used based on your machine locale setting.
:	Time separator used to separate hours, minutes, and seconds in time values. Other characters may be used based on your machine locale setting.
/	Date separator used to separate years, months and days in data values. Other characters may be used based on your machine locale setting.
E-, E+, e-, e+	Scientific format used to display exponential values. For example, 2.3^{13} would be expressed as 2.3E+13 when using the format string "###.###E##".
- + ( )	Displays a literal character.
\	Displays the next character in the format string. For example The format string "\Z\e\r\o" can be used to display the word "Zero". If you want to display a back slash, you need to double it in the string: For example, "\\\Z" will display "\Z".
"ABC"	Displays the characters in quotation marks as a string within your expression.

Format string special characters for numeric type values

Format string in Date/Time Values

Only one section exists in this string and the following table specifies the characters that can appear in the format string for numeric values.

Character	Description
:	Time separator used to separate hours, minutes, and seconds. When specified, time values will be formatted. For example, the time value "10.5" will be expressed as "10:30:00". However, the actual character appearing in the time value will depend on the locale system settings.
/	Date separator used to separate days, months and years.
c	Displays date and time in the format ddddd and ttttt respectively. See examples of these formats later in the table.
d	Displays a date format as the day of the month with no leading zeros: 1 – 31
dd	Displays a date format as the day of the month with leading zeros: 01 – 31
ddd	Displays the day name as three letters, Mon through Sun.
dddd	Displays the whole name of the day: Monday through Sunday.
ddddd	Displays the date as m/d/yy (short format). Depending how your system setting defines short format to be, the data will be displayed according to that format. For instance, if the system setting for short format is "dd/mm/yy" then the date will be displayed as "13/1/01"; and if the system setting for short data is "dd/mm/yyyy" then the date will be displayed as "13/1/2001". The system setting for short dates can be set in the Widows Control Panels' Regional Settings applet. (See figure below) 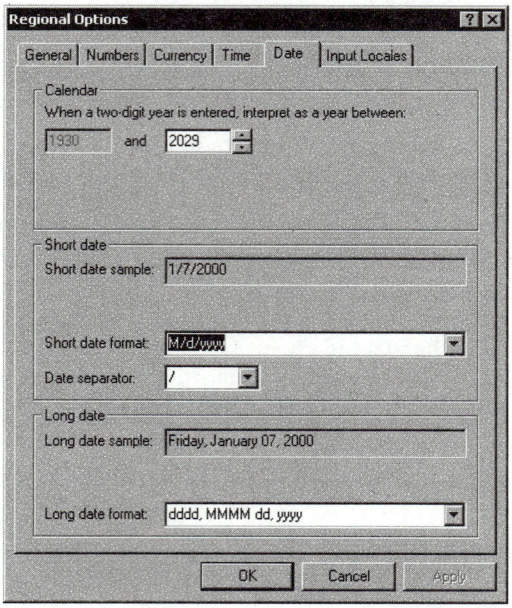 *Setting the short and long date formats for the system*

Character	Description
dddddd	Displays the date as long format (mmmm, dd, yyyy). Long date format can also be set in the Control Panel as shown in the figure above. An example of long date format is: January 1, 2001.
w	Displays the number of the day in the week (1 for Sunday and 7 for Saturday).
ww	Displays the number of the week in the year (1 to 52).
m	If this character does not follow the h/hh characters, it displays the month as a number without leading zeros from 1 to 12. 1 for January, and 12 for December.
mm	Displays the month number with leading zero if needed: 01 – 12. January being represented by 01 and December by 12.
mmm	Displays the month name as a three characters, Jan – Dec.
mmmm	Displays the full name of the month: January – December.
q	Displays the quarter of the year as a number: 1 – 4.
y	Displays the day of the year as a number from 1 to 366.
yy	Displays the year as two digits (00 to 99).
yyyy	Displays the year as four digits (0000 to 9999).
h, hh	Displays the hour of the day with or without leading zero (0 – 23) or (00 – 23).
n, nn	Displays the minute with or without leading zero (0 – 59) or (00 – 59).
s, ss	Displays the seconds with or without leading zero (0 – 59) or (00 – 59).
ttttt	Displays time as h:mm:ss. An example is: 12:34:32
AM/PM, am/pm	Displays upper or lower case AM or PM based on 12 hour cycles.
A/P, a/p	Displays A or P for AM and PM respectively in upper or lower case based on a 12-hour cycle.
AMPM	Uses the 12-hour clock. Displays the AM or PM string literal as defined by your system. AMPM can be either uppercase or lowercase, but the case of the string displayed matches the string as defined by your system settings. For Microsoft Windows, the default format is AM/PM.

Format string special characters for date/time type values

MDX Cube Slicers

As we saw in Chapter 7, slicers are defined in the WHERE clause of the MDX statement. Slicers and axes are similar in many ways. Actually, if you choose to eliminate slicers in your statements, you can do so and still limit your returned dataset to the values it would have if the slicer were used. For example, the following two queries return the exact same datasets:

```
SELECT
    {[Measures]. Members} ON COLUMNS
    {[TIME].Members ON ROWS
FROM SalesCube
WHERE ([ProductCategory].[Dairy Products], [Store].[Detroit, Michigan])
```

and

```
SELECT
    {[Measures]. Members} ON COLUMNS
    {[TIME].Members ON ROWS
{[ProductCategory].[Dairy Products], [Store].[Detroit, Michigan]} ON PAGES
FROM SalesCube
```

The first one of the two queries above uses a slicer in the WHERE clause to limit the resulting dataset to dairy products and Detroit, Michigan. The second statement does not use the slicer, but adds a third axis that, by intersecting the other two axes, defines the resulting dataset to be the same as in the first query.

You might ask then why do we even bother with slicers, and why don't we just specify everything in the statement using axes? The answer is that you can do that, but slicers make it more intuitive and easy to construct the statement and understand it. The calling clients will also be able to interpret the statement's dataset better and faster if slicers are used. Clients will interpret the first query as a two-dimensional array, whereas the second one as a three-dimensional array.

Beefing Up MDX Cube Slicers

Just like slicers may include simple members from the cube, they can also include calculated members from different dimensions including the measures. For example, it is safe to write:

```
WHERE ([Measures].[Average Sales Per Product Category], [Time].[Sum YTD])
```

Or even include MDX expressions and functions (see MDX Expressions later in the chapter):

```
WHERE (Descendants([Dairy Products], [Brands]),
BottomPercent([Geography].[States].Members, 25, Sales))
```

The seemingly complex slicer above limits the returned dataset in the query it is used in to the descendant brands of the dairy products category, and to the states corresponding to the bottom 25% sales. To make this clearer, the descendants of the Dairy Products will include members such as: cheese, milk, etc. As for the states, to get the states that contributed the bottom 25% sales volume, some sorting of the states according to their sales figures will take place. The sales for the sorted states will be added up from the bottom up until we hit the 25% of total sales. The states included in the count are the ones included in the slicer. For detailed information on the `Descendants()` and `BootomPercent()` functions, refer to Appendix C, MDX Function Reference.

In the examples above, you notice that the slicer defines sets of multiple tuples. Although you can write your slicer to include such sets, OLAP Services will aggregate the result and return one tuple. In other words, the sets participating in the slicer above are `{Dairy, Cheese, Milk, ...}` and `{California, Michigan, New York, ...}`.

Joining Cubes in the FROM Clause

Although the current release of MDX supports only one cube in the FROM clause, some OLE DB for OLAP providers may support joining multiple cubes together in the future. This can be done by simply listing the names of the cubes in the FROM clause separated by commas. Unlike relational databases, where joins on tables have to be explicitly defined in the SQL statement either in the WHERE clause, or in the FROM clause using the Join operators, MDX does not require such joins to be explicit. The fact that two cubes have shared dimensions allows for implicit join between them if listed together in the FROM clause.

Note: Two cubes are said to have common dimensions if and only if the dimensions have the same DIMENSION_UNIQUE_NAME property.

The following are notes on joining cubes along their common dimensions:

- If two cubes have a common dimension, but do not have any common members in this dimension, the two cubes cannot be joined. For instance, the first cube has a geographic dimension, just as the second cube, but the members of that dimension for the first cube are countries and cities in Europe, while the members of the dimension in the second cube are countries and cities in South America, then the two cubes cannot be joined.
- If two cubes with a common dimension have identical sets of members of that dimension, the two cubes can be joined and the resulting cube will have the total number of dimensions from both minus the common dimension. To clarify this further, take the example of the previous bullet. If the geographic dimension in both cubes had the same countries and cities in Europe, then these two cubes can be joined along this dimension. If the first cube had 3 dimensions and the second had 4, then the resulting cube from the join operation will have 3 + 4 –1 = 6 dimensions.

To better understand the last point, consider the example of cube A and cube C with dimensions (X, Y, Z) and (Z, W) respectively. Dimension Z is the common dimension between the two cubes. Assuming that members of the common dimension are identical for both cubes, the resulting cube AB will have the dimensions (X, Y, Z, W), and the following statements apply:

```
SELECT AB.X ON COLUMNS, AB.Y ON ROWS, AB.Z ON PAGES
WHERE (W.[ALL])
```

Is the same as the cube `A(X, Y, Z)`.

And the dataset:

```
SELECT AB.Z ON COLUMNS, AB.W ON ROWS
WHERE (X.[ALL], Y.[ALL])
```

Is the same as the cube `B(Z, W)`.

This type of join is referred to as the natural join. Providers have the freedom to expand it in the future to make it as sophisticated as they wish.

Empty FROM Clause

OLE DB for OLAP allows for derivation of a cube name from the MDX statement. This is considered an optional feature that providers can take advantage of. If the provider chooses to support this feature, then a cube name can be derived from the specified axis and slicer dimensions. In this case, the cube does not have to be included in the FROM clause. For example, with support for this feature, you will be able to write a statement like the query below:

```
SELECT
  {Product.Members}, {[Measures].[Costs]} on columns
  [Store].[Michigan].[Cities].Members on rows
WHERE ([1998])
```

If the OLE DB for OLAP provider supports this feature, then it will derive the cube name from the axis dimensions: Product and Store and from the slicer dimensions: Time and the Cost measure, even though no FROM clause is included.

Checking the MDPROP_MDX_JOINCUBES property of the data source helps determine if the provider supports this feature. The MDPROPVAL_MJC_IMPLICITCUBE bit will be set if the provider supports this feature.

Using Outer References in an MDX Query

In many cases, data you want to retrieve in your MDX query is segmented in different cubes. For example, a cube may hold actual costs data, whereas budgeted costs may reside in another cube. Your query may need to reference tuples or members in the cube that does not appear in the FROM clause. For instance, you may want to retrieve the actual costs of products that exceeded their budgeted costs. The query would look like:

```
SELECT
FILTER (Product.Members, [Measures].[Costs] >
          [Budgeted Costs Cube].[Measures].[Cost]) on columns
          [Store].[Michigan].[Cities].Members on rows
FROM  [Actual Costs Cube]
WHERE ([1998])
```

The query above will filter the resulting set retrieving only tuples where costs exceeded their budgeted values grouping the results by city in the state of Michigan for the year 1998. The Filter function will be explained later in the chapter, or you can refer to Appendix C for more explanation about it.

Using Property Values in MDX Queries

Frequently you want to query based on a property value, rather than the dimension member itself. For instance, assume that you have a cube containing vehicle information for an auto manufacturer and you want to limit your query only to cars that have automatic transmission, convertibles, and have V6 engines, which are member properties of the Model Year level of the Product dimension as shown in the next figure.

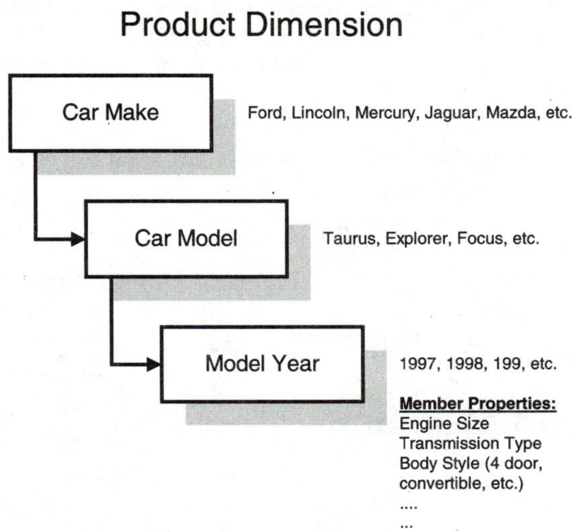

Representation of the member properties for the model year level

The MDX query would look like this:

```
SELECT [Measures].[Sales] ON COLUMNS,
   Filter(Product.MEMBERS, ([Model Year].[Engine Size] = "V6" AND
                            [Model Year].[Transmission] = "Automatic" AND
                            [Model Year].[Body Style] = "Convertible")) ON ROWS
FROM [Vehicle Cube]
WHERE ([1998])
```

The query will retrieve all sales in 1998 for all models and model years where the engine size is V6, the transmission is automatic, and the body style is convertible.

A query like this would be very helpful when used in a search engine. This search engine could be used as the basis to search inventory in a data warehouse directly from a web page.

Overriding the WHERE Clause

In MDX expressions, individual sets, members, tuples, or numeric functions execute in the larger context of the entire statement. If some information is missing in the definition of any of these items, the missing information is inferred from the context of the whole statement. In some cases, a coordinate is specified in both the WHERE clause and another part of the MDX statement, such as a Filter. In this case, coordinates obtained in the WHERE clause are overridden by any coordinates obtained in axis specification. As an example, consider the following MDX statement.

```
SELECT
   FILTER({USA.Children}, ([1997], ActualSales) > 10000) ON COLUMNS
   Quarters.Members on ROWS
FROM SalesCube
WHERE ([1998], ActualSales, [Products].ALL, [Salespersons].ALL)
```

The statement returns actual sales in 1998 where the actual sales exceeded a certain value in 1997 as determined by the filter. The WHERE clause, already includes all the actual sales for 1998. In this case the filter overrides the WHERE clause specification and only 1998 sales where the 1997 sales exceeded the 10000 threshold are returned.

In other words, the WHERE clause in the statement above includes all the sales of 1998 as [1998] as part of the that clause. However, the Filter function overrides this by only including the 1998 sales where the actual sales for the previous year were greater than 10000.

For example, if the first quarter sales were $12000 in 1998, and only $9000 in 1997, then the $12000 contributed in the first quarter of 1998 will not be tallied as the 1998 year sales in the query because the 1997 sales are less than the filter criteria ($10000).

Default Hierarchy and Member

As we have seen in previous chapters, each dimension has a default hierarchy. Each hierarchy has a unique member as well. These defaults become significant in the following situations:

- If your query specifies that a dimension, such as the `Time` dimension, will be positioned on one of the axes, such as the X-Axis, but does not choose any members from that dimension to occur along the specified axis. In this case, the provider chooses a hierarchy and member as the defaults and places them on the axis.
- If your query indicates that a dimension, such as the `Time` dimension, must be a slicer dimension but does not choose a member as the slicer. In this case, the provider uses a default slicer (such as Year), which yields the default member (such as current year).
- If the OLE DB interface, IMDFind::FindCell, does not specify a member for one of the constituent dimensions of an axis, the provider uses the default member for that dimension.
- If the OLE DB interface, IMDFind::FindTuple, does not specify a member for a constituent dimension on the axis, the provider uses the default member for that dimension.

Note: IMDFind is an OLE DB interface. This interface is an optional interface on the dataset object, and has methods to find the ordinal number of a cell in the dataset and the ordinal number of a tuple on the axis. It is no surprise that these two methods are: FindCell and FindTuple respectively. To find a cell with the FindCell method, you need to specify an array of members and a starting ordinal position. To find a tuple using the FindTuple method, you need to specify the array of members and a starting ordinal and axis identifier.

You can explicitly select the default member and default hierarchy by using the expressions: `Dimension.DefaultMember`, and `Hierarchy.DefaultMember`. It is also safe to assume that the default member of a dimension is the default member of the default hierarchy of the dimension.

Empty Cells:

MDX queries can sometimes return sets that might have empty cells. For instance, if you are trying to find out the sales of vehicles per dealer per model for a two-month period, chances are one particular model or models are not sold at a particular dealership, which results in an empty cell. The following sections discuss some of the issues associated with empty cells beginning with how they can be formed, NULL and invalid members, how empty cells can be handled and how they can be counted.

NULLs, Invalid Members, and Invalid Calculations

When performing MDX queries, you need to be aware of situations where invalid calculations are used. You also need to be aware of Null members and Nulls in your calculations that may result in empty cells. Microsoft OLAP does not treat errors, like division by zero, as an empty value; instead, it may return a bogus value. Some external function libraries, if used in your queries, may detect such errors and raise an ActiveX error that you can trap. However, it is best if you test for conditions of floating point overflow and the like when building your expressions to avoid these bogus results.

Null values usually lead to empty cells in the resulting cubes from the MDX queries. If you think of cross joining several dimension tables in your query, and each table includes several Null values, the resulting cube will have far more empty cells than the dimension tables' Null values, which leads to the data sparsity problem in OLAP systems. Sparsity does not always result from Null values in dimension tables. Empty cells can actually result from absence of rows corresponding to other dimension values. For example, if we are cross joining the geography and time dimensions on one axis, selecting all cities in the state of Michigan to return the sales of a certain product (the other axis) will result in empty cells when the product is not sold to start with in a certain city. So, if brand XYZ of cheese is not sold in Grand Rapids during the period specified on the Time dimension, an empty cell corresponding to the intersection of the two axes will result at this city and for this brand of cheese. This empty cell results from the lack of a row in the sales fact table corresponding to this situation.

MDX provides a function, `IsEmpty()` to check whether a cell is empty, and Microsoft OLAP provides the NULL operator to express missing values. The OLE DB for OLAP specification states that empty cells are treated in a similar fashion to zeros in numerical expressions, and a zero length string in string expressions. Boolean types are not allowed for cell values in MS OLAP services, and if you try to insert a Boolean value using a function to return it, the value will not parse. In OLAP Services, the contents of a cell are either numeric or strings.

Unlike other programming languages, in OLAP services two variables that are Null in value are considered equal (Null = Null), and the expression (Null <> Null) is always false. (This is unlike other programming languages such as Visual Basic; if variables A and B are both Null then we cannot say that A = B. We have to say that A <> B) To further discuss Nulls in MDX and OLAP services, let's discuss the following example. If you are trying to find the percentage difference between the sale price and cost, you may write:

```
100 * ([measures].[sales] - [measures].[cost]) / [measures].[cost].
```

If the sales value is Null, but the cost is not Null, then the expression evaluates to `100 * (0 - [measures].[cost]) / [measures].[cost]`, which is –100%. However, if the cost is Null and the sales are not, then the expression results in an overflow due to the division by zero. OLAP services returns a bogus value in the string "–1.INF". If both the cost and sales were Null, then OLAP Services will result in an empty value. This example gives you an idea of how you may get incorrect results when dealing with Nulls and that you always have to guard against such situations.

Another way you can get empty values for your cells is when you reference invalid members or tuples. Invalid members can occur in several ways. For instance referencing the children of a leaf level member will yield an empty value because there are no children of leaf levels in OLAP hierarchies. Thus, assuming that the leaf level for the geography dimension is City, the expression `[Seattle - Washington].Children` will yield an empty cell, and using this expression as part of a tuple or set will also yield an invalid tuple or set. Thus the set: { `[Seattle - Washington].Children, [1998]` } includes only empty tuples.

It is particularly important to check for invalid members when using the range operator, the colon. The reason this is important is because if a range is specified, and one of the two values specifying its boundaries is invalid, OLAP services returns a range that extends to the edge of the database, with the ordering of members on the same level as the valid member.

For example, if we take the range: `[December].NextMember:[July]`, the second member `(July)` will be valid. However, `December.NextMember` will be invalid. OLAP Services, in this case returns the range: { `[January]:[July]` }.

On the other hand, if you were to specify the range, `[July]:[January].PrevMember`, with the invalid member on the right, the resulting set would be: { `[July]:[December]` }. If both sides of the range specify invalid members, the resulting set will be empty.

To test and guard against these situations, you can use either the `IsEmpty()` function, or you can be more creative in using the `IIF()` function. For example, if you are calculating a three-month total sales moving average, you need to make sure at least three months exist for the period over which you are calculating your results. To do this, you can write:

```
IIf(
    COUNT( LastPeriods(3, [Time]), INCLUDEEMPTY) >= 3,
    Avg(LastPeriods(3, [Time]), [Measures].[TotalSales]),
    Null
    )
```

In the example above, we are checking the count of periods to make sure we have at least three going backward before we do the calculation. If we don't have three or more periods, we return a Null for the moving average. As another example, if you want to find the sum of total sales for a particular range of time and you suspect that the left side of the range could be empty or invalid, you can check for this conditions using the `IsEmpty()` function:

```
IIf(
  NOT IsEmpty( [Time].CurrentMember.Lag(12)),
  SUM([Time].CurrentMember.Lag(12):[Time].CurrentMember, [Measures].[TotalSales]),
  Null
  )
```

One last note is that the colon is not the only way you can construct ranges. You can build your ranges using functions like `ParallelPeriod()` and `Cousin()`. The same principle also applies to dealing with invalid members to these ranges. For a detailed explanation of these functions, please refer to Appendix C, MDX Function Reference.

The COALESCEEMPTY Function

Another way to find out about empty cells and handle them is by using the `COALESCEEMPTY` function. As the name implies, this function coalesces the value of an empty set to a number or a string. Support for this function is mandatory and all OLE DB providers for OLAP should support it. The structure for this function is:

```
COALESCEEMPTY(value_expression, value_expression [, value_expression] ...)
```

As a result, an empty cell will end up with some non-empty values. For example, `COALESCEEMPTY(Value1, Value2)` returns Value1 if Value1 is not empty, and Value2 if Value1 is empty. The function `COALESCEEMPTY(Value1, Value2, Value3, ....Valuen)` returns the first non-empty values of the arguments passed to it.

The `COALESCEEMPTY` function is similar to using a `CASE` expression. Thus `COALSECEEMPTY(Value1, Value2)` is similar to saying:

```
CASE
WHEN NOT ISEMPTY(Value1) THEN Value1
ELSE Value2
END
```

Which means that if Value1 is not empty, the CASE statement will return Value1, otherwise, it will return Value2.

Taking this even further, `COALESCEEMPTY(Value1, Value2, Value3, ....Valuen)` is the same as saying:

```
CASE
WHEN NOT ISEMPTY(Value1) THEN Value1
ELSE  COALESCEEMPTY(Value2, Value3, ..., Valuen)
```

Which can be expanded further to read:

```
CASE
WHEN NOT ISEMPTY(Value1) THEN Value1
ELSE
    CASE
    WHEN NOT ISEMPTY(Value2) THEN Value2
    ELSE COALESCEEMPTY(Value3, Value4, ..., Valuen)
```

Counting Empty Cells

Many MDX functions, such as COUNT and AVERAGE, evaluate the count of cells. All MDX functions, except for the COUNT function, ignore empty cells. The COUNT function has an optional parameter, INCLUDEEMPTY, which, if provided, results in including empty cells in the count process. In general, counting empty cells is a little tricky and has to be done with caution. For example, if you are presenting the sales of automobile models at dealerships across a certain region, you may want to show all the dealerships in that region, even if the sale of a particular model was nil in that dealership (which corresponds with empty cells). On the other hand, if you are calculating average sales of automobile models per dealer per region, you may not want to include the dealerships that did not sell the model of interest because including it would decrease the average.

Empty Cells in a Dataset and the NON EMPTY Keyword

As we saw at the beginning of the Empty Cells section above, MDX queries might result in empty cells as part of the returned set. Just like any other cell, an empty cell is associated with a set of tuples. Sometimes the tuple itself is said to be empty "empty tuple" when every cell is empty at the intersection of this tuple and any other tuple in all of the other axes.

End-user applications may choose to show or hide empty cells from the dataset. MDX provides the keyword NON EMPTY to provide for this capability. This keyword is usually provided at the axis level. If provided, NON EMPTY forces the result to exclude empty tuples along an axis from the dataset. The NON EMPTY keyword fits in the MDX statement as follows:

```
MDX_Statement ::= SELECT axis_specification
                         [, axis_specification...]
                      FROM cube_specification
                      WHERE slicer_specification
axis_specification ::= [NON EMPTY] set_expression ON axis_name
```

As you can see, NON EMPTY is an optional keyword. The default is not to provide it, which means returning all cells including empty tuples.

If you think about it, you can still get empty cells even if NON EMPTY is specified in the MDX statement for all axes. As an example, let's say that the dealer named Jackson Cars did not sell any Ford or Lincoln cars in the first and second quarter of 1998. Let's say that in the third and fourth quarter he sold specifically Lincoln cars, but still no Ford cars. Now, consider the following query:

```
SELECT
   NON EMPTY CROSSJOIN({Jackson Cars, Anderson Vehicles}, {[Ford], [Lincoln]})
      ON COLUMNS,
   NON EMPTY {[1998], [1999]} ON ROWS
FROM Sales
WHERE (Sales)
```

This results in the following dataset:

	Jackson Cars		**Anderson Vehicles**	
	Ford	**Lincoln**	**Ford**	**Lincoln**
1998		$250,000	$1,023,900	$567,450
1999	$350,940	$780,000	$1,125,000	$612,900

You notice in this example that the cell corresponding to Jackson Cars/Ford/1998 is empty because this dealer did not sell any Ford cars in 1998. The reason this cell was still empty in the resultset despite the NON EMPTY operator is that it does not represent an empty tuple, and the NON EMPTY operator filters out only completely empty tuples.

More ON Named Sets and Calculated Members

As you might recall from the previous chapter, you can define named sets and calculated members using the WITH operator. Let's take a look at the example you saw in Chapter 7:

```
WITH
     MEMBER  [Measures].[Profit] AS
    '[measures].[Sales] - [measures].[Cost]',
     SOLVE_ORDER = 1
     MEMBER  [Time].[October - November Change] AS
    '100 * ([TIME].[November-1998] - [Time].[October-1998])/[TIME].[November-
1998]',
     SOLVE_ORDER = 2
SELECT
    { [Measures].[Sales],
      [Measures].[Cost],
      [Measures].[Profit] } on columns,
    { [Time].[Calendar].[October-1998],
      [Time].[Calendar].[November-1998],
      [Time].[October - November Change] } on rows
FROM EmployeeCube
WHERE ( [Stores].[City].[ Troy, Michigan ] )
```

You notice here that we have multiple formulae to evaluate. It matters which formula is evaluated first on the resulting set. The table below results from the evaluation of the members according to the provided SOLVE_ORDER.

	Sales	**Cost**	**Profit**
October, 1998	$120,000	$69,000	$51,000
November, 1998	$150,000	$71,000	$79,000
Percent Change	25%	3%	55%

As we saw in Chapter 7, the shaded value in the table above, is particularly sensitive to this solve order. The following rules define the semantics of SOLVE_ORDER:

- Evaluation of expressions with solve order values specified is always done before the evaluation of expressions and members which don't have a solve order. The evaluation among members with solve order takes place from the lower SOLVE_ORDER to the higher SOLVE_ORDER.
- Solve orders must always be greater than or equal to 0.
- The default solve order of a formula is 0.

Let's revisit, for a moment, a topic we met in the last chapter – lifetime and scope of named sets and calculated members. If the scope of these values is not identified in their formula, the scope defaults to the formula itself, and the values don't exist outside the formula. Named sets provide a powerful mechanism to preserve state during a session and for all sessions as well. To define a custom scope for a named set or calculated member, you may write:

```
Create-Formula_Statement := [Scope]  formula_specification
```

The `formula_specification` is the same as the formulae used to create the set and/or member. The `[Scope]` operator, can be used to extend the lifetime and scope of the set or member. The value of this operator can be set to either:

- **GLOBAL:** The entity created with this specification will be visible to all sessions and queries from all of these sessions can use it.
- **SESSION:** The entity created with this specification will only be visible to queries in the session in which it is created. The session is started by connecting to the OLAP Server, and ends by disconnecting from it.

If the scope value is not defined, it defaults to the session value.

The name of the entity, named set or calculated member has to qualify with the cube name to which it belongs. You can also have two named sets or calculated members with the same name qualified by the same cube name as long as each exists in a different session from the other.

An example of creating a named set with session scope is:

```
CREATE SET SESSION SalesCube.RowsAxisSet AS {Qtr1.CHILDREN, Qtr2, Qtr3,
Qtr4.CHILDREN}
```

Or:

```
CREATE SET SalesCube.RowsAxisSet AS {Qtr1.CHILDREN, Qtr2, Qtr3, Qtr4.CHILDREN}
```

And, as an example of creating a named set with a global scope:

```
CREATE SET GLOBAL SalesCube.RowsAxisSet AS {Qtr1.CHILDREN, Qtr2, Qtr3,
Qtr4.CHILDREN}
```

MDX Expressions

An MDX statement contains expressions that operate on different items of the OLAP schema. These expressions deal with sets, tuples, members, numbers, and strings. A detailed listing of these expressions and functions is provided in Appendix C. This section, therefore, will present certain issues that have to do with particular expressions, which warrant more explanation beyond the definitions and examples provided in the appendix.

Set Value Expressions

As we discovered previously, a set is a collection of tuples, which are in turn a collection of members from different dimensions. Set expressions operate on the different levels of the set elements starting with the set as a whole, and continuing to the individual members of its tuples. Drill-down and drill-up operations are some of the most common operations in applications with graphical user interfaces that present OLAP data in a hierarchical fashion. Drilling operations can be conducted on the member or the level basis. For example, take the set `{1998, 1999}`. You might want to obtain a set that contains 1998, 1999, and all the children of 1998. This is a sample of drilling down by member. On the other hand, consider the set `{1998, 1999}` and let's try to get a set that contains 1998, 1999, and all the quarters in 1998, which is an example of a drill-down operation by level. MDX allows you to combine any of these drilling operations with a top or a bottom condition. For example, consider the set `{1998, 1999}` and return a set that includes 1998, 1999, and the top two quarters of 1998 based on Sales.

Please note that MDX functions that perform drill-up and drill-down operations require a set that is formed from a single dimension. In other words, the set used as an argument to these functions cannot be the result of a CROSSJOIN operation. Functions that have this restriction include: DRILLDOWNMEMBER, DRILLUPMEMBER, DRILLDOWNMEMBERTOP, DRILLUPMEMBERTOP, DRILLDOWNLEVEL, DRILLDOWNMEMBERBOTTOM, DRILLDOWNLEVELTOP, DRILLUPLEVEL, DRILLDOWNLEVELBOTTOM, DRILLUPMEMBER, and TOGGLEDRILLSTATE.

To better understand the following functions, let's take a look at the hierarchy of the product dimension presented in the following figure:

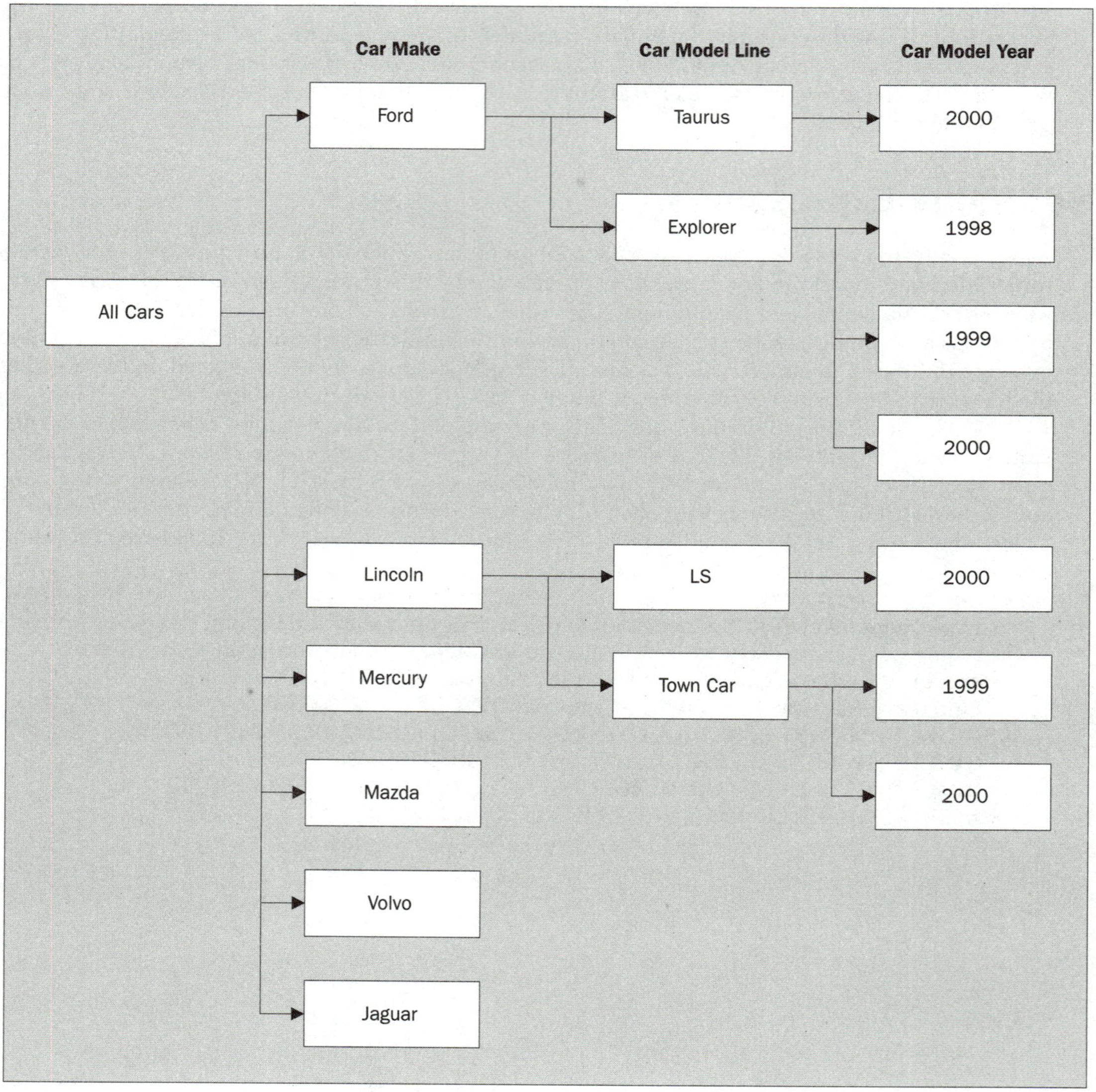

A sample product hierarchy used to explain the drilling functions

Drilling by Member

The first function to discuss is the `DRILLDOWNMEMBER()` function, which is used to drill down by a member. The syntax for this function is:

```
DRILLDOWNMEMBER(Set1, Set2 [, RECURSIVE])
```

This function drills down the members of the set `Set1` that are present in `Set2`. If the word `RECURSIVE` is provided, then the drilling continues beyond the first next level of these members. Since Microsoft OLAP only accepts complete hierarchies as we saw in Chapters 2 and 3 earlier, the RECURSIVE keyword will cause the drill down to go all the way to the leaf level of the dimension hierarchy.

For example, the function:

```
DRILLDOWNMEMBER({Ford, Lincoln}, {Ford, Honda})
```

will yield the result `{Ford, Taurus, Explorer, Lincoln}`.

Providing the optional RECURSIVE flag will yield the set:

```
{Ford, Taurus, [Taurus-2000], Explorer, [Explorer-1998], [Explorer-
1999], [Explorer-2000], Lincoln}
```

The way this function works is as follows:

- The member "Ford" from Set2 is inspected to see whether it is present in Set1. The inspection yields a positive result; therefore, it is drilled down to yield the set that has Ford, all models in Ford (in this example), and Lincoln as the result set.
- The second member of Set2, Honda, is inspected to see whether it is present in Set1 result. It is not; therefore, Washington is not drilled down any further, and the set result is still the same. If Honda were to be part of Set1, then it would have also been drilled and the resulting set would have been joined in a union operation to the first result.

This process is sensitive to the order of the members in Set2. This becomes clearer if we were to have another member in Set2 that is also present in Set1.

This function is typically used in applications with a graphical user interface that allows users to click on a "+" sign, for instance, to expand the contents of a branch. In this case, the function is called with the parameters: `DRILLDOWNMEMBER(Set1, {m})`, where `{m}` is the member that was clicked. More sophisticated applications allow for drilldown of multiple members and for recursive drilldowns as well.

The `DRILLDOWNMEMBERTOP` function is a variation of `DRILLDOWNMEMBER`. Instead of including all children (or descendants) of a member, it includes only the top n children (or descendants) based on the evaluation of a numeric expression. The syntax of this function is as follows:

```
DRILLDOWNMEMBERTOP(Set1, Set2, Index [, [numeric_expression][,
RECURSIVE]])
```

The desired number of children (or descendants) is specified by Index, and <numeric_expression> gives the criterion. For example, the call

```
DRILLDOWNMEMBERTOP ({[Lincoln LS], [Ford Explorer], [Ford Taurus]},
{[Ford Explorer], [Honda Accord], [Lincoln LS]}, 2, Sales)
```

returns the following set:

```
{[Ford Explorer], [Ford Explorer - 1998], [Ford Explorer - 1999],
[Lincoln LS], [Lincoln LS - 2000], [Ford Taurus]}
```

In this case, the top two model years of the Ford Explorer and Lincoln LS in sales were included in the result set. For Lincoln LS, since only the 2000 model year is available in our example, only this model year was returned.

Use of the `RECURSIVE` flag has an effect similar to its effect in `DRILLDOWNMEMBER`.

The function `DRILLDOWNMEMBERBOTTOM` is similar, except that the bottom condition is applied instead of the top condition.

To drill up by a member, use the `DRILLUPMEMBER` function. The syntax is as follows:

```
DRILLUPMEMBER(Set1, Set2)
```

Drills up the members in `Set1` that are present in `Set2`. To understand this function, let's take a look at the following example:

```
DRILLUPMEMBER({Ford, Taurus, [Taurus-2000], Explorer, [Explorer-1998],
[Explorer-1999], [Explorer-2000], Lincoln}, {Taurus, Explorer, [Honda
Accord]})
```

The result is the set:

```
{Ford, Lincoln, Taurus, Explorer}
```

In this example, the car model line level was rolled up (drilled up) for the model lines in Set2 that exist in Set1.

> *Note that there is no RECURSIVE flag for the DRILLUPMEMBER function. This is because when a member is drilled up, all the descendants (not just the immediate children) are removed. In other words, drilling up is usually recursive in nature and does not need to be explicitly specified to be so.*

Finally, a useful function that combines both the `DRILLDOWNMEMBER` and `DRILLUPMEMBER` is the `TOGGLEDRILLSTATE` function. The syntax for this function is:

```
TOGGLEDRILLSTATE(Set1, Set2[, RECURSIVE])
```

This toggles the drill state for each member of `Set2` that is present in `Set1`. If a member `m` of `Set2` that is present in `Set1` is drilled down (that is, has a child or descendant in `Set1`), then OLAP Services applies the function `DRILLUPMEMBER(Set1, {m})`. On the other hand, if the member `m` is already drilled up (there is no descendant of `m` that immediately follows `m` in Set1), then OLAP Services applies the function `DRILLDOWNMEMBER(Set1, {m}[, RECURSIVE])` to `Set1`. If the `TOGGLEDRILLSTATE` function were called with the optional `RECURSIVE` flag, the `DRILLDOWNMEMBER` is also called with that flag.

For example, the function:

```
TOGGLEDRILLSTATE({Ford, Taurus, [Taurus-2000], Explorer, [Explorer-
1998], [Explorer-1999], [Explorer-2000], Lincoln}, {Taurus})
```

Will be the same as running the function:

```
DRILLUPMEMBER({Ford, Taurus, [Taurus-2000], Explorer, [Explorer-1998],
[Explorer-1999], [Explorer-2000], Lincoln}, {Taurus, Explorer, [Honda
Accord]})
```

This is because m which corresponds to {Taurus} is already drilled down in the first set (it has the child: [Taurus-2000]).

Drilling by Level

The first function to discuss here is the DRILLDOWNLEVEL function. The syntax for this function is:

```
DRILLDOWNLEVEL(Set [,Level])
```

The function drills down the members in Set to one level below Level, if it is specified. If Level is not specified, it defaults to the lowest level in Set. Using the same product hierarchy presented in the figure we saw previously, we can build the following example on this function:

DRILLDOWNLEVEL({Ford, Lincoln}, [Car Make]) will yield the set:

```
{Ford, Taurus, Explorer, Lincoln, LS, Town Car}
```

In this example, the level below the car make level is the car model. Therefore, OLAP services drills down the members in set to that level. In real-life applications, the application allows the user to select a level to which they want to drill down the set members to from something like a drop-down list.

A number of functions similar to the drilling by member functions are also available to allow for drilling by level while only including the top or bottom m number of members in the resulting set. These functions include, DRILLDOWNLEVELTOP and DRILLDOWNLEVELBOTTOM. Similar to their member drilling counterparts, these functions take an index that determines the number of members to return after the drilling operation, and a numeric expression the result of which is used to order members in a level in an ascending or descending order.

> *Notice that there is no RECURSIVE flag with these functions, that is because we specify the exact level we want to drill to (or it is specified by default) and the RECURSIVE flag makes no sense in this situation, since the function does not go beyond the specified level.*

Just like there is a DRILLUPMEMBER function, there is a parallel one for the level case. The function is called, DRILLUPLEVEL, and has the syntax:

```
DRILLUPLEVEL(Set [, Level])
```

A practical use of this function may explain what it means and does. Imagine having a graphical user interface that shows an expanded hierarchy of products, similar to the figure below. Clicking the "-" sign at any level will drill-up the members of the hierarchy immediately below the "–" sign to the level at which the sign is located. However, to drill up all the members to the level of your interest, you may want to select a level from a drop-down list.

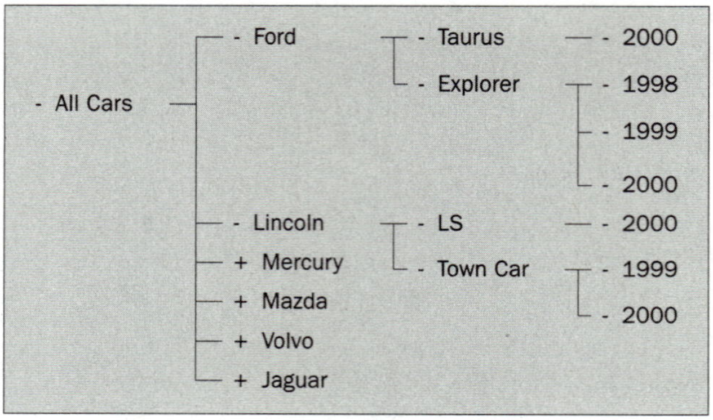

An expanded view of the Ford make of car

For example, to rollup the set to the Ford car make level, click the "-" next to the Ford make. The result will be similar to the figure shown below:

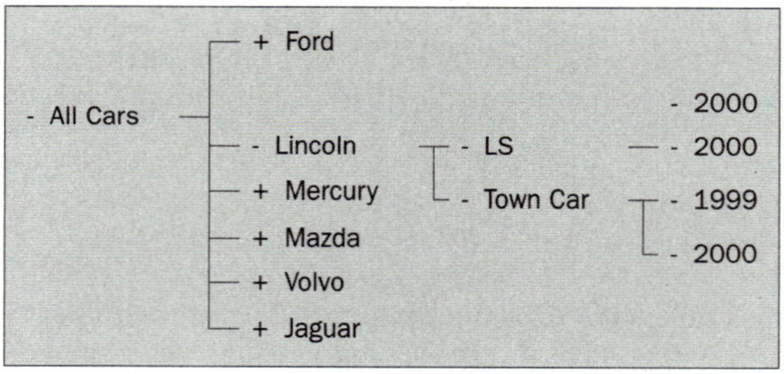

The Ford cars drilled up to the Ford make member using the DRILLUPMEMBER function.

This is equivalent to using the `DRILLUPMEMBER` function as follows:

```
DRILLUPLEVEL({Ford, [All Ford Models and Model Years], Lincoln, [All Lincoln
Models and Model Years], Mercury, Mazda, Volvo, Jaguar}, {[Ford]})
```

On the other hand, the following figure shows the difference between this result and the result of applying the DRILLUPLEVEL function as follows:

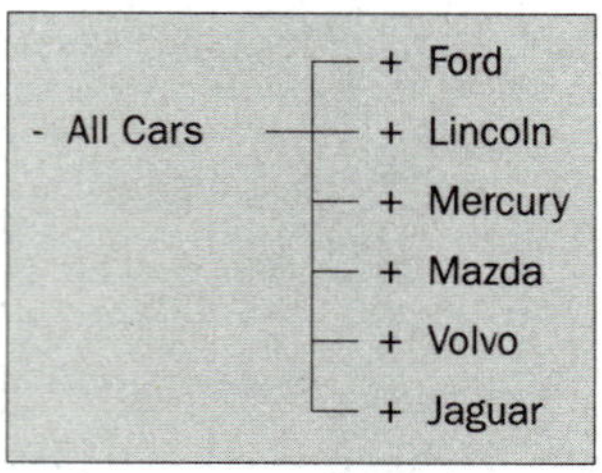

Drilling up to the car make level using the DRILLUPLEVEL function

```
DRILLUPLEVEL({Ford, [All Ford Models and Model Years], Lincoln, [All Lincoln
Models and Model Years], Mercury, Mazda, Volvo, Jaguar}, [Ford Models])
```

Preserving State During UI Operations

Many OLAP applications allow users to drill up and down data sets to view the data. In order to avoid re-writing the query to perform drill operations, MDX provides a powerful way to preserve state of these queries using the DRILLUP and DRILLDOWN functions. The way this works is by representing each axis expression by a named set. The named sets can then be represented in the drill functions, such as `DRILLDOWNMEMBER, DRILLDOWNLEVEL`, etc.

For example, as you saw earlier, we can create a set with global scope with a statement like:

```
CREATE SET GLOBAL SalesCube.RowsAxisSet AS {Qtr1.CHILDREN, Qtr2, Qtr3,
Qtr4.CHILDREN}
```

Or:

```
CREATE SET GLOBAL SalesCube.Q1Childern AS {Qtr1.CHILDREN}
```

This named set can then be used in the Drilldown/Drillup functions, which will make these functions have the same scope as the set. For example, using the two named sets above in the following function will cause the function to persist.

```
DRILLUPLEVEL(SalesCube.RowsAxisSet, SalesCube.Q1Childern)
```

Finally, when you use the function above in the MDX query below, you persist the query.

```
SELECT DRILLUPLEVEL(SalesCube.RowsAxisSet, SalesCube.Q1Childern) on rows
FROM SalesCube
```

Of course this is a simple query, and if it were more complex, you might end up using many named sets and Drill functions along the different axes of the query.

Conditional Expressions

MDX includes some conditional expressions that enrich it and make even more powerful. These expressions include:

- If Statements.
- Simple Case Expressions.
- Searched Case Expressions.

But, before we start explaining these expressions and bring up some samples of how they can be used, let's look at the comparison, logical, and conditional operators provided by MDX. MDX provides the following comparison operators:

Operator	Description
<	Less than (a < b)
>	Greater than (a > b)
<=	Less or equal (a <= b)
>=	Greater or equal (a >= b)
=	Equal (a = b)
<>	Not equal (a <> b)
`IsEmpty(Exp)`	Returns True if Exp is NULL

MDX also provides some logical operators, such as the AND, OR, NOT, and XOR operators.

XOR is called Exclusive OR (or logical exclusion). The syntax for it is: A XOR B. In simple terms it means either A or B can be true, but not both or neither. The following table summarizes the results it can return based on the values of A and B:

A	B	A XOR B
True	True	False
True	False	True
False	True	True
False	False	False

If Clause

The If clause is used in MDX in the form ***IIF***. This clause allows you to search on a certain condition and returns one of two value expressions based on the search result. The general syntax for the IIF clause is:

```
IIF(Search Condition, True_Value_Expression1, False_Value_Expression)
```

If the search condition is true, the `True_Value_Expression` is returned. Conversely, if the search condition is false, the `False_Value_Expression` is returned. The two value expressions, `True_Value_Expression` and `False_Value_Expression` must be of the same data type. for example, they can either both be strings or both be numeric.

The following is an example on how the IIF clause can be used in MDX queries. The query in the example returns the sales, the goals and the difference between the actual sales and the goal of automobiles for two car dealerships. The IIF statement ensures that no negative values are returned.

```
WITH MEMBER [Measures].[Diff] AS
    IIF(IIF ((Sales > Goal), (Sales - Goal), (Goal - Sales))
SELECT
   {Sales, Goal, Diff} ON COLUMNS,
   CROSSJOIN(  {[Jackson Cars], [Anderson Vehicles]},
               {[Q1-1998], [Q2-1998], [Q3-1998], [Q4-1998]}) ON ROWS
FROM Sales
WHERE ([1998], [Cars].[Ford])
```

This results in the following dataset (sales in thousands of dollars):

	Jackson Cars			**Anderson Vehicles**		
1998	**Sales**	**Goal**	**Diff**	**Sales**	**Goal**	**Diff**
Q1	125	100	25	207	150	57
Q2	131	110	21	143	150	7
Q3	119	120	1	181	145	36
Q4	123	115	8	190	145	45

Simple Case Expression

The case expression comes handy in many situations when writing MDX queries. The general syntax for this expression is:

```
CASE Case_Value_Expression
    WHEN  When_Value_Expression  THEN Then_Value_Expression
    ...
    ...
    ...
    ELSE  Else_Value_Expression
END
```

The dots in the code above indicate that the WHEN clause can be repeated several times. This expression returns the `Then_Value_Expression` corresponding to the first `When_Value_Expression` that evaluates to True. In other words, even if more than one of the `When_Value_Expressions` is True, the statement will return the first one of these True expressions in the list. If none of the `When_Value_Expressions` evaluates to True, the `Else_Value_Expression` is returned. It is important to note that the data type of the `When_Value_Expression`, `Then_Value_Expression` and the `Else_Value_Expression` is VARIANT. The Else part of the statement can be left out. In this case, if none of the When expressions evaluates to True, the statement returns an empty cell value (basically does nothing). The following example demonstrates the use of this function.

```
WITH MEMBER [Measures].[Rating] AS
    CASE ([Measures].[PerformanceRating)
            WHEN   5  THEN  "Excellent"
            WHEN   4  THEN  "Very Good"
            WHEN   3  THEN  "Good"
            WHEN   2  THEN  "Poor"
            WHEN   1  THEN  "Very Poor"
            ELSE   "NA"
    END
SELECT {[Measures].[Sales], [Measures].[Rating]} ON COLUMNS,
   Dealerships.MEMBERS ON ROWS
FROM Sales
WHERE ([1998], [Geography].[States].[MI], [Products].[All])
```

The MDX query above returns the sales amount together with a performance rating for car dealerships in Michigan. The rating value is decided based on the value of `[Measures].[PerformanceRating]`. A Case expression is used for this purpose to return the appropriate value for the performance rating.

Searched Case Expression

The Searched Case Expression takes the simple case expression a step further by making the `When` operands search conditions themselves. In the example presented in the previous section, a performance rating is evaluated based on a rating value from 1 to 5. What if the evaluation is based on the percentage of sales above target sales. For example, if the salesperson exceeds their target sale (the value of the named member in the query below is higher than 100%), then the rating is 5. To express this logic in the MDX statement, you can write:

```
WITH MEMBER [Measures].[PerformanceTemp] AS
   ([Measures].[Sales] - [Measures].[TargetSales])/
   [Measures].[TargetSales]*100
MEMBER [Measures].[Rating] AS
   CASE
      WHEN [Measures].[PerformanceTemp] > 100 THEN 5
      WHEN [Measures].[PerformanceTemp] > 50  THEN 4
      WHEN [Measures].[PerformanceTemp] > 0   THEN 3
      WHEN [Measures].[PerformanceTemp] > -25 THEN 2
      ELSE 1
   END
SELECT {[Measures].[Sales], [Measures].[Rating]}
   ON COLUMNS,
   Dealerships.MEMBERS ON ROWS
FROM Sales
WHERE ([1998], [Geography].[States].[MI], [Products].[All])
```

The example above shows the same results as the simple case expression example, except that the performance rating is evaluated based on ranges of values of the percent exceedance of targeted sales for Michigan dealerships in 1998.

Note that the When clauses have to be in the order presented above in order for this case expression to work (same is true for the simple case example too). This is because we are using the ">" operator rather than bracketing the values between "<" and ">" operators. In other words, if we were to express the When clauses as:

```
WHEN [Measures].[PerformanceTemp] > 100 THEN 5
WHEN ([Measures].[PerformanceTemp] > 50  AND
[Measures].[PerformanceTemp] <100) THEN 4
WHEN ([Measures].[PerformanceTemp] > 0
AND [Measures].[PerformanceTemp] < 50) THEN 3
WHEN ([Measures].[PerformanceTemp] > -25 AND
[Measures].[PerformanceTemp] < 0) THEN 2
```

Then we would not have to keep the same order of these When clauses.

More MDX Functions and Operators

MDX provides a rich set of built-in functions and operators to handle all situations from specifying cells and tuples, to performing numerical calculations and aggregations, to filtering operators, ordering functions, and hierarchy-preserving functions to name but a few. Appendix C provides a detailed list of all the built-in functions and operators, with explanations and examples on each of them. Appendix C also lists functions available to OLAP Services and MDX that are available in Visual Basic for Applications (VBA), and Microsoft Excel.

The MDX SampleApplication

To make writing MDX statements easier and avoid syntax problems, Microsoft shipped a sample MDX application to help write such statements. The application is installed with the OLAP Services installation. The application is written in Visual Basic and its code is provided in the folder located at <Drive Letter>:\Program Files\OLAP Services\Samples\MDX Sample. If you are a seasoned VB programmer, you may want to consider looking closely at the code, or even modifying it to fit you needs. The MDX sample application can be launched from the same OLAP Services group in the Start menu. Once launched, you are prompted to enter an OLAP server name to connect to, and an OLE DB Provider for OLAP to use. The defaults are your local OLAP Server, and the OLE DB Provider for Microsoft OLAP (MSOLAP). Although the application is anything but as sophisticated as the query-by-example (QBE) tools provided in MS Access and MS Visual Studio, it still serves as a good start to get familiar with the MDX syntax and avoid such errors when building your expressions.

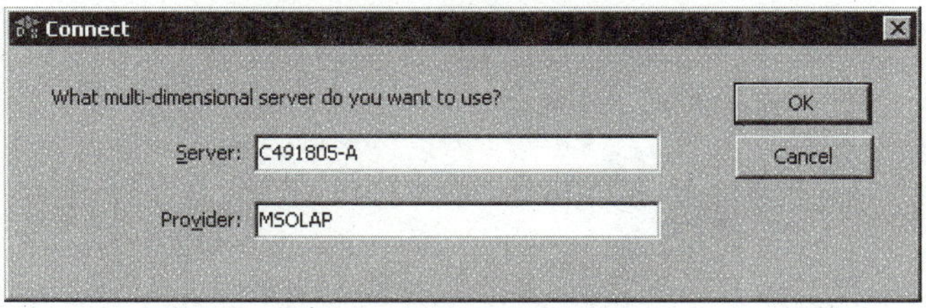

Connecting to the OLAP server in the MDX sample application

The main application screen after passing the connection dialog box, shown in the above figure, is shown in the following screenshot. In this screen, you can select an OLAP database from the DB drop-down menu, select a previously saved query to work with, and select one of many views provided to make building the MDX statement and testing it easy.

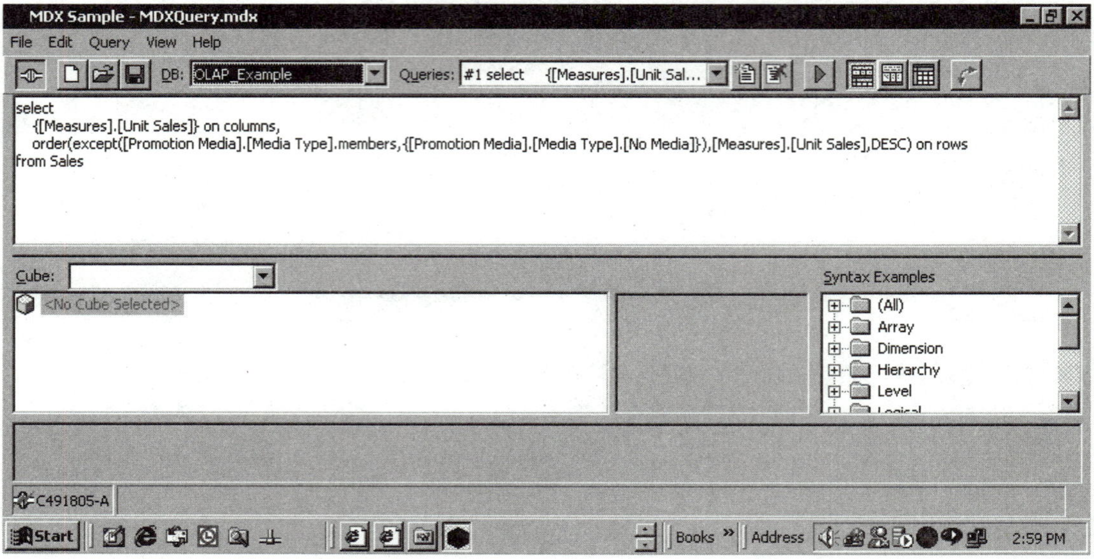

The main screen of the MDX sample application

The main screen is composed of a number of ActiveX controls that allow you to view the OLAP database cubes, the cube metadata, write your query against the OLAP database, view and select from a list of available functions, and view the results after running the query. We will not go into the details of the VB applications and the individual user controls that comprise the application; instead, We will simply look at how you can write a sample OLAP query with this tool.

In the example, we will be using the FoodMart database that ships with OLAP Services and build a query that retrieves the percentage store profits for the different departments, ordering the results based on the profit rate in descending order. The query that accomplishes this is shown below:

```
WITH member [Measures].[Store Profit Rate] as
             '([Measures].[Store Sales]-[Measures].[Store Cost])/
                [Measures].[Store Cost]', format = '#.00%'
SELECT
    {[Measures].[Store Cost],[Measures].[Store Sales],
      [Measures].[Store Profit Rate]} on columns,
    Order([Product].[Product Department].members,
      [Measures].[Store Profit Rate], BDESC) on rows
FROM Sales
where ([Time].[1997])
```

You can either type the query in the query section of the MDX Sample Application screen, or you can build it using the functions and tools available to you. Let's see how you can build it making sure the syntax is correct.

1. First define your calculated member with the WITH clause. Type "WITH MEMBER " and double click the Measures dimension in the cubes metadata tree.

2. Give a name to the calculated member as [Store Profit Rate] and type AS.

3. As a definition of the calculated member, type the formula shown in single quotes dragging and dropping the measure dimension members from the tree view whenever possible.

4. Use the FORMAT operator to format the string resulting as the calculation of the specified member as format = '#.00%'. This will format the member as a percentage with two decimal digits. So far, the screen should look as shown below:

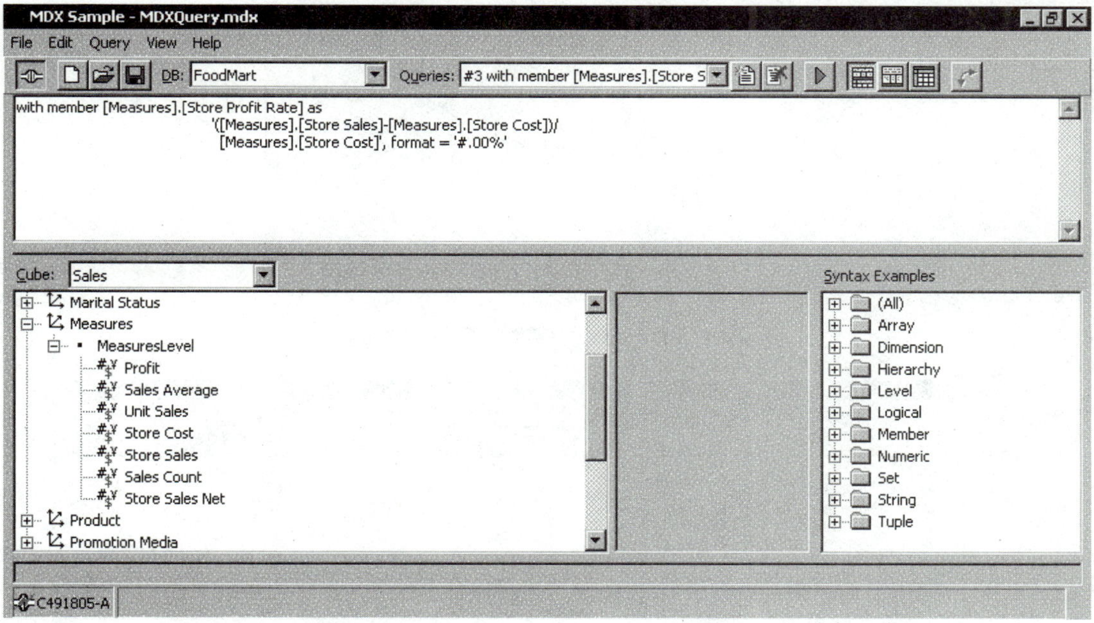

Specifying the named member in the MDX sample query

5. Next, you can type the SELECT statement, or type the keywords and drag and drop the members and dimensions from the tree view onto the query section.

6. What is worth mentioning here is that when adding the Order function, select it from the function list found under the Syntax Examples, then drag and drop it onto the query pane. The function provides you with a guidance of what needs to go as its arguments. Replace the different sections showed in the next diagram with measures, dimensions, etc. that you drag and drop from the Cube metadata tree view.

7. After you finish building the rest of the query, you can run it to view the results (below).

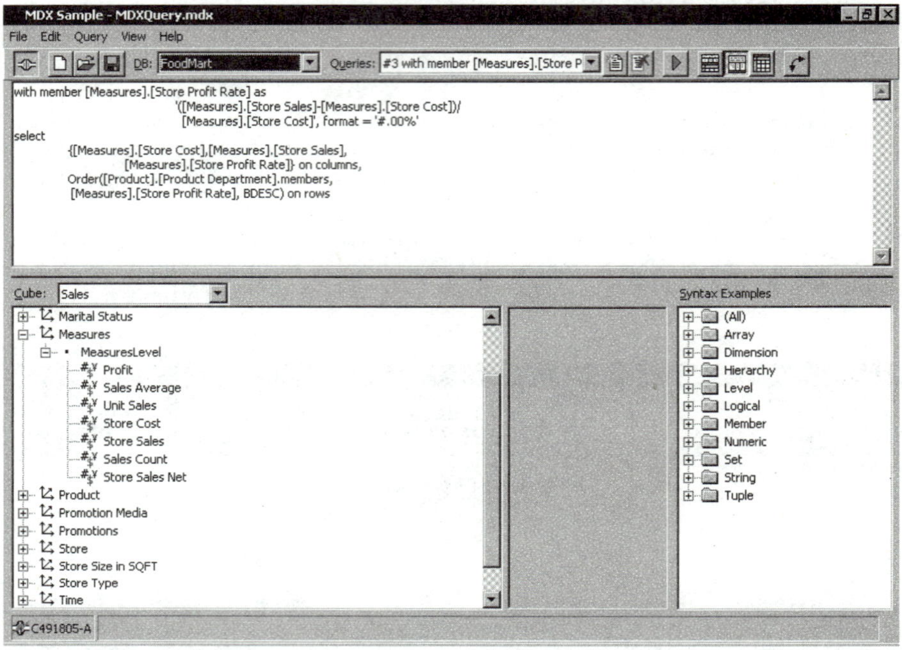

Adding the Order Function to the query pane.

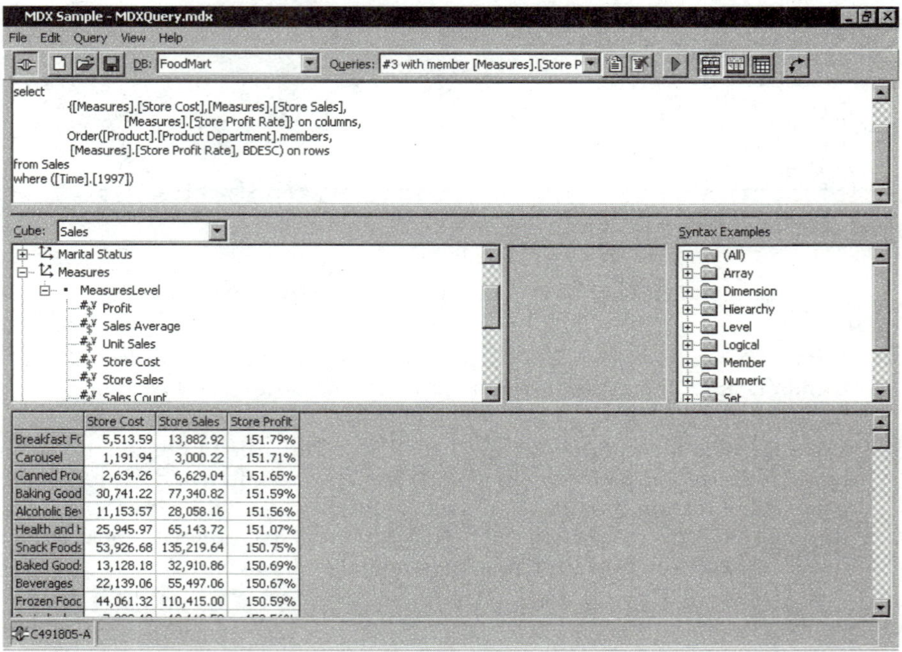

Results of the MDX sample query

Summary

Unfortunately, the first release of MS OLAP Services did not include the comprehensive documentation of MDX with the samples that one would like to see. Hopefully, the following release of OLAP Services that might accompany the release of SQL Server 2000, will include more comprehensive documentation. This chapter introduced you to some of the powerful concepts and features of MDX. Together with Chapter 7, you should be on your way to using this language to build queries that you can use in your OLAP applications. Appendix C can serve as a reference for all the built-in functions and expressions provided with MDX. Finally, the sample MDX application provided with OLAP Services can be of great help to familiarize you with the language syntax. The next chapter marks the end line of the OLAP solution design and implementation. The chapter discusses the end-user part of this solution – the reporting tools that deliver the data to the use in the form that benefits them most.

9

Data Analysis and Presentation

We have seen how to design and build a data warehouse, and even build an OLAP solution based on the massive amounts of data held in the data warehouse. So, what benefit does this give to the regular end-user? These users are not interested in fancy technical jargon and terminology. Instead, they are interested in getting answers to their questions from the accumulated data in the data warehouse in a clear, easy to understand way. These users will not be writing MDX queries, nor will they be writing regular SQL queries. Instead, they want the results of these sorts of queries put in simple tables and graphs that they can understand and use them in their decision-making process.

This chapter presents the way Microsoft handled the issue of delivering the solution to the end user. In particular, we will concentrate on three tools: The Microsoft OLAP Manager and its ability to present data, the Microsoft Pivot Table service, the corner stone for such delivery, and a Microsoft ActiveX control that allows applications written in other languages to mimic the OLAP Manager's functionality (OLAP Manager's Cube Browser). Hence, the topics covered in this chapter include:

- OLAP Client Architecture.
- The OLAP Manager as a data presentation tool.
- The PivotTable Service as a cornerstone for data reporting in MS OLAP Services.
- The OLAP Manager's Cube Browser ActiveX control with a sample application on how it can be used.

OLAP Client Architecture

The goal of the OLAP client is to help the OLAP solution developer get the data to the end user in the simplest, most effective, and efficient manner. The end user wants to access the data as "canned" reports that they could inspect on a regular basis, or on an ad hoc basis that allows them to get data summaries with a few mouse-clicks selecting certain criteria for the report. For instance, the user may select a city from the customer drop-down list, a time period, such as the third quarter of 1999 from a time drop-down list, and a particular product category from the product drop-down list. They would expect in return to see the sales, costs, and profits, besides other measures, plotted for them in a table, or a graph that is easy to read.

To fulfill end-user requirements, Microsoft built in a complex but powerful architecture for the OLAP services. As we saw previously, the OLAP Server pre-builds the aggregations of the data in the data warehouse based on the existing dimensions and stores these aggregations in the multi-dimensional database in MOLAP and HOLAP storage types, and in summary tables in the relational database in the ROLAP case. The PivotTable service carries client requests to the OLAP Server. The OLAP Server processes these requests and builds the dataset from the pre-stored aggregates, if possible, or from processing new aggregations based on the parameters passed to it. The OLAP Server then sends back the dataset to the client via the same service that carried the request.

When Microsoft wanted to build a tool that allows client applications to access OLAP data, it looked at a technology it already had working for years with some of the Microsoft Office products. This technology is the Pivot Table technology. Microsoft Excel has incorporated Pivot Tables since version 5.0, and Microsoft Access incorporated another form of this technology, crosstab queries, with the last few versions (since version 2.0). Pivot Tables proved to be a reliable and efficient way to access data and present it in an easy-to-understand and intuitive way. Therefore, it was natural to take advantage of this technology and expand it to fit the Microsoft OLAP. Hence was the birth of the PivotTable service.

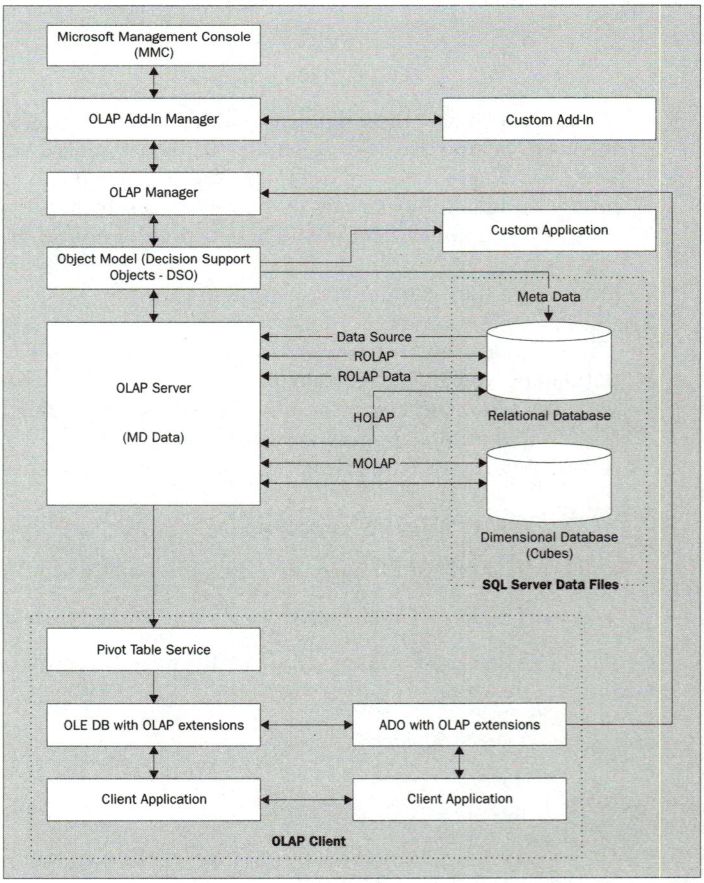

The OLAP client architecture in relation to the OLAP Services architecture

The figure previously shows a schematic of the OLAP Services architecture and how the client architecture fits in the whole picture. The figure shows the clear interaction between the client pieces of this architecture and the other pieces. The main point of such communication is the PivotTable service. This service is the link between client applications and the OLAP Server, which is eventually responsible for delivering the data, and aggregations the client applications are asking for.

In the figure below, we zoom in on the client pieces of the OLAP Services client and look at how the interaction between the PivotTable service and the OLAP server takes place. Client applications connect to the PivotTable service using OLE DB with the OLAP extensions. Clients can connect to the service via OLE DB, or via ADO, which uses OLE DB to make the connection, as shown in the figure. Client requests for multi-dimensional data are then transferred to the PivotTable service, which pulls the requested data from the OLAP Server.

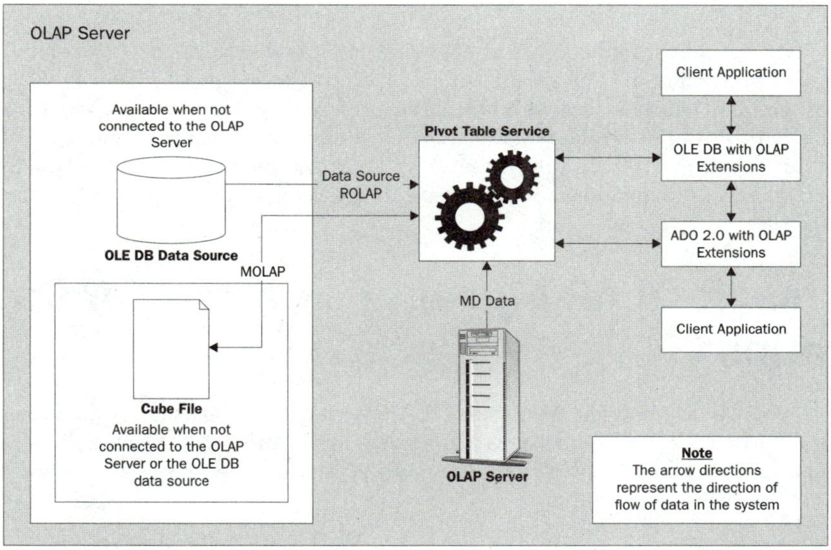

Schematic of the PivotTable Architecture

The PivotTable service also allows client applications to access local OLE DB data sources when the connection to the OLAP server is not available. These data sources are usually partial replicas of operational databases or data marts that reside locally on the client machine. The PivotTable service also allows for creating and accessing local cubes on the client, which facilitates disconnected and mobile analysis.

The previous figures and discussions clearly show that the PivotTable service is the center of the Microsoft OLAP client architecture. This service is now a companion to OLAP Services that provides client access to OLAP data for custom applications. The PivotTable service has great features that make it uniquely important in the Microsoft OLAP architecture and Microsoft data warehousing strategy as a whole. Some of these features include:

- The PivotTable service has a caching ability on the client, which improves the performance of client applications accessing the OLAP data.
- The same PivotTable service is incorporated in Microsoft Excel 2000, which makes Excel a powerful tool for OLAP data presentation.

- With The PivotTable service, one can create client-side cubes which allow for conducting analyses on mobile computers while disconnected from the network and the main data source. Client side cubes are usually stored in cube files on the client machine. These files can be opened and read by the OLAP Manager as we will see later in the chapter.
- Since The PivotTable service is installed on client machines, such as when Microsoft Excel is installed, developers can build applications using any programming language they feel comfortable with to access OLAP data or even relational data sources using the OLE DB technology.
- The PivotTable service is optimized to work with OLAP services as an integral part of the whole architecture of these services. Therefore, PivotTable service allows for multiple clients to access the same cubes by automatically dividing processing among these users and using a complex, but efficient, caching system.

Client applications as shown in the figure above – *Schematic of the PivotTable Architecture* – are built for user analysis and presentation. OLAP data can be developed to use the Desktop PivotTable Service. Integration of the PivotTable service with other Microsoft technologies such as Microsoft ActiveX controls and Microsoft Office implementations makes it easy to create applications that provide powerful graphical user interfaces. Another service, the Microsoft Desktop Data Cube Service, also provides interfaces that independent software vendors are using to develop third-party applications.

The Microsoft OLAP Manager as a Tool for Data Presentation

In this section, you will see how the Microsoft OLAP Manager can be used for data presentation and reporting. OLAP Manager in this context is just a client application that uses the PivotTable service to access the multidimensional data provided by the OLAP server. The sample FoodMart database that ships with OLAP services will be used in this section.

Getting Started

To start viewing multidimensional data in Microsoft OLAP Manager, you need to select a cube in the tree view pane and click on the Data tab in the detailed web page pane. In the following figure, for example, you can see the data page of the Sales cube in the FoodMart sample database. The figure below shows the measures and calculated members of the cube along the columns of the data grid (x-axis), including:

- Unit Sales
- Store Cost
- Store Sales
- Sales Count
- Store Sales Net
- Profit
- Average Sales

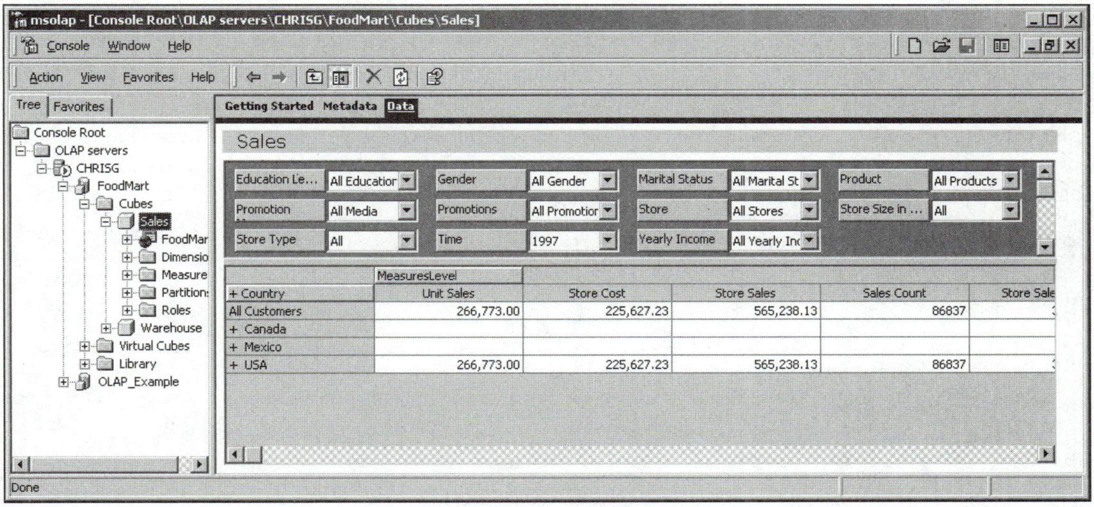

The data page for the Sales cube

The cube has 10 different dimensions besides the measures dimension, and two member properties. The dimensions include:

- Product
- Store
- Time
- Customers
- Education Level
- Gender
- Promotion Media
- Yearly Income
- Marital Status
- Promotions

The two member properties are:

- Store Size in sq. ft.
- Store Type

In this example, the `Customer` dimension is actually a geographic dimension, and is represented on the y-axis as the row of the grid. The reason I say "a geographic dimension" is that there is another dimension that has a geographic nature in the scope of this example – the `Store` dimension. The rest of the dimensions, including the `Store` dimension, and member properties are represented on the top as drop-down lists. These drop-down lists allow you to drill to any level in the dimension it represents. For example, in the figure below, you can see the `Product` Dimension selected with the levels expanded to the `Brand` level allowing us to select the Booker cheese brand as the `Product` dimension member at which we need to perform our aggregations.

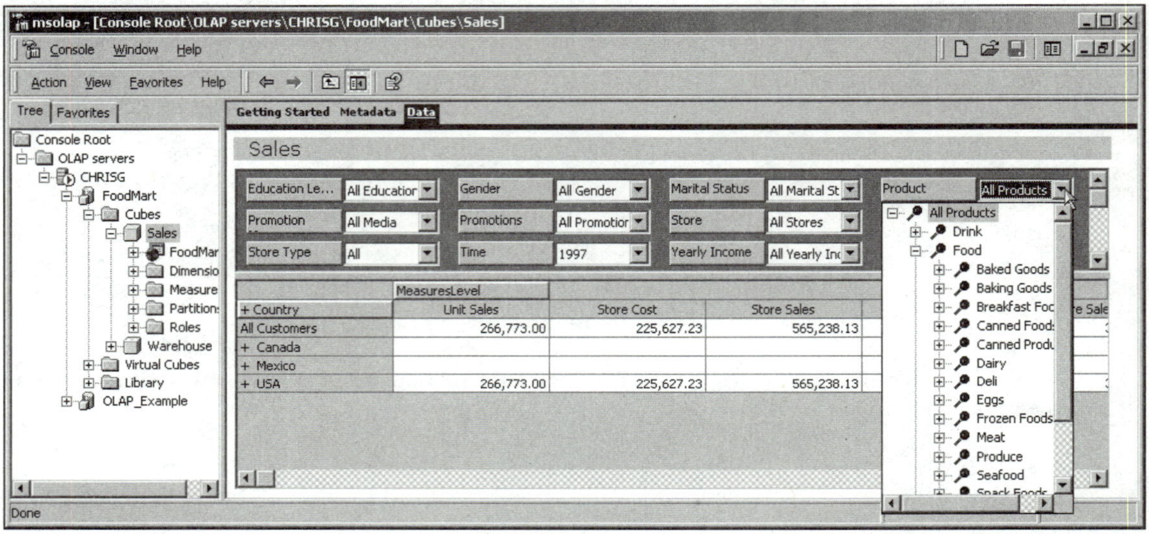

The OLAP Manager's Data page with the Product dimension selected

Once you select a member from a dimension, or a combination of members from several dimensions from the drop-down lists, the data grid gets updated and the corresponding measure and calculated member aggregations are recalculated. Expanding the levels of the `Customers` dimension on the y-axis shows the calculated measures for these expanded levels. For example, the next figure shows the values of the different measures with the Customers dimension expanded to show aggregations at the customer city level for the state of Washington in the USA.

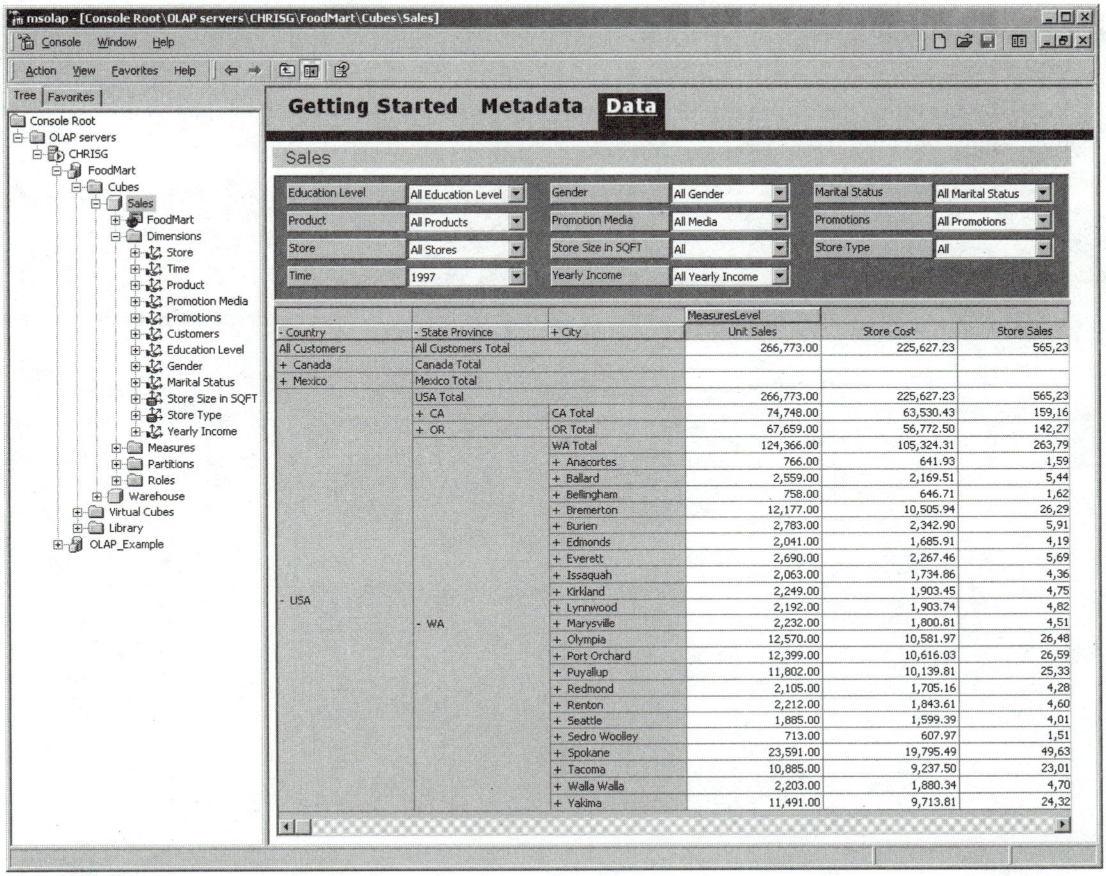

The OLAP Manager's Data page with an expanded view of the Customer dimension

Data Analysis

You can drag and drop dimensions from the top of the grid to the left, adding these dimensions to the y-axis. The next figure shows the results you get when you drag and drop the Gender and Marital Status dimensions onto the y-axis.

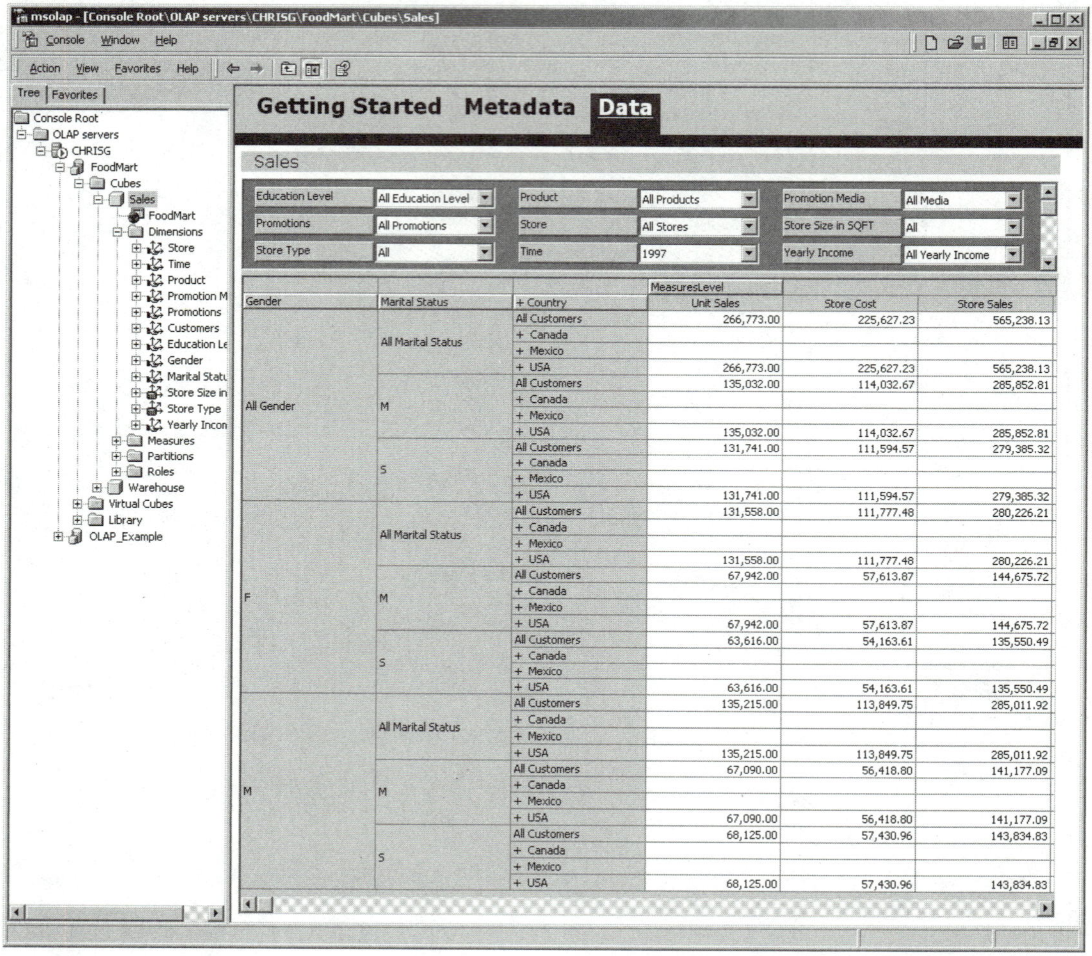

The Data page showing the Gender, Martial Status, and Customer dimensions along the y-axis.

The ability to do this gives you great flexibility in the way you view and analyze the data. This also serves in discovering aspects about your data that were not known before, such as the relationships between these dimensions. For instance, you notice in the previous figure that married people contributed more to the values of the dimensions and calculated members than single people, it did not matter whether these married people were males or females. You can flip the relationship by dragging the Marital Status dimension to the area in front of the Gender dimension so that the aggregations get calculated for the marital status first, then to the gender. Doing so shows you that males generally contributed slightly higher values to the measures and calculated members, except for the case of married females who contributed slightly more to these measures and calculated members than unmarried females (See figure oppsite).

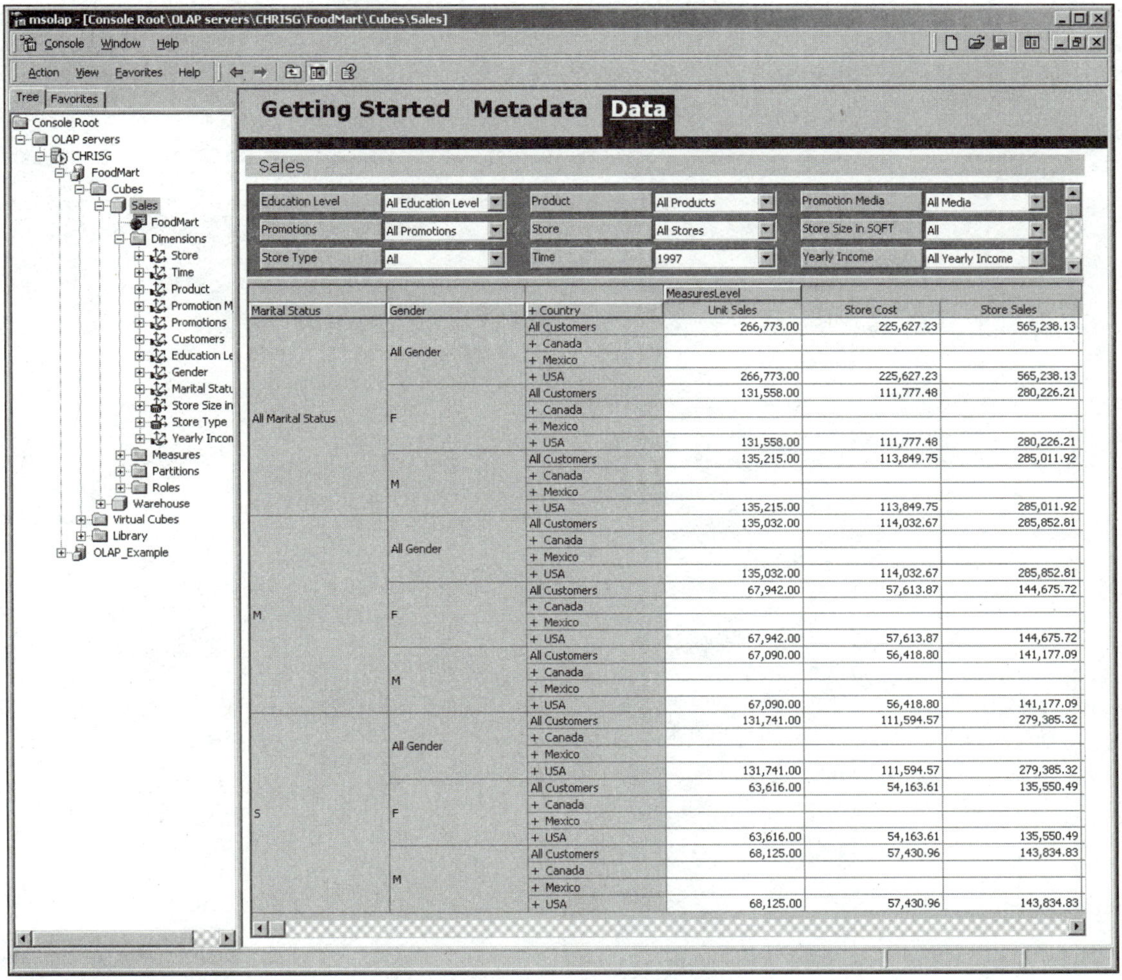

Flipping the order of two dimensions may show different sides of the relationships between the two dimensions

Another example of conducting such visual analysis is looking at the relationship between promotion types and customer gender. The figure below shows the data page with these two dimensions listed along the y-axis, and the remaining dimensions set to their default values with the ALL level selected when possible. The figure shows that certain promotion types have different effects on people based on their gender. For instance, females contributed to most measures and calculated members more than males did when presented with promotions such as radio ads, in-store coupons, etc. Males, on the other hand, contributed more to the sales and other measures than females when presented with promotions such as daily paper/radio, and product attachments. These results could help the marketing department of the FoodMart company adjust its marketing schemes to make the most of their promotional campaigns.

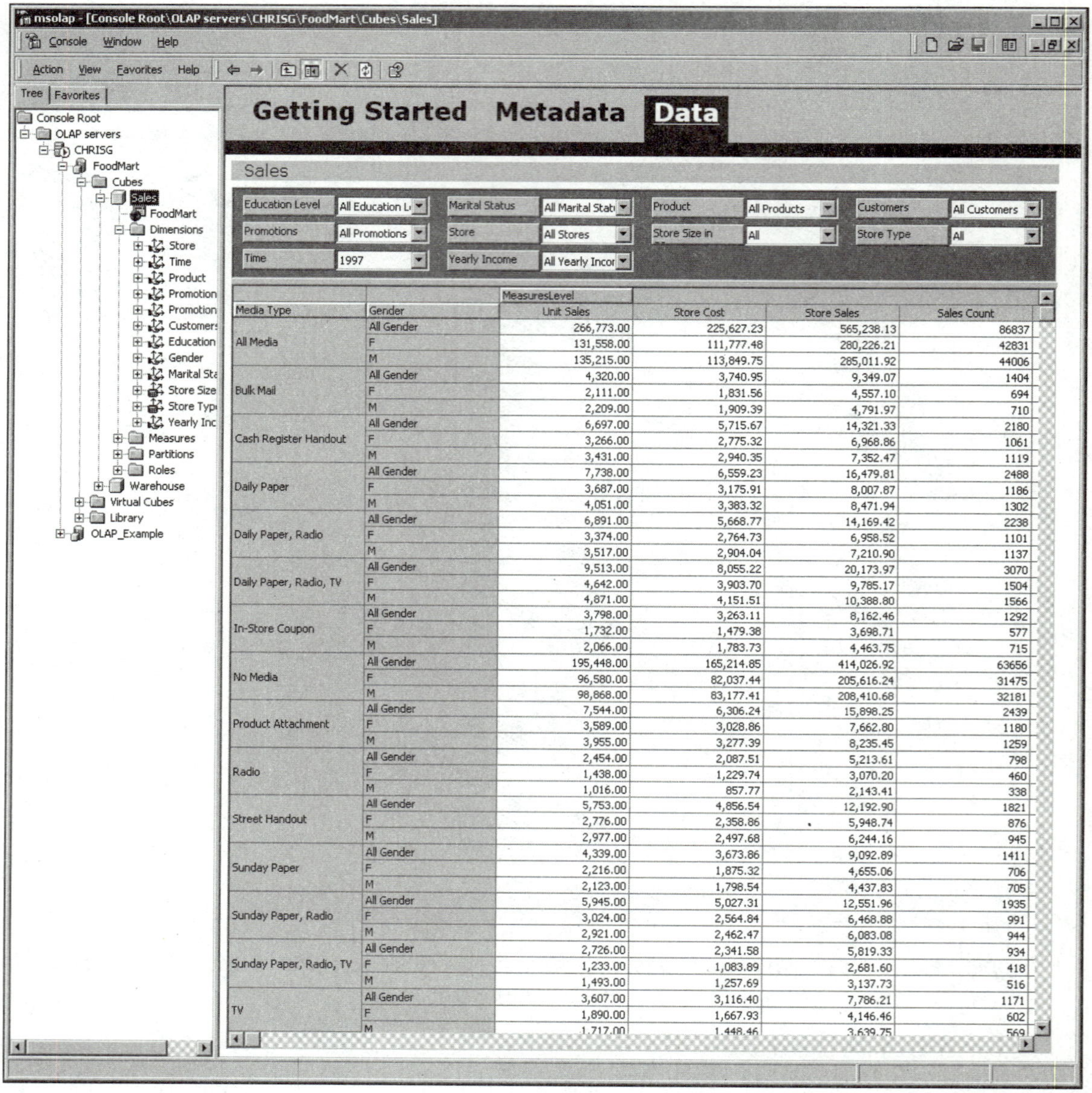

Media Type	Gender	Unit Sales	Store Cost	Store Sales	Sales Count
All Media	All Gender	266,773.00	225,627.23	565,238.13	86837
	F	131,558.00	111,777.48	280,226.21	42831
	M	135,215.00	113,849.75	285,011.92	44006
Bulk Mail	All Gender	4,320.00	3,740.95	9,349.07	1404
	F	2,111.00	1,831.56	4,557.10	694
	M	2,209.00	1,909.39	4,791.97	710
Cash Register Handout	All Gender	6,697.00	5,715.67	14,321.33	2180
	F	3,266.00	2,775.32	6,968.86	1061
	M	3,431.00	2,940.35	7,352.47	1119
Daily Paper	All Gender	7,738.00	6,559.23	16,479.81	2488
	F	3,687.00	3,175.91	8,007.87	1186
	M	4,051.00	3,383.32	8,471.94	1302
Daily Paper, Radio	All Gender	6,891.00	5,668.77	14,169.42	2238
	F	3,374.00	2,764.73	6,958.52	1101
	M	3,517.00	2,904.04	7,210.90	1137
Daily Paper, Radio, TV	All Gender	9,513.00	8,055.22	20,173.97	3070
	F	4,642.00	3,903.70	9,785.17	1504
	M	4,871.00	4,151.51	10,388.80	1566
In-Store Coupon	All Gender	3,798.00	3,263.11	8,162.46	1292
	F	1,732.00	1,479.38	3,698.71	577
	M	2,066.00	1,783.73	4,463.75	715
No Media	All Gender	195,448.00	165,214.85	414,026.92	63656
	F	96,580.00	82,037.44	205,616.24	31475
	M	98,868.00	83,177.41	208,410.68	32181
Product Attachment	All Gender	7,544.00	6,306.24	15,898.25	2439
	F	3,589.00	3,028.86	7,662.80	1180
	M	3,955.00	3,277.39	8,235.45	1259
Radio	All Gender	2,454.00	2,087.51	5,213.61	798
	F	1,438.00	1,229.74	3,070.20	460
	M	1,016.00	857.77	2,143.41	338
Street Handout	All Gender	5,753.00	4,856.54	12,192.90	1821
	F	2,776.00	2,358.86	5,948.74	876
	M	2,977.00	2,497.68	6,244.16	945
Sunday Paper	All Gender	4,339.00	3,673.86	9,092.89	1411
	F	2,216.00	1,875.32	4,655.06	706
	M	2,123.00	1,798.54	4,437.83	705
Sunday Paper, Radio	All Gender	5,945.00	5,027.31	12,551.96	1935
	F	3,024.00	2,564.84	6,468.88	991
	M	2,921.00	2,462.47	6,083.08	944
Sunday Paper, Radio, TV	All Gender	2,726.00	2,341.58	5,819.33	934
	F	1,233.00	1,083.89	2,681.60	418
	M	1,493.00	1,257.69	3,137.73	516
TV	All Gender	3,607.00	3,116.40	7,786.21	1171
	F	1,890.00	1,667.93	4,146.46	602
	M	1,717.00	1,448.46	3,639.75	569

Dimension relations can be clearer when put side by side with other dimensions set at their default levels.

In summary, the OLAP Manager's Data view is a powerful tool that allows you to conduct quick visual evaluations of the results and aggregations in the OLAP database. The data is pulled into this view using the PivotTable service behind the scenes. However, since not many people have access to the OLAP Manager's screens and usually decision makers couldn't care less about learning how to use a "new" tool like the OLAP Manager, you often find yourself having to use more popular and commonly accepted tools for reporting purposes, such as Microsoft Excel, in combination with the PivotTable.

A Closer Look at the PivotTable Service

As I mentioned earlier in the OLAP client architecture section, the PivotTable service allows clients to send requests for data to the OLAP server, and carries the datasets back to the client. This service also allows the clients to format the data and present it in many flexible ways. Actually, the PivotTable service doesn't just do these functions. It is also an OLE DB provider that supports the optional OLE DB for OLAP extensions introduced in OLE DB 2.0 and ADO 2.0. It even goes beyond being a simple client service to be a more sophisticated in-process desktop OLAP server that provides online and offline data analysis, and online access to OLAP data.

The PivotTable service conducts data analyses, cube building on the client end, and cache management while presenting the data to the end user in tabular format. This service not only provides functionality to view the data, but also to manipulate it. PivotTable service is designed with great flexibility. It can store data locally on the client computer for offline analysis and offers connectivity to the multidimensional data managed by OLAP Services, other OLE DB-compliant providers, and to non-OLAP relational data sources.

The following is a discussion of the different aspects of this service and how it serves as the centerpiece in the Microsoft OLAP Services architecture.

PivotTable Service Installation

OK, you might ask if this service is installed on your server or machine automatically when you install SQL Server OLAP services. The answer is both yes and no. Yes, the service is installed during the installation of OLAP services, but no, it is not installed by default. You have to select the client components in the Select Components dialog box (see Appendix B, Installing OLAP Services).

What Exactly Is It Used For?

I feel that it is important to know, from a developer's perspective, what this tool can do for me, and how to make the best use of it. PivotTable service was built for the following purposes:

- To connect to the OLAP server as a client of MS OLAP services. This makes the PivotTable a bridge between client applications and the OLAP Services. By connecting to the PivotTable services, these applications also connect to the OLAP Services. Client applications also connect to PivotTable service to do local, disconnected analysis, in stand-alone desktop analysis applications.
- Supports a subset of the Structured Query Language, SQL, allowing it to be a tabular data provider.
- Supports Multidimensional Expressions Language, MDX, allowing it to be a multi-dimensional data provider.
- Accesses relational data sources allowing for the implementation of multi-dimensional functionality and exposing the OLE DB interfaces with the optional OLAP extensions.

- Allows client applications to create cubes locally, directly from a relational data source.
- Allows users to retrieve data from data sources and store the retrieved data in multi-dimensional structures on the local computer for offline analysis. With this, the PivotTable service acts more like a mobile client.
- The PivotTable service offers data definition language (DDL) statements that allow you to create new local cubes and populate them with data, maintain calculated members, user-defined sets, and cache.

Well, you might well be asking your self "what is the catch? Is there anything that this service will not be able to do?" The answer to this question is yes. The following are some limitations of the PivotTable service:

- The PivotTable service can work with only a single local cube partition for cubes stored locally on the client, and does not implement an internal aggregation management system, like the OLAP Server does (see Chapter 2, OLAP Services Architecture), for defining and storing aggregations.
- As the previous bullet implies, the performance of the PivotTable service is closely tied to the amount of data it manages.
- Even though the PivotTable service does offer DDL statements, it does not offer DBA-type activities, such as managing users and groups, and data access rules.

PivotTable Service Clients

You might well ask, "I thought that the PivotTable service was a client. How come it has clients?" Well, it is true that PivotTable service can be a client to the OLAP Services, but it can also be a server that offers the services mentioned above to many clients that take advantage of these services. The PivotTable service can be used by custom applications to access multi-dimensional OLAP data, perform some analyses, and present the data summaries. Microsoft, third party vendors, or even you can write these custom applications.

Web-based applications can use the PivotTable service to display and browse data summaries, analyses, and aggregates on web pages. When used to create local cubes that can be browsed and analyzed offline, tools used to view the cube, including the OLAP Manager are considered clients of the PivotTable Service.

Microsoft Office 2000 applications can be powerful clients to the PivotTable service using it to retrieve data from multi-dimensional data sources, analyze the data, and create local cube files. Of particular importance are Microsoft Excel and Microsoft Access because these two products already implement some forms of this service.

Using the PivotTable Service

Now you know what the PivotTable Service is all about, you might be wondering how it can be used. This section shows you how you can use this service to accomplish the tasks that it is intended for, including creating local cubes, populating local cubes, retrieving data from OLAP servers, and viewing and refreshing data from such servers and local cubes.

Creating Local Cubes

When creating a local cube, you can define its storage to be either Multidimensional OLAP (MOLAP), or Relational OLAP (ROLAP) storage (see Chapters 1 and 2 for definition of MOLAP, HOLAP, and ROLAP). If you want the local cube storage to be MOLAP, you can use the CREATE CUBE statement and the INSERT INTO statement (see the following sections for explanation of these two statements) to populate it with dimension members and measure data. Once created, you can connect to the local cube and view its data for offline analysis.

If, on the other hand, you elected the ROLAP storage type for your cube, you can still use the same CREATE CUBE and INSERT INTO statements to create the local cube and insert dimension members into it. However, you need to use the option OPTIONS DEFER_DATA with the INSERT INTO statement. This is because with ROLAP storage, cube structure is created and dimension members are populated, but measure data is not saved into the cube. Once created, you can connect to the local cube to view and analyze its data, but you still need to be connected to the cube's data source (not to the OLAP Server).

The option, DEFER_DATA, causes the query to be parsed locally and executed only when necessary to retrieve data to satisfy a user request. This option fits the ROLAP storage mode since you still need to have connection to the data source to view the local cube data.

As you might expect, local cubes saved with the MOLAP option will take longer to create and will take much larger disk space to store than cubes created with the ROLAP option. This is the trade-off of having the data ready locally for quick and effective analysis. Since ROLAP-based local cubes don't store the measure data, queries against these cubes take longer to execute compared to the same queries on MOLAP-based local cubes.

The created cubes are saved as files on the local machine with the extension `.cub`. (You cannot use PivotTable services to create cubes on the OLAP Server.) Also, when creating local cubes, the data source must be a tabular data provider, such as Microsoft SQL Server, or Microsoft OLAP Services, which can act as a tabular data provider. The cube name is specified in the DBPROP_INIT_DATASOURCE property, which is a special property of the OLE DB data source.

It is recommended that you use unique filenames for your local cubes. If you choose a filename for your local cube that is already used for another cube, the other cube file will be overwritten, unless you set the OLE DB source special property: DBPROP_MSMD_USEEXISTINGFILE to "T" (True), "Y", or a non-zero number. The DBPROP_MSMD_USEEXISTINGFILE property is used in the connection string as the "Use Existing File" section, and cannot be changed once the session has been established. This property determines whether a cube file is to be over-written or just appended to.

The CREATE CUBE Statement

The CREATE CUBE statement defines the structure of a new local cube. This statement looks similar to the CREATE TABLE statement in SQL92, with specifics to the cube. The following is the syntax for this statement.

> **SQL92 (or SQL2) is the standard for the structured query language (SQL) set by the International Standards Organization (ISO) and the American National Standards Institute (ANSI) in 1992. A new standard, SQL3 (or SQL99) has been established by the same bodies above and other ones to enhance the SQL92 standard and incorporate new features that catch up with SQL implementations and exceed them in certain instances. For more details about the SQL92 and the SQL3 standard, you may refer to** http://www.sql-99.org/.

```
CREATE CUBE cube_name (
  DIMENSION dimension_name [TYPE TIME],
    Hierarchy_def [hierarchy def...]
    [{, DIMENSION dimension_name [TYPE TIME],
    hierarchy_def [hierarchy def...]}...] ,
  MEASURE measure_name measure_function_def [measure_format_def] [measure_type_def]
    [{, MEASURE measure_name measure_function_def [measure_format_def] [measure_type_def]}...]
    [,COMMAND expression]
    [,COMMAND expression...]
  )
```

As an example:

```
CREATE CUBE SalesCube
(
DIMENSION TimeDim TYPE TIME,
   HIERARCHY [Fiscal],
      LEVEL [Fiscal Year] TYPE YEAR,
      LEVEL [Fiscal Qtr] TYPE QUARTER,
      LEVEL [Fiscal Month] TYPE MONTH OPTIONS (SORTBYKEY, UNIQUE),
   HIERARCHY [Calendar],
      LEVEL [Calendar Year] TYPE YEAR,
      LEVEL [Calendar Month] TYPE MONTH,
DIMENSION ProductsDim,
      LEVEL [All Products] TYPE ALL,
      LEVEL Category,
      LEVEL [Sub Category],
      LEVEL [Product Name],
DIMENSION GeographyDim,
      LEVEL [World] TYPE ALL,
      LEVEL Region,
      LEVEL Country,
      LEVEL City,
MEASURE [Sales]
   FUNCTION SUM
   FORMAT 'Currency',
MEASURE [Units Sold]
   FUNCTION SUM
   TYPE DBTYPE_UI4
)
```

Populating Local Cubes

To populate a local cube that has already been created, you can use the INSERT INTO statement. If the OLE DB special property DBPROP_INIT_DATASOURCE does not exist, it will be created during the processing of the INSERT INTO statement.

The INSERT INTO statement maps cube elements (levels and measures) to columns in the cube's data source, populates the structures of the cube dimensions, and populates the cube with data.

Populating the data in the cube structure can take place in one of two modes:

- Immediate population (MOLAP cubes) (default mode): With this mode, all the tables are read from the data source when the local cube is created. Data is transferred and persisted in the local cube file. At that point there is no need to keep the connection to the data source, hence the connection is dropped. This method of population produces a local MOLAP (multidimensional OLAP) cube.
- Deferred population (ROLAP cubes): With this mode, data is sent to the client computer only on demand to fulfill a request such as a query from the client application. The only thing that is persisted in the cube definition is the dimension structureThe OPTIONS DEFER_DATA clause is used in the INSERT INTO statement to specify deferred data population.

INSERT INTO Statement

This statement populates the cube with dimension members, and, if the cube storage is of the MOLAP type, it also populates it with measure data. The syntax for the statement is:

```
INSERT INTO target-clause
  [options-clause] [bind-clause] source-clause
target-clause = cube-name open-paren target-element-list
  close-paren
target-element-list = target-element[, target-element-list]
target-element = [dim-name.[hierarchy-name.]]level-name
    | time-dim-name
    | [Measures.]measure-name
    | SKIPONECOLUMN
```

It is important to note that the following are explanations of some of the parts of the statement.

```
optionsClause = option [, options-list] (option-list = option1, option2, etc.)
option = defer-options | analysis-options
defer-options = DEFER_DATA | ATTEMPT_DEFER
analysis-options = PASSTHROUGH | ATTEMPT_ANALYSIS
```

Also it is important to note the following points about the INSERT INTO statement:

- Elements in the INSERT INTO statement correspond to levels and measures. These names are sometimes qualified with the dimension name or the keyword `Measures`.
- Each level and each measure in a cube corresponds to a column in the SELECT clause from which it is derived.
- The columns specified in the associated SELECT clause must correspond to the elements of the INSERT INTO statement in the same order as a one-to-one basis.
- A level can be derived from two columns, name column and key column. The two columns must be in the same table. The suffix .NAME or .KEY should be used in the INSERT INTO statement after the level name if there are two columns associated with the level.
- Unused columns from the data source (the SELECT clause) can have placeholders by specifying the keyword SKIPONECOLUMN in the INSERT INTO statement. This key word can be used more than once in the INSERT INTO statement.
- A dimension of TYPE TIME can be specified by the name of the dimension, which correlates the entire dimension with a single column in the source table that contains data with a date/time data type. The levels, of TYPE level_type, identified for the time dimension in the CREATE CUBE statement cause the time information to be extracted from the source column specified in the SELECT clause.
- The BIND clause is used to bind level and measure names specified in the INSERT INTO statement with column names used to create rowsets. For example, the BIND statement can be used to bind the profit measure to the Profit column in the source table.
- The AS alias-name syntax is not supported for local ROLAP cubes.

Please note that the Measures keyword is case-sensitive in binary comparisons. If you use binary comparison, use Measures as shown with only "M" in upper case.

The following are two examples on the INSERT INTO statement:

```
INSERT INTO SalesCube (Year, Month.Name, Month.Key, [Product Group],
  [Product Name], Country, Sales, Cost)
OPTIONS DEFER_DATA
SELECT tblSales.Year, tblSales.Month, MONTH(tblSales.Month), tblSales.ProdGroup,
  tblSales.ProdName, tblSales.Country, tblSales.Sales, tblSales.Cost
FROM tblSales
WHERE tblSales.SalesRep = "Michael" and tblSales.CustomerGroup = "Household"
```

The statement above inserts the `year` level; the `month` name and key from the `time` dimension; the product group, and product name from the `product` dimension; country level of the `geography` dimension, and the sales and cost as the measures. A restriction is placed on the data retrieved by setting the sales rep. Value to `Michael`, and the customer group to `Household`. Notice the use of the prefix, `Month`, because we have a month name and key.

Another example on the INSERT INTO statement is:

```
INSERT INTO SalesCube (Year, Month, [Product Group], [Product Name], Country,
  Sales, Cost)
OPTIONS PASSTHROUGH SELECT tblSales.Year, TblSales.Month, tblSales.ProdGroup,
  tblSales.ProdName, tblSales.Country, tblSales.Sales, tblSales.Cost
FROM tblSales
WHERE tblSales.SalesRep = "Michael" and tblSales.CustomerGroup = "Household"
```

The statement above is similar to the previous statement except that it uses the PASSTHROUGH option to pass the query as is to the data source for execution.

The Options clause includes one of the following options:

- `PASSTHROUGH`
- `DEFER_DATA`
- `ATTEMPT_DEFER`
- `ATTEMPT_ANALYSIS`

Notice in the example above the use of the option PASSTHROUGH. This option passes the SQL statement to the data source unaltered. The PivotTable service, in this case, does not parse the statement. The DEFER_DATA is used with ROLAP storage and causes the query to be parsed locally and data is retrieved on demand from the data source. The ATTEMPT_DEFER option makes the PivotTable service try to parse the query and get the data on demand. If this is not successful, the query is passed through to the data source. The ATTEMPT_ANALYSIS option will cause the PivotService to try to parse the query and formulate a set of optimized queries. If the query parsing at the PivotTable service level is not successful, the service passes the query to the data source as a pass-through query giving it another chance to run as a native query to the data source before raising an error. If the data source still cannot parse the query and raises an error, the error is relayed to the client through the PivotTable service.

Connecting to the PivotTable Service

OLE DB interfaces are the link that connects client applications to the PivotTable service. A number of special OLE DB data source properties that are set when connecting to the PivotTable service. These properties are summarized below by their property IDs (property names are given in parentheses):

- `DBPROP_AUTH_PASSWORD` (Password): reserved for future use.
- `DBPROP_AUTH_USERUID` (User ID): reserved for future use.
- `DBPROP_INIT_ASYNCH` (Asynchronous Processing): Initializes asynchronous processing.
- `DBPROP_INIT_LCID` (Locale Identifier): Locale ID of preference for the client.
- `DBPROP_INIT_PROVIDERSTRING` (Source OLE DB Provider): name of server computer or local cube file on the client machine.
- `DBPROP_MSMD_AUTOSYNCHPERIOD` (Auto Synch Period): determines the frequency at which the local cubes should be refreshed, or synched with the server in milliseconds.

- `DBPROP_MSMD_CACHEPOLICY` (Cache Policy): reserved for future use.
- `DBPROP_MSMD_COMPARECASENOTSENSITIVESTRINGFLAGS` (CompareCaseNotSensitiveStringFlags): when specified adjusts case-insensitive string comparisons for a specified locale.
- `DBPROP_MSMD_COMPARECASESENSITIVESTRINGFLAGS` (CompareCaseSensitiveStringFlags): when specified adjusts case-sensitive string comparisons for a specified locale.
- `DBPROP_MSMD_CREATE_CUBE` (CREATECUBE): `CREATE CUBE` statement used to create local cubes on client machines.
- `DBPROP_MSMD_DATA_CHACHE_SIZE` (Client Cache Size): controls the amount of memory allocated for the local cache that holds variable and other downloaded data from the OLAP Server.
- `DBPROP_MSMD_DEFAULT_ISOLATION_MODE` (Default Isolation Mode): controls whether the isolation level is determined by the cursor type of the rowset, or whether the isolation level "is isolated".

Isolation levels in SQL Server and in SQL92 are introduced when locking is used as the mechanism to control concurrent users accessing the same database resource (table, row, page, etc.) Isolation levels keep each transaction against the database in isolation from other transactions. Four isolation levels are supported by SQL92 and SQL Server. These levels are from the least to the most restrictive: `Read Uncommitted`, `Read Committed`, `Repeatable Reads`, *and* `Serializable`. *Isolation levels determine the degree to which one transaction must be isolated from other transactions. A lower isolation level increases concurrency but at the expense of data correctness. Conversely, a higher isolation level ensures that data is correct, but can negatively affect concurrency. The isolation level required by an application determines the locking behavior SQL Server uses. For data warehousing purposes, we are not concerned with transactions that change the data in the data warehouse, and can live with the SQL Server default of* `Read Committed` *isolation level. This level guarantees reading committed transactions to the database by all users. For detailed explanation of isolation levels, refer to the SQL Server Books Online, or to the Wrox book: Professional SQL Server 7.0 Programming, ISBN 1861002319.*

- `DBPROP_MSMD_EXECLOCATION` (Execution Location): determines the location of query resolution, client, server, or both.
- `DBPROP_MSMD_INSERT_INTO` (INSERTINTO): The INSERT INTO statement used to populate local cubes that are created with the CREATE CUBE statement.
- `DBPROP_MSMD_LARGE_LEVEL_THRESHOLD` (large level threshold) determines the point at which a level is said to be large, based on the number of members in that level. The default is 1000 members more in a level would make it a "very large" level. You can change this value to control aggregations, as we will see in Chapter 14.
- `DBPROP_MSMD_READ_ONLY_SESSION` (Read-only session): reserved for future use.
- `DBPROP_MSMD_SOURCE_DSN` (Source DSN): This is used to specify OLE DB connection string, ODBC connection string, or ODBC data source name (DSN) for the source database (used only with local cubes).

- `DBPROP_MSMD_SOURCE_DSN_SUFFIX` (SOURCE_DSN_SUFFIX): specifies a string that is appended to the Source DSN property when connecting to a local cube.
- `DBPROP_MSMD_USEEXISTINGFILE` (Use Existing File): if specified when creating a cube and inserting data in it using the CREATE CUBE and INSERT INTO statements, prevents overwriting an existing file with the same name as the created cube. Instead, it forces you to use the existing file.
- `DBPROP_MSMD_WRITEBACK_TIMEOUT` (Writeback Timeout): a client sometimes communicates data to the server by writing the data to a writeback table on it. This property controls the length at which the client should wait for communicating with the server to perform this write process in seconds.

Retrieving, Viewing, and Refreshing Cube Data

Data can be retrieved after connecting to OLAP data sources using SQL queries, or multi-dimensional expressions (MDX) queries. As for viewing the data, PivotTable service does not provide a user interface to view the data. It is the responsibility of the client applications to come-up with their own user interfaces in the form of data grids, tabular controls, or HTML tables for presenting and formatting the data.

To refresh cube data, you can use the REFRESH CUBE statement, which causes the memory cached on the client to be synchronized with the server. The syntax for this statement is:

```
REFRESH CUBE CubeName
```

For example:

```
REFRESH CUBE SalesCube
```

Will refresh the local copy of the `SalesCube` cube.

Defining Calculated Members for Client Cubes

A calculated member can be defined with one of three scopes. These scopes are defined below:

- Query scope: As we saw in Chapter 7, MDX has a WITH clause that is used to define calculated members, named sets, etc. If a calculated member is defined in the WITH block, it will be available for use only by the query containing the WITH clause
- Session scope: MDX allows you to create a calculated member with the CREATE MEMBER statement (see Chapters 7 and 8). If the calculated member is created with this statement, it will be visible to all queries in the session in which it is created.
- Global scope: The calculated member can be used by any query and session connected to the server. The calculated member definition is stored (but its data is not).

To persist a calculated member in a local cube, the COMMAND clause of the CREATE CUBE statement should have a CREATE MEMBER statement specified in it. For example:

```
CREATE CUBE LOCALSALE
(
DIMENSION ...
... ,
COMMAND [CREATE MEMBER [LOCALSALE].[MEASURES].[STOREPROFIT]
        AS '[MEASURES].[SALES] - [MEASURES].[COST]']
)
```

Sample ASP Pages Using the PivotTable Service

This section presents a Web page in the form of an active server page (ASP) that uses the PivotTable service to connect to a data source, create a new cube, and populate it. The ASP page uses the sample FoodMart database that ships with SQL Server OLAP Services.

First, let's declare some variables that we will use in our code later on. Of particular importance is the `cnCube` variable that will be our connection object to the FoodMart database. This exercise assumes that you already have a DSN (ODBC data source name) defined as FoodMart. Setting up the DSN is beyond the scope of this book. If you want to learn about connecting or dealing with databases from Visual Basic code, or even ASP code, you may want to consider the books: Beginning ASP Databases, ISBN 1861002726, or Professional VB6 Databases, ISBN 1861002025.

```
<%@ Language=VBScript %>
<%
  Dim cnCube
  Dim s
  Dim strProvider
  Dim strDataSource
  Dim strSourceDSN
  Dim strNewCube
  Dim strInsertInto

  On Error Resume Next

  Set cnCube = server.CreateObject("ADODB.Connection")

  'Add Provider that will process the connection string.
  '-------------------------------------------------------

  strProvider = "PROVIDER=MSOLAP"

  'Add DataSource, the name of the cube file (.cub)
  'that will be created.
  '-------------------------------------------------------
  strDataSource = "DATA SOURCE=c:\newcube.cub"

  'Add Source DSN, the connection string for where the data comes from.
  strSourceDSN = "SOURCE_DSN=FoodMart"
```

Notice that in the code above, we will save the created cube in a file named newcube.cub on the c: drive. Also notice that we are using the Microsoft OLE DB provider for OLAP to create this cube. Next, lets build the string we will use as the statement to create the cube, named "newcube". We are using the special OLE DB properties listed earlier in the chapter to create the cube. In particular, we are setting the value of the special property "CREATECUBE" in the code below to the following string, and that defines the dimensions, levels of each dimension, and measures of the cube.

```
strNewCube = "CREATECUBE=CREATE CUBE newcube( "
```

Add the dimensions: Product, Store, Time, and Warehouse. Notice that for the Time dimension, we are specifying the hierarchy to use as well.

```
StrNewCube = strNewCube & "DIMENSION [Product]," & _
                          "LEVEL [All Products]  TYPE ALL," & _
                          "LEVEL [Product Family] ," & _
                          "LEVEL [Product Department] ," & _
                          "LEVEL [Product Category] ," & _
                          "LEVEL [Product Subcategory] ," & _
                          "LEVEL [Brand Name] ," & _
                          "LEVEL [Product Name] ," & _
                          "DIMENSION [Store]," & _
                          "LEVEL [All Stores]  TYPE ALL," & _
                          "LEVEL [Store Country] ," & _
                          "LEVEL [Store State] ," & _
                          "LEVEL [Store City] ," & _
                          "LEVEL [Store Name] ," & _
                          "DIMENSION [Store Type]," & _
                          "LEVEL [All Store Type]  TYPE ALL," & _
                          "LEVEL [Store Type] ," & _
                          "DIMENSION [Time] TYPE TIME," & _
                          "HIERARCHY [Column]," & _
                          "LEVEL [All Time]  TYPE ALL," & _
                          "LEVEL [Year]  TYPE YEAR," & _
                          "LEVEL [Quarter]  TYPE QUARTER," & _
                          "LEVEL [Month]  TYPE MONTH," & _
                          "LEVEL [Week]  TYPE WEEK," & _
                          "LEVEL [Day]  TYPE DAY," & _
                          "HIERARCHY [Formula]," & _
                          "LEVEL [All Formula Time]  TYPE ALL," & _
                          "LEVEL [Year]  TYPE YEAR," & _
                          "LEVEL [Quarter]  TYPE QUARTER," & _
                          "LEVEL [Month]  TYPE MONTH OPTIONS (SORTBYKEY) ," & _
                          "DIMENSION [Warehouse]," & _
                          "LEVEL [All Warehouses]  TYPE ALL," & _
                          "LEVEL [Country] ," & _
                          "LEVEL [State Province] ," & _
                          "LEVEL [City] ," & _
                          "LEVEL [Warehouse Name] ,"
```

Notice that in the next section, we define the measures of the new cube. These measures include: Store Invoice, Supply Time, Warehouse Cost, Warehouse Sales, Units Shipped, and Units Ordered.

```
StrNewCube = strNewCube & "MEASURE [Store Invoice] " & _
                          "Function Sum " & _
                          "Format '#.#'," & _
                          "MEASURE [Supply Time] " & _
                          "Function Sum " & _
                          "Format '#.#'," & _
                          "MEASURE [Warehouse Cost] " & _
                          "Function Sum " & _
                          "Format '#.#'," & _
                          "MEASURE [Warehouse Sales] " & _
                          "Function Sum " & _
                          "Format '#.#'," & _
                          "MEASURE [Units Shipped] " & _
                          "Function Sum " & _
                          "Format '#.#'," & _
                          "MEASURE [Units Ordered] " & _
                          "Function Sum " & _
                          "Format '#.#')"
```

The next section will insert members in some levels of some of the dimensions in the cube. In particular, the code will insert members at different levels of the `product`, `store`, `time`, and `warehouse` dimensions of the cube. The code will also insert data into the fact table corresponding to the measures: `store invoice`, `supply time`, `warehouse cost`, `warehouse sales`, `units shipped`, and `units ordered`. First the code lists these dimensions, levels and measures, and then (in the next section) it populates the data accordingly.

```
'Inserting the data:
'--------------------

strInsert = strInsert & "INSERTINTO=INSERT INTO newcube " & _
               "(Product.[Product Family], " & _
               "Product.[Product Department]," & _
               "Product.[Product Category], "  & _
               "Product.[Product Subcategory]," & _
               "Product.[Brand Name], " & _
               "Product.[Product Name]," & _
               "Store.[Store Country], " & _
               "Store.[Store State], Store.[Store City]," & _
               "Store.[Store Name], " & _
               "[Store Type].[Store Type], [Time].[Column]," & _
               "[Time].Formula.Year, [Time].Formula.Quarter, " & _
               "[Time].Formula.Month.[Key]," & _
               "[Time].Formula.Month.Name, " & _
               "Warehouse.Country, Warehouse.[State Province]," & _
               "Warehouse.City, Warehouse.[Warehouse Name], " & _
               "Measures.[Store Invoice]," & _
               "Measures.[Supply Time], " & _
               "Measures.[Warehouse Cost], Measures.[Warehouse Sales]," & _
               "Measures.[Units Shipped], Measures.[Units Ordered] )"
```

The following shows the actual population of the data as a series of SELECT statements that pulls data from the source FoodMart database to the new cube.

```
'Add some options to the INSERT INTO if we need to.
'---------------------------------------------------

strInsert = strInsert & _
    "SELECT product_class.product_family AS Col1," & _
    "product_class.product_department AS Col2," & _
    "product_class.product_category AS Col3," & _
    "product_class.product_subcategory AS Col4," & _
    "product.brand_name AS Col5," & _
    "product.product_name AS Col6," & _
    "store.store_country AS Col7," & _
    "store.store_state AS Col8," & _
    "store.store_city AS Col9," & _
    "store.store_name AS Col10," & _
    "store.store_type AS Col11," & _
    "time_by_day.the_date AS Col12," & _
    "time_by_day.the_year AS Col13," & _
    "time_by_day.quarter AS Col14," & _
    "time_by_day.month_of_year AS Col15," & _
    "time_by_day.the_month AS Col16," & _
    "warehouse.warehouse_country AS Col17," & _
    "warehouse.warehouse_state_province AS Col18," & _
    "warehouse.warehouse_city AS Col19," & _
    "warehouse.warehouse_name AS Col20," & _
    "inventory_fact_1997.store_invoice AS Col21," & _
    "inventory_fact_1997.supply_time AS Col22," & _
    "inventory_fact_1997.warehouse_cost AS Col23," & _
    "inventory_fact_1997.warehouse_sales AS Col24," & _
    "inventory_fact_1997.units_shipped AS Col25," & _
    "inventory_fact_1997.units_ordered AS Col26 " & _
    "From [inventory_fact_1997], [product], " & _
    "[product_class], [time_by_day], [store], [warehouse] " & _
    "Where [inventory_fact_1997].[product_id]" & _
    " = [product].[product_id] And " & _
    "[product].[product_class_id] = " & _
    "[product_class].[product_class_id] And " & _
    "[inventory_fact_1997].[time_id] = " & _
    "[time_by_day].[time_id] And " & _
    "[inventory_fact_1997].[store_id] = " & _
    "[store].[store_id] And " & _
    "[inventory_fact_1997].[warehouse_id] " & _
    "= [warehouse].[warehouse_id]"
```

Next, it is time to run the statements enclosed in the string variables above. To do this, we open the connection object, cnCube, which we created earlier.

```
cnCube.Open strProvider & ";" & _
               strDataSource & ";" & _
               strSourceDSN & ";" & _
               strNewCube & ";" & _
               strInsert & ";"
```

The next four lines of code check if errors occurred. If no errors occurred, the message Cube Created will be printed in the Web page. Otherwise, the error number and description will be written to the page.

```
    If err.number <> 0 Then
      Response.Write "Error: " & err.number & "<BR>" & err.description
      Response.End
    End If
  %>

  <HTML>
  <HEAD>
  </HEAD>
  <BODY>

  <P> </P>
  Cube Created ...
  </BODY>
  </HTML>
```

Before running the script above, make sure your OLAP Manager, if open, is not connected to the same database used by the script. Running the script with the connection open will cause an error due to locking issues, which will prevent you from creating the cube. You can easily expand this example by adding another ASP, or maybe even using the same ASP to view the data in the cube. This example is available in full at the Wrox website http://www.wrox.com.

Using the OLAP Manager Cube Browser ActiveX Control

At the beginning of this chapter, I mentioned that Microsoft ships an ActiveX control with the OLAP services that can be used from other development tools, such as Visual Basic to view and analyze multi-dimensional data in OLAP cubes. This section describes, through a sample application written in Visual Basic 6.0, how this control can be used to build custom client applications that access the OLAP data.

Creating the Project

First, open the Visual Basic development environment and create a new EXE project in the New Project dialog box. Name the Project OLAPBrowser.vbp and save it in some directory on your system, such as <Drive Letter>:\OLAP Samples\VB\OLAPBrowser.

From the Project menu, select the Components menu command (you can use the shortcut *Ctrl* + *t*, or right-click in the toolbox and select the Components menu item from the context-sensitive menu). The Components dialog box looks like the figure to the right.

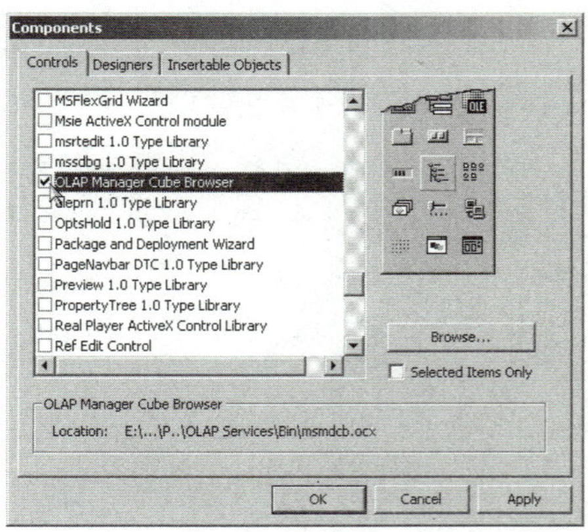

In the components dialog, scroll until you find the "OLAP Manager Cube Browser" ActiveX control. Select the control and click OK to close the dialog. If everything went right, an icon representing the added control should show up on your toolbox.

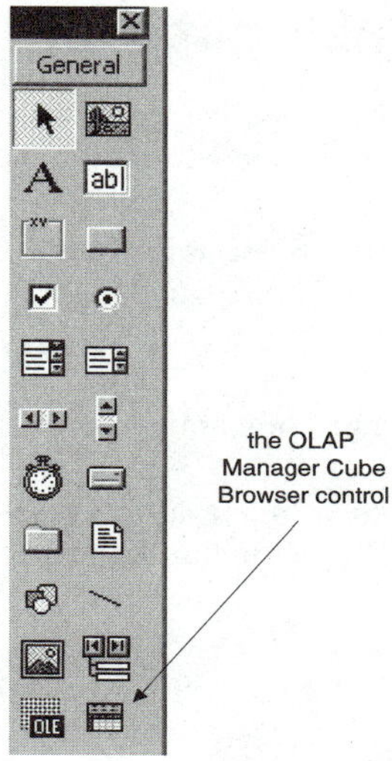

OLAP Manager Cube Browser control in the VB toolbox

Building the Form

Next, we need to build a form to present the OLAP data. Let's start with the form created with the project by default. Rename the form to `frmCubeBrowser`, set its caption property to "OLAP Cube Browser Control ...", and save it as `frmCubeBrowser.frm` in the same folder as the project file.

Select the OLAP Manager Browser control (referred to as the OLAP control from now on) icon from the toolbox and place it on the form. Make sure you expand the width and height of the form to allow for a large view of the control. Expand the control to fill the majority of the form area as you can see in the figure below.

Select the OLAP control and rename it to `CB1`, instead of CubeBrowser1 for simplicity. Add a command button, name it `cmdClose`, and set its caption property to "`&Close`" as shown in the figure.

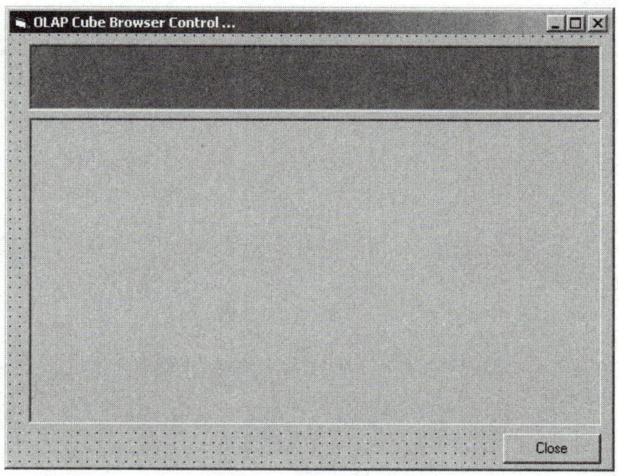

The cube browser form in design mode

Making It Work

Now you have your form ready with all the controls you need on it. Let's make it work. First, write the code below for the Click event of the cmdClose command button:

```
Private Sub cmdClose_Click()
  Unload Me
End Sub
```

The code above causes the form to unload, ending the session we are working with.

Next, make sure you set a reference to the ADO library from the **References** menu option of the **Project** menu, and add the following code in the Load event of the form.

```
Private Sub Form_Load()

  'declare connection object variable and
  'connection string variable:
  '------------------------------------------
  Dim cn As ADODB.Connection
  Dim strConnection As String

  On Error GoTo EH

  'Instantiate the connection object and set its connection string value:
  '----------------------------------------------------------------------
  Set cn = New ADODB.Connection
  strConnection = "Provider=MSOLAP;" & _
                  "User ID=sa;" & _
                  "Location=C491805-A" & _
                  ";Initial Catalog=FoodMart;"

  cn.ConnectionString = strConnection

  'Open the connection to the OLAP database:
  '-----------------------------------------
  cn.Open

  'Connect the cube browser control using the connection object
  'you have just created and opened:
  '-------------------------------------------------------------
  CB1.Connect cn, "Sales"

Sub_Exit:
  Set cn = Nothing
  Exit Sub

EH:
  'Print error message to the immediate window:
  '--------------------------------------------
  Debug.Print "Error: " & Err.Number & vbCrLf & Err.Description
  Resume Sub_Exit

End Sub
```

In the code previously, we declare an ADO connection object and set its connection string before we open it. The connection string uses the MSOLAP OLE DB provider, which is the OLE DB provider for OLAP. The location parameter in the connection string is the host name where the OLAP database resides. The initial catalog parameter points to the database to be used in the example, which is the FoodMart database. These parameters can be seen in the line (please note that for your case, you need to change the location to your OLAP server name):

```
strConnection = "Provider=MSOLAP;" & _
                    "User ID=sa;" & _
                    "Location=C491805-A" & _
                    ";Initial Catalog=FoodMart;"
```

The next step is to connect the OLAP control to the same database using the connection we have just created. To do this, we use the `Connect()` method of the OLAP control:

```
CB1.Connect cn, "Sales"
```

In the code line above, we passed the cube name we want to establish the connection to, which in this case is the `Sales` cube.

Notice that the ADO connection object is not kept alive after connecting the OLAP control. Keeping the connection object alive will allow us to refresh the cube data dynamically if the data ever changes on the server. However, in systems like this, OLAP data is not likely to change often, and hence, it makes sense to free the resources taken up by the connection object before exiting the function. You might say: well just exiting the function will make the object go out of scope and will destroy it. The answer to this is that you cannot always trust that VB conducts proper "garbage collection".

It was that simple

Believe it or not, we are done. That's all the code we had to write. Run the program from the Run menu or the toolbar. The form will open and the OLAP control will show the contents of the `Sales` cube with its dimensions and measures (See next figure). If the view in the figure below looks familiar, this is because it is the same view you see in the OLAP Manager, when you select the Data tab in the Detail pane with the cube of interest selected.

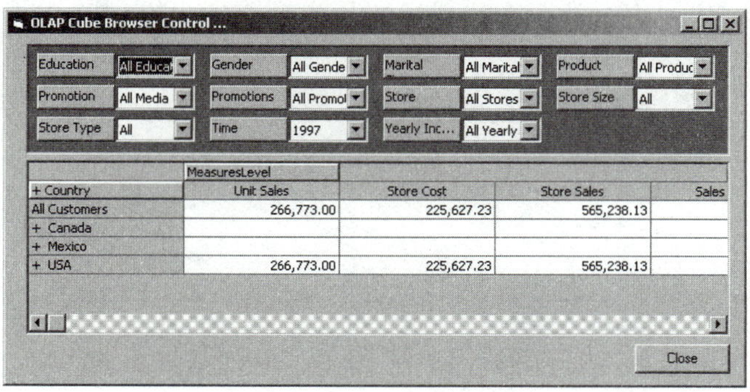

The OLAP Manager Cube Browser control in action.

You can manipulate the view of the cube the way you want by moving dimensions from one axis to another, or expanding dimensions on the y-axis, or even selecting certain level for dimensions on the x-axis (on top), similar to the procedure we used at the beginning of this chapter with the OLAP Manager's data view.

Accessing OLAP Data From Microsoft Excel

Microsoft Excel 2000, one of the most popular desktop spreadsheet programs, can be used to access OLAP data allowing managers and decision makers to use a tool they are likely to be familiar with to analyze their data. In this section, I will show you how you can use the PivotTable wizard in Microsoft Excel to access OLAP cubes on OLAP servers, or created locally with the PivotTable Service.

Launching the PivotTable Wizard

In Microsoft Excel, you can launch the PivotTable wizard from the Data menu by selecting the PivotTable and PivotChart Report menu command. Doing so, will launch the wizard shown in the next figure:

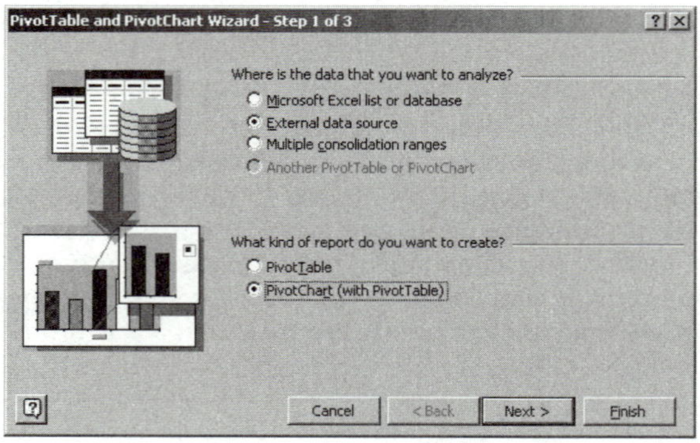

The PivotTable and PivotChart wizard in Microsoft Excel

As you can see from the figure above, you can analyze data existing locally in the Excel workbook, externally in some database, or multiple consolidated ranges in the workbook. The second option, external data source, is the one we are interested in using to access our OLAP data. You can also select an option that enables you to view your data in a table, or chart format.

Select the External Data Source and Pivot Chart options and click the Next button. The second step in the wizard, shown below, allows you to get the external data specifying the source by clicking the Get Data... button.

Second step of the wizard

Clicking the Get Data... button will open the Choose Data Source dialog (See next image). This dialog allows you to choose a database, a query, or an OLAP cube as your data source. If you want to use a local cube, you can browse to it with the Browse button. So, if you wanted to use the `newCube.cub` file we created earlier in the chapter, this is where you can use it. Let's select the OLAP Cubes tab and double click the <New Data Source> list item.

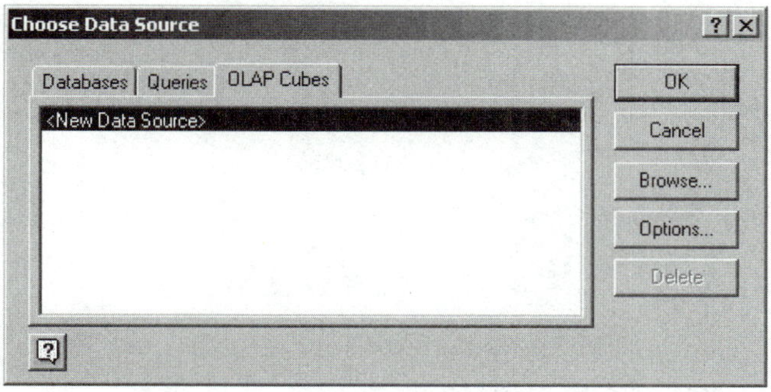

Choosing a data source

The Create New Data Source dialog will be displayed. In this dialog, you need to specify a name for the new data source, a provider, and connect to an existing OLAP server and database. To do the connection, click the Connect button and follow the steps in the resulting wizard to specify your OLAP server and the FoodMart database.

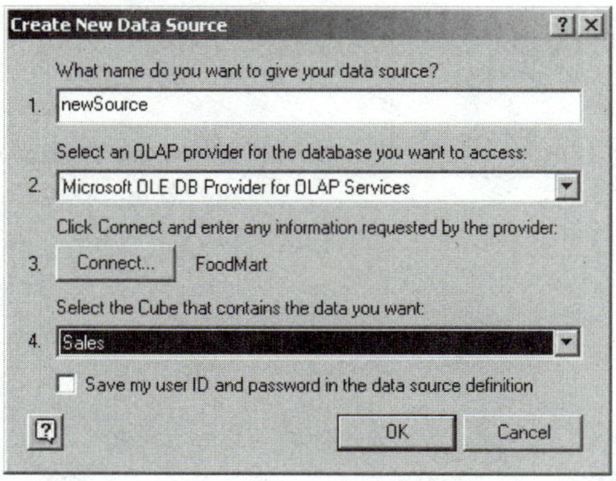

Creating a new data source

You can then select the cube, or cubes, that you want to analyze. Select the Sales cube and click OK. When you go back to the new data source dialog, select the newSource data source we have just created and click OK. This will take you back to the second step of the PivotTable and Chart wizard. Click Next to move to the third and final step. The final step allows you to specify which worksheet to use for the data analysis. Click the Finish button.

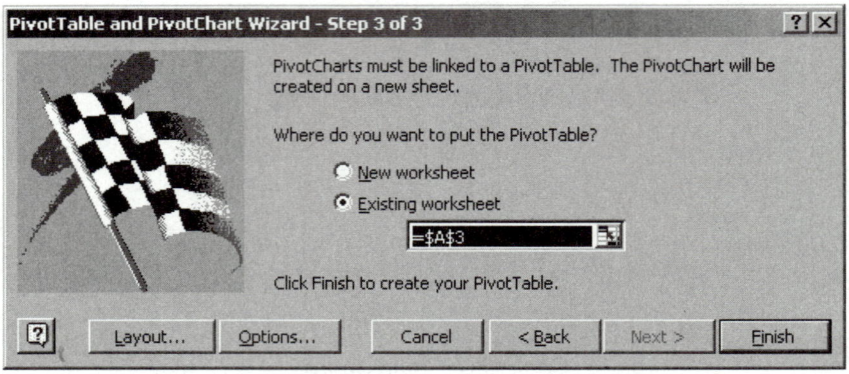

The last step in the Wizard

Once you've finished, you can drag and drop dimensions and measures to the appropriate locations on the chart. For example, the chart below shows the net sales for the four quarters of 1997 for stores in three states of the USA.

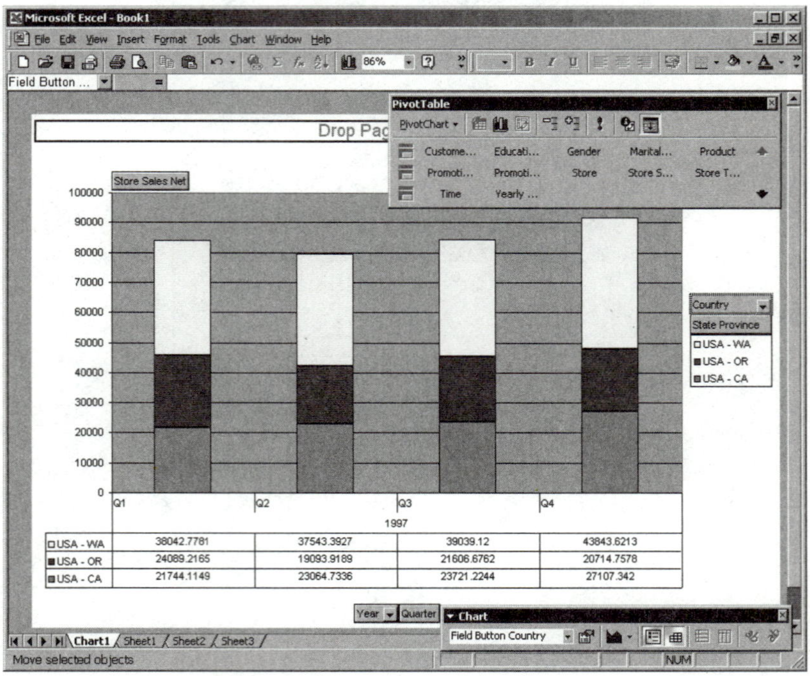

Please note on the figure above that the floating PivotTable box (shown on the upper right corner) contains the dimensions and measures that you can drag and drop onto the axes of the chart changing what the chart is representing with great ease.

Summary

OLAP Services came with a great and powerful presentation service in the PivotTable service. This service, together with other Microsoft data access technologies, make it fairly easy to view OLAP data and conduct simple analyses directly from the OLAP Manager, or from custom applications you create. You can even use desktop applications to access OLAP data, for example, Microsoft Office products, which can access OLAP data programmatically using ADOMD (multi dimensional ADO), or the PivotTable wizard in Microsoft Excel.

10

Data Marts

The data warehouse, although a great concept and inventory for the enterprise data, has had many disappointments when it comes to meeting certain requirements. It has traditionally cost a great deal of money to build viable data warehousing solutions. Data volume is also an issue in data warehousing. Collecting all the enterprise data in one place will generate huge repositories. Building queries and reports based on such repositories caused them to explode in volume in some cases (see Chapter 3, the section titled: *The Potential of Database Explosion*). Centralization of data in the data warehouse caused some flexibility problems, especially for applications built to be used by people who are on the move.

All of these issues, and others I will mention in the chapter, made it easy for data marts to gain wide acceptance in the corporate world. This chapter is not specifically about Microsoft data warehousing. It is a more generic chapter that discusses, for the most part, data marts, their benefits, drawbacks, design, and implementation. I will also mention why Microsoft SQL Server and the OLAP Services can be great tools for building dynamic and efficient data marts.

Topics covered in this chapter include:

- What are data marts?
- Why do we need to have data marts?
- Data mart models
- Design considerations – things to watch for
- Microsoft data warehousing strategy and data marts

What is a Data Mart?

A data mart is a decentralized repository of subject-oriented data that is either extracted from a data warehouse, or exists by itself as a stand-alone repository. A data mart is built to support the unique business unit requirements of a specific decision support system. For instance, a data mart can support the human resources data for a company, while another data mart may support all sales in a specific region, North America, for example. The figure below illustrates some of the business areas a data mart may support.

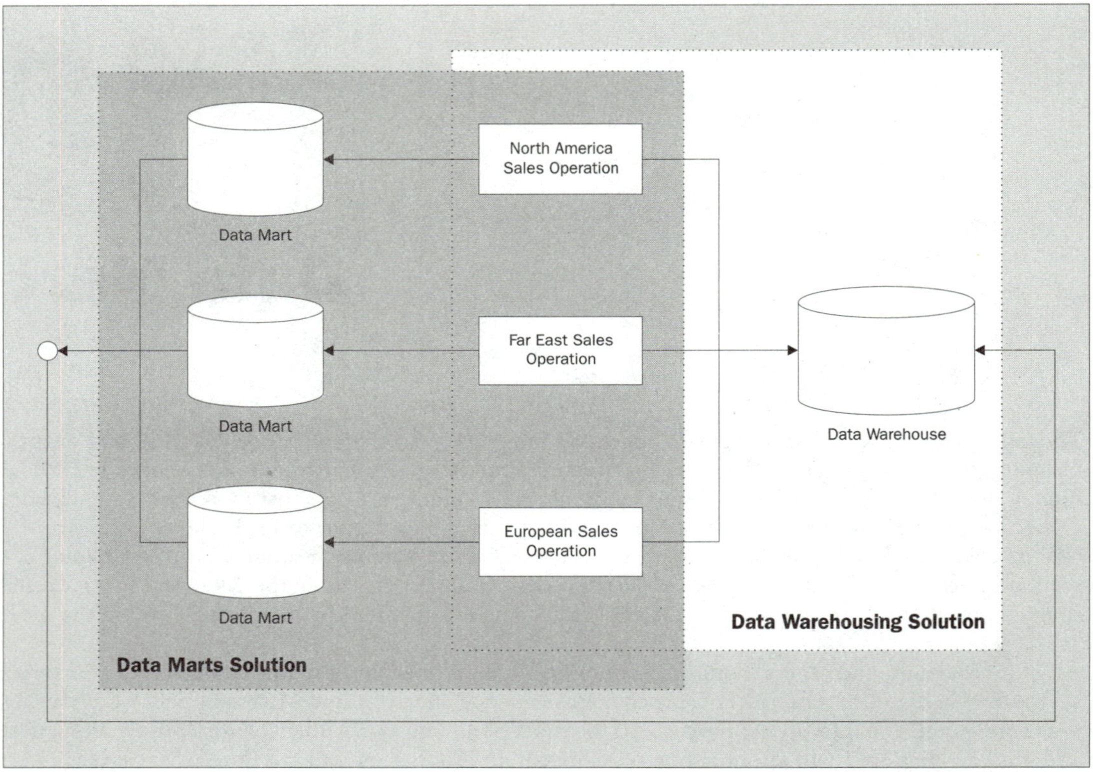

Illustration of data warehouse and data mart solutions

Above, you can see that the data warehouse has a bigger scope. It encompasses the sales operations in North America, the Far East, and Europe. The three data marts to the left have the smaller regional scope, in this case. The arrows coming out of the data marts and eventually leading to the data warehouse illustrate that sometimes, smaller data marts are used to build a larger data warehouse.

Now we have a basic idea of what a data warehouse is, and how a data mart differs from a data warehouse, lets see in more detail how data marts relate to data warehouses.

The first thing that jumps at you when relating or comparing data warehouses and data marts is that data warehouses are repositories of corporate data which are comprehensive in scope. They encompass several functional business areas, up to the entire enterprise. A data mart, on the other hand is usually built to handle a single functional business process or unit.

Data warehouses have a much more elaborate architecture and a long planning horizon. Data warehouses can be built as one giant structure, which is the unlikely scenario, or built in small increments, such as adding data to them on a monthly, quarterly, or annual basis. Data is usually added to them following standardized guidelines for technology, data standards, toolsets, data integration, boundaries (scope), project management and operations. Data marts, on the other hand, are simpler in structure, since they have a more focused scope. They are, therefore, easier to design and build, which leads to a significantly smaller cost compared to the data warehouse. According to the META Group, a company that conducts research and analyses in the information business, data mart costs run on the order of $100,000 to $300,000 compared to $3,000,000 dollar average cost for data warehouses. But these figures can be a bit misleading, since if you were to add up the individual costs of the individual data marts that may exist as a replacement of the enterprise data warehouse, they could add up to quite a large cost.

Data warehouses are traditionally used to collect and house large amounts of historical data. They are built to analyze transaction data, looking for trends or patterns, which can provide business insight. Data warehouses provide the basic environment to conduct data mining. Data marts, on the other hand, cannot provide the same insights to conduct extensive data mining and finding trends in the business if handled as stand alone units. They can however, serve as a good environment for trend analysis and data mining (discussed in detail in Chapter 11, Data Mining) if linked together in a coherent manner.

Data warehouses can be configured as a data staging area, in which the principal warehouse task is to collect, clean and format data for subsequent distribution to data marts. Such data marts are called "dependent", meaning they are populated from a centralized data warehouse rather than each managing its operations. In such configurations, the data warehouse may or may not offer any access to end-users. Data marts, in this case, are just partial replicas of the data warehouse where the data marts are refreshed every time new data is dumped into the data warehouse. Thus, in this scenario, data mart data is as good as the data in the data warehouse. The figure on the next page illustrates the architecture of this scenario.

In some corporations, a data warehouse simply cannot capture all the business sides and facets of the organization. It is likely that there is a business unit or process here or there that works independently; it probably works best that way, and incorporating its data in the corporate data warehouse is a wasted effort. Therefore, in situations like this, a stand-alone data mart may be the best fit for this business unit or operation. Some links may still be established between the data mart and the enterprise data warehouse(s) when it comes to certain aspects of the business as a whole. For instance, employee records and information for this independent unit will still be in the human resources database, which may be feeding the data warehouse. A link between the data mart and the data warehouse that verifies consistent data relating to these employees in the two entities is definitely helpful.

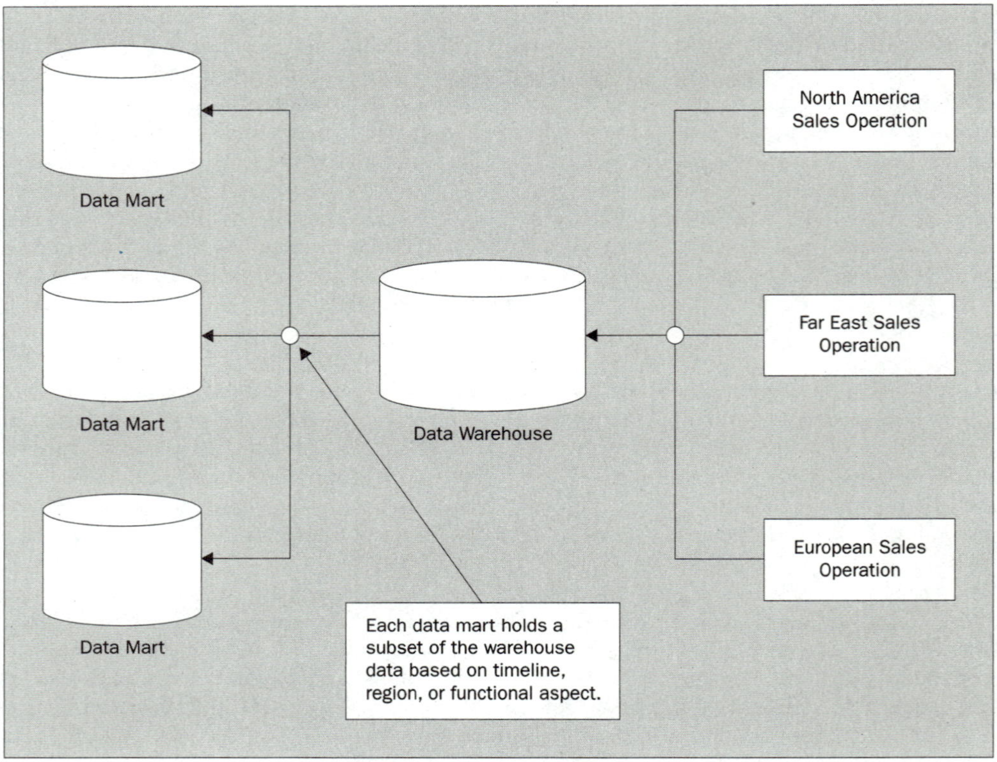

A data warehouse serving as a staging point that feeds smaller data marts

We can safely say that a data mart is a data warehouse, but with a smaller business scope or a single subject area. The smaller scope does not imply that data marts are always small in size. Data marts can have millions of rows of data; hence, they are small in scope, not number of rows.

When data marts are built independently from one another, they can present a big problem when you want to consider them as a group, or want to integrate some of their data for the purposes of some analyses and data mining. The problem is ensuring consistent and reliable data from an enterprise viewpoint in this case.

Do We Need to Have Data Marts?

Having read the previous section, you should have a feeling of why you would choose one solution versus the other. The data warehouse solution versus the data mart solution. To solidify this feeling, let's see what drives corporations to rush to building data marts nowadays.

The data warehousing revolution raised the expectation that it will provide the decision makers of an organization easy access to integrated, consistent, accurate and timely information helping them make better informed business decisions. These expectations have really fueled the tremendous growth of data warehousing solutions among enterprises.

In practicality, when companies tried to build enterprise-wide data warehouses, they were faced with many issues, including:

- Long delivery schedules of a year or more. This is because the design, implementation, and collection of data from the whole enterprise was proving to be a lengthy process.
- High capitalization on the order of millions of dollars. Again, the META Group estimated the average data warehouse in 1996, to cost on the order of $3,000,000.
- Costly overruns of time and money.
- Lower return on investment than projected. This is partially from inadequate designs, or due to inadequate utilization, or maybe simply over-inflated user expectations.
- Reduced functionality. This is partly due to the difficulty of achieving consistency and consensus for a common metadata model for the entire organization amongst the various lines-of-business contributing data to the data warehouse, which resulted in:
    - Lack of flexibility in responding to windows of opportunity.
    - Early obsolescence of delivered function due to changed business circumstances.

The current world economic climate and the global nature of competition demands quick solutions that allow organizations to respond rapidly to changing business conditions, and to be able to predict emerging business opportunities, and leverage current investments to exploit these opportunities. Solutions that result in long delivery schedules cannot meet the criteria necessary to address these challenges.

Thus, organizations began to search for data warehouse solutions that provided flexibility, low capital and operating costs, and rapid returns on investment. They were also searching for a solution that allowed them not to sacrifice control, or cause integration or synchronization problems in the future. As a result of the search, many organizations saw the development and deployment of independent data marts on low-cost server platforms using inexpensive packaged software as a way of addressing many of the drawbacks associated with building the enterprise data warehouses.

These developments and trends drove many data warehousing vendors to offer low-cost data mart implementation technologies that generally include hardware, software and services to enable customers to rapidly design, develop, and deploy independent data marts.

There is a big debate still raging among data warehousing technology professionals, on whether the data mart approach has really solved the issues it was supposed to resolve, or whether it created new issues and headaches. While data marts offer a number of advantages, data mart design, development, and deployment may have the following potential disadvantages:

Integration issues can arise down the road from widely implementing independent data marts. These issues will arise between the various disparate data marts and a future enterprise data warehouse, which creates the same problem data warehouses were designed to solve in the first place. Examples of inconsistencies that may result in integration problems include differences in business terminology and semantics, data formats and representations, system of record, and attributes missed in the data models. The two main reasons for these inconsistencies to happen would be using different vendors to build the different data marts, and the lack of communication among the teams implementing the various data marts, and failing to counter future integration requirements in their designs. Therefore, one would hope that sticking with one vendor, and establishing better communication channels in the company may alleviate the problem to a great degree.

There are a group of users that require seamless access to different independent data marts. These users may find it necessary to implement a distributed data mart configuration due to time and cost pressures. Distributed data mart systems involve building multiple independent data marts connected via hub servers, which act like a gateway that provides seamless access to distributed data marts, and even an enterprise data warehouse by insulating the user from their physical location. Hub servers can also provide other benefits such as providing enhanced security, business views, and performance metrics for tuning the environment.

In summary, data marts are warranted in today's business economy due to what they offer to fix the problems with implementing enterprise-wide data warehousing solutions. Implementation of data marts, should however, be done with great care to reduce the probability of causing integration problems down the road when the need arises to connect them and maybe even build an enterprise data warehouse. So, if your organization cannot afford to pay the big bucks at the present time, nor can it afford to wait for a long time to implement a data warehouse, it should consider building data marts, at least as a first step. Also, if your organization is not centralized and business units have a great deal of independence in the way they conduct their operations, or don't have the hardware that supports building a huge data warehouse, then you may also consider building data marts.

Data Mart Models in Enterprise Decision Support Systems (DSS)

Three models exist when building enterprise decision support systems involving data marts. These systems are:

- The bottom up approach
- The top to bottom approach
- The independent "islands" of data approach.

Let's start by discussing the last, and least favorable of these approaches, then let's take a closer look at the other two approaches in the next sections.

Independent Data Marts – Islands of Data

This approach of building enterprise DSS systems was a direct result of the high cost of developing a comprehensive data warehousing solution. Many corporations that found it hard to justify spending the money on the bigger and more integrated solutions, followed it as a shortcut. The model involves building independent data marts that handle individual business processes. These marts are directly connected to the operational sources of data and open to the end-users for querying purposes. The next figure illustrates this approach.

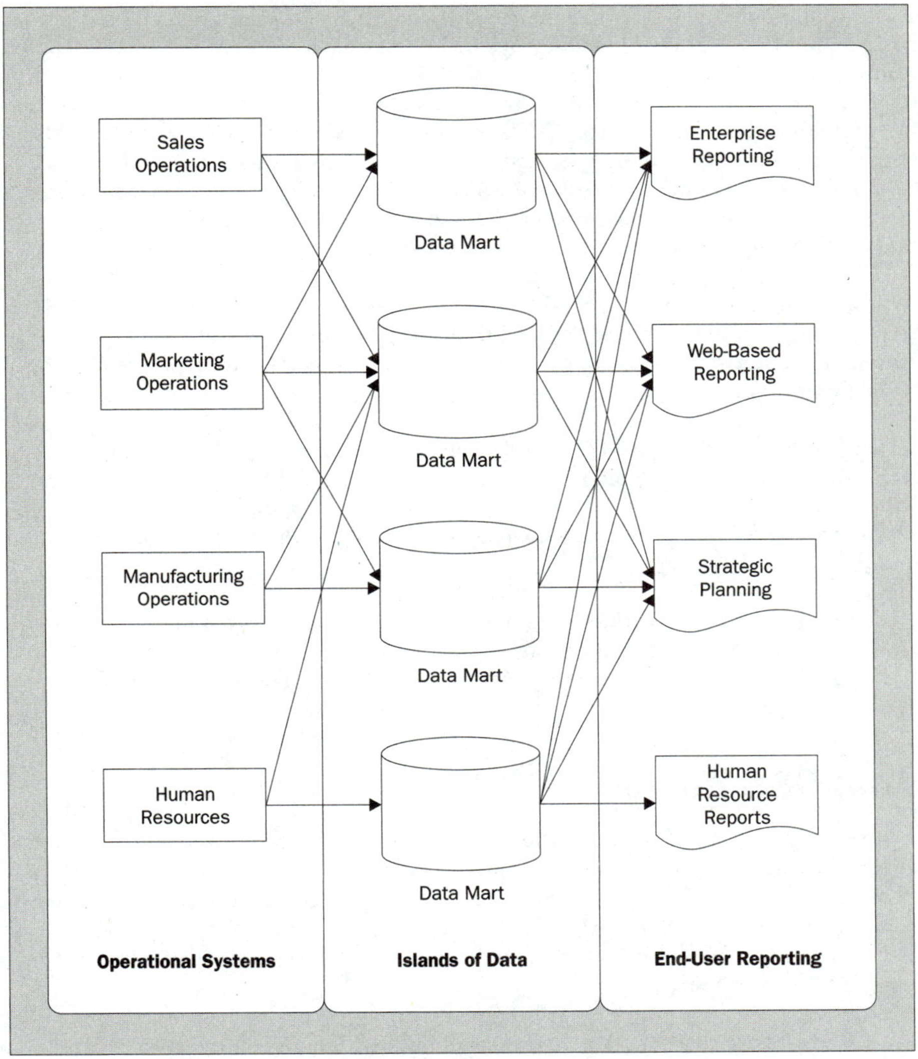

Illustration of the "Islands-of-Data" DSS approach

The figure above shows that, even though the data marts handle specific areas of the business operations, they still interact with multiple operational systems to gather their data. On the reporting end, chances are all of the data marts can be used at a particular point by an end user, which creates the "spaghetti-like" shape of this approach for the whole enterprise decision support system. If you add up the cost of building the individual islands of data, you might be surprised to find that it could exceed the cost of the well-designed Enterprise data warehousing solution these islands were trying to shortcut.

The main disadvantages to building a decision support system (DSS) based on independent data marts are redundant data, redundant processing, lack of integration, and scalability.

As the number of these independent data marts grow, and their use grows, the amount of redundant data increases within them. This redundancy occurs because each of the independent data marts requires its own, typically duplicated copy of the detailed corporate data. Also, data processing, such as cleansing, scrubbing, etc. will be duplicated for each data mart. With a centralized data warehouse scenario, all of these activities and processes take place only once in the data warehouse. One reason for duplicate processing in the case of independent data marts is that separate teams will typically build each of the independent data marts in isolation. As a result, these teams do not take advantage of information gathered, lessons learned, or standards set by other teams, which results in repeating the same work that someone else has already done.

Another byproduct of implementing completely independent data marts is that autonomous teams may select different tools, software and hardware. With this they deprive the company of the benefits and savings of standardization, and force the enterprise to retain employees with all the skills needed to cover these technologies.

As for scalability, each data mart will connect directly to the operational system and collect the data it needs, which is usually loaded in batch updates. These data loads will contain great amounts of overlaps that cause the whole decision support system to suffer from the scalability point of view. This is because most operational systems have limited batch windows, such as two hours during the night and cannot support numerous extracts.

Also, as a result of disconnected work on building these independent data marts, reports extracted from these data marts may produce different results. For instance, in a college system, finding the number of students with specific criteria may return different numbers to the end-user depending on the data mart that was queried for the data.

Top-Bottom DSS Model

This model assumes that you are planning the decision support system for the whole organization and that in building the solution, you build an enterprise data warehouse that interacts directly with operational systems. Smaller, data marts are built based on specific business processes. These data marts are usually populated from the data warehouse. End users issue their reports and queries against the data in the data marts and may also do that directly against the data warehouse. This scheme is illustrated in the following figure.

The pros for this model are that the data marts are all built within an enterprise-wide data management strategy, allowing them to be more integrated and allowing querying across several data marts at times. Redundancies in data and processes found with the independent data marts model are absent in this model, since the data marts have a single source for their data, and the same data transfer techniques. In this model, data is organized extensively because it is all transformed using the same methods and staged in one big repository before it can be divided among the data marts.

However, you might say that this model is really expensive and will take a while before the company can materialize its benefits. This is because the data marts will not be built until after the data warehouse is built. Therefore, data warehousing scholars and researchers recommend that the data marts be built with the global enterprise strategy in mind, allowing the organization to utilize the data marts during the time they are building the data warehouse. Data marts, in this situation, should be built with flexibility that allows loading them from the data warehouse as opposed to the operational systems, once the data warehouse is built. The system described here is usually referred to as staged data warehousing strategy.

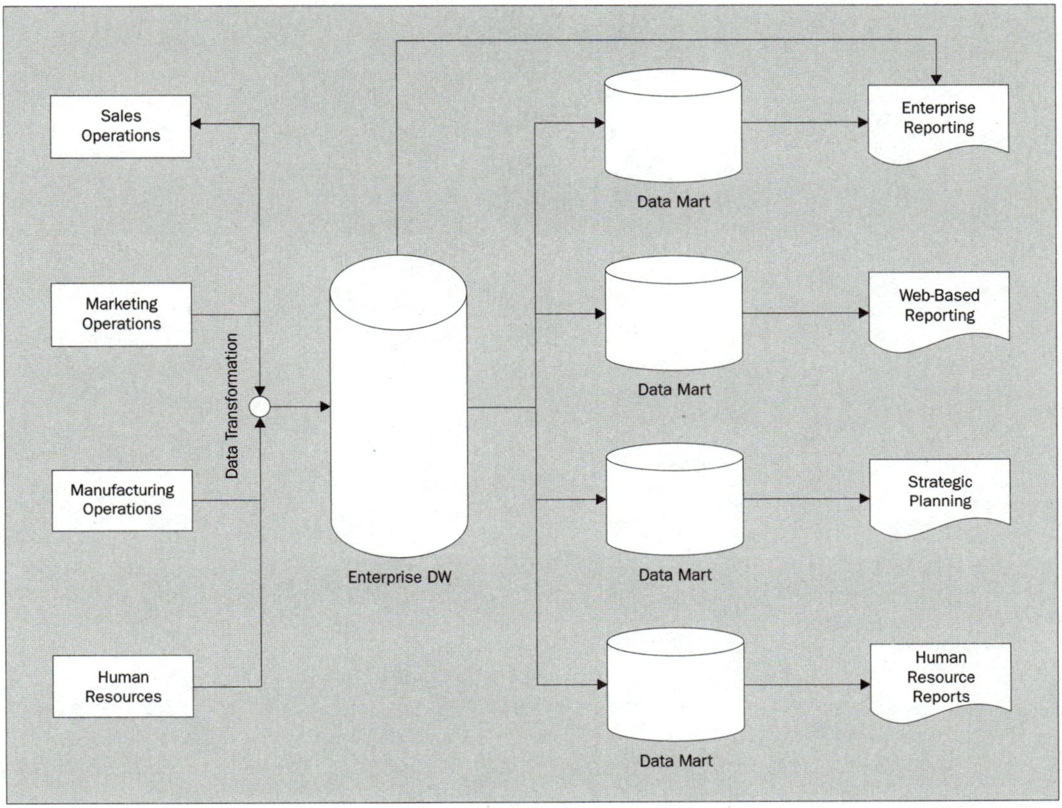

The Top-down model for building an Enterprise DSS system

Bottom-Top DSS Model

This system is somewhat similar to the staged data warehousing strategy described in the previous section. The difference is that after the Enterprise data warehouse is built, in the staged system, data marts will be populated from data in that warehouse, rather than being populated directly from operational systems.

In contrast, in the bottom-top model, data marts are built with the Enterprise as a whole in mind to facilitate interaction between these data marts and integrating them into an Enterprise data warehouse (see figure on next page). The data marts will continue to be the source of data for the data warehouse after it is built. Data transformations are conducted using standardized procedures and operations when the data marts are populated.

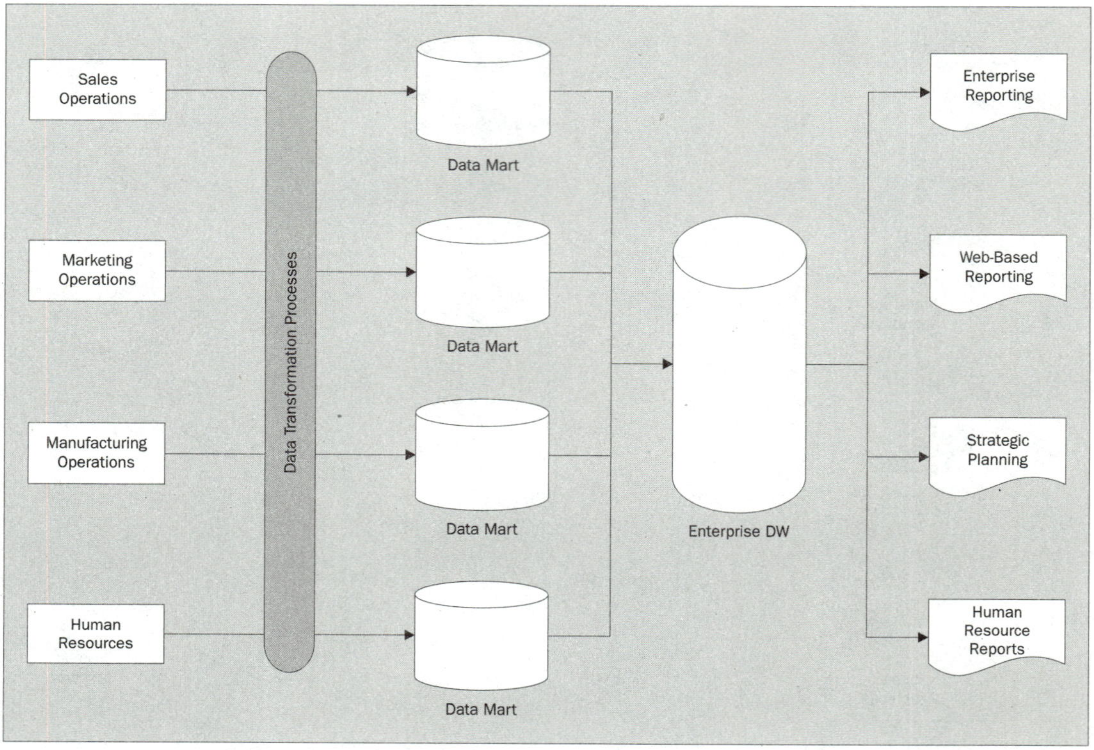

An illustration of the bottom-up DSS model

Design Considerations – Things to Watch For

When building data marts as part of the Enterprise-wide decision support system, you need to take special consideration to some issues. These issues are related to the fact that data marts should work together in tandem allowing querying across while still representing separate functional business units. The following are some of the issues you need to be aware of when building your data warehousing solution.

Minimize Duplicate Measure Data

In the data mart models described above, the top-bottom and the bottom-top models try to minimize any duplication of measure data by making the data marts very specific to individual subject areas. It is the measure data that makes up most of the size of the data mart. The descriptive, textural, and dimension data surrounding the measures is very small in size compared to the measure data, hence we can afford to have such dimension data duplicated across data marts.

Allow for Drilling Across and Down

With the two models described in the previous paragraph, the data marts usually add up to the whole data warehouse. In this case, these data marts must function together so we can drill across data marts to assemble integrated views of the enterprise. Drilling across, similar to drilling down, has a very specific technical interpretation. For example, if we were to line up some measures across a line in a report that spans several of these data marts, we need to make sure the dimensions in these different marts correspond to the same entities and concepts. Hence, when one data mart defines a geographic region as the northeastern region, this region should exist in the other data marts participating in the query, and should mean the same thing too. These issues have to be addressed before the data marts are built and outlined in an enterprise DSS strategy that results in a unified metadata that can be used for all of these data marts.

Build Your Data Marts with Compatible Tools and Technologies

The data marts that eventually comprise the Enterprise data warehouse and the building blocks of the organization's decision support strategies, should be implemented with the same or compatible technologies. You cannot afford to have these small units built with diverse incompatible technologies such as different hardware and software. Allowing this to happen will make it a nightmare to integrate data and reports from these various data marts.

Take into Account Locale Issues

Many design issues arise from spreading the geographic reach of the data warehousing solution across time zones and international boundaries. These issues include currency rates, time issues, and language.

To synchronize multiple time zones, it seems tempting to store each underlying transaction with an absolute timestamp and leave it up to the application to sort out issues of local times. Although this is a somewhat conservative and safe approach, it does not solve the problem of time zone synchronization; instead, it just transfers it to the application programmer. You need to come up with a really good design that uses the capabilities of the database engine to take care of the majority of the problem, rather than delegating it with all the complexities associated with it to the application developer.

> *As an example of solving multiple time zone issues, you can represent the time in the database as absolute time, such as Eastern Standard Time (EST). Given that the geographical location is also known, you can have an additional field in the geographical dimension table (or the geographical lookup table in case of operational relational databases). This column can hold the offset from the standard time for all locations. When you build your queries, you can use these two date/time columns to present the result with sufficient accuracy according to any time you want.*

Another issue arises when considering multiple national calendars with different holidays for different cultures. Your design should take this into consideration when building the time dimension and the fact table.

Multiple currencies may create one of the biggest challenges to you in the process of your design. This is because exchange rates are so dynamic and fluctuate almost constantly. Usually, operational systems provide the data in local currencies. The data has to be transformed to a standard currency when saved in the data warehouse or data mart because reporting will be in the standard currency. The easiest way to handle this is by storing the values in two fields, local currency and standard currency while using a daily agreed-upon exchange rate that also gets stored if needed. The solution will mean more storage space requirement, but will alleviate many issues when time comes to report profits and sales across branches of the organization in multiple countries.

Another important issue that arises with multi-national data marts is harmonizing the character data sets in SQL Server. By making sure that every national system uses the same character set, all sorts of problems can be avoided. For instance, it is not possible to do a straightforward data dump from one SQL server database to another if they have different character sets specified. It is also not possible to change the character set of an SQL server installation at a later date without a complete re-install.

Finally, another issue that arises from extending the data warehousing solution across international boundaries is multinational names and addresses. Address standards are different from one country to another, and your design should find a way to incorporate the different standards while minimizing storage and empty cells in the fact table.

Microsoft Data Warehousing Framework and Data Marts

Microsoft data warehousing framework (DWF) supports both data warehouses and data marts. To add to this, SQL Server, the database engine, has been well tested and proven to work very well with small and medium sized databases, which would be a good fit for data marts. With the latest release, SQL Server 7.0, promises to handle very large databases (on the order of terabytes) very smoothly. Other technologies that accompanied SQL Server 7.0, such as data transformation services help make this happen.

OLAP Services supports dealing with data marts and data warehouse. OLAP Services is able to query data within the data warehouse at any level of detail possible. It can also drill down in a data mart just like it does in a data warehouse. Some features, such as virtual cubes, make OLAP Services able to drill across several data marts if needed making it easy to query decision support systems designed with multiple data marts that add up to the Enterprise data warehouse.

Many case studies can be found on the Microsoft Web site at http://www.microsoft.com/sql/productinfo/olap.htm, that handle situations where the clients opted to having data marts as the building block of their DSS systems.

Summary

In summary, data marts are an integral part of decision support systems. They can be independent or dependent in getting their data from the Enterprise data warehouse. Data marts are quicker to build, more focused on certain subject areas of the business, and cost considerably less than data warehouses to design and build. Many considerations should be taken into account when building data marts. These considerations have to do with building different data marts with the whole enterprise decision support system in mind. Data marts should be built with compatible technologies, reduce redundancies in both data and loading operations, and allow for lateral drilling across them by using the same consistent metadata. Microsoft SQL Server and the Microsoft OLAP Services support building data marts, both independent and dependent, and provide the tools to build these data marts appropriately as part of the whole Enterprise strategy for data management.

11

Data Mining

Using data mining technologies is an effective way to extract value from data marts, data warehouses, and sometimes even operational databases. Data mining is starting to become a big player in helping organizations to better understand their customers and their behavior, retain customers, forecast inventories with greater accuracy, optimize selling practices, as well as many other benefits that can provide a greater competitive advantage. Data mining sifts through tons of marketing, production, inventory, customer, production and financial data using special techniques. The goal of data mining is usually to find hidden, but meaningful patterns and relationships, that can lead to increased sales and healthier profits, that might otherwise take tens of man-years to find. In other words, the main difference between data mining techniques and conventional database querying techniques is that with the conventional techniques, the databases are passive, and are simply used to dump enormous amounts of data for retrieval at a later date. With data mining, on the other hand, the database is no longer passive. It can give you invaluable information about how you should run your business in the future.

In this chapter, we will cover data mining principles, and discuss whether Microsoft OLAP Services supports data mining. Topics to be covered include:

- What is data mining?
- Data mining techniques and methodologies.
- Success factors.
- Deploying data mining solutions.
- Data mining and the web.

What is Data Mining?

With mountains of data piling up everywhere and everyday as organizations and government agencies go about their own business, data mining becomes the art and science of finding hidden treasures in these piles of data. These treasures are meant to improve the process of transforming the data to information and knowledge that will increase the organization's competitive advantage.

Historical Perspective

Computerized data collection started in the 1960's. Collected data fueled queries that retrieved facts about the businesses generating such data. The collected data was stored in database management systems that evolved from the flat file to the network and hierarchical databases. Relational database systems were established in the 1970's and 80's as one of the best ways to store and access data during everyday operation of the different systems.

In the 1990's corporations began to transfer operational data to data warehouses to be used for decision support. Thus, OLAP and data warehousing started to evolve strongly throughout the 1990's. These systems provided powerful tools to look at the data from different perspectives and drill down to specific levels. For instance, using OLAP tools, a CEO can drill down to the sales of their company in Chicago, or roll-up the sales by region, such as sales in the Midwest, and sales in the Northwest.

In the late 1990's, new requirements started to emerge. In order for companies to stay competitive, they needed to find the key success factors in the data that they collected through their operational systems. They needed to know things that were not obvious, and were hidden in the large amounts of data; rather, they had to extract it using special methodologies. Thus, data mining was born. Data mining implements complex statistical and mathematical calculation in analyzing the data in the warehouse to reach the proper decisions. With data mining, the CIO can now ask a question of why a certain product sells better in Detroit, and does not sell as well in New York.

The diagram below shows the evolution of data mining as the last step of data acquisition and analysis. The diagram shows the initial stages of data collection in the 1960's, followed by the database management systems (DBMSs) in the 1970's and 1980's. It also shows how these systems evolved into data warehouses and OLAP systems, and eventually how data mining is now the cream of the pie when it comes to data management and analysis.

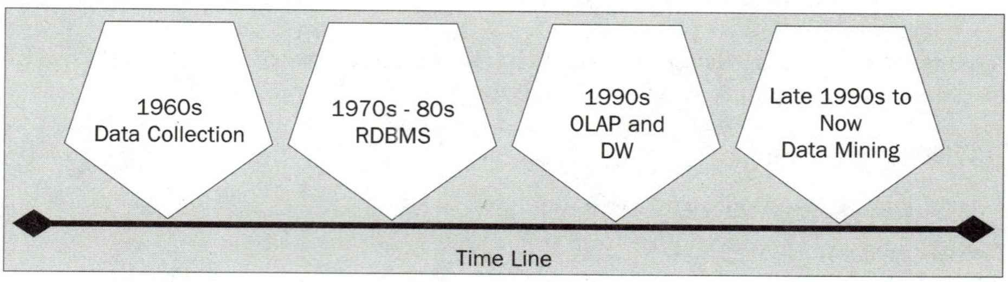

Progression from data collection in the 1960s to data mining in the late 1990s

Definition

Data mining is the process of finding new patterns and trends in data. As organizations continue to pile up their data as a result of functional operations, the need increases to use the data as raw material from which information about the organization's status in the market, and how it can be improved, can be drawn. Some researchers also use the term Knowledge Discovery in Databases (KDD) interchangeably with "data mining".

With traditional querying tools, you might easily find the answer to a question like: How many customers bought my product last month? However, you might ask a question like: What is the likelihood that the customer will switch to a competing product? or: What would make the customer stick with my product and not go to competitors? These kinds of questions cannot possibly be answered with traditional querying tools, even if the answer lies right in the data itself. On the other hand, data mining with its sophisticated techniques, can come up with logical predictions based on the data, and hence can find answers to these questions.

With traditional queries, you issue the query with some idea of how the answer will look like already in your mind. So, when you query the database about the number of customers who bought your new product last month, you can look at the data and know that a simple query, such as "`SELECT Count(*) FROM SalesTable Where Product = 'ABC'`", will directly tally the result for you. If, on the other hand, you need to know about fraudulent insurance claims, then looking at the data, or using a simple query, such as "`SELECT [Fraudulent Claims] FROM ClaimsTable`", will not give you the answer because there is no such field or attribute as `[Fraudulent Claims]` in your table. You need to implement some analyses way beyond the simple query to get the answer you want.

Data mining is still considered an evolving technology. Implementation of this technology will become mandatory in the future if organizations are to remain competitive. Compare this to data warehousing, which has matured to a great extent over the last ten years. Data warehousing has always delivered a competitive advantage to organizations implementing them, and is now considered a competitive imperative. Data mining, on the other hand, is still in its early stages, and yet many of its early adopters are seeking and realizing a competitive advantage. The reaction time between securing an advantage and simply staying in the status quo will vary from industry to industry, but you need to realize that someone could already be using it to compete against your products on the market. Hence, the market space is already attempting to use data mining.

In the course of using data mining, you can identify many trends and relationships. Some of these relationships are obvious relationships and do not require data mining. An example of an obvious relationship is that new parents are likely to buy formula milk, and diapers. This relationship is what makes retail stores place these items, almost everywhere in the baby's sections and other child-related sections in the store. However, hidden relationships would include: what other products could the customer buy and what variables may result in my losing the customer to competition?

How Does Data Mining Work?

Data mining took great advantage of the incredible growth of the computer industry and the increasing power of the computer chips on the market. If it were not for this advancement, data mining would still be wishful thinking, because it requires a lot of resources. Why, you might ask? The answer is because of the way it works. Data mining sorts through the huge amounts of data in the database and tries to discover patterns and relationships that are not obvious to the unaided observer. Therefore, data mining requires fast processors in order to return the results quickly enough to the user. In the next sections, I will describe the functions that data mining performs as it goes about doing its business.

Discovery of Relationships

You may not fully understand the significance of this fact when you are first confronted with it, but the fact is that relationships between different items of data have to be discovered. Usually, the data in the datawarehouse, or even the operational database, piles up without indicating clearly what relationships exist within. Data mining uncovers these relationships and brings them up to the surface.

Take automobiles, for example. The vehicle identification number, know as the VIN #, if deciphered, can tell you a good deal of information about the particular vehicle it is attached to. Looking at the VIN itself will not make much sense. However, looking at the VIN in context of what it represents starts to make much more sense. Take marketing, as another example, how many times have you received unsolicited promotional material (junk) in the mail? And how many times you did not even bother opening the mail before discarding it in the bin? However, there must have been a few times when you opened some of this mail and found that the contents were either useful or interesting. Why do you think you received the unsolicited mail? The senders must have conducted extensive research and analyses of data collected from previous promotions to find the people who would most likely respond to their campaign. To get to their findings, they established and stumbled across many hidden relationships in the collected data.

Hidden Relationships

Many relationships among objects are obvious, but this does not mean that all relationships between such objects are clear. Sometimes, you have to dig to find a relationship between two things, or better yet, you may uncover such a relationship purely by accident while working on other aspects of the data. For example, take banks and other financial institutes. You probably keep getting letters offering you certain services and products. These letters may include a sentence like: "our records show that you have a mortgage with an interest rate higher than 8%..." A little later in the letter, you will receive a solicitation for a home equity loan, or a home improvement loan, etc. The bank did not simply send you the letter because you have a mortgage, they sent it because they conducted many analyses and correlated certain groups with specific demographic and credit characteristics with the potential of refinancing or getting a loan, etc.

When you go to the grocery store, chances are that you might well end up buying some of the items positioned by the cash register. Placing such items near the cash register is based on identified relations between what people buy from the store and what they buy at the cash register, even if these items may seem completely unrelated.

Hidden Patterns

With pattern discovery, data miners can find out about behavioral patterns or the possibility of some activity to be carried out in conjunction with another activity. In other words, if activity X is carried out, chances are activity Y will also be carried out. Patterns have a temporal element to them. The longer the pattern is observed, the more credible it becomes and decisions based on it are usually more sound.

Take, for example, movies and popcorn. The fact that most people like to eat popcorn while watching a movie caused many video stores to place microwave popcorn near the cashier to make it easy for you to pick up some on your way out. The activity of watching a movie usually occurs in conjunction with eating popcorn. This pattern has been well established over a long period of time, and the decision resulting from it, placing popcorn near the cash registers in video stores is a sound decision.

Data Mining Benefits

Data mining present great benefits for organizations and government agencies. It allows for a focused perception of real facts. This perception leads to the right decisions being made that cut costs and maximize benefits and profits. Generally speaking, data mining contributes to the following areas:

- Identifying new clients likely to buy your products, which helps focus promotional campaigns and save marketing cost, while maximizing profits because of increased sales.
- Anticipating demands on inventory, which helps keep the right amount of inventory most of the time, and minimizes the amount of wasted products that haven't been sold, or were sold below cost.
- Predicting buying habits of customers, which gives you the chance to prepare the right tools and products, which can also lead to an increase in profits.
- Mapping market developments allowing you to anticipate new trends in the market that can have direct impact on your current functions or can spur new ideas for new business arenas.
- Calibrating customer loyalty, giving you a clear picture of who would be long-term clients, and who would be short-term clients that are likely to switch to the competition at any time.
- Finding perpetrators of fraud, mostly in the insurance business, which yields many benefits to the insurance company saving it a great deal of cost, and to the consumer saving them a great deal of premium cost.
- Allocate resources more efficiently.

The benefits described above lead to giving the company, which is implementing data mining in its business practice, a competitive edge in the market.

Techniques and Methodologies

The process of transferring data to information begins with OLAP and reporting. However, OLAP and reporting from the data warehouse and data mart fall short when it comes to making crucial decisions. Don't get me wrong; OLAP and reporting are a good start for data analysis that will lead to enterprise planning and decision-making. However, these techniques only tell you what has happened in the past. They do not really tell you why it happened, or the likelihood that it will happen in the future. For example, you can use OLAP and reporting tools to find out the sales of a specific product in a specific region over a period of time. The data you get is already there; you just aggregated it and displayed it in a different format.

If you want to get real information or knowledge about things you did not know before from your data, you need to use more advanced analysis techniques, and that is what data mining offers you. Advanced data analysis through data mining has gained a great deal of popularity recently because they yield quality information for decision-making, they deliver the information in a more usable form, and they finally yield a faster generation of actionable results.

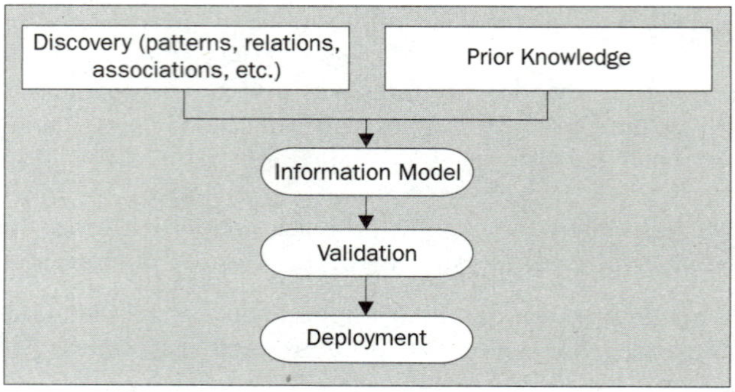

Steps to implement data mining

The above figure shows the steps involved in building a data mining solution. These steps include compiling and assembling prior knowledge, adding discovered patterns, relations, associations, etc., to the solution to come up with an information model. The model is then validated via extensive analysis and testing of the data before the solution is deployed.

Many techniques are followed in data mining. Most of these techniques fall into two categories: data-driven techniques, and theory-driven techniques (usually referred to as hypothesis testing). A brief description of these techniques is presented in the following sections.

Data-Driven Techniques

With data driven-techniques, data compiled over time is analysed in many different ways. This analysis is usually focused on visualizing the data, categorizing, and grouping it. Unlike theory-driven techniques, which build the model first and validate it through analysis and testing, data-driven techniques build the model based on found patterns, relations, and associations. The following is a description of the main data-driven techniques, including:

- Visualization
- Decision trees
- Clustering
- Factor analysis
- Neural networks
- Association rules
- Rule induction

Data Visualization

Humans are more receptive to pictures than words and numbers. Sometimes, a picture can summarize what you would say in a few pages or a big table of numbers. For example, a linear trend in data might not be evident from a table of data. On the other hand, a scatter plot showing a series of points lined up on a straight line provides immediate insight into data relations. A pie chart showing the sales of a product by region is sometimes much more effective than presenting the same data in a text or tabular form (See next figure).

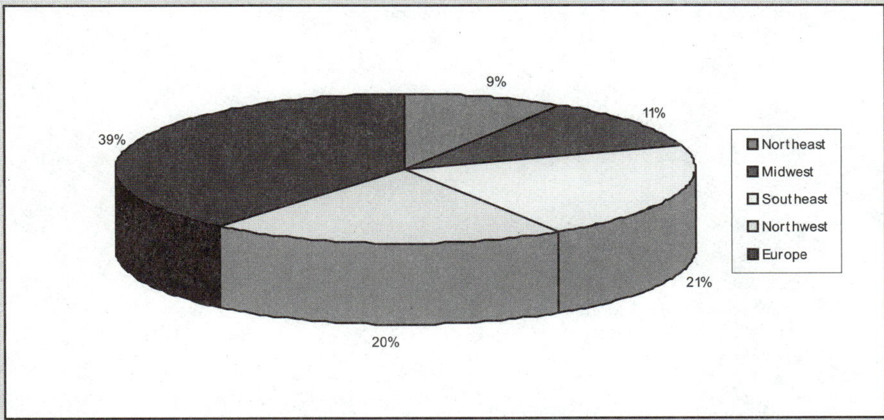

Region	Sales ($1000)
Northeast	453
Midwest	232
Southeast	235
Northwest	124
Europe	98

The power of visualization in data mining cannot be disputed

With high power computer graphics, visualization tools can also be effective presentation tools. Once a discovery is made, the analyst must convey that discovery using an easily accessible language such as pictures. Some visualization tools even go beyond the three-dimensional limit of graphs by using other characteristics such as color, shapes of data points, and even angles to express information at higher dimensions.

Decision Trees

Decision trees are tools that have been in common use for a long time, even before data mining, to find out a series of characteristics or rules and the effects of these rules on a target variable. For example, if you want to find out the characteristics of the person who is most likely to respond to a direct mail, you may translate these characteristics into a set of rules.

Let's say, for example, that you are designing a direct mail campaign to introduce a new car dealership to an area and induce more sales. Knowing who is most likely to respond to the direct mail will help build a more focused campaign and cut down on the costs associated with it. To start the campaign, you would first analyze combinations of demographic variables distinguishing potential responders, the figure below shows the decision tree you would follow to determine who will most likely respond to your direct mail.

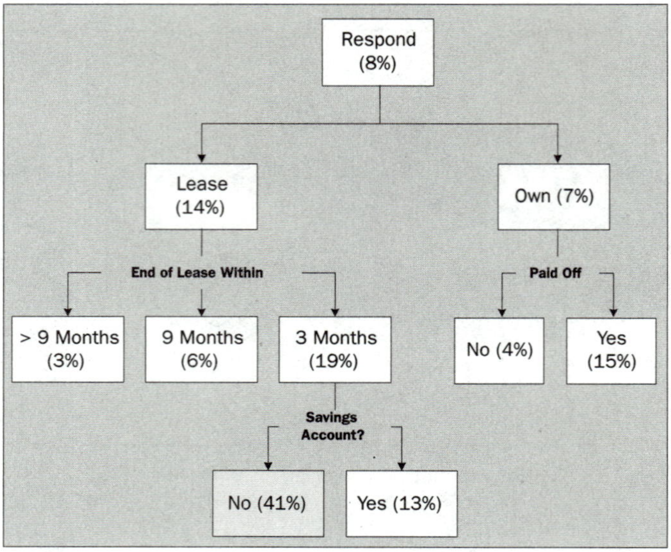

Decision tree analysis for direct mail campaign for an auto dealership

Typically, looking for combinations of demographic variables that best distinguish those households who responded to previous similar promotions from those that did not, a process known as "Data Segmentation or Segmentation Modeling", is followed to accomplish this goal.

In the diagram shown in the figure above, we can see that 8% of all people who received a direct mail piece responded to the promotion. However, if we split the group into those who own their cars versus those who lease them, we can see that 14% of people who lease responded to the piece whereas only 7% of owners responded. We can continue separating the group into segments to find a segment most likely to respond. This segment can then be expressed as a rule such as "If the recipient leases, and has less than 3 months left for the lease term, and does not have a savings account, then that recipient is likely to respond with probability of 41%." Or more simply, 41% of the segment with those characteristics is likely to respond to a direct mail piece. On the other side of the equation, we can identify that those who own their vehicles and have them paid off are likely to respond with the low probability of 4%. Maybe we can introduce more rules on the owners' side to better segment the group, like age of car, etc.

Hence, you can see that decision trees are a useful tool to automate the process of finding our best target market. Using tests of statistical significance, we can sub-group our data in mutually exclusive and exhaustive segments that differ significantly in terms of response rate to our promotion. Finally, decision trees are not only useful in locating the best markets, but they are a good tool for analyzing attrition (otherwise known as churn, which is a decrease or erosion in number of customers, sales, or even employees), finding cross-selling opportunities, performing promotions analysis, analyzing credit risk or bankruptcy, and detecting fraud.

The statistical significance of a test result is an estimated measure of the degree to which the result is "true". In other words, how truly does the result represent the population on which the test was conducted? For instance, a test may yield that if event A takes place, then event B will happen with a 95% statistical significance. This can be translated as: we are 95% confident that event B will happen when event A occurs.

Cluster Analysis

Cluster analysis is a data reduction technique which groups together either variables or cases based on similar data characteristics. Similarities are usually identified leading to segmentation of large datasets made up of similar members with certain characteristics. This technique is useful for finding customer segments based on characteristics such as demographic and financial information or purchase behavior.

For example, suppose a car dealership wants to find segments of customers based on their income. A cluster analysis gave three groups of customers as shown in the diagram below. The three groups are: people with high income (>$80,000), people with medium income ($25,000 to $80,000), and people with low income (less than ($25,000). After identifying the three groups, you will add the characteristics of each group, such as marital status, have children, currently owns or leases a car, last car purchased or leased was a new car, etc. You combine these characteristics with the groupings to find out their distribution among the group.

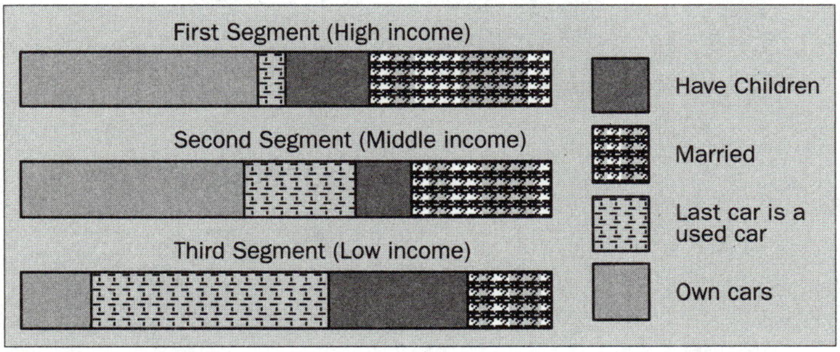

Example of clustering as a data mining technique

The first segment consists of more married people than the other categories, and seems to have a larger proportion of people owning their own vehicles than the other two segments. The third segment, on the other hand, has a larger proportion of unmarried people, people with children, and people who are more likely to drive a used car. With such analysis, the dealership might then look for other differences in behavior, especially attrition, between the segments, and might then treat the segments differently based on these characteristics.

Factor Analysis

Factor analysis is another data reduction technique. However, unlike cluster analysis, factor analysis builds a model from data. The technique finds underlying factors, also called "latent variables" and provides models for these factors based on variables in the data. As an example, let's say that your software company is conducting a survey to find out the nine most perceived attributes of one of your products. You might be able to categorize these products in categories such as service for technical support, availability of training, and a good help system embedded with the product. This technique can be very helpful in finding important underlying characteristics which might not otherwise be observed, but which might be found as manifestations of variables that are observed.

Factor analysis is also used for grouping together products based on a similarity of buying patterns. This is a method vendors may use in their cross-selling tactics and bundling of several products as one to sell them together at a lower price than their added individual prices. In the example presented in the next figure, a bookseller is conducting factor analysis to determine which products can be sold together. The analysis tells us we have four distinct groupings of books: VB programming, SQL Server, Web development, and operating systems. A table is then constructed similar to the one in the figure to list all products and then shows you which factor (or group) each product belongs to. The products in our example are the books that are sold by the bookseller, and are represented on the left-hand side of the graph. An inspection of the factors in this picture suggests that these factors make conceptual sense.

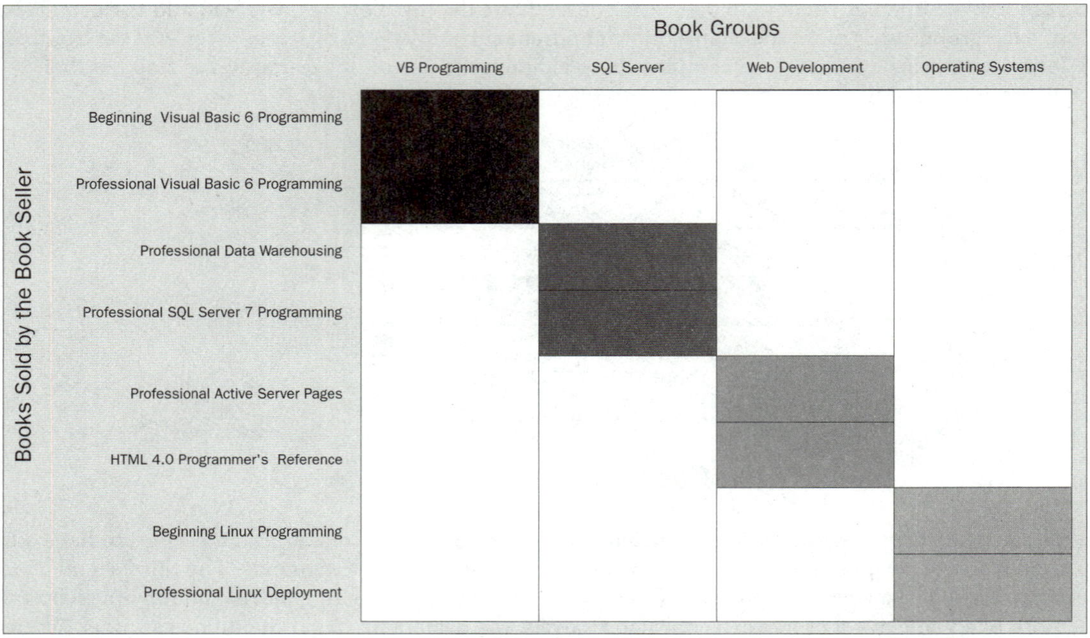

Factor analysis as a data mining tool

With these product groupings you can now design packages of products, or attempt to cross sell products to customer in each group who may not be currently enrolled in the other products in the product group.

Neural Networks

Neural networks mimic the function of the human brain. Similarly to how the brain is composed of neurons that are interlinked and interact with each other on a constant basis, neural networks are composed of three layers; the input layer, the middle layer, and the presentation layer. The input layer is the layer where model parameters are entered. Initially, no model would be set. Parameters entered into the input layer, together with the processing that takes place in the middle layer, helps determine this model. Input parameters are usually flexible and they can be changed during the modeling process until you reach the most appropriate model.

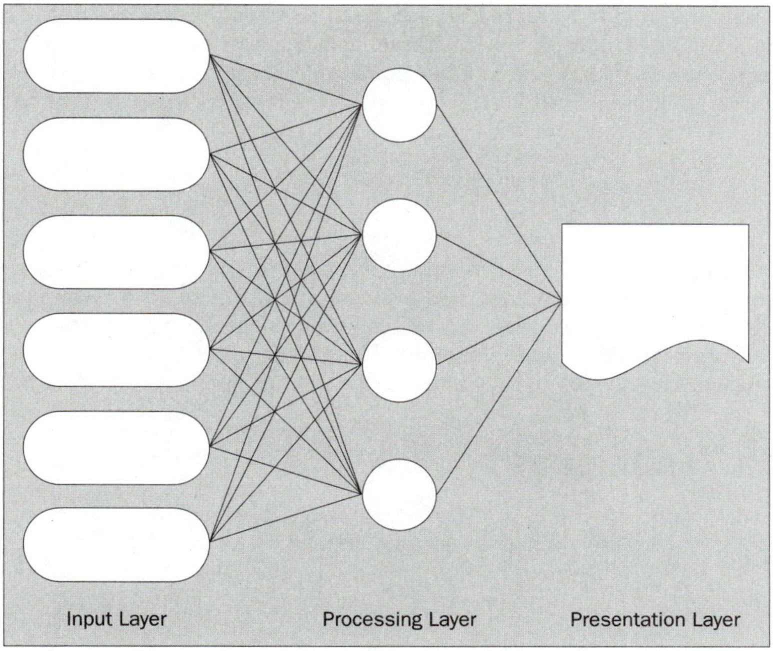

The three layers of the Neural Networks technique

The middle layer is the layer where most of the processing takes place. The presentation layer, on the other hand, is the layer where the results are shown. These results help determine if some of the parameters entered into the input layer need to be changed. The net result of this process is finding a pattern of the data being analyzed.

Although neural networks are non-linear by design, they differ from non-linear regression in that they don't require explicit specification of a functional form, such as quadratic or cubic. This simplification makes it possible to start with no model in mind when you start your analysis and allows neural networks to find interaction effects, such as effects from the combination of age and gender, which must be explicitly specified in regression. However, the simplification of not having an explicit specification of a functional form makes it harder to interpret the resultant model with its layers of weights and arcane transformations.

Neural networks are useful in predicting a target variable when the data is highly non-linear with interactions, but they are not very useful when these relationships in the data need to be explained. They are usually used for forecasting, credit scoring, response model scoring, and risk analysis.

Association Rules

Association models are models that examine the extent to which values of one field depend on, or are predicted by, values of another field. With this technique, you can find rules about items that appear together in an event such as a purchase transaction. The rules have user-stipulated support, confidence, and length. The rules find things that "go together", which is different than "predicted by". Again, by looking at the things that go together, we don't mean the obvious things such as bread and butter; instead, it means things we cannot imagine that would go together, only to find out that they do. For instance, you might find that many men buy shaving cream when they buy diapers for their babies (this is just a fictional example).

These models are often referred to as Market Basket Analysis when they are applied to retail industries to study the buying patterns of their customers. These models are widely used, especially in grocery and retail stores that issue their own credit cards. Charging against these cards gives the store the chance to associate the purchases of customers with their identities, which allows them to study associations among other things.

Rule Induction

This is a powerful technique that involves creating a large number of rules using a set of "`If...Then`" statements in its pursuit of all possible patterns in the dataset. For instance, if the customer is a male then, if he is between 30 and 40 years of age, and his income is less than $50,000 and more than $20,000, he is likely to be driving a car that was bought as new. The amount of rules generated with this method makes it cover almost all possible situations. This can be overwhelming at times, especially if many of the rules, which are independent in nature, contradict each other.

Theory-Driven Techniques

These techniques are usually referred to as hypothesis testing. They require the user to provide the model and apply statistical tests to validate its accuracy. Theory-driven techniques include:

- Correlations
- t-Tests
- Analysis of Variance (ANOVA)
- Linear Regression
- Logistic Regression
- Discriminant Analysis
- Forecasting Methods

Correlations

If you ever took a statistics course, chances are you were exposed to the concepts of correlation. Actually, this concept is so important for research, scientific, and academic studies, that it is covered in many non-statistics books in some way or another. Correlation measures the relation of two variables. For instance, customers who buy chips and tortillas tend to buy cheese. Hence, a correlation can be inferred between the sales of the two items. Correlation is usually visualized as scatter plots like the one shown in the following figure:

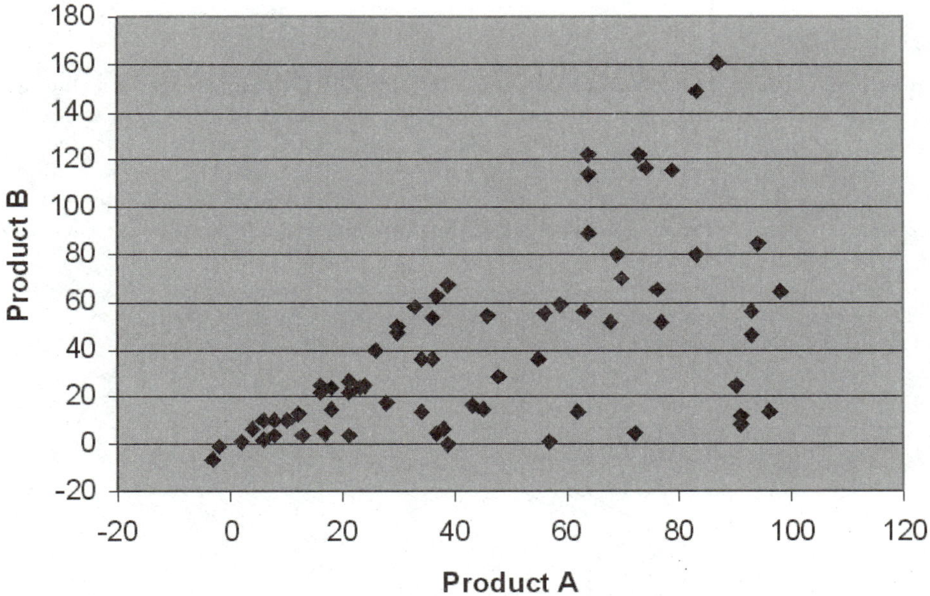

Correlation between sales of Product A and Product B represented as a scatter plot

Of course, correlation does not always depict a positive relationship. The relationship it depicts could very well be an inverse one. This is represented usually by a negative correlation. For instance, as interest rates go down, home prices go up indicating a stronger home buying market. Positive correlations are useful for finding products that tend to be purchased together. Negative correlations, on the other hand, can be useful for diversifying across markets in a company's strategic portfolio.

t-Tests

This statistical test examines if two or more variables are statistically significant. We are not going to go into the details of this test. Instead, we will simply accept that it is one of the most frequently used tests in what is called non-parametric statistical evaluations. This test examines whether the two variables have the same mean, variance, or entire distribution if the variance is not known. An example of using this test is that you may want to study whether the level of education of customer service reps has any effect on repeat business of their customers. In other words, does a sales rep with a college degree tend to have more repeat customers than a sales rep with only a high school diploma, as an example?

ANOVA

ANOVA, which stands for Analysis of Variance, is another powerful statistical test, which examines the differences in mean values. For example, to find out the difference in sales per sales person for three different branches, you may consider conducting this test. Interaction between the different variables is an important factor that may affect the results of an analysis.

Linear Regression

Linear regression is a method that fits a straight line through data. If the line is upward sloping it means that an independent variable such as the size of a sales force has a positive effect on a dependent variable such as revenue. If the line is downward sloping there is a negative effect. The steeper the slope, the more effect the independent variable has on the dependent variable. The point at which the line intersects the y-axis is called the intercept and represents the initial value of the dependent variable represented on the y-axis when the value of the independent variable (represented on x-axis) is zero.

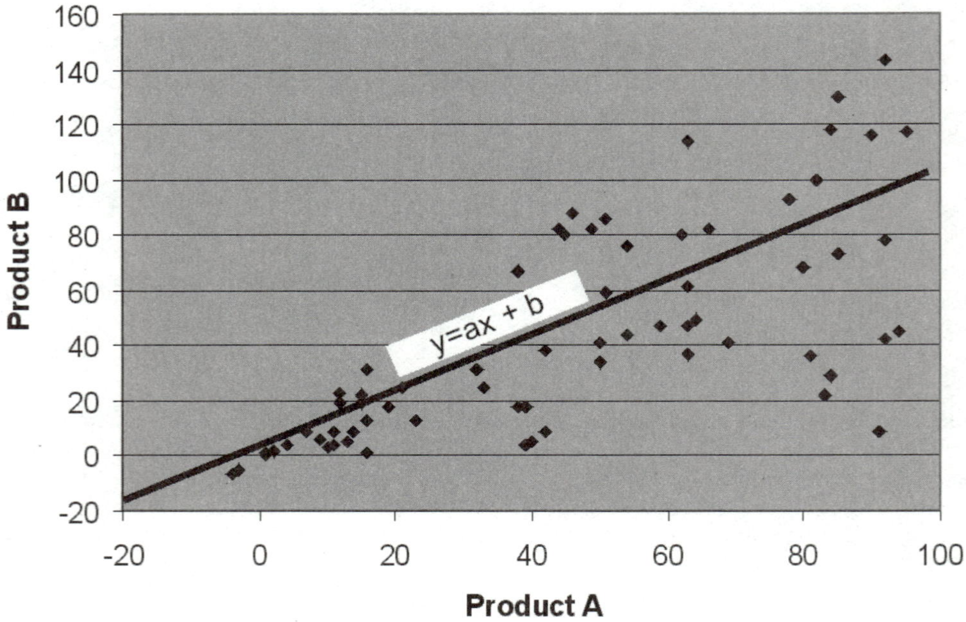

Linear regression example

Logistic Regression

In this technique, the probability of one event is estimated based on other events happening or not happening. For example, the probability of someone defaulting on a mortgage may be found to be relevant to the person's income and mortgage amount. Logistic regression could then be conducted to verify this theory and support it if possible. The result of this analysis would then help banks determine limits on age and amount to be loaned to customers.

Discriminant Analysis

Discriminant analysis is a classification method that measures the importance of factors determining membership within a category. For example, we might want to test the factors leading to the non-renewal of a book or music CD. If we are able to identify the right factors, our model should be able to use these factors to "discriminate" between those likely to renew and those likely to not renew.

Forecasting Methods

Forecasting is one of the most common uses of data mining. In forecasting, a user takes past data on a given variable, such as sales, and projects that variable into the future. Forecasting can help an organization plan appropriate strategies for long-term growth. There are numerous methods of forecasting including time-series regression techniques and neural networks. Many of these techniques can pick up not only long-term linear trends, but also short-term cyclical fluctuations.

Data Mining Success Factors

Data mining does not succeed by default. Careful planning and implementation are critical for its success. The business problem that needs to be solved needs to be clear as a first step. Data should be available in sufficient quality and quantity. Without the data, no data mining can take place. In summary, in order for data mining to succeed, several factors have to be established as discussed below.

Clear and Legitimate Business Problem

The business problem has to be clearly articulated in order for data mining to be considered as a viable technology for it. Keep in mind though that the problem has to be legitimate. In other words, the problem has to be worth solving because it is either a source of difficulties to the organization, or it is seen as an opportunity.

You have to know how to ask the questions that are worth taking the effort of data mining. For example, if you ask yourself, what is my most profitable product, the answer to the question may lie in the recordset returned from a SQL query, or a very simple analytical processing. However, if you ask, what are the characteristics that make this product very profitable? Then you might be laying your hands on a prime candidate for data mining.

Direct Access to the SQL Server

SQL Server 7 is the repository of data mining efforts in the case of data mining for data collected in SQL Server based data warehouses. Therefore, direct, quick, and easy access to the data in SQL Server is a must.

Quality and Quantity of Data Associated with the Problem

Without data, no data mining can be done. You may want to extend this to say: without good quality data available in abundant amounts, no data mining can be conducted. Data is the raw material that fuels data mining. Therefore, it had better be available in good quantities and of good quality. The first thing you need to do when considering data mining for a certain problem is assessing the data you have at hand and see if it is adequate for your research and analysis. The type of data available has to have great relevance to the problem. If you are, for instance, studying insurance fraud, you need to collect data about previous fraud that was discovered so you can establish your characteristics and patterns.

Know How to Manage the Data Mining Project

Data mining projects are unique in many ways. They differ from traditional projects in that you cannot restrict them very tightly to certain rules, schedules, and milestones. The whole purpose of data mining is discovery of new patterns and relationships in the minds of those conducting it. This discovery cannot be easily bound by rules and schedules. On the other hand, data mining projects cannot be left open-handed according to the business managers. You still have to have some degree of definition of deliverables and a framework that determines the budget and other management requirements.

Balancing the two views is a delicate matter that eventually makes the results of the analysis relative and anything but absolute. This means that if you say that the analyst will analyze the collected data for two weeks before they give us the predictive model, then the data has been analyzed for two weeks and the model corresponds to this level of analysis. It is not by any means the final model or the optimum model sought after. It is just the best model for a two-week analysis.

Just like any other projects, the more experience you have with data mining, the better you will get at assessing the minimal time intervals needed to come up with a viable model for a certain problem. Experience will also teach you to break down the project scope into small tasks separated by checkpoints. The checkpoints serve as guards against major hurdles that might impact the flow of the whole project, such as the need for more data to conduct a certain evaluation, or the need to do different data manipulation from what had been done up to that checkpoint, etc. If everything seems to be OK at the checkpoint, you may proceed with the next tasks leading to the next checkpoint, and so on.

Know the Limits of Data Mining and Always Accept and Learn from its Results

Your attitude when conducting data mining should be that you know that the analysis may not yield the expected results. After all, data mining is not magic. It is still a new discipline that is gaining more popularity and acceptance as an important practice for the survival of organizations in a highly competitive market. Hence, if your project fails, you need to know some of the reasons why it did. Is the data not quite adequate for the problem being analyzed, or is it the high degree of complexity of the business problem that caused this failure to happen. No matter what the reason is, it should always be regarded as a learning experience.

Future of Data Mining

Microsoft described data mining as the "digital nervous system" for the technological future of the enterprise. This really sums up what data mining will become. With data mining proving itself as a great tool for transferring data into information and knowledge used by organizations to gain the competitive advantage, more of these organizations are considering it as an important business tool used to maximize profitability and minimize risk. The new trend in data mining is that organizations are bringing it to the desktop, to the regular employees, empowering them to explore and discover relationships in valuable corporate data.

Mainly, three areas are worth elaborating on when it comes to advancements in data mining technologies leading to the future: better and more standardization of data mining methods, the increase in volume of data being collected from the corporate world, and the phenomenal growth of the Internet as the main new arena for commerce and conducting business.

Better Tools, Standards and Methods For Data Mining Bringing It to the Desktop

Recent technological changes, combined with improvements in data mining techniques, are only reinforcing it as a technology of choice that provides decision-makers with the information they need to make decisions quicker and easier. Technological changes that had an impact on data mining include improved standardization across data mining vendors, improved performance of data mining tools, and accessibility of data mining applications due to relatively lower cost of deployment. By wrapping data mining methods in solutions-oriented applications, technical and non-technical decision-makers can capture, store and analyze business data more effectively.

A recent report by International Data Corporation (IDC) predicts that, worldwide, the revenue generated by statistical and data mining software will grow at a compounded annual growth rate of 23.6 percent during the next five years, reaching $2.2 billion by 2003. If anything, this is an indicative of the growing demand for data mining applications as organizations realize the importance of data mining to their position on the market in the future.

When data mining started in the early 1990s, large mainframe computers and professional technical analysts were needed to run time-intensive data mining applications. Corporations were also reluctant to share database information throughout the organization. In other words, data mining was, at that point, inaccessible, expensive and unavailable to non-technical decision-makers.

Things have changed tremendously since then. Personal computers and their applications spread throughout corporations, leading to better productivity in the workplace and fueling more competition. Competition made information flow more freely and quickly throughout an enterprise, because quick reactions to changing markets made a big difference. Sophisticated data mining tools are providing enterprises with the resources they need to make intelligent, accurate decisions in a timely manner.

PCs and their software are becoming more powerful by the day, including data mining, analysis, and visualization software. Not only did PCs and software become better, but also became more affordable and accessible to key decision-makers. Data mining applications are offering greater visualization features. Data "wizards" offer decision-makers an easy-to-use tool for entering or importing data for analysis. Seamless integration with Microsoft Office, Excel and other best-selling business software helps decision-makers import data more accurately and communicate results more effectively. Today, companies are using data mining for various purposes, from detecting fraudulent use of their services to predicting the buying patterns of their customers.

More and More Data

Data loads are growing at staggering rates. With more online transactions and data collection applications, enterprises must store, capture and analyze thousands of customer business transactions each day. The increasing volume of data available for analysis provides enterprises with greater opportunity to learn from the information and to make actionable decisions using leading data mining applications.

The growth of data was fortunately accompanied by vastly improved data storage capabilities. That combined with advances in user friendly, PC-based data mining tools and enterprise-wide solutions are driving growth in the data mining implementation. Data mining applications are providing enterprises with the resources they need to capture, store, process and analyze this data to make confident decisions.

Data Mining Tools

In this section, some of the main data mining products and tools on the market as well as the Microsoft contributions to data mining now and in the future. Let's start with the Microsoft status regarding data mining.

SQL Server 7.0 is a good database to use with data mining because it allows for fast access to and retrieval of vast amounts of data. With the improved support for very large databases in SQL Server 7.0, its support for data mining as a backend database has only become better.

However, when it comes to data mining tools that dig through the data and perform the statistical analyses and present the findings in an easy and understandable format, Microsoft has yet to come up with a professional quality product that performs such tasks and handles gigabytes of data. However, through partnering with other companies that are established in the field, or maybe even acquisition, Microsoft will probably add data mining capabilities to its OLAP tools. For now, you may consider Excel as the best representative of the Microsoft products in this regard, especially since many of the leading data mining tools in the industry have interfaces to Excel, allowing end users to see the data using a tool they are most familiar with. Also, Excel has its own data analysis capabilities with a large library of statistical and mathematical functions, and several add-ins (such as Solver), that help conduct analyses and statistical tests on smaller amounts of data.

Some of the main contributors to data mining are presented in the table below along with their flagship product in the field.

Company	Tool	Web Address
SPSS	SPSS Clementine Data Mining Systems	http://www.isl.co.uk/topclem.html
Knowledge Discovery, Inc.	KD Data Mining Suite	http://www.datamining.com/dmsuite.htm
RightPoint (now a division of E.piphany, Inc.)	DataCruncher	http://www.datamind.com/products/datacruncher.html
SAS Institute	Enterprise Miner	http://www.sas.com
IBM	Intelligent Miner	http://www-4.ibm.com/software/data/iminer

Company	Tool	Web Address
Cognos	4Thought & Scenario Visualizer	http://www.cognos.com/scenario/data_mining.html
Silicon Graphics, Inc. (SGI)	MineSet	http://www.sgi.com/software/mineset/overview.html
Alta Analytics	NETMAP For Claims	http://www.altaanalytics.com/products.html
Syllogic	Syllogic Data Mining Tools	http://www.syllogic.com/aboutsyllogic/productsindex.html
Data Mining Technologies, Inc.	Nuggets	http://www.data-mine.com/products.htm
WizSoft	WizWhy	http://www.wizsoft.com
PilotSoft	Discovery Server	http://www.pilotsw.com
Oracle Corporation	Darwin	http://www.think.com

Data Mining and the World-Wide Web

The Internet has entered our lives in a very strong way. It has actually changed the way many business transactions and methodologies are conducted. Many companies saw their birth and tremendously fast growth on the virtual media. From booksellers to online automobile dealerships, to powerful bidding houses, business, as we knew it, has changed for good. Barriers between corporations and competitors are disappearing. E-commerce companies are competing significantly with established businesses by operating more quickly with today's next-generation technological tools. Intelligent enterprises are implementing innovative data mining solutions to acquire knowledge about their customers and products for greater profitability.

The Internet entered the corporate world in the form of intranets, which are smaller versions of the Internet that are specific to the organization, surrounded by a stiff security system, often referred to as fire wall, and connected to the larger Internet through certain bridges only. Intranets have evolved tremendously over the past five years. They have evolved from merely billboards for company information to a powerful medium to run company-wide applications. Enterprises are offering intranet-based solutions that deploy powerful data analysis tools to employees' desktops throughout an enterprise. With these tools, business decision-makers can perform data analysis within a familiar web-browser environment, customize web pages for data analysis and standardize reports.

Another profound effect of the Web and Internet on the way business is conducted and the way analyses are conducted is that the Web allowed corporations to access a larger number of people and collect more data through their Web sites or e-Commerce applications. This data is only adding to the reservoir of knowledge and information the company is building after it is analyzed.

Summary

Data mining is proving to be the "digital nervous system" of the future with its powerful tools, techniques and results on improving corporate sales, customer management and satisfaction, employee management, and corporate profits. Data mining solutions are becoming easier and more convenient to use. Corporate-wide deployment of data analysis software will bring data mining to employees' desktops, allowing them to make critical business decisions in real time.

The growth of the Internet and corporate intranets along with better, more user-friendly analysis tools and software that is adapted to run in the Web browsers, will only emphasize the role of data mining as a critical tool for the success of any organization in the future.

12

Data Warehouse Security

Data collected over the years is the most important asset for an organization. Unfortunately, intruders are always trying to hack their way to corporate data and use the data for their own purposes. Therefore, security is an essential part of any business application. Obviously, I'm not claiming that you can make something 100% secure, but at least you can minimize the chances that someone will break into your system, view, or tamper with your data.

In this chapter, we will look at the basic security scheme for your data warehousing application. This scheme spans several levels; the operating system on which you are running your solution, the database serving as the storage space for the data warehouse or data marts, and the OLAP data.

Topics covered in this chapter include:

- Windows NT and Windows 2000 Security
- SQL Server 7.0 Security
- OLAP Services Security

Overview of Windows NT 4.0 Security

Windows NT was built with plenty of security checks. Actually, anything you do in the NT environment undergoes a security check to validate your right to doing whatever it is you are trying to do. Starting from the point of logging on to the NT machine to the simple task of trying to open a file, or even rename it, a security check will occur. Security checks will also occur when you try accessing the machine remotely from another machine, or even if you try to run a program from another machine. These are just some examples of situations where security checks will occur, since many more examples can still be brought up.

When you use NT as your desktop operating system and log on as an administrator or someone with administrative privileges, you do not see any of these checks, because you already have permissions to do almost anything you want on the system.

Windows NT provides several functions that allow you to control access to the enterprise data and applications. These functions include:

- **User and group management**: controls network logon and logoff rights for local and remote users.
- **Security policy definitions**: defines user and group access rights, such as password aging, default access permissions, etc.
- **File and object access**: protects the files and folders on the system including files used to run the Windows NT system, and files used for applications and corporate data on both fixed and removable media.
- **Windows registry access**: protects registry settings from unwanted intervention.

The functions listed above are designed to protect several types of objects. These objects include:

- Local or remote Windows NT file system (NTFS) files and directories, in addition to remote FAT disk volumes.
- Processes and threads.
- Console screen buffers.
- File-mapping objects.
- Registry keys.
- Local or remote printers.
- Windows NT network shares.
- Windows NT Services.
- Inter-process synchronization objects.
- Other objects such as mail slots and access tokens.

Windows NT 4.0 Network Domains

Windows NT networks implement the concept of domains. A domain is a grouping of a set of resources on the network that are connected together. These resources may include computers, printers, and other shared devices. Each domain has one computer that controls information about the domain users, computers, logins, and other network resources. This computer is called the Primary Domain Controller (PDC). One or more Windows NT servers can be assigned to be Backup Domain Controllers (BDC) that take over some of the tasks for the PDC and may get promoted to PDC level in case of PDC failure. The diagram on the next page, demonstrates the principle of using domains to control the NT network.

Both the PDC and BDC must be running the Server version of Windows NT. Other computers on the domain may be running another system of your choice, such as Windows 9x, or Windows NT Workstation. Computers running Windows NT Server but are neither a PDC or a BDC are called member servers.

Domains can be connected to each other with "trust" relations. Trust relations between domains can be one-way or two-way relations. Trusting domains may allow access to users and user groups on trusted domains to the trusting domain's resources. For instance, in the diagram below, if a computer in Domain B were to access the SQL Server database in Domain A, Domain A must trust Domain B via a trust relationship, and the Domain B user should be added to a group that has access to the SQL database in Domain A. This group could be the SQL Server operators group local to the SQL Server machine.

These principals are very important to be understood by developers who build applications for the Windows NT platform. They are also important for users who run services on this platform, such as users who use Microsoft SQL Server. As a developer or database administrator, you are not required to know the intricate details of how security and trust relationships work. It is enough to know they are there, and what they mean if you were to use them as part of your application security model.

User and Group Management

To put it simply, Windows NT controls user access to resources on the system or the machine by implementing user accounts, user groups, user-rights policies, and program access control. The following is an overview of each of these items.

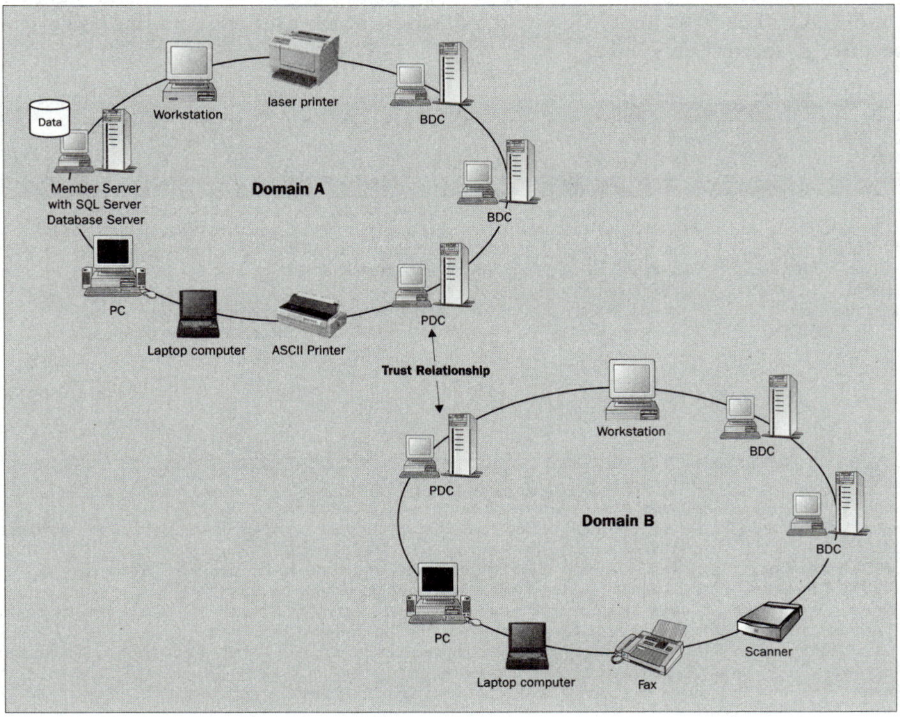

The concept of domains in the Windows NT platform

User Accounts

User accounts basically identify who can log on to the system, and who cannot. If you cannot log on to the system locally or remotely from another machine, you will not have access to anything on it. User accounts are the cornerstone on which NT security is built. A user account consists of a user name and password. Several guidelines determine what a valid user account and password are. However, I am not going to get into that much detail in this chapter.

The Windows NT User Manager for Domains on the domain controller can be used to administer domain user accounts. The User Manager is a similar tool that allows for local administration of user accounts on a machine running Windows NT (workstation or member server) in the domain. With these tools, you can create, delete, or disable user accounts. You can create as many accounts as needed, and then restrict user access to your application and any Windows NT resource on a per-account basis. The User Manager for Domains allows you to do this on the domain level, whereas the User Manager allows you to this for the local machine only. In any case, properly configured user accounts play a significant role in allowing users access to your application and operating system resources. User Manager is shown below, and can be launched from the Start|Administrative Tasks|User Manager menu item.

Two types of users exist in the Windows NT networks: local user accounts, and domain user accounts. The local users are, as the name implies, local to the machine and a list of the local users is kept at that machine. Domain users, on the other hand, are users who are registered with the domain controllers, the PDC and BDCs. The PDC and BDCs hold a database of the user names and passwords and what domain security properties they have.

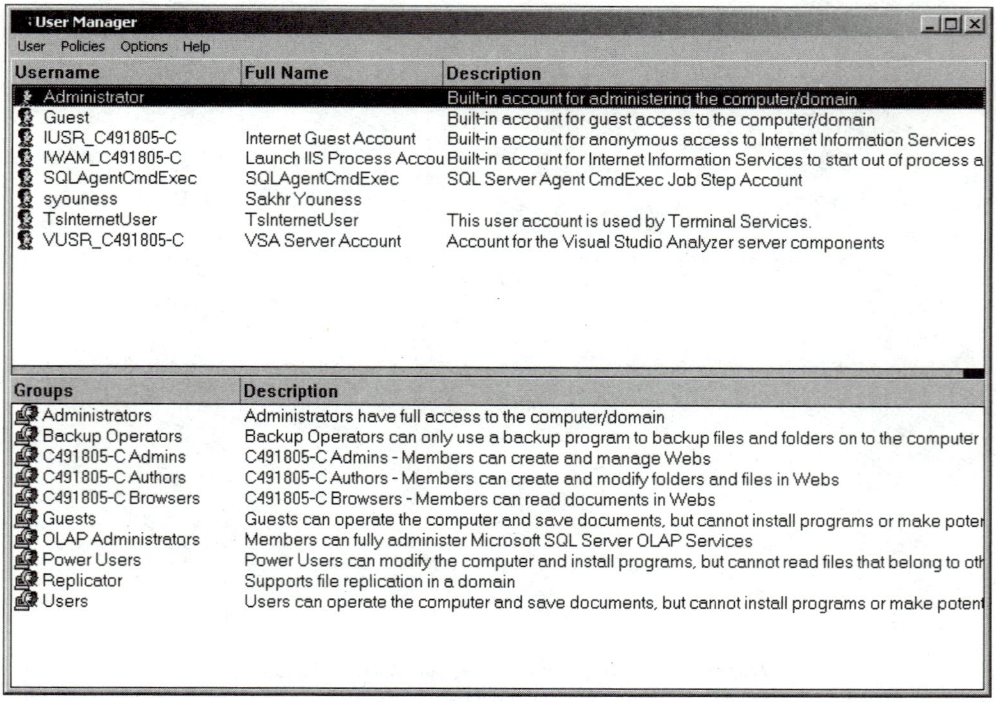

User Manager for Domains

User Groups

Windows NT users can join groups created on the NT machine. Again the User Manager for Domains program can be used to manage these groups and the user accounts contained in each of them. Group members have equal rights and privileges in general. However, a user account can join more than one group. By collecting user accounts into groups, Windows NT simplifies administration of user access. For example, granting access to a designated network resource to a user group will grant these access privileges to all the members of the group. Hence, to allow certain users access to certain folders, you should create a group, add the users you want to it, then grant permissions to the group instead of the individual users.

User groups help you define your application security model in a better way. Certain groups will have access to a given set of application permissions, while other groups will have access to other permissions. To build such a security model you need to identify the different sets of functionality that people can access, create corresponding groups, and add the users to these groups after you grant the proper access permissions to them.

Just as there are local and domain users, there are also local and domain user groups. The domain groups are called "global groups," which are stored on the domain controllers. Global groups can be added to local groups to allow domain users who are members of these groups to have the same access permissions or members of the local group to local resources. Local groups, on the other hand, cannot be added to global groups, because local groups are stored locally, and not on the domain controllers.

User Rights Policies

With user rights policies, you can impose restrictions on users and groups as to what they can access and do on the system. For instance, you can allow certain users to log on the system locally, or access the computer from the network. You can also restrict the password to expire within a given period of time. Just like you can administer user accounts and user groups, you can set user-rights policies from the User Manager for Domain application.

Program Access Control

Sometimes you may not be satisfied with the NT security and you need to go to the application level applying security programmatically to allow users certain access rights to your application. Windows NT helps you do this by making NT authentication option available to you. After the user is authenticated from the system, your application can then control user access in any way you want. For example, you can set roles and permissions on component interface levels on COM objects running in Microsoft Transaction Server (MTS). You can also control user access to certain pages in your web site by using the session object in ASP to verify user rights at the page level.

This is particularly important when dealing with access to SQL Server from the network with both SQL Server and NT security working together. This case is discussed in more detail later in the chapter, in the SQL Server Security section.

File and Object Access

Windows NT provides a choice of either the old file allocation table (FAT) or Windows NT file system (NTFS).

FAT

File Allocation Table (FAT or FAT16) is the old system used with DOS, Windows 3.x, and later Windows 95a. This file system does not allow for setting any security on the files located on a volume formatted according to this system (although it allows for primitive permissions on the directories). Therefore, if you have access to one file on the machine that is configured with the FAT system, you will have access to all the files on any FAT partition on the system. A new system, FAT32, was introduced with Windows 95b and Windows 98. This system has a lot in common to the NTFS system, even though they are fundamentally incompatible.

FAT32 system is not compatible with Windows NT, but is supported by Windows 2000

NTFS

Windows NT with NTFS provides more security options because NTFS supports access control and ownership rights not available with the FAT file system. Windows NT ensures data and system protection through its ability to define file access control on both the file and folder levels. The NTFS file system can effectively prevent users from damaging key system or application files.

The best and most convenient tool to use when setting file access permissions is Windows Explorer. With this tool, you can set file permissions on a file-by-file basis, or for folders. By selecting the file or folder of interest, right clicking, and selecting the Properties menu item on the menu, you can open the file (or folder) properties dialog. The figure below shows this dialog with the Security tab selected.

In the security page of the file properties dialog, you can allow or deny certain permissions on the selected object for the user selected in the Name list box of the dialog. You can also add more users to the list of users allowed to have permission on the object, or even a whole user group by clicking the Add button and selecting the appropriate user/group from the Select Users and Groups dialog. The Advanced button in the file properties dialog givers you even more options to control the file/folder access.

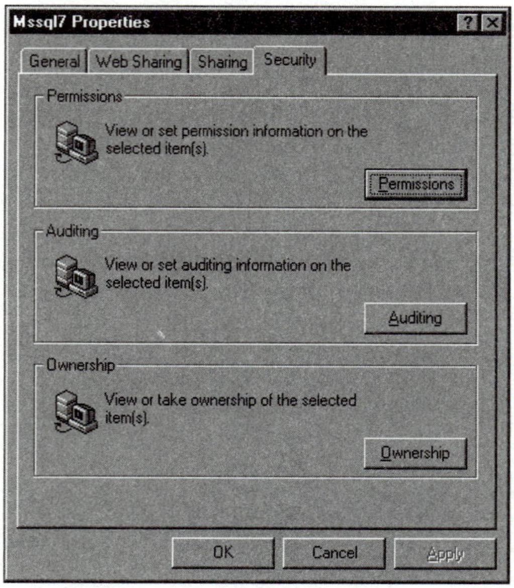

The security page of the file/folder properties dialog

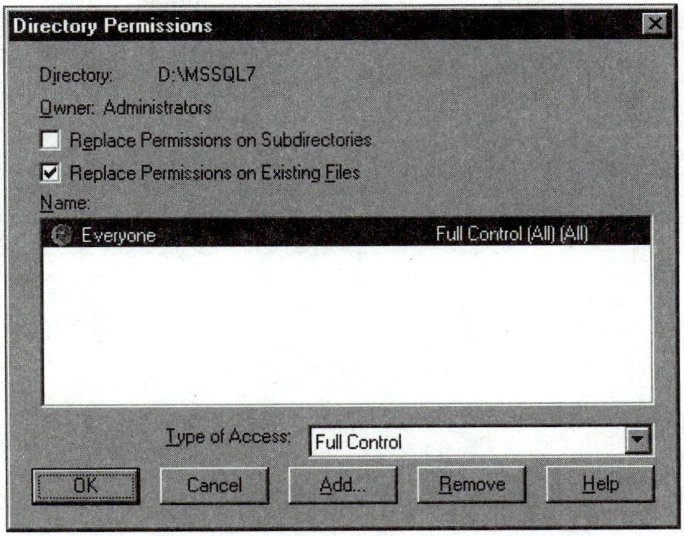

The User and Group selection dialog.

Windows Registry Access

The Windows NT registry is a database with information about the applications on your computer and their configurations. Protecting it is a must if you want your applications to function properly. Registry protection is conducted against remote access. By default, any user with administrator privileges can access the registry on your server, and make changes to it. To eliminate this possibility, you must create the following key on every workstation that uses your application:

```
HKEY_LOCAL_MACHINE\SYSTEM\CurrentcontrolSet\Control\SecurePipeServers\winreg
```

Then you should edit the registry permissions of the `winreg` key to grant or revoke specific access privileges. This can be done using the `regedt32.exe` program. You can start this program from the command line or from the Start|Run window. This program opens the registry with each of the main hives in its own child window. The Security menu on the menu bar allows you to set permissions for the different registry keys as shown in the following figure.

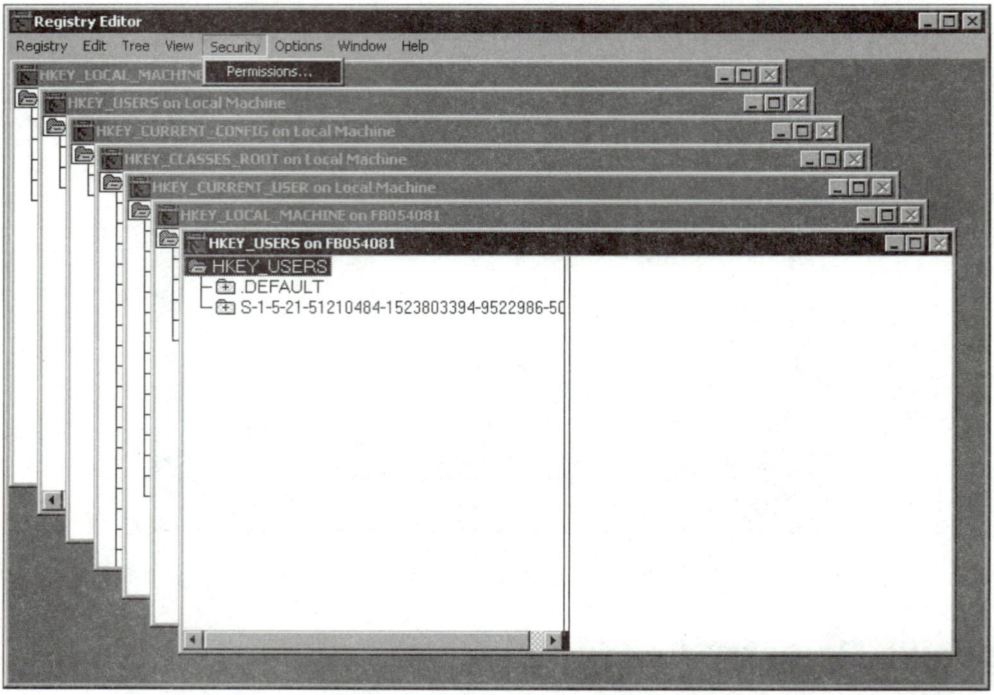

The regedt32.exe program screen can be used to set permissions on registry keys

Protecting the registry against remote access is not quite enough to prevent tampering with it by specific people. You must also protect the registry files located in the Winnt\System32 directory by setting the proper security privileges on that folder.

SQL Server 7.0 Security

SQL Server 7.0 security starts with user authentication. Users are authenticated against stored login accounts within SQL Server, or against Windows NT user accounts. Logins within SQL Server can be assigned privileges allowing them access to different aspects of the server functionality. The following sections describe the SQL Server security model starting with authentication modes, and ending with Server and Database Roles.

Authentication Modes

Just like any other security, SQL Server security starts with authenticating the user who is trying to access the server by querying their name and password. Authentication in SQL Server 7.0 can take one of three options: Windows NT-Mixed mode, SQL Server mode, or Windows NT mode. These three modes are described below.

SQL Server Authentication Mode

With native SQL Server security, you create a SQL Server login ID. It does not matter how you were authenticated into the network or local computer, the login ID allows you to access the server and its databases based on permissions granted to this login. Permissions are usually granted directly to a login, or to a role, then the login is assigned to the role.

Prior to SQL Server 7.0, this option was presented separately in the SQL Server security dialog. In SQL Server 7.0, this option is no longer presented as a separate option in the security dialog. However, it is still a valid option through the NT-Mixed security option (see figure below), when you use SQL Server logins to log onto the server from your applications.

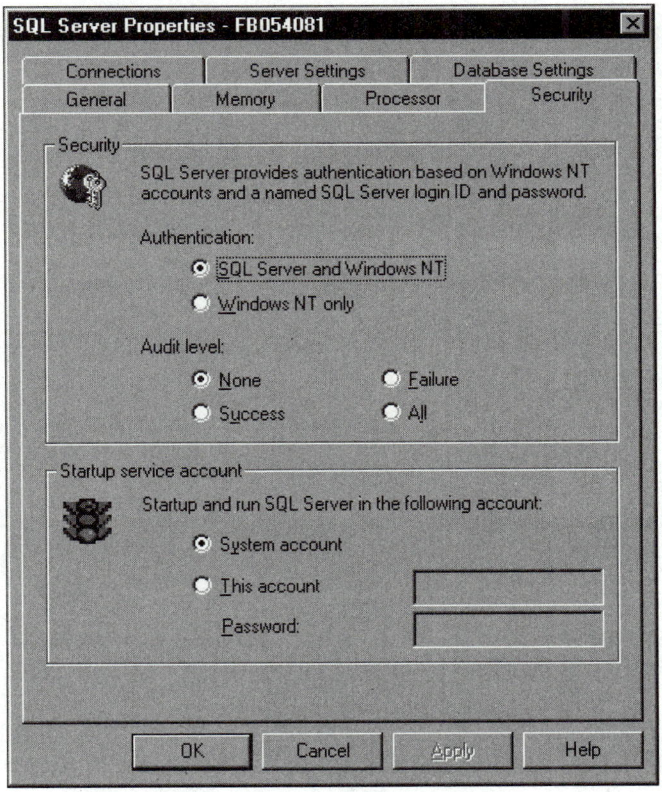

SQL Server 7.0 Properties-Security dialog

NT Authentication Mode

Security of Window NT or Windows 2000 allows for mapping logins from trusted NT domains into the SQL Server. This is what is usually referred to as integrated security. This is a really powerful principle that solves many connectivity problems to the database server.

Integrated security has many benefits, such as:

- Maintaining user access to many resources from one place.
- Granting SQL Server rights is simple. You just need to add the user granted these rights to the appropriate NT user group, sparing you from doing this from within the SQL Server tools.
- Users will be using a single login to get into these resources with a single password.
- Integrated security allows for applications to access the SQL Server and its databases by using generic NT login IDs. For instance, web based applications written for Internet Information Server (IIS) will connect to the SQL Server using the *IUSER_machinename* account if the anonymous option is turned on in IIS for the particular site, and the *IUSER_machinename* is made a domain account.

NT Mixed Authentication Only

This mode uses a combination of the previous two modes. With this mode, the login is checked to see if it is a SQL Server login. If it is, the user is authenticated with the SQL Server login ID and password as we have seen in the SQL Server authentication mode above. If the login ID is not a SQL Server login, connection is attempted using the NT account of the current user. The decision flowchart shown on the next page describes the authentication process into SQL Server for both NT and Mixed modes.

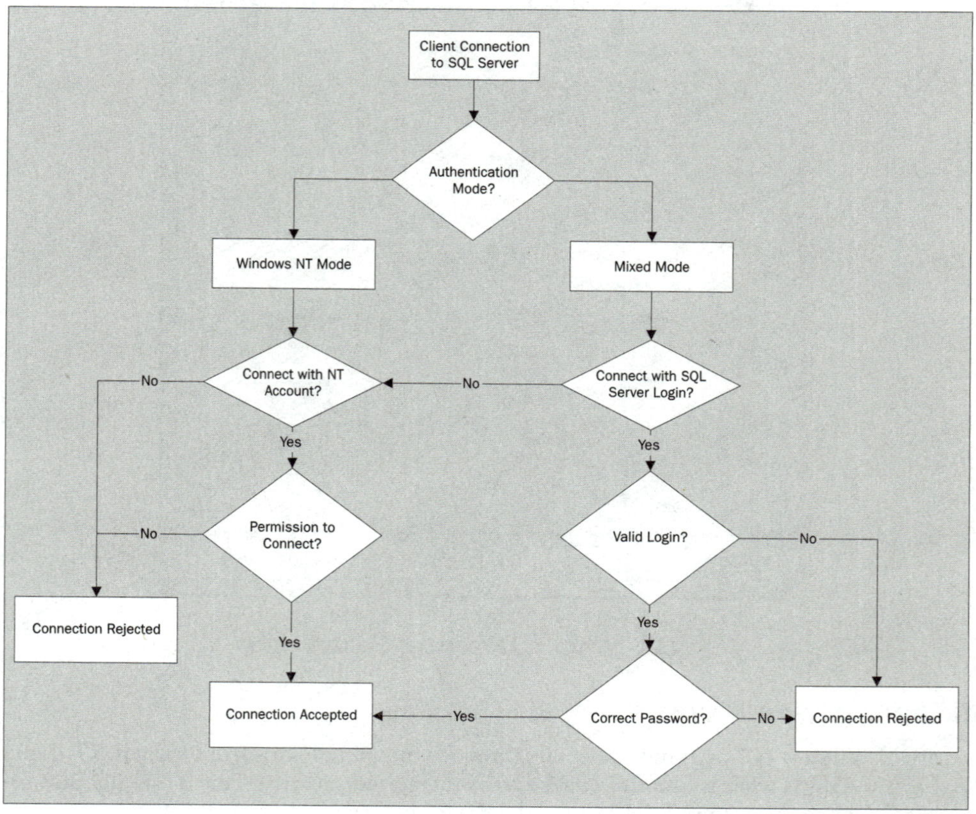

Flowchart of authentication process to SQL Server 7.0

The figure above shows that after a client application requests a connection to SQL Server, depending on the type of authentication it is configured with, the server will follow one of two paths. If the server is configured with mixed authentication mode, it will check if the client is logging in with a SQL Server login. If this is the case, it checks the validity and credentials of the login; based on the results of this check, it either accepts or rejects the connection.

With NT only mode, or mixed mode where no SQL Server login is used, the server checks if the current NT domain user trying to login has permissions to connect. If it does, the connection is accepted. If not, it is rejected.

Microsoft SQL Server supports several methods and network protocols to communicate between client applications and the server. When the application is on the same computer as SQL Server, Windows Interprocess Communication (IPC) components, such as local named pipes or shared memory, are used. When the application is on a separate client, a network IPC is used to communicate with SQL Server by default. Therefore, when using Named Pipes, the user must have permission to connect to the Windows NT Named Pipes IPC, \\<computername>\IPC$. With the Named Pipes connection protocol, a user cannot connect to the SQL Server if the user does not have permission to connect to it. However, to work around this you can do one of two things:

- make sure the Windows NT guest account on the computer is enabled (it is disabled by default),
- make sure that the permission "access this computer from the network", which is found on the user policies dialog in the NT User Manager for Domains dialog, is granted to EVERYONE.

Logins, Roles, and Access Privileges

With the SQL Server authentication mode, SQL Server logins are checked for validity. These logins are a type of SQL Server-specific user accounts. They have a name and password and are saved on the server in the logins table in the master database, which is a default database that is installed with every SQL Server installation. Logins are usually granted permissions to access one or more databases on the server, or even to access specific objects within these databases, as you will see later in the chapter.

When you install SQL Server 7.0, six databases are usually installed by default. These databases include: master, model, msdb, Northwind, Pubs, and tempdb. Discussing these databases is beyond the scope of this book. If you want to know more about them, you may want to refer to the Wrox book: *Professional SQL Server 7.0 Programming, ISBN 1861002319.*

It is not my intent to show you how to create SQL Server logins and maintain them. Many good SQL Server books already discuss this in great detail. However, suffice to say that to create SQL Server logins, you can either use the SQL Server Enterprise Manager, or the system stored procedure, `sp_addlogin`. You can also use SQL Distributed Management Objects (SQL DMO) to accomplish this goal.

SQL-DMO is a collection of objects encapsulating Microsoft SQL Server database and replication management. With SQL-DMO, you can automate repetitive or commonly performed SQL Server administrative tasks, SQL Server object creation and administration, creation and administration of SQL Server Agent jobs, alerts, and operators, and SQL Server replication installation and configuration.

Advantages of using SQL Server logins include:

- The user does not have to be an NT domain user in order to gain access to the SQL Server.
- User information is stored in the SQL Server, which allows for more control over that information directly by database administrators.

Disadvantages of using SQL Server logins are:

- Users have to login twice, once to the network, and once to the SQL Server for each connection they create.
- Maintenance of logins is an added task when considering the ability to use already maintainable NT domain accounts.
- Using SQL Server logins, you need to assign passwords. More passwords only mean potential trouble due to forgetting them.

Now you know what logins are, you might ask what roles are, and why are they needed? Roles are very important in two aspects:

- They can be used on a group of users who have the same permissions.
- If the certain users with the same permissions do not belong to a Windows NT group, or you do not have access to Windows NT user and group administration, a role you create and assign them to will help you administer permissions to all of these users at once.

Roles are just a way of grouping users and logins within SQL Server. Of course, the greatest advantage to this is ease of administration. For example, if you decide that you want to grant permission later on to this group of users on a certain table, you only need to grant that permission to the role assigned to them.

User-defined roles have some characteristics. These characteristics include:

- A user can have more than one database role at the same time.
- You can assign Windows NT users and groups, SQL Server logins, and even other roles to a role, provided that all of these elements exist in the current database.

Two types of roles exist in SQL Server 7.0, server roles, and database roles. User-defined roles fall into the larger category of database roles, as you will see later in the chapter.

User Rights

In order to determine what a user can access and do with the resources they access on the SQL Server and its databases, Microsoft added the concept of user rights. User rights start with the right to login, to the right to access a specific database, and even to perform specific actions on objects within the database.

Granting Access to Databases

Access to a database is usually granted to the SQL Server login using the Enterprise Manager or the system stored procedure, `sp_grantdbaccess`.

When you grant access to a database using the system-stored procedure, `sp_grantdbaccess`, you need to specify which database to grant access for by using the T-SQL command, `use dbName` before using the stored procedure. If you don't do this, the access will be granted for the current database. This system-stored procedure can also be used to grant access to NT domain users. When doing so, however, you need to make sure the domain name is included as part of the user name. For example, to grant database access to the SQL Server login "`mylogin`" and to the NT user "`myDomain\myUser`" to the Northwind database, you write:

```
USE Northwind
EXEC sp_grantdbaccess 'mylogin'
EXEC sp_grnatdbaccess 'myDomain\myUser'
```

Conversely, the system stored procedure; `sp_revokedbaccess` can be used to revoke access of a login or user to a database. This procedure has the same syntax as the `sp_grantdbaccess`, but it reverses its action.

Object Permissions

SQL Server not only allows you to grant permissions on the database level. It also allows for granting these permissions on individual objects within the databases. These objects include anything you can think of, such as tables, views, and stored procedures. SQL Server allows for controlling several types of rights on the individual objects. These rights are listed in the table below:

User Right	Description
SELECT	Allows for viewing the object data and properties. For example, a SELECT granted on a table called `myTable`, allows the grantee to issue SQL queries that return read-only recordsets from the table.
INSERT	Allows the user to run INSERT statements against tables in the database, inserting new records into these tables.
UPDATE	This user right allows for updating existing records in the database using the UPDATE SQL statement.
DELETE	Allows the user to delete records in specific tables using the DELETE statement.
REFERENCES	When inserting new records in a table that has foreign key constraints, the foreign key references another table that the user may not have access to. In this case this permission allows the user to still insert records in the table of concern.
EXECUTE	Allows users to execute stored procedures.

To grant permissions to these objects, you can use T-SQL commands, or the Enterprise Manager. Using the Enterprise Manager is usually easy and recommended unless you want to automate the process of granting such user rights to a large number of users and logins. In this case, it is probably better to use T-SQL commands.

When using the Enterprise Manager to grant permissions to objects, you need to get to the object permissions dialog from the object's properties window. For example, to assign permissions to current users who have access to the Northwind database for the `Products` table, the permissions dialog box looks as follows.

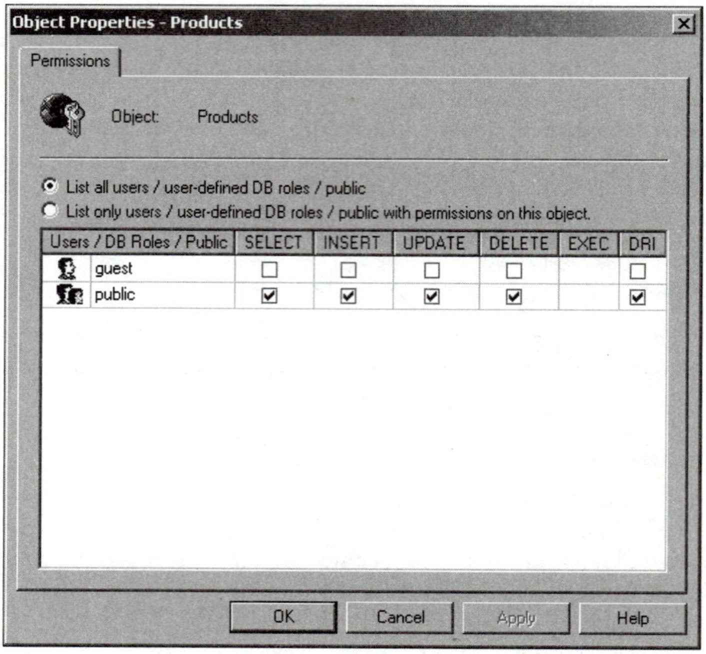

Granting and revoking permissions on a table using the Enterprise Manager

Using T-SQL to control database object permissions requires getting familiar with a number of T-SQL commands, such as, `GRANT`, `DENY`, and `REVOKE`. These keywords are explained below:

GRANT

This command gives a user or a role access to an object in the database. The syntax for this keyword is:

```
GRANT
    {ALL [PRIVILEGES] | permission[,...n]}
    {
        [(column[,...n])] ON {table | view}
        | ON {table | view}[(column[,...n])]
        | ON {stored_procedure | extended_procedure}
    }
TO security_account[,...n]
[WITH GRANT OPTION]
[AS {group | role}]
```

The `ALL` keyword causes all applicable rights for the object to be granted. If you don't specify the `ALL` option, you have to explicitly specify the permissions you want to grant. The keyword `PRIVILEGES` is only introduced for more compatibility with the SQL-92 standard. `ON` and `TO` keywords specify what objects to include in the permissions, and the user or role the permissions are granted to respectively. The `WITH GRANT OPTION`, if specified, allows the grantee to grant similar permissions to other users, logins, and roles. The `AS` keyword is used when permissions on an object are granted to a group or role, and the object permissions need to be further granted to users who are not members of the group or role. Hence, this keyword specifies the optional name of the login in the current database that has the authority to execute the `GRANT` statement.

Below is an example using this statement to grant `SELECT`, and `UPDATE` access to a login called `myLogin` to the `Products` table in the Northwind database:

```
GRANT SELECT, UPDATE
ON Products
TO myLogin
```

DENY

This statement overrides any `GRANT` statements issued for access to an object. If a user belongs to multiple roles with some of the roles granted access privileges to an object and other roles having a `DENY` set for the same object, then the `DENY` always wins and access to the object is denied. The syntax for this statement is:

```
DENY
   {ALL [PRIVILEGES] | permission[,...n]}
   {
      [(column[,...n])] ON {table | view}
      | ON {table | view}[(column[,...n])]
      | ON {stored_procedure | extended_procedure}
   }
TO security_account[,...n]
[CASCADE]
```

The `ALL` keyword, `ON` and `TO` phrases are similar to their counterparts in the `GRANT` statement. It is worth noting, however, that the `CASCADE` option causes the effect of the `DENY` statement to cascade to logins and users granted the same denied privilege by the user being denied with this statement.

REVOKE

This statement reverses the effect of the `GRANT` statement. It removes any permission granted to a user or role on a database object. The syntax for this statement is:

```
REVOKE [GRANT OPTION FOR]
   {ALL [PRIVILEGES] | permission[,...n]}
   {
      [(column[,...n])] ON {table | view}
      | ON {table | view}[(column[,...n])]
      | {stored_procedure | extended_procedure}
   }
{TO | FROM}
   security_account[,...n]
[CASCADE]
[AS {group | role}]
```

The `GRANT OPTION FOR` phrase specifies that `WITH GRANT OPTION` permissions are being removed. You can use the `GRANT OPTION FOR` keywords with `REVOKE` to remove the effects of the `WITH GRANT OPTION` setting specified in the `GRANT` statement. This does not prevent the user or role from accessing the object. It only prevents them from granting access to the object to other users and role. If you specify the `GRANT OPTION FOR` in the `REVOKE` statement when the `WITH GRANT OPTION` is not specified in the `GRANT` statement, the `GRANT OPTION FOR` clause is ignored.

The following example uses the `REVOKE` statement to reverse certain permissions granted to the user `myUser` and role, `myRole`.

```
REVOKE CREATE TABLE, CREATE DEFAULT, CREATE VIEW
FROM myUser, myRole
```

Server and Database Roles

In addition to the user-defined roles that SQL Server allows you to create and manage, it also introduced a special set of role that have specific privileges on the server level, called Server Roles, and on the database level, called Database Roles. These special roles are described below.

Server Roles

The table below summarizes the SQL Server roles, which are fixed and created when you install SQL Server.

Server Role	Description
sysadmin	This role has the same privileges as the special sa login. Users with this role can perform any activity on the SQL Server. This role is introduced as a replacement to the sa admin, which, with this role in place, can now be abandoned. It is worth noting that the Windows NT administrator on the SQL Server machine is automatically mapped to this role. This means that anyone belonging to the Administrators group on the NT server has sa privileges on the SQL Server. You can remove the NT administrators from the sysadmin role if you need to tighten security.
serveradmin	This role is limited in scope. It can perform things like server configuration and shut down of the server.
setupadmin	This role manages startup procedures and linked servers.
securityadmin	This role allows users assigned to it to manage logins, read error logs, and manage `CREATE DATABASE` permissions.
processadmin	Manages processes running on the SQL Server. For instance, if a process has been running for a long time (hanging), users with this role can kill that process.
dbcreator	Creates and alters database structures.
diskadmin	Manages files and file groups assigning them to databases.

In real life, it is rare to use more than the `sysadmin` and `securityadmin` roles. However, you can mix and match these roles to give specific logins certain privileges that are combinations of the privileges provided by these roles.

Database Roles

You have already seen earlier in the chapter that user-defined roles are considered to fall under database roles. Actually, database roles do not only span user-defined roles, but also "fixed" database roles, which are a set of roles that perform database-specific activities. These fixed roles are summarized in the table below.

Fixed Database Role	Description
db_owner	This role encompasses the rest of the fixed database roles. A user with this role can perform any activity on the database the user is assigned to.
db_accessadmin	Acts like the server role, securityadmin, except that the scope of its function is limited to the database it is assigned to. For example, a user with this role can create new database users, but cannot create server logins and roles. It also can add existing logins and roles to the database, and can even add NT users and user groups into the database.
db_datareader	This roles is allowed to retrieve data from any table in the database it is assigned to using `SELECT` statements.
db_datawriter	This role can insert new data, change, or delete existing data in the database tables it is assigned to by issuing `INSERT`, `UPDATE`, and `DELETE` statements respectively.
db_ddladmin	This role can add, modify, and drop objects in the database.
db_securityadmin	Similar to the `db_accessadmin`, except that it cannot create new database users. This role can manage roles and members of database roles, and statement and object permissions in the database it is assigned to.
db_backupoperator	This role is capable of backing up the database.
db_denydatareader	This role is denied access to any user tables in the database.
db_denydatawriter	This role denied permissions to change data in the database.

Now you know about database roles and that user-defined roles are part of these database roles, let's see how such user-defined roles fit within the scheme of SQL Server security, and how they can be created.

To create a new role, you can use the SQL Server Enterprise Manager, a T-SQL statement, or the SQL-DMO. To add the role using the Enterprise Manager, you need to right-click the **Roles** item in the tree view for the database of concern, and select **New Database Role** from the pop-up menu. This will open the dialog shown below.

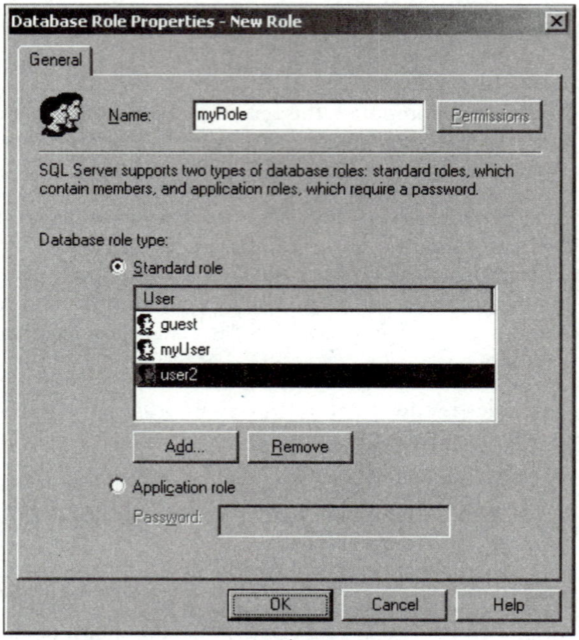

Adding a new database role with the Enterprise Manager

Notice how the Permissions button is disabled. SQL Server will not allow you to assign permissions at the moment you create the roles. Instead, after creating the role and adding some users to it, you need to close the dialog shown and double click the newly added role in the list of database role available in the HTML (right pane) pane of the Microsoft Enterprise Manager. This will open a dialog with the Permissions button enabled. This dialog is very similar to the dialog above, except that you cannot change the role type. You also notice an additional button, the Apply button on the new dialog that puts whatever changes you made into effect without closing the dialog.

Clicking the Permissions button will open the Permissions window that allows you to manage permissions for the role on any database object. Notice how in the screenshot on the next page, we grant `SELECT` permission but deny `INSERT`, `UPDATE`, and `DELETE` for the role on the `Products` table.

You don't need to explicitly deny access to stop someone from having permissions to a certain object in the database. You only need to do this when a user is assigned to multiple roles. If one role gives the permissions, while another role denies it, then you need to use the deny option for the user.

To create the same role using T-SQL and assign the same permissions to it, you can write the following T-SQL statements:

```
USE Northwind
-- Create the role
EXEC sp_addrole 'myRole'
-- Grant SELECT privilege to Products table
GRANT SELECT ON  Products TO myRole
-- Deny INSERT, UPDATE, and DELETE privileges to Products table
DENY INSERT, UPDATE, DELETE ON Products TO myRole
```

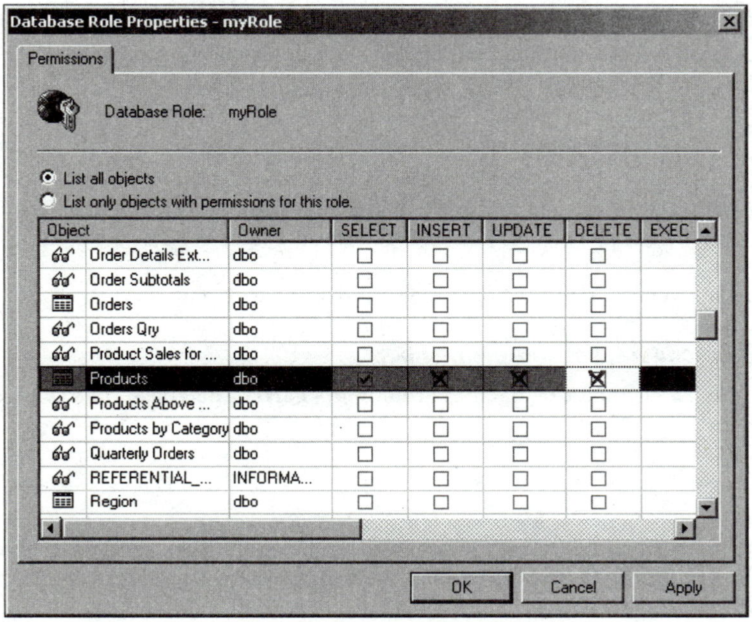

Assigning permissions to a database role

To remove a user-defined database role using Enterprise Manager, you MUST remove all users added to it, and then delete it by right-clicking its name and selecting the DELETE command from the menu. The same rule applies to removing the role using the system-stored procedure, `sp_droprole`. You have to empty the role from any users added to it first using the system-stored procedure, `sp_droprolemember`.

```
Use Northwind
-- Remove users belonging to the role:
EXEC sp_droprolemember myRole, guest
EXEC sp_droprolemember myRole, myUser
EXEC sp_droprolemember myRole, user2
-- Drop the role:
EXEC sp_droprole myRole
```

In the last few examples, I used a number of system-stored procedures to perform the same tasks that were possible to perform with the Enterprise Manager. If you are not familiar with system stored procedures, they are a number of built-in procedures that are compiled and stored in the database and perform many administrative tasks of the server and the databases. Since these procedures are compiled, they run faster, and using them for bulk administrative jobs is much more efficient than using the Enterprise Manager. Besides, system stored procedures can be accessed directly from applications designed to perform some administrative tasks for the SQL Server through OLE DB or ODBC. A detailed discussion of system-stored procedures is beyond the scope of this book. You can either refer to the Books-On-Line (BOL), or to one of many good SQL Server 7.0 books on the market for such a detailed discussion. For our purposes, I will only briefly explain the three procedures I used so far, `sp_addrole, sp_droprole, and sp_droprolemember`, in addition to the procedure `sp_addrolemember`.

The System Stored Procedure, sp_addrole

This stored procedure can be used to add a database role to the current database. The syntax of this procedure is:

```
sp_addrole [@rolename =] 'role' [,[@ownername =] 'owner']
```

The arguments of this procedure are simply the role name and the owner name. The owner name has to be a valid login, which could be a SQL Server login, or an added Windows NT user.

This stored procedure returns 0 in case of success, and 1 in case it fails.

The System Stored Procedure, sp_addrolemember

This procedure adds an account to a database role in the current database. The syntax for the procedure is:

```
sp_addrolemember [@rolename =] 'role', [@membername =] 'security_account'
```

Arguments passed to this procedure are simply the role name and the user name. These two identifiers must be valid in order for the procedure to succeed. This stored procedure returns 0 in case of success, and 1 in case it fails.

The System Stored Procedure, sp_droprolemember

Simply speaking, this stored procedure removes a user from a role membership in the current database. The syntax for this procedure is:

```
sp_droprolemember [@rolename =] 'role', [@membername =] 'security_account'
```

Arguments passed to the procedure include the role name and user name. These two arguments have to be valid identifiers in order for the procedure to succeed. This stored procedure returns 0 in case of success, and 1 in case it fails.

The System Stored Procedure, sp_droprole

This stored procedure removes an EMPTY role from the current database. The syntax for this procedure is:

```
sp_droprole [@rolename =] 'role'
```

The role name passed to the procedure must be a valid role in the database. It must also be empty, i.e. all users who are members of the role must be removed before the role can be dropped. This stored procedure returns 0 in case of success, and 1 in case it fails.

Application Roles

This type of role is used for application security as the application accesses the database. You may often run into situations where you would like a user to have a separate set of rights depending on how they are accessing the database. Usually these situations occur when you want the user to access the database from an application. With application roles you can have a great flexibility in what exactly the user can do with the database under different contexts. For example, your user can have only `SELECT` access to the tables in the database, yet by adding them to an application role, they may be able to do more things, such as updating a table, from within the confines of an application.

Application roles differ from regular user-defined database roles in that you can assign a password to them when you create them. Speaking of creating them, the easiest way to do so is in the Enterprise Manager. If you look back at 'Adding a new database role with the Enterprise Manager', you will notice that you can specify the role type as being an application role. Selecting this option will activate the Password text box allowing you to enter a password for the role.

You can also create the application role using the system-stored procedure, `sp_addapprole`. This procedure takes the role name and password as arguments as it create a new application role in the current database. The syntax for this procedure is:

```
sp_addapprole [@rolename =] 'role', [@password =] 'password'
```

How Do Application Roles Work?

Application roles serve a great purpose of giving the SQL Server user special access rights and privileges within a certain context. This works in the following way:

- Application users log into the SQL Server interactively through a login screen provided by the application, or implicitly through a system account.
- The login is validated and the user is given whatever rights the login has.
- Next, the application issues a call to the stored procedure, `sp_setapprole`, providing a role name and password.
- Upon validation of the application role, the connection is switched to the context of this application role replacing any rights the user has through the login with the rights assigned to the application role, which may or may not be more restrictive than the login rights.
- It is important to note that the user cannot go back to using the rights of the login until the connection is closed and they re-connect to the server.

Setting Up Application Roles

Application roles do not become active until the applications using them activate them by calling the system-stored procedure, `sp_setapprole`. This procedure takes a role name and password as some of its arguments. The syntax for this procedure is:

```
sp_setapprole [@rolename =] 'role' ,
   [@password =] {Encrypt N 'password'} | 'password'
   [,[@encrypt =] 'encrypt_style']
```

The password can either be supplied directly or encrypted using the ODBC canonical `Encrypt` function. When you use the `Encrypt` function, you must precede the password by a capital "N" to convert it to a Unicode string. Notice the use of the curly braces around the keyword `{Encrypt N 'password'}`, rather than regular parentheses.

SQL Server Security Considerations

Other SQL Server security considerations that may affect the way users deal and interact with SQL Server include, using views as an effective way to restrict user access to data in the database, disabling the Guest account, and making sure the sa login password is different from the default blank password.

Using Views and Stored procedures

Views provide snapshots of the data at the time they are used. They also provide a great way for you to limit what the users can access. If you want your users to view the employee information table minus the `BirthDate` field, you can simply create a view that includes all the columns of the `Employee` table except for the `BirthDate` field, practically preventing them from viewing the data in it. For example, the code to create this view based on the Northwind sample database that is installed with the SQL Server installation is:

```
CREATE VIEW dbo.EmployeesMinusDOB
AS
SELECT   EmployeeID,
   LastName,
   FirstName,
   Title,
   TitleOfCourtesy,
   HireDate,
   Address,
   City,
   Region,
   PostalCode,
   Country,
   HomePhone,
   Extension,
   Photo,
   Notes,
   ReportsTo,
   PhotoPath
FROM   Employees
```

The same can be said about stored procedures. You can use those, not only to limit viewing certain fields, but also to limit the users to updating certain fields, or inserting into certain tables only if certain conditions are met, etc.

Another advantage views and stored procedures offer is performance enhancement. Views are stored in the database and their execution plan is stored in the procedure cache and will not be removed unless the view structure is changed. Hence, the database engine does not have to try a large number of execution paths and plans every time you run the view. Stored procedures are pre-compiled and saved in the database, which also makes them very fast and efficient in responding to client requests.

Guest Account

The Guest account provides default access to a number of default databases that are created when SQL Server is installed. These databases include: master, msdb, Northwind, Pubs, and tempdb. Newly-added logins have the same security rights as the Guest account. Therefore, new logins might sometimes end up with more rights and privileges than you intended for them, creating a security hole. Therefore, it is recommended that this account be disabled completely and not be used unless there is a very pressing need to it.

Sa Account Password

One of the things that many people who install SQL Server don't bother changing is the sa account password. This password is empty by default, and leaving it unchanged poses a great security risk simply because this account has godly rights on both the server and the databases in it. Leaving the password blank will allow unwanted access to the data on your server, which by itself should be a strong-enough incentive for you to change this password.

In SQL Server 7.0, a server role that allows the same level of rights as the sa account is the sysadmin server role. With this role, it is recommended that you dump the sa account altogether. Instead, you can add a user or two to the sysadmin role to limit sa-type access to these two users.

How Does SQL Server Security Apply To The Data Warehouse?

Now that you have seen an overview of the SQL Server security, you might be wondering exactly how does all this apply to the data warehousing scheme of things. Well, the information you learned in this chapter so far is very relevant to the data warehouse security. You can use this information to customize user and group access to the data in the SQL Server database serving as the database of the data warehouse. For instance you can start by creating some logins and a data warehouse administrator role, call it `dwadmin`:

```
EXEC sp_addlogin 'SQLuser1'
EXEC sp_addlogin 'SQLuser2'
EXEC sp_addlogin 'SQLuser3'
go

Use DWDatabase          -- the database of the data warehouse
EXEC sp_addrole 'dwadmin'
```

Next, you can add users to this role and assign access privileges to the role. These users can be NT users or SQL Server logins:

```
EXEC sp_addrolemember 'dwadmin', 'SQLuser1'
```

Then, you might create more logins, more roles corresponding to some departments in your organization and add users to these roles as necessary:

```
EXEC sp_addlogin 'marketing1', 'password'
EXEC sp_addlogin 'marketing2', 'password'
EXEC sp_addlogin 'marketing3', 'password'
EXEC sp_addlogin 'finance1', 'password'
EXEC sp_addlogin 'finance2', 'password'
EXEC sp_addlogin 'finance3', 'password'

-- Add some roles:
EXEC sp_addrole 'marketingMGR'
EXEC sp_addrole 'marketingUser'
EXEC sp_addrole 'financeMGR'
EXEC sp_addrole 'financeUSR'

-- Add some members to the marketing roles:
EXEC sp_addrolemember 'marketingMGR', 'marketing1'
EXEC sp_addrolemember 'marketingUser', 'marketing2'
EXEC sp_addrolemember 'marketingUser', 'marketing3'
-- Add some members to the finance roles:
EXEC sp_addrolemember 'financeMGR', 'finance1'
EXEC sp_addrolemember 'financeUser', 'finance2'
EXEC sp_addrolemember 'financeUser', 'finance3'
```

Now you have your roles and members setup, you can grant the privileges you want to the database objects to the roles you created. For example:

```
GRANT ALL ON Employees TO dwadmin, financeMGR
GRANT SELECT ON Employees TO financeUser, marketingMGR, marketingUser
```

You can, of course continue building this security scheme, maybe even adding application roles to change the privileges of the users based on the context of the application accessing the database. In summary, with the SQL Server security tools and methods, you have a wealth of powerful tools to secure and customize user access to the server and the databases.

Windows 2000 Security

Windows 2000 security has many new features that simplify domain administration, improve performance, and integrate Internet security technology based on public-key cryptography. The main features in Windows 2000 security services include:

- Windows 2000 security is integrated with Windows 2000 Active Directory services (explained later in the chapter), which provides flexible and scalable account management for large domains. This integration also provides better access control and delegation of administration.
- Windows 2000 integrates the Kerberos version 5 authentication protocol (explained later in the chapter). This protocol is a mature Internet security standard, which is implemented as the default protocol for network authentication. This protocol provides a foundation for authentication interoperability allowing a single sign-on to the network to allow access to all resources the user has rights to access, including resources on NT or UNIX servers.
- Incorporation of public-key certificates and providing secure channels based on Secure Sockets Layer (SSL) 3.0, and Crypto API (Application Programming Interface) to deliver industry-standard protocols for data integrity and privacy across public networks.

In the following sections, I will provide a brief high-level overview of the main features and basic components of the Windows 2000 security model.

Main Elements of the Windows 2000 Security

Windows 2000 security is integrated with the Active Directory through logon authentication and access control to objects in the directory. Integration of the Kerberos authentication protocol (explained later in the chapter) allows for a single network logon. This provides administrators with the ability to manage directory data and organization throughout their network. Also, with this single logon, authorized network users can access resources anywhere on the network. Windows 2000 also supports policy-based administration, which makes management easy even for complex networks. The following sections briefly explain some of the basic elements of the Microsoft Windows 2000 security.

Active Directory

First let's define what a directory is. A directory is a hierarchical structure that stores information about objects on the network. For instance, user accounts, servers, etc. can all be saved in a structured directory.

Second, let's define what a directory service is. A directory service is a service in Windows that provides methods for storing directory data and making this data available to network users and administrators.

Windows 2000 Active Directory (referred to as the Active Directory hereafter) is a directory service that stores information about Windows 2000 and Windows NT network resources, including user accounts and other objects relating to the large network domains as well as the different members of the Back Office family of products (including SQL Server). For example, the Active Directory stores information about user accounts, such as names, passwords, phone numbers, and so on, and enables other authorized users on the same network to access this information.

Other features provided by the Active Directory include:

- Stores all domain security policy and account information.
- Provides replication and availability of account information to multiple Domain Controllers
- Available for remote administration.
- The Active Directory supports a hierarchical name space for user, group, and computer account information. Accounts can be grouped by organizational units, rather than the flat domain account name space provided by earlier versions of Windows NT.
- Administrator rights to create and manage user or group accounts can be delegated to the level of organizational units. Access rights can be granted to individual properties on user objects to allow, for example, a specific individual or group to have the right to reset passwords, but not to modify other account information.
- Active Directory replication allows account updates at any domain controller, not just the primary domain controller (PDC). Multiple master replicas of the Active Directory at other domain controllers, which used to be known as backup domain controllers (BDCs), are updated and synchronized automatically.

Kerberos 5 Authentication Protocol

In ancient Greek mythology, Kerberos was a three-headed dog that guarded the under-world. Today's kerberos is an authentication protocol that guards against unauthorized access to network resources. The principle behind Kerberos is simple. The authenticated party presents a proof of privilege to the authenticating party guarding the needed resource in the form of a secret that only the latter party knows. If the secret turns out to be the correct one, the authenticated party is allowed access to the resource.

The way this simple protocol is accomplished is very complex, but boils down to using an encryption/decryption key by the authenticated party. The authenticated party encrypts a message with the key and presents it to the authenticating party. The latter party decrypts the message with its copy of the key (the mechanism by which the authenticating party gets its copy is very complex). If the message is decrypted successfully, that means both parties have the same key and the authentication succeeds.

Windows 2000 integrates the latest version of the Kerberos protocol, and uses it as its primary authentication protocol. In Windows 2000, this protocol doesn't provide authorization to services or databases; it establishes identity at logon (the encryption/decryption key), which is used throughout the session.

The integration of the Kerberos protocol allows, for the first time, for a single sign-on to the network. With this protocol, a user can sign-on to the network in the morning and continue to work with any resources they have rights to access without ever having to sign-on again. These resources may span several Windows 2000 domains, or even may be located on a UNIX network.

Access Control List (ACL)

Each object on the Windows 2000 network has a unique security descriptor that includes an access control list (ACL). An ACL is a list of entries that grant or deny specific access rights to individuals or groups. The Windows 2000 Server object-based security model lets administrators grant access rights to a user or group-rights that govern who can access a specific object, a group of properties, or an individual property of an object. The definition of access rights on a per-property level provides the highest level of granularity of permissions.

As an example of how easy it is to manage ACLs in Windows 2000, you can open the Windows Explorer, right click a file or folder (in our case we selected a folder named 'Security') and select the Properties pop-up menu item. This will show you the properties dialog for the selected file or folder. In the dialog, select the Security tab, shown in the following figure:

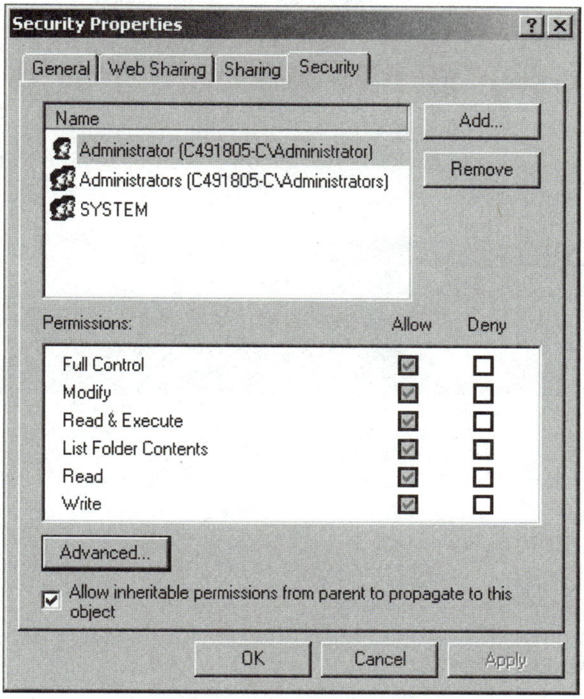

The Security Tab of the selected file in Windows 2000

The Security page shown above allows you to set permissions for the users who have access permissions to the file or folder. If you click the Add button, the dialog shown below will appear.

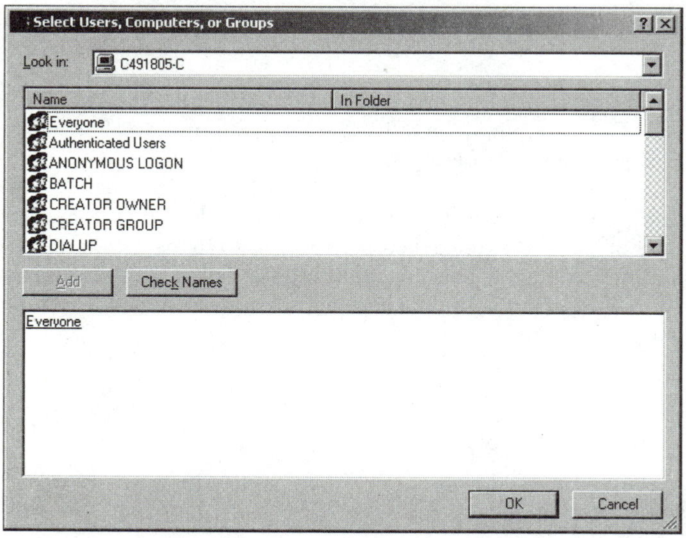

Adding new users to access the resource

The dialog above allows you to add new users who have access to the file or folder by either typing their name, or selecting them from the list. Let's add the Everyone user for example.

If you close the dialog above, you return to the security page of the selected file. In this page, you can specify precisely we are allowing some rights (read, list folder contents, and read & execute), and denying others (write access). If you click the Advanced button below the Permissions list, you get the Access Control dialog shown below:

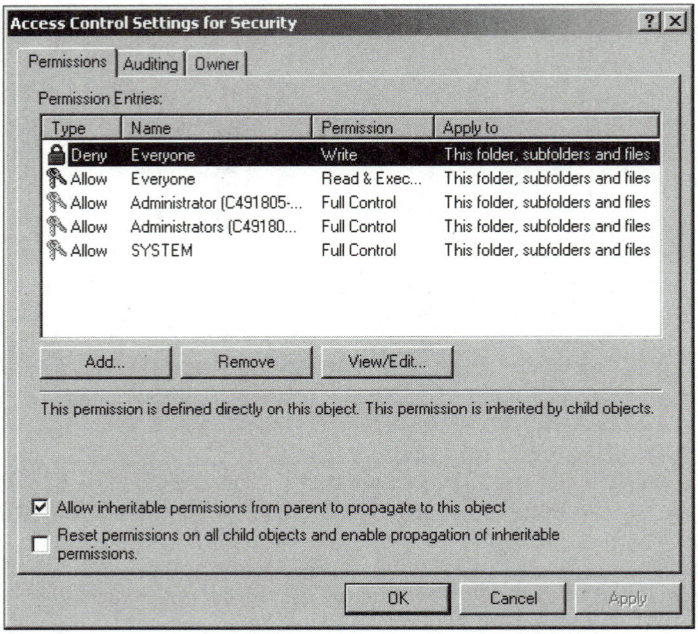

Access Control Dialog for the selected file or folder

The dialog above provides you with tremendous flexibility in setting the granularity level to which you want to set permissions. For example, if you click the View/Edit button after selecting the newly added resource, you get the dialog shown below.

The dialog below allows you to set further permissions to the selected object. You can even set permissions beyond the object and extend such permissions to items within the object, such as subfolders, files within the folder, etc. This is done using the Apply Onto drop-down list. The dialog can also allow you to change the person with the given permissions to someone else by clicking the Change button.

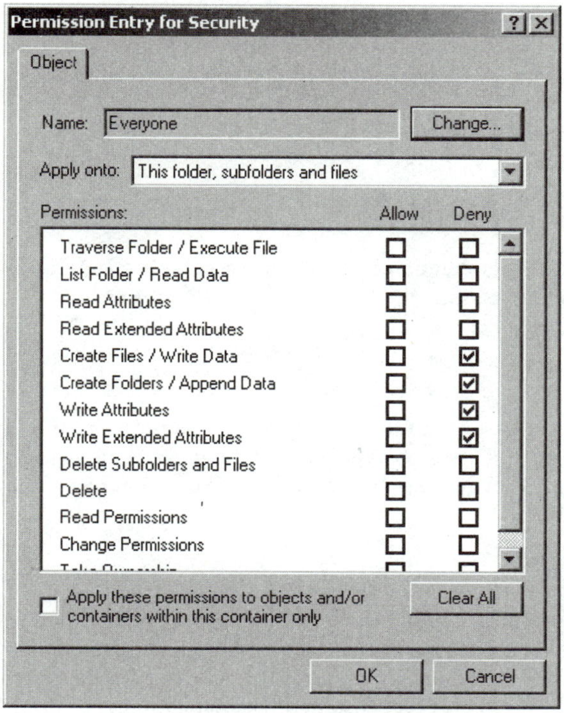

Permission Entry Dialog for the selected folder

Policy-Based Administration

Group Policies are configuration settings applied to computers or users as they are initialized. For example, when you create a new user, you can select a group policy for them, which will set all the security permissions and properties very quickly. Group policy settings determine access to directory objects and domain resources, what domain resources (such as applications) are available to users, and how these domain resources are configured for use. These settings are saved in Group Policy Objects (GPO), and applied to active directory sites, domains, or organizational units.

How does SQL Server Security Integrate with Windows 2000 Security?

The next release of SQL Server, SQL Server 2000, will rely on Active Directory to simplify the management of large enterprise deployments. As a database server, SQL will use the directory to centralize configuration, location and maintenance information. This information will include user accounts, logins, roles, registered servers, databases on the servers, user and role privileges to the databases and servers, etc.

With SQL Server 2000, Active Directory will serve as a central hub for registering servers, finding databases, subscribing to replication services, and keeping applications and databases in sync. When installed, SQL Server 2000 will automatically register in Active Directory, which will let database administrators search for SQL Servers and databases without knowing a location or name.

With integration with Windows 2000 security, authentication to SQL Server will take place through the Kerberos identity that was given to the user when they first logged into the network. If the user does not have the privileges to access a database on the SQL Server, they will still have a chance to use a native SQL Server login.

OLAP Services Security

The third level of security is implemented at the OLAP cube level. As I promised back in Chapter 5, I will explain in the following sections the role-based OLAP cube security.

Cube Security

OLAP cube security is role-based. In other words, you create roles in the OLAP database for the cube of concern, add users to it, and assign privileges to these users. This scheme is somewhat similar to the SQL Server security scheme in general, but it adds the protection of another layer at the OLAP cube data and aggregations level.

Authentication

With OLAP Services, authentication occurs at the operating system level when a user logs on to a Windows NT domain. This is because OLAP Services supports an integrated security authentication scheme. Hence, access to OLAP Services requires the user to be a member of the same domain as the user account under which the server was installed. Users belonging to domains trusted by the mentioned domain can also access the OLAP Services on your server.

Access Control

Access control determines which users can access the OLAP data and exactly what they can do with it. Access controls are only active for servers installed on NTFS volumes, and not supported on FAT volumes. With access control, you can limit user's rights to read, read/write, and administer the OLAP server.

The read access level supports viewing the data and the metadata of the OLAP cubes without allowing the user granted this right to modify the data. The read/write access level provides the privileges of the read access level in addition to allowing the user assigned to it the right to modify cube data and metadata for write-enabled cubes. The Admin access level allows for all privileges for the previous levels besides allowing the user with this right to process the OLAP data (process dimensions and cubes, etc.). A Windows NT group, OLAP Administrators, is usually created when you install the OLAP services. The user who installs the services is automatically added to this group. Users of this group have the admin access control level.

Roles

Similar to SQL Server roles, OLAP Services roles group NT users and user groups before assigning access rights and privileges to them. Roles are created and managed at the database level. Roles can be assigned to specific cubes within the database. The following is a description of how they can be created and managed.

To create a new role in the OLAP Manager:

- Expand the Library tree item in the tree view pane and right click the Roles item on the tree.

- Select New Database Role from the context-sensitive menu to open the Create a Database Role dialog.

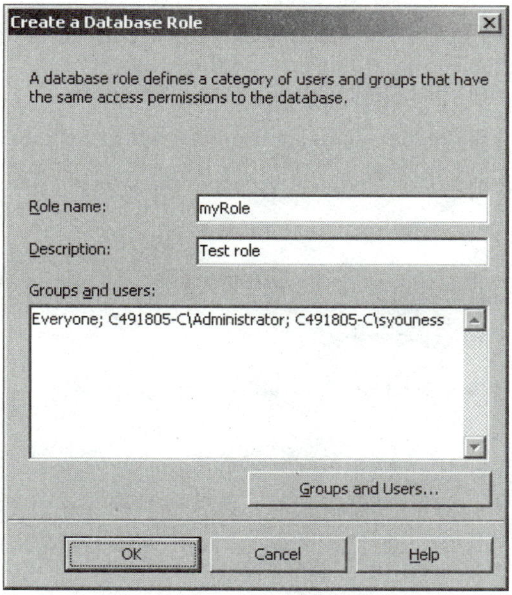

Creating a new OLAP database role

- Type a name and description for the role, then click the Groups and Users... button.
- A dialog "Add Users and Groups" opens to allow you to add NT users and groups to the new role.

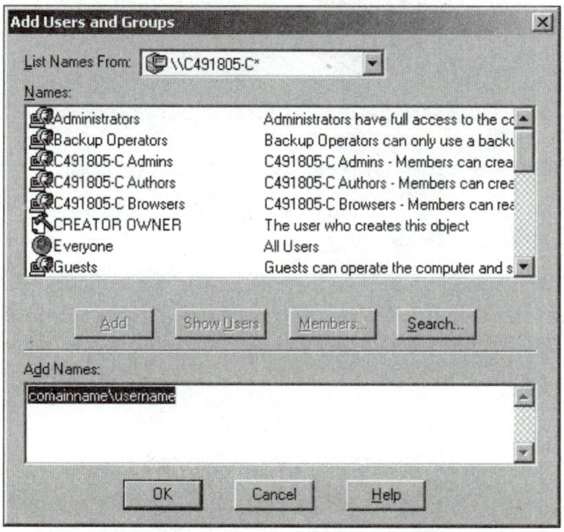

Adding users and groups to the new role

- Select the users and groups you want to add to the new role, and click OK.
- Now, to add the new role to the Sales cube, right click the roles folder under the appropriate cube and select Manage Roles from the context sensitive menu.
- This will open the Manage Roles dialog, (see below). You notice in the figure that the new role we created is in the left-hand side list, the Database Roles list. You can add it to the cube access list (on the right-hand side) by clicking the ">" button.
- Notice that you can also create a new role from this dialog by clicking the New Role button.
- Finally, you can grant read/write control access to the selected roles by checking this option in the dialog box.

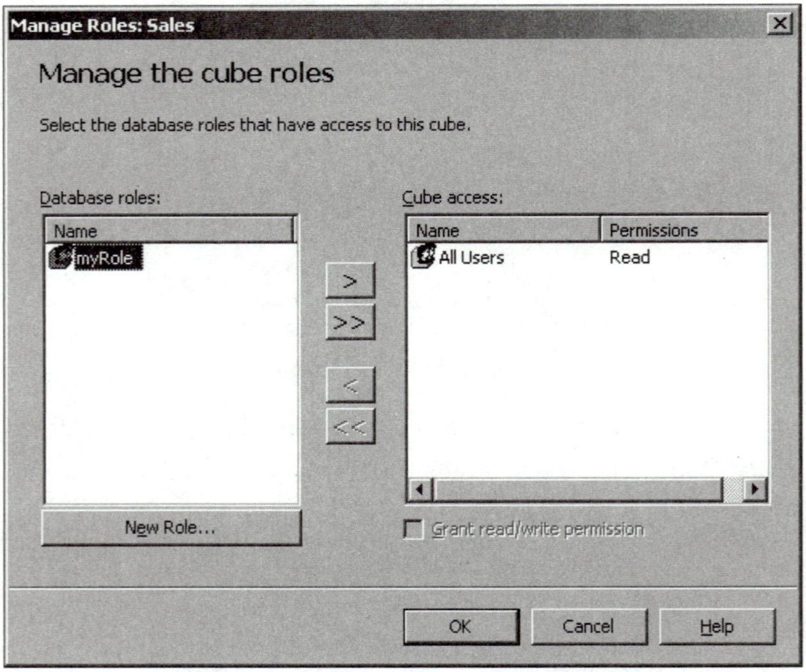

Adding the newly created role to the Sales cube.

A Few Words About Virtual Cubes

Similar to views in relational databases, virtual cubes allow for viewing the data from specific angles restricting unwanted access to sensitive data. Virtual cubes can combine multiple cubes in one view, or can only expose selected subsets of measures and dimensions within one cube. Therefore, you might want to consider using virtual cubes where you want to restrict certain users from accessing all the data in your cubes.

Cell-Level Security

Microsoft introduced a new feature in Service Pack 1 of OLAP Services, cell-level security. This feature will be part of the next release of SQL Server (SQL Server 2000). Cell-level security provides a finer degree of control over the OLAP cubes. With this feature, users can be granted or denied permission to access data down to individual cells within a cube.

Cell-level security is optional. If it is not specified, end users will see the data in all the cells of the cubes they are authorized to access. If a cube is write-enabled, end users cannot update cell values. If one or more of a virtual cube's component cubes are write-enabled, end users cannot update the virtual cube's cell values.

Cell-level security is implemented through MDX statements. These statements are used to define rules that define whether an access is allowed or denied to a cell in a cube. The MDX statements are saved in the cube role's collection. Cell-level security falls into three main categories:

- **Readable cells**: These cells are readable through direct or indirect queries (through calculated members) if the permissions set on them evaluate to True. On the other hand, if these permissions evaluate to False, the cells become unreadable. A cell derived from a protected cell does not follow the rules of the original cell. For example, if `Cell2` is derived from `Cell1` and `Cell1`'s security rules evaluate to False, then `Cell2` will still be readable if its security rules for `Cell2` evaluate to True.
- **Contingent Readable cells**: Security rules for these cells apply only to calculated members. The rules are almost the same as those for the standard readable cells, except for the case of derived cells. Hence, if the security rules for a contigent readable cell evaluate to True, the cell will be readable. If these rules evaluate to False, the cell will not be readable. Derived cells, however, follow different rules. If `Cell2` is derived from `Cell1` in this scenario, and `Cell1`'s security permisions evaluate to False, then `Cell2` will NOT be readable regardless of how its own permissions are. But, if `Cell1`'s security permissions evaluate to True, then `Cell2` will be readable only when its own security rules evaluate to True.
- **Write-Enabled cells**: With this rule, cells will be changed if their security rules evaluate to True, and will not be changed if these rules evaluate to False. If a cell's security rule evaluates to False according to this scenario, the changes made to the cell will be allowed in the cube, but will not be comitted to the data source. Also, users with read-only access will be able to change the content of the cells which enables them to conduct "What If" scenarios. Their changes, however, will not be committed to the data source.

Example of Establishing Read Permissions

The following is an example that shows how cell security is set programmatically by using MDX through Visual Basic:

- Create a user called `CellTest` and add it to the `Users` group of your Windows NT groups.
- Make sure the OLAP Server is running.
- Create a new application using Visual Basic.
- Add a reference to the Microsoft Decision Support Objects in the Project References dialog box

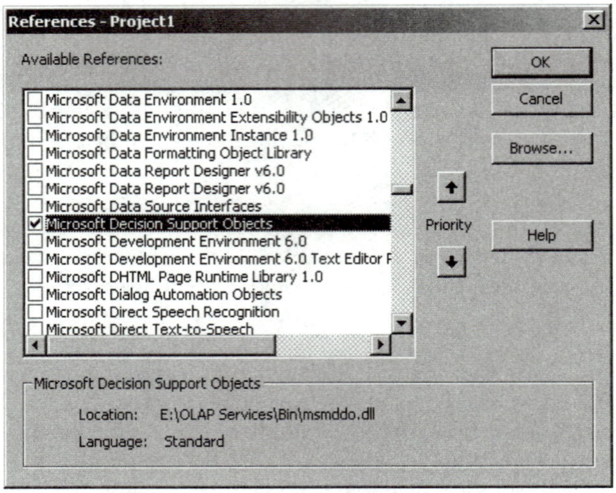

❑ In the `Form_Load` event procedure, add the code below.

```
Private Sub Form_Load()
    Const NEW_ROLE = "Test Role"
    Dim dsoSrv As DSO.Server
    Dim dsoDB As DSO.MDStore
    Dim dsoCube As DSO.MDStore
    Dim dsoRole As Role
```

❑ Connect to the OLAP Server, then set the database to be OLAP_Example and the cube to be "Sales of 1998" (or any database and cube you have on your machine, as long as you reflect that in the following code)

```
    Set dsoSrv = New DSO.Server
    dsoSrv.Connect ("LocalHost")

    'Set the database and cube:
    Set dsoDB = dsoSrv.MDStores("OLAP_Example")
    Set dsoCube = dsoDB.MDStores("Sales of 1998")
```

❑ Add the new role to the database, and add the user `CellTest` as a member of the role.

```
    If Not dsoDB.Roles.Find(NEW_ROLE) Then
        dsoDB.Roles.AddNew (NEW_ROLE)
        Set dsoRole = dsoDB.Roles(NEW_ROLE)
        dsoRole.UsersList = "CellTest;"
        dsoRole.Update
    End If
```

- Add the new role to the cube and construct the MDX statement to set the permissions:

```
    If Not dsoCube.Roles.Find(NEW_ROLE) Then
      dsoCube.Roles.AddNew (NEW_ROLE)
    End If

    Set dsoRole = dsoCube.Roles(NEW_ROLE)

    'This is where the security rule is defined!
    dsoRole.SetPermissions "CellRead", _
      "iif(Measures.CurrentMember.Name = ""Store Cost"", 1, 0)"
```

- You need to remove the role "All Users" from the cube, because it contains everyone and has full permissions which will override our permissions:

```
    If dsoCube.Roles.Find("All Users") Then
        dsoCube.Roles.Remove ("All Users")
    End If

    dsoCube.Update

    dsoSrv.CloseServer
    Set dsoCube = nothing
    Set DsoDB=nothing
    Set dsoSrv = Nothing
End Sub
```

When you run the code, the security permissions will be set. You can verify that by opening your OLAP_Example database and checking the existence of the role "Test Role" on the indicated cube, and that the user `CellTest` exist under that role and that it is the only user to be listed.

DTS Package Security

The last topic we will cover regarding security of the data warehouse is the security implemented at the DTS package level. We saw in Chapter 6, Microsoft Data Transformation Services, DTS packages provide two levels of security: owner and user. The figure on the next page reminds you that when a package is saved it can be assigned an owner password, a user password, or both.

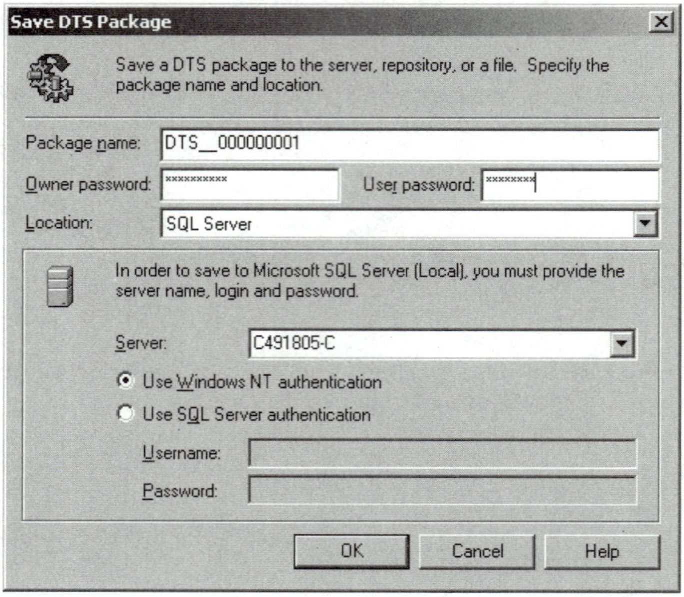

Assigning owner and user passwords for the DTS package

Assigning passwords for the owner or user will result in prompting the user to enter either password when they try to edit the cube or execute it. Assigning the passwords will also result in saving the package in an encrypted format. When a DTS package or version is encrypted, all of its collections and properties are encrypted, except for the DTS package Name, Description, ID, VersionID, and CreationDate properties.

Summary

In this chapter, we learned about the different levels of security (defense) that can be used to control access to the SQL Server data warehouse and the OLAP data. One of the most powerful features that stands out in the security scheme of SQL Server and the OLAP Services, is the integration of their security with the operating system security, Windows NT. This integration allows for users to login once to the system, and have immediate access to the SQL Server or the OLAP cubes without having to login again when they try to access these resources. Although Microsoft promises full compatibility between the Windows 2000 operating system and Windows NT 4.0, it remains to be seen how the new security features introduced by Windows 2000 will affect SQL Server and OLAP security when the next version is released.

13

Administration and Maintenance

Your job as a data warehouse professional does not end with creating and populating the data warehouse. The data warehouse has to be maintained and nursed on a daily basis so that it can continue to receive new data, as old data that is no longer (or rarely) used for reporting and decision-making can be dealt with or archived asnecessary. It will probably take a few months after you rollout your data warehouse to get it to a stable state (where only regular maintenance and administration is needed). This chapter addresses the following points:

- Developing backup and recovery strategies for the data warehouse and for the OLAP aggregations, once the cubes have been processed.
- Archiving old data that is no longer needed for decision support.
- Replication, as a way to build data marts based on data existing in a data warehouse.
- Automating the data warehouse administration tasks (using the SQL Agent).
- Responding to events.

What Should We Do After We Roll Out the Data Warehouse?

Before you can claim full control over the data warehouse after rolling it out, and before you get to the stage where only regular maintenance and administration work is needed to make sure it continues to serve its purpose, there will be a period of more intensive monitoring of all aspects of the data warehouse. In particular, the areas you need to monitor include usage, process, and infrastructure.

What Tools Do We Use For Monitoring?

SQL Server provides many tools that help you monitor its performance and usage. These tools are explained in more detail in Chapter 14, Optimization. One such tool is the **SQL Profiler**, which creates traces of the activities conducted on the server, and allows you to customize these traces to certain activities. For instance, you can trace the execution of queries from a certain application, or issued by a certain user.

SQL Server also provides a **Query Analyzer** tool that allows you to analyze your queries and see their execution path. The Query Analyzer is a great tool because it points out the bottlenecks that will consume most of the resources in the query execution.

As part of the Query Analyzer, SQL Server provides an **Index Analyzer**. This tool optimizes indexes for better performance of your queries.

You can also use SQL Server's rich library of system and extended stored procedures to monitor almost every aspect of the system. The discussion of these stored procedures is beyond the scope of this book. Many SQL Server books discuss them in detail; for example, *Professional SQL Server 7.0 Programming (Wrox Press, ISBN 1-861002-31-9.*

Usage Monitoring

Even though we gathered the requirements from the user, designed the data warehouse and built it according to the client needs (and better yet, we conducted piloting and intensive testing before we rolled it out to the users), we will still need to monitor the usage of the data warehouse to make sure the users will use it according to expectations. In particular, we need to pay close attention to the user queries, reports, use of aggregates, effectiveness of the indexes, etc.

We need to look for the pattern of ad hoc queries issued against the data warehouse, which will give us a clue as to what additional aggregations are needed. For instance, when we processed the OLAP cubes, we processed them up to certain levels of aggregates. However, as the users start using the system, we may notice that the queries use certain aggregates built at run time that is they are not pre-calculated. We may want to add these aggregates to improve the performance of these queries.

Indexes in a data warehouse consume a large amount of the direct access database storage. This is because we try to increase the number of indexes in the beginning to make sure performance will not suffer. In addition, we know that we have relative freedom to do so since the data warehouse will not be subject to online transactions that cause its data to be updated or deleted, or cause new data to be directly inserted into it. However, as the users use the data warehouse, we will see that some of the indexes are not contributing any performance gain. We learn this by monitoring the user queries and reports. Identifying the indexes that do not contribute to query performance and dropping them will free large spaces that may be very valuable and better filled with data and aggregates.

When we roll out the data warehouse, we usually get a feel of a "best guess" as to what aggregates to pre-calculate and store. We get this feeling from interviewing users and gathering requirements. However, as users start using the real system, we will need to adjust the aggregates we designed initially, to reflect what the users really use most. This is crucial for optimal performance of queries and reports used against the data warehouse.

Infrastructure Monitoring

When building a data warehouse, it is important that we conduct pilot tests before rolling it out. The infrastructure needed for these tests is usually much less than what is needed for the data warehouse when it is rolled out. Of course, it would be foolish to rollout the data warehouse with the just the hardware and network configurations needed for the pilot tests. We need to rollout the data warehouse with much more resources than that.

After the data warehouse (or data mart) becomes available to the users, we need to monitor the infrastructure and make sure we do not lack any piece that may cause a detrimental effect on its performance. One thing we need to watch is disk space usage. We should have additional disk space available that can be used immediately as soon as it is needed.

In the case of data marts, in particular, we need to watch for disk fragmentation. We may have much more space than we really need, but if disk space is fragmented, queries and reports against the data mart (or data warehouse) will suffer badly. The reason data marts are more prone to this problem is that they are usually subjected to more frequent data archival and replacement.

RAM is essential for the success of the data warehouse and data mart. Many of the aggregations performed at runtime are kept in memory. Therefore, memory usage should be monitored to make sure it never becomes a bottleneck for the optimal performance of the system.

We also need to monitor the usage of the network and the available bandwidth. This is important, especially with data marts. Many of these data marts are populated by partially replicating data in the data warehouse over the company's wide area network. Monitoring the use of this network will identify bottlenecks that need to be addressed for fast replication of the data and thus to ensure that the data warehouse and the data marts are in synch.

By monitoring and the modifying the system, we will reach the stage at which the system is stable. At this point, we can say that the system is now ready for regular use, and only regular monitoring, administration and maintenance are needed.

Backup and Recovery

Two of the most important maintenance operations of the data warehouse and OLAP data are backup and recovery. Backup simply means creating extra copies of snapshots of the data warehouse somewhere outside the database on different storage devices or even different storage media, such as backup on tape. Data warehouses are characteristically large in size. A SQL Server 7.0 database can theoretically be as large as 1,048,516 terrabytes (Tb) (there is no way we can verify this Microsoft claim at this time). Knowing that a terabyte is 1,099,511,627,776 bytes, you can imagine how big such storage is. If a data warehouse database is 1 Tb in size and for some reason it is lost, it might take days, if not weeks to reconstruct it and repopulate it (assuming that the operational data that fed the original database is still available in some way, shape or form).

With an available backup of the data warehouse, recovery is much faster, probably a matter of hours instead of days or weeks (depending on the hardware used for backup, and the size of the database). Also, an organization cannot afford to keep a data warehouse down for an extended period of time, especially if many decisions are made based on its data. A good backup strategy will guarantee that a data warehouse will not be down for long.

A backup of the transaction log is usually conducted along with backing up a database in SQL Server. The transaction log is a serial record of changes made to the database and which transactions caused these changes. In an Online Transaction Processing (OLTP) system, where database modifications are common, it is important to take the transaction log into account when backing up the database. In any case, if the transaction log is backed up, then all uncommitted transactions will be rolled back to maintain database consistency.

In a data warehouse, or data mart scenario, where modifications to data are rare, you still need to worry about backing up the transaction logs. This is because most backups take place during the night when the usage of the data warehouse is minimal. Well, it is usually during that time that data is fed into the data warehouse through tools like data transformation services (DTS). Such feeds can take a long time since they bring data from several data sources and perform data cleansing and scrubbing before dumping it in the warehouse. As a good strategy to coordinate the two processes, you may do a differential backup at the beginning of the night, say at 8:00 PM, and a transaction log backup every 3 to 4 hours during the night.

SQL Server allows for several backup methods: full backup, differential backup, transaction log backup, and file and filegroup backup. With a full backup, the whole database is backed up to the backup media. With differential backup, only changes that occurred since the last full backup will be written to the backup media. With transaction log backup, committed transactions in the log will be written to the backup media. Finally, with file and filegroup backup, you can elect to backup only certain tables that are located on certain data files or data filegroups.

What to Backup?

Now that we have determined we should implement a backup and recovery strategy for the data warehouse, we will ask about what exactly to backup. Do we only backup the database that hosts the data warehouse, or do we also need to backup some system databases with it as well?

When we install SQL Server, several databases are created by default. These databases are: master, tempdb, msdb, model, Pubs, and Northwind databases. As the figure below shows, some of these databases are **system databases** (master, tempdb, msdb, and model), and others are **user databases** (Pubs and Northwind). Another system database that is created when the server participates in replication is the Distribution database. System databases must be backed up periodically (except for tempdb, for reasons you will see in the following sections). Actually, it would be a good idea to include backing up these databases as part of the backup and recovery strategy of the data warehouse. With this, your backup strategy should include:

- The user databases of concern (the data warehouse database).
- Database logs (if you think this is necessary).
- The system databases indicated in the following sections.

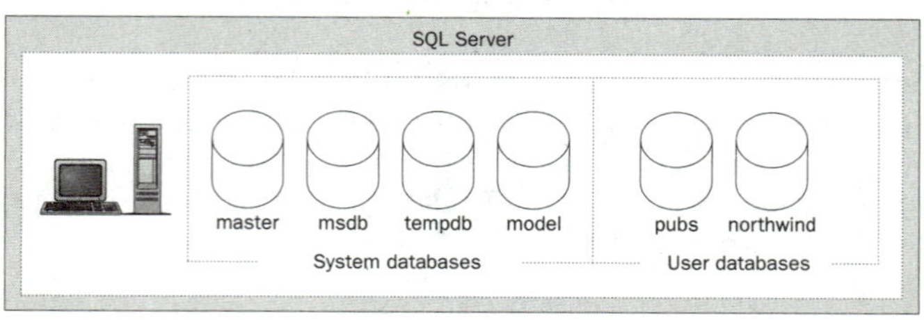

The master Database

The master database records system information for SQL Server, including:

- All login accounts.
- All system configuration settings.
- The existence of all other databases.
- The location of the primary files that contain the initialization information for the user databases.
- The initialization information for SQL Server.

> **The master database has to be backed up periodically to maintain the system information when database recovery is needed.**

The tempdb Database

The tempdb database is created when the SQL Server starts, and is destroyed when it is shut down to be reconstructed the next time the server is restarted. This database plays an important role since it:

- Holds all temporary tables and temporary stored procedures.
- Fills any other temporary storage needs, such as work tables generated by SQL Server.
- tempdb is a global resource; the temporary tables and stored procedures for all users connected to the system are stored there.

> **tempdb autogrows by default since its initial size is very small (default is 8 Mb for the data file and 0.5 Mb for the log file). Each time the system is started, tempdb is reset to its default size. You can avoid the overhead of having tempdb autogrow by using ALTER DATABASE to increase the size of tempdb.**
>
> **Since tempdb is recreated when the server starts, there is no need to include it in the backup plan for the user and system databases.**

The model Database

The model database serves as a template for creating other databases on the system. Each time you create a database, a copy of the model database is created and used as a starting point for your database. The model database has to exist on the SQL Server system if you want to successfully create new databases.

> **The model database needs to be backed up to ensure its existence when we conduct any recovery.**

The msdb Database

The msdb database is used by the SQL Server agent to store scheduled jobs and alerts and recorded operators. It is also used to store DTS packages (as we have seen in Chapter 6, Data Transformation Services) when we choose to store them in the SQL Server or the repository.

> **The msdb database also needs to be backed up when we build our backup and recovery plan to avoid loss of saved alerts and scheduled jobs, and to ensure that the SQL Agent will still work properly.**

The Distribution Database

This database maintains all the settings for replication when the server is participating in replication. The database actually also holds the data that is replicated and is waiting to be distributed to other replication participants, thus the name "Distribution". This database does not have to exist when starting the server, but must exist if the server is participating in replication.

The Pubs and Northwind Databases

These two databases are sample user databases that are shipped with SQL Server. They do not need to be included in our backup and recovery plan, because losing them will not affect server functionality, nor will it hurt other user databases.

Files and Filegroups

Before version 7.0, all databases and log files mapped to database devices, which were mapped to physical files in the file system. SQL Server 7.0 changed this by mapping databases and log files directly to physical files in the file system. Each database has at least one data file and one log file. SQL Server 7.0 takes this a little further, allowing us to logically group data and log files into logical groupings called **filegroups**.

The importance of using filegroups is that SQL Server 7.0 allows for file and filegroup based backup. This allows us to separate our data into static data that we know will never change, such as the sales transactions for last year, and data that will likely be replenished and maybe has the remote possibility of being modified, such as this year's sales transactions. The diagram shows this situation.

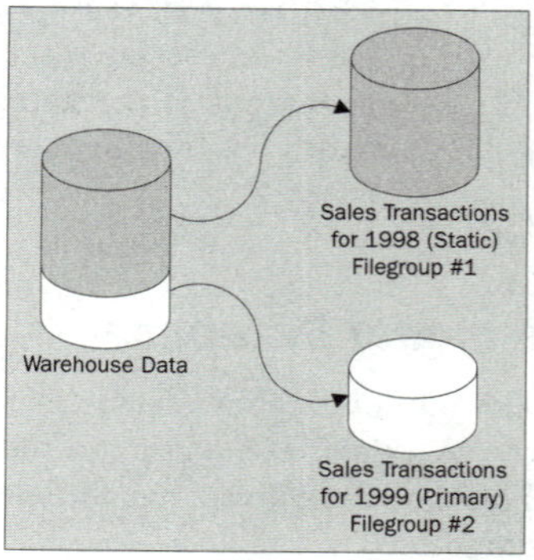

The obvious benefit from separating your data into different filegroups according to the diagram above is that backing up the static data becomes an easy task since it does not need to be included in the backup every time. Such data is only backed up once, or maybe several times a year with considerable time between backups.

You can create filegroups using the Enterprise Manager or T-SQL commands. The following figure shows how you can use the Enterprise Manager to create multiple database files and add them to such filegroups. To open the dialog in the figure below, select the database and edit its properties.

In the dialog, to create the second file, just type the information shown on the screen for the `OLAP_Static` file, and type the word **Static** in the filegroup combo box. This will create the filegroup, `Static`, and add the new data file, `OLAP_Static`, to it. Set the data file size and other properties according to the dialog before you click the **Apply** or **OK** buttons to actually create the file and filegroup.

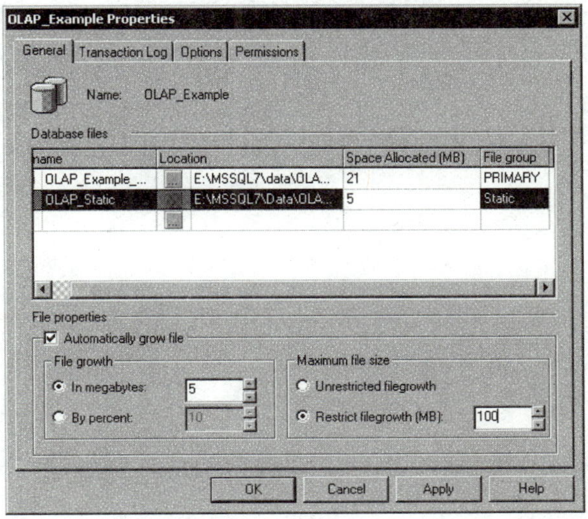

Adding files and filegroups using the Enterprise Manager

To do the same thing in T-SQL, you can type the following in the Query Analyzer:

```
Alter database OLAP_Example
Add filegroup static
Go
Alter database OLAP_Example
Add file
( name = 'OLAP_Static',
  filename='<your file path>\OLAP_Static.ndf',
  size = 5mb,
  maxsize = 100mb,
  filegrowth = 5mb)
to filegroup static
go
```

The SQL Server will echo the following message if everything goes well:

```
Extending database by 5.00 MB on disk 'OLAP_Static'
```

Once you have created the file and filegroup, you can assign which tables will be assigned to them by selecting the table and using the Action | Design Table menu command. This command will open the following Design Table window (shown for the Sales_Fact_1997 table):

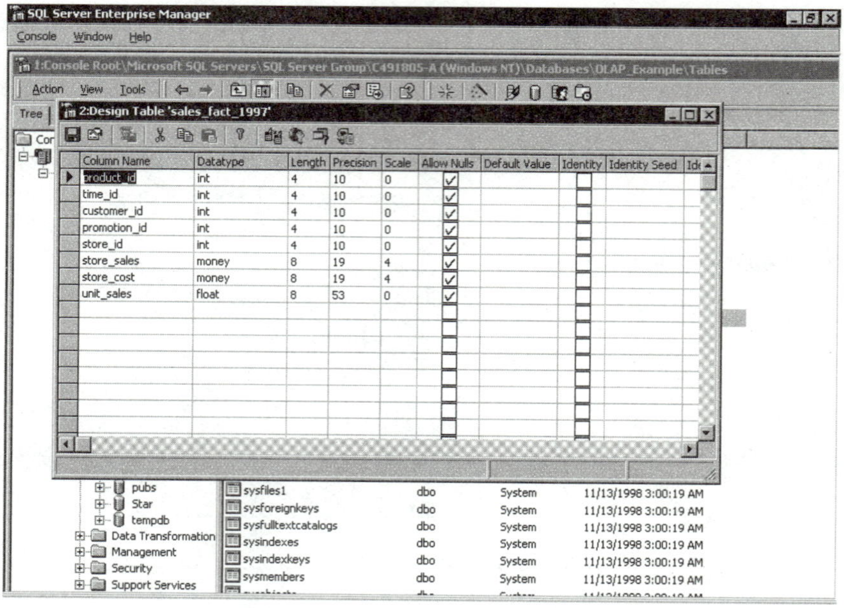

The Design Table Window

Clicking the Table and Index Properties toolbar button in the window above will open the dialog shown below. Make sure you select the appropriate filegroups from the dropdown lists for the **File Group Name** and **Text File Group** lists.

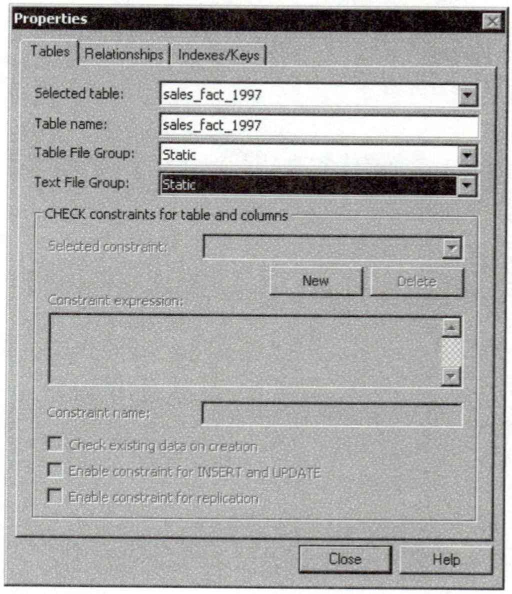

Table and Index Properties dialog box

In summary, using filegroups gives us a great advantage in controllinghow much data needs to be backed up and in the frequency of such backups. You can divide your tables any way you like to perform such backups. Files and filegroups can also be invaluable when archiving data that is no longer needed to be in the warehouse, as we will see in the data archival section later in the chapter.

Defining the Backup Device

SQL Server uses three types of backup devices: **disk**, **tape**, and **named pipes**. Disk and tape backup devices are usually created using the Enterprise Manager. Named pipes devices are usually created with third party tools, allowing vendors to use specialized backup and recovery software. Examples of third party backup tools that can create such devices include the Seagate Backup and Computer Associates Arcserve backup.

Named pipes are the default network libraries that ship with SQL Server, allowing clients to communicate with the server on a one-to-one basis. The named pipe library uses inter-process procedure calls (RPCs) in Windows NT to establish the communication between the client and the server. With named pipe backups, the data is backed up over the network using this library to a remote storage location.

To add a backup device in Enterprise Manager, you need to expand the Management folder on the tree pane and right-click the Backup item underneath it. From the pop-up menu you can then select New Backup Device. This will open the dialog shown below.

The tape backup device should be physically attached to the SQL Server. It is not possible to perform backups to remotely located tape drives.

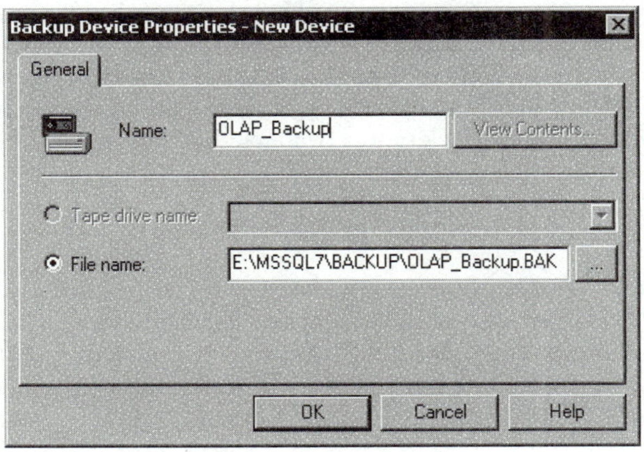

New Backup Device dialog

In the dialog above, you can select a name for the backup device and a path (if you want to define it as a disk device). If you want to specify the backup device as a tape device, you need to select the Tape Drive Name from the appropriate drop-down list. In the figure above, this option and menu are disabled because the computer used to generate the dialog is not physically linked to a tape drive.

When you choose the backup device to be a disk device, make sure the device is not physically on the same disk as the database files. This is because disk failure will kill both the database and the backups, preventing you from recovering the database later on.

You can use T-SQL script to define the backup device. For example, the following script the tape as the backup media for the OLAP_Example database, and chooses "OLAP_Backup" as the name for the backup.

```
use OLAP_Example
exec sp_addumpdevice {'tape', 'OLAP_Backup', '\\.\tape0'}
```

Had we wanted to use disk or pipe backup instead of the tape backup used in the script above, we would have replaced the keyword 'tape' with 'disk' or 'pipe'. We also would have replaced the tape name '`\\.\tape0`' with the path of the backup device. For example, for disk backup, the script would become:

```
use OLAP_Example
exec sp_addumpdevice {'disk', 'OLAP_Backup', '\\SQLBackups\Backups\December30.bak'}
```

Managing Backup Media

Managing backup media involves selecting the right media for the backup and establishing a plan to accommodate full and differential backups. The plan calls for reuse of the media when it is full in a way that allows full recovery in cases of failure. You should always have one full backup, and all differential backups since that full backup, accommodated on the backup media. For example, if you conduct a full backup every week, and the last full backup was conducted on Friday night, you need to have that full backup and all differential backups since Friday night.

Backup Media

Although SQL Server allows for backups on disk, it is recommended that backups be performed on removable storage media. In fact, only small backups are warranted on disk. Removable storage media nowadays ranges from 650 Mb recordable CD-ROMs to 70 Gb digital linear tapes (DLTs). For Datawarehousing, small media are not recommended. You need to use fast, high capacity, and economical media.

Generally the best media that meets the criteria we are looking for are tape devices. In order for these devices to perform quickly, you need to use tape drives that support Small Computer System Interface (SCSI) interfaces. These interfaces provide a fast way for transferring data (up to 40 Mb per second) and can connect to multiple tape, disk, or CD-ROM devices (up to 14). Some of the mostly used tape drives are listed below:

Quarter Inch Cassette and Travan Drives

These are mostly used for system backups, such as the Jumbo 250 that can store 250 Mb on a single tape. With the Travan technology, the capacity can be increased to 2 Gb. However, these drives are slow (throughput around 500 Kb/second) and not too reliable. Therefore, they are not recommended for use in data warehouse backups

4mm Digital Audiotape (DAT)

These tapes have been in use for several years. They can store 12 Gb of uncompressed data on one tape. The storage capacity doubles when implementing hardware compression of the data. Transfer rate for these drives is around 1 Mbits/second. This is a good and economical option for smaller databases (around 20 Gb) and if you are not too concerned about speed of backup.

8mm Tape

These use the same technology as VCR tapes, except they are digital. They are comparable to the 4mm digital audiotapes in storage size, but slightly faster (throughput around 1.2 Mb/second). These tapes are not used as much nowadays because the 4mm tapes present a cheaper yet comparable option.

Digital Linear Tape (DLT)

These tapes come with various capacities, up to 70 Gb of compressed data. Transfer speed can reach 10 Mbits/second making this a very fast option for backing up large databases in shorter periods. Tape changers and libraries can be used with this option to increase the storage capacity to the terabyte order of magnitude. For example, the TimberWolf 9710 DLT works with multiple platform environments employing advanced rotational robotics and a camera-based vision system that offer fast data transfer and up to 20.58 tb of data storage (uncompressed).

For more information on DLT tapes, visit the Web site: http://www.dlttape.com.

Advanced Intelligent Tape (AIT)

This is the newest format of tape drives and is based on the 8mm tape technology. These tape drives provide capacities on the order of 50 Gb of compressed data and transfer speed around 6 Mbits/second. These devices, along with DLT devices are perfect for large data warehouse backups with the size of the warehouse in terabytes since they can both implement tape changers and libraries that tremendously increases the storage capacity offered by them.

For more information on AIT tapes, visit the Web site: http://www.aittape.com.

Be aware when using hardware compression in your tape backups. Such compression is usually proprietary and one compression format may not be compatible with all brands of tape drive. Therefore, if you use compression with your backup, make sure that the drives you use to recover data understand the compression format of the drive used to create the tape backup.

Rotating Backup Tapes

Cost is usually an important factor to consider when backing up the data warehouse. The cost of tapes will limit the number of tapes that you can use in your backing up. Such tapes, therefore, will be rotated and used as a set.

Implementing full backups every time is not a good idea because it takes longer and wears down the tape quicker. Besides, let's say all you have is a full backup from last night, and you find out that the database (or parts of it) is corrupted. You need to recover to a backup that does not have the corrupted data. If all you have is last night's backup, you are in trouble.

The ideal solution is to have a combination of a full backup and a number of differential backups taken since that full backup. Many SQL Server administration books present good information on using such tape rotation schemes. One scheme that fits data warehouse backups and allows for even use of the tapes while allowing for fast reliable recovery is the Grandfather/Father/Son rotation scheme. Grandfather stands for monthly backups; Father, stands for weekly backups (usually on Friday night); and Son for daily backups. This system rotates the tapes so each tape will be used in each of the backup types above and allows access for backups for each day in the previous week, and each week in the previous 10 weeks. The tape rotation according to this system is presented in the table below:

Week	Mon	Tue	Wed	Thu	Fri
0					Tape 10 – Full
1	Tape 1 - Diff	Tape 2 - Diff	Tape 3 - Diff	Tape 4 - Diff	Tape 5 – Full
2	Tape 1 - Diff	Tape 2 - Diff	Tape 3 - Diff	Tape 4 - Diff	Tape 6 – Full
3	Tape 1 - Diff	Tape 2 - Diff	Tape 3 - Diff	Tape 4 - Diff	Tape 7 – Full
4	Tape 1 - Diff	Tape 2 - Diff	Tape 3 - Diff	Tape 4 - Diff	Tape 8 – Full
5	Tape 2 - Diff	Tape 3 - Diff	Tape 4 - Diff	Tape 5 - Diff	Tape 6 – Full
6	Tape 2 - Diff	Tape 3 - Diff	Tape 4 - Diff	Tape 5 - Diff	Tape 7 – Full
7	Tape 2 - Diff	Tape 3 - Diff	Tape 4 - Diff	Tape 5 - Diff	Tape 8 – Full
8	Tape 2 - Diff	Tape 3 - Diff	Tape 4 - Diff	Tape 5 - Diff	Tape 9 – Full
9	Tape 3 - Diff	Tape 4 - Diff	Tape 5 - Diff	Tape 6 - Diff	Tape 10 – Full

Notice in the table above that if the system crashes on Wednesday of week 8, then you can restore the database using the full backup from the previous Friday on tape 8 and the differential backup on tape 3. If you fear data corruption during week 8, you can restore all the way from Tape 6 in week 5 and restore the database to the way it was each day of the previous week.

It is recommended that grandfather backups be full backups and the tapes on which they were stored never be reused (or at least not for a year or two). This is because the database may get infected with viruses that lay dormant or unnoticed for several months. Therefore, having the grandfather backup from the period prior to infection or data corruption will help recover the database to a stable state.

With this backup rotation scheme, you end up using 10 tapes with each tape used evenly 17 times in an 11 month period.

How To Do a Backup

You can conduct a database backup using Transact-SQL commands or using the SQL Server Enterprise Manager (EM). With Transact-SQL, you use the `BACKUP DATABASE` command. This command is explained in detail below. With EM, you can use the Backup Database dialog or the Backup wizard. You can also use SQL DMO to backup a database from within an external application written in a different language, such as Visual Basic or Visual C++. SQL DMO usage for backing up the database is not discussed in this book. You can read more about it in the SQL Server Books-Online, or in the Wrox book *Professional SQL Server 7.0 Programming* ISBN 1861002319.

The BACKUP DATABASE Command

You can use the Transact-SQL command, `BACKUP DATABASE` to create the database backup. With this command, you specify the name of the database to back up, and the backup device where the database backup will be written. You can optionally specify whether you want to overwrite the backups on the backup media using the `INIT` clause. You can even choose to overwrite the data in the backup media even if such backups have not yet expired. Finally, you can choose to initialize the backup media and overwrite any existing header with the `FORMAT` clause.

> **You need to use extreme caution when using the `FORMAT` or `INIT` clauses of the `BACKUP` statement. This is because they will result in permanently loosing any backups previously stored on the backup media.**

As an example, the following command will perform full backup of the OLAP_Example database to the backup device called OLAP_Device, with append (not overwriting any existing data on the backup media):

```
USE OLAP_Example
GO
BACKUP DATABASE OLAP_Example
    TO TAPE = '\\.\Tape0'
    WITH NOINIT,
    NOUNLOAD,
    NAME = 'Full Backup of OLAP_Example'
GO
```

Backup With The Enterprise Manager

With the Enterprise Manager, you can create backups by selecting the Backup Database menu command. This command is available from All Tasks submenu of the context-sensitive menu that pops-up when you right-click the database name in the tree view of the Enterprise Manager. The command is also available from the Tools menu on the menu bar. Once the command is selected, the SQL Server Backup dialog appears as shown in the figure below.

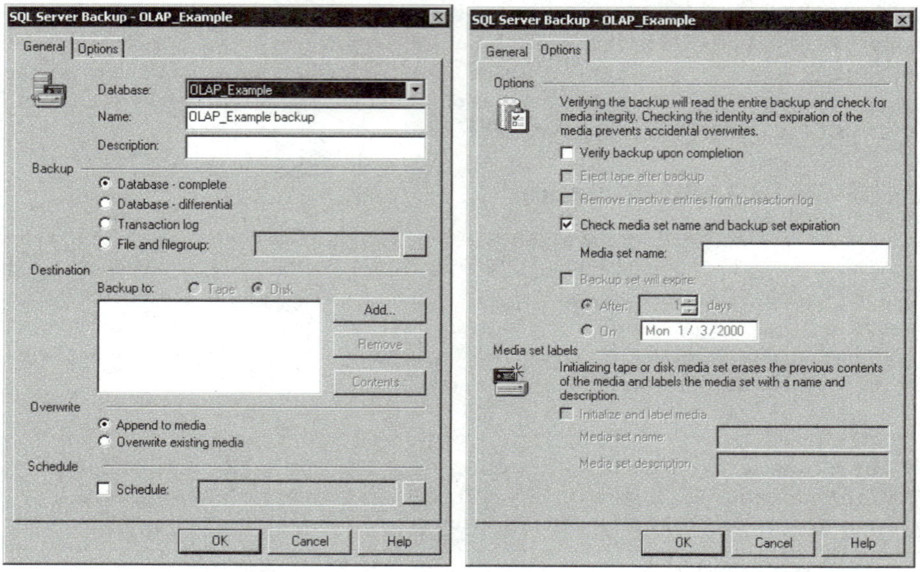

The Backup Database dialog box

As you see in the figure above, you can specify the database you want to backup from the Database drop-down menu. You can also specify a name for the backup and add a description that would remind you of certain things you need to remember about this backup. Backup options available through this dialog include:

- Type of backup (full, differential, transaction, or filegroup backup).
- Destination: disk or tape. This is where you can add the backup devices you need to use in the backup.
- Options on whether you want to append the data to the backup media, or overwrite whatever is on the media.
- An option to set a schedule for the backup. Scheduling and automating tasks will be discussed later in the SQL Agent section of the chapter.
- You can also choose to have SQL Server verify the backup which checks for media integrity prevents accidental loss of data.
- You can also set the media set name.
- You can set the expiration data and time for the backup.
- Finally, you can choose to initialize the backup media, which is equivalent to using the `FORMAT` clause in the `BACKUP DATABASE` T-SQL command.

Enterprise Manager also provides a wizard that leads you through most of these tasks listed above. However, the backup wizard will not allow you to perform filegroup backup. I will not discuss the backup wizard since it is very straightforward, and if one knows how to use the Backup Database dialog shown above, it would be easy to use the wizard.

Database Restoration

Database restoration will return the database to its condition at the time the backup was created. When restoring a database from backup, the data is copied from the backup media to the database, and committed transactions in the transaction log backup are also copied and stored in the database. Uncommitted transactions are rolled back to maintain database consistency.

Database restoration from backups is not always needed in crisis situations; rather, we may use it in a variety of different situations, including:

- Migrating the database to a new server, you can use backups to restore the database after you create it from scripts on the new server.
- Disk failure caused complete loss of the databases on the server. Backups come to the rescue in this crisis situation.
- Natural disasters may strike, such as a flood, fire, or tornado, causing permanent damage to the server and forcing us to rebuild the server after emotional recovery from the natural disaster.

These are only a few examples of possible situations – you may encounter many others that require restoration from backups.

Rebuilding System Databases

System databases (master, msdb, model, and distribution) can be restored from a backup if you have one, or can be rebuilt if you don't have a backup. To rebuild the system databases, you need to run the command-line utility `rebuildm.exe`, located in the `binn` directory under the SQL Server installation or on the SQL Server CD. Before you run this utility, you need to make sure that the SQL Server services are stopped.

Restoring Databases with the RESTORE DATABASE command

T-SQL provides a command, `RESTORE DATABASE`, that allows for database restoration. The command takes several arguments, including: database name, backup device to restore from. A host of other optional arguments can be specified. These arguments are explained in detail in the Books-On-Line under the T-SQL command: Restore Database.

As an example of restoring a full database:

```
RESTORE DATABASE OLAP_Example
    FROM OLAP_Backup
```

An example on restoring full and differential backups is:

```
RESTORE DATABASE OLAP_Example
    FROM OLAP_Backup
    WITH NORECOVERY
RESTORE DATABASE OLAP_Example
    FROM OLAP_Backup
    WITH FILE = 2
```

In the example above, the `OLAP_Example` full backup is recovered with the `NORECOVERY` option. This option causes uncommitted transactions not to be rolled back. The full restore is followed by differential restore. The backup set #2 on the storage media is used during the recovery of the differential backup.

The following example backs up and restores the `OLAP_Example` database virtually making a copy of it:

```
BACKUP DATABASE OLAP_Example
    TO DISK = 'c:\OLAP_Example.bak'
RESTORE FILELISTONLY
    FROM DISK = 'c:\OLAP_Example.bak'
RESTORE DATABASE TestDB
    FROM DISK = 'c:\OLAP_Example.bak'
    WITH MOVE 'OLAP_Example' TO 'c:\test\testdb.mdf',
    MOVE 'OLAP_Example_log' TO 'c:\test\testdb.ldf'
```

In the example above, the `BACKUP DATABASE` command creates the `OLAP_Example.bak` file. The `RESTORE FILELISTONLY` returns a list of the database and log files contained in the backup set. The subsequent commands create a new database, testdb, by creating a copy of the OLAP_Example database.

Finally, the following example shows how to restore certain files or filegroups:

```
RESTORE DATABASE OLAP_Example
    FILE = 'OLAP_Example_data_1',
    FILE = 'OLAP_Example _data_2',
    FILEGROUP = 'new_customers'
    FROM 'OLAP_Example _Backup
    WITH NORECOVERY
-- Restore the log backup.
RESTORE LOG 'OLAP_Example
    FROM 'OLAP_ExampleLog1
```

To restore the database, the system administrator restoring the database must be the only person using it.

Restoring with Enterprise Manager

In the Enterprise Manager, you can right-click a database name and select the Restore Database command from the All Tasks submenu of the pop-up menu. The figure below shows the dialog box you get when you do so.

In this dialog, you can specify the database name, and type of restore (database, file or filegroups, or restore from a device). Each selection will result in slightly different options in the subsequent sections of the dialog. For instance, if you were to specify filegroup or files restore, the first backup to restore dropdown list will disappear.

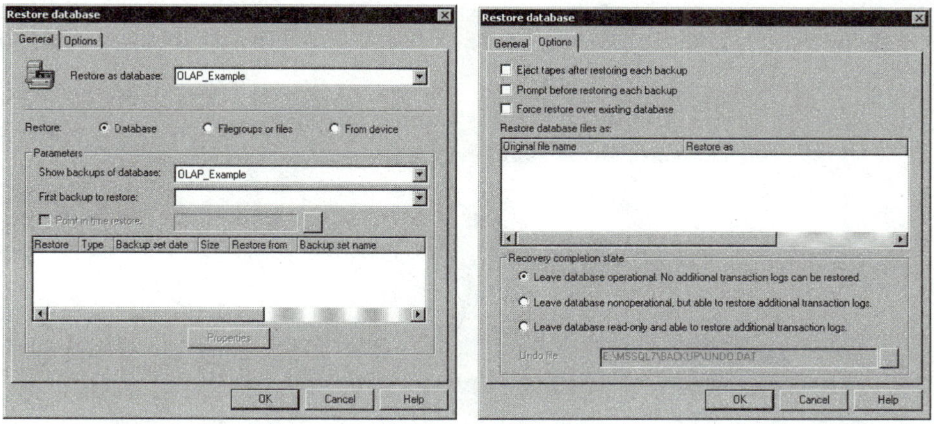

The Restore Database Dialog box

Data Archival

As more data is added into the data warehouse, the size of the database increases enormously. The size of pre-calculated aggregates also increases to a great size threatening the efficiency of the queries issued against the data. To avoid this problem, we usually prioritize the data in the data warehouse and the OLAP cubes. Data that is not used (or is used very infrequently) is then archived to different media. Data archival is a special case of data backup, except that the data is not copied to new media; instead, it is moved into the new media, making its space in the original database available for new data and new aggregations.

Data archival should be part of the planning for the data warehouse. Several criteria could determine how and when such archival takes place. The criteria could be based on the time the data is collected (e.g. we might say that all data that is five years or older should be archived). It could also be based on usage (e.g. all data that has not been used in the last year should be archived). Another criteria could be functional (e.g. if a department is closed and its services are no longer offered, you might want to archive all data related to it in the data warehouse, since data from this department is not likely to be included in decision making processes). A combination of these criteria could also sometimes be used.

Archival is usually done to tape, CD ROM, or DVD, these being some of the cheapest storage media. It is recommended that more than one copy of the archived data be stored on separate archive media and saved in physically different safe locations, just in case a tape goes bad and becomes inaccessible.

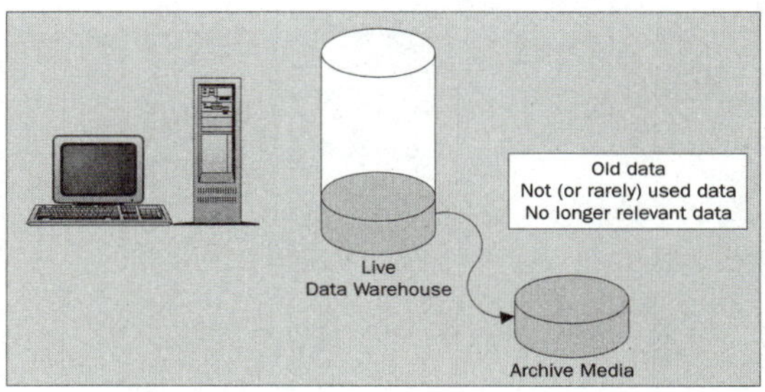

Data Archival Scheme

Data archival is done in several ways. Since archival involves picking up data from different tables, a straight table backup will not work. Archived data needs to be moved first to one or more archive tables. The data is usually moved into these tables using DTS or ActiveX programming, or even simple SQL scripts. These tables should be located in their own separate filegroups (see the discussion of filegroups earlier in the chapter). Using the SQL Server filegroup backup method will then allow us to archive the separated data. After the backup is successfully completed, the archive tables can be emptied with the `TRUNCATE` T-SQL command. The scheme described here is presented in the figure below:

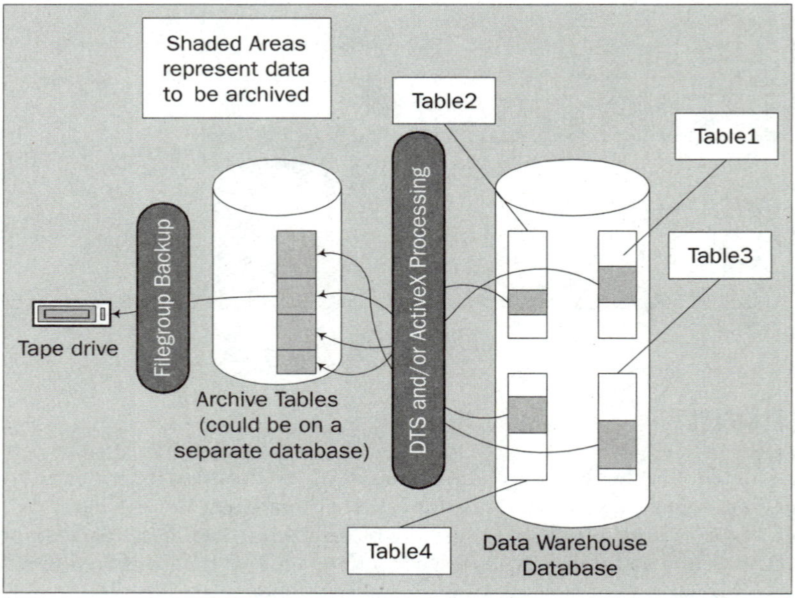

Representation of archival process

In any case, an archive plan should be established as part of the data warehouse design. An example of such a plan is presented in the flowchart below that consists of the following steps:

1. The database is searched for data older than a certain time limit.

2. If old data is found, it is moved to an archive table in the same database, or in a different database.

3. The database size is checked to see if it exceeds a certain threshold set by the user.

When estimating database size, you don't really need to estimate to the last byte, you just need a rough estimate using a consistent method to calculate it every time. The SQL Server Administrator Companion, which is part of the SQL Server documentation, lists detailed methods to do accurate estimates of database size in Appendix E.

For a quick estimate of the size for a database, perform this calculation for each database table, except for the archive table (you may actually only count the large tables, such as the fact tables and aggregation/summary tables, since they contribute most of the database size): add the number of bytes for the table row. For varchar columns, use half of the maximum length (e.g. a field with varchar(200) yields 100 bytes) as an average, for date/time columns, use 8 bytes, and for integer columns, use 4 bytes. Multiply the row length by the number of rows in the table. Finally, add another 20 percent to account for table overhead and indexing.

4. If the database size (minus archive table if it is in the same database) exceeds the threshold, data that has not been used in queries and reports any time sooner than the threshold is moved to the archive table.

5. Steps 3 and 4 are repeated with a certain reduction of the time threshold until database size (minus archive table if it is in the same database) is below the database size threshold.

6. If the database size does not exceed the time threshold, a filegroup backup is conducted to backup the archive table data to the destination archive media.

7. Archive table is `TRUNCATE`d.

Please notice that tracking record usage is not an easy task. You might need to either use the SQL Sever Profiler, which imposes a large overhead, and might reduce your query speed, or implement a database-tracking method, such as adding a table that lists the key values of records returned in queries and the date they were returned. This table has to be updated every time a query is issued against the database, which means that these queries or reports will be generated as part of some program that implements this strategy, and any queries issued directly against the database will not count, because they will not result in updating this table. In most cases, you might want to take the easy way by conducting surveys among users to ask them about the data they no longer care about in the data warehouse.

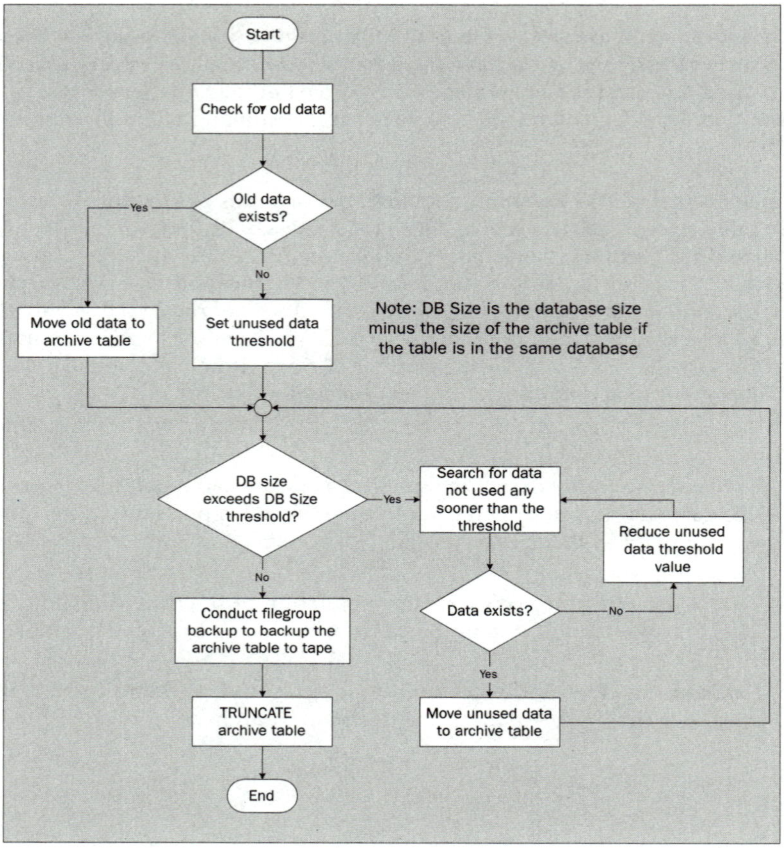

Flowchart showing an example archive plan

Replication

More and more applications are now built to fit in a distributed environment. Many companies distribute their applications and data to branch offices, or even to mobile offices (people traveling with laptop computers). Data warehouse applications are no exception. With the increasing need of having the data distributed across the enterprise in a timely manner, more data warehousing applications are using replicated data marts to accomplish this goal. You would, for instance, see regional salespeople in Europe having access only to the data they care about. Such data is replicated to them from the enterprise data warehouse (see following figure).

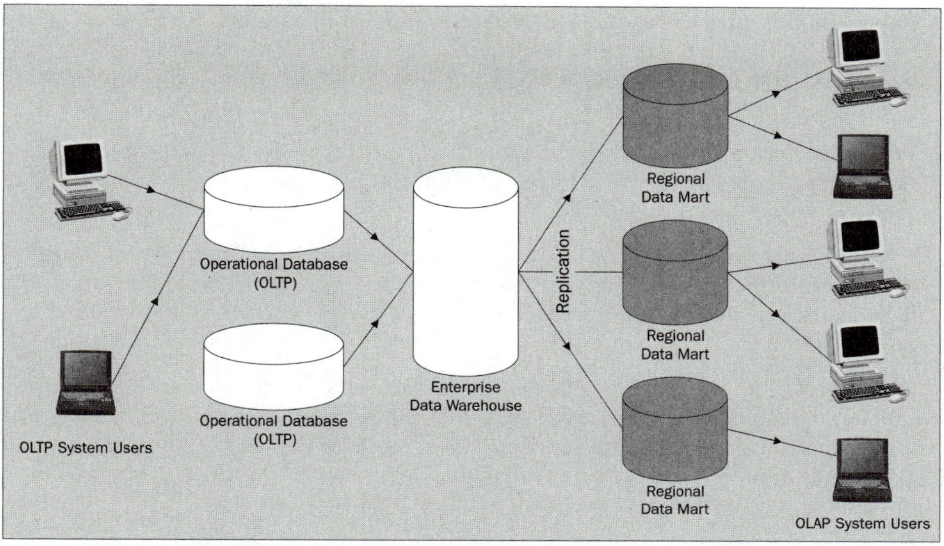

Using Replication to populate data marts from the Enterprise Data warehouse

Microsoft SQL Server 7.0 has improved and powerful replication capabilities that allow database application designers to achieve the following goals. The following section describes the replication model in SQL Server 7.0 including the different components of the model.

> **Replicated data can also serve as a useful 'hot' backup. However, it should never be used as the only form of backup.**

SQL Server 7.0 Replication Model

SQL Server's replication model is a replica of real life magazine publication. Just like with magazine publication where you find a publisher, subscribers, and distributors who all handle the publication, in SQL Server similar components exist. These components are described below:

- **Publisher**: This component in the replication model is a server that is responsible for making replication data available to other servers. This server keeps track of the data that changed in order to propagate such changes when needed.
- **Subscribers**: This component is one or more servers, often referred to as replicas, that store the replicated data, and receive updates to the data. SQL Server 7.0 allows Subscribers to make updates to data. In the SQL Server 7.0 replication model, the same server can be a subscriber and a publisher to other subscribers at the same time.
- **Distributor**: This component is a server that holds the distribution database. The role of this component is different depending on the type of replication, as we will see later in the chapter. The same computer can be both a publisher and distributor, or the distributor can also be one of the subscriber servers.

- **Publication**: Replicated data is collected in groups, called articles. A collection of such articles forms the publication. An article can contain any of the following: a whole table, certain columns of a table using "vertical filter", certain rows in the table using "horizontal filter", or a stored procedure in some cases.

- **Pull Subscription**: This is a subscription in which replicas are updated based on the subscribers' requests. This type of subscription is suitable for a large number of subscribers, such as Internet-based subscribers, that need to control when their data is updated.

- **Push Subscription**: Unlike the Pull Subscription, in this kind of subscription, data updates are controlled by the publisher rather than by subscriber requests. With this kind of subscription, data can be updated as the updates take place, or based on a schedule controlled by the publisher.

- **Snapshot Agent**: This component runs on the distributor and connects to the publisher to prepare the tables and stored procedures that will be included in the publication. From these it prepares a snapshot publication file on the distributor and stores information about the synchronization in the distribution database. Don't worry now if you don't yet grasp the function of this agent, it will be explained in detail later.

- **Log Reader Agent**: One type of database replication in SQL Server 7.0 is transactional replication. In this type of replication, the log reader agent, which runs on the distributor, moves transactions marked for replication in the transaction log from the publisher to the distributor.

- **Distribution Agent**: This component moves the transactions and snapshot jobs held in the distribution database tables to the subscribers. Depending on the type of replication, this agent can run on the distributor or on the subscriber. This component runs under the SQL Server Agent, and as we will see later, can be administered from the Enterprise Manager.

- **Merge Agent**: This component moves and reconciles incremental data changes that occurred after the initial snapshot was created.

- **Two-Phase Commit**: Changes to the database are committed in two phases across the distributed servers to ensure that data is in synch among these servers. If at any stage a server fails to commit, all participating servers in the replication will also fail to commit. In other words, the two-phase commit (2PC) is all or nothing for all servers participating in the replication.

Don't worry if you cannot visualize how these components relate to and interact with each other in the replication mode. This all will make much more sense as we look at the different types of replication supported by SQL Server and how these components fit into each of these types in the following sections.

Types of Replication

Each application requiring replication as part of its design has its own unique requirements. Some applications require that the replicas are always as up-to-date as possible. Some applications can live with periodic updates of the replicas, rather than instant updating as the publisher data is changed. SQL Server replication supports both ends of the spectrum by supporting different types of replication: snapshot replication, transactional replication, and merge replication. In the next few sections we will look at these three types with brief explanations of what they mean.

Snapshot Replication

This is the simplest type of replication, in which the distribution agent (which is located on the distributor), prepares a new set of the data comprising the replica and sends the complete set to the subscribers as shown in the figure. The publisher is a SQL Server that contains the data to be replicated to the subscribers. The distributor is the server that contains the snapshot agent, which is responsible to connecting to the publisher, collecting the data that needs to be replicated, and moving it into the distribution database on the distributor. The distributor could be the same machine as the publisher, one of the subscriber machines, or a separate server by itself.

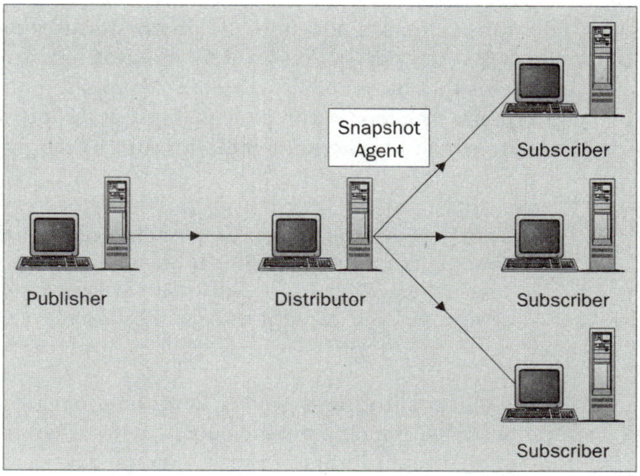

The snapshot agent then records information about the synchronization process in the distribution database.

How does this model work with data warehousing applications? The answer to this question lies in the figure opposite. As you can see, the publisher is usually the SQL Server that hosts the data warehouse database (in the example, the data warehouse is located in New York). The distributor is the SQL Server computer that manages the distribution of the replicated data to the proper subscribers. Although three distributors are shown in the figure, the same distributor may be able to handle the replication jobs for all subscribers in North America, Europe, or Asia Pacific.

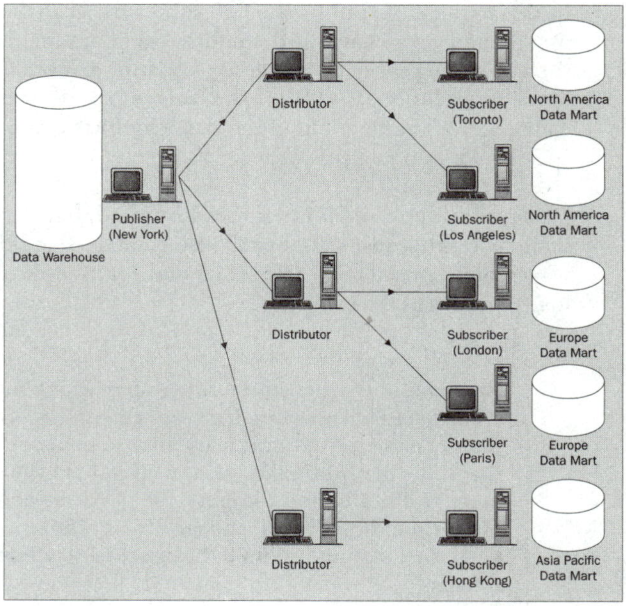

The subscribers are servers located in Toronto, Los Angeles, London, Paris, and Hong Kong. Each subscriber gets the appropriate data replicated to through the distributor.

Transactional Replication

With transactional replication, the distributor uses the log reader agent to monitor changes to the publisher at the transaction level by monitoring the transaction logs. All insert, update, and delete operations that have been successfully committed on the server are prepared for distribution to the subscribers. The monitored data changed at the publisher is distributed to the subscribing servers continuously or at scheduled intervals to subscribing servers.

> **This type of replication can possibly lead to near-real-time propagation of data changes from the publisher to the subscribers. However, in order for this to happen, subscribers will need a continuous network connection to the Publisher, which is not always possible in data warehouse/data mart scenarios.**

This type of replication is used in data warehousing applications when data marts need to be updated periodically with incremental changes, rather than rebuilding their database. We may consider using transactional replication to refresh regional data marts shown in the previous figure just after we get new loads into the data warehouse. This will cause considerably smaller amounts of data to move across the network than snapshot replication.

Merge Replication

In this replication, publishers and subscribers can work independently and reconnect periodically to merge their data changes. If conflicts occur among data from the different subscribers and the publisher, such as having more than one site updating the same data values, merge replication provides automatic conflict resolution. Conflicts are resolved based on assigned priorities, which server first submitted the change, or a combination of the two. Conflicts can be detected and resolved at the row level, or at a specific column in a row.

This type of replication is very sophisticated, but is not likely to be used in data warehousing applications because data warehouse databases and data marts are only updated in a tightly controlled way, which is usually by importing new loads of data at scheduled intervals, and scarcely archiving loads of unused data.

> **Replication frequency is a function of many factors including the amount of data to be transferred across the wire between servers, availability of network (or sometimes, phone) connections, and feasibility to the operator to perform a synchronization with the publisher. For example, the operator in the field, who has a replica of the data mart on their laptop computer, may not be able to perform a synchronization until night time. In all cases, and just to minimize network traffic, it is a good practice to keep the amount of data to be synched to a minimum by performing more frequent synchs.**

Replication Wizards

SQL Server 7.0 provides several wizards that make conducting and managing replication an easy task. These wizards include the following:

- The Configure Publishing and Distribution Wizard helps you specify a server to use as a Distributor and other replication components you may need.
- The Create Publication Wizard helps you create a publication from the data in your database.
- The Disable Publishing and Distribution Wizard helps you disable publishing, distribution, or both on a server.
- The Pull Subscription Wizard helps you "pull" a subscription to a publication on one server into a database on another server. For instance, if you have two servers S1 and S2, the wizard will help you pull a publication on S1 to a database on S2.
- The Push Subscription Wizard helps you "push" a subscription from a publication on one server to one or more servers or server groups.
- The Microsoft Replication Conflict Viewer: this tool is not a wizard; rather it helps you view the manner in which conflicts were resolved and make changes to these resolutions.

These wizards are available by clicking the Wizards button on the toolbar, and expanding the Replication section in the resulting dialog. This will show you a list of available replication wizards that you can choose from, as shown in the figure:

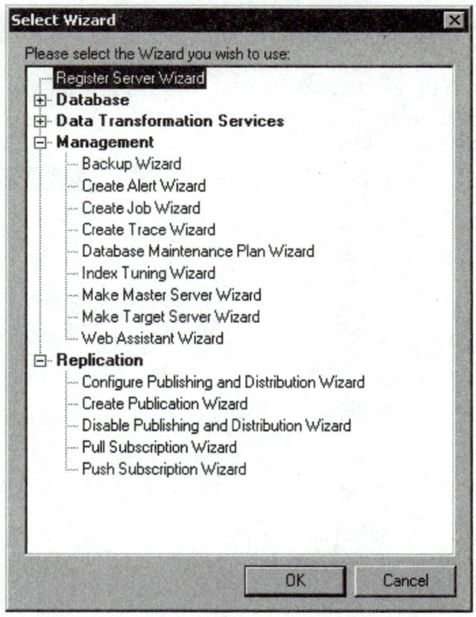

The Configure Publishing and Distribution Wizard

This wizard allows you to configure a server as a distributor, or to specify the current server as a publisher, among other things. The opening window in this wizard is shown below:

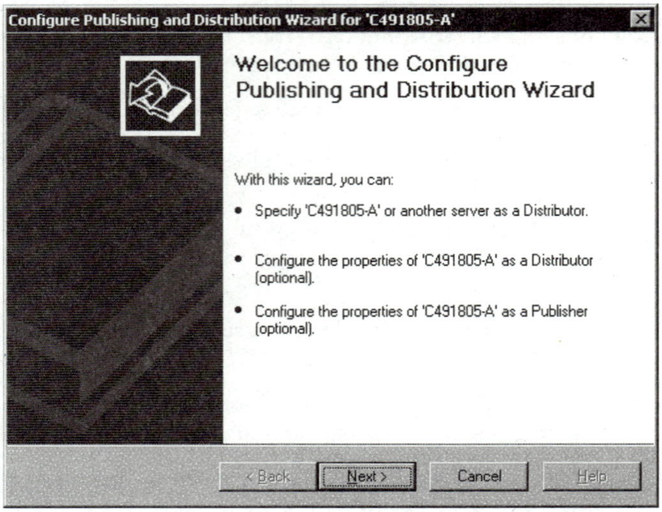

The next screen in the wizard allows you to choose a distributor. The screen allows you to register a remote server in the Enterprise Manager in case you need to specify one that is not registered.

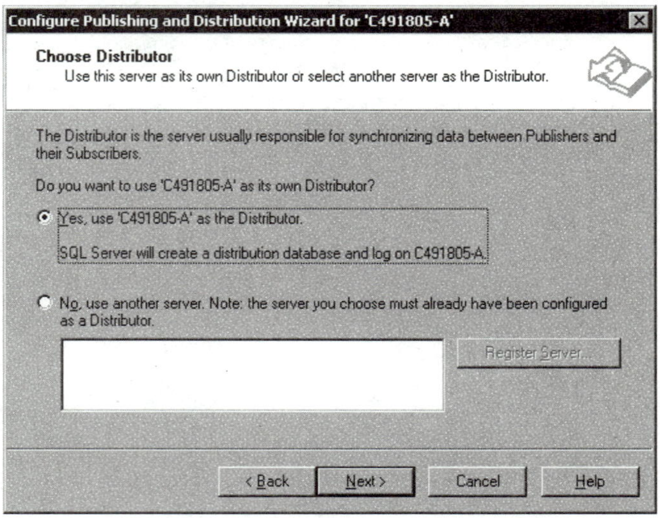

Please note that you need to have the SQL Server Agent service startup account different from the system account "sa". Having SQL Agent start under the system account will cause replication to fail. If you have the system account setup as the startup account, you will be prompted to change it when you try to move to the next step in the wizard.

The next step in the wizard presents you with default settings for the distributor, the publisher, the distribution database location, and a list of the participating subscribers corresponding to the list of registered servers. You can keep these defaults, or change them, as shown in the next figure.

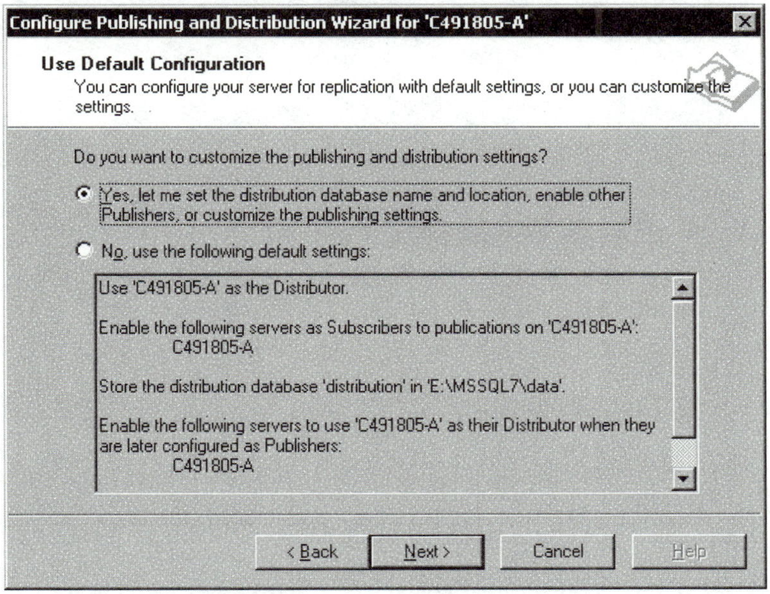

If you choose to change the default settings, the next screen allows you to set the distribution database name and location, as shown in the figure below.

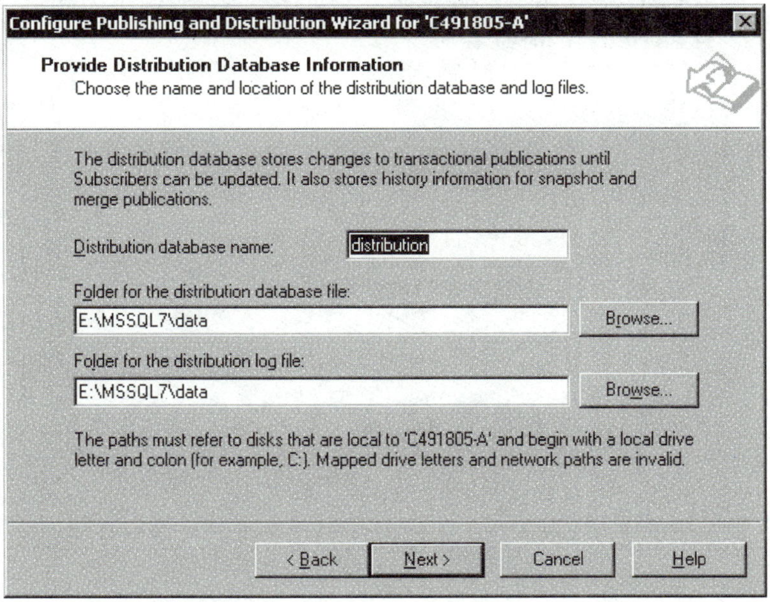

The next screen allows you to enable a server as a publisher that contributes publications that need to be propagated to the distributors.

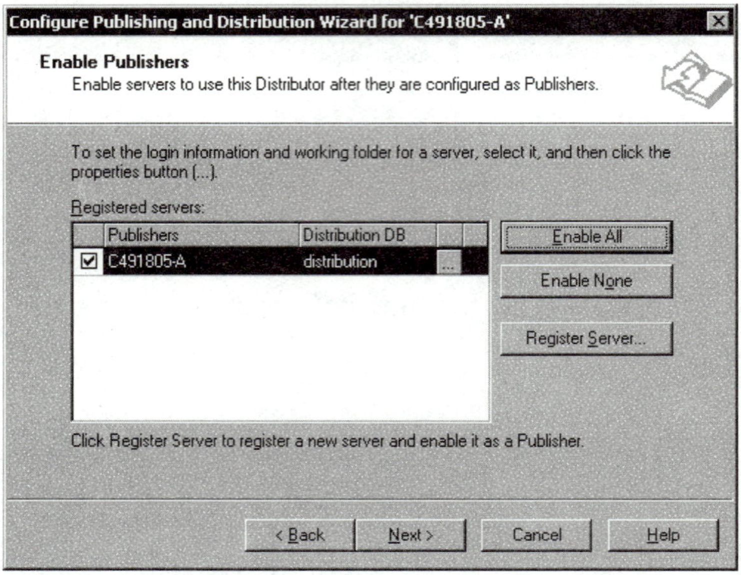

The next screen allows you to choose which databases you need to include in the publication, and the type of replication they will participate in: transactional (including snapshot replication), or merge replication.

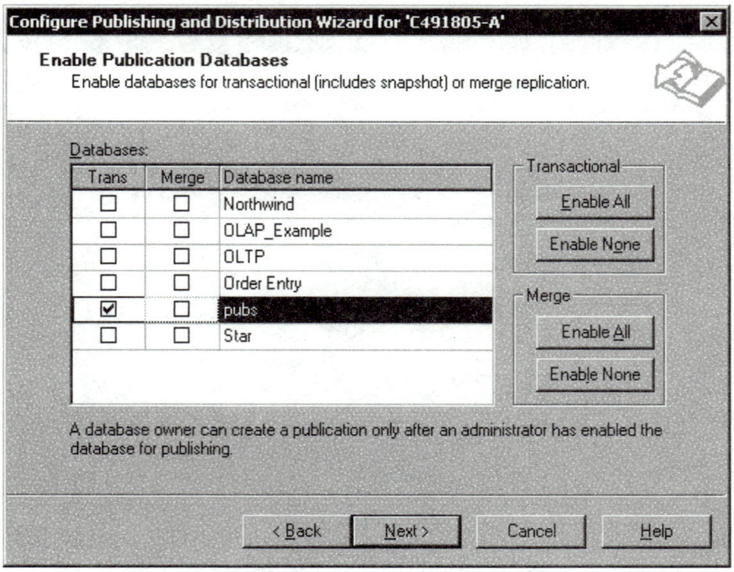

The next screen allows you to choose the servers that will act as subscribers in the replication model.

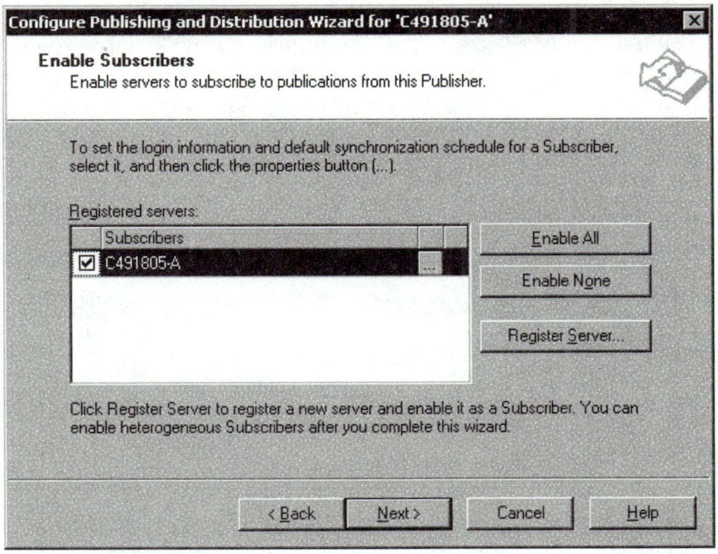

The next screen, which is the last screen, presents you with your choices so far. You can examine the choices you have made. If you think you need to change some of them, you can use the Back button to go to the appropriate step that allows you to make your changes.

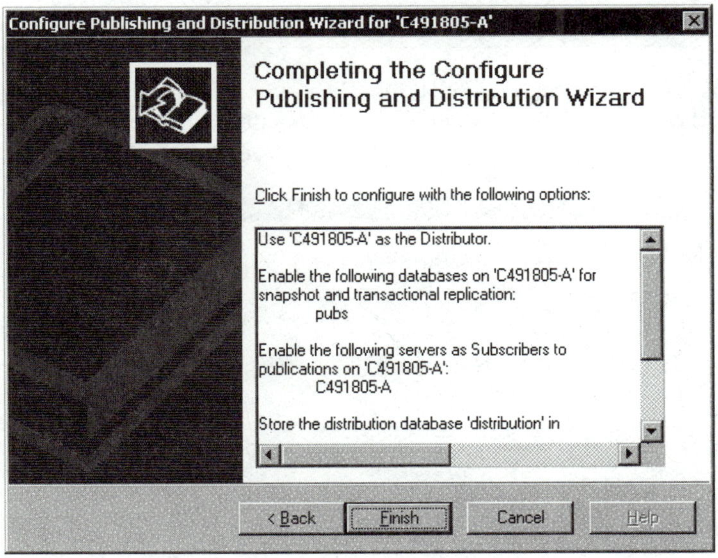

The Create Publication Wizard

When you launch this wizard, a screen will be presented to you to allow you to select a database for publication. Once you make your selection, the rest of the wizard will allow you to specify which tables to include in the publication, and what type of replication you will use: snapshot, transactional, or merge replication. The wizard will also allow you to specify the subscribers, giving you the option to include non-SQL Server subscribers. The following is a description of some of the important screens in the wizard.

In the dialog that allows you to select a database for publication, select the database you want and click the Create Publication button.

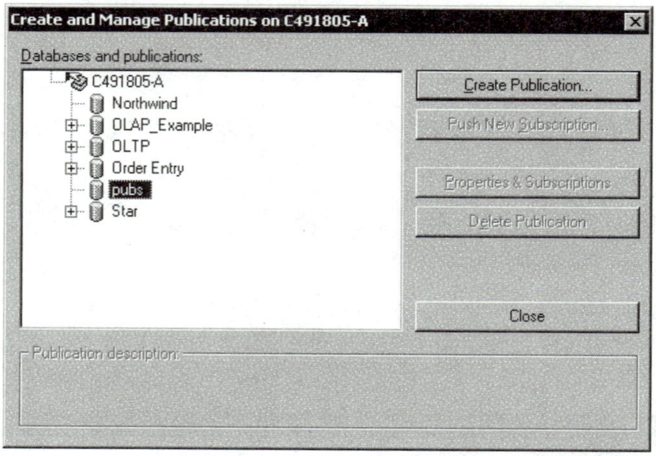

The next screen is just a welcome screen that introduces the remaining steps. A page that allows you to select a distributor, in case you do not want to use the default distributor selected by the wizard, follows the welcome screen.

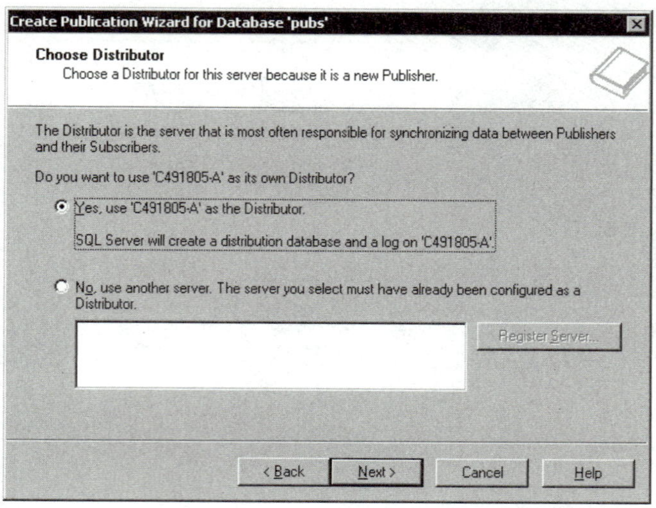

The next screen, shown below, allows you to select the type of replication to use: snapshot, transactional, or merge replication.

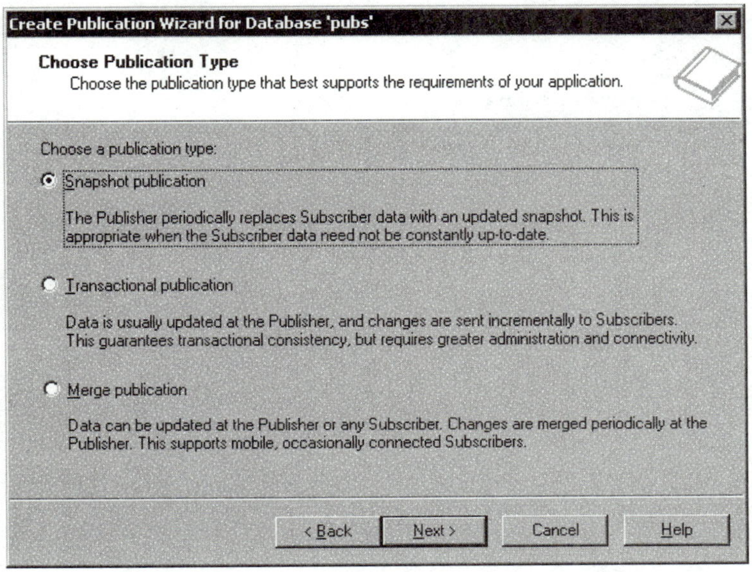

Following this screen will be a page that allows you to set whether you need to have immediate updates done to the subscribers as soon as changes take place on the publisher. For the purposes of data warehousing applications, this is not necessary; therefore, we will go with the default, which is not to have immediate updates. The next screen allows you to specify the subscriber type: SQL Server, or non-SQL Server subscriber, as shown in the figure below.

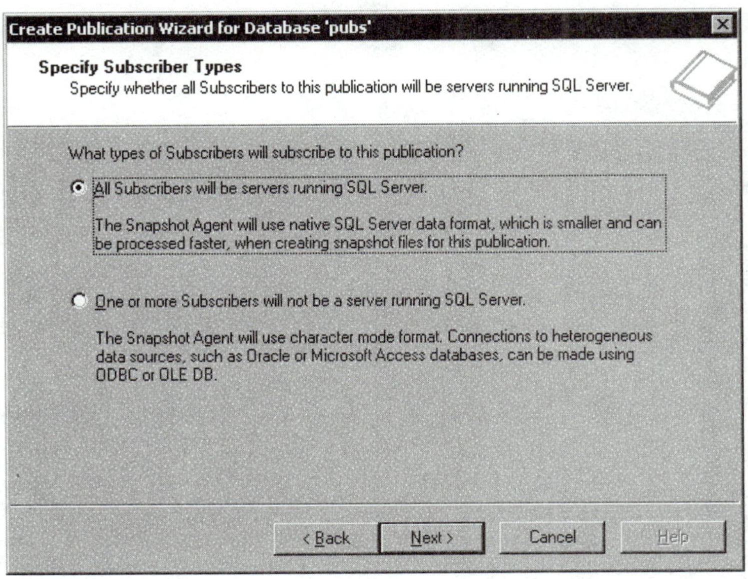

The next screen allows you to specify an article for publication. The article is either a database table, or a stored procedure.

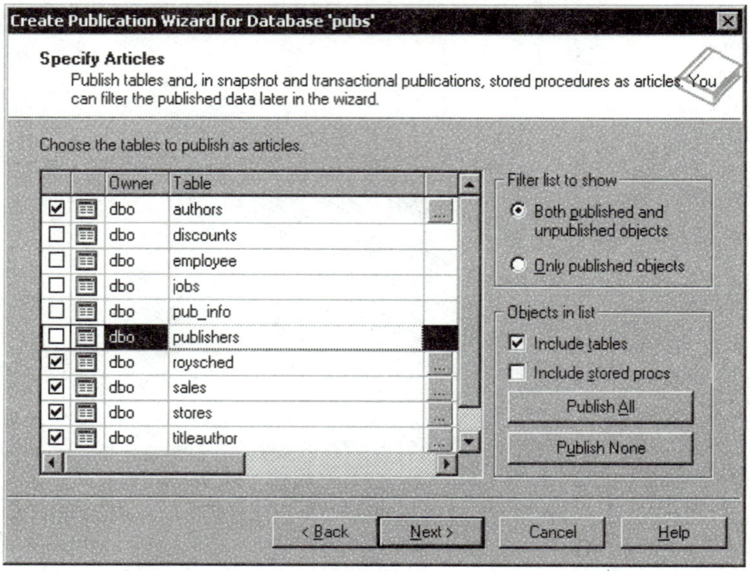

Notice that when you select an article for publication, an ellipsis "..." button appears next to it. This button opens the properties dialog for the selected article, as shown below. The properties dialog allows you to set the article name, set the destination table name and table owner, as well as options related to dropping and recreating the table, versus, deleting the data and repopulating it. It also provides the ability to specify whether to copy indexes to the subscribing database.

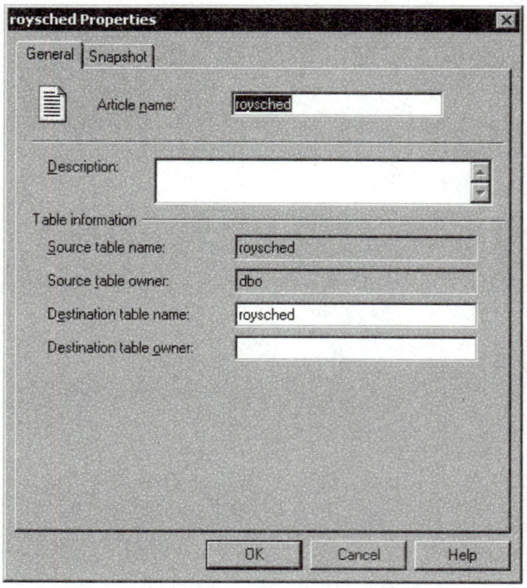

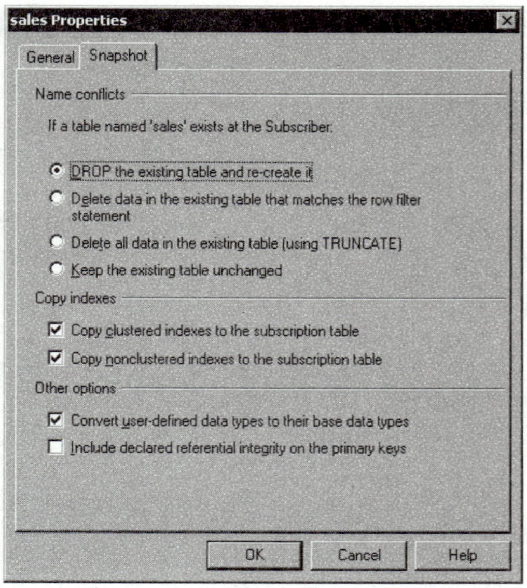

The remaining screens in the wizard are straightforward. They allow us to specify a name for the publication, set filters on the articles that were included in the publications, and even set a schedule for the snapshot agent.

The remaining wizards are all relatively straightforward and I will leave it to you to find out how they work and contribute to the SQL Server replication model.

Automating the Data Warehouse Administration Tasks – SQL Agent

SQL Server 7.0 provides powerful tools to automate administrative tasks that are repetitive or tedious in nature. An example of automation of such tasks is the act of backing up the database servers every night. Let us say that Darren the database administrator is responsible for backing up the database servers of the company every night. Darren performs the following tasks so he can leave work at 5:00pm and still have the servers backed up on schedule:

- Darren defines himself and his manager, Lewis, as operators and defines Lewis as the failsafe operator. The failsafe operator is just a backup for the primary operator.
- Darren then sets up a non-production server as the master server. The master server is the primary server in a multi server administration scheme.
- Darren enlists the servers he needs to have backed up as subordinates to the master server.
- Darren creates a backup job with T-SQL to perform the backup. Jobs and steps will be explained later in the chapter.
- Darren schedules the job to start at 9:00pm every night.
- Darren remembers that the backup might sometimes not go as scheduled for a variety of reasons. Therefore, he defines the job to notify him by pager, write to the Windows NT event log a message with the problem description, and page the failsafe operator.
- Finally, Darren starts the SQL Server Agent service, which is the tool that automates administrative tasks.

With this, Darren can leave work at 5:00pm confident that the backup will take place according to schedule. If anything wrong happens, the SQL Server Agent will page him letting him know of the problem. If he is not available, the failsafe operator will be also informed via pager of the problem.

Multi Server Administration

Multi server administration involves automating administration tasks of more than one SQL server over the network. Besides the ability to manage several servers from a central location at the same time, this process allows us to schedule information flows between enterprise servers for data warehousing.

Multi server administration involves having at least one master server and more than one target servers. The master server stores a central copy of the job definitions for jobs that need to run on target servers. The master server then distributes the jobs to the enlisted target servers while receiving events from these target servers. The target servers connect periodically to the master server and update their list of jobs to perform. If a new job exists for the target server, it downloads it and disconnects from the master server. The target server will connect again to the master server when it finishes executing the job to upload the job status to the master server. The figure below shows basic architecture of multi server administration.

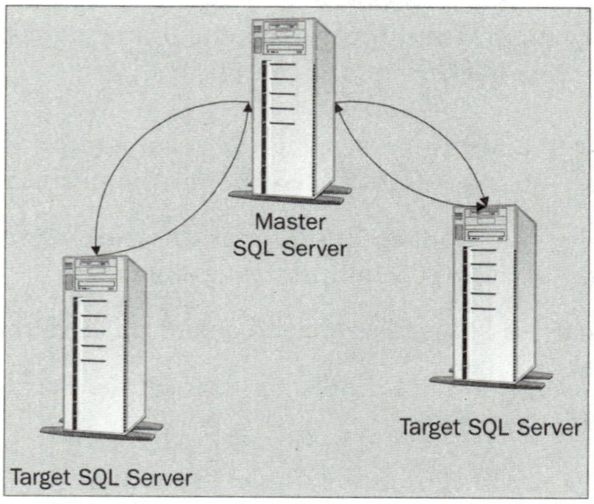

Multi server administration architecture

In the figure above, if you need to perform the same automated task for company servers, you can write that task as a job and deploy it on the master server. All servers that need to run the same job are then enlisted as target servers in the multi server configuration, which will make the job run on all of them.

> **Creating and running jobs on the master server in multi server configurations can be done by the sysadmin role of the master server. Users with sysadmin roles on the target servers will not be able to change the job or its steps. With this security measure, accidental changes of jobs or their steps or schedules are avoided in this configuration.**

Defining Master and Target Servers

Now we know what master and target servers are, let's see how they can be defined in SQL Server 7.0. To define the Master server, follow these steps:

- To ensure that you do not affect the performance of applications running on production servers, it is recommended that you choose a non-production server for your master server.
- Expand the Enterprise Manager's tree view for the server you want to make as the master, making sure the Management item is expanded.
- Underneath this item, you will see the SQL Server Agent. Right click it and select Multi server Administration|Make this a Master... from the popup menu. This will launch the Make MSX Wizard, which will help you define a master server operator (called MSXOperator). The first two screens of the wizard are shown below. Follow the steps of the wizard to create the MSXOperator under which the master server will operate.

> **Make sure the account under which the SQL Server Agent service runs is a Microsoft Windows NT domain account for each of the master and target servers participating in the multi server administration. Also, make sure all target servers and the master servers are running SQL Server 7.0.**

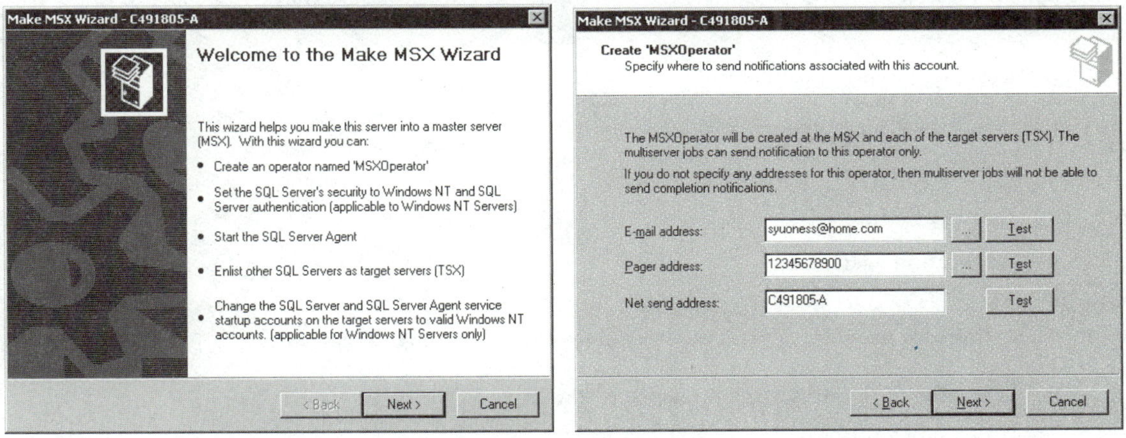

The wizard provided by Enterprise Manager to define master servers

To define target servers, you can use the previous wizard, or expand the server that will be enlisted as target server in the tree view of the Enterprise Manager (assuming that it is registered in the Enterprise Manager) and right clicking the SQL Server Agent tree branch. After this, you need to select the Multi Server Administration|Make this a Target ... menu item from the popup menu. This will launch the "Make TSX" wizard, which will help you to enlist the server as a target server with a master server.

It is worth noting that a target server can be enlisted with only one master server. So if you need to enlist a certain server with another master server, you will need to break its enlistment with the first master server first. Also, if the computer name of the target server changes, you need to first break its enlistment with the master before changing its name, then re-enlist it afterwards. Finally, if the NT domain account under which the SQL Server Agent service on a target server is run is changed, you also need to break the enlistment with the master before you change the domain account for the SQL Server Agent on the target server.

Automatic Administration Components

In this section we will see what jobs, operators, and alerts are after they have already been mentioned several times in the sections above. These three items are the basic components of automatic server administration and are explained below.

Jobs

Jobs are used to define administrative tasks once, and running them one or more times afterwards manually or automatically according to a defined schedule. These jobs can be executed on the local server or on several remote servers participating in a multi server administration configuration. **Alerts**, which are explained a little bit later in the chapter, can be used to trigger the execution of jobs. Each job is made up of one or more steps, each defining a particular task.

Job steps provide a powerful and flexible tool for administrators because they can be any of the following:

- Executable programs
- Windows NT commands
- T-SQL statements or stored procedures
- ActiveX Script
- Replication agents

Job scheduling also provides several options, including scheduling the job to run:

- When the SQL Server Agent service is started
- When CPU utilization is at a level defined as idle
- At one point in time
- On a recurring schedule
- When an alert occurs

To define a new job, you need to right-click the **Jobs** item on the tree view in the Enterprise Manager, and select **New Job** from the pop-up menu. This will open the **New Job Properties** dialog shown in the following figure.

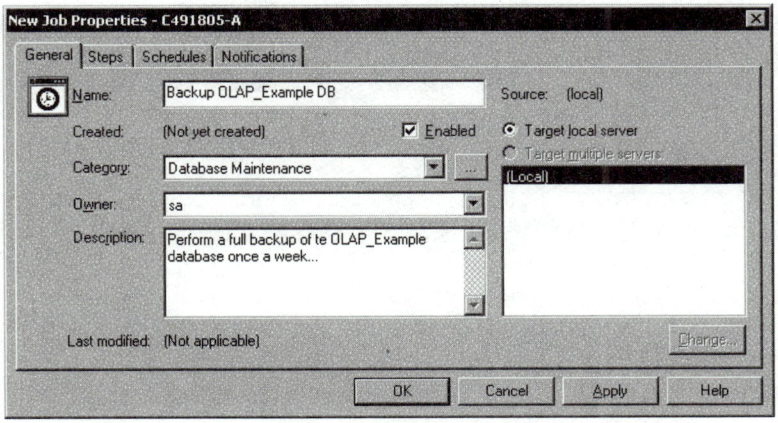

The New Job Properties dialog

The figure above shows that the job will perform a full backup of the `OLAP_Example` database. In the **Steps** tab, we can specify a new step by clicking the **New** button, which will open the **New Step Properties** dialog shown below:

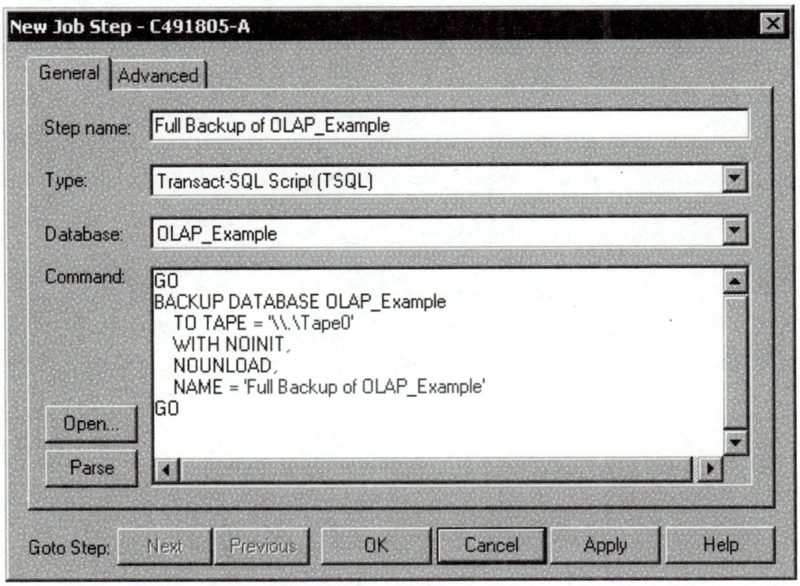

The New Step Properties Dialog

In the **New Step Properties** dialog, you can specify the name and type of step to be executed. You can also specify the database on which the step will be executed as well as the command to be executed in the step. I selected the step type to be Transact SQL script and the command is the same script we saw earlier in the chapter that performs a full backup of the `OLAP_Example` database.

The Job Properties dialog we saw earlier allows us to manage steps, editing them, inserting new steps, or prioritize them to run in a certain order.

The Schedule tab of the new job properties dialog allows us to schedule the job to run according to the possibilities mentioned earlier. In our example, the job will run indefinitely every Friday at 9:00pm.

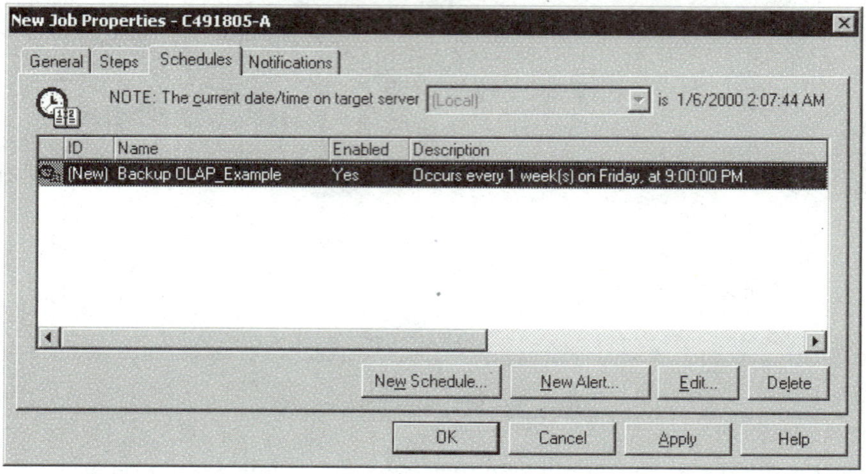

Setting job schedules in the New Job Properties dialog

The Notifications tab allows us to send email, page, or network message notification in case of failure (or success or completion) to designated operators. It also allows us to send a message to the Windows NT event log.

Operators

An **operator** is a person who conducts maintenance tasks for the SQL Server. An operator is usually the Database administrator (DBA). SQL Server Agent, along with SQL Mail, allows us to notify operators when alerts happen via email, pager, or network messages. SQL Server agent allows to rotate responsibilities among several operators so that if the database backup fails in the first week of the month, Joe will be notified, while if the failure happens in the second week, Darren will be notified, and so on. Fail-safe operators can also be assigned so that they too are notified in case notifications to the main operator(s) fail.

The dialog box below shows how you can define operators using SQL Server Agent. To open the dialog, right-click the Operators item on the tree view of the Enterprise Manager and select New Operator from the popup menu.

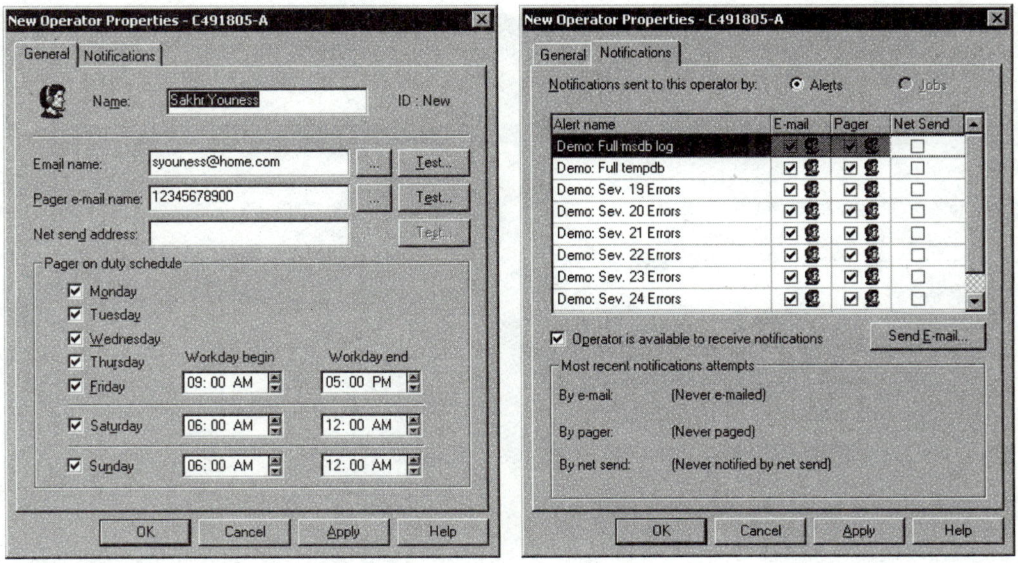

Defining a New Operator

Alerts

An **alert** is an event that takes place when one or more SQL Server events happen. The alert definition also includes the response that should be taken when the alert occurs, such a response is usually a predefined job. The alert definition also includes a list of operators to which the alert should be forwarded.

The following are some of the events that trigger alerts in SQL Server:

- Specific error numbers.
- Severity level of errors.
- User problems, such as an application being unable to connect to a specific database.
- Performance issues with the SQL Server.

The severity level of an error message provides an indication of the type of problem that Microsoft SQL Server has encountered. Messages with a severity level of 10 are informational messages. Severity levels from 11 through 16 are generated by the user, and can be corrected by the user. Severity levels from 17 through 25 indicate software or hardware errors. The system administrator should be informed whenever problems that generate errors with severity levels 17 and higher occur.

To define an alert, you can use the New Alert Properties dialog shown below. This dialog can be opened by right-clicking the Alerts tree branch in the tree view of the Enterprise Manager and selecting New Alert from the popup menu.

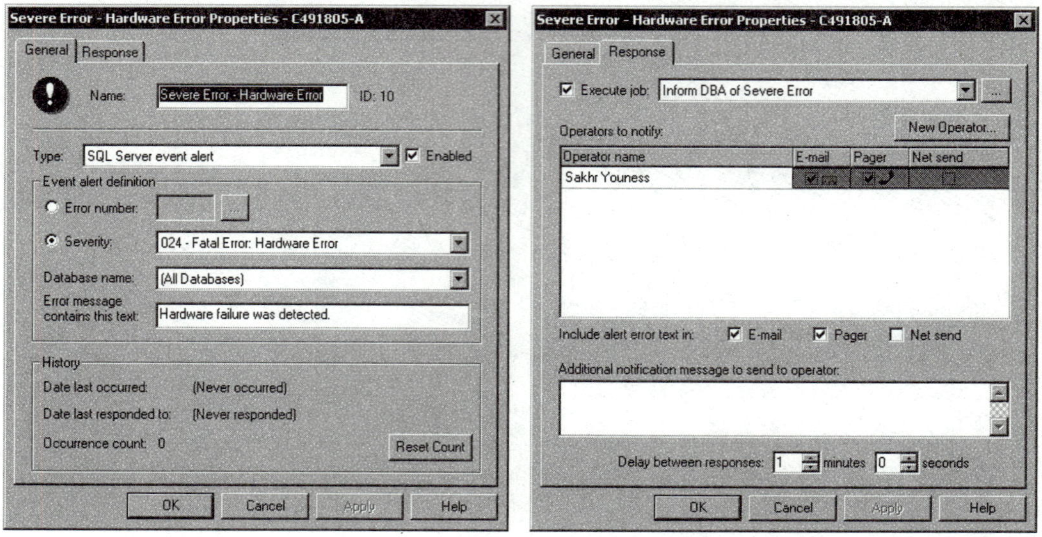

Defining a new alert

The figure above shows an example alert that executes a job "Inform DBA of severe error" when server error 24 (hardware failure) occurs. As you can see in the dialog box above, you can specify the alert name and type, in our example they are: "Sever Error: Hardware Failure" and "SQL Server event alert" respectively. The type can be either a SQL Server Event alert or a SQL Server Performance Condition alert. With the SQL Server event alert, you can define the event as a specific error number or a specific severity of the error that took place, we are using the latter in the example shown in the figure above. You can also define the database and an error message for the event. In our case, error 24 is not database-specific, thus the "All Databases" is selected in the Database Name drop-down list. The error message we chose to display when the DBA is informed is shown in the "Error message contains this alert" text box.

In the case of a SQL Server performance condition alert, you need to identify the object that caused the alert and the counter, such as free space scans/second. You need to also identify a value for the counter at which, under which, or above which the alert occurs. For example, you may specify that an alert will occur if the number of full scans/second exceeds 10.

The response page of the alert dialog allows you to specify the operators who will receive the alert and the way they should be notified (pager, email, or network message). This page also allows you to specify what job to run in response to the alert.

Summary

In this chapter, we looked at some of the main maintenance and administration issues of the SQL Server data warehouse. These issues included backup and recovery planning of the warehouse database, archiving unused data, using replication as a means for populating data marts from enterprise data warehouses, and finally, automating administration tasks using the SQL Server Agent. Each one of these topics could easily justify at least one chapter in itself. Nevertheless, I tried to discuss the main issues that matter to us when designing and building the data warehouse. In the next chapter, we will examine performance issues of the data warehouse and how to plan for optimal performance.

14

Optimization and Tuning

Performance optimization is an essential part of the different stages of the Data warehouse design and implementation. From the early design stages, you must think with optimum performance in mind. As you build the Data warehouse and use it, you need to make sure it remains optimized by monitoring it and tuning it as needed. Optimization takes place at several levels: the data source level, the processing and aggregation of OLAP data level, and the data querying and reporting level. The goal of performance optimization is to use minimal disk resources, have speedy processing of the data cubes, and have fast return on your queries and reports.

This chapter discusses performance optimization issues. These issues are divided into two main categories: optimizing the OLAP services, and optimizing the Data warehouse. The topics covered in this chapter include:

- Optimizing the Data warehouse: Under this title, you will see issues related to optimizing the performance of the SQL Server database used as the Data warehouse database. The issues discussed here include indexes, views, partitions, file groups, etc.
- Optimizing the OLAP Services: Under this title, I will discuss issues related to populating OLAP dimensions and aggregations, optimizing storage options, and optimizing MDX queries.
- Monitoring SQL Server 7.0 performance: Including a brief discussion of the Windows NT/2000 Performance Monitor, SQL Server Profiler, Query Analyzer, and Index Analyzer.

Optimizing the Data warehouse

Optimizing the Data warehouse database is the first step towards getting highly optimized OLAP services, which is the ultimate goal for efficient data analysis and fast reporting. If the SQL Server database used as the source for the OLAP operations is not performing well, data retrieval to create and populate dimensions and aggregations will be slow, resulting in slow retrieval of information critically needed for decision-making. This section discusses the issues surrounding SQL Server database performance optimization as it relates to Data warehousing and OLAP systems. We shall not go into optimizing everyday activities on the SQL Server, which is usually the case for online transaction processing (OLTP) systems. Therefore, in this discussion, we won't be discussing multi-user issues found in these systems, such as data locking and blocking, etc.

Using Database Indices... To Index or Not to Index...

It is not unusual for people seeking help from database experts on optimizing their database performance to be confronted with the question: Does your database have adequate indices? The keyword here is "adequate". Although it has been proven over time that indices improve query performance, indexing should not be done arbitrarily from the practical sense. You should design these indices with extreme care in order for you to get the benefits you want from your database system. So, let's see what considerations should be taken into account when indexing the Data warehouse?

What Columns Do I Index?

You might think, "Why not index all the fields in the table, since this way I don't have to worry if a field is indexed when I build my queries?". Of course, it might be tempting to do so, but if you remember that additional indexes mean additional space needed in the database, then you may think again, especially when you learn that indexing all fields in the tables might increase the storage size needed for them by up to 50%. A stronger reason for avoiding such practice, especially in OLTP systems, is that updates, deletes, and sometimes inserts, conducted on the table, will often result in rebuilding the index, which adversely affects performance. At least for the Data warehouse, where little if any updates and deletes are expected, you can index more fields than you were able to in OLTP systems, especially if these fields are used to build dimension tables in the OLAP database.

Stay away from indexing Boolean fields. You may have heard this advice over and over as the first rule of thumb for establishing good indexes on your database tables. Actually, this rule stems from the principle that indexed fields must have as many distinct values as possible. In other words, the selectivity of a single row in the table must be a minimum. Selectivity, in this case, is the inverse of the number of distinct values in the field of the table. Therefore, this rule also implies that fields such as Gender should, in general, not be indexed.

In short, the best way to choose your fields is to look at the SQL queries and analyze the fields that will exist in the WHERE clause. These fields are usually good candidates for your indexing. One time I was called on to investigate a means to improve the performance of queries running on a SQL Server database. I noticed that the tables in the database had a flag field that was set to True when anything changed in the field. This Boolean field was used to allow for processing new records by an application that synchronizes the database with another databases, transferring to it only changed and inserted records. As soon as a field was synchronized with the other database, the flag is set to False.

At first, you might think, this is a Boolean field, and so should not be indexed. However, when we analyzed the data in the field of one of the critical tables that had hundreds of thousands of records, we noticed that only a few records had the flag set to True every day when the synchronization application is run. The portion of these fields was consistently less than 0.5%. So, when we indexed that particular field for testing purposes, we immediately noticed an enormous improvement in query response time. The query was now taking less than a minute compared with about 10 minutes before.

In summary, you need to balance the different rules when you decide which field to index. Even if one rule makes it unfavorable, you still need to check the other rules and conduct some pilot testing before you make your final conclusion.

Key Column Constraints

When Microsoft OLAP Services populate dimension tables and cube partitions, it relies heavily on the key fields that are defined for dimensions. It uses these key fields to build the SQL statements necessary to populate these structures. Therefore, indexing the key fields (or using primary key constraints) as well as the join fields in dimension tables (or using foreign key constraint), is very important for fast retrieval of data from the database management system to OLAP Services. Generally speaking, you should index all member key columns in dimension tables, and in the fact table you should create an index on the combined dimension columns for each fact table.

How About Using Database Views?

Views offer you a great flexibility in designing your cubes and dimensions. However, you need to make sure these views are optimized before you use them in your designs. You optimize the views by optimizing the SQL code used to create them. For instance, you may want to reduce the number of joins used in the view to a minimum. You also need to make sure the view does not perform its selections based on non-indexed columns. Instead, you need to use fewer joins and more indexes on the columns used by the view to filter the resultset.

Views used to create dimension tables should not be a big concern. If the views used in this respect are inefficient, they will only affect the processing time for the dimension. OLAP services will store all the metadata connected to these dimensions internally, and use the metadata to process cubes and MDX queries.

Of more importance, however, are the views used to create fact tables for OLAP cubes, especially when you are using ROLAP or HOLAP storage for the cube partitions. If the view used to build the fact table in a MOLAP storage environment is inefficient, it will only affect the processing time of the cube. Once the cube is processed, queries made against its data and aggregations will be efficient because OLAP Services will no longer use the inefficient view. However, for ROLAP- and HOLAP-based storage, queries against a cube partition may result in using the inefficient view to build the aggregations requested for, which will result in slow and inefficient queries. To work-around using views in ROLAP and HOLAP systems you might consider the use of partitions, and/or multiple fact tables.

RAID (Redundant Array of Independent Disks) is a disk system comprised of multiple disk drives that form an "array". This system is used to provide higher performance, reliability, fault tolerance, storage capacity, and lower cost. RAID systems are categorized in six levels, 0 through 5. Each level uses a different algorithm to implement fault tolerance. RAID is not a part of Microsoft SQL Server. However, its implementation can directly affect SQL Server's performance.

How Can File Groups Be Used To Improve the Database Performance?

SQL Server 7.0 allows you to place your tables on a specific file group (see Chapter 13 for an explanation of filegroups) different from the default file group. This feature gives you great flexibility in optimizing your I/O for enhanced query performance. For example, a query going against a table located on a specific file group that has several files distributed over several disks, each with its own controller device (see following figure), will perform considerably better than the same query if the table is located on a file group with all the files on the same disk. This is because when the files are located on different disks, all the controllers will work in parallel to scan and retrieve the results. You can get the same performance gain if you use a single file on a redundant array of independent disks (RAID) level 0, 1, or 5 devices. RAID systems are discussed in detail in Appendix D.

Microsoft SQL Server creates a database using a set of operating system files:

- **Primary File**: This file contains the startup information for the database and is used to store data. Each database has only one primary data file.
- **Secondary Files**: Generally, these files are not needed if the primary file holds all the data. However, you can still create multiple secondary files to distribute the data among them and the primary file.
- **Transaction Log Files**: These files hold the log information used to recover the database. Each database must have at least one transaction log file.

Microsoft SQL Server allows you to group your database files in file groups for administrative and data allocation/placement purposes. One benefit of using multiple files and file groups for your databases is that if your database exceeds the maximum size for a single Microsoft Windows file, you can use secondary data files to allow your database to continue to grow.

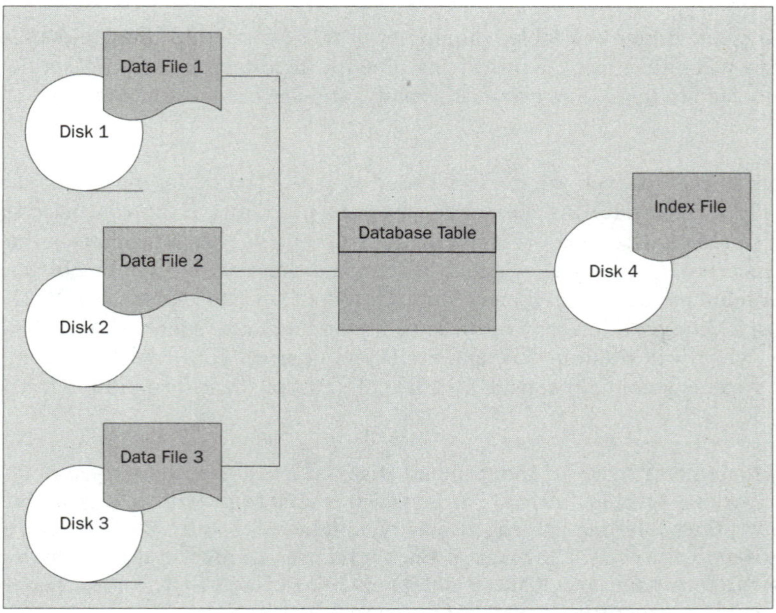

Illustration of using files and file groups in SQL Server 7.0 to improve query performance

You can further enhance query performance with a file group spanning multiple disks when you have multiple processors. This is because these processors will scan the files in parallel. When the table is accessed sequentially, separate threads will be created for each file in the file group, which allows for reading the data in parallel. Similarly, when a query joins tables on different filegroups, each table can be read in parallel, thereby improving query performance.

Another thing to consider when utilizing file groups to enhance query performance is placing "big" fields, such as text, ntext, and image fields within a table on a separate file group than the one containing the rest of the table fields.

> **Please note that if there are too many files in the file group, you will reach a point where you have too many parallel threads causing bottlenecks in the I/O subsystem. You may therefore, experiment with the number of files to use until you reach an optimal value. The performance monitor in Windows NT/2000, explained later in the chapter, can help you identify such bottlenecks.**

When dealing with file groups, you may also consider including indices into the picture. Non-clustered indexes in SQL Server can be located on different files than the tables they are related to. Doing so will also speed the scanning of the data and queries in general.

Is Database Partitioning a Good Option Too?

Partitioning the database involves dividing big tables that hold too many records into smaller tables. With smaller tables, queries will perform faster and be more efficient. This is because the queries will not have to scan all the data in the table; instead, they will scan the smaller partitions. Partitioning can be done at the physical level or logical/physical level. Physical partitioning is actually done through using files and file groups and placing a table on several files spanning multiple disks that have their own controllers, or by using a RAID system, as you saw in the previous section. Logical partitioning, however, is done in one of two ways, horizontal partitioning and vertical partitioning.

Horizontal Partitioning

Horizontal partitioning divides the table into a number of smaller tables each having the same structure and columns as the original table. The figure below shows an illustration of how this is done. In the figure the sales table is divided into three tables with fewer number of rows. The tables were partitioned based on the sales region: `Northeast`, `Northwest`, `South` region.

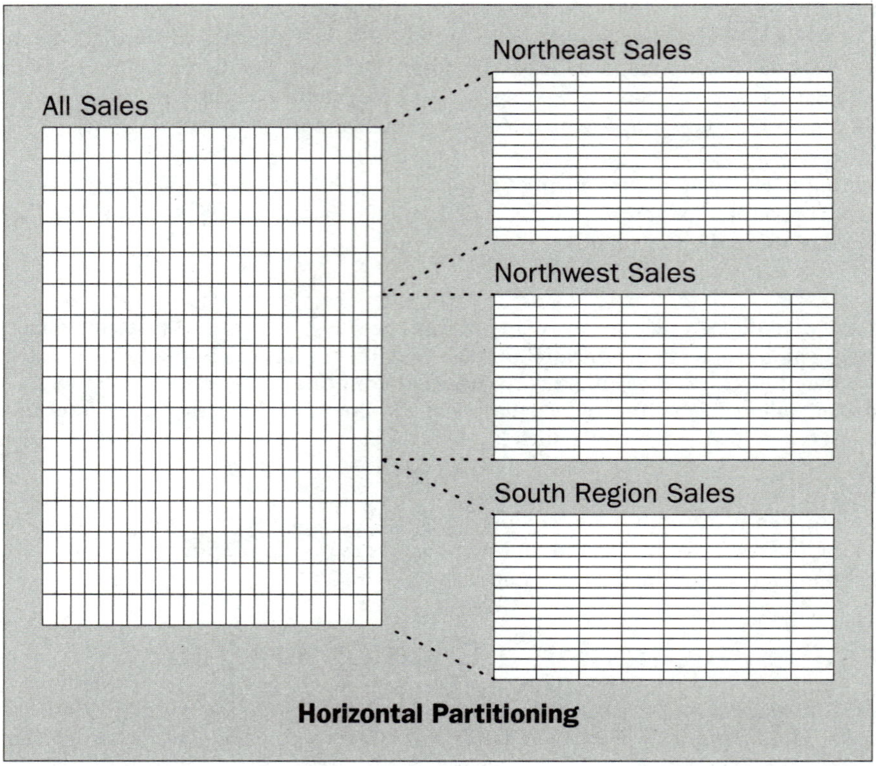

With this type of partitioning, a query concerned only with `Northeast` sales data will only go against the `Northeast` sales table, which has a much smaller number of rows than the original `All Sales` table. This will result in a performance gain and the results of the query will be returned much faster. On the other hand, if a query needs to return sales data for both the `Northeast` and `South` Region, the query has to perform a UNION between the two corresponding tables.

Generally speaking, you should partition your tables in a way that minimizes UNION joins. Such joins, when used excessively, will adversely impact query performance. One common way to partition data is based on age. For example, a sales table may contain data for the last five years, but only the current year sales are frequently queried. In this case, it makes sense to partition the table based on year.

Vertical Partitioning

Unlike, horizontal partitioning, vertical partitioning results in smaller tables that have fewer columns than the original table, but the same number of rows. Vertical partitioning has two types: normalization and column splitting.

With column splitting, a table is split into two or more smaller tables by separating out some columns and adding fields that join the tables together. The next figure shows an illustration of this technique. This technique is mostly useful when you have a field or two in a table that are particularly big in size (text, ntext, image). It is a good idea to separate these fields out in their own table.

With normalization (see Chapter 3), redundant data is removed from the table into one or more smaller tables that have a primary key linked to a foreign key in the original table. The figure on the next page shows an illustration of vertical partitioning via normalization. In that figure, the table `BigOrders` is partitioned into three tables: `Orders`, `Order Details`, and `Products`. Notice that in the `BigOrders` table, the same product information is repeated in each order detail record that points to that particular product. With the partitioning, the only field that is repeated is the `ProductID`, which is a foreign key in the Order Details table.

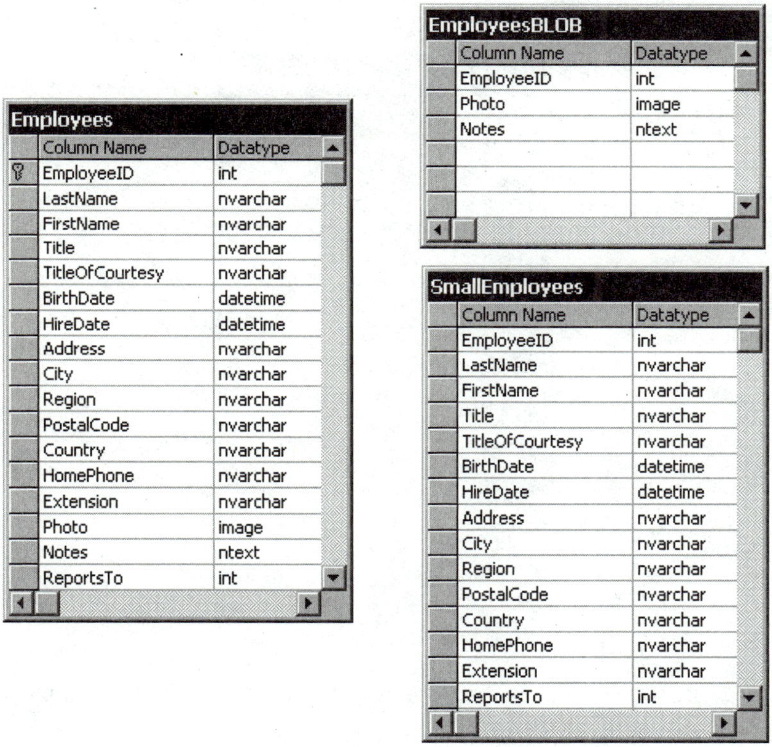

Illustration of Column Splitting as a means of vertical table partitioning

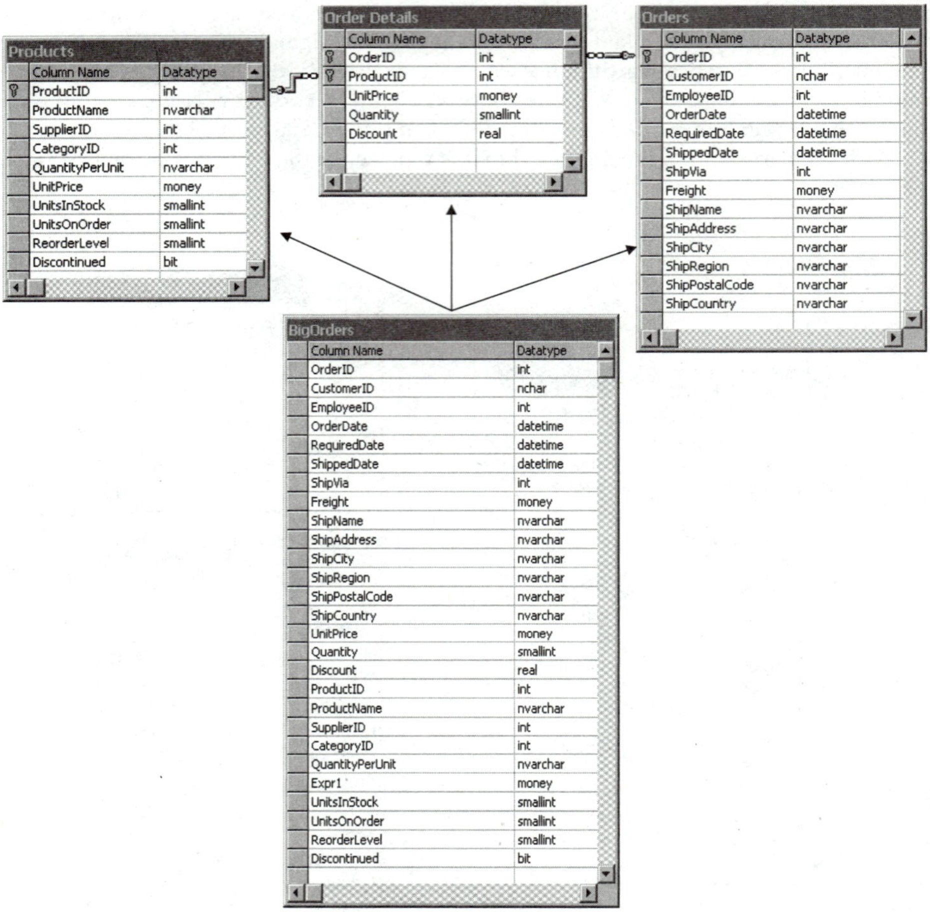

Illustration of normalization as a means of vertical table partitioning

Optimization of OLAP Services

Assuming that you had already built and optimized your Data warehouse, you still need to optimize the way it is used in your OLAP applications. This section presents some of the performance optimization issues you need to be concerned with when you use Microsoft OLAP Services to build decision support systems.

Designing Optimal Dimensions and Cubes

A good design of dimension and cube schema results in good performance. So, what are the factors that lead to a good dimension and cube design? The answer to this question lies in the following points:

Efficient Table Joins

Make sure that not only key columns in your dimension tables are indexed, but also that join columns are. This will optimize data joining and retrieval from these tables.

Key Data Type and Size

Dimension level key data type and size impacts the amount of storage needed for the aggregations made over these levels. It is more efficient, for instance, to have the key as a four-byte integer than an eight-byte character string. These effects become more visible in ROLAP storage than in MOLAP and HOLAP storage. This is because OLAP Services compresses the data stored in the later two types of storage.

Make sure you verify the key data type and size properties for dimension levels before you process the dimension or cube. If you change these properties after such processing, you will end up redoing it.

Unique Level Members: It is possible to have several members at a dimension level with the same name. For instance, you can have a city of Jackson in the state of Mississippi as well as the state of Delaware. However, make sure that the member key values are unique for each member. For example, if the key value for Jackson, Mississippi is 121, then make sure the key for Jackson, Delaware is not 121. The reason for this is that having non-unique key members will force Microsoft OLAP Services to refer to the higher levels in the dimension (for instance if the current level in the Store dimension is the City level, OLAP Services will try to qualify the city with the State level) to reference the non-unique members when it processes the dimension. This will result in significantly longer processing periods.

Be careful when you set the Unique Members property for a dimension level. If you set this property to True while you really have non-unique members in the level, the dimension processing will fail. In other words, OLAP Services will not refer to upper levels if you specify that a level is unique when it finds the data not to be unique; instead, it will simply fail (see figure below). It will only refer to higher levels in the dimension when you set the Unique Member property of the level to False.

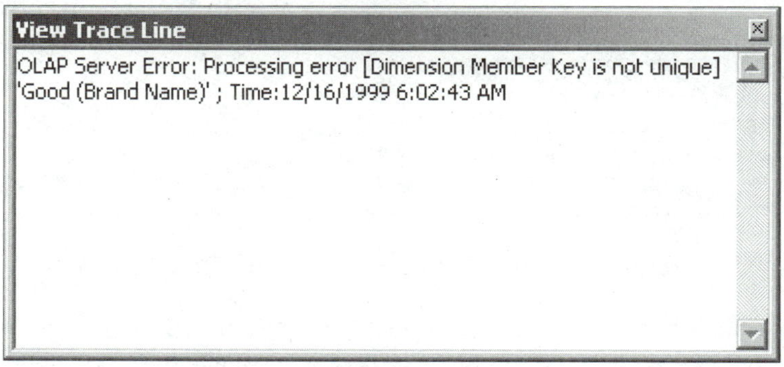

A sample error message when OLAP Services finds non-unique members in a level that is identified to have unique members through the Unique Member property

Level Aggregations

As we saw in Chapter 5, OLAP Manager allows you to set the property Aggregation Usage in the Cube Editor. The values possible for this property are:

- **Standard (All Levels):** causes OLAP Services to create aggregates for all levels of the dimension when the cube is processed.
- **Top Level Only:** causes OLAP Services to create aggregates for only the top level of the dimension when the cube is processed.
- **Bottom Level Only:** causes OLAP Services to create aggregates for only the leaf level of the dimension when the cube is processed.
- **Custom:** Allows you to specify which levels you want OLAP Services to create aggregates for when the cube is processed.

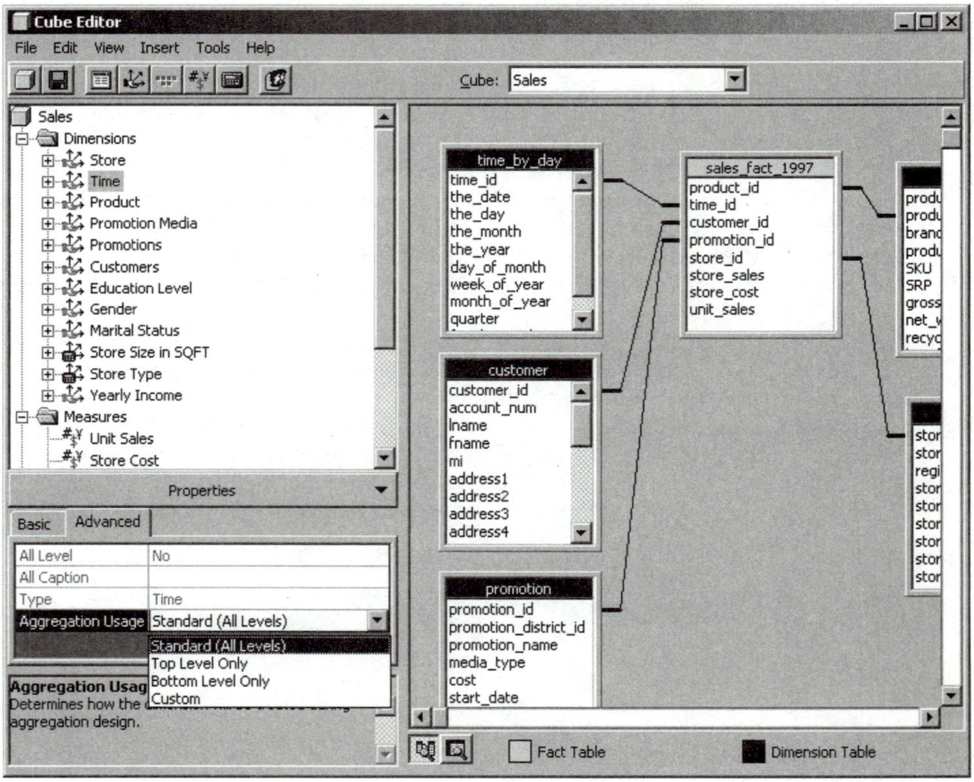

The Cube Editor allows you to set the value of the Aggregation Usage property for a dimension

There are other ways to specify aggregations for a cube partition with even more flexibility. These ways involve using decision support objects (DSO), which are explained in Appendix A. However, for the purpose for this discussion, I will stick to the aggregation boundaries as defined by the cube editor.

You might ask how this property helps us to optimize OLAP Services. Well, for example, if you know that all queries involving a specific dimension will always result in aggregations at the leaf level only, then you will be better off setting the Aggregation Usage property to "Bottom Level Only". As an example, MDX queries requesting information about sales of a product category, or brand, or any level of the product dimension, will always find the products sold under that brand or category, etc. then they will return the number of such products. In this case, you know that all MDX queries will be using aggregations at the leaf level, and aggregations at higher levels will not be of any business significance (for example, it does not make much sense to ask about the number of product categories sold by stores in West Virginia in October, 1999. It makes more sense to ask about the number of products sold in that state for that particular month). Specifying Only Bottom Level will result in faster processing of the cube, and will ensure that all queries using these aggregations will run fast because the aggregations are pre-calculated and saved in the database.

OLAP Storage Options

As we discovered earlier, there are three storage options offered by Microsoft OLAP Services: MOLAP, HOLAP, and ROLAP. We learned that with ROLAP, the relational database management system creates, populates, and holds all the aggregations, but it does occupy more disk space and takes longer to process its cubes and dimensions. MOLAP, on the other hand, when compared with HOLAP will take longer to process and occupy more disk space because it stores aggregations and leaf data at the same time. When it comes to query processing, however, MOLAP will be the fastest, followed by closely by HOLAP, while ROLAP comes a distant third according to benchmark and performance tests conducted by Eric Thomsen (Microsoft OLAP Solutions – published John Wiley & Sons, 1999).

In general when you query data stored in Microsoft OLAP Services structures (MOLAP and HOLAP cases), these queries perform much faster than queries against data stored in summary tables in the RDBMS (ROLAP). This is just due to the fact that OLAP Services structures are optimized to handle such aggregations and queries.

You may be asking yourself by now, "If ROLAP is slower in processing, requires more disk space to store aggregations, and is slower in responding to queries, then why bother consider it in the first place?" Well, ROLAP offers a really nice advantage with big databases, that is the ability of distributing the partitions and cubes across a number of servers, which allows for parallel processing of queries, hence the benefits of such distributed processing.

Your decision as to which storage option to use should finally rely on the combination of several factors. These factors are:

- Number of queries to be executed and the nature of such queries.
- Available disk storage (MOLAP still takes more storage space than ROLAP because it stores leaf data).
- Amount of fact data available.
- Number of aggregations, which, along with the amount of fact data may be used to determine the needed storage for the aggregations.
- Accessibility to multiple servers for distributed storage.

So, when deciding which storage option to go with, you need to weigh up these factors and come up with a subjective weight that will help you determine which to use.

Designing For Optimal Aggregations

As we saw in Chapter 5, OLAP Services allow you to design the storage and aggregations of a cube when you create it, before you save it or afterwards. The figure below shows one way to start the storage and aggregation design wizard through the menu bar of the Cube Editor.

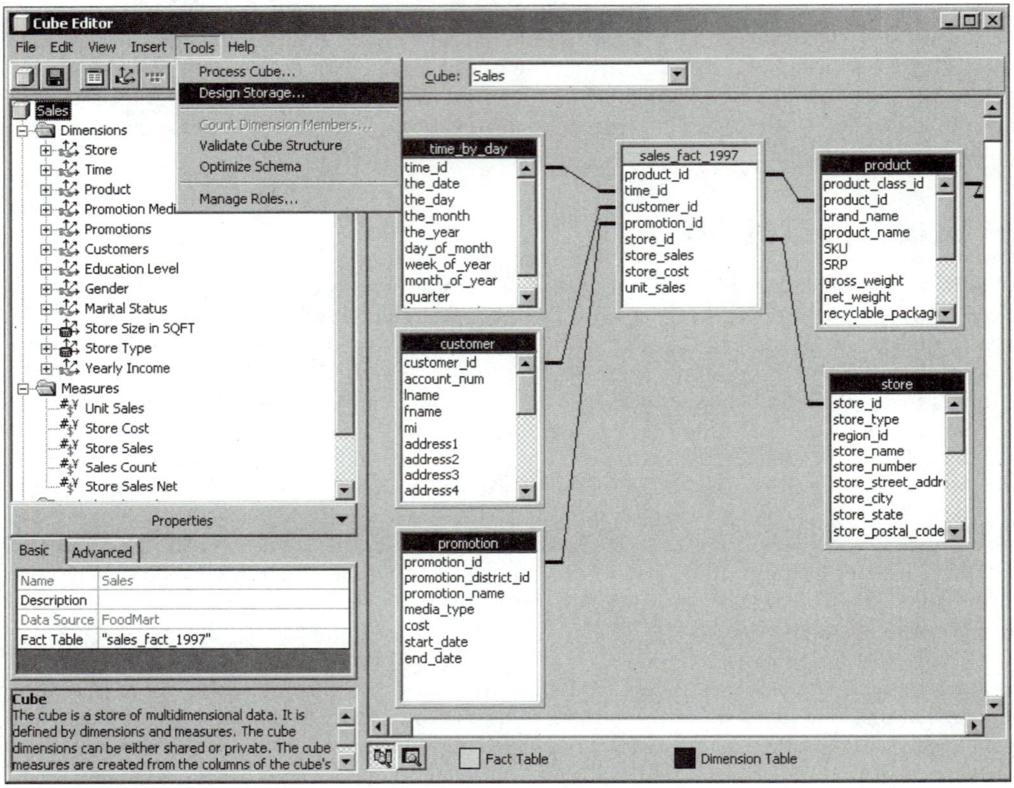

Starting the Storage and Aggregation Wizard

The number of aggregations performed when the cube is processed and determined by the aggregation designer in OLAP Services is the same for all three types of storage: MOLAP, HOLAP, and ROLAP. The aggregation designer, which is part of the Storage Design Wizard in the OLAP Manager (see next page), drives the process of creating the aggregations and stops as soon as the requested size or performance targets are reached, or as soon as 100% performance gain is achieved (or if you choose, until you press the STOP button).

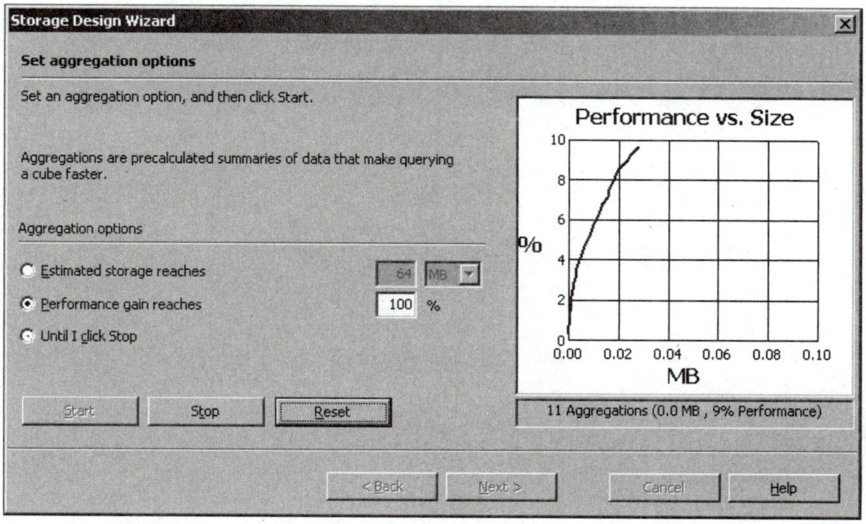

The storage design wizard calculating cube aggregations

When you issue a query against the OLAP data, OLAP Services resolves the query in the order shown in the flowchart shown on next page. The figure shows two steps that are labeled 1 and 2. The step labeled 1, is performed relatively fast at runtime, whereas the step labeled 2, is much slower. Usually OLAP Services will be able to resolve the query and build the aggregation at runtime from other existing aggregations if you have enough aggregations saved when you processed your cube. Therefore, it is not important, from query performance perspective, to get all possible aggregations resolved and saved when you process the cube. However, it is important to get enough of these aggregations pre-calculated. To determine what is an adequate number of aggregations to pre-calculate, determine the levels you will usually query against and have OLAP Services do the aggregations up to these levels only.

The intricate details of how the Aggregation Analyzer, which is the engine that drives creating the aggregations behind the scenes, creates these aggregations are beyond the scope of this book. Especially, that some of the rules used are heuristic and may change in future releases of Microsoft OLAP Services. Suffice it to say, that as a result of the rules used by the aggregation analyzer, OLAP Services may create less aggregations than you would like to, or may create useless aggregations that you do not need. You can, however, trick OLAP Services into creating more aggregations by increasing the fact table size property in the cube editor, this is because one of the heuristic rules used by the aggregations analyzer is based on this property.

The Aggregation Analyzer is the engine that performs the aggregations of the cube data based on the available dimension members and the number of records in the fact table. This analyzer can be accessed by Decision Support Objects (DSO), and is also driven by the Storage Wizard when you design the cube aggregations.

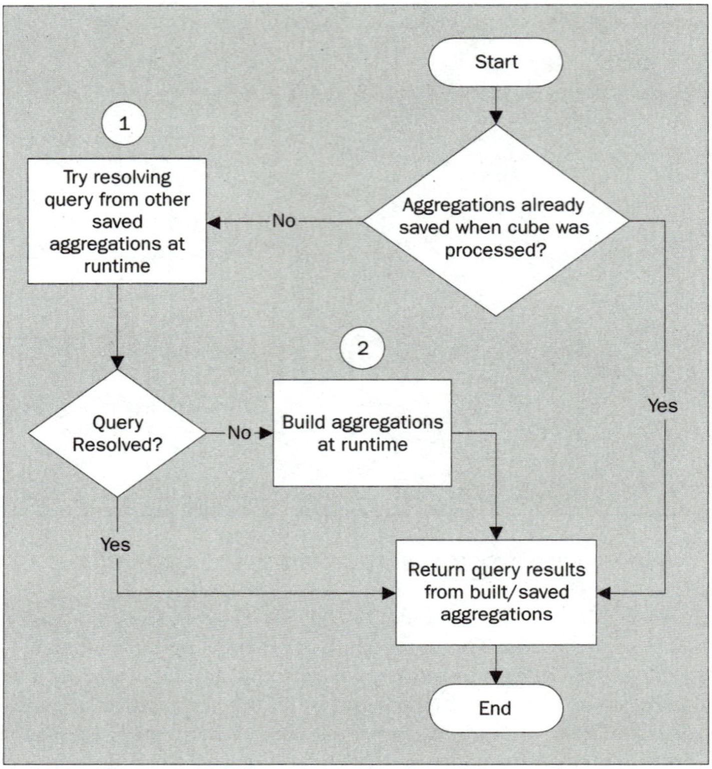

Illustration of how OLAP Services builds aggregations

The Fact Table Size property of a cube defaults to the size of the fact table when you first create and process the cube. However, if you change the fact table for the cube, OLAP Manager does not change the value set for the property, which may significantly affect the aggregations calculated by OLAP Services when you reprocess the cube. One situation where this will be significant is if you initially design your cube based on test data, which is much smaller than the final fact data. In this case, when you switch to the actual fact table, OLAP Services will greatly underestimate the number of aggregations it needs to create. Therefore, always base the value of the Fact Table Size on the estimated size of the fact table in production.

Tracking MDX Queries

OLAP Services tracks queries issued against OLAP data by logging them into an MS Access database, `msmdqlog.mdb`, which is installed with OLAP Services. The default setting on the tracking is one query in every ten. However, you can change this setting to anywhere between all queries, and one every 10,000. To change this setting, right-click the server name in the OLAP Manager and select the Properties menu item from the context-sensitive menu. The Query Log tab in the Properties dialog allows you to set the frequency of the query logging, and also allows you to clear the current log.

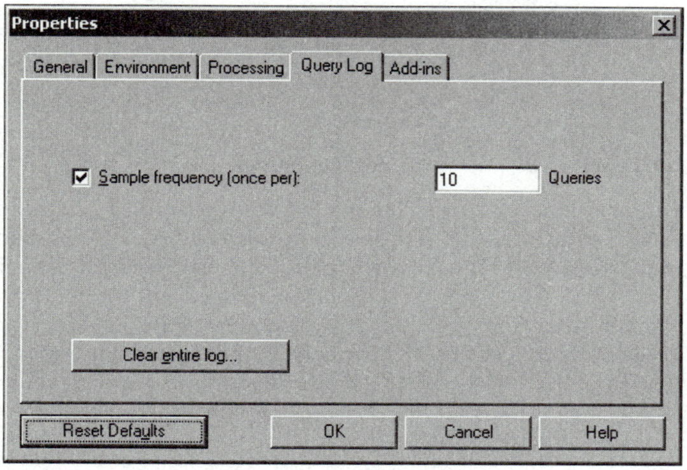

Setting Query Log parameters in the Server Properties dialog

If you are familiar with MS Access, you can open the database and view the query log. You can even build reports based on the log. However, if you are not familiar with MS Access, you can use the Usage Analysis Wizard provided by OLAP Services. You can launch this wizard by right-clicking any cube or partition in the Tree view of the OLAP Manager, and selecting the Usage Analysis menu item.

If you open the `msmdqlog.mdb` database, you will find one table in it. The table is called `QueryLog` and has the structure shown in the figure below:

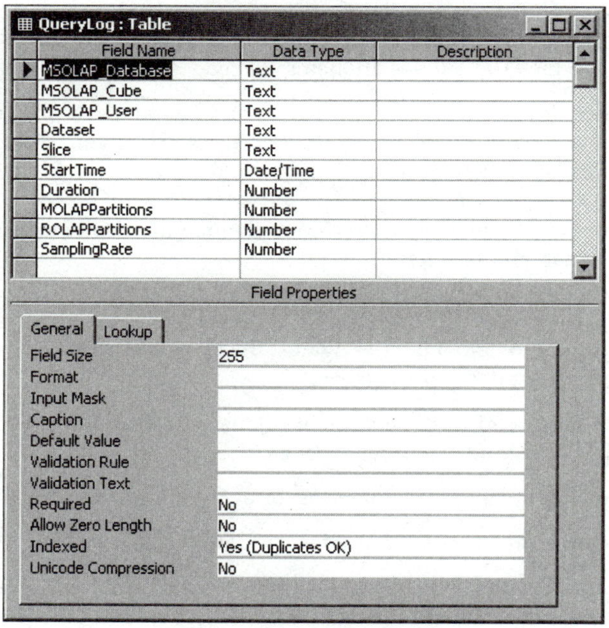

Query log table structure

The fields in the table structure correspond to the following items from top to bottom:

- OLAP database name: against which the query is issued.
- OLAP cube: against which the query is issued.
- The logged on user name (including domain name).
- The aggregation number (Dataset): the number is given to the aggregation according to the ordinal number of the level that was used in the aggregation for each dimension. For example, in the FoodMart sample database, if you query the Sales cube data with all dimensions at the All level, except for the `Store` dimension, at the `City` level and the `Customer` dimension at the `State` level, the number of the resulting aggregation will be: 411112111111. Each digit of this number corresponds to a dimension in the cube, and the value of the digit represents the level at which the query was run. In this case, the number shows that query was at the 4th level of the `Store` dimension, which corresponds to the `City` level. The number also shows the rest of the dimensions to be all at the first level (the ALL level), except for the `Customer` dimension, which is at the `State` level (level 2).

The ordinal number of the level of a dimension used in calculating the aggregation number corresponds to the location of the level in the tree view of the OLAP Manager for that dimension.

- Data slice, if any, identified by the dimension that defines it.
- Duration of the query execution in seconds.
- Start data and time of query execution.
- The number of the MOLAP partition involved in the query.
- The number of the ROLAP partition involved in the query.
- The frequency at which the queries are being logged.

Again, if you are proficient at using MS Access, you can build all kinds of printable reports from the logged data. However, if you are not proficient with MS Access, then you can use the Usage Analysis Wizard to obtain information on the following:

- A table of the runtime of queries ordered from the one that took longest to execute to the one that took the least amount of time.
- A table of the frequency of each query ordered from the most to the least frequent.
- A table of the users who issued queries against the system ordered from the user with the most to the one with the least number of queries.
- A histogram-like graph showing the number of queries based on the response time expressed in time intervals: 0-5 seconds, 6-10 seconds, etc.
- A bar graph showing the number of queries for every hour of the day.
- A bar graph showing the number of queries per date.

We won't go into detail on how to use the Usage Analysis Wizard, since it is relatively straightforward. It is however, worthy to note that none of the reports built by the wizard are in printable format.

Usage-Based Optimization Wizard

OLAP Services provides a usage-based optimization wizard that can be launched by right-clicking any cube or dimension and selecting the Usage-Based Optimization menu option. This wizard is a combination of the Usage Wizard and the Storage and Aggregation Design Wizard; therefore, we won't go into great detail explaining all of its screens. The first part of the wizard allows you to view the queries from the query log based on dates, uses, duration of queries, frequency, and the type of storage of the partition involved in the query (MOLAP, ROLAP, HOLAP). The next figure shows you the screen that allows you to make your selections.

Although the wizard will replace your existing aggregations, it still asks you in the next screen whether you want to replace the existing aggregations or just add new ones. It also tells you the storage type, the space occupied by the aggregations, and the number of aggregations available. The screens that follow are similar to the Storage Design Wizard screens, where they allow you to change the storage type, set aggregations options, and process the cube. You may also notice when you run the Usage-Based Optimization wizard that in the step where you set the aggregation options, the default Storage and Performance goals are set instead of the actual values based on the existing aggregations. Although the Beta release of SQL Server OLAP Services 2000 still shows the defaults for this step and still replaces your aggregations, I hope by the time the final product is released, these two issues will be fixed.

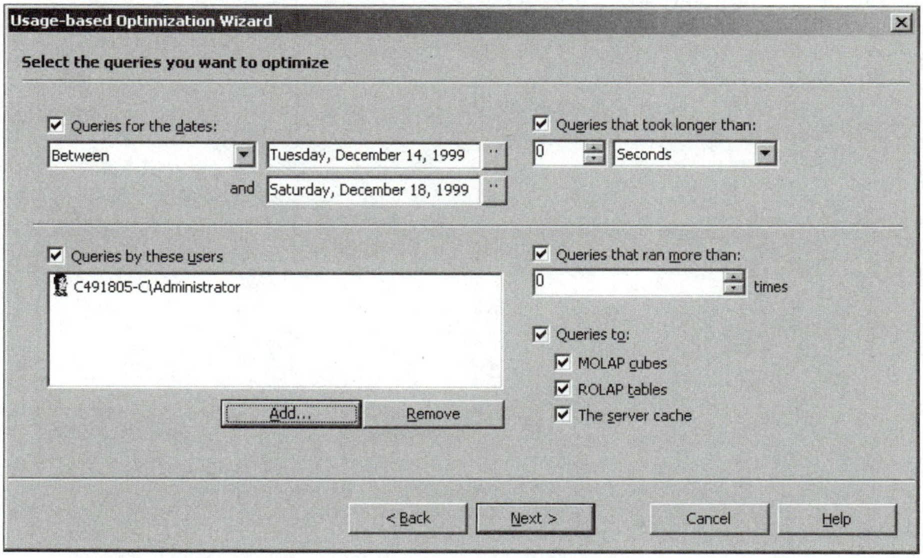

Making query criteria selection in the Usage-Based Wizard

In summary, the Usage-Based Optimization Wizard does not do much more than let you redesign your storage and aggregations, and the logged queries don't seem to play any role in determining what the wizard does with the existing aggregations, or how the existing queries will affect the calculation of the new aggregates.

Optimizing MDX Queries

It is important to understand how OLAP Services parses the queries issued to it in order to optimize the performance of such queries. The steps involved in such processing are:

- A client application issues an MDX query or a statement, such as CREATE SET statement.
- The PivotTable Service parses the query or the statement.
- The Query is divided into smaller internal queries, each against one of the partitions that will contribute data to the resultset. ROLAP partitions are queried serially, while MOLAP and HOLAP partitions are queried in parallel. This is due to the fact that MOLAP and HOLAP data is saved in multi-dimensional structures which allow such parallel processing, while ROLAP data is stored in summary tables the relational database itself.
- Results of these queries are combined wherever the calculations are conducted before returning them to the application.

You notice that the last bullet above did not specify the location where the calculations are conducted. This is because they can be conducted either at the OLAP Server, or at the PivotTable client depending on the value of the Large Level property of the server environment. This value is set in the Properties dialog box of the server in the Environment tab. This value defaults to 1000 members.

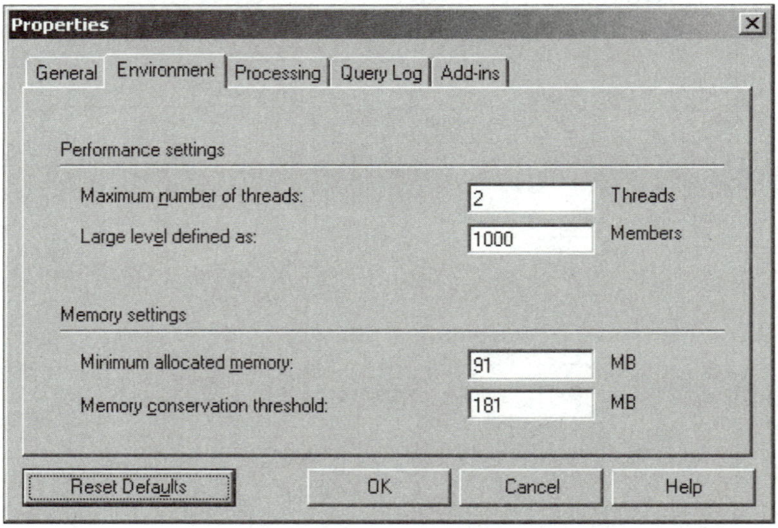

Setting the Large level property of the server environment

Large level server environment property determines the minimum number of members a dimension level must contain to be processed as a "large level".

Large levels are processed at the server and are not sent to the client unless they are specifically requested, but small levels are sent to the client to be processed even if the entire level is not requested. By changing the value of this property (in the dialog above), you can control how many queries are actually processed at the client and how many are processed at the server. Each of these two cases has its benefits and drawbacks. For example, if your query is processed at the server, it will consume more memory and resources and take longer processing by the server. However, the query results will be cached on the server so that requests for the same query by other client applications are readily available. On the other hand, if the query is processed on the client, the server will not use much processing power and resources; whereas the client will be responsible for supplying such resources, and the query will be cached on the client. Of course another issue that comes to mind when large amounts of data is downloaded from the OLAP Server to the client is the increased network traffic generated during the download process. Such traffic can adversely affect other applications running on the network reducing their performance as well.

How Does OLAP Services Handle Large Levels?

An interesting issue arises when a client issues a query to the OLAP Services. This issue arises when some levels of a dimension used in the query are identified as large levels (see previous section for definition of large levels). In this case the server hands the dimension members to the client for the small levels, but not for the large levels. The reason for this is that the large levels are considered to be expensive in terms of load time, memory consumption, hashing, and so on. As a result of handling small level members, but not large level members from the server to the client, some members that are not fully qualified may not be recognized on the client because of missing members of one or more of their higher levels.

The server hands dimension members to the client because the client, who is the PivotTable Service in this case, is supposed to perform some or all of the processing of the query.

Fully qualified members are members who are referenced by their name and the names of their ancestors in the dimension levels. For instance, the customer John Doe is fully qualified when expressed as: `[USA].[Michigan].[Detroit]. [John Doe].`

The issues stemming from this OLAP Services behavior are:

- **Referring to member names**: For members of some dimension levels that don't have unique names, how can these members be referred to if they happen to be on a large level, or one of the dimension levels above them is large?
- **Listing user-defined properties**: How can we get the list of the user-defined properties defined at a given level that may be large?

You might then say, "Why not always have the clients fully qualify members in an MDX query?" Alternatively, why not always use unique names for dimension members? This may seem a simple solution to the problem, but it is not always possible to accomplish. For instance, an application may refer to a customer as John Doe, instead of fully qualifying his name by country, state and city. Also, it is not possible to guarantee unique members for some levels. The example in this case is the city name "Jackson" which can be found in the states of Michigan, Alabama, and Delaware.

One viable solution to this problem is to force the query parsing and execution to take place on the server. This is because in this case, all levels will be loaded on the server and all members will be identified, even if they are not fully qualified. You must be thinking now: How can I force the query parsing to occur on the server? Using the OLE DB property `ExecutionLocation`, which specifies where the query will be resolved, can do this. This property can have any of the following values:

- 0 (default)
- 1 (automatic)
- 2 (client)
- 3 (server)

The execution location can be set either at the query level (for each query) or at the connection level (for each connection) as the default execution location in the connection string. As an example, the connection string below satisfies these conditions.

```
"Provider=MSOLAP; ... ;Execution Location=3; ..."
```

The second step of the solution to the problem is to defer the binding of the member by using the MDX function `StrToSet()`. See Appendix C, MDX Function Reference, for a detailed description of this function. Binding the member means associating it with an object on the dimension tree corresponding to the text specified by the client application. The reason you need to defer binding the member until the execution phase of the query is that if a member is not found during this stage, OLAP raises an error.

After you are done with the previous two steps: setting the execution location and deferring the member binding, don't forget to reset the execution location to the previous value.

The following is an example of how this situation is handled using Visual Basic. The code uses Microsoft ActiveX Data Objects (Multidimensional) (ADO MD), which needs to be referenced in the Project|References menu item in the Visual Basic project. The code is written to get the member unique name for an ambiguous specified member at a large level without loading the level. The example uses the FoodMart database, which is installed with OLAP Services.

```
Dim cn As ADODB.Connection
Dim cset As ADOMD.Cellset
Dim intOriginalLocation
CONST EXEC_LOCATION_SERVER = 3

Set cn = New ADODB.Connection
Set cset = New ADOMD.Cellset

' Connect to the server.
cn.Open "Provider=MSOLAP; Data Source=localhost; Initial Catalog=Foodmart;"
Set cset.ActiveConnection = cn

' More code here
' ...

' Set execution location to 3 (server).
intOriginalLocation = cn.Properties("Execution Location")
cn.Properties("Execution Location") = EXEC_LOCATION_SERVER

' Execute query.
cset.Open "SELECT StrToSet(""{[John Doe]}"") ON COLUMNS FROM [Sales]"
Debug.Print cs.Axes(0).Positions(0).Members(0).UniqueName
```

```
' Restore execution location property.
cn.Properties("Execution Location") = intOriginalLocation

' More code here
' ...

' Done
cs.Close
cn.Close
```

The code above prints something like the following as a representation of the ambiguous member:

```
[Customers].[All Customers].[USA].[MI].[Detroit].[John Doe]
```

More discussions and other solutions to the problems caused by large levels are presented in a white paper that can be found on the Microsoft OLAP Web site at:

`http://www.microsoft.com/sql/productinfo/olap.htm.`

The title of the paper is: "Working with Large Levels in SQL Server 7.0 OLAP Services White Paper".

Tuning MDX Expressions

In my experience with relational databases, I find that you get the biggest bang for your buck by tuning the SQL Statements. This rule also applies to some extent with MDX expressions. The way these expressions are constructed plays a big role in affecting the overall performance of the OLAP applications. In this section, I will discuss some of the most important topics related to getting optimal performance from your MDX expressions.

The most important issue is to monitor and adjust your query text based on resource use both at the client and at the server. Consider this case for instance: you have a query that uses small levels; hence the query is likely to be parsed on the client. However, this does not mean the query cannot be expensive for the client resources. As an example, consider the following query:

```
TopCount(Geography.Cities.Members, 5, Sales)
```

The query will return the top 5 cities in sales volume. The query will be evaluated on the server if the number of members in the level `Geography.Cities` is less than the threshold that determines a Large level. Let's assume for now the number of members in this level is 800, which is below the Large level default limit of 1000. Let's also say that the query is modified to return the top 5 city/product category in sales. In this case, the query becomes:

```
TopCount(CrossJoin(Geography.Cities.Members, Product.Category), 5, Sales)
```

Although the query only returns 5 tuples, it will generate a much larger number of product category/city combinations. For instance, if the number of product categories is 50, the number of generated combinations will be 50 x 800 = 40000 combinations. Depending on how much available resources you have available on your client, this can be considered expensive and resource-intensive.

You may think in this case, why don't I have the server perform the calculations, since chances are it will have much more available resources. This is true, but there is no direct way to make the server do the calculation. You must specify this, as you saw in the previous section, in the connection string of the data source. Besides, if the server receives so many queries like this at the same time, its resources may be exhausted faster than you think.

One solution to this problem lies in changing the way you write the MDX statement. For instance, the previous query can be re-written as:

```
TopCount(
   Generate(Geography.Cities.Members,
      TopCount(CrossJoin(Geography.Cities.CurrentMember,
         Product.Category
         ), 5, Sales
      )
   ), 5, Sales
)
```

As you notice, in the query above, we used the `Generate` function to figure out the top five tuples resulting from cross-joining the cities and product categories for the current city. Then we coupled the results with the remaining members of the `City` level. Hence the number of combinations in this case is: `1 x 400 + 5 x 800 = 4400`. This is a significant reduction of `40000 - 4400 = 35600` combinations over the original query, which means this last query will reduce the resource use on the client (or the server) by `35600 x 100/40000 = 89%` reduction. It is amazing what simple rewording of the MDX query can do.

The example above is just one example of how you can tune your MDX expressions to get the maximum performance gain from them. I strongly recommend in cases of performance problems to start with the MDX statements. After you are done tuning them to the maximum you think possible, think of other solutions (which will probably be more costly, like adding memory, etc.).

The following are some rules that will help you optimize your MDX expressions:

- You can use the Large Level limit to force more or less queries to be executed and parsed on the server. When you do so, you need to take into account the resources available on the client and the server.
- You can replace complex `CrossJoin()` statements with a combination of `Generate()` and `CrossJoin()`. The rule here is that: `CrossJoin(X, Y) = Generate(X, CrossJoin(X.CurrentMenmber, Y)`, or `CrossJoin(X, Y) = Generate(CrossJoin(X, Y.CurrentMenmber), Y)`
- Use the commutative nature of the functions: `SUM`, `MAX`, `MIN`, and `TopCount`. For instance: `SUM(CrossJoin(X, Y), m) = SUM(X, SUM(Y, m))`
- For Count operations, the following applies: `COUNT(CrossJoin(X, Y)) = SUM(X, COUNT(Y))`

Monitoring SQL Server 7.0 Performance

Besides the Windows NT/2000 Performance Monitor, SQL Server 7.0 comes with many tools that are designed to allow you to fine-tune and improve the performance of your server. These tools are described briefly in the following sections. I do not intend to go into the details of each tool, since this will require writing at least one chapter for each. Many SQL Server books are available and discuss the tools in more detail in case you want to learn beyond what is presented about them here. Some of these books include: Professional SQL Server 7.0 Programming by Robert Vieira, published by Wrox Press, and SQL Server 7.0 Unleashed which is published by Sams.

Performance Monitor

Windows NT and Windows 2000 have a neat utility that allows you to monitor the performance of the server or some of its resources in a graphical or report format. This utility, referred to as the "Performance Monitor" from now on, allows some server applications to integrate with it adding counters that can be monitored by it. The next figure shows this utility in Windows 2000 Advanced Server. It is clear that in Windows 2000 this tool runs as a snap-in under the Microsoft Management Console (MMC).

You can add SQL-Server related counters to monitor using the Add Counters dialog box, which is launched by clicking the "+" button on the toolbar or by right-clicking the graph and selecting Add Counters from the context-sensitive menu. You can add counters related to the following areas with Windows 2000 and SQL Server (These items can be found in the Performance Object drop-down list on the Add Counters dialog):

- Access methods
- Backup device
- Buffer manager
- Cache manager
- Databases
- General statistics
- SQL Server latches
- SQL Server locks
- SQL Server memory manager
- Replication agents
- Replication distribution
- Replication log-reader
- Replication merge
- Replication snapshot
- SQL statistics
- User set-table

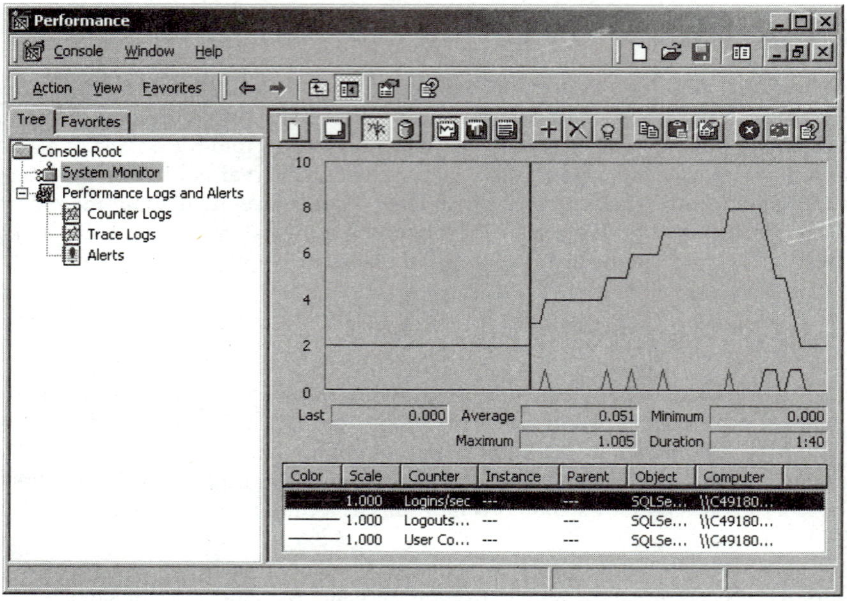

Performance Monitor snap-in in Windows 2000/Advanced Server

Each one of the performance objects listed above has several counters that can be monitored. These counters can be found if the "Select Counters from List" option is selected in the drop-down list below this option. For example, the SQL Server Replication Merge Performance object has the following counters:

- Conflicts per second.
- Downloaded changes per second.
- Uploaded changes per second.

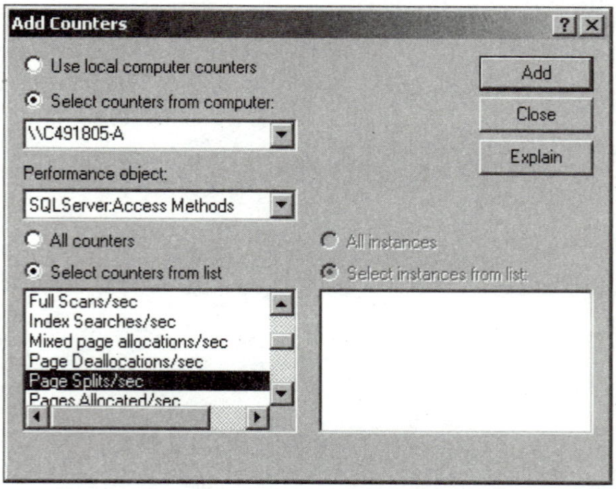

The Add Counters dialog box

Some of the counters even have instances that you can select from. These instances can be found in the drop-down list located below the Select Instance from the List option button. For example, under the SQL Server Locks performance object, average wait time counter, you can find the following instances:

- Database
- Extent
- Key
- Page
- RID
- Table

These instances can help you narrow down the areas you want to monitor even further.

Once you make your selections from the performance objects, counters, and instances, you can monitor these items graphically as a histogram or a graph; or you can view the monitoring results in a report format.

Performance Monitor is an excellent tool that helps you locate excessive resource usage areas or bottlenecks in the system. It is best used when you are accessing the SQL Server via client applications that have other services involved, such as using ActiveX scripting or COM objects to access the SQL Server DTS Services to populate the Data warehouse. Performance Monitor can help you find out which of these services is acting as the bottleneck when you notice performance degradation.

SQL Server Profiler

SQL Server Profiler is a graphical tool that is included with SQL Server 7.0 that allows you to monitor and collect server events.

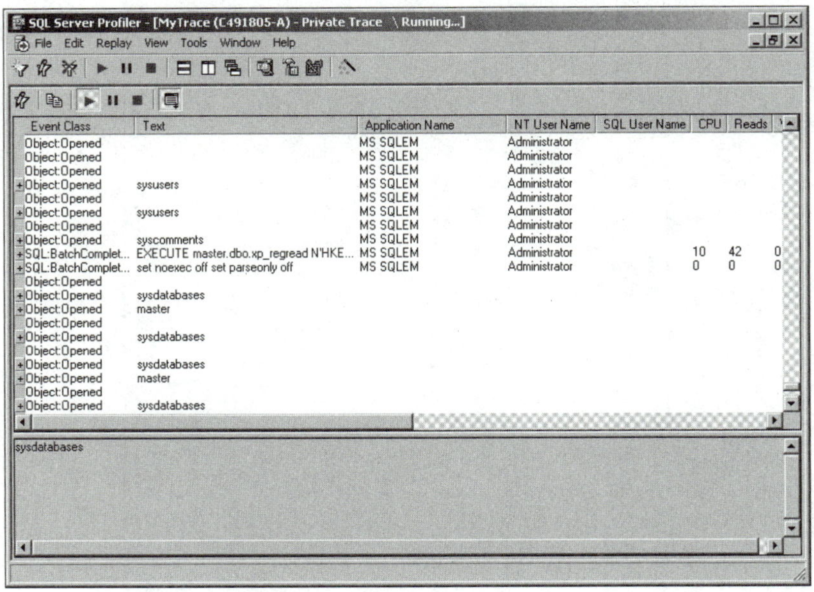

The SQL Profiler in action

Examples of these events include:

- Server connect and disconnect events (e.g. SQL Server name and user logging on and performing activities on the SQL Server).
- Transact-SQL batch jobs (e.g. SQL:BatchCompleted).
- The execution of stored procedures statements (e.g. text inside the procedures and the SQL statements being executed).
- Deadlocks (e.g. users involved in the deadlock).
- Error logging to the SQL Server error log (e.g. severity of errors).
- Duration of SQL Server and other types of events.

You have three options to view and store the results of the tracing activities. These options include:

- Displaying the information in SQL Server Profiler.
- Storing the information in trace files.
- Saving the collected information in a Microsoft SQL Server table that you specify.

Based on the events you are tracing, information captured by the profiler can be overwhelming, especially if numerous users are accessing the server at once. However, you can apply filters to the data you want traced so that you don't have to track data that is irrelevant to your need. For example, you can trace SQL:BatchCompleted with duration more than one second, or you can perform traces for a certain login or application. You can specify all these parameters and others from the Trace Properties dialog box.

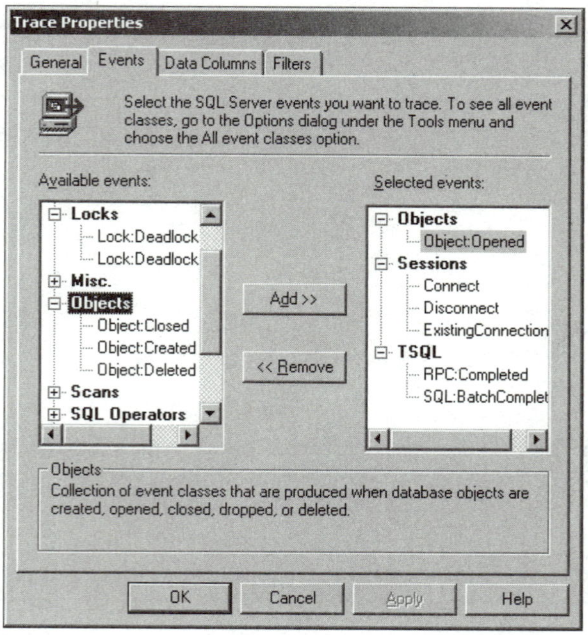

The Trace Properties dialog

As you get more familiar with the SQL Server Profiler, you will find it a very handy tool, for both developers and database administrators, to do things like:

- Monitor the performance of SQL Server.
- Debug Transact-SQL statements and stored procedures.
- Identify slow-executing queries.
- Capture error information in the context of the queries being executed.
- Identify scans of large tables.

Query Analyzer

Query Analyzer is a graphical tool provided by SQL Server 7.0 to help execute and test Transact-SQL statements, batches, and scripts interactively. The tool can be launched from the SQL Server Group in the Start|Programs menu, or it can be called from SQL Server Enterprise Manager itself.

The Query Analyzer graphical user interface has different parts each with a different function. These parts include:

- Query pane, which is a text editor for keying in Transact-SQL statements, or opening Transact-SQL code previously saved in text files. This editor is color-coded which makes reading the code easier and checking syntax validity.
- Results Pane: This window presents the results of the query in either a grid or a text form.
- Query Plan Page: This is a graphical diagram of the showplan information showing the logical steps of an execution plan of a Transact-SQL statement, or a batch of such statements. This particular diagram is invaluable since it allows the users to pinpoint parts of the query that are causing the performance to suffer.

SHOWPLAN is used by SQL Server to describe the method chosen by the SQL Server query optimizer to execute the query and retrieve the data. You can activate this feature by using the Transact-SQL command: SET SHOWPLAN_ALL, which causes SQL Server to return detailed information about how the SQL statements are executed and estimates of the resource requirements for running them. The statements themselves are not executed though. Therefore, this can be used as a query tuning tool for database administrators and developers. Finally, the Query Analyzer hides the complexities associated with the direct use of the SET SHOWPLAN_ALL command by allowing you to execute this command interactively through its graphical user interface.

- The query analyzer also includes an Index Tuning Wizard that can be used to determine the effectiveness of using indexes in Transact-SQL queries.

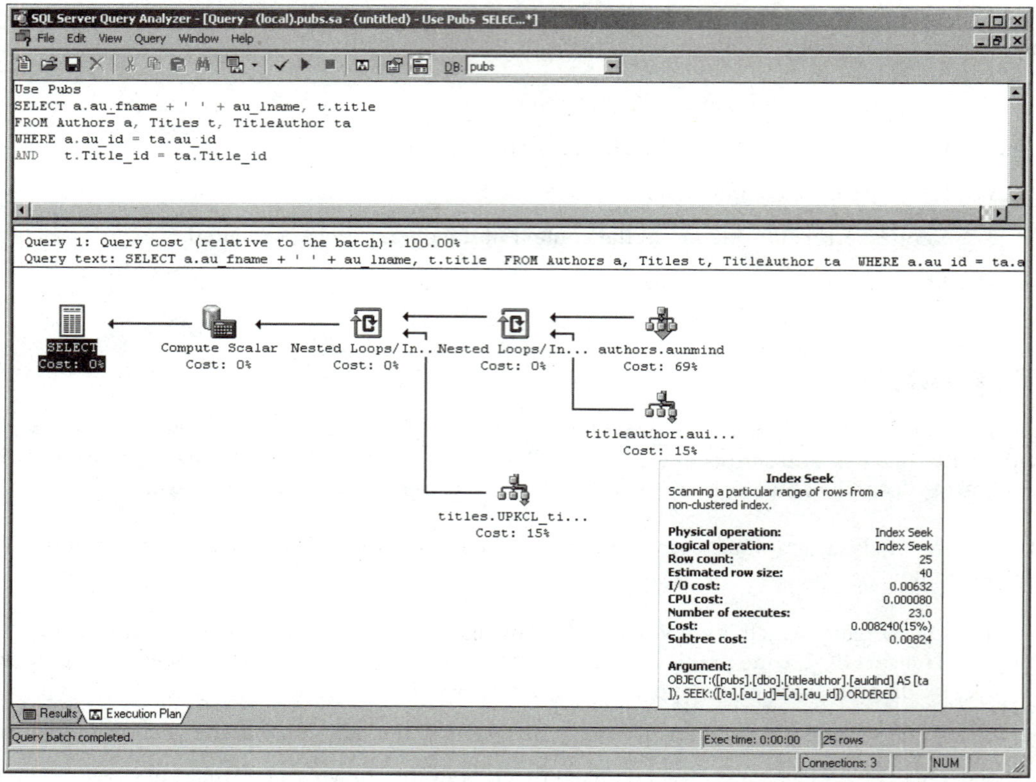

The SQL Server Query Analyzer in action

As an example on using the Query Analyzer, let's take the following query:

```
Use Pubs
SELECT   a.au_fname + ' ' + au_lname,
    t.title
FROM     Authors a,
    Titles t,
    TitleAuthor ta
WHERE    a.au_id = ta.au_id
AND      t.Title_id = ta.Title_id
```

The following are the steps you need to follow to execute it interactively in the Query Analyzer, and display both its results and the execution plan:

- In the Query Analyzer query pane, enter the query text as shown above.
- The Query menu has several toggle items. Selecting them will toggle their status between active and inactive. Make sure the Show Execution Plan toggle option is activated, by selecting it so that the icon to the left of it looks depressed. Also, make sure the Results In Grid menu option is also activated, so that we can see the results in a grid instead of plain text format.

- Click the Execute option on the Query menu or click the  button on the toolbar.
- The query will run next and the results along with the execution plan will be displayed as a two-tabbed page, one tab for the results, and one for the execution plan. The previous page shows the execution plan page, while the figure below shows the results page.

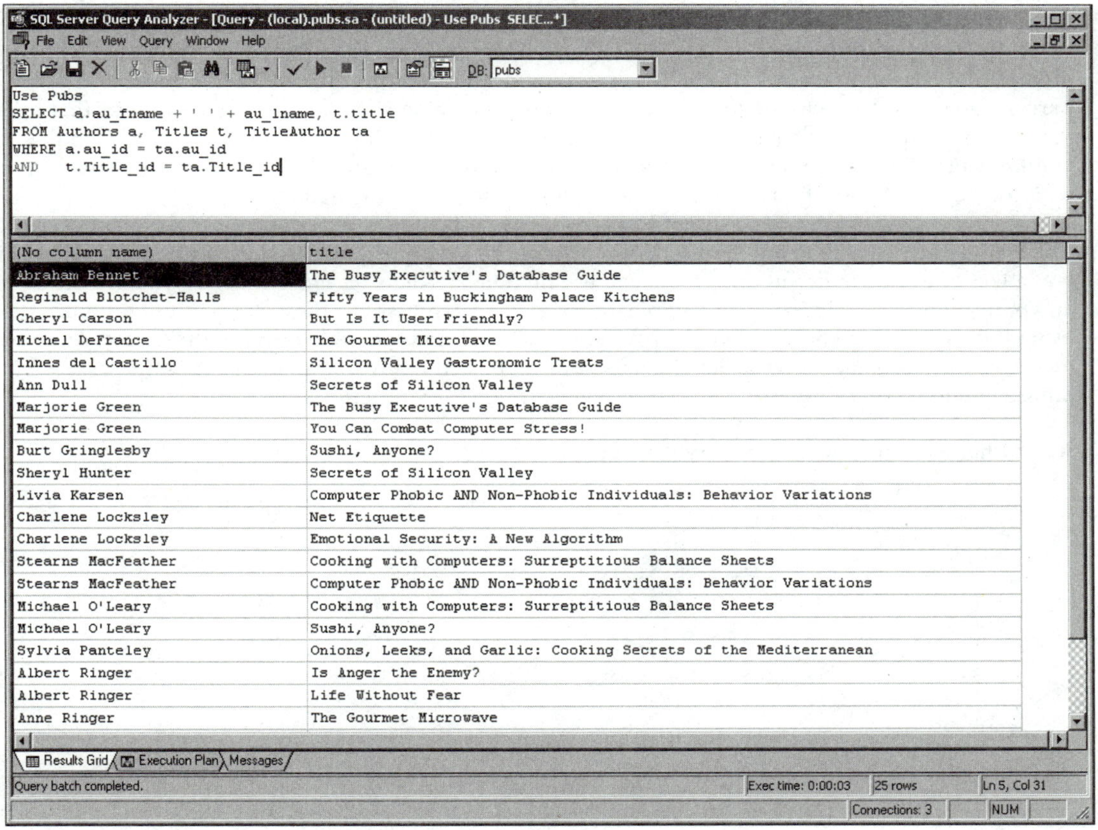

Query Analyzer screen with the results page.

You can notice that the results view introduces an additional tab: the Messages tab. The corresponding page includes error messages, or simply the number of rows returned by the query, unless you disabled the row count property by issuing the Transact-SQL command: `set nocount on`. *Disabling the row count feature is recommended if you are issuing batches of SQL statements or stored procedures. This is because when this feature is enabled, it makes the SQL Server communicate to the client the number of rows returned as a result of executing every statement, which increases network traffic between the client and the server.*

Execution Plan

In the previous figure, titled 'The SQL Server Query Analyzer in action', you notice a big rectangle with information about the step of the execution. This is actually a tooltip that shows up when you move the mouse over the object being analyzed. The significance of this tooltip is that it includes detailed information about the costs associated with this step (index scan in our example).

The Query Analyzer uses a special set of icons to represent execution steps. These icons can be looked up in the SQL Server Books On Line. The Query Analyzer connects these icons using arrows that indicate the execution direction. The labels used under these icons indicate the step name and the percentage cost relative to the total cost of the query. The plan shown in that figure tells us that most of the cost of the query was spent scanning the `aumind` index which is a non-clustered index on the authors table. The nested loops in that figure represent the inner joins between the three tables involved with the query. Obviously the cost associated with these joins is negligible.

The whole idea from showing the execution plan of the example above in a little more detail is to give you a feel of what wonderful things you can use the Query Analyzer for. Let us say you are developing an application that includes some complex queries. You can first test these queries and optimize them using this tool before you use them in your application. This is possible because the Query Analyzer made possible and easy to visualize the execution steps and really focus on areas that need improvement in query performance to the highest value for your efforts.

As another example on using Query Analyzer, consider the query:

```
SELECT   titles.title,
    SUM(CONVERT(int, sales.qty)),
    SUM(sales.qty * titles.price),
    stores.state,
    stores.city
FROM     sales INNER JOIN
    stores ON sales.stor_id = stores.stor_id INNER JOIN
    titles ON sales.title_id = titles.title_id
GROUP BY
    titles.title,
    stores.city,
    stores.state
```

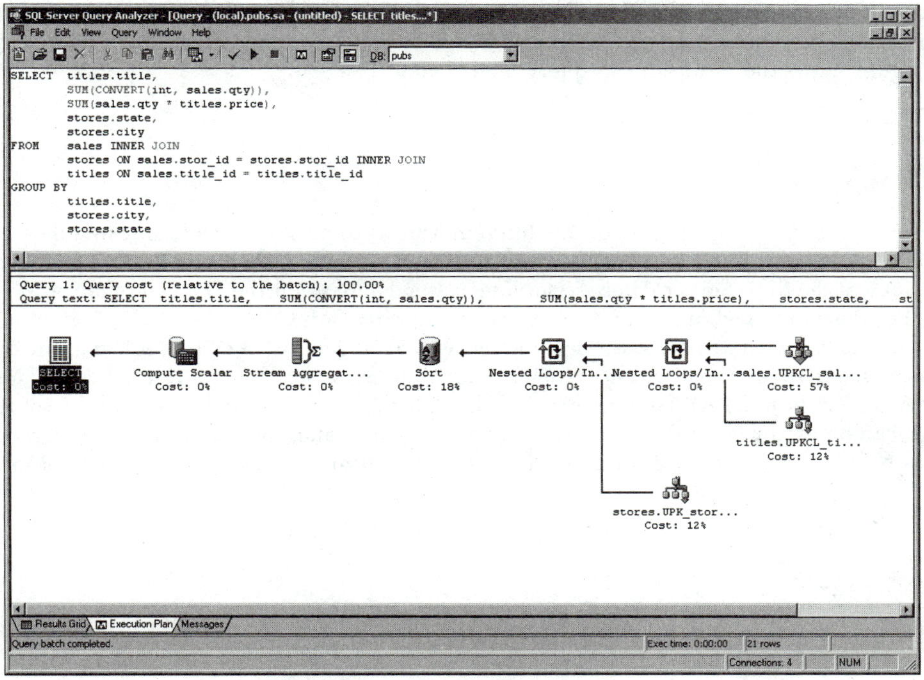

Execution plan of a query that has grouping functions

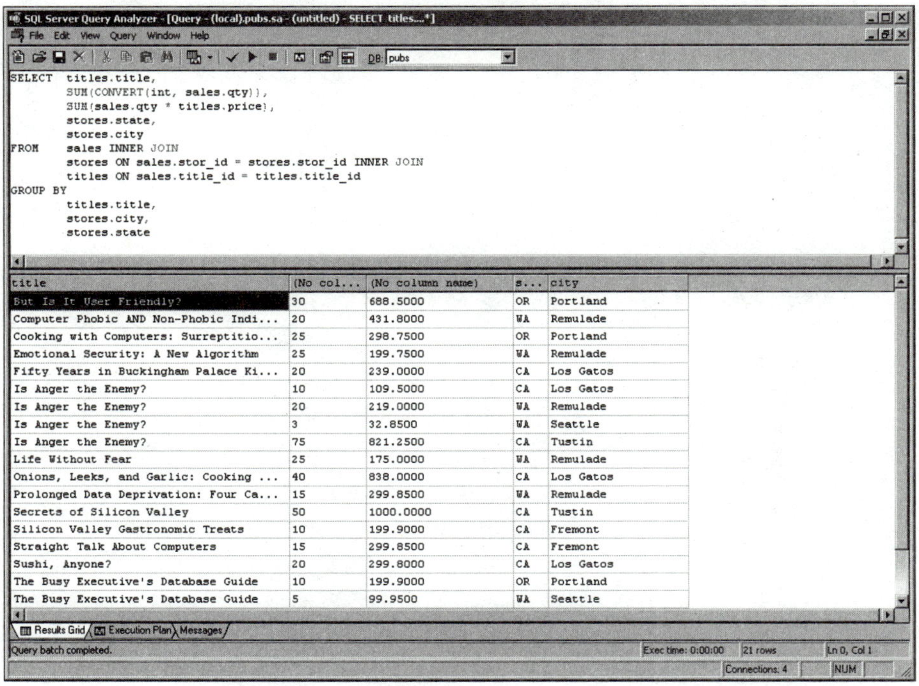

The results of the previous query in grid format

This query involves using the grouping function, SUM. The top figure shows the execution plan for it. You may notice that the sorting operation associated with the grouping took 18% of the resources. The bottom figure shows the results of this query in grid view.

Summary

This chapter presented to you some of the different aspects of performance tuning of a data warehouse and OLAP application. We looked at how indices, views, and file groups can be used to improve the performance of the SQL Server database serving as the database for the Data warehouse. We also looked at optimization techniques and issues regarding Microsoft OLAP, by using efficient table joins, the right key data type and size, and selecting the right aggregations. We also looked at the differences in performance between the different OLAP storage options, as well as how to track MDX query performance, and how OLAP Services handles "large levels". Finally, we looked at some of the useful tools that can be used with SQL Server 7.0 to fine-tune your database, including the integration with the Windows NT/2000 Performance Monitor, the SQL Server Profiler and the Performance Monitor.

A

Overview of Decision Support Objects (DSO)

Microsoft OLAP Services includes an object model called Decision Support Objects (DSO), accessible from other programming languages which allows you to build your own applications to manipulate your OLAP services, the connections within these services, and the different objects available from it. This tool is so powerful and extensive that it warrants a book for itself, or a large section of a book. In this appendix I will introduce you to this tool and show you how it can be used to perform specific tasks.

Topics covered in this appendix include:

- An overview, including the DSO object model and discussion of the DSO objects and interfaces.
- Using DSO including an example on how to use DSO from within Visual Basic to create connections, databases, cubes, and other OLAP Services objects.

DSO Overview

Let's start by looking at the DSO object model. The model exposes OLAP Services objects in a hierarchical form that mimics that of OLAP Services. In other words, the hierarchy starts at the top with the Server level, followed by the Database, Cubes, Partitions, and Aggregations. The following diagram shows this hierarchy in the form of interfaces and corresponding classes that are used programmatically.

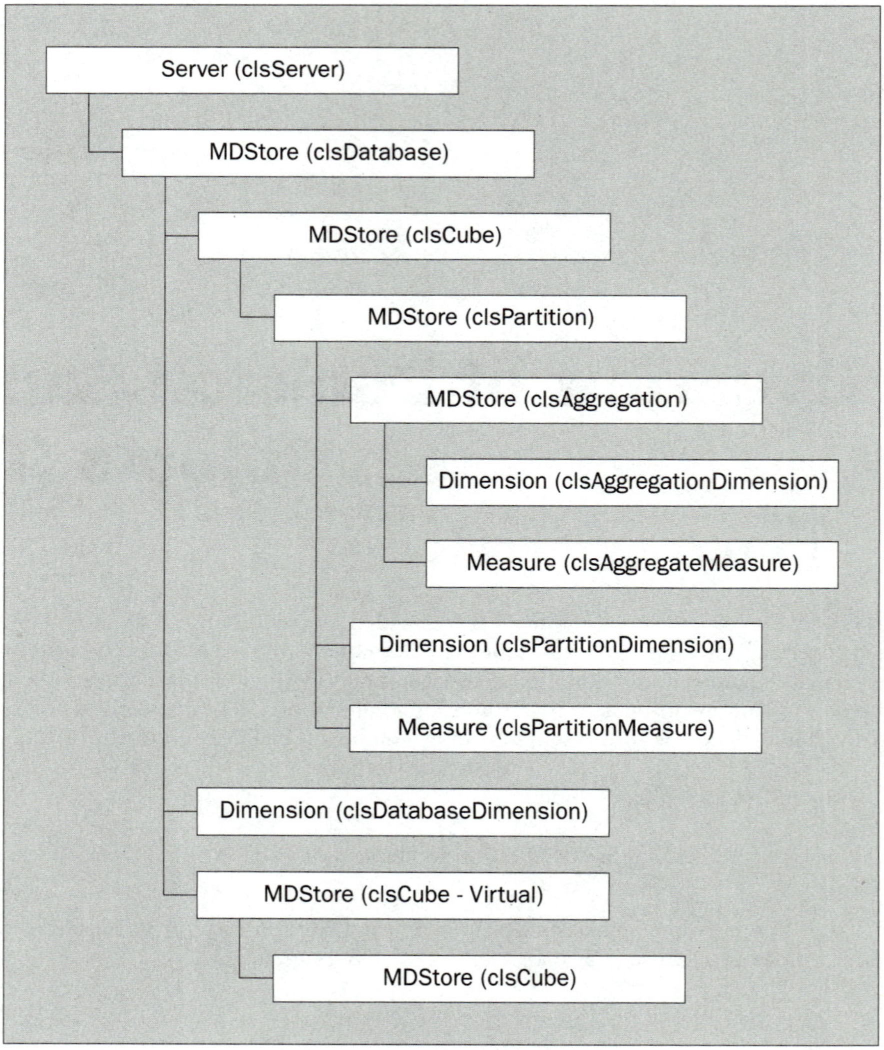

DSO object model hierarchy

Examining the DSO object model presented in the above figure, you can notice that each object in the hierarchy contains a set of other objects. The server object, which resides at the top of the hierarchy, for instance, contains groups of objects that define OLAP databases. Each one of the database objects contains groups of objects representing cubes, shared dimensions, and virtual cubes. Each one of these objects, in turn, contains other objects that support the OLAP Services hierarchy.

DSO Objects and Interfaces

DSO objects are classified as either one of the following classifications:

- Objects that can be accessed and managed directly. These objects have their own collections, methods and properties, and include the following:
    - clsCubeAnalyzer
    - clsPartitionAnalyzer
    - clsDataSource
    - clsServer
    - clsMemberProperty
- Objects that implement a DSO interface. The objects cannot be manipulated directly. Instead, the interfaces corresponding to them should be used. The table below lists these objects and their interfaces.

Interface	Implementing Objects (Classes)
Command	clsDatabaseCommand clsCubeCommand
Dimension	clsDatabaseDimension clsCubeDimension clsAggregationDimension clsPartitionDimension
Level	clsDatabaseLevel clsCubeLevel clsAggregationLevel clsPartitionLevel
MDStore	clsDatabase clsCube clsPartition clsAggregation
Measure	clsCubeMeasue clsPartitionMeasure clsAggregationMeasure
Role	clsDatabaseRole clsCubeRole

The following is a description of the different DSO objects and how they correspond to the OLAP Services hierarchy.

DSO Database Object

The database DSO object contains several collections:

- `Dimensions`, including shared and private dimensions and their levels.
- `Levels` collections of the database dimensions.
- `DataSources` applicable to all subordinate objects in the database.
- `Roles`, which is a collection of Role objects that control access to databases and cubes.
- `Commands`: this collection is not currently used; but is reserved for future use.
- `Custom` properties, a collection that allows you to add your own custom property objects to fullfill specific needs.
- `MDStore` collection of cubes and virtual cubes.

Databases are themselves contained in MDStore collections under the server object (clsServer).

DSO Cube Objects

A DSO cube object contains the following collections and objects:

- `Dimensions`: including shared dimensions defined at the database level and added to the cube's `Dimensions` collection, and private dimensions.
- `Measures`: collection of cube measure associated with the cube.
- `DataSources`: a collection that contains the datasource used for the cube, or its partition. Only one data source is allowed for the cube.
- `Roles`: contains `Role` objects that exist in the `Roles` collection at the database level, and are passed to the cube.
- `Commands`: a collection that includes the MDX commands and statements used to specify the data to be used in the cube.
- `Custom` Properties.
- `MDStores`: collections that carry one or more partitions in the cube.

DSO Partition Objects

Every cube has at least one partition, the default partition, and if you are running the Enterprise version of OLAP Services, then you can have multiple partitions for a single cube. Each partition consists of the following objects and collections:

- `Dimensions`: the cube dimensions stored in the partition.
- `Measures`: These are the measures of the cube included in the partition.
- `DataSource`: The data source for the partition. Unless defined seperately, it usually is the same as data source of the cube.

- `Custom` properties.
- `MDStores`: a collection that contains aggregations associated with the partition.

DSO Aggregations

Aggregations contain collections of:

- `Dimensions`: a collection of dimensions used by the aggregation and their subordinate levels.
- `Measures`: a collection of measures used by the aggregation calculations.
- `DataSources`: collection of locations of data to be aggregated.
- `Custom` Properties.

DSO Virtual Cubes

Virtual cubes are used in a similar way to views in relational databases. Virtual cubes combine several cubes together and allow you to specify roles and permissions that would let someone who does not have permissions on the individual cubes to view their data through the virtual cube. Also, please note that virtual cube dimensions and measures are limited to those in their underlying cubes.

DSO virtual cubes consist of the following collections and objects:

- `Dimensions`: a collection of the dimensions used in the virtual cube. These dimensions must exist in the underlying cubes.
- `Measures`: a collection of the measures used by the virtual cube. Like the dimensions, these should also exist in the underlying cubes.
- `Roles`: This is a collection of permissions granted to the virtual cube. These roles must be defined on the virtual cube's database level.
- `Commands`: these are a collection of MDX expressions and statements that define the data used by the cube.
- `Custom` Properties.
- `MDStores`: This is a collection of one or more cubes.

DSO and the Repository

DSO manages the metadata stored by the repository. DSO can access the metadata, which is stored in msdb, a relational system database on the SQL Server. DSO can query the metadata, add to it, update it, or even delete from it. This can be done through using the DSO objects and their properties and methods.

Using DSO Objects

Given that you are already familiar with basic object-oriented programming and know how to use objects and classes in a language like Visual Basic, the previous introduction to the DSO objects and interfaces should be enough to understand the examples presented in this section. In the section, I will show you how you can use DSO objects to connect to an OLAP server, create a database, and add a data source. You can do a lot more with DSO, however at this stage, I just want to introduce you to how the DSO objects and interfaces are used and how powerful they can be.

Connecting to the Server

Open a new Visual Basic 6 project and create a new Standard EXE project. Save the project as `DSOExample.vbp` in a distinct folder on your hard disk. When prompted to save the blank form, name it and save it as `frmDSO` in the same folder you selected for the project file. Set the caption for the form to "`DSO Example`".

- Add a command button to the form and set its name to `cmdConnect`, and its caption to "`Connect`".
- In the Project|References menu item, add a reference to the Microsoft Decision Support Objects library.
- Add the following code for the form and the Click event of the `cmdConnect` command button:

```
Option Explicit

Dim dsoSrv As DSO.Server
Dim dsoDB As DSO.MDStore
Dim dsoCube As DSO.MDStore


Private Sub cmdConnect_Click()
   On Error GoTo EH

   Dim intClassType As Integer
   Dim strClassType As String

   'Initialize global objects
   Set dsoDB = Nothing
  Set dsoCube = Nothing

   'Create instance of server and connect.
   '"LocalHost" will default to the
   'local Windows NT Server where the
   'OLAP server is installed.
   Set dsoSrv = New DSO.Server
   dsoSrv.Connect ("LocalHost")

   'Get the class type and describe it.
   intClassType = dsoSrv.ClassType
```

```
    Select Case intClassType
        Case clsServer
            strClassType = "Server"
        Case Else
            strClassType = "Invalid Class Type"
    End Select

    'Show the server's information to the user.
    Print vbCr & "Server Properties:"
    Print "----------------------------" & vbCr
    Print "Name: " & vbTab & vbTab & dsoSrv.Name
    Print "ClassType: " & vbTab & dsoSrv.ClassType & "  -  " & strClassType
    Print "Description: " & vbTab & dsoSrv.Description
    Print "machine: " & vbTab & dsoSrv.Machine
    Print "Service State: " & vbTab & dsoSrv.ServiceState
    Print "Server State: " & vbTab & dsoSrv.State

    Exit Sub

EH:
    Debug.Print "Error connecting to server"
    Debug.Print Err.Number, Err.Description, Err.Source
    Err.Clear
    Debug.Assert False
End Sub
```

❑ To disconnect from the server, add another command button, set its name property to `cmdDisconnect` and its caption to `Disconnect`. Then, add the following code for its Click event:

```
Private Sub cmdDisconnect_Click()
    If Not dsoSrv Is Nothing Then
        On Error Resume Next
        dsoSrv.CloseServer
        Set dsoDB = Nothing
        Set dsoCube = Nothing
        Set dsoSrv = Nothing
    End If
End Sub
```

Running the code and clicking the `Connect` button should show the form and the printed results:

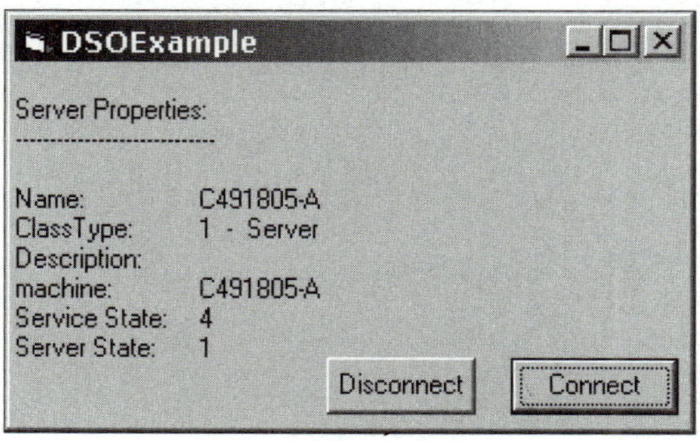

Running the code for connecting to the OLAP server

Working with OLAP Databases

In this section, you will see how you can use DSO to list databases available on a server, add a new database to the server, and remove an existing one.

First let's change our Print commands in the Connect to Server section to Debug.Print. This is because we don't want to print those lines on the form every time we connect, now that we verified that we could actually connect to the OLAP Server.

- ❑ Add a list box and set its name to `lstDB`.
- ❑ Add a command button and set its name property to `cmdListDB` and its caption to `List DBs`.
- ❑ Add a command button with the name property `cmdAddDB` and the caption `New DB`.
- ❑ Add a command button with the name property `cmdRemoveDB` and its caption to `Remove DB`.
- ❑ Rearrange the buttons to look like the following screen shot.

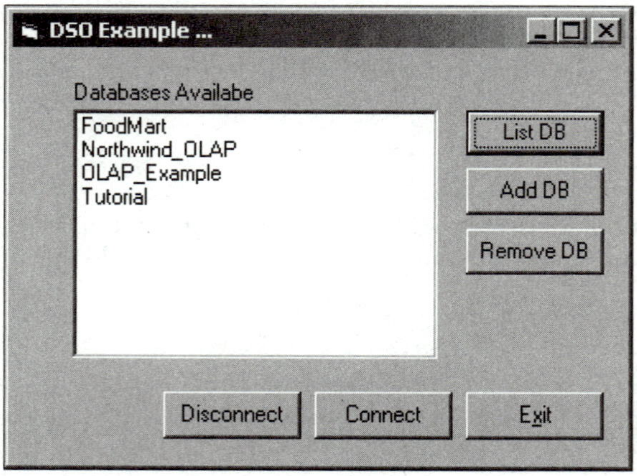

The form used with the DSO sample application at run time

- ❑ Add the following code to the form module to correspond exactly to the names of the controls you placed on the form.

```
Private Sub cmdListDB_Click()

    Dim dsoTempDB As DSO.MDStore
    Dim Counter As Integer

    On Error GoTo EH

    'If no server is assigned use the local one
    If dsoSrv Is Nothing Then
        cmdConnect_Click
    End If
```

```
    'If connection to the server is not established,
     establish it.
    If dsoSrv.State <> stateConnected Then
        cmdConnect_Click
    End If

    'Clear the list box of databases:
    lstDB.Clear

    'For each database on the server, print its name.
    For Counter = 1 To dsoSrv.MDStores.Count
        Set dsoTempDB = dsoSrv.MDStores(Counter)
        lstDB.AddItem dsoTempDB.Name
    Next Counter
    Exit Sub

EH:
    Debug.Print "Error listing databases:"
    Debug.Print Err.Number, Err.Description, Err.Source
    Err.Clear
  Debug.Assert False
End Sub

'Add the new database to the server
Private Sub cmdAddDB_Click()

    On Error GoTo EH

    'Declare and allocate local string variables
    'for use by the MDStore object.

    Dim strDBName As String
    Dim strDBDesc As String

    'Ask the user for a name for the database
    strDBName = InputBox("Enter a Unique DB Name", _
                        "Adding New Database")

    'Is this new database name blank?
    If strDBName = "" Then
        MsgBox ("You must enter a database name")
        Exit Sub
    End If

    'Query the server to see if there already is a
    'database by this name. Notice the use of the Find method
    'of the MDStores object.
    If dsoSrv.MDStores.Find(strDBName) Then
        MsgBox (strDBName & " already exists")
        Exit Sub
    End If

    'Add new database to server object collection
    'Using the AddNew method from MDStores.
    Set dsoDB = dsoSrv.MDStores.AddNew(strDBName)
```

```
    'Ask the user for a description for the new database
    strDBDesc = InputBox("Enter a Description", _
                            "Adding New Database")

    'Assign this description to the MDStore's
    'Description property, and call the Update method.
    dsoDB.Description = strDBDesc
    'Commit updates to the database properties
    dsoDB.Update


    'Add new databse to the list box.
    cmdListDB_Click
    Exit Sub
EH:
    Debug.Print "Error adding new Database"
    Debug.Print Err.Number, Err.Description, Err.Source
    Err.Clear

End Sub
```

```
'Remove the database selected in the list
Private Sub cmdRemoveDB_Click()

    Dim strDBName
    Dim bResult As Boolean

    'Make sure a database is selected from the list
    strDBName = lstDB.List(lstDB.ListIndex)
    If strDBName = "" Then
        MsgBox "Please select a database from the list.."
        Exit Sub
    End If

    'If the database can't be found on the server, inform the user.
    If Not dsoSrv.MDStores.Find(strDBName) Then
        MsgBox (strDBName & "database not found on this server")
        Exit Sub
    Else
        Set dsoDB = dsoSrv.MDStores(strDBName)
    End If

    'Ask users if they are sure they want to delete this DB
    bResult = MsgBox("Are you sure you want to remove " & dsoDB.Name, _
                        vbYesNo, "Remove Database")

    If bResult = True Then
        strDBName = dsoDB.Name
        dsoSrv.MDStores.Remove strDBName
        Set dsoDB = Nothing
```

```
            'Update list box:
            cmdListDB_Click
        Else
            MsgBox ("Canceled - Database not removed")
        End If

    End Sub
```

As a closing note, you can easily expand this sample project to add data sources, cubes, dimensions, levels, measures, and even process the added dimensions and cubes. I will leave this to be an exercise that will familiarize you with DSO. At any rate, a complete code listing for the project with the added functionality mentioned here will be available on the Wrox web site at: http://www.wrox.com

B

Installing OLAP Services

This appendix is designed to guide you through the process of installing the Microsoft OLAP Services, if you haven't already done so, and start working with them. The appendix shows you how to easily install Microsoft OLAP services, presenting you with the minimum and practical system requirements, installation options, and a description of the installation process. Additional material covered in this appendix includes removing OLAP services and reinstalling them.

If you have already installed OLAP services from the SQL Server CD you could skip this appendix, unless you want to know more about the installation process beyond running the installation wizard.

Microsoft OLAP Installation

If you have already installed SQL Server 7.0, some of the pieces needed to for this book have already been installed. To be specific, your installation of SQL Server 7 installs the data transformation services (DTS), which is described in some detail in Chapters 6 and 7.

The following sections lead you into the installation process of Microsoft OLAP services, as well as the installation of the English Query part.

Installation Pre-requisites

The following pre-requisites assume that you have already installed SQL Server 7 and met its installation pre-requisites. Before you start the installation process of the Microsoft OLAP Services, make sure you have met the following requirements.

Processor:

SQL Server and OLAP Services should be run on either a DEC Alpha AXP and compatible systems, or on an Intel-based (or compatible) systems with a minimum of 133 MHz clock speed. If you are using an Intel-based computer, it is recommended that you use at least a Pentium Pro or Pentium II CPU chip.

Memory:

Microsoft recommends at least 64 MB of RAM to run Microsoft OLAP services, even though it claims that 32 MB is the bare minimum. However, try to run OLAP services with a 32MB of RAM and you will see that this is totally unpractical. To run these services comfortably on an NT system with SQL Server installed, you will probably need 128 MB of RAM.

Disk Space:

Depending on whether you install all the pieces of OLAP Services on your machine, you need around (30 – 50 MB) of disk space. If you include the common files, documentation, and samples, you will need around 85 MB of disk space. Of course, you will need to have a CD ROM drive to install Microsoft OLAP services, or to run the components that you haven't installed from the CD.

Operating System and Other Software Requirements:

Microsoft OLAP Services need to run on an NT 4.0-based system with service pack 4 or later. The indicated service pack is provided on the SQL Server installation CD. Microsoft OLAP Services can be installed on either an NT 4.0 Server, or NT 4.0 Workstation or later, including Windows 2000 Professional, Server, and Advanced Server editions.

Client components can also be installed on systems running Windows 9x with the following conditions: If you install client components on a Windows 95 or Windows 95 with service release 2 (OSR2), you need have DCOM95 installed before installing the Microsoft OLAP client software. You can download DCOM95 free from the Microsoft Web site at: http://microsoft.com/com/dcom/dcom95/download.asp. However, if you have Windows 98 installed, you don't need to install DCOM95.

You also need to make sure you have a Windows-based network with transmission control protocol/Internet protocol (TCP/IP) protocols installed to run OLAP Services and client tools.

Internet Explorer 4.01 with service pack 1 or later (IE) is needed for the Microsoft Management Console (MMC), and for viewing the product documentation and help files. Minimum install of IE is required and it is not required to be the default browser on your system. IE 4.01 with service pack 1 is included on the SQL Server 7.0 disk. If you install OLAP Services on Windows 2000 platform, you don't have to worry about this requirement, since IE 5.0 is an integral part of the this Windows system.

> **Please note that installing the OLAP server requires logging on the server with administrative privileges.**

Setup Components

OLAP Services are composed of two main components: server components and client components. The server components are called the Microsoft OLAP Server and can only be installed on a Windows NT4.0-based system or later. The client components include tools such as OLAP Manager, Pivot Table Service, etc. Client components are installed on the OLAP server by default when OLAP services are installed. Client components allow for remote access to the OLAP server so that reports can be generated from its repository on these machines.

Installation Wizard

The installation wizard for OLAP services can be launched in two ways: from the installation wizard of SQL Server, or from the SQL Server CD ROM.

When you install SQL Server 7.0, one of the options you are presented with in the installation wizard is installing the OLAP Services. Selecting this option after you have installed SQL Server 7.0 will launch the OLAP Services installation wizard.

Launching the OLAP Services installation wizard from the SQL Server installation wizard

To launch the OLAP installation wizard from the CD ROM, you need to run the program `setup.exe` located in the directory `\MSOLAP\Install\setup.exe` on the SQL Server 7.0 CD ROM. Launching the OLAP installation wizard will present you with the screen as shown below.

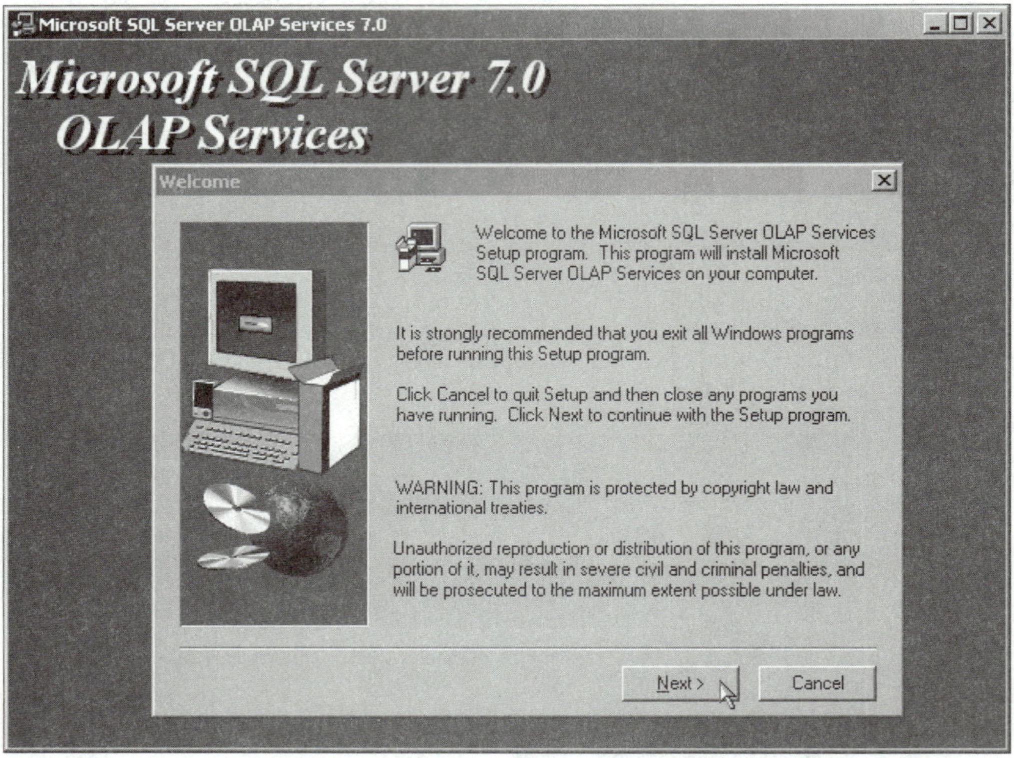

OLAP Services installation wizard start page

Clicking the Next button in the screen will lead you into the next wizard screen that presents you with the license agreement. Read the whole agreement carefully and click the Yes button if you agree with what you read.

The next screen, shown below, presents you with a default location for the installation on your hard disk. You can change this destination by clicking the Browse... button and selection a different path.

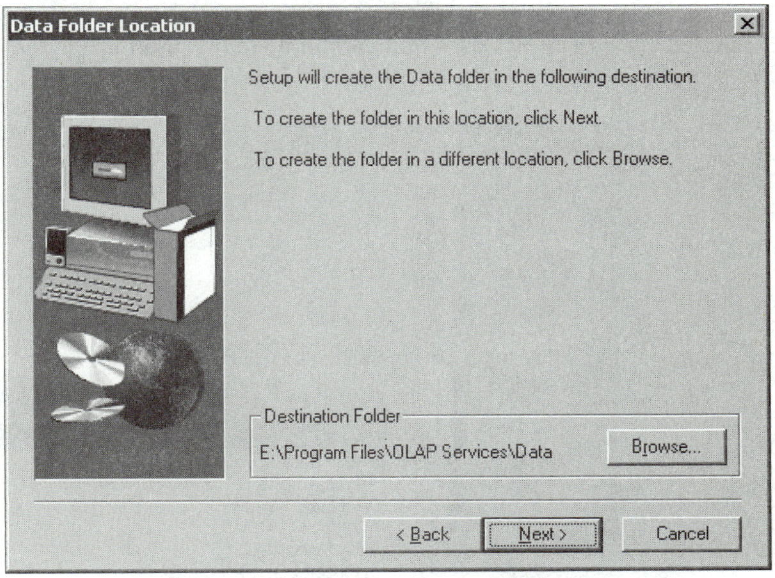

Selecting the installation path for OLAP Services

Clicking the Next button will lead you into the screen in which you select the components you want to install. By default, all components are selected, including the sample applications. Make sure you select the right components (see Setup Components above) and click the Next button.

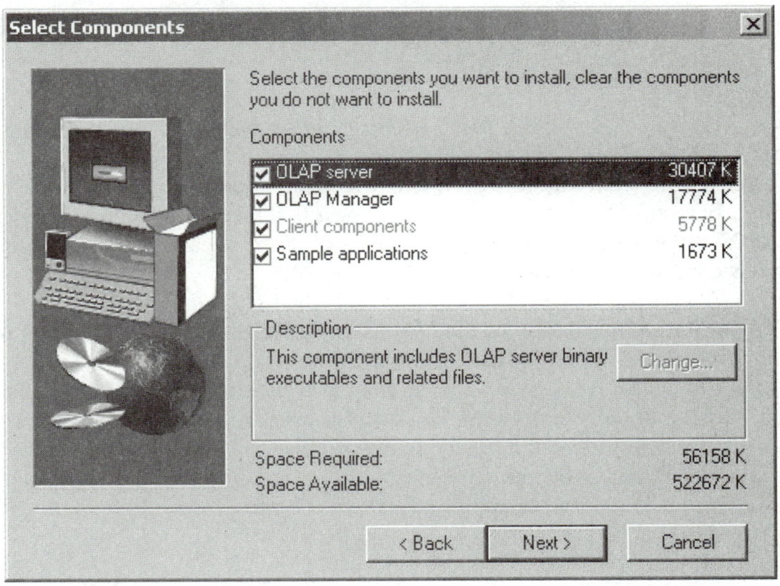

Selecting the OLAP Services components to install

The next screen allows you to select the program group in which the OLAP Services components will be located and can be launched from on the Windows' Start menu. By default, the Microsoft SQL Server group is used to house the OLAP Services components.

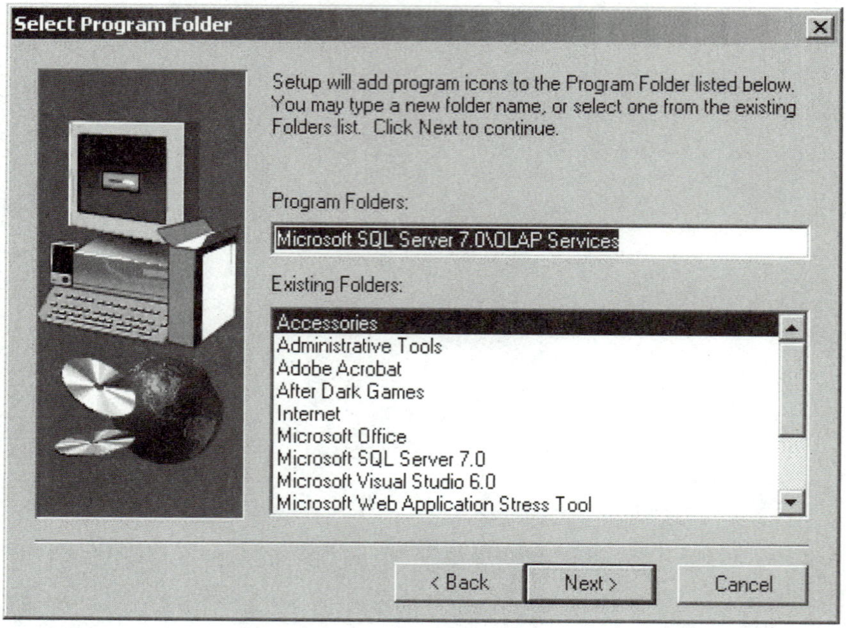

Selecting the OLAP Services program folder on the Start menu

Clicking the Next button will initiate the installation of the Microsoft Data Access tools (MDAC), and the Microsoft OLAP Services. This process will take a few minutes depending on the speed of your CD ROM drive and your computer. At the end of the wizard you are presented with the option of restarting your computer because some of the changes made to your system will not take effect until then.

To verify the installation of the Microsoft OLAP Server, start the Windows Control panel and select the Services applet. Look for the MS SQL Server OLAP Service in the list of services. If you find it, make sure it is started. In this applet, you may also determine how the service will be started. You can choose to start it manually every time you want to use it conserving with that some server resources when you really don't want to use it. You can also choose to have it started automatically when the NT server is restarted. Finally, you can choose to disable the service if you know that you will not be using it for some time. The Services applet also allows you to determine the login ID used when the service is started.

In Microsoft Windows 2000, the Services applet becomes one of the administrative functionalities and can be reached by selecting "Administrative Tasks" from the Windows Start menu.

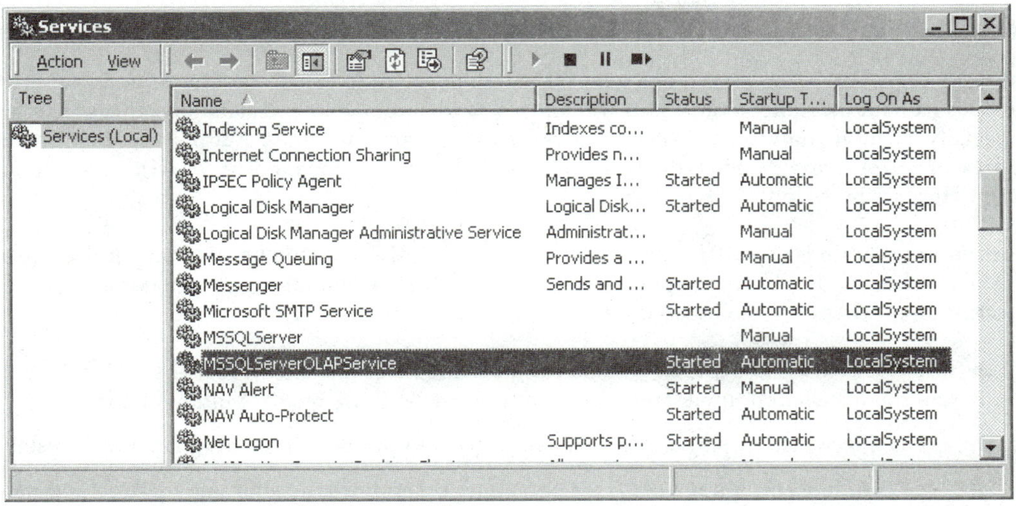

MS SQL Server OLAP Services in the Services applet

You can also verify the OLAP Services installation by selecting the SQL Server 7.0 folder and then the OLAP Services folder from the Windows Start menu, as shown below

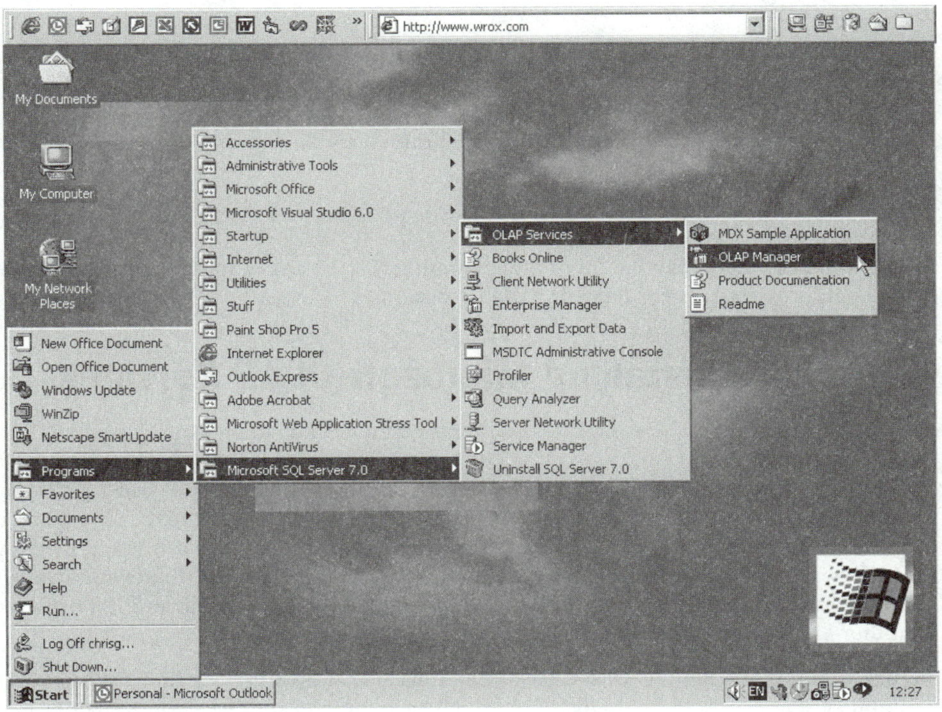

OLAP Services program folder on the Start menu

OLAP Services Silent Installation

You can use set-up parameters along with the set-up program to install the Microsoft SQL Server OLAP services without user interaction. This will allow you to automate the installation process and becomes especially useful if you want to install these services on many machines. Automating the installation process requires writing a batch file that can be run from the command line, or writing a Windows Script Host script to do the job.

The set-up program is usually located in the path (\MSOLAP\Install\setup.exe) on your SQL Server CD. The following is a list of the parameters that can be used with the set-up program, with a description of what they can be used for:

- `-r` can be used to generate a silent response file (with the extension `.iss`). This file records all the installation input, and is created in the default Microsoft Windows folder.
- `-s` is the switch, or parameter, that can be used to performs a silent (unattended) installation.
- `-f1<path\ResponseFile>` This parameter determines the alternate location and name of the response file (`.iss` file). The default location of this file, if this option is not used, is the same folder as the set-up program.
- `-f2<path\LogFile>` This parameter determines the alternate location and name of the log file. By default, the `Setup.log` log file is created and stored in the same folder as that of `Setup.exe`.

The `-r` option allows you to create a record of any desired installation scenario. This record can then be used to perform a silent installation.

As an example on using the set-up program and its parameters, the command

```
Setup.exe -s -f1C:\temp\setup.iss
```

initiates a silent (unattended) installation of the components specified in the `setup.iss` response file. This file had been previously recorded using the `-r` option.

Removing and Reinstalling Microsoft OLAP Services

You have to be aware of several issues when you remove the OLAP services:

- When you remove the SQL Server OLAP Services, the repository file (`msmdrep.mdb`), which contains cube metadata will be deleted. It is recommended that you make a backup copy of this file before you remove OLAP Services. The reason for this is that if you reinstall the OLAP Services, you can still import the old file, restoring with that whatever cubes and objects you had before the uninstall. Or you may take the backup file and import it from another OLAP Server to recover the OLAP cubes contained in it.
- When you remove the OLAP services some files are marked for deletion the next time the computer starts since they are likely to be in use when you run the de-installation. Because of this, if you intend to remove and reinstall these services, you will need to restart your system before you reinstall.

- If, for any reason, you get errors indicating failure of the removal of the OLAP services, reinstall OLAP Services, and then restart the removal process. There is the possibility that you may have to manually delete some remaining files and folders after running the Add/Remove Programs application in Control Panel.

Reinstalling the OLAP services involves running the set-up program again from the CD ROM. If you install OLAP services over an existing installation, even though the reinstallation does not delete the repository file which contains the cube metadata, you still need to process all dimensions and cubes after the reinstallation process.

English Query Installation

As mentioned earlier, English query is a client component that can be used to query the OLAP database in an easy way. Installation of this component is separate from that of Microsoft SQL Server. The installation files, however, are located on the same CD ROM.

The installation process is straightforward and starts with the SQL Server Installation wizard. Selecting English Query in that screen will launch the set-up program.

You can manually start the set-up program from the \MSEQ\X86 directory on the SQL Server CD ROM.

English Query Components

English Query has two components:

- English Query domain editor (`Mseqdev.exe`), which creates an English Query application.
- English Query engine which uses the application to translate English queries into SQL.

Depending on your needs, you may install both components, or just the English Query engine. For instance, to build an English Query application, you must install the domain editor. However, if you want to use an existing English Query application with a client user interface (as an example, Active Server Pages or a Visual Basic program), you need only install the English Query engine.

Operating System and Disk Space Requirements

The English Query domain editor and engine require:

- Microsoft Windows 95 or later
- Microsoft Windows NT, version 4.0 or later

The minimum Disk Space requirement is 12 megabytes of free disk space to install the domain editor and engine. You need to have a minimum of 7 megabytes to install the engine only.

Supported Databases

The English Query engine generates SQL for Microsoft SQL Server version 6.5 or later. Queries generated by English Query may not run on other databases, such as Microsoft Access.

There are two sample English Query applications provided with the English Query installation:

- `Pubs.eqp` is an application for the `Pubs` sample database, distributed with Microsoft SQL Server.
- `Northwind.eqp` is an application for the `Northwind` sample database, distributed with Microsoft SQL Server 7.0.

Both of these samples exist in the Samples directory.

C

MDX Function Reference

Multidimensional Expressions (MDX) language includes many functions that make it flexible and able to perform its job. Chapters 7 and 8 discussed the language and how it can be used. In the process of the discussion in these two chapters, many of the important operators and functions were discussed and used. This Appendix provides a reference for the MDX functions that you can refer to quickly when you encounter a situation that warrants using them.

The functions you can use with MDX are divided into several categories:

- Built-in MDX functions that help define complex calculated members . A list of these functions is available in the Cube editor's Calculated Member Builder.
- VBA Functions that help with string manipulations, numeric evaluations, and data type conversions.
- Excel functions that allow for statistical analyses, conducting Excel-type financial, and other calculations.

Built-in MDX Functions:

There are around 100 built-in MDX functions that are divided into the categories below:

- Array functions
- Dimension functions
- Hierarchy functions

- Level functions
- Logical functions
- Member functions
- Numeric functions
- Set functions
- String functions
- Tuple functions

Array Functions

SetToArray()

This function converts one or more sets into an array that can be used by the user in user-defined functions. The syntax for this function is:

```
SetToArray(Set [, Set]...[, Numeric Expression])
```

The members of the array can either be sets or numeric expressions. The dimension of the resulting array is equal to the number of sets passed to the function. The following is an example of using this function:

```
SetToArray({[Geography].[States].Members}, {[Time].[1998 Quarters].Members})
```

Elements of the resulting two-dimensional array would include:
(MI, Q1) (MI, Q2) (MI, Q3) (MI, Q4) (CA, Q1) (CA, Q2) (CA, Q3) (CA, Q4), etc.

Dimension Functions

Dimension functions are available to return a dimension of a level, hierarchy, or member, or simply to return the dimension given its name or ordinal position.

Dimension

This function returns the dimension that includes a certain member, level, or hierarchy. The function is expressed as: `Member.Dimension`, `Level.Dimension`, or `Hierarchy.Dimension`. Examples of using this function are:

`[1998].Dimension`	returns the Time dimension
`[States].Dimension`	returns the geography dimension
`[Fiscal Year].Dimension`	returns the fiscal hierarchy of the Time dimension

Dimensions()

The function syntax is:

```
Dimensions([numeric expression] or [string expression])
```

This function returns the dimension whose ordinal position is indicated by the numeric expression or name of the dimension passed to the function. For example, `Dimensions(0)` will return the measure, `Dimension(2)` may return a Region dimension.

Hierarchy Functions

One hierarchy function is available to return the hierarchy of the level or member involved.

Hierarchy

This function returns a hierarchy that includes a certain member or level. The syntax for this function is:

```
Member.Hierarcy,
```

or:

```
Level.Hierarchy.
```

Level Functions

Three level-related functions exist in MDX. These functions are explained below.

Level

This function returns the member level if preceded by a member name. For example, `December.Level` returns the `Month` level of the `Time` dimension.

Levels()

This function may take a numeric expression as an argument, or a string. If a numeric expression is passed to this function it returns the level of the dimension corresponding to the ordinal location calculated by the expression. If a string is passed, the string should be the name of a level in the dimension, and the function returns that level.

For example, assuming that the `Time` dimension has the levels: `All`, `Year`, `Quarter`. `Month`. Then the function `Time.Levels(1)` returns the `Year` level. Also, the function `Time.Level("Month")` returns the `Month` level of the dimension.

Logical Functions

One logical function, `IsEmpty`, is available with MDX:

IsEmpty()

This function determines whether an expression evaluating to a cell value returns an empty cell. If the cell is empty, the function returns `TRUE`, and otherwise returns `FALSE`. For example:

```
IsEmpty([Measures].[CurrentMember])
```

returns `TRUE` if the cell is empty

Member Functions

The current release of MDX contains almost 20 functions that return members of dimension levels, or deal with such members. These functions are listed below.

Ancestor()

This function returns the ancestor of a member in a hierarchy at a specified level. The syntax for the function is:

```
Ancestor(member, level)
```

For example:

```
Ancestor([Milk], [Product Category])
```

may return `dairy products`.

ClosingPeriod()

This function returns the last sibling among the descendants of a member at a certain level. If no level is used, the level below the specified member is used. Also, if no level is used, the dimension defaults to the Time dimension. If a level is passed to the function, the dimension of the level is used. If no level or time are used, the default will be `[Time].CurrentMember`. For example:

```
ClosingPeriod([Month], [1998])
```

will return `[1998].[December]`.

Cousin()

This function returns the member with the same relative position under a member as the member specified. The syntax of the function is:

```
Cousin(Member1, Member2)
```

The function looks for the position under Member1 and finds the matching member at the similar position of Member2. For example:

```
Cousin([1998].[April], [1999])
```

will return `[1999].[April]` if the number of months before each of the two members is equal.

CurrentMember

This function returns the current member of a dimension along an iteration. The syntax for the function is shown through the following example:

```
[Time].[Year].CurrentMember
```

may return `[1999]`. This function may be used to return the members of a dimension iterating through the dimension levels in a loop.

DefaultMember

The default member in a dimension is usually the `All` level. If there is no `All` level, then the default member is ambiguous. This function, when issued, returns the default member of a dimension.

```
[Time].DefaultMember
```

returns `ALL TIME`.

FirstChild

This function returns the first child of a member in the next level. For example, if the `Time` dimension includes the levels `Year`, `Quarter`, `Month`, then

```
[Time].[1998]. FirstChild
```

will return the first quarter: `[1998].[First Quarter]`.

FirstSibling

This function returns the first child of a parent of a member. Depending on the member passed and its position in the level, it could return the same member.

```
[Time].[1998].FirstSibling
```

may return `[Time].[1991]` if this is the first member in the `Year` level of the `Time` dimension.

Item

This function returns a member from a tuple or a tuple from a set.
Syntax for this function is presented below:

```
Tuple.Item(numeric expression) or
Set.Item(string expression [,string expression]..|Index)
```

The first case returns the member of the tuple indicated by the result of the numeric expression. In the second case, the function returns the tuple of the set corresponding to the string expressions passed, or whose position corresponds to the index value. For example:

```
[Time].[Year].Item(0)
```

may return [1991]

```
{[Time].[Year], [Geography]}.Item([1996],[USA])
```

returns the ([1996], [USA]) tuple.

Lag

This function returns the member that is located at a specified number of positions prior to a specified member along the member's dimension.

For example, returning the second member before the member [1998].[April] will yield [1998].[February], and the function used to return it is:

```
[1998].[April].Lag(2)
```

Please note that passing negative numbers to this function will return members ahead of the current member along the dimension. For example, Member.Lag(-1) is equivalent to Member.NextMember.

LastChild

This function returns the last child of a member. For example, if the time dimension includes All, Year, Quarter, Month, Week, and Day levels, then the following function:

```
[1998].LastChild
```

returns [1998 - Fourth Quarter], and:

```
[1998 - Fourth Quarter].LastChild
```

returns December.

LastSibling

This function returns the last child of a parent of a member. For example, [January].Lastsibling returns March assuming that the parent level is Quarters.

Lead

This is the mirror function for the Lag function, except it returns the member a number of places ahead of the current member along the member's dimension.

For example, if the Time dimension includes Year and Month levels, then, [June].Lead(2) returns [August]. A negative number passed to this function makes it act exactly like the Lag function with the same number with a positive sign. For example:

```
[June].Lead(-2) = [June].Lag(2)
```

and both functions return [April].

Members()

This function returns the set of members in a dimension, level, or hierarchy, or the member whose name is specified by a string. For example,

```
[1998].[Quarters].Members
```

returns { [Quarter1, 1998], [Quarter2, 1998], [Quarter3, 1998], [Quarter4, 1998] }, which are the members of the Quarters level. The following:

```
[Fiscal 1998].Quarters.Members
```

returns the fiscal members of the hierarchy.

When passing a string expression to it, the expression is usually a user-defined function (UDF) that returns a string representing a set or member.

NextMember

This function returns the next member in the level that includes the current member.

For example, if a year level includes 1991, through 1999, then:
[1997].NextMember returns [1998]

OpeningPeriod()

This function is similar to ClosingPeriod function, except that it returns the first sibling instead of the last one. See the ClosingPeriod function for more details.

ParallelPeriod()

This function returns a member from a prior period in the same relative position as a specified member, for example the same relative month in the previous quarter. With this, the function looks similar to the Cousin function, except that it is more closely related to time series. The syntax for this function is:

```
ParallelPeriod([Level [, Numeric Expression [, Member]]])
```

All the parameters of this function are optional and default to the following values if not passed:

- Level defaults to the level of the parent of Member
- Numeric Expression defaults to the value 1
- Default Member value is [Time].CurrentMember

The following are examples on using this function:

ParallelPeriod(Year, 3, [98 Quarter 3]) returns [85 Quarter 3]

ParallelPeriod(Year, 3) assuming that the current member of the time period is Time.CurrentMember = [July - 1999], the function will return [July - 1996]

ParallelPeriod(Year) returns the current member of the same level from last year, that is if the Time.CurrentMember is [July - 1999], then the function returns [July - 1998].

And finally, ParallelPeriod() is a little tricky. If the time dimension includes Year, Quarter, and Month levels, then assuming the Time.CurrentMember is [July - 1999], then the function will return [April - 1999]. The way this is calculated is as follows: the immediate parent of [July - 1999] is [Quarter 3, 1999]. The prior sibling to that is [Quarter 2, 1999], from which the parallel to July is April.

Parent

This function returns the parent of a member. For example, [Milk].Parent returns [Dairy Products].

PrevMember

This function returns the previous member in a level that contains a specified member. For example: [April].PrevMember returns [March].

ValidMeasure()

This function a valid measure in a virtual cube. It does so by forcing inapplicable dimensions to their top level (usually the ALL level). The syntax for the function is:

```
ValidMeasure(tuple)
```

Knowing that in a virtual cube you can have dimensions that are not common for all cubes underlying the virtual cube, the measure values for such dimensions are usually calculated only for the top level of these dimensions. This function returns the measure value from the cell at the "ALL" level coordinates for such dimensions.

For example, the following two expressions are equal:

```
ValidMeasure(State.MI) = (State.MI, ALL Products, ALL Time)
```

Numeric Functions

Many numerical functions are provided with MDX to allow for aggregation and calculating members. The following is a list of the available numerical functions for the first release of MDX.

Aggregate()

This function returns a calculated value using an appropriate aggregate function based on the aggregation type of the member. The syntax for the function is:

```
Aggregate(Set [, Numeric Expression])
```

As an example:

```
WITH MEMBER Geography.Total AS  'AGGREGATE({USA, Canada})'
SELECT {Measures.SumSales, Measures.MaxSales} ON COLUMNS,
      {USA, Canada, Total} ON ROWS
FROM SalesCube
WHERE ([1999])
```

The calculated member `Total` is calculated once using the `SUM` function and once again using the `MAX` function.

Avg()

The syntax of this function is:

```
Avg(Set [,Numeric Expression]).
```

The function evaluates the average value of the numeric expression over the cells of the provided set. The count of cells is calculated only for non-empty cells. To force counting empty cells in the calculation of the average, you need to use the `CoalesceEmpty() function`. For example:

`Avg({[Bread], [Dairy Products], [Meat]}, Sales)` will evaluate the average sales value for the product categories: `bread`, `dairy products`, and `meat`.

CoalesceEmpty()

This function coalesces the value of an empty cell to a string or number and returns the coalesced value. The syntax of the function is:

```
CoalesceEmpty(value expression1 [,value expression2])
```

In other words, the function evaluates the value of the cell by evaluating the value expressions passed to it. If the evaluation returns non-empty value, the function returns that value. If the evaluation returns an empty value, the function returns the value `expression2` passed to the function. Value `expression1` and value `expression2` have to be of the same type, either numeric, or character types. For example:

```
CoalesceEmpty(Geography.CurrentMember, "USA")
```

In the example above, the function will return "USA" if the `Geography.CurrentMember` evaluates to an empty cell, otherwise, it will return the value of the expression.

Correlation()

This function returns the correlation of two series evaluated over a set. The syntax of the function is:

```
Correlation(Set, Numeric Expression1 [, Numeric Expression2])
```

The function evaluates `Set` against Numeric `Expression1` to get the values of the y-axis. Numeric `Expression2` is optional. If it is provided, the function evaluates Cell against it to get the values of the x-axis. If Numeric Expression2 is not provided, the values of `Set` are used for the x-axis.

This function ignores empty cells and cells with logical or string values. However, cells with zeros are included in the evaluation.

Count()

This function returns the number of tuples in a set. The syntax for the function is:

```
Count(Set [,EXCLUDEEMPTY}INCLUDEEMPTY])
```

The flag EXCLUDEEMPTY causes empty cells to be excluded from the Count evaluation. INCLUDEEMPTY, on the other hand, causes such cells to be counted in the evaluation. If the flag is not included, the default is to include empty cells.

For example, if the `Time` dimension includes three years at the year level, then:

```
Count([Time].[Quareters].Members)
```

will return the value `12`.

Covariance()

This function calculates the covariance of two series evaluated over a set using the biased calculation (divides by the number of elements in the sample, N). The syntax for this function is:

```
Covariance(Set, Numeric Expression1 [, Numeric Expression2])
```

The function evaluates `Set` against `Numeric Expression1` to get the values of the y-axis. `Numeric Expression2` is optional. If it is provided, the function evaluates `Cell` against it to get the values of the x-axis. If Numeric Expression2 is not provided, the values of `Set` are used for the x-axis.

This function ignores empty cells and cells with logical or string values. However, cells with zeros are included in the evaluation.

CovarianceN()

This function is similar to the `Covariance()` function, except that it used the unbiased population formula (divides by N-1).

IIF()

This function returns one of two passed values based on the result of a logical test. The syntax for this function is:

```
IIf(Logical expression, value expression1, value expression2)
```

If the logical expression evaluates to TRUE, the function returns the first value expression, value `expression1`. Otherwise, the function returns value `expression2`. For example:

```
IIF(IsEmpty([Measures].CurrentMember), 0, 1)
```

In the example above, the function will return 0 if the expression `Measures.CurrentMember` evaluates to an empty cell. Otherwise, the function will return 1.

LinRegIntercept()

This function evaluates the linear regression of a set retuning the intercept `b` of the linear regression line `y = b + ax`. This regression equation is derived using the least-square method. In the equation, `a` is the slope of the best fitting line to the sample data, and `b` is the intercept of this line with the y-axis.

The syntax of this function is:

```
LinRegIntercept(Set, Numeric Expression1 [, Numeric Expression2])
```

The function evaluates `Set` against `Numeric Expression1` to get the values of the y-axis. `Numeric Expression2` is optional. If it is provided, the function evaluates `Cell` against it to get the values of the x-axis. If `Numeric Expression2` is not provided, the values of `Set` are used for the x-axis.

This function ignores empty cells and cells with logical or string values. However, cells with zeros are included in the evaluation.

For example, to find the trend in sales for the last 12 periods, the functions below will return the values for `a` and `b` respectively.

```
LinRegSlope(LastPeriods(12), Sales)
LinRegIntercept(LastPeriods(12), Sales)
```

LinRegPoint()

This function evaluates the linear regression of a set and returns the value of y in the linear regression line
`y = b + ax` that corresponds to a given value for x. The syntax for this function is:

```
LinRegIntercept(Numeric Expression1, Set, Numeric Expression2 [, Numeric
Expression3])
```

This function ignores empty cells and cells with logical or string values. However, cells with zeros are included in the evaluation.

The last three arguments to this function evaluate the linear regression line. `Numeric expression1` represents the `x` coordinate for which the function will return the value of `y` using the resulting regression line. For example,

```
LinRegPoint(10, LastPeriods(15), Sales)
```

returns the sales for the fifteenth period.

LinRegR2()

This function calculates the linear regression of a set and returns the coefficient of determination, R^2. The syntax for the function is:

```
LinRegR2(Set, Numeric Expression1 [, Numeric Expression2])
```

The function evaluates `Set` against `Numeric Expression1` to get the values of the y-axis. `Numeric Expression2` is optional. If it is provided, the function evaluates `Cell` against it to get the values of the x-axis. If `Numeric Expression2` is not provided, the values of `Set` are used for the x-axis.

This function ignores empty cells and cells with logical or string values. However, cells with zeros are included in the evaluation.

LinRegSlope()

This function is similar to the `LinRegIntercept()` function, except that it returns the slope (a) of the linear regression function. The syntax of this function is:

```
LinRegSlope(Set, Numeric Expression1 [, Numeric Expression2])
```

The function evaluates `Set` against `Numeric Expression1` to get the values of the y-axis. `Numeric Expression2` is optional. If it is provided, the function evaluates `Cell` against it to get the values of the x-axis. If `Numeric Expression2` is not provided, the values of `Set` are used for the x-axis.

This function ignores empty cells and cells with logical or string values. However, cells with zeros are included in the evaluation.

For example, to find the trend in sales for the last 10 periods, the functions below will return the values for the slope `a`, and the intercept `b`, respectively.

```
LinRegSlope(LastPeriods(10), Sales)
LinRegIntercept(LastPeriods(10), Sales)
```

LinRegVariance()

This function is similar to the `LinRegIntercept()` function, except that it returns the variance of the linear regression function. The syntax of this function is:

```
LinRegVariance(Set, Numeric Expression1 [, Numeric Expression2])
```

The function evaluates `Set` against `Numeric Expression1` to get the values of the y-axis. `Numeric Expression2` is optional. If it is provided, the function evaluates `Cell` against it to get the values of the x-axis. If `Numeric Expression2` is not provided, the values of `Set` are used for the x-axis.

This function ignores empty cells and cells with logical or string values. However, cells with zeros are included in the evaluation.

Max()

This function returns the maximum value of a numeric expression evaluated over a set. For example, to return the maximum sale for a set of regions, we can write:

```
Max({Northeast, Southeast, Midwest, Northwest}, Sales)
```

Assuming the sales for these regions are respectively: $55,000, $32,000, $67,000, and $110,000, the function will return the value, 100,000.

Median()

This function returns the median value of a numeric expression evaluated over a set. For example, to return the median sale for a set of regions, we can write:

```
Median({Northeast, Southeast, Southwest, Midwest, Northwest}, Sales)
```

Assuming the sales for these regions are respectively: $26,000, $55,000, $32,000, $67,000, and $110,000, the function will return the value, 55,000.

Min()

This function returns the minimum value of a numeric expression evaluated over a set. For example, to return the minimum sale for a set of regions, we can write:

```
Min({Northeast, Southeast, Southwest, Midwest, Northwest}, Sales)
```

Assuming the sales for these regions are respectively: $26,000, $55,000, $32,000, $67,000, and $110,000, the function will return the value, 26,000.

Ordinal()

This function returns the zero-based ordinal value associated with a level. The syntax of this function is: `Level.Ordinal`. For example:

```
[Time].[Quarters].Ordinal
```

returns the ordinal value for this level. If, for example, it is 2, then it corresponds to the third quarter.

Rank()

This function returns the one-based rank of a tuple in a set. The syntax for this function is:

```
Rank(Tuple, Set)
```

For example:

```
Rank((1998, Canada), {(1998, USA), (1997, USA), (1998, Canada), (1997, Canada)})
```

Will return 3.

Stddev()

This function returns the standard deviation value (unbiased) of a numeric expression evaluated over a set. For example, to return the standard deviation of sales for a set of regions, we can write:

```
StdDev({Northeast, Southeast, Southwest, Midwest, Northwest}, Sales)
```

Assuming the sales for these regions are respectively: $26,000, $55,000, $32,000, $67,000, and $110,000, the function will return the value 33519.

StddevP()

This function returns the standard deviation value (biased) of a numeric expression evaluated over a set. For example, to return the standard deviation of sales for a set of regions, we can write:

```
StdDevP({Northeast, Southeast, Southwest, Midwest, Northwest}, Sales)
```

Assuming the sales for these regions are respectively: $26,000, $55,000, $32,000, $67,000, and $110,000, the function will return the value 29980.

StDev()

Same as `Stddev()`

StDevP()

Same as `StddevP()`

Sum()

This function returns the sum of a numeric expression evaluated over a set. The syntax for this function is:

```
Sum(Set, Numeric Expression)
```

For example, to return the sum of sales for a set of regions, we can write:

```
Sum({Northeast, Southeast, Southwest, Midwest, Northwest}, Sales)
```

Assuming the sales for these regions are respectively: $26,000, $55,000, $32,000, $67,000, and $110,000, the function will return the value 290,000.

Value()

This function returns the value of a measure. It is worth noting that this is the default property of a measure. Hence, referring to `Sales.Measure.CurrentMember.Value` is equivalent to referring to it as: `Sales.Measure.CurrentMember`.

Var()

This function returns the variance value (unbiased) of a numeric expression evaluated over a set. For example, to return the variance of sales for a set of regions, we can write:

```
Var({Northeast, Southeast, Southwest, Midwest, Northwest}, Sales)
```

Assuming the sales for these regions are respectively: $26,000, $55,000, $32,000, $67,000, and $110,000, the function will return the value 1123500000.

Variance()

Same as `Var()` function.

VarianceP()

This function returns the variance value (biased) of a numeric expression evaluated over a set. For example, to return the variance of sales for a set of regions, we can write:

```
VarianceP({Northeast, Southeast, Southwest, Midwest, Northwest}, Sales)
```

Assuming the sales for these regions are respectively: $26,000, $55,000, $32,000, $67,000, and $110,000, the function will return the value 898800000.

VarP()

Same as `VarianceP()` function.

Set Functions

Many of the built-in MDX functions fall into this group (around 40 functions). These functions facilitate the conduction of set operations and evaluations.

AddCalculatedMembers()

This function adds calculated members to a set. The calculated members have to be siblings in the set. As an example on this function, examine the following figure:

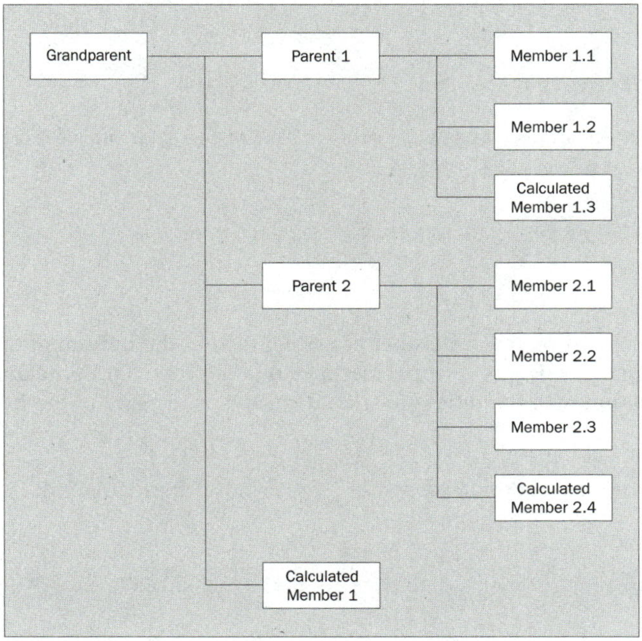

A hierarchy with calculated members at two levels

Based on the figure, the functions below have the following return values:

`AddCalculatedMember({Grandparent.Children})` returns the set `{[Parent1], [Paren2], [Calculated Member 1]}`

`AddCalculatedMember({Parent1.Children})` returns the set `{[Member 1.1], [Member 1.2], [Calculated Member 1.3]}`

`AddCalculatedMember({[Member2.2]})` returns the set `{[Member 2.2], [Calculated Member 2.4]}`

BottomCount()

This function returns a specified number of items from the bottom of the set. The function may order the set before returning its value. The syntax for the function is:

```
BottomCount(Set, Count [, Numeric Expression])
```

For example:

```
BottomCount([geography].[states].Members, 3, Sales)
```

returns the three states with the least amount of sales.

BottomPercent()

This function sorts a set and returns a number of items from the bottom of the set whose cumulative total for a numeric expression is less or equal to a specified percent value. The syntax for the function is:

```
BottomPercent(Set, Percent, Numeric Expression)
```

For example, to return the states whose total sales is 25% of the total sales for all states from the bottom of the given set, you can write:

```
BottomPercent([Geography].[States].Members, 25, Sales)
```

BottomSum()

This function sorts a set and returns a number of elements from the bottom of the set whose total for the provided numeric expression is less or equal to s specified number. This function is similar to the `BottomPercent` function with the difference that it calculates the sum of the items in the set rather than the percentage.

To return the items from the bottom of the `States` set whose cumulative sales is less than or equal to a $200,000, we write:

```
BottomSum([Geography].[States].Members, 200,000, Sales
```

Children

Returns the children of a member. The syntax is:

```
Member.Children
```

For example:

```
[Quarter1 - 1998].Children
```

returns { `[January-1998], [February-1998], [March-1998]` }

CrossJoin()

Returns the cross product of two sets. The syntax is:

```
CrossJoin(Set1, Set2)
```

For example,

```
CrossJoin({[1998], [1999]}, {[[USA], [Canada]})
```

will return: { `[1998-USA], [1998-Canada], [1999-USA], [1999-Canada]` }

Descendants()

This function returns the set of descendants of a member at a specified level. Using a special flag, you can include or exclude descendants in other subsequent levels. The syntax for this function is:

```
Descedants(member, level [, Desc_Flag])
```

The optional `Desc_Flag` can have the values outlined in the table below:

Flag	Description
SELF	This is the default flag. It returns the descendant members of the level provided to the function. If the level specified is the same level of the member passed to the function, then the member will also be returned.
AFTER	Returns all descendant members from the ALL levels subordinate to the specified level.
BEFORE	Returns all descendant members of all levels between the specified level and the level of the specified member, not including the members of the specified level
BEFORE_AND_AFTER	Returns the union of all the descendants returned using both the AFTER and BEFORE flags.

Flag	Description
SELF_AND_AFTER	Returns the union of all the descendants returned using the SELF and AFTER flags
SELF_AND_BEFORE	Returns the union of all the descendants returned using the SELF and BEFORE flags
SELF_BEFORE_AFTER	Returns descendant members from all levels subordinate to the specified member.

As an example, assuming the levels to be `Product Family`, `Category`, `Subcategory`, and `Brand`:

`Descendants([Dairy Products], [Brands])` returns all brands in the dairy products food subcategory. This would be the same as the result of `Descendants([Dairy Products], [Brands], SELF)`

Distinct()

This function eliminates duplicate tuples in a set. The syntax for the function is:

```
Distinct(Set)
```

For example:

```
Distinct({(USA, 1998), (Canada, 1998), (USA, 1998)}
```

returns `{(USA, 1998), (Canada, 1998)}`

DrillDownLevel()

This function drills down the members of a set to one level below the lowest level represented in the set. Or, if a level of a member is represented in the set, it drills down to one level below that level. The syntax for the function is:

```
DrillDownLevel(Set [, Level])
```

An alternate syntax is: `DrillDownLevel(Set, , Index)`

If, in the first syntax, no level is specified, the function drills down to the lowest level represented by the members of the set. If the level is specified, but no member in the set is at that level, the function returns the set itself.

In the alternate syntax, the index is the ordinal location of the dimension in the set. For instance, if the tuples in the set look like `(USA, Drink, 1998)` then the first dimension represented is the store dimension and has the index zero. The second dimension represented would be the product dimension and has the index 1. The time dimension is the third one in the tuple and has the index 2. For example:

DrillDownLevel({USA, Canada, France, Michigan}) is the same as DrillDownLevel({USA, Canada, France, Michigan}, [State or Province]) and the result of the drill down would be (assuming that the next level after [State or province] is [City]: DrillDownLevel({USA, Canada, France, Michigan, All Cities in Michigan})

DrillDownLevelBottom()

This function drills down a specified number of members of a set from the bottom and which are a certain level one level below that. The syntax for the function is:

```
DrillDownLevelBottom(Set, Count [, Level[, Numeric Expression]])
```

This function orders the members of a set and picks a number of these members specified by the Count parameter at the specified level "level" and drills these members one level below their current level.

As an example,

```
DrilldownLevelBottom({[Country].Members},2, ,[Sales])
```

returns the set: {Canada, <bottom two provinces in Canada>, Mexico, <bottom two states in Mexico>, ..., USA, <bottom two states in USA>}.

DrillDownLevelTop()

This function drills down a specified number of members of a set from the top and which are a certain level one level below that. The syntax for the function is:

```
DrillDownLevelTop(Set, Count [, Level[, Numeric Expression]])
```

This function orders the members of a set and picks a number of these members specified by the Count parameter at the specified level "level" and drills these members one level below their current level.

As an example,

```
DrilldownLevelTop({[Country].Members},2, ,[Sales])
```

returns the set {Canada, <top two provinces in Canada>, Mexico, <top two states in Mexico>, ..., USA, <top two states in USA>}.

DrillDownMember()

This function drills down members in a specified set that exist in another specified set. The syntax for the function is:

```
DrillDownMember(Set1, Set2 [,RECURSIVE])
```

Set1 is usually a subset of Set2. If the RECURSIVE flag is specified, the function continues the drill down replacing Set1 with the drilldown results and performing the drill down for these results against Set2 again.

For example,

```
DrillDownMember({[1999], [1998]}, {Time.Year.members}), where Time.Year.Members is
a set {[1990] .. [1999]}.
```

The return from the function is: `{[1999], [Q1-1999], [Q2-1999], [Q3-1999], [Q4-1999], [1998], [Q1-1998], [Q2-1998], [Q3-1998], [Q4-1998]}`

DrillDownMemberBottom()

This is similar to `DrillDownMember`, except that it limits the result to a specified number of members. The syntax for the function is:

```
DrillDownMemberBottom(Set1, Set2, Count [, Numeric Expression [,RECURSIVE]])
```

The resulting set of this function is limited to the bottom "count" based on the numeric expression. For example:

```
DrilldownMemberBottom({USA, Canada, Mexico}, {USA, WA, Mexico}, 2, [Unit Sales])
```

returns the set `{USA, bottom two states in USA, Canada, Mexico, bottom two states in Mexico}`

DrillDownmemberTop()

This is similar to `DrillDownMember`, except that it limits the result to a specified number of members. The syntax for the function is:

```
DrillDownMemberTop(Set1, Set2, Count [, Numeric Expression [,RECURSIVE]])
```

The resulting set of this function is limited to the top "count" based on the numeric expression. For example:

```
DrilldownMemberTop({USA, Canada, Mexico}, {USA, WA, Mexico}, 2, [Unit Sales])
```

returns the set `{USA, top two states in USA, Canada, Mexico, top two states in Mexico}`

DrillupLevel()

This function drills up the members of a set that are below a specified level. The syntax of the function is:

```
DrillupLevel(Set [, Level])
```

If no level is specified it defaults to the level below the lowest level represented by the members of the passed set. For example:

```
DrillUpLevel({USA, CA, [San Francisco], MI, Detroit, Canada, BC})
```

returns the set {USA, CA, MI, Canada, BC}

and

```
DrillUpLevel({USA, CA, [Los Angeles], MI, Detroit, Canada, BC},[Store.Country])
```

returns the set {USA, Canada }.

Drillupmember()

This function drills up members in a specified set that exist in another specified set, which is usually a subset of the first specified set. The syntax is:

```
DrillupMember(Set1, Set2)
```

For example:

```
DrillUpLevel({USA, CA, [San Francisco], MI, Detroit, Pontiac, Ann Arbor, Canada,
BC}, {MI})
```

Returns: {USA, CA, [San Francisco], MI, Canada, BC}

Except()

This function returns the difference between two sets. In other words, it returns the tuples in a set that do not exist in another set. A flag (ALL) can be used to allow for duplicates in the resulting set. It has the following syntax:

```
Except(Set1, Set2 [,ALL])
```

For example:

```
Except({USA, Canada, Germany, Italy}, {USA, France})
```

will return: {Canada, Germany, Italy}

Extract()

This function is the opposite of the `CrossJoin()` function. To understand it, take a look at its syntax and the example below:

```
Extract(Set, Dimension1 [, Dimension2 …])
```

```
Extract({([1998], Detroit), ([1998], Washington DC), ([1999], Seattle)}, Time)
```

returns the set: { [1998], [1999] }

Filter()

This function filters a set based on a search condition and returns the set resulting from the filtering process. The syntax is:

```
Filter(Set, Search Condition)
```

For example:

```
Filter({[Store].[States].Members, (Population, [1998]) > 10000000)
```

Generate()

This function generates a new set as a result of a union of the sets resulting from applying one specific passed set to another. The syntax of the function is:

```
Generate (Set1, Set2 [,ALL])
```

The ALL flag results in including duplicates in the resulting set. To understand this function, consider the following example:

```
Generate({USA, Canada}, Descendants(Store.CurrentMember, Cities))
```

The function above will apply the results of the `Descendants()` function to each of USA and Canada in `Set1`. This will result in all cities in the USA and all cities in Canada. This is a situation where `Set2` is a result of a set expression, and `Set1` is related to this set expression. If `Set1` is not related to the set expression, the resulting set will simply be a replication of the set implied by the set expression.

```
Generate({[USA], [Canada]}, {[Detroit], [New York]}, ALL)
```

will result in the set: `{[Detroit], [New York], [Detroit], [New York]}`. If the ALL flag is omitted, the result will be `{[Detroit], [New York]}`.

Head()

This function returns the first specified number of tuples in a set. The syntax of the function is:

```
Head(Set [, Numeric Expression])
```

If the numeric expression is not passed, it defaults to 1. For example:

```
Head({[USA], [GB], [Canada], [France]}, 3) returns {[USA], [GB], [Canada]},
```

and

```
Head({[USA], [GB], [Canada], [France]}) returns {[USA]}
```

Hierarchize()

This function orders the members of a set into a hierarchy format. The function accepts one argument, the specified set.

```
Hierarchize (Set)
```

Members in a level will be sorted in their natural order. Members across a dimension will be stored in their natural order, unless otherwise specified. This function will always include duplicates.

Intersect()

This function returns the tuples shared by two sets (intersect of the two sets). An optional flag (ALL) can be used to include duplicates in the resulting set. The syntax of this function is:

```
Intersect(Set1, Set2 [,ALL])
```

For example:

```
Intersect({[USA], [GB], [Canada], [France]}, {[GB], [Germany], [Canada], [Russia]}
```

returns `{[GB], [Canada]}`

LastPeriods()

This function returns a set of periods prior to and including a member. The syntax for this function is:

```
LastPeriods(index [, member])
```

If no member is specified, the default member is used, which is: `Time.CurrentMember`. If the index is zero, an empty set will be returned.

Examples:
`LastPeriods(3, [July-1998])` returns `{[May-1998],[June-1998],[July-1998]}`
`LastPeriods(-3, [July-1998])` returns `{[July-1998],[August-1998],[September-1998]}`

Members

This function returns the set of members in a dimension, level, or hierarchy, or the member whose name is specified by a specified string. Examples on using this function include:

`Time.Members` returns a set of all the time dimension members.
`Members(UDF())`, where `UDF()` is a user defined function evaluating to a string. The `members` function returns the member defined by the return value of the UDF function.

MTD()

This function is similar to `PeriodsToDate()` except that it specifies the level to be `Months`. Hence, `Mtd([Member])` is equivalent to `PeriodsToData(Month, [Member])`

Order()

This function arranges members with the option of breaking the hierarchy or maintaining it. The syntax of the function is:

```
Order(Set, {String Expression | Numeric Expression} [, ASC | DESC | BASC | BDESC])
```

PeriodsToDate()

This function returns a set of periods (members) of a specified level and ending with a particular member. The syntax for the function is:

```
PeriodsToDate([Level[, Member]])
```

The default value for member is `Time.CurrentMember`, and the default value of the level is the level of the parent of the specified member.

Qtd()

This function is similar to `PeriodsToDate()` except that it specifies the level to be quarters. Hence, `Qtd([Member])` is equivalent to `PeriodsToData(Quarter, [Member])`

StripCalculatedMembers()

This function removes calculated members from a set. The function is the opposite of `AddCalculatedMembers`, since it removes calculated members added using that function. A single parameter is passed representing the set.

StrToSet()

This function builds a set from a string expression. For example, it can convert the string: `"Product.Members"` to a set `{[ Product].Members}`.

SubSet()

This function has the syntax `SubSet(Set, Start [,Count])`. It returns the subset that starts at the member indicated by Start of the specified set. The length of the returned set is defined by the `Count` parameter. Please note that `Count` defaults to 1 if not passed. For example,

```
SubSet({[USA], [Canada], [Japan]}, 1) will return {[Canada]}
```

Tail()

This function returns a subset from the end of a set. The syntax for the function is:

```
Tail(Set [, Count])
```

If `Count` is not specified, it defaults to 1. If `Count` is less than 1, an empty set is returned. If `Count` is greater than the number of members in the set, the whole set is returned.

Example:

`Tail({[USA], [Canada], [Japan]})` is the same as `Tail({[USA], [Canada], [Japan]}, 1)` which returns the value `{[Japan]}`

ToggleDrillState()

This function is a combination of `DrilUpMember` and `DrillDownMember` functions. It toggles the drill state of members. The syntax for the function is:

```
ToggleDrillState(Set1, Set2 [, Recursive])
```

The function looks for members of Set2 that are present in Set1 and toggles their drill state. If their drill state is drill down (the member has descendants), The `DrillUpMember` is applied to Set1

TopCount()

This function returns a specified number of items from the top of the set. The function may order the set before returning its value. The syntax for the function is:

```
TopCount(Set, Count [, Numeric Expression])
```

For example:

```
TopCount([geography].[states].Members, 3, Sales)
```

returns the three states with the highest amount of sales.

TopPercent()

This function sorts a set and returns a number of items from the top of the set whose cumulative total for a numeric expression is less or equal to a specified percent value. The syntax for the function is:

```
TopPercent(Set, Percent, Numeric Expression)
```

For example, to return the states whose total sales is 25% of the total sales for all states from the top of the given set, you can write:

```
TopPercent([Geography].[States].Members, 25, Sales)
```

TopSum()

This function sorts a set and returns a number of elements from the top of the set whose total for the provided numeric expression is less or equal to s specified number. This function is similar to the `TopPercent` function with the difference that it calculates the sum of the items in the set rather than the percentage.

To return the items from the top of the `States` set whose cumulative sales is less than or equal to a $200,000, we write:

```
TopSum([Geography].[States].Members, 200,000, Sales
```

Union()

This function returns the union of two sets, optionally retaining duplicates. The syntax is:

```
Union(Set1, Set2 [,ALL])
```

The ALL flag determines that duplicates are to be retained when added. The alternate syntax to using this function is using:

```
Set1, Set2 or Set1 + Set2
```

When using alternate syntax, the duplicates area is always retained.

VisualTotals()

This function dynamically totals the members of a parent member in a set. The function uses a pattern to construct the label for the total field. The syntax for the function is:

```
VisualTotals(Set, Pattern)
```

In the pattern, the asterisk (*) is used as a placeholder for the parent member. If you want to display an asterisk in the label, you need to use the escape sequence of two asterisks in a row. The function totals the member values in the set only. It does not add the child members outside the specified set. For example:

```
SELECT
{[Measures].[Unit Sales]} on columns,
{VisualTotals({[Product].[Food].[Meat],
   [Product].[Food].[Meat].[Turkey],
   [Product].[Food].[Meat].[Fish]},
    "**SubTotal - *")
} on rows
FROM SalesCube
```

The result of this query would look like:

*SubTotal	Unit Sales
Turkey	5000
Fish	3000

Wtd()

This function is similar to `PeriodsToDate()` except that it specifies the level to be `Weeks`. Hence, `Wtd([Member])` is equivalent to `PeriodsToData(Week, [Member])`

Ytd()

This function is similar to `PeriodsToDate()` except that it specifies the level to be `Years`. Hence, `Ytd([Member])` is equivalent to `PeriodsToData(Year, [Member])`

String Functions

Several string functions are built into MDX to allow for conversion between MDX structures and strings, such as converting a tuple to a string and vice versa. Other functions simply return string values.

CoalesceEmpty()

See the `CoalesceEmpty()` function in the numeric functions section above.

IIF()

This function takes a logical test and two values. Based on the result of the logical test, one of the two values is returned. The syntax for the function is:

```
IIF(Logical Expression, Value Expression1, Value Expression2)
```

For example:

```
IIF(IsEmpty([Measures].CurrentMember), 0, 1)
```

In the example above, the function will return 0 if the expression `Measures.CurrentMember` evaluates to an empty cell. Otherwise, the function will return 1.

Name

This function returns the name of a dimension, hierarchy, level, or member. The syntax for the function is:

```
[Dimension|Hierarchy|Level|Member].Name
```

SetToStr()

This function returns a string based on a set. For example,

```
SetToStr({[USA], [France]}  returns: "{[Store].[USA], [Store].[France]}"
```

TupleToStr()

This function returns a string based on a tuple. For example, the function:

```
TupleToStr(USA, 1998)
```

returns: `"([Store].[Country].[USA], [Time].[1998])"`

UniqueName

This is a handy function that returns the unique name of a dimension, level, or member.

Tuple Functions

Three functions return tuples or members from tuples. These functions are discussed below.

Current

This function returns the current tuple from a set during an iteration.

Item

This function returns a tuple from a set, or a member from a tuple. For example,

```
{([1998], USA), ([1999], USA), ([1998], Canada)}.Item(1)
```

returns the tuple `([1999], USA)` whereas:

```
([1999], USA).Item(0)
```

returns `[1999]`

StrToTuple()

This function converts a string expression to a tuple. The syntax for the function is: `StrToTuple(String Expression)`. For example,

```
StrToTuple("(Sales, [1998])") returns the tuple (Sales, [1998])
```

VBA and Excel Functions

OLAP Services is designed to use functions available in Visual Basic for Applications (VBA), and many spreadsheet functions available in Microsoft Excel. Support for these functions, especially, the Microsoft Excel ones, adds a great feature to OLAP Services in that it can use powerful well-established function libraries to perform sophisticated mathematical, statistical and other calculations. The current release of OLAP Services does not support all functions in VBA and Excel. The table below shows the VBA functions currently supported, followed by a table that shows the supported Excel functions. Discussing these functions is outside the scope of this book.

Microsoft OLAP Services Supported VBA Function			
Abs	DateSerial	LeftB	Sgn
Asc	DateValue	Len	Shell
AscB	Day	LenB	Sin
AscW	DDB	Log	SLN
Atn	Environ	LTrim	Space
CBool	Exp	Mid	Sqr
CByte	FileDateTime	MidB	Str
CCur	FileLen	Minute	StrComp
CDate	Fix	Month	String
CDbl	Format	Now	SYD
Chr	FV	NPer	Tan
ChrW	Hex	Oct	Time
CInt	Hour	Pmt	Timer
CLng	IIf	PPmt	TimeSerial
Cos	InStr	PV	TimeValue
CSng	InStrB	QBColor	Trim
CStr	Int	Rate	TypeName
CurDir	IPmt	RGB	UCase
CVar	IsDate	Right	Val
CVDate	IsError	RightB	Weekday
Date	IsNull	Rnd	Year
DateAdd	IsNumeric	Round	
DateDiff	LCase	Rtrim	
DatePart	Left	Second	

Microsoft OLAP Services Supported Excel Function			
Acos	FDist	Median	Search
Acosh	Find	Min	SearchB
And	FindB	MIrr	Sinh
Asc	FInv	Mode	Skew
Asin	Fisher	NegBinomDist	Sln
Asinh	FisherInv	NormDist	Slope
Atan2	Fixed	NormInv	Small
Atanh	Floor	NormSDist	Standardize
AveDev	Forecast	NormSInv	StDev
Average	FTest	NPer	StDevP
BetaDist	Fv	Npv	StEyx
BetaInv	GammaDist	Odd	Substitute
BinomDist	GammaInv	Or	Sum
Ceiling	GammaLn	Pearson	SumProduct
ChiDist	GeoMean	Percentile	SumSq
ChiInv	HarMean	PercentRank	SumX2MY2
ChiTest	HypGeomDist	Permut	SumX2PY2
Choose	Intercept	Pi	SumXMY2
Clean	Ipmt	Pmt	Syd
Combin	Irr	Poisson	Tanh
Confidence	IsErr	Power	TDist
Correl	IsError	Ppmt	Text
Cosh	IsLogical	Prob	TInv
Count	IsNA	Product	Transpose
CountA	IsNonText	Proper	Trim
Covar	IsNumber	Pv	TrimMean
CritBinom	Ispmt	Quartile	TTest

Microsoft OLAP Services Supported Excel Function			
Days360	IsText	Radians	USDollar
Db	Kurt	Rate	Var
Dbcs	Large	Replace	VarP
Ddb	Ln	ReplaceB	Vdb
Degrees	Log	Rept	Weekday
DevSq	Log10	Roman	Weibull
Dollar	LogInv	Round	ZTest
Even	LogNormDist	RoundDown	
ExponDist	Match	RoundUp	
Fact	Max	RSq	

D

Using Redundant Array of Independent Disks (RAID) With SQL Servers

One of the main challenges to performance of computer systems is its I/O (Input/Output) throughput. I/O capabilities of disk drives has improved dramatically in the recent years. However, these capabilities still lag behind those of CPUs or computer memory. Accessing data on hard disks is still much slower than accessing the data in memory.

Another issue with disks and disk drives is reliability. Usually, disk drives fail after usage for an extended period of time threatening the loss of data stored on them. In data warehousing, this issue and the data retrieval speed become especially important. With disk failure, historical data stored in the warehouse may be lost and will be very difficult to recover. Even if a backup is available for recovery, the vast amount of data makes the recovery process a very slow one.

The issues presented above lead to the development of Redundant Array of Independent Disks (RAID) technology. A RAID system is a collection of hard drives (disk farm), one or more controller cards, and embedded software to increase the reliability and redundancy of data storage on hard drives. With RAID, data is saved on multiple disks with redundancy. Failure of one disk in the RAID disk set will not lead to permanent loss of the data. Also, having the data spread over multiple disks improves retrieval since multiple disk controllers will be working in parallel for such retrieval to occur.

RAID Levels

RAID comes in multiple flavors offering improved performance and/or improved data reliability. These flavors are known as the RAID levels. The most common RAID implementations are 0, -1, and 5.

RAID Level 0 – Disk Striping

With this level, data is split among several disks allowing multiple controllers to work in parallel for data retrieval, which considerably improves I/O performance. This level does not address redundancy. Therefore, if fault tolerance is to be considered, this level should never be used alone. It is usually used with level 1 forming what is called as RAID level 10.

RAID Level 1 – Disk Mirroring

As the name implies, with this level, the data is stored on multiple disks called mirror set. This allows for data redundancy, which improves the fault tolerance of the I/O system and allows for easy data recovery. This level is usually used with Level 0 as I mentioned earlier.

RAID Level 2

This is a proprietary disk array patented by Thinking Machines, Inc. With this level, data is split on a bit level among several drives with additional drives providing parity information. This level requires a large number of disks, and since it is proprietary to one company, it is generally incompatible with many widely used disk drives. This level is not being used for the most part.

RAID Level 3 – Data Striping With Parity

This level provides redundancy and improved performance. The data is shared across multiple drives with and additional drive providing parity information. Data striping improves performance but requires simultaneous reads as the array is accessed. The drive with the parity information can be used to reconstruct the data should one of the data disks fail. This level is usually used with three data drives and one parity drive. One drawback of this level is that small random writes are generally slow, as the parity drive must be accessed for each write.

RAID Level 4 – Data Striping With Dedicated Parity

This RAID level is similar to RAID 3 except that larger data blocks are striped. Also, this level does not require the participation of each drive for each data access. The parity drive is accessed for each data access.

RAID Level 5 – Striping And Parity (Independent Disk Access)

This is the most common RAID implementation. With this level, both the data and parity information is striped across multiple drives with each drive holding both data and parity information. The additional drive that was holding the parity information and acting as the bottleneck is no longer needed. Should any one drive fail, the remaining drives contain sufficient information to allow recovery. This level provides complete redundancy with improved performance. The smallest RAID 5 implementation requires three drives though more can be used for improved performance.

Using RAID With SQL Server

When storing SQL Server data on a RAID array, make sure you follow the following two rules:

- Always store the data files of the application databases on RAID level 5 to guarantee the best redundancy and performance.
- Store the temporary database (tempdb) and the log files of all databases (these files have the highest write I/O rates) on the combination of RAID levels 0 and 1 (level 10).

Software vs. Hardware RAID

RAID levels are provided by software that can be located either in the disk storage system (hardware RAID) or within the computer itself (software RAID). In hardware RAID, the disk storage system performs the operations on behalf of the I/O requests. In software RAID, Windows NT/2000 uses some of the computer system CPU power to perform RAID operations.

The main advantage of hardware RAID is that RAID operations are transparent to the computer. Thus, SQL Server can use all the CPU power. The disadvantage is that it is more costly than software RAID.

E

Microsoft Data Warehousing Alliance and MS OLAP-Related Third Party Tools

http://www.data warehouse.com/posters/ms_poster/index.html
http://www.microsoft.com/industry/bi/business/partners/profiles.stm

This appendix presents the work done by many third-party vendors to add to the Microsoft data warehousing tools. These third-party vendors are mostly members in the Microsoft Data Warehousing Alliance (DWA). These vendors embrace the Microsoft data warehousing framework (DWF) and provide solutions that extend the data warehousing capabilities of Microsoft SQL Server 7.0 and the business intelligence functionality provided in Office 2000. Many of the products offered by these vendors target the OLAP client applications allowing better and more extensive analysis while maintaining ease of use.

Microsoft DWF is built to support integration and extension of its capabilities with those of other products. Some of the features offered by the Microsoft DWF that allow this to happen include:

- full-featured functionality
- consistent design and usability standards
- ease of management
- open architecture supported by Microsoft DWA members
- scalability
- flexibility

The DWA members as of December 1999 include the following vendors:

- Members Contributing Query, Reporting, and Analytical Tools
- Members Contributing Building and Management Tools
- Members Contributing Analytical Applications

The following tables list the members of each of these groups at the time of this writing.

Members Contributing Query, Reporting, and Analytical Tools:

Company	Products	URL
Appsource	Wired for PLAP 4.1 Wired for OLAP 5.0	http://www.appsource.com
Arcplan	Insight dynaSight	http://www.arcplan.com
Business Objects	Business Objects	http://www.businessobjects.com
Cizer Software Corporation	Cizer	http://www.cizer.com/index.html
Cognos	NovaView PowerPlay	http://www.cognos.com
ComShare	DecisionWeb	http://www.comshare.com
Decision Support Panel International AB	DS Panel	http://www.dspanel.com
European Management Systems PLC	ActiveAnalyst	http://www.activearchitect.com
FRx Software Corporation	Alytix	http://www.frxsoft.com
Knosys	ProClarity	http://www.knosysinc.com
Lawson Software	Analytic Workbench	http://www.lawson.com
Maximal Innovative Intelligence	Max	http://www.maxsw.com
OLAP@Work	OLAP@Work for Excel OLAP@Work for Office	http://www.olapatwork.com

Company	Products	URL
PolyVista Software	PolyVista	http://www.ployvista.com
Portola Dimensional Systems	Coronado	http://www.portola.com
Revelwood Inc.	SmartSite	http://www.revelwood.com
Seagate Software	Seagate Info	http://www.seagate.com
TopTier Software	Enterprise Integration Portal	http://www.toptier.com
Visual Insights	Advisor/2000 Advisor	http://www.visualinsights.com

Members Contributing Build and Management Tools:

Company	Products	URL
AppsCo Software Ltd.	AppsMart	http://www.appsco.com
Ardent Software	Data Stage Suite	http://www.ardent.com
Artech	GeneXus	http://www.genexux.com
Cognos	DecisionStream	http://www.cognos.com
DataMirror	Transformation Server for SQL Server	http://datamirror.com
Datawatch	Monarch Data Pump	http://www.datawatch.com
Informatica	PowerCenter	http://www.informatica.com
	PowerMart	
MetaEdge	C-Insight	http://www.metaedge.com

Members Contributing Analytical Applications:

Company	Products	URL
Adaytum Software	e.Planning	http://www.adaytum.com
Baan Company	Baan Business Intelligence Suite	http://www5.baan.com/cgi-bin/bvisapi.dll
Best Software	Best! Imperativ Action Planner	http://www.bestsoftware.com
BI Logix	The BI Solution	http://www.bilogix.com
Broadbase Software	Broadbase EPM	http://www.broadbase.com
Changepoint Corporation	Changepoint	http://www.changepoint.com
Citicorp Information Technology Industries Limited (Citicorp Information Technology)	FLEXCUBE Information Center	http://www.citibank.com/citil
Decision.ism	.COM Analysis	http://www.decisionism.com
Epicor Software	Business Performance Suite	http://www.epicor.com
Harmony Software, Inc.	Harmony 360°	http://www.harmony.com
Infinium Software	BIAS	http://www.infinium.com
Information Builders, Inc.	SmartMart	http://www.informationbuilders.com
Manugistics Corporation	Manugistics Supply Chain Analytics	http://www.manugistics.com
MIS Technologies GmbH	MIS Alea Decisionware	http://www.mstechnologies.com
NetAcumen	WebVision	http://www.netacumen.com
Sagent Technology	Sagent Solution 4.1	http://www.sagent.com
Silvon Software	DataTracker	http://www.silvon.com
	DecisionMar	

Index

Symbols

A

B

D

G

H

I

K

L

M

N

O

P

Q

R

T

U

V

W

Y

Professional Data Warehousing with SQL Server 7.0 and OLAP Services - Registration Card

Name ______

Address ______

______

______

______

City ______ State/Region ______

Country ______ Postcode/Zip ______

E-mail ______

Occupation ______

How did you hear about this book? ______

- ☐ Book review (name) ______
- ☐ Advertisement (name) ______
- ☐ Recommendation ______
- ☐ Catalog ______
- ☐ Other ______

Where did you buy this book? ______

- ☐ Bookstore (name) ______ City ______
- ☐ Computer Store (name) ______
- ☐ Mail Order ______
- ☐ Other ______

What influenced you in the purchase of this book?

- ☐ Cover Design
- ☐ Contents
- ☐ Other (please specify) ______

How did you rate the overall contents of this book?

- ☐ Excellent ☐ Good
- ☐ Average ☐ Poor

What did you find most useful about this book? ______

What did you find least useful about this book? ______

Please add any additional comments. ______

What other subjects will you buy a computer book on soon? ______

What is the best computer book you have used this year?

______

Note: This information will only be used to keep you updated about new Wrox Press titles and will not be used for any other purpose or passed to any other third party.

2815 **Check here if you DO NOT want to receive support for this book** ☐ **2815**

NB. If you post the bounce back card below in the UK, please send it to:

Wrox Press Ltd., Arden House, 1102 Warwick Road,
Acocks Green, Birmingham B27 6BH. UK.

Computer Book Publishers

NO POSTAGE
NECESSARY
IF MAILED
IN THE
UNITED STATES

BUSINESS REPLY MAIL

FIRST CLASS MAIL PERMIT#64 CHICAGO, IL

POSTAGE WILL BE PAID BY ADDRESSEE

WROX PRESS INC.
29 S. LA SALLE ST.
SUITE 520
CHICAGO IL 60603-USA